Scandinavia in Social Science Literature

West European Series / Indiana University

Scandinavia in Social Science Literature 〈〈〈✕〉〉〉 An English-Language Bibliography

by Sven Groennings

for the International Affairs Center

INDIANA UNIVERSITY PRESS

Bloomington & London

Library of Congress catalog card number: 69-16997

Manufactured in the United States of America

ISBN 253-39800-2

Scope and Organization

This bibliography lists English-language literature, including unpublished theses, on Denmark (and Greenland), Finland, Iceland, Norway, and Sweden in the fields of economics, education, geography, history, international relations, law, political science, and sociology. *The organization,* first by discipline and thereafter by common subheadings under each country heading, is intended to promote comparative analysis.

There are three statements to be made about inclusion and classification. First, entries are listed not on the basis of meeting social science standards, but on the basis of covering topics relevant to social science; the interpretation of relevance has been liberal. Secondly, scholarly works are not always classified under the discipline of the author, but rather under that discipline which has dominated the research on the topic.

Thirdly, the listing is almost exclusively of *twentieth century sources* and within this time span is based on a systematic and thorough search for all the years through 1963. The bibliography is intended to include all the major works of this period. It is meant to be comprehensive with regard to books, dissertations, articles in academic journals, and articles in the principal non-academic journals devoted to the area. The biblibliography is select with regard to additional materials. In order to increase the usefulness of the listing, hundreds of items published during the years 1964-1967 were added as they happened to cross the compiler's desk.

The *purpose* of undertaking this compilation was originally to stimulate comparative research on teaching about Scandinavia. A bibliography also has other functions, one of which is to serve as an indicator of past research emphases and current gaps in the literature. Another function is to provide indications and evaluations of the quality of that which is available to us. In a listing as extensive as this one, the quality of the entries will vary greatly, and annotation of all items would be a herculean if not impossible task. Nevertheless, some guidelines are provided: the user will find brief *introductions to the literature* under each discipline heading. The purpose of these introductions is to lead the user quickly to some of the standard and most significant sources or "places to begin" and to indicate some obvious gaps or subjects on which he can expect to find little or nothing that is worthwhile. These introductory orientations are limited to books and dissertations; they do not include articles.

With very few exceptions, *each source is listed only once.* Therefore, the user will have to consult several headings in order to exhaust this bibliography's potential for suggesting literature relevant to his interest. The introductory sections indicate relevant headings found elsewhere in the bibliography.

Note on *alphabetical ordering:* the Scandinavian letters Å, Ä, AE, and Ø or ö have been integrated with the letters A, E and O on the grounds that the differentiations have often been dropped in the publications cited, as well as on the grounds of presumedly greater convenience for users unfamiliar with these letters.

Those who seek access to the *parliamentary debates* of any of the Scandinavian countries will find an appendix listing those libraries not in the five countries which hold these documents. This listing was completed in September, 1960.

Acknowledgments

Bibliographic work is not at all joyous. It is excruciatingly slow and frustrating, inherently painstaking and tedious. This bibliography was begun in 1958, completed in 1968. The sources have been found scattered across many libraries; the daily harvest has been irritatingly small, eyes have become sore, and one typist after another has quit in utter despair. Moreover, frequent discoveries that journals have been inconsistent and that skilled bibliographers have overlooked sources and made errors have led to the understanding that this work cannot possibly include everything of significance or be entirely free of error. The endeavor was sustained by the conviction that this bibliography was needed and would be very useful.

During most of the period 1963-1966, Erwin and Carol Welsch were really the mainstays of the project. Mr. Welsch was the History Librarian at Indiana University. The Welschs contributed to every aspect of the undertaking — the search, the checking, the organization, the technical aspects, the employment of helpers and typists, and even the typing. Their contributions have been invaluable if not indeed crucial to the completion of the bibliography.

For financial assistance I wish to express thanks to Indiana University and its West European Studies Program, whose grants of 1964 and 1967 provided for clerical assistance, travel to Midwestern libraries, and all typing expenses.

The search for sources was conducted in the libraries of Indiana University, Stanford University, the University of California at Berkeley, the University of Wisconsin, the University of Minnesota, and the Norwegian parliament.

Sven Groennings
Bloomington, Indiana

February 1, 1968

Abbreviations

Months

Ja	Ap	Jl	O
F	May	Aug	N
M	Je	S	D

Cities

Copenhagen: Coph. Philadelphia: Phila.
Helsinki: Hels. Reykjavik: Rey.
London: Lond. Stockholm: Stock.
New York: N.Y. Washington, D.C.: Wash.
Kristiania (former name of Oslo): Kra.

Journals, Serials, and Analyzed Monographs:

AcAr	Acta Archaeologia
ACNWA	Current Notes on World Affairs (Australia)
AcPsy	Acta Psychologica
AcSoc	Acta Sociologica
AdEd	Adult Education (A combination in 1951 of Adult Education Bulletin and Adult Education Journal)
AgHist	Agricultural History
AlpineJ	Alpine Journal
AmAnthro	American Anthropologist
AA	American Archivist
ABAJ	American Bar Association Journal
AER	American Economic Review
AHR	American Historical Review
AJCL	American Journal of Comparative Law
AJES	American Journal of Economics and Sociology
AJIL	American Journal of International Law
AJPH	American Journal of Public Health
AJS	American Journal of Sociology
AmPers	American Perspectives
AmT	American Teacher Magazine
APNS	Acta Psychiatrica et Neurologica Scandinavica
APSR	American Political Science Review
ASM	American Swedish Monthly
ASR	American-Scandinavian Review
ASEER	American Slavic and East European Review
AmSocR	American Sociological Review
ASIB	American-Swedish Institute Bulletin
AnColEc	Annals of Collective Economy
Annals	Annals of the American Academy of Political and Social Sciences
AAAG	Annals of the Association of American Geographers
ArbLJ	Arbitration Law Journal
Archiv	Archiv; An International Documentary Research Service
Arv	Arv; Tidskrift för Nordisk Folkminnesforsking
BoWP	Background on World Politics.

	Now: Background; Journal of the International Studies Association
BC	Baltic Countries. Continued after D, 1936 as:
BSC	Baltic and Scandinavian Countries
BR I	Baltic Review (Stock.). Superceded by:
BR II	Baltic Review [Free Estonia Committee] (N.Y.).
BFMB	Bank of Finland Monthly Bulletin
BdofTradeJ	Board of Trade Journal
BJS	British Journal of Sociology
BSMS	British Survey (Main Series)
BYIL	British Yearbook of International Law
BIFD	Bulletin for International Fiscal Documentation
BIN	Bulletin of International News
CGJ	Canadian Geographical Journal
CG	Canadian Geographer
CHistR	Catholic Historical Review
CEF	Central European Federalist
ChHist	Church History
Classica	Classica et Mediaevalia
Comm	Commentary
ComRep	Commerce Report
CGQ	Coop Grain Quarterly
CompEdR	Comparative Educational Review
CoR	Cooperative Review
CR	Contemporary Review
C&C	Cooperation and Conflict: Nordic Studies in International Politics
CPR	Cooperative Productive Review
CH	Current History
ACNIA	Current Notes on World Affairs (Australia)
CurSoc	Current Sociology
DFOJ	Danish Foreign Office Journal
DO	Danish Outlook
DF	Democracy in Finland (Hels.: Finnish Political Science Assoc., 1960). 104 p.
DeptStateBul	Department of State Bulletin
EBE	Economic Bulletin for Europe
E&W	East and West
EW	Eastern World
EG	Economic Geography
EconaHist	Economics and History

EcHistR	Economic History Review
EconJ	The Economic Journal
EdD	Education Digest
EdFor	Educational Forum
EdRes	Educational Research
EdRChina	Educational Review of China
EdYrbk	Educational Yearbook (Columbia University Teachers College, International Institute)
EkT	Ekonomisk Tidskrift
ElSchJ	Elementary School Journal
En	Encounter
EHR	English Historical Review
EEH	Entrepreneurial History
EFTA Bull	European Free Trade Association Bulletin
EFTA Rep	European Free Trade Association Reporter
EY	European Yearbook
FBIR	Federation of British Industries Review
Fennia	Fennia; Suomen maantieteelinen seurd; Sailskapet för Finlands Geografi
BFMB	Finlands Bank, Helsingfors. Monthly Bulletin. (Bank of Finland Monthly Bulletin)
FFP	Finnish Foreign Policy (Hels.: Finnish Political Science Assoc., 1963). 232 p.
FTR	Finnish Trade Review (Known as Finnish Trade, Ja 31, 1925-D 31, 1927; and as Finnish Trade Bulletin, Ja 31, 1928-D 31, 1929). M 1930—.
Focus	Focus (American Geographical Society)
Folk	Folk: Dansk etnografisk tidsskrift
Folk-Liv	Folk-Liv; Journal for European Ethnology and Folklore
F&A	Food and Agriculture
FA	Foreign Affairs
ForAg	Foreign Agriculture
ForComWk	Foreign Commerce Weekly
FED	Foreign Educational Digest
FPR	Foreign Policy Reports
FSJ	Foreign Service Journal
FT	Foreign Trade
Fortid og Nutid	Fortid og Nutid; Tidsskrift for Kulturhistorie og Lokalhistorie
Forum	Forum
Fremtiden	Fremtiden; Tidsskrift for international orientering
GT	Geografisk Tidsskrift

GeoA	Geografiska Annaler		Fiske Islandic Collection
GeogJ	Geographical Journal		at Cornell University
GeoM	Geographical Magazine	JAirLawCom	Journal of Air Law and
GeoR	Geographical Review		Commerce
Geog	Geography	JCEA	Journal of Central European
Gogelle	Gogelle; International Jour-		Affairs
	nal for Mass Communica-	JCL	Journal of Comparative
	tion Studies		Legislation
HER	Harvard Educational Review	JCH	Journal of Contemporary
Heimen	Heimen; Journal of the		History
	[Norwegian] National As-	JofDoc	Journal of Documentation
	sociation for County and	JofEH	Journal of Ecclesiastical
	Town History		History
Historian	Historian; Phi Alpha Theta	JEH	Journal of Economic History
Humaniora	Humaniora Norvegica; The	JofEd	Journal of Education (Lond.)
Norvegica	Year's Work in Norwegian	JES	Journal of Educational So-
	Humanities		ciology
HumRel	Human Relations	JFE	Journal of Farm Economy
IcR	Iceland Review	JFor	Journal of Forestry
IQ	India Quarterly	JofGeo	Journal of Geography
ILRR	Industrial and Labor Rela-	JofHEd	Journal of Higher Education
	tions Review	JHE	Journal of Home Economics
IndRel	Industrial Relations	JIA	Journal of International Af-
Ind	Industry		fairs
I&L	Industry and Labor	JKCGS	Journal of King's College
IPMJ	Institute of Personnel Man-		Geographical Society
	agement Journal	JM	Journal of Marketing
IA	International Affairs (Lond.)	JMH	Journal of Modern History
IAF	International Affairs	JPE	Journal of Political Economy
	(Moscow)	JP	Journal of Politics
IFLAP	International Federation of	KOPER	Kansallis-Osake-Pankki
	Library Associations Pub-		Economic Review
	lications	Ki	Kierkegaardiana
IGCong	International Geographical	L&N	Labor and Nation
	Congress, Papers	LM	Labor Monthly
IntJ	International Journal	LandEc	Land Economics. Until 1924
ILR	International Labor Review		published as: Journal of
IM	International Markets		Land and Public Utility
IO	International Observer		Economics
IOrg	International Organization	LCP	Law and Contemporary
IRAS	International Review of Ad-		Problems
	ministrative Sciences	LCQJ	Library of Congress Quar-
IntRevAg	International Review of		terly Journal
	Agriculture	LibJ	Library Journal
IntRE	International Review of	LibW	Library World
	Education	Libri	Libri; International Library
IRSH	International Review of		Review
	Social History	LBR	Lloyds Bank Review
ISSB	International Social Science	LSG	Lund Studies in Geography
	Bulletin. After v. 10		A: Physical Geography
	(1957) becomes:		B: Human Geography
ISSJ	International Social Science		C: General and Mathe-
	Journal		matical Geography
ISSAssoc	International Social Security	Lychnos	Lychnos (Uppsala); Annal of
	Association Bulletin		the Swedish History of Sci-
IYEd	International Yearbook of		ence Society
	Education	MilitaryR	Military Review
Islandica	Islandica; An Annual Relat-	MT	Monetary Times
	ing to Iceland and the	MLR	Monthly Labor Review

NGeogM	National Geographic Magazine	ScPolSt	Scandinavian Political Studies
NatObs	National Observer	ScSt	Scandinavian Studies
NIR	Nordisk immateriellt rättskyld	ScStCrim	Scandinavian Studies in Criminology
NoAmRev	North American Review	ScStL	Scandinavian Studies in Law
NorAmCom	Norwegian-American Commerce	Sc	Scandinavica; An International Journal of Scandinavian Studies
NMR	National Managerial Review	ScSl	Scando-Slavica
NT	Nationalokonomisk Tidsskrift	Sch&Soc	School and Society
		SchR	School Review
NTJ	National Tax Journal	SciS	Science and Society
New Eur	New Europe (Lond.)	SciM	Scientific Monthly
NiCen	Nineteenth Century and After	SGM	Scottish Geographical Magazine
Nord	Le Nord; Revue Internationale des pays du nord	SBQR	Skandinaviska Banken Quarterly Review
Nord. Tids. for Int. Ret	Nordisk Tidsskrift for International Ret	SlR	Slavic Review; American Quarterly of Soviet and East European Studies
NBB	Norges Bank Bulletin	SEER	Slavonic and East European Review
Norseman	The Norseman 1943-1958. Periodical of same name began publication in 1960 without volume numbering.	SocRes	Social Research
		SoCo	Socialist Commentary
		SocRur	Sociologia Ruralis
		SR	Sociological Review
NGT	Norsk Geographisk Tidsskrift	S&SR	Sociology and Social Research
Nor-Am	Norwegian-American Historical Association Publications	SC	Soil Conservation
		SAQ	South Atlantic Quarterly
		SSSQ	Southwestern Social Science Quarterly
NSN	Norwegian Shipping News	SPT	Soviet Press Translations
OISB	Bulletin of the Oxford University Institute of Statistics	SHI	Svenska Handelsbanken Index
		SRWA	Swiss Review of World Affairs
		TBR	Three Banks Review
PPT	Paedogogisk Psykologisk Tidsskrift	TCP	Town and Country Planning
ParAf	Parliamentary Affairs	TIBG	Transactions, Institute of British Geographers
PDK	Phi Delta Kappan	T	Triangle
PolQ	Political Quarterly	Unitas	Unitas Nordisk Föreningsbanken; Quarterly Review Describing Trade Conditions in Finland.
PSQ	Political Science Quarterly		
PolS	Political Studies		
PopSt	Population Studies		
PC	Problems of Communism		
PubFin	Public Finance	UNB	United Nations Bulletin, 1946-1954. Superceded by United Nations Review, 1954—.
POQ	Public Opinion Quarterly		
QJSA	Quarterly Journal of Studies on Alcohol		
Res	Research (Council of Europe Publications)	USNIP	U.S. Naval Institute Proceedings
RofES	Review of Economic Studies	WestSocTrans	Westermarck Society Transactions
RofER	Review of Educational Research	WPQ	Western Political Quarterly
		WA	World Affairs (Wash.)
RIC	Review of International Cooperation	WAI	World Affairs Interpreter
		WAQ	World Affairs Quarterly (Lond.)
RevPol	Review of Politics	WorldAg	World Agriculture
RS	Rural Sociology	WAAEB	World Association for Adult Education Bulletin
ScPP	Scandinavia Past and Present (Odense, 1959). 3 vols.	WP	World Politics
		WT	World Today
SEHR	Scandinavian Economic History Review	Yrbk of Ed	Yearbook of Education

Contents

ECONOMICS

INTRODUCTION

The entries in this section include both descriptions of segments of national economies and works of economic analysis. In both cases, the literature is plentiful and the contributors have been numerous. "Economics" is one of the largest sections in this bibliography; however, it is the least comprehensive. The listing of some journals' articles must be regarded as suggestive rather than exhaustive, because it has not been possible to review all the volumes of the numerous English-language bank and commercial journals which are published in Scandinavia. Regularly featured series of articles have usually been noted.

It may be useful to know that the statistical bureaus of the various governments regularly publish bulletins and occasionally publish lengthy surveys. Also, there are occasional OECD booklets of a survey character. Some other sections of this bibliography are relevant for the student of national economies, for example, the section on Law. For listings on social welfare, look under Sociology. For entries on economic geography, see Geography, and for additional entries concerning Nordic union, see International Relations. Sources on economic history will be found here under Economics, not under History.

Scholarly journals are *The Scandinavian Economic History Review*, whose every article is listed here, and *The Swedish Journal of Economics*, which tends to be highly theoretical and includes few articles of interest

to regional specialists. The Swedish *Skandinaviska Banken Quarterly Review* is excellent. Also good is *Svenska Handelsbanken Index*. Each issue of *The Swedish Economy*, published quarterly by the National Institute of Economic Research in Stockholm, covers foreign trade, the credit market, investments, production, the labor market, and economic prospects. One should also be aware of the *Swedish Monthly Economic Survey*, published by Göteborgs Bank. For Finland there are three bank journals of high quality: *Bank of Finland Monthly Bulletin, Kansallis-Osake-Pankki Economic Review*, and *Unitas*, the quarterly review of Nordiska Föreningsbanken. Articles on the Northern Countries appear in nearly every issue of the *EFTA Bulletin* and the *EFTA Reporter*. *Norwegian Shipping News* carries articles on all these countries. Its articles are almost always very short, and this bibliography contains entries from only a couple of representative years. Articles on economic conditions in Scandinavia appear frequently in *The American-Scandinavian Review, The Danish Foreign Office Journal, The Norseman*, and *The American-Swedish Monthly*. For current events, one may wish to consult the popular magazine, *The Scandinavian Times*.

There is no single volume on the development and structure of the region's economy, but whoever seeks an introduction might well begin by reading in *Scandinavia Between East and West* (1950), edited by Henning Friis, or by reviewing articles in the three magnificent volumes of *Scandinavia*

Past and Present (1959). Each article in these books is listed in this bibliography. One might also read Marquis Childs' *Sweden, the Middle Way* (1936, 1947), which is now available in paperback (1961). While the literature is particularly excellent on Sweden, it is also excellent on Norway. Only on Iceland is it very weak: there is only one book, William Chamberlin's *The Economic Development of Iceland Through World War II* (1947). For literature on problems pertaining to Icelandic fisheries, look under International Relations.

There is no survey book introducing the Danish economy, but there are commendable books on Danish labor and agriculture: Walter Galenson, *The Danish System of Labor Relations* (1952); Kristen Skovgaard, *Survey of Danish Agriculture* (1946); Einar Jensen, *Danish Agriculture, Its Economic Development: a Description and Economic Analysis Centering on the Free Trade Epoch, 1870-1930* (1937); there is also Einar Petersen's long description, *Danish Dairying: Production, Manufacture, Organization and Marketing* (1956, 1964), and N. Heigham's recent thesis, *Agricultural Ideas and Practice and Social Conditions in Denmark* (1964). On the export of agricultural commodities there is one unpublished dissertation, John Murphy's *Long-Term Contracts for the Export of Denmark's Butter and Bacon* (1955). These two other unpublished dissertations also focus on foreign trade: W. Beckerman's *Some Aspects of Monopoly and Monopsony in International Trade as Illustrated in Anglo-Danish Trade, 1921-1938* (1952), and Hans Jensen's very long and much broader *Foreign Trade, Institutional Change and Economic Development in Denmark* (1961). Finally, there are three published studies of Danish pricing, two of them clearly historical: Astrid Friis and Kristoff Glamann, *A History of Prices and Wages in Denmark, 1600-1800* (1959); *An Analysis of Price Behaviour during the Period 1855-1913* (1938) by Pedersen and Petersen; Bjarke Fog, *Industrial Pricing Policies: an Analysis of Pricing Policies of Danish Manufacturers* (1960).

On Finland there are numerous fine scholarly articles, but there is no introductory survey book. The historical depth of Carl Erik Knoellinger's superb *Labor in Finland* (1960) help it to qualify as a general survey, but one may prefer to turn to the works in economic geography by William Mead, most of which are listed under Geography, or to John Wuorinen's *A History of*

Finland (1965). Wuorinen presents chapters on "Economic Trends Before 1914," "The Economic Scene, 1918-1939," and "Economic Developments Since 1945." In Wuorinen's book economic developments can be seen in the context of developments in domestic politics and foreign relations. For the period immediately following World War I there are two thin books: *Effects of the War on Economic and Social Life in Finland* (1933) by Leo Harmaja, and *Economic Theory and Policy in Finland, 1914-25* (1958) by Erin Jucker-Fleetwood. The only monograph other than Knoellinger's which covers the period since World War II is like Knoellinger's in that it reviews economic problems in previous decades: Kaarlo Larna, *The Money Supply, Money Flows and Domestic Product in Finland, 1910-1956* (1959). There is a recently published dissertation on one of the most significant factors in Finnish economic life since World War II, Bartell Jensen's *The Impact of Reparations on the Post-war Finnish Economy: An Input-Output Study* (1966). There is no book on Finnish foreign trade.

Several economists have written books on aspects of Norway's comprehensive economic planning after World War II. The basic book, which is excellent, is Alice Bourneuf's *Norway, The Planned Revival* (1958). Complementary are Petter Bjerve's *Planning in Norway 1947-1956* (1959), and Mark Leiserson's *Wages and Economic Control in Norway, 1945-1957* (1959). Also complementary are three unpublished dissertations: Allen Barton, *Sociological and Psychological Problems of Economic Planning in Norway* (1957); Donald Syvrud, *Post-war Norwegian Financial Problems and Policies: A Study of the Monetary, Banking and Foreign Exchange Problem of Norway During the Post-War Years 1945-1949* (1956); Joseph Grunwald, *National Economic Budgeting in Norway* (1951). There are later dissertations on budgeting and on the demand for money: Henry Peskin's *The Norwegian Budget Model* (1965) and Edward Syring's *The Demand for Money in Norway: an Econometric Analysis* (1966). Lee Soltow's *Toward Income Equality in Norway* (1965) spans a century and is based on study of the cities in Vest Agder and Østfold counties. Two publications of the Norwegian Central Bureau of Statistics should also be mentioned: Arthur Stonehill's *Foreign Ownership in Norwegian Enterprises* (1965), and the volume edited by Odd Aukrust, *Norges økonomi etter krigen; The Norwegian Post-War Economy* (1965). For those who read Norwegian, the latter is the best broad survey of post-war economic development. It contains a summary in English. There is no book on Norwegian foreign trade.

On Norwegian labor there is a fine book, Walter Galenson's *Labor in Norway* (1949), nicely complemented by Herbert Dorfman's *Labor Relations in Norway* (1958). On cooperatives, see the books by O. B. Grimley, *Cooperatives in Norway* (1950) and *Agricultural Co-operatives in Norway* (1950). There are two books on Norway's industries: Kaare Peterson's history, *The Saga of Norwegian Shipping* (1955), and the descriptive volume edited by Olge Adamson, *Industries of Norway, Technical and Commercial Achievements* (1952). There is also an unpublished dissertation on the fishing industry, Lawrence Sommers' *The Norwegian Fishing Industry as Exemplified by Møre og Romsdal County* (1951). By the geographer Vincent Malmström there is a dissertation on transportation, *A Study of Land Transport in Norway* (1954). Finally, for students of early economic history one should mention John Gade's *The Hanseatic Control of Norwegian Commerce During the Late Middle Ages* (1951).

Sweden has produced many economists of wide renown, among them Gustav Cassel, Eli Heckscher, Erik Lindahl, Erik Lundberg, Gunnar Myrdal, and Knut Wicksell. There are two books on Wicksell, namely Torsten Gärdlund's *The Life of Knut Wicksell* (1958), and Carl Uhr's *Economic Doctrines of Knut Wicksell* (1960). There is also a dissertation by Benjamin Caplan, *The Wicksellian School: a Critical Study of the Development of Swedish Monetary Theory, 1898-1932* (1942). The purpose of this bibliography, however, is not to list Swedish contributions to economic theory, but to present writings about Sweden. Fortunately, these writings are extensive and include many studies of high quality. However, there is no survey book, analytical as well as descriptive, introducing the development and structure of the Swedish economy.

A popular introduction is Marquis Childs' *Sweden: the Middle Way* (1961 ed.). Journalist Wilfrid Fleisher's *Sweden, the Welfare State* (1956) is a popular survey of social and economic conditions, but hardly an academic treatment. Many non-Scandinavians have been particularly curious about the Swedish government's involvement in the economy. One aspect of this involvement, the scope and management of public enterprise, is well covered in *Public Enterprise*

in Sweden (1959) by Douglas Verney. On taxation there is an immense and encyclopedic work by Harvard University's International Program in Taxation entitled *Taxation in Sweden* (1959). There is also an unpublished dissertation by Lawrence Myers, *Taxation of Income and Property in Sweden* (1954). Although most of the literature on cooperatives was published in the 1930's, there are two post-war books: J. W. Ames, *Cooperative Sweden Today* (1952), and Åke Gullander, *Farmers' Co-operation in Sweden* (1948). On housing, see Leonard Silk, *Sweden Plans for Better Housing* (1948). For the development of Stockholm, look under Geography.

Eli F. Heckscher's *An Economic History of Sweden* (1954) is superb and easily read, but ends with the First World War. Heckscher died two years prior to this book's publication. His son, political scientist Gunnar Heckscher, contributed a supplementary chapter on "The Disintegration of Nineteenth-Century Society," and there is a thirty-page preface by Alexander Gerschenkron on the scholarly contributions of Eli Heckscher. *Wages, Cost of Living and National Income in Sweden 1860-1930* (1933, 1935, 1937) is an immense three-volume work by a group of Sweden's foremost economists. Closely parallel in its historical dimensions is O. Johansson's *The Gross Domestic Product of Sweden and Its Composition 1861-1955* (1967). For the growth of industry, see Arthur Montgomery, *The Rise of Modern Industry in Sweden* (1939); Lennart Jørberg, *Growth and Fluctuations of Swedish Industry, 1869-1912* (1961); Gunnar Löwegren, *Swedish Iron and Steel: an Historical Survey* (1948); Howard Smith, *The Development and Present Scope of Industry in Sweden* (1953). Sune Carlson has studied the behavior of modern managers: *Executive Behavior, a Study of the Work Load and the Working Methods of Managing Directors* (1951). A very able presentation not only of a major bank but also of the role of banking in developing industry between 1856 and 1914 is Olle Gasslander's *History of Stockholm Enskilda Bank to 1914* (1962). For policy in the inter-war period, see Arthur Montgomery, *How Sweden Overcame the Depression, 1930-1933* (1938). There is also an unpublished dissertation on this period, Ralph Holben's *Swedish Economic Policy and Economic Stability, 1927-1938* (1951). Economic adjustments during World War II are reviewed in Daniel Edwards' dissertation, *Process of Economic Adaptation in a World War*

II Neutral Country: a Case Study of Sweden (1961). On post-war monetary policy, see Reuben Miller's dissertation, *Swedish Monetary Policy in the Postwar Period, 1945-1961* (1966). On fiscal policy as an instrument for achieving growth and stability, see Henry Andersson's dissertation, *Effects of Swedish Fiscal Policy on Economic Growth and Stability, 1930-1964* (1966). Two very recent analyses of Sweden's economic growth, each an unpublished American dissertation, are Richard Park's *An Econometric Model of Swedish Economic Growth, 1861-1955* (1966) and Maurice Wilkinson's *Swedish Economic Growth: a Model of the Long Swing* (1965). Another recent analysis, overwhelmingly mathematical, is the book by B. Höglund and L. Werin, *The Production System of the Swedish Economy: an Input-Output Study* (1964).

With regard to foreign trade, the available book literature fails to provide a good overview. There are three books: Gunnar Fridlizius, *Swedish Corn Export in the Free Trade Era, Patterns in the Oats Trade, 1850-1880* (1957); Ernst Söderlund, Annagreta Hallberg, and Jan Sanden, *Swedish Timber Exports, 1850-1950* (1952); Erin Fleetwood, *Sweden's Capital Imports and Exports* (1947). There is one unpublished dissertation on the balance of payments, Marcus Bruhn's *Sweden's Balance of Payments 1920-1950* (1955).

Sweden is well known for its peaceful labor relations, and the books on this subject are numerous. The most recent books are Thomas Johnston's *Collective Bargaining in Sweden, a Study of the Labour Market and Its Institutions* (1962), and Folke Schmidt's *The Law of Labour Relations in*

Sweden (1962). Older books are: Marquis Childs, *This Is Democracy: Collective Bargaining in Scandinavia* (1938); James Robbins, *The Government of Labor Relations in Sweden* (1942); Paul Norgren, *The Swedish Collective Bargaining System* (1941); Charles Myers, *Industrial Relations in Sweden: Some Comparisons with American Experience* (1951). Closely related to these books is John Wounsch's unpublished dissertation, *The Contribution of the Swedish Labor Movement 1940-1950 to Industrial Relations* (1953). There are three additional unpublished American dissertations on the organization of labor and employment policy: Richard Underhill, *Centralization in the Swedish Labor Market* (1965); Ludwig Wagner, *The Wage Policy of the Swedish Trade Unions under Full Employment and Full Unionization* (1955); Walter Langway, *The Employment Security Program in Sweden and Its Possible Applications to the United States* (1965). Finally, there are two older books: Harrison Clark, *Swedish Unemployment Policy, 1914 to 1940* (1941), and Carl Ratzlaff, *The Scandinavian Unemployment Relief Program* (1934).

In conclusion, the literature on Scandinavia's economic systems is best with regard to organized labor. It is very weak on foreign trade, on public finance, and on agricultural economics. There is no good introductory book which presents the development and structure of a national economy both descriptively and analytically. While there is ample literature to serve as the basis for comparative analysis, there are no landmark comparative studies.

SCANDINAVIA

Ames, J. W. "The Scandinavian Wholesale Society," AnColEc, 26 (1955), 243-49.

Angus, J. Houston. "The Geography of Power: Its Sources and Transmission," GeogJ, 118 (1952), 251-61.

Bjerve, Petter J. "Government Economic Planning and Control," in Henning Friis, ed., Scandinavia Between East and West (Ithaca, 1950), 49-111.

Bliss, G. L. "Impressions of Housing in Scandinavia," Savings and Loan Journal (Aug 1953), 18-20+.

Boardman, A. G. "A New Look at Northern Europe," Dun's Review (F 3, 1951), 27+.

Bolin, Sture. "Tax Money and Plough Money." SEHR, 2 (1954), 3-21.

Bonow, Mauritz. "Economic Democracy," in J. A. Lauwerys, ed., Scandinavian Democracy (Coph., N.Y., 1958), 261-79.

Carlson, Sune. "Management of State-Owned Industries: Some Scandinavian Experiences," SBQR, 41 (1960), 81-90.

Columbia University, School of Business. Scandinavian Banking Laws: a Translation of the Acts and Regulations Governing the Central Banks. N.Y., 1926. 122 p.

Comstock, Alzada. "Recovery in Scandinavia," CH, 19 (Jl 1950), 1-4.

"Co-ordination of Wage Statistics in the
Scandinavian Countries and Finland," ILR,
63 (1951), 279-86.

Davey, Harold W. "Formulating the Federal
Government's Economic Program: the
Experience of Other Countries," APSR,
42 (1948), 295-306.

Delegations for the Promotion of Economic
Cooperation Between the Northern Countries. The Northern Countries in the
World Economy: Denmark, Finland,
Iceland, Norway, Sweden. Hels., 1937.
240 p.; 2d ed. 1939, 183 p.; 3d ed. 1952,
240 p.

Drachmann, Povl. The Industrial Development and Commercial Policies of the
Three Scandinavian Countries (Carnegie
Endowment for International Peace Publications). N.Y., 1915. 130 p.

Economic Conditions and Banking Problems.
Saltsjöbaden, Sweden, 1950. 281 p.

"EFTA Success Stories in Scandinavia,"
EFTA Rep (F 20, 1967), 4-5.

Empson, E. "Housing Abroad," CR, 26
(1952), 254-57, 284-85; 27 (1953), 14-15.

"Family Allowance Schemes in 1947: I,"
ILR, 57 (1948), 315-33.

Holmstedt, Gustaf. "Social Expenditures in
Scandinavian Countries," SBQR, 33 (O
1952), 96-100.

Hovde, Brynjolf J. "Economic Developments in Post-War Scandinavia," ASR,
36 (1948), 342-47.

International Monetary Fund, Research De-
partment, Statistics Division. Papers on
International Financial Statistics. No. 2,
Survey of Money and Banking Statistics,
Denmark; 1951. No. 28, Survey of Money
and Banking Statistics, Finland; 1952.
No. 30, Banking in Norway; 1953. Wash.

Jensen, Adolph L. O. "The Scandinavian
Nations," in A History of Banking in All
the Leading Nations, v. 4 (N.Y., 1896),
373-406.

Kjaer Hansen, Max. Selling Costs and Advertising Expenditure in Scandinavia: an
Analysis and Evaluation of the Costs of
Commercial Advertising in Denmark,
Finland, Norway and Sweden (Federation
of Nordic Marketing Associations Publications, no. 1). Coph., 1956. 40 p.

Krefetz, Gerald, and Ruth Marossi. "Scan-
dinavia and Finland," in their, Investing
Abroad: a Guide to Financial Europe
(N.Y., 1965), 203-25.

Kristensen, Thorkil. "State Intervention and
Economic Freedom," in J. A. Lauwerys,

ed., Scandinavian Democracy (Coph.,
N.Y., 1958), 192-218.

Laursen, Svend. "The Scandinavian Coun-
tries in a Changing World Economy," in
Henning Friis, ed., Scandinavia Between
East and West (Ithaca, 1950), 23-47.

Leppo, Matti. "The Double-Budget System
in the Scandinavian Countries," PubFin,
5 (1950), 137-46.

Lundberg, Erik. "Stability Problems in the
Scandinavian Countries During the Post-
war Period," AER, 51 (1961), 378-89.

Martinez, Orlando. "Automation and Scandinavia," Norseman, 16 (1958), 86-90.

Montgomery, Arthur et al. "Contemporary
Scandinavia: Historical Forward," by
Arthur Montgomery; "Main Trends in
Norway's Economy," by Wilhelm Keilhau;
"Post-War Economic Problems in Den-
mark," by Carl Iversen. LBR, (Ap-O
1948), 13-34; 21-33; 22-38.

Moritzen, Julius. "The Perils of Scandinavia," NoAmRev, 205 (1917), 228-37.

———. "Scandinavian and European Reconstruction," CH, 9 (1945), 308-10.

———. "Scandinavian Renaissance," CH, 8
(1945), 330-35.

Morstein Marx, Fritz. "The Divided Budget
in Scandinavian Practice," NTJ, 8 (1955),
186-200.

Myhre, J. F. Handbook of Leading and Dis-
charging Ports with Special Regard to the
Timber Trade in Sweden, Finland, Norway, Denmark, Faroe Islands, Iceland,
Poland, Germany, Germany (Russian
Zone), Netherlands, Belgium, Great Britain, Northern Ireland, Erie, Russia. 10th
ed. 1950. [Title varies]

"National Budgets in Europe — Post War Experiments in National Income Forecasting
in the United Kingdom, the Netherlands
and Scandinavia," EBE, 5 (1952-53), 63-82.

"Neutral Flags: the Scandinavian-American
Line," ASR, 4 (1916), 106-10.

Nordic Council. Yearbook of Nordic Statistics. 1962—.

"Not Feeding Germany," ASR, 5 (1917),
201-205.

O'Dell, Andrew C. "The Hinterland Areas
of Scottish and Scandinavian Ports in Relation to Industrial Development," IGCong,
17th (1952), 161-64.

Oersted, H. C. "Employers' Organizations
in the Northern Countries," ILR, 8 (1923),
333-44.

Organization for European Economic Cooperation. Economic Condition in: Denmark, Iceland, Norway and Sweden. 1953-
1961. N 1961 became OECD. Each year

contains articles and statistics by country, including basic statistics, government, living standards, trade, etc. Each
booklet 37-60 p.
——. Europe and the World Economy. 11th
Annual Economic Review. Paris, 1960.
138 p.
——. Policies for Sound Economic Growth.
10th Annual Economic Review. Paris,
1959. 133 p.
Ovesen, Liv. "Consumer Protection in
Scandinavia," AnColEc, 28 (1957), 88-95.
——. "Consumer Protection in Scandina-
via" [Norway's measures, compared with
those of Sweden and Denmark], Cartel, 6
(Ap 1956), 38-43.
Paulsson, Thomas. Scandinavian Architec-
ture: Buildings and Society in Denmark,
Finland, Norway, Sweden from the Iron
Age until Today. Lond., 1958; Newton
Centre, Mass., 1959. 256 p.
"Recent Developments in Scandinavia," Sta-
tist, International Banking Section (N 18,
1950), 22-24.
Raymond, William L. "The Strength of the
Viking Nations," in his, National Govern-
ment Loans (Boston, Lond., 1925), 159-
75.
Scandinavian Year Book: a Comprehensive
Guide to Commerce, Industry and Tour-
ism in Denmark, Norway and Sweden.
Lond., 1952——.
Some Notes on the Scandinavian Market.
Stock., 1963. 57 p.
Svennilson, Ingvar. Growth and Stagnation
in the European Economy. Geneva, 1954.
342 p.
Tait, Alan, and J. F. Due. "Sales Taxation
in Eire, Denmark, and Finland," NTJ, 18
(1965), 286-96.
Tanner, Väinö A. "Some Economic Prob-
lems in the North," Nord, 1 (1938), 274-
80.
Thorelli, Hans. "Anti-Trust in Europe:
National Policies After 1945," University
of Chicago Law Review, 26 (1959), 222-36.
Twentieth Century Fund. Europe's Needs
and Resources: Trends and Prospects in
Eighteen Countries. By J. Frederic Dew-
hurst, John O. Coppock, P. Lamartine
Yates, and Associates. N.Y., 1961.
1198 p.
Voskuil, W. H. "Scandinavia's Fuel Problem," SciM, 51 (1940), 466-69.

MONETARY POLICY

Keilhau, Wilhelm C. "The Monetary Problem of the North," ASR, 21 (1933), 151-56.

Lester, Richard A. "Recent Scandinavian
Experiments," in his, Monetary Experi-
ments, Early American and Recent Scan-
dinavian (Princeton, 1939), 173-283.
Meissner, Frank. "Scandinavia Rediscovers
Monetary Policy," Norseman, 13 (1955),
368-76.
Wicksell, Knut. "The Scandinavian Gold
Policy," EconJ, 26 (1916), 313-18.

NORDIC AND EUROPEAN ECONOMIC INTEGRATION

Belinfante, Johan F. E. "The Oslo Conven-
tions," BSC, 4 (1938), 43-46.
Bellquist, Eric C. "Inter-Scandinavian Co-
operation," Annals, 168 (1933), 183-96.
Boeg, Nils V. "Scandinavian Interchange,"
ASR, 7 (1919), 50-52.
Clift, A. Denis. "North Sea Gas: a Case
Study in International Cooperation," WT,
23 (1967), 146-52.
European Free Trade Association. EFTA
Bulletin (1960——) and EFTA Reporter
(1953——). Frequent short articles.
——. Building EFTA: a Free Trade Area
in Europe. Geneva, 1967. 150 p.
——. The European Free Trade Associa-
tion Today and Tomorrow. Geneva, 1964.
43 p.
——. The Importance of the EEC Market
to EFTA Countries. Geneva, 1966. 24 p.
——. The Importance of the EFTA Market
to the Six Member Countries of the EEC.
Geneva, 1965. 12 p.
"Free Trade in EFTA," EFTA Bull, special
issue, 8 (1967, no. 1), 36 p.
Free Trade in Western Europe. A Joint
Statement by the Industrial Federations
and Employers' Organizations of Austria,
Denmark, Norway, Sweden, Switzerland,
the United Kingdom. Paris, Ap 14, 1958.
Coph., 1958. 16 p.
Gormsen, Marius. "The Oslo Conventions,"
BSC, 4 (1938), 39-42.
Hatt, Gudmund. "The Potentialities of Inter-
Northern Commerce," Nord, 1 (1938),
143-62.
Ingstad, Helge. "Scandinavian Co-operation
in the West Greenland Fisheries," Norse-
man, 13 (1955), 222-29.
Jonsson, Per Olof. "The Scandinavian Cus-
toms Union and the Marshall Plan," SSSQ,
47 (1966), 287-98.
Karjalainen, Ahti. "Plan for the Expansion
and Improvement of Economic Coopera-
tion in the Nordic Countries," BFMB, 31
(1957, no. 12), 18-21.
Lambert, J. R. "Enlargement of the Common

Market: Denmark, Norway, and Iceland," WT, 18 (1962), 350-60.

Lange, Gunnar. "EFTA's Contribution to Scandinavia," EFTA Rep (O 25, 1965), 4-5.

Leistikow, Gunnar. "Scandinavian Collaboration; What It Was — What It May Be," ASR, 30 (1942), 15-23.

Lundgren, Nils. "Nordic Common Market, For and Against," EFTA Bull, 7 (1966, no. 2), 1-7; (no. 3), 10-15. Partially reprinted: "A Nordic Common Market? Pros and Cons," EFTA Rep (M 28, 1966), 6-7.

Martinez, Orlando. "Scandinavian Cooperation," CR, 197 (1959), 300-303.

Meissner, Frank. "Scandinavian Customs Union," Norseman, 12 (1954), 246-54.

Meyer, Frederick V. The Seven: a Provisional Appraisal of the European Free Trade Association. Lond., 1960. 140 p.

Montgomery, Arthur. "Economic Fellowship, Past and Present Between Finland and Sweden," Nord, 3 (1940), 81-93.

——. "From a Northern Customs Union to EFTA," SEHR, 8 (1960), 45-70.

"Nordic Council Calls for Closer EFTA Cooperation," EFTA Bull, 9 (1968, no. 3), 2-4.

"Nordic Countries Bid for EEC Membership," EFTA Rep (Aug 28, 1967), 4-6.

Nordic Economic Cooperation Committee. "Plan for Closer Economic Cooperation," in Nordic Economic Cooperation; Report. Coph., 1958. 143 p.

——. Nordic Economic Cooperation; Supplementary Report. Coph., 1959. 43 p.

Ohlin, Bertil. "Some Aspects of the European Economic Integration — A View from the North," C&C (1965, no. 1), 74-78.

Olsson, Bertil. "The Common Employment Market for the Northern Countries," ILR, 68 (1953), 364-74.

Procopé, Hjalmar G. "Cooperation and Competition in the North," BSC, 5 (1939), 9-11.

——. "Economic Cooperation Between the Northern Countries and the Joint Delegation for Its Promotion," Nord, 1 (1938), 48-58.

Sandberg, Ole R. "Free Trade in Agricultural Products?" EFTA Bull, 9 (1968, no. 3), 16-18.

"A Scandinavian Customs Union," SHI (M 1948), 18-24.

Scott, Franklin D. "An 1813 Proposal for a Zollverein," JMH, 22 (1950), 359-61.

The Seven. Stockholm Plan for a European Free Trade Association (Chamber of

Commerce Booklet no. 2 [G.O.T.]). Written by Lewis Payne in consultation with R. L. Wills. Lond., 1959. 24 p.

Suviranta, Bruno K. "Economic Cooperation Between the Northern Countries," BC, 1 (1935), 183-85.

Wuorinen, John H. "Scandinavia Looks at European Unity," CH, 42 (1962), 160-65.

SCANDINAVIAN AIRLINES SYSTEM (SAS)

Bahr, Henrik. "The Scandinavian Airlines System (SAS): Its Origin, Present Organization and Legal Aspects," Arkiv for Luftrett, 1 (1961), 199-253.

Heistein, B. John. "United Nations of the Air," ASIB, 8 (1953), 9-21.

Medbøe, Odd. "Jet Trails Around the World: Sometimes Called the 'United Nations of the Air,' SAS is Today the Sixth Largest Airline in the World," Norseman (1960, no. 2), 25-27.

Nelson, Robert A. Scandinavian Airlines System: a Study in International Cooperation. Thesis (Ph.D.), Clark University, 1954. 281 p.

——. "Scandinavian Airlines System: Cooperation in the Air," JAirLawCom, 20 (1953), 178-96.

Throne-Holst, H. "Scandinavian Airlines System," ScPP, III, 373-78.

FOREIGN TRADE

"America, Scandinavia and Russian Trade," New Eur, 16 (1920), 307-10.

Boston National Shawmut Bank. Scandinavia and Its Trade Opportunities. Boston, 1919. 12 p.

Cowie, Donald. "Scandinavia and the Dominions," Norseman, 1 (1943), 386-92.

European Free Trade Association. EFTA Trade 1959-1964. Geneva, 1966. 98 p.

Flinn, Michael. "Scandinavian Iron Ore Mining and the British Steel Industry, 1870-1914," SEHR, 2 (1954), 31-46.

Giordano, Antonio. "Baltic and Scandinavian Trade with the Balkans During the First Half of 1938," BSC, 5 (1939), 42-46.

——. "The Economic and Maritime Penetration of the Baltic and Scandinavian Countries in the Mediterranean," BSC, 4 (1938), 64-67.

——. "Trade and Shipping Relations Between Italy and the Baltic Countries," BC, 3 (1937), 77-81.

Goldstein, E. Ernest. American Enterprise and Scandinavian Anti-Trust Law. Austin, Texas, 1963. 391 p.

Hambro, Johan. "They Circle the Globe,"
Norseman (1961, no. 6), 27-30.

Hartogsohn, S. "Scandinavia and the Sterling
Area," in Economic Conditions and Banking Problems (Saltsjöboden, Sweden,
1950), 129-43.

Humlum, Johs. "The World Crisis in the
Baltic Trade" [Summary of Danish arti-
cle], GT, 40 (1937), 53-57.

International Markets, 1953, features Scandinavia.

Johnston, N. D. Trading Opportunities in
Scandinavia. Ottawa, 1922. 184 p.

Keuster, Joseph de. "Competition Between
Antwerp and Rotterdam in Their Relations with the Baltic," BSC, 4 (1938),
53-57.

Morgenstierne, Bredo. "The Commercial
Policy of Scandinavia," ASR, 5 (1917),
9-13.

Moriarty, Daniel J. "Scandinavian Foreign
Trade in Fresh Fruits," ComRep, 32
(1928), 343-47.

"Nordic Trade Important for U.S.," EFTA
Rep (Ap 15, 1968), 2-3.

Organization for European Economic Cooperation. Foreign Trade Statistical Bulletin, 1950—.

Polkowski, Boleslaw. "The Foreign Trade
of the Baltic Countries in 1935," BSC, 3
(1937), 296-304.

Rutkowski, Stanislaw. "Dispersion of Baltic
and Scandinavian Foreign Trade," BSC, 4
(1938), 198-203.

"Scandinavia and Asia," EW (M 1952),
40-48.

Scandinavia, U.S.A. — 1960. 8th Annual ed.
East Norwalk, Conn. [Title varies]

Schwedtman, Ferdinand C. V. The Development of Scandinavian-American Trade
Relations. N.Y., 1921. 125 p.

Sweden, Union of Cooperatives. "Scandinavian Cooperative Export Society,"
AnColEc, 26 (1955), 250-52.

Tabak, Boleslaw. "The Significance of the
Rhine for the Baltic and Scandinavian
Countries," BSC, 4 (1938), 58-63.

Thoman, Richard S. Free Ports and Foreign
Trade Zones. Cambridge, Md., 1956.
203 p.

United States, Bureau of Foreign and Domestic Commerce. Automotive Markets
of Scandinavian Countries and Finland
(Trade Information Bull. no. 629). Wash.,
1929.

FOREIGN TRADE IN EARLIER ERAS

Bamford, P. W. "French Shipping in Northern European Trade, 1660-1789," JMH,
26 (1954), 207-209.

Christensen, Aksel E. "Scandinavia and the
Advance of the Hanseatics," SEHR, 5
(1957), 89-117.

Fredrickson, J. William. "American Shipping in the Trade with Northern Europe,
1783-1860," SEHR, 4 (1956), 109-25.

Hinton, Raymond W. K. The Eastland Trade
and the Common Weal in the Seventeenth
Century. Cambridge, 1959. 244 p.

Hitchcock, Frank H. Our Trade With Scandinavia, 1890-1900 (U. S. Dept. of Agriculture, Section of Foreign Markets, Bull.
no. 22). Wash., 1901. 124 p.

Lewis, Archibald R. The Northern Seas:
Shipping and Commerce in Northern Europe A.D. 300-1100. Princeton, 1958.
498 p.

Malowist, Marian. "The Baltic and the
Black Sea in Medieval Trade," BSC, 3
(1937), 36-42.

Öhlberg, Arne. "Russia and the World Market in the Seventeenth Century," SEHR, 3
(1955), 123-62.

Rasch, Aage. "American Trade in the
Baltic, 1783-1807," SEHR, 13 (1965),
31-64.

Tonning, Ole. Commerce and Trade on the
North Atlantic, 850 A.D. to 1350 A.D. Including England, Ireland, Iceland, Greenland, Scotland, and Norway. Thesis (Ph.D.),
University of Minnesota, 1935. 325 p.

United States, Department of Agriculture, Division of Foreign Markets. Norway, Sweden, and Russia as Markets for Packing
House Products; Imports from Principal
Countries, 1895-1904. Wash., 1906. 21 p.

INDUSTRY, SHIPPING

Daugherty, William T. Chemical Industries
and Trade of Norway and Denmark (U.S.
Bureau of Foreign and Domestic Commerce. Trade Information Bull. no. 780).
Wash., 1931. 32 p.

"The Era of Light Metals," ASR, 7 (1919),
202-205.

"Industrial Home Work," ILR, 58 (1948),
735-51.

Kiaer, A. N. "Historical Sketch of the Development of Scandinavian Shipping." JPE
(1892), 329-63.

Knee, Derek. "Retailing in EFTA: Scandinavia," EFTA Bull, 5 (1964, no. 6), 2-5.

Lien, Marie E. The Scandinavian Organization for the Promotion of Home Industries
in Arts and Crafts. Thesis (Ph.D.), Columbia University, 1944. 135 p.

Magnússon, Eiríkr. Notes on Shipbuilding and Nautical Terms of Old in the North. Lond., 1906. 56 p.

Nordell, Bengt. "The Steel Industry in EFTA," EFTA Bull, 5 (1964, no. 6), 2-5.

"Small-Scale Rural Industries in Northern Europe," ILR, 19 (1929), 704-708.

Talvitie, Y. "Chemical Industries of the Scandinavian Countries and Finland," Chemical Trade News, 5 (1953), 67-75.

United States, Bureau of Mines, Foreign Minerals Division. "Mineral Production and Trade of Denmark, Finland, Norway and Sweden," Foreign Minerals Quarterly, 2 (1939), 1-74.

Vaigo, A. C. "Scandinavia's Response to the Science Boom," New Scientist, 30 (1966), 600-601.

Wilson, C. F. et al. "Fur-Production in Scandinavia," Foreign Trade (Canada), 108 (D 21, 1957), 11-14.

HOUSING

Abrams, Charles. "Housing," in Henning Friis, ed., Scandinavia Between East and West (Ithaca, 1950). 169-98.

Graham, John. Urban and Rural Housing in Scandinavia. Chapel Hill, N. C., 1940. 223 p.

United States Congress, House Committee on Banking and Currency. Cooperative Housing Abroad. Wash., 1950, 47 p.

——. Cooperative Housing in Europe. Wash., 1950. 112 p.

LABOR, LABOR RELATIONS, UNEMPLOYMENT

Baude, Annika, and Per Holmberg. "The Positions of Men and Women in the Labour Market," in Edmund Dahlström, ed., The Changing Role of Men and Women (Lond., 1967), 105-34.

Childs, Marquis W. This is Democracy: Collective Bargaining in Scandinavia. New Haven, 1938. 169 p.

"Collaboration of the Northern European Labour Movements," ILR, 52 (1945), 424-26.

"Conditions of Domestic Employment in the Scandinavian Countries," ILR, 41 (1940), 614-33.

Galenson, Walter. "The Labor Movement and Industrial Relations," in Henning Friis, ed., Scandinavia Between East and West (Ithaca, 1950), 113-38.

——. "The Scandinavian Labor Movement," in his, Comparative Labor Movements (N.Y., 1952), 104-72. Reprint no. 40, Institute of Industrial Relations, University of California.

Holter, Harriet. "Disputes and Tensions in Industry," in J. A. Lauwerys, ed., Scandinavian Democracy (Coph., N.Y., 1958), 219-60.

——. "Women's Occupational Situation in Scandinavia," ILR, 93 (1966), 383-400.

"The Influx of Young People into the Employment Market in Western and Northern Europe," ILR, 75 (1957), 335-53.

Lange, Halvard M. "Scandinavia," in Hilary A. Marquard, ed., Organized Labour in Four Continents (Lond., N.Y., 1939), 229-86.

Montgomery, Bo Gabriel. British and Continental Labour Policy: the Political Labour Movement and Labour Legislation in Great Britain, France and the Scandinavian Countries, 1900-1922. Lond., 1922. 575 p.

Ratzlaff, Carl J. The Scandinavian Unemployment Relief Program. Phila., 1934. 211 p.

"Seafarers' Welfare, Some Post-War Development," ILR, 58 (1958), 625-36.

"Statistics of Occupied Population in Different Countries (Finland, Sweden)," ILR, 36 (1937), 264-70.

"Survey of Wages in Denmark, Norway, Sweden," MLR, 34 (1932), 942-69.

"Unemployment in Scandinavian Countries," ILR, 18 (1928), 249-55.

"Unemployment Insurance, Agreement between the Nordic Countries: Crediting of Contributions and Employment Periods," I&L, 23 (1960), 413-14.

United States, Bureau of Labor Statistics. Labor-Management Relations in Scandinavia. Wash., 1952. 25 p.

Thorsell, Siv. "Employer Attitudes to Female Employees," in Edmund Dahlström, ed., The Changing Role of Men and Women (Lond., 1967), 135-69.

Waris, Heikki. "Workers' Participation in Management in Scandinavian Industry," AcSoc, 4 (1959), 1-6.

COOPERATIVES

Hillman, Arthur. "Relationships of the Cooperative and Labor Movements," S&SR, 6 (1951), 399-405.

Hirsch, Edith J. "Producer and Consumer Cooperatives," in Henning Friis, ed., Scandinavia Between East and West (Ithaca, 1950), 199-223.

Örne, Anders E. Cooperative Ideals and

Problems. Manchester, 1926. 143 p.
Rev. ed. Manchester, 1937. 157 p.

Parker, Florence E. "Scandinavia and Finland," Part 2 of "Cooperatives in Postwar
Europe," MLR, 66 (1948), 386-91.

Peel, Roy V. "Consumers' Cooperation in
the Scandinavian Countries," Annals, 191
(1937), 165-76.

"Some Examples of Cooperative Organization Among Fishermen," Part III: Denmark, 336-40; Part VI: Norway, 347-51.
AnColEc, 11 (1935).

Tanner, Väinö A. "The Consumers' Cooperative Movement in the Northern Countries," IO, 1 (1936/37), 63-78.

AGRICULTURE

"Agricultural Conditions and Labour Agreements in Denmark and Sweden," ILR, 2
(1921), 97-118.

"Agricultural Policy in Scandinavian Countries," ILR, 81 (1960), 25-46.

Bjurling, Oscar. "The Barons' Revolution"
[Agricultural reform in Denmark and
Sweden in the late 18th and early 19th
centuries], EconaHist, 2 (1959), 19-37.

"Conditions of Work and Productivity in
North-European Agriculture," ILR, 67
(1957), 173-78.

European Free Trade Association. Agriculture in EFTA. Geneva, 1965. 147 p.

——. Annual Review of Agricultural Trade
1964. Geneva, 1964. 44 p.

——. Annual Review of Agricultural Trade
1965. Geneva, 1965. 38 p.

Food Research Institute, Stanford University. "The Wheat Situation in Scandinavia," Wheat Studies of the Food Research
Institute, 7 (1931, no. 7), 347-404.

Koht, Halvdan. "Self-Assertion of the Farming Class," Mélanges d'Histoire Offerts à
Henri Pirenne (Brussels, 1926), 271-78.

Nellemann, George. "Theories on Reindeer
Breeding," Folk, 3 (1961), 91-103.

Whyte, R. O., R. L. Crocker, and Martin
Jones. Farming Systems and Post-War
Problems in the Northern Countries.
1948. 6 p. Reprinted from Agriculture:
the Journal of the Ministry of Agriculture
[Great Britain], 55 (1948), 242-47.

——. Grass Farming in the Northern
Countries. 1947. Reprinted from Journal of the British Grassland Society, 2
(1947), 195-205.

FORESTRY, FOREST INDUSTRIES

Champion, H. G. "Scandinavian Forestry,"

Empire Forestry Review, 25 (1946), 169-
79.

"Forestry Legislation in the Scandinavian
Countries," IntRevAg, 20 (1929), Part II:
Monthly Bulletin of Agricultural Eco-
nomics and Sociology, 125-30.

Handbook of the Northern Wood Industries:
Timber, Woodpulp, Paper. Sweden, Norway, Finland. Stock., irregular.

Ilvessalo, Yrjö. "A Comparison Between the
Forest Resources of the Northern Countries," BFMB, 8 (1931), 22-28.

Lagerloef, Eric G. "Scandinavian Pulp and
Paper Industries — Their Past, Present,
and Future," ForComWk, 15 (1944),
5-11+.

Liersch, J. E. "Observations on Forestry
Practice in Scandinavia," JFor, 50 (1952),
299-302.

Lyrholm, T. L. Handbook of the Northern
Wood Industries. Stock., 1934.

Marsh, Raymond E. Public Policy Toward
Private Forest Land in Sweden, Norway,
and Finland. Wash., 1954. 80 p.

Salger, Michael. "Where the Green Gold is
Minted: the Forests of Norway and Sweden," GeoM, 33 (1960/61), 635-42.

Spencer, Arthur. "Scandinavian Timber,"
Magazine of the Future, 4 (1949), 31-37.

United States, Office of International Trade.
Pulp and Paper Developments in Sweden,
Norway, and Finland (World Trade in
Commodities, pt. 10, v. 7, no. 34). By O.
K. Krogfose. Wash., May 1950. 8 p.

DENMARK

Bernhard, John T. "Empirical Collectivism
in Denmark," JP, 13 (1951), 623-46.

Bjerke, K. "The National Product of Denmark, 1870-1952," in S. Kusnets, ed., Income and Wealth, series V (Lond., 1955),
123-51.

Copenhagen Institute of Economics and History. Economic Conditions in Denmark.
Ap/Je, 1927+. English summaries of articles in Økonomi og Politik.

Currie, James. Denmark: Economic and
Commercial Conditions in Denmark,
April, 1955. Lond., 1955. 105 p.

Danmarks Nationalbank Monetary Review.
Quarterly, May 1962—. [Consists of economic tables relating to the Bank and to
general economic conditions]

Denmark, Information Office. Economic and
Commercial Conditions in Denmark.
N.Y., 1948. 5 p. Mimeographed.

Denmark, Economic Secretariat. The Danish

Economy in 1958 and Prospects for 1959: a Summary of the Economic Survey of Denmark, 1959. 14 p.
——. Economic Survey of Denmark, 1949. Annual. Coph., 1949—. 45-95 p.
Denmark, Ministry of Foreign Affairs. Danish Foreign Office Journal and Danish Commercial Review. Quarterly. Coph., 1920—.
——. Economic and Commercial Conditions in Denmark. Coph., 1948. 5 p.
Denmark, Ministry of Foreign Affairs and Danish Statistical Department. Denmark. Coph., 1924—.
——. Factors in Danish Economic Life. 1934. 50 p.
Denmark, National Committee on Technical Assistance. Denmark and the United Nations Expanded Program of Technical Assistance. Coph., 1956. 23 p.
"Denmark's Buying Power," Triangle, 1 (1947), 8-11.
"Denmark: Return to Prosperity," Petroleum Press Service, 20 (1953), 326-28.
Denmark, the Centre of Trade with Centuries of Tradition. Coph., 1953. 34 p.
"Denmark Today: Political and Economic Problems," WT, 3 (1947), 477+.
"Economic Conditions in Denmark: Report on the Economic and Employment Position," ICFTU Economic and Social Bulletin (S 1953), 6-8.
"Economic Destruction of Denmark," ASR, 29 (1941), 125-28.
"Economic Post-War Problems in Denmark," ILR, 53 (1946), 186-94.
"Economic Review," DFOJ quarterly feature.
"Economic Review of 1949," DFOJ (1950, no. 1), 28-32.
"Economic Survey for 1946," DFOJ (1947, no. 1), 31-35.
"Economic Survey for 1947," DFOJ (1948, no. 1), 31-35.
Financial Denmark, Past and Future. Coph., 1919. 96 p.
Financial Denmark and the War. Coph., 1918. 78 p.
Glamann, Kristof. "Industrialization as a Factor in Economic Growth in Denmark Since 1700," in Contributions to the First International Conference of Economic History, Stockholm, 1960 (École pratique des hautes études: 6e section, sciences économiques et sociales. Congrès et colloques, I) (Paris, 1960), 115-28.
Gøtrik, Hans P. Danish Economic Policy, 1931-1938. A Report to the Twelfth International Studies Conference, Bergen,

1939 (Danish Memorandum no. 1). Coph., 1939. 74 p.
Great Britain, Department of Overseas Trade. Report on Economic and Commercial Conditions in Denmark. Lond., 1920. Irregular, up to 100 p.
Horne, H. J. "Danish Economic Conditions Show Improvement in Current Year," FT, 4 (1948), 1252-55.
"Institute of Economics and History, Copenhagen," ISSB, 4 (1952), 140-43.
Iversen, Carl. "Economic Development and Economic Policy in Denmark," SBQR, 36 (1955), 42-51.
Jensen, Hans E. Foreign Trade, Institutional Change and Economic Development in Denmark. Thesis (Ph.D.), University of Texas, 1961. 904 p.
Johansen, Hans Chr. "J. G. Büsch's Economic Theory and His Influence on the Danish Economic and Social Debate," SEHR, 14 (1966), 18-38.
Jones, Hugh. Modern Denmark, Its Social, Economic and Agricultural Life. Lond., 1927. 83 p.
Krag, Jens O. "Prospects for Danish Economy," DFOJ (1948, no. 4), 1-2.
Leistikow, Gunnar. "Denmark's Creeping Crisis" [Armament and foreign exchange], FA, 33 (1955), 473-83.
——. "Denmark's Economy at the Crossroads," ASR, 46 (1958), 135-44.
Lester, Richard A., and C. L. Christensen. "The Gold Parity Depression in Norway and Denmark, 1925-1928," JPE, 45 (1937), 433-65, 808-15.
MacDonald, S. G. "Economic Conditions in Denmark Showed Upward Trend Last Year" [1949]; "Policy of Monetary Retrenchment Ended by Denmark in Past Year"; "Industrial Production in Denmark Reached New High in Past Year"; "Total Trade of Denmark Rises but Trade with Canada Lower"; FT, 8 (Jl, Aug, S 1950), 178-82; 234-37; 349-51; 422-26.
Monthly Review of the Economic Situation in Denmark. Coph.
O'Donnell, Thomas. A Trip to Denmark. Dublin, 1908. 48 p.
Pedersen, Jørgen. Economic Conditions in Denmark after 1922. Coph., 1931. 52 p.
——. "Review of Danish Economic Conditions," BC, 1 (1935), 62-64.
——. "A Review of Danish Economic Conditions," BC, 2 (1936), 219-21.
Schmidt, E. I. "The Impact of the Rearmament on Denmark," PubFin, 7 (1952), 164-75.
United States, Bureau of Foreign Commerce,

World Trade Information Service. Basic Data on the Economy of Denmark (Economic Reports, pt. 1, no. 57-11). By Robert P. Donogh. Wash., 1957. 18 p; 1960 ed. (Economic Reports, pt. 1, no. 60-26). By Marion Anderson and Ann C. Holmes. Wash., 1960. 15 p.

——. Economic Developments in Denmark, 1954 (Economic Reports, pt. 1, no. 55-31). Wash., 1955. 9 p.; 1956 ed. (Economic Reports, pt. 1, no. 57-8). By Robert P. Donogh. Wash., 1957. 8 p.; 1958 ed. (Economic Reports, pt. 1, no. 59-14). By Ann C. Holmes. Wash., 1959. 5 p.; 1960 ed. (Economic Reports, pt. 1, no. 61-33). By Ann C. Holmes. Wash., 1961. 4 p.

United States, Bureau of International Commerce. Basic Data on the Economy of Denmark (Overseas Business Reports, OBR-63-112). Wash., 1963. 18 p.

Wehrwein, George S. "The Message of Denmark," ForGeo, 12 (1913/14), 58-60.

Westergaard, Harald L. Economic Development in Denmark Before and During the World War (Publications of the Carnegie Endowment for International Peace, Division of Economics and History). Lond., N.Y., 1922. 106 p.

White, John B. Denmark in 1935, Her Economic Position. Lond., 1936. 63 p.

——. Denmark Revisited. Lond., 1939. 47 p.

GREENLAND, FAEROE ISLANDS

Christiansen, Hans C. "Denmark's Biggest Assignment: Occupational Conditions of Greenland," DFOJ, no. 36 (1961), 18-22.

Denmark, Greenland Government. Summary of Statistical Information Regarding Greenland. Coph., 1942-47.

Dunbar, M. J. "Greenland During and Since the Second World War," IntJ, 5 (1950), 121-40.

Friis, Herman R. "Greenland: a Productive Artic Colony," EG, 13 (1937), 75-92.

Hansen, H. J. "Greenland Builds," ASR, 49 (1961), 279-88.

Kampmann, Per. "Greenland's Lead Mountain," ASR, 44 (1956), 32-37.

Marcus, G. J. "The Greenland Trade-Route," EcHistR, new series, 7 (1954/55), 71-80.

Nyman, Anders. "Hay Harvesting Methods on the Faeroe Islands," Folk-Liv, 21/22 (1957/58), 101-106.

Petersen, Robert. "Family Ownership and Right of Disposition in Sukkertoppen District, West Greenland," Folk, 5 (1963), 269-81.

——. "Some Regulating Factors in the Hunting Life of Greenlanders," Folk, 7 (1965), 107-24.

Sveistrup, P. P. Economic Principles of the Greenland Administration Before 1947 (Denmark, Commission for Scientific Investigations in Greenland. Meddelelser om Grønland, v. 150, no. 1). Coph., 1949. 215 p.

Therkelsen, Kjeld R. "Greenland Looks Ahead," GeoM, 33 (1960/1961), 545-55.

ECONOMIC PLANNING

Denmark, Information Office. The Long-Term Program of Denmark [Submitted to the Organization for European Economic Development]. Rev. ed. Coph., 1948. 76 p.

Denmark, Ministry of Foreign Affairs. Denmark and the Marshall Plan: 11th Report. Coph., 1951. 20 p.

——. Denmark and the Marshall Plan; Final Survey by the Danish Government of Operations and Progress under the European Recovery Program, 1948-1952. Coph., 1952. 52 p.

Krag, Jens O. "European Recovery and Its Relation to Danish Economy," T, 5 (1949), 11-14.

Organization for European Economic Cooperation. General Memoranda on the 1950-51 and 1951-52 Programmes: Denmark. Paris, 1950. 23 p.

PUBLIC FINANCE, MONETARY POLICY

Bolin, Sture. "Tax Money and Plough Money," SEHR, 2 (1954), 3-21.

Carroll, M. B. "Income Tax Convention Between the U.S. and Denmark," BIFD, 3 (1949), 182-90.

Dahl, Basil D. "The Course of Monetary Stabilization in Denmark," U.S. Commerce Reports (Dept. of Commerce), (F 28, 1927).

"Danish State Finances: the Developments of a Decade," DFOJ, no. 172 (1935), 63-67.

Denmark, Ministry of Finance. Summary of Current Danish Legislation Concerning Taxation of Income and Capital. Coph., 1961. 35 p.

Denmark, Ministry of Foreign Affairs. Summary of the Current Danish Legislation Concerning Income and Capital Taxation. Coph., 1957. 21 p.

Hansen, E. Alban. "A Non-discriminatory Consumer Tax," DFOJ, no. 61 (1968), 12-13.

Hansen, H. C. "Denmark's Financial Position," DFOJ (1948, no. 2), 1-3.

Herler, Povl. "The Danish-American Convention for the Avoidance of Double Taxation in Relation to the Danish Taxation Rules," BIFD, 3 (1949), 27-29.

Hiort-Lorenzen, S. "The Struggle Against Tax Evasion: the Situation in Denmark," BIFD, 7 (1953), 8-15.

Jacobsen, Johan. The Collapse of Our Monetary System, March 1932. Coph., 1932. 28 p.

Kristensen, Thorkil. "Danish Financial Policy," ScPP, III, 468-76.

———. "Denmark's Financial Position," DFOJ (1947, no. 1), 1-3.

———. "Speech in the Danish Lower House 2nd July 1948," DO, 1 (1948), 76-86.

Lando, Z. D. "The Danish Krone," Banker's Magazine, 179 (1955), 140-45.

Røgind, Sven. "Present-Day Problems of Taxation in Denmark," Nord, 7 (1944), 249-58.

Spang-Thomsen, V. "Recent Developments in Danish Taxation," BIFD, 13 (1959), 263-75.

"The State Financial Situation in Denmark," DFOJ, no. 157/158 (1934), 17-22.

Svendsen, Knud Erik. "Monetary Policy and Theory in Denmark, 1784-1880." SEHR, pt. 1, 10 (1962), 38-77; pt. 2, 11 (1963), 3-26.

United States, Department of the Treasury. Preliminary Study of Certain Financial Laws and Institutions: Denmark. By Nelson Lacione. Wash., 1944. 707 p.

Warming, Jens P. "The Taxation of Real Property in Denmark," PSQ, 39 (1924), 414-31.

PRICES AND WAGES

Friis, Astrid, and Kristof Glamann. A History of Prices and Wages in Denmark, 1600-1800. Lond., 1959. v. 1, 350 p.

Johnson, Dudley W. "Are Cost-of-Living Escalator Clauses Inflationary? Economic Experience of Denmark and Australia," LIJ, 11 (1960), 891-902.

———. "Wage Escalators and Inflation in Denmark, 1945-55," JPE, 68 (1960), 175-82.

Pedersen, Jørgen, and O. S. Petersen. An Analysis of Price Behaviour during the Period 1855-1913. Oxford, 1938. 268 p.

PERSONAL INCOME AND CONSUMPTION

Hamtoft, H. Tobacco Consumption in Denmark. I. The Danish National Morbidity Survey of 1950 (Communication no. 8). Danish Medical Bulletin, 2, 213-20.

Hess, Charles F. Selected Specific Impacts of Consumer Behavior in the Retail Service Area of Greater Aalborg, Denmark. Thesis (Ph.D.), Michigan State University, 1964.

Lemberg, K. "Redistribution of Income in Denmark," in Alan T. Peacock, ed., Income Redistribution and Social Policy (Lond., 1954).

"Recent Family Budget Enquiries: the Danish Family Budget Enquiry of 1931," ILR, 36 (1937), 688-99.

"Report of a Commission on National Pensions in Denmark," ILR, 75 (1957), 354-68.

"Saving Capital Gain and Composition of Personal Wealth in Copenhagen in 1949," OISB, 22 (1960), 117-30.

FOREIGN TRADE, EUROPEAN ECONOMIC INTEGRATION

"American Interest in Danish Brown Leghorns," DFOJ (1946, no. 3), 15-17.

Andersen, P. Nyboe. "Danish Economic Life," ScPP, III, 465-67.

———. "Denmark's Foreign Trade," ScPP, III, 736-40.

———. "European Market Integration," DFOJ, no. 41 (1962), 15-17.

Beckerman, W. Some Aspects of Monopoly and Monopsony in International Trade as Illustrated in Anglo-Danish Trade, 1921-1938. Thesis (Ph.D.), Cambridge University, 1952.

———. "Some Aspects of Monopoly in Anglo-Danish Trade, 1921-38," NT, 89 (1951), 256-64.

Boetius, Povl. "Danish Industrial Exports," DFOJ (1947, no. 3), 1-3.

———. "Denmark: Its Industrial Exports," IM (Ap 1952), 20-22.

———. "Industrial Goods in Danish Exports," DFOJ, no. 23 (1957), 21-23.

Carstens, Einar. "The Importance of the EEC Market to EFTA Countries: Denmark," EFTA Bull, 6 (1965, no. 6), 2-4.

Christiansen, Christian. "Fishing as an Export Industry," DFOJ (1948, no. 1), 1-4.

"Danish Export Trade," Archive, 1 (1948), 46-47.

Denmark, Agricultural Council. The Agricultural Export of Denmark. 1939. 42 p.

Denmark, Ministry of Foreign Affairs. Investment of Foreign Capital in Denmark. Coph., 1956. 30 p.; 2d ed. 1957. 29 p.

Denmark, Ministry of Foreign Affairs and
Ministry for Industry, Commerce and
Shipping. Danish Export Firms. Danish
Export Articles. Coph., 1927. 109 p.;
1931 ed., 113 p.
Denmark Exports. Coph., Annual.
"The Exporting Wood Industry in Denmark,"
DFOJ, no. 173 (1935), 78-85.
Great Britain, Foreign Office. Agreement
Between the Government of the United
Kingdom and the Government of Denmark,
Relating to Trade Commerce. Lond.,
1949. 5 p.
Haekkerup, Per. "EFTA-A Danish View,"
EFTA Bull, 5 (1964, no. 1-2), 5-6.
Heckscher, Kay. "Danish Trade with Rus-
sia," CR, 187 (1955), 266-69.
——. "Denmark's Dilemma" [EFTA], CR,
192 (1957), 193-96.
"How Denmark Helps Exporters," EFTA
Rep (Ja 23, 1967), 7.
"How Denmark Secured Fuel Supplies during
the War," DO, 1 (1948), 127-30.
"Import and Foreign Currency Exchange
Regulations: Progressive Developments
in Danish Legislation," DFOJ, no. 206
(1938), 41-43.
"The Indefinable Attraction...the Fourth
Largest National 'Export' Trade," DFOJ,
no. 23 (1957), 11-14.
Jensen, P. Koch, ed. Denmark Exports,
1958-1959. Coph., 1958. 160 p.
Jürgensen, Dethlef. Danish Trade Problems
in Wartime. 1940. 22 p.
Korst, Mogens. "The Danish Economy Faces
Freer Trade," DFOJ, no. 47 (1964), 24-
26.
Kristensen, Axel. "Denmark's Need of For-
eign Supplies," DFOJ (1947, no. 2), 1-3.
Kristensen, Thorkil. "Denmark's Economy
and Anglo-Danish Trade," Norseman, 5
(1947), 244-49.
Krosby, H. Peter. "Denmark, EFTA and
EEC," IntJ, 21 (1966), 508-20.
Lassen, Niels. "Export Assistance to Danish Firms," EFTA Bull, 7 (1966, no. 8),
2-4.
Made in Denmark, 1948-49. Coph.
MacDonald, I. V. "Denmark's Industries In-
crease Their Exports," ForTrade (Canada), (F 2, 1957), 6-7.
——. "What Denmark Buys Abroad,"
ForTrade (Canada), (O 27, 1956), 2-4.
Merchants' Guild of Copenhagen. General
Review from the World Markets and Denmark during 1928-1938. By Jens Vest-
berg. Coph., 1929-1939. 1939 annual
(1940), 33 p.; 1947 (1948), 40 p.; 1949
(1950), 48 p.; 1955 (1956), 54 p.

Murphy, John Carter. "Danish Long-Term
Export Contracts and Agricultural Pro-
duction," NT, 95 (1957), 272-88.
——. "The Development of Centralized
Exporting in Danish Agriculture," South-
ern Economic Journal, 23 (1957), 363-79.
——. Long-Term Contracts for the Export
of Denmark's Butter and Bacon. Thesis
(Ph.D.), University of Chicago, 1955.
334 p.
Mutter, J. L. "Denmark Alters Its Trading
Pattern," FT (Aug 29, 1953), 2-5.
Nash, Eric F., and E. A. Attwood. The Ag-
ricultural Policies of Britain and Den-
mark; a Study in Reciprocal Trade.
Lond., 1961. 94 p.
New York University, Institute of Interna-
tional Finance. Credit Position of Den-
mark, 1938 (Bull. no. 97; Supplement to
Bull. no. 78 of May 29, 1935). N.Y., 1938.
25 p.
Østergaard, S. "Danish Potatoes: Rising
Exports of Seed and Ware Potatoes,"
DFOJ (1948, no. 3), 15-18.
Rønne, Torben. "Danish Concern over
World Trade Changes," EFTA Rep, no.
138 (M 28, 1966), 3-4.
Thygesen, I. C. "Industry for the World
Market," DFOJ, no. 41 (1964), 24-25.
Traberg, J. "Denmark's Exports of Dressed
Poultry," DFOJ (1948, no. 4), 13-15.
"Trade with the United Kingdom and U.S.A.,"
DFOJ (1946, no. 1), 5-6.
Tsiang, S. C. "The 1951 Improvement in the
Danish Balance of Payments," Interna-
tional Monetary Fund Staff Papers, 3
(1953), 155-70.
United States, Bureau of Foreign Commerce,
World Trade Information Service, Licens-
ing and Exchange Controls: Denmark
(Operations Reports, pt. 2, no. 60-57).
Wash., 1960. 5 p.
Waerum, E. "Economic Collaboration with
the Oslo Group," DFOJ, no. 206 (1938),
37-41.
——. "Danish Trade Policy After the Lib-
eration," DFOJ (1947, no. 1), 4-6; 34-35.

FOREIGN TRADE IN EARLIER ERAS

Dalgaard, Sune. "Danish Enterprise and
Mauritius Ebony, 1621-1624," SEHR, 4
(1956), 3-16.
Denmark, Colonial Council for St. Thomas
and St. Jan. Provisional Ordinance Con-
cerning Custom House and Ship Dues in
St. Thomas and St. Jan, 30th May, 1914.
St. Thomas, 1914. 11 p.
Glamann, Kristof. "The Danish Asiatic

Company, 1732-1772," SEHR, 8 (1960), 109-49.

Hill, Charles E. The Danish Sound Dues and the Command of the Baltic. Durham, N.C., 1926. 305 p.

Jorgensen, Johan. "Denmark's Relations with Lübeck and Hamburg in the Seventeenth Century," SEHR, 11 (1963), 73-116.

Leitgeber, Boleslaw. "The Dardanelles and the Sound," BSC, 3 (1937), 71-76.

Skade, Hans N. "The East Asiatic Company, Copenhagen," BC, 2 (1936), 214-18.

Westergaard, Waldemar C. The Danish West Indies Under Company Rule (1671-1754). N.Y., 1917. 359 p.

SHIPPING, FISHING

Bramsnaes, Frode. "Danish Fishery Products," DFOJ (1948, no. 3), 3-10.

"Danish Mercentile Shipping," DFOJ, no. 181 (1936), 15-19.

Denmark, Ministry of Trade and Shipping. Notification Containing Detailed Regulations as to the Survey of Sailing Ships etc. Coph., 1910. 11 p.

———. Notification Containing Detailed Regulations as to the Build and Equipment, etc. of the Ships and Vessels Coming within the Law of the Survey of Steam Ships and as to the Government Survey of Such Ships and Vessels. Coph., 1912. 80 p.

Harhoff, Christian. "Danish Shipping Today," DFOJ (1946, no. 3), 1-7.

Maegaard, Eilert. "Danish Shipping," ScPP, III, 705-11.

Skaaning, Preben. "A Maritime Masterpiece," DFOJ, no. 41 (1962), 34-36.

Taning, Aage V. "Danish Fisheries and Fishery Research," ScPP, III, 575-82.

Wenzell, Victor. "Danish Shipping During the Post-War Period," NSN (1960), 142, 145-46.

BANKING, CREDIT SOCIETIES

Blem, M. P. The Danish Credit Societies. Coph., 1913. 8 p. Reprinted from Denmark Abroad.

Bramsnaes, C. V. The National Bank During the German Occupation of Denmark. Coph., 1948. 18 p.

"Danish Credit Association," DFOJ, nos. 157-158 (1934), 27-30; no. 172 (1935), 68-70.

"Danmarks Nationalbank," DFOJ, no. 183 (1936), 47-49.

Flux, Alfred W. Cooperative Credit in Denmark. Lond., 1936. 22 p.

Glindemann, Paul. "The Banking System of Denmark," in H. Parker Willis and B. H. Beckhart, eds., Foreign Banking Systems (N.Y., 1929), 589-621.

Green, Johannes. "Danish Banks," ScPP, III, 825-30.

Hansen, S. "The Danish Banking System," Banker's Magazine, 178 (1954), 498-506.

Krogstrup, Erik. "Some Characteristics of Banking in Denmark," Banker's Magazine, 189 (1960), 27-31.

Thomsen, M. The Danish Savings Banks and Their Social Activity. 54 p.

Thorsteinsson, Thorstein. "The Danish Credit Associations," Nord, 5 (1942), 134-55.

———. Mortgaging of Real Estate in Denmark. 2d ed., Coph., 1960. 45 p.

INDUSTRY, BUSINESS

Bailey, Richard. "Nine Hundred Million Green Bottles: Beer from Denmark," GeoM, 33 (1960/61), 643-48.

Banke, Niels. "Restrictive Practices: Danish Legislation," Cartel, 5 (Ap 1956), 44-47.

Barfod, Börge. Local Economic Effects of a Large-scale Industrial Undertaking. Coph., Lond., 1938. 74 p.

Bjerge, Torkild. "The Danish Atomic Energy Research Center," ASR, 48 (1960), 15-23.

Christensen, Knud. "Insurance in Denmark," ScPP, III, 859-62.

Christensen, V. A., and O. V. Maegaard. The Businessman's Guide to Denmark. Coph., 1939. 46 p.

Danish Employer's Confederation. The Danish Employers Confederations. Coph., 1956. 20 p.

"The Danish Machine Tool Industry," DFOJ, no. 214 (1938), 145-53.

Danish Publishers Association. The Book Trade in Denmark: a Short Guide on Its History, Organization and Functions. N.Y., 1953. 32 p.

Danish Wholesale and Retail Trade Study. An English Summary and Conclusions. Coph., S 1952. 15 p.

Denmark, Atomic Energy Commission. Risö, the Research Establishment of the Danish Atomic Energy Commission. Coph., 1958.

"Denmark's Chemical Industry," Chemical and Rubber Industry Report, 7 (1960), 20-29.

Fog, Bjarke. Industrial Pricing Policies:
an Analysis of Pricing Policies of Danish
Manufacturers. Amsterdam, 1960. 229 p.

Foss, Alexander. "Industrial Denmark,"
ASR, 1 (1913), 5-14.

Glamann, Kristof. "Beer and Brewing in
Pre-Industrial Denmark," SEHR, 10
(1962), 128-40.

Great Britain, Board of Trade. Hints to
Business Men Visiting Denmark (Hints to
Business Men Series). Lond., 1961. 32 p.

Hartz, M. G. E. "Danish Industry After the
War," DFOJ (1946, no. 2), 6-10.

———. The Industry of Denmark. Coph.,
1931. 24 p.

———. "The Industries of Denmark," DFOJ,
no. 191 (1936), 137-53.

Holler, S. A/S Det Danske Gaskompagni
1853-1953. The Danish Gas Company.
1953. 80 p. [Danish and English text]

Jensen, Jørgen. "Danish Industry," ScPP,
III, 659-76.

———. "Danish Industry and European Reconstruction," DO, 1 (1948), 103-106.

Kjaer-Hansen, Max. Cost Problems in Modern Marketing. Amsterdam, Coph., 1965.
131 p.

———, ed. Readings in the Danish Theory of
Marketing. Coph., 1966. 325 p.

Kjaer-Hansen, Ulf. Trends in Danish Advertising Expenditures. Coph., 1963.
33 p.

Lind, C. Statistical Investigations into the
Economy of Retailing; The Provision
Trade. Coph., 1935. 52 p.

Michelson, Borge. "National Developments
Based on Science: the Case of Denmark,"
Impact, 4 (Spring 1953), 29-52.

Møller, Sten. "Danish Furniture," DFOJ
(1947, no. 3), 13-18.

Nygaard, Georg. "C. F. Tietgen, a Centenary," ASR, 17 (1929), 397-405.

Rasmussen, Erik. "The History of Industry
in Denmark" [Review of 3 vol. Danish
study by Aksel Christensen, J. O. Bro
Jörgensen, and Axel Nielsen], SEHR, 4
(1956), 94-103.

Robinson Richard J. Personnel Practices in
Denmark and Holland: an Environmental
Analysis. Thesis (D.B.A.), University of
Washington, Seattle, 1966.

Rostock, Xenius. The Royal Copenhagen
Porcelain Manufactory and the Faience
Manufactory Aluminia, Past and Present.
Coph., 1939. 76 p.

Schou, Erik. "Danish Experiments with
Wind Power," ASR, 9 (1921), 562-63.

Short, S. L. "Observations on the Danish
Co-Operative Productive Societies,"
CPR, 27 (1952), 128-29.

Sörensen, Just. "Research and Danish Industry," EFTA Bull, 7 (1965, no. 3), 12-
14.

Strøyberg, Ole. "Factories on the Sea Bed,"
DFOJ, no. 41 (1962), 37-38.

Taaning, Tage. "Three Danish Beverages of
World Renown," DFOJ (1947, no. 2), 10-
14. Followed by other articles about this
industry.

Thorsteinsson, Thorstein. Mortgaging of
Real Estate in Denmark. Coph., 1949.
39 p.

Trotter, Parsons. "Bookselling in Denmark:
from Publisher to Buyer; Training and
Techniques," Publishers Weekly, 158
(1950), 2553-56; 2617-20.

United States, Economic Cooperation Administration, ECA Mission in Denmark. How
to do Business in Denmark: a Manual and
Directory to Assist the Businessman in
Trading with Denmark. Wash., 1950.
125 p.

United States, International Cooperation Administration. Danish Marketing and Distribution on Seminar Team Report (Special Country Reports, no. 5). By Hal M.
Chase. Wash., 1954.

vonDer Recke, Karin. "Five Generations at
Kählers," ASR, 29 (1941), 138-43.

HOUSING

Bjerregaard, M. K. "Copenhagen Municipal
Housing Measures Since 1916," DFOJ,
no. 225 (1939), 168-79.

Boldsen, M. F. C. "Housing in Denmark,"
DFOJ, no. 176 (1935), 121-26.

Bryner, Edna. "How Denmark is Solving the
Housing Problem," Nation, 2 (Ja 12,
1921), 41-43.

Christensen, Aage. "Cooperative Supply of
Housing Materials and Equipment,"
AnColEc, 24 (1953), 382-84.

———. "Non-Profit and Cooperative Housing
in Denmark," RIC, 44 (1951), 129-33.

Denmark, Ministry of Labour and Social Affairs, International Relations Division.
Housing (Danish Social Structure Pamphlet no. 10). Coph., 1957. 21 p.

Hiort, Esbjørn. Housing in Denmark Since
1930. Coph., 1952. 112 p.; Lond., 1953.
111 p.

Housing Conditions of Large Families in
Copenhagen. Coph., 1946.

Langkilde, H. E. "Danish Housing Develops
New Types," DFOJ (1948, no. 1), 5-9.

Leistikow, Gunnar. "Prefabricated Housing
in Denmark," ASR, 53 (1965), 394-98.

Tejsen, J. Ström. "Co-operative Home-
Building," ASR, 13 (1925), 476-80.

TRANSPORTATION

"The Danish State Railways," DFOJ, no. 180 (1936), 1-5.

Denmark, Ministry of Foreign Affairs. Opening Tomorrow's Airways: Danish Aviation from Ellehammer to SAS. Coph., 1956. 44 p.

"Denmark and Civil Aviation," DFOJ, no. 181 (1936), 22-23.

Gregersen, Knud. "Danish Air Services After the War," DFOJ (1946, no. 3), 8-14.

Pedersen, F. P. "Transport in Denmark," Journal of the Institute of Transport, 28 (1959), 204-209.

LABOR, UNEMPLOYMENT

Andersen, N. A. "Industrial Relations in Denmark," SoCo, 14 (Ja 1950), 21-23.

"A Danish Industrial Peace Act," ILR, 43 (1941), 192-94.

Danish Institute. Employers and Workers: Development and Organization of the Danish Labour Market. Coph., 1956. 38 p.

Denmark. Summary of the Report of the Danish Government, Committee on Technical and Scientific Personnel. Coph., 1959. 45 p.

——. "Industrial Relations in Denmark: Basic Collective Agreements and Laws on Labour Disputes," Socialt Tidsskrift (1947), 32 p.

Drachmann, F. "Safety on the Job," DFOJ, no. 33 (1960), 11-13.

Egan, Maurice F. "Teamwork in Denmark," The Youth's Companion (1914).

"Employment Situation in Denmark in 1959," I&L, 13 (1960), 439-41.

Foster, J. B. "Danish Office Employees and Vacation Laws," Comparative Law Series, 2 (Ja 1939), 33-37.

Galenson, Walter. The Danish System of Labor Relations. Cambridge, Mass., 1952. 321 p.

——. "Some Aspects of Industrial Relations in Denmark," in Industrial Relations Research Association, Proceedings, 1949 (Champaign, Ill., 1950), 230-41.

Hersch, L. "Seasonal Unemployment in the Building Industry in Certain European Countries," Part III: Denmark. ILR, 19 (1929), 358-70.

Jensen, Holger. "Denmark Has Lived Through a General Strike," Free Labour World (Je 1956), 19-23.

Larsen, Helge. "Organization of the Danish Labor Market," ScPP, III, 803-11.

"The New Danish Apprenticeship Law," DFOJ, no. 214 (1938), 154.

Philip, Allan. "Commercial Arbitration in Denmark," Arbitration Journal, 13 (1958), 16-22.

"Recent Wage Changes in Various Countries: Denmark," ILR, 18 (1928), 93-97.

"The Regulations of Wages in Denmark," ILR, 46 (1942), 203-206.

Robinson, Joan. "Obstacles to Full Employment," NT (1946), 169-78.

Røgind, Sven. "Unemployment, a Radical Proposition Launched in Denmark," ASR, 19 (1931), 358-64.

Schou, Kai. "A Capital Without Newspapers for Four Months" [The typographers' strike in Copenhagen], Norseman, 5 (1947), 304-306.

"Statistics of Occupied Population in Different Countries: Denmark," ILR, 35 (1937), 263-66.

"Unemployment in Denmark from 1910 to 1925," ILR, 15 (1927), 454-57.

"Unemployment Insurance in Denmark During the Year 1923-1924," ILR, 13 (1926), 740-41.

"Vocational Training in the Iron and Metal Industry in Denmark," ILR, 13 (1926), 741-42.

"Work Committees in Denmark," ILR, 57 (1948), 365-67.

COOPERATIVES (see also Agriculture)

"Co-operation in Denmark," CoopR, 20 (N 1946), 218.

The Co-operative Movement in Denmark. 3d rev. ed., Coph., 24 p.

Drejer, Aage A. Cooperation in Denmark. Coph., 1947. 38 p.

——. "Co-operation in Denmark," DFOJ, no. 195 (1937), 33-39.

——. "The Co-operative Movement in Denmark," RIC, 44 (O 1951), 230-36.

——. "Cooperative Movement in Denmark," Nord, 3 (1940), 165-73.

——. "The Danish Co-operative Movement," ScPP, III, 776-86.

Groes, Ebbe. "Danish Consumers' Societies: a Plan for Rationalisation," RIC, 46 (Aug 1953), 184-88.

"A Group Training Course on Cooperation in Denmark," AnColEc, 27 (1956), 34-68.

Hemmingsen, Bernice. "Danish Cooperative Group Promotes Arts and Crafts," ForComWk (Je 25, 1951), 3-4+.

Hensley, H. C. "Cooperation: the Danish Way," NFC (S 1946), 12-15.

Howe, Frederic C. Denmark: A Cooperative Commonwealth. N.Y., 1921. 203 p.

——. Denmark, The Co-operative Way.

N.Y., 1936. 277 p. [Rev. and enl. ed. of preceding entry]

"Industrial Co-operation in Denmark," AnColEc, 19 (1948), 343-47.

Jørgensen, Alfred Th. Cooperation in Denmark between Public and Voluntary Relief Work. Coph., 1936. 30 p.

Johannson, Björn. "Where Individualists Cooperate," ASR, 29 (1941), 218-24.

Manniche, Peter. "Co-operation and Other Aspects of Danish Life," IO, 1 (1936), 20-25.

National Travel Association of Denmark. Cooperative Denmark. Coph., 1951. 8 p.

Pedersen, Thor. Urban Co-operation in Denmark. Coph., 1948. 56 p.; 2d ed., Coph., 1950. 55 p.

——. "Urban Co-operation in Denmark," RIC, 44 (O 1951), 240-46.

——. "The Workers' Co-operative Movement in Denmark," CPR, 26 (1951), 172-73.

Ravnholt, Henning. The Danish Cooperative Movement (Danish Information Handbook). Coph., 1st ed., 1947, 107 p.; 1950 ed., 102 p.

"Twenty-five Years of Det Kooperative Faelesforbund," RIC, 40 (1947), 158-62.

AGRICULTURE

Aakjaer, Svend. "Land Measurement and Land Valuation in Medieval Denmark," SEHR, 7 (1959), 115-49.

Alkjaer, Ejler. The Market for Agricultural Machinery and Implements in Denmark (Market Handbooks). Coph., 1953. 42 p.

Bergsmark, Daniel R. "Agriculture in Denmark, a Land of Specialized Farming and Cooperation," ForGeo, 37 (1938), 129-42.

Bording, Kr. "Better Prospects for Danish Agriculture," DFOJ (1948, no. 3), 1-3.

Branson, Eugene C. "Denmark," in his, Farm Life Abroad. (Chapel Hill, N. C., 1924), 303 p.

Bredkjaer, N. "Denmark's Cultural and Agricultural Enlightenment," DFOJ, no. 192 (1937), 1-6.

Bunting, B. T. Danish Agriculture: a Revaluation from the Standpoint of Cultural Geography. Thesis (M.A.), Sheffield University, 1957.

Childs, Marquis W. "Denmark Organizes the Farm," in his, Sweden, the Middle Way (New Haven, 1936), 133-44.

Christensen, Chris L. Agricultural Cooperation in Denmark. (U.S. Dept. of Agriculture Bull. no. 1266). Wash., 1924.

——. "Linking the Farm and the Market: What an American Can Learn from Danish Cooperative Agriculture," ASR, 15 (1927), 350-56.

Danish Agriculture. Denmark as a Food Producer. Coph., 1954. 94 p.

Denmark, Agricultural Council. Denmark: Agriculture. Coph., 1935. 324 p.

Denmark, Institute of Farm Management and Agricultural Economics. Thirty Years of Farm Accounts and Agricultural Economics in Denmark, 1917-1947. Coph., 1949. 80 p.

Denmark, Ministry of Foreign Affairs. Proposals for Technical Assistance to Agriculture in Denmark. Coph., 1950. 69 p.

——. Summary and Conclusions of Report on the Agricultural Information Service in the U.S.A. (TA 36-75). Coph., 1953.

——. Summary and Conclusions of Report on the Growing of Fodder Crops and Maize. (TA 36-115). Coph., 1953.

Denmark, Research Council for Plant Culture. Danish State Experiments and Research in Plant Culture. Coph., 1949. 12 p.

"Denmark's Agriculture," DO, 1 (1948), 40-46.

European Free Trade Association. "Denmark," in Agriculture in EFTA (Geneva, 1965), 27-41.

Exeter University, Department of Economics (Agricultural Economics). Agricultural Co-operation in Denmark and the British Farm. By J. Bradley and J. E. Harrison. 1962.

Faber, Harald. Agricultural Production in Denmark. Lond., 1924. 75 p.

Friedmann, Karen J. "Agriculture and Food in Denmark," ForAg, 8 (1944), 110-20.

——. "Denmark's Agricultural Policy," ForAg, 16 (1952), 39-43.

Geary, Francis J. Denmark and Ireland: Some Facts for the Irish Farmer. Dublin, 1925. 110 p. Reprinted from Irish Independent, appearing S, O 1925.

Haggard, Sir Henry R. Rural Denmark and Its Lessons. N.Y., 1911. 335 p.; new ed., 1913.

Hart, John F. "Vestergaard: a Farm in Denmark," in Richard S. Thoman and Donald J. Patton, eds., Focus on Geographic Activity (N.Y., 1964). 45-48.

Hauch, H. "The Present Position of Danish Agriculture," DFOJ (1946, no. 2), 1-5.

Heckman, J. H., and A. E. Wheeler. "Danes Build Strong Coops on Their Own," News for Farmer Cooperatives, (N 1952), 11-13.

Heigham, N. Agricultural Ideas and Practice and Social Conditions in Denmark. Thesis (D. Phil.), Oxford University, 1964.

Hertel, Hans. Cooperation in Danish Agriculture. Adapted by Harald Faber from Andelsbevaegelsen i Danmark. N.Y., 1918 ed., 176 p.; 1931 ed., 188 p.

———. A Short Survey of Agriculture in Denmark. Coph., 1925. 69 p.

Howe, Frederic C. "The Most Complete Agricultural Recovery in History," Annals, 172 (1934), 123-29.

———. The Most Complete Agricultural Recovery in History, the Example of Denmark (U.S. Agricultural Adjustment Administration, G-11). Wash., 1934. 14 p.

International Institute of Agriculture. The First World Agricultural Census, Bull. no. 19: Denmark. Rome, 1936. 19 p.

Jacobsen, A. P. "Advisory Service in Danish Agriculture," F&A, 3 (Ap 1950), 68-74.

Jensen, Einar. Danish Agriculture, Its Economic Development: a Description and Economic Analysis Centering on the Free Trade Epoch, 1870-1930. Coph., 1937. 417 p.

Kaarsen, A. C. "The Crisis as It Affects the Danish Farmer," ASR, 21 (1933), 157-62.

———. "The Danish Farmer and His Creditors," ASR, 22 (1934), 46-50.

Kampp, Aa. H. "The Agro-geographical Division of Denmark and the Time Factor," GT, 66 (1967), 36-51.

———. "Some Types of Farming in Denmark," Oriental Geographer, 3 (1959), 17-32.

Kernel, Willy. "The Farm of the Future," DFOJ, no. 34 (1960), 16-20.

———. "Quality is Their Aim" [Food production], DFOJ, no. 41 (1962), 21-23.

"Labour Costs in Danish Agriculture," ILR, 17 (1928), 856-59.

Lund, Hans. "Danish Agriculture," ScPP, III, 503-14.

Meyer, Raphael. "Where Denmark Teaches Agriculture," ASR, 10 (1922), 98-100.

Michelsen, Peter. Danish Wheel Ploughs: an Illustrated Catalogue (Publications from the International Secretariat on the History of Agricultural Implements, no. 2). Coph., 1959. 116 p. [70 plates]

Minneman, P. G. "Denmark's Agriculture as Affected by War," ForAg, 4 (1940), 301-26.

Moltesen, P. A. "Some Post-war Problems for Danish Agriculture," Journal of the Proceedings of the Agricultural Economics Society, 7 (1947), 160-72.

Pedersen, Sigurd. "Developments in Danish Agriculture During Post-War Years," World Crops, 7 (1955), 483-87.

Perry, Enos J. Among the Danish Farmers. Danville, Ill., 1940. 191 p.

Røgind, Sven. "Danish Agriculture and the Crisis," ASR, 20 (1932), 158-61.

Sinclair, John F. Agricultural Cooperation in Denmark (Illinois Circular no. 259, IDA). Springfield, Ill., 1918.

Sinha, K. P. "Agricultural Co-operation in Denmark," All India Co-operative Review, 21 (1955), 21-23.

Skovgaard, Kristen K. Survey of Danish Agriculture. Coph., 1946. 168 p.

Swaminathan, V. S. "Agricultural Denmark," CGJ, 41 (1950), 120-29.

Thygesen, J. V. "Importance of Freedom in Agriculture," European-Atlantic Review, 11 (1961, no. 4), 44-46.

Tsu, Sheldon. "Financial Assistance to Agriculture in Denmark," Foreign Agricultural Economics (U.S. Department of Agriculture) (N 1963), 3-5, 7-10.

United Nations, Food and Agriculture Organization, Danish National FAO Committee. Report from the Danish National FAO Committee to the Food and Agriculture Organization of the United Nations (FAO). Coph., 1947, 59 p; 1948, 70 p.; 1951, 107 p.

United States, Farm Credit Administration. Agricultural Credit in Denmark. Wash., 1940. 71 p.

Warming, Jens P. "Danish Agriculture With Special Reference to Cooperation," Quarterly Journal of Economics, 37 (1923), 491-509.

———. "Trends in Agricultural Production in Denmark," in George H.L.F. Pitt-Rivers, ed., Problems of Population (Lond., 1932) 55-61.

World Agriculture [A Denmark number]. 1922.

DAIRY, POULTRY AND SWINE INDUSTRIES

Frederiksen, L. P. "Danish Butter Production," DFOJ (1947, no. 4), 4-10.

———. "Danish Cheese Production," DFOJ (1947, no. 1), 7-12. Followed by other articles on cheese industry.

Gasser, E. "Present State of the Dairying Industry in the Various Countries: Denmark," IntRevAg, 27 (1936), 189-96.

Haavelmo, Trygve. "A Dynamic Study of

Pig Production in Denmark," Nordisk
Tidsskrift for Teknisk Økonomi (Oslo), 5
(1939), 177-214. Reprinted: Studier fra
Aarhus Universitets Økonomiske Institut,
no. 4. 1939. 48 p.

Kock, W. A. "Danish Eggs: Why They Are
So Good and Why There Are So Many,"
DFOJ (1948, no. 2), 19-24.

Møller, Halvdan. "Danish Case in Production," DFOJ (1947, no. 3), 11.

Mulgrue, J. "Dairy Industry in Denmark:
Product and Organization Highly Effi-
cient," Quarterly Review of Agricultural
Economics, 5 (1952), 116-19.

Petersen, Einar O. Danish Dairying: Production, Manufacture, Organization and
Marketing. Coph., 1956. 198 p. 2d ed.,
1964.

Petersen, F. Haagen. "Danish Bacon,"
DFOJ (1948, no. 2), 6-10.

Shaw, Earl B. "Swine Industry of Denmark,"
EG, 14 (1938), 23-37.

"The Story of Danish Milk: Organized Supply Ensures High Quality at Low Cost,"
DFOJ (1951, no. 3), 3-13.

LAND UTILIZATION AND TENANCY

Anskov, Lauritz T. Small Holdings in Denmark; 25 Years Legislation. Coph., 1924.
24 p. Reprinted from DFOJ.

Bergsmark, Daniel R. "Agricultural Land
Utilization in Denmark," EG, 11 (1935),
206-14.

Bunting, B. T. "Problems of Land Improvement and Reclamation in Denmark," Geog,
40 (1955), 119-20.

———. "Recent Trends in Land Utilization in Denmark," Geog, 43 (1958),
53-54.

Ede, R. "Small Farms in Denmark,"
Advancement of Science, 10 (1953),
45-50.

Flensborg, C. E. The Danish Heath-Society,
with Special View on Planting. Viborg,
1939. 16 p.

Gade, Ole. Land Reclamation and the Cultivation of Reclaimed Waste Lands in Denmark. Thesis (M.A.), Florida State University, 1964.

Hansen, Poul. "Corn Will Wave Where
Heather Grows; How Jutland Reclaimed
Her Moors" [Excerpt], DFOJ (1951, no.
1), 11-15.

Heigham, N. Plans for Agrarian Reform in
Denmark, 1767-1772. Thesis (B.Litt.),
Oxford University, 1958.

Kampp, Aa. H. "The Field Rotation in Different Regions in Denmark," Tidsskrift
for Landøkonomi (1956), 393-412.

Kristensen, J. H. Danish Small-Holders.
Coph., 1932. 22 p.

Kristensen, K. J. "Public Guidance in Rural
Land Utilization in Denmark," Annals,
150 (1930), 230-37.

Lange, Leila. "The Social Significance of
the Small Holding in Denmark," IO, 1
(1936/37), 117-25.

Lökken, Thomas O. "Reclaiming the Great
Wild Bog" [Store Vildmose], ASR, 31
(1933), 393-400.

"Peat: Millions of Acres of It, Unsurveyed,
Unexploited," Scope (D 1948), 104-106+.

Skrubbeltrang, Fridlev S. Agricultural Development and Rural Reform in Denmark
(United Nations Food and Agriculture Organization Agricultural Study 22). N.Y.,
1953. 320 p.

———. "Developments in Tenancy in
Eighteenth-Century Denmark as a Move
Towards Peasant Proprietorship," SEHR,
9 (1961), 165-75.

United States, Department of Agriculture,
Resettlement Administration, Land Utilization Division, Land Use Planning Section. Recent Policies Designed to Promote Farm Ownership in Denmark (Land
Use Planning Publication no. 15). By
Elizabeth R. Hooker. Wash., 1937.

Wasserman, Louis. "Denmark: Land, Politics and Single Tax Sentiment," ASES, 22
(1963), 363-77.

FORESTRY

Benson, J. L. "A Visit to Denmark," Quarterly Journal of Forestry, 12 (Jl 1960),
2-7.

Champion, H. G. "Scandinavian Forestry;
IV, Denmark," Empire Forestry Review,
27 (1948), 44-47.

"The Forests of Denmark," DO, 1 (1948),
120-27.

Grøn, Alfred H. "Forestry in Denmark,"
DFOJ, no. 173 (1935), 75-77.

———. "Forestry in Denmark," ScPP, III,
559-62.

Kraemer, J. Hugo. "Forest Resources and
Lumber Industry of Denmark," JFor, 45
(1947), 799-803.

Sabroe, Axel S. Forestry in Denmark: a
Guide to Foreigners. Coph., 1946. 110
p.; 2d ed., 1947. 114 p.; 3d ed., 1954. 118
p. [Title varies]

FINLAND

Aarnio, Paavo. "Economic Organization in Finland," BFMB, 25 (1951, no. 5/6), 25-29.

Alho, K. O. "The Economic Position in Finland in 1947," BFMB, 22 (1948, no. 1), 22-26. Similar articles in the first issue of 1946, 1950, 1952, 1953, 1954, each reporting on the previous year.

Bank of Finland, Institute for Economic Research. Year Book, 1951. (32d annual). Hels., 1952. 56 p.

Clausen, O. G. "Finland-Gasping in an Ursine Hug," Canadian Business (F 1954), 30-32+.

"Economic Development in Finland in 1961," KOPER (1962), 14-38.

"The Economic Situation" [30-40 p. survey in each issue of Unitas]. Quarterly.

Fieandt, R. von. "Post-War Problems in Finland," in Economic Conditions and Banking Problems (Saltsjöbaden, Sweden, 1950), 144-66.

Finland, Ministry of Finance, Division for Economic Affairs. Economic Survey. Prepared annually as supplement to the budget proposal to parliament, 1949—. 70-110.

Finland: Some Aspects of Economic Life. Selected articles from the Finland Year Book, 1947. Hels., 1948. 135 p.

"Finland: A Survey, 1957-60," WT, 17 (1961), 12-24.

Finland, An Economic Survey. By The Statist. Lond., Ap 1955. 50 p.

"Finland's Perplexities: Deepening Difficulties Cloud Republic's Economic Future," ForComWk (O 10, 1942), 12-13+.

"The Finnish Market Review," Quarterly feature of BFMB, 17-20 p.

Fougstedt, Gunnar. "Equilibrium in Our National Economy," Unitas, 27 (1955), 79-82.

Fredrickson, J. William. "The Economic Recovery of Finland Since World War II," JPE, 68 (1960), 17-36.

"From the Finland Station" [Problems of reconstruction, reparations, foreign relations], Economist, 191 (May 30, 1959), 853-54.

Great Britain, Department of Overseas Trade. Economic and Commercial Conditions in Finland. Lond., 1921. (1949 ed. By W. J. S. Laing. 100 p.)

Gröland, Paavo. "The National Income of Finland 1960-1965," BFMB, 39 (1965, no. 10), 18-20.

——. "The National Income of Finland 1963-1966," BFMB, 40 (1966, no. 10), 18-20.

——. "Structural Changes in the Finnish Economy, 1948-1965," BFMB, 41 (1967, no. 3), 18-22.

Gupta, S. N. Economic Rehabilitation in Finland (UNRRA Operational Analysis Papers, 18). Rev. and ed. by Barbara Todd and Mary Redmer. Lond., 1947. 41 p.

——. UNRRA Aid to Finland (UNRRA Operational Analysis Paper 5). Rev. and ed. by William G. Welk. Lond., 1946. 15 p.

Helelä, Timo. "The Outlook for Growth in the Next Few Years," BFMB, 39 (1965, no. 2), 18-21.

Jalava, Jorma. "Stabilization in Finland," RIC, 42 (1949), 74-76.

Jutikkala, Eino K. The Economic Development of Finland Shown in Maps (1950). Reprinted from Proceedings of the Finnish Academy of Science and Letters, 1948 (Hels., 1950), 159-66.

Kahra, Eljas. "Reconstruction in Finland," ILR, 43 (1941), 501-13.

Kaira, Kurt. "A Review of Reconstruction Legislation," Unitas, 13 (1941), 3-9.

Karjalainen, Ahti. A National Economy Based on Wood: What Finland Lives on and How. Hels., 1953. 85 p.; 2d ed., 1956. 84 p.

Kärkkäinen, Hannu. "The Structure of Finnish Internal Trade," BFMB, 39 (1965, no. 1), 18-22.

Korpelainen, Lauri. "The Finnish Economy in 1962," BFMB, 37 (1963, no. 3), 18-23.

——. "The Finnish Economy in 1966," BFMB, 41 (1967, no. 4), 18-22.

Krusius-Ahrenberg, Lolo. "A Finnish Textbook in Economic History" [Review of text by Eino Jutikkala], SEHR, 3 (1955), 112-16.

——. "The Political Power of Economic and Labor-Market Organizations: a Dilemma of Finnish Democracy," in Henry W. Ehrmann, ed., Interest Groups on Four Continents (Pittsburgh, 1958), 33-59.

Laatto, Erkki. "The Finnish Economy in 1957," BFMB, 32 (1958, no. 2), 18-22.

——. "The Finnish Economy in 1958," BFMB, 33 (1959, no. 2), 18-22.

Laisaari, Mauno. "Compensation for Property Lost in the War of 1941-1944," BFMB, 21 (1946, no. 10-12), 22-26.

Laurila, Eino H. "Finland's National Income After the War," BFMB, 23 (1949, no. 7/8), 28-33.

——. "The National Income of Finland, 1954-1956," BFMB, 31 (1957, no. 11), 18-21.

——. "The Trend of Finland's National Income," Unitas, 26 (1954), 43-48.

Lindblom, Seppo. "Fixed Capital Formation in Finland During 1958-1961," BFMB, 37 (1963, no. 2), 18-22.

Lindblom, Seppo, and Kari Puumanen. "The Finnish Economy in 1965," BFMB, 40 (1966, no. 4), 18-20.

Lindgren, Verner. "Supply of Commodities in Finland After the Outbreak of the War in 1939, in the Light of Available Statistics," Unitas, 13 (1941), 57-66.

Linnamo, Jussi. "A Forecast of Economic Development in Finland 1960-1970," BFMB, 34 (1960, no. 5), 18-21.

Louko, Aimo. "Gross Fixed Capital Formation in Finland, 1948-1957," BFMB, 32 (1958, no. 11), 18-22.

Mead, William R. "Reconstruction in Finland," Norseman, 5 (1947), 397-406, map.

Mickwitz, Gösta. "A New Pattern of Trade Cycles in Finland?" Unitas, 38 (1966), 127-39.

——. "Rising Trends and Economic Recovery," Unitas, 35 (1963), 173-81.

Modeen, Gunnar. "Our Present Standard of Living," Unitas (1950), 35-40.

"National Production in Finland Reaches Its Pre-War Level," FTR (D 1948), 7-8+.

Niitamo, O. E. "The National Income of Finland, 1956-1957," BFMB, 32 (1958, No. 9), 18-22.

——. "The National Income of Finland in 1957-1959," BFMB, 33 (1959, no. 10), 18-23.

——. "The National Income of Finland in 1959-1961," BFMB, 35 (1961, no. 10), 18-23.

——. "The National Income of Finland in 1959-1962," BFMB, 36 (1962, no. 10), 18-23.

——. "The National Income of Finland in 1960-1963," BFMB, 37 (1963, no. 10), 18-23.

——. "The National Income of Finland in 1961-1964," BFMB, 38 (1964, no. 10), 18-23.

"On the Threshold of Economic Reconstruction: Finland's Good Resources for Continued Economic Progress," Unitas, 12 (1940), 3-6.

Paunio, J. J. "The Finnish Economy in 1959," BFMB, 34 (1960, no. 2), 18-21.

——. "The Finnish Economy in 1960," BFMB, 35 (1961, no. 3), 18-22. Articles covering the years 1961 and 1964, also by Paunio, appear in issues 3 of 1962 and 4 of 1965.

Pipping, Hugo E. "Finland's Economy and

Employment in Review," ScPP, III, 489-500.

——. "Finland's Way to Peace Economy," Nord, 7 (1944), 174-83.

"Recent Developments" [And statistical section], BFMB, 32 (1958), 1-16.

A Review of the Economic Development in Finland: the Third Quarter of 1957," KOPER (1957), 190-218. A similar review appears for each quarter of each year.

"A Review of the Economic Development in Finland in 1958," KOPER (1959), 22-48.

Rossi, Reino. "The Finnish Economy Today," TBR, 24 (1954), 3-15.

——. "The Finnish Economy in 1955," BFMB, 30 (1956, no. 2), 18-21.

Sletholt, Erik. "Finland Today," IntJ, 6 (1951), 118-26.

"Statistics on Finnish Economy," KOPER (1949), 31-40. Feature of each issue.

Suviranta, Bruno K. "The Finnish Economy During the Last Ten Years," SBQR, 35 (1954, no. 4), 97-101.

"Tasks and Problems of Reconstruction," Unitas, 13 (1941), 28-40.

Three-Monthly Economic Review [of] Finland. Lond., 1953.

Törnqvist, Erik. "The Growth of the National Income of Finland," BFMB, 29 (1955, no. 12), 20-26.

Tudeer, Alf E. "The Finnish Economy in 1954," BFMB, 29 (1955, no. 1/2), 29-33.

Tuominen, Leo et al. "Finland: a Statist Survey: an Economic Survey," Statist, 184 (May 1, 1956), 356+.

United States, Bureau of Foreign Commerce, World Trade Information Service. Economic Developments in Finland, 1954 (Economic Reports, pt. 1, no. 55-44). Wash., 1955. 7 p.

United States, Bureau of International Commerce. Basic Data on the Economy of Finland (OBR 64-19). Prepared by Harold A. McNitt. F 1964. 15 p.

Vartiainen, Henri J. "The Finnish Economy in 1963," BFMB, 38 (1964, no. 4), 18-24.

Viita, Pentti. "The Finnish Economy in 1956," BFMB, 31 (1957, no. 2), 18-21.

"War Conditions Dominate Finland's Economy," ForComWk, 3 (Je 21, 1941), 16-17.

Waris, Heikki. "Economic Growth and Social Welfare," BFMB, 36 (1962, no. 12), 18-21.

——. "Last Year in Retrospect," BFMB, 38 (1964, no. 1), 18-20.

——. "A Retrospective View of the Past Year," BFMB, 37 (1963, no. 1), 18-20.

——. "Structural Changes in Finnish

Prices," BFMB, 21 (1946, no. 4-6), 29-35.

DEVELOPMENT PRIOR TO WORLD WAR II

Bank of Finland. Finland: Diagrams of Economic Conditions. Hels., 1925. 46 p.

Cajander, Aimo K. Finland's Progress as an Independent State. Hels., 1939. 40 p.

Eichholz, Alvin C. Finland: an Economic Review. (U.S. Bureau of Foreign and Domestic Commerce, Trade Information Bull. no. 681) Wash., 1930. 49 p.

Ekholm, Miriam. "Economic Recovery in Finland Since 1931," BFMB, 16 (1936, no. 11), 22+.

Essen, Georg von. "Economic Progress in Free Finland," ASR, 28 (1940), 34-38.

Finland, Central Statistical Bureau. The Republic of Finland; an Economic and Financial Survey. Hels., 1920. 76 p.

Frederiksen, Niels C. Finland: Its Public and Private Economy. Lond., 1902. 306 p.

Halme, Veikko. "Finland's Economy During the Period of the Gold Standard" [Review of Heimer Björkqvist. Prisrörelser och penningvärde i Finland under guldmyntfotsperioden 1878-1913], SEHR, 6 (1958), 195-200. Bank of Finland Institute for Economic Research Publications, B:19, Hels., 1958.

Harmaja, Leo. "Economic Progress in Finland After the Great War, Compared with Other Northern Countries," Unitas, 3 (1931), 81-91.

——. Effects of the War on Economic and Social Life in Finland (Carnegie Endowment for International Peace, Economic and Social History of the World War [Translated and abridged series]). New Haven, 1933. 125 p.

——. "The Position of Different Trades in the National Economy of Finland: a Statistical Investigation," Unitas, 8 (1936), 2-8.

Hourwich, I. A. "Situation in Finland," JPE, 11 (1902/3), 290-99.

Jucker-Fleetwood, Erin E. Economic Theory and Policy in Finland, 1914-25 (Basle Centre for Economic and Financial Research Publications, series B, no. 1). Oxford, 1958. 109 p.

Jutikkala, Eino K. "The Distribution of Wealth in Finland in 1800," SEHR, 1 (1953), 81-104.

Lindberg, Valter. "An Estimate of the National Income of Finland," Unitas, 7 (1935), 65-69.

Lindgren, Verner. "Twenty Years of Economic Reconstruction in Finland" [1917-1937], Unitas, 10 (1938), 87-146. Reprinted, Hels., 1938. 59 p.

Suviranta, Bruno K. "Economic Policy in Recovery," Unitas, 6 (1934), 57-61.

——. Finland and the World Depression [A summary of two studies made for the Economic Council in Finland and published in its series: Taluodellinen asema (The Economic Situation), D 1929, and Suomi ja maailman talouspula (Finland and the World Crisis), M 1931]. BFMB (1931, no. 4), Supplement, 48 p.

Tuthill, Richard L. "An Analysis of Post-War Finland," JofGeo, 39 (1940), 356-61.

REGIONAL DEVELOPMENT

Alanen, Aulis J. "Maritime Trade and Economic Development in South Ostrobothnia," SEHR, 1 (1953), 127-32.

Aunola, Toini. "The Indebtedness of North Ostrobothnian Farmers to Merchants, 1765-1809," SEHR, 13 (1965), 163-85.

Helin, Ronald A. Economic-Geographic Reorientation in Western Finnish Karelia, a Result of the Finno-Soviet Boundary Demarcations of 1940 and 1944. Thesis (Ph.D.), University of California at Los Angeles, 1961. 284 p. National Research Council, Publication 909. Wash., 1961.

Kiiskinen, Auvo. "The Economic Growth by Regions in Finland 1926-1952" [English summary], in Taloudellinen Kasvu alueittain Suomessa vuosina 1926-1952 (Taloudellinen Tutkimuskeskus, Julkaisusarja A, 3). Hels., 1958. 397 p.

——. "Regional Economic Growth in Finland, 1880-1952," SEHR, 9 (1961), 83-104.

Lloyd, Trevor. Norwegian Collaboration in the Economic Development of Arctic Finland (Technical Report ONR 438-03-03, Ja 1956). Hanover, N.H., 1956. 8 p. Mimeographed.

Mannermaa, Kauko. "The Regional Structure of the Finnish Economy," BFMB, 39 (1965, no. 3), 18-21.

Mead, William R. "Frontier Themes in Finland," Geog, 44 (1959), 145-56.

MONETARY SYSTEM

Bank of Finland. The Currency Reform of 1963 and the New Currency Act. Hels., 1962. 8 p. Reprinted from Bank of Finland Year Book 1961.

Fieandt, R. von. "The Recent Devaluation in Finland," BFMB, 31 (1957, no. 10), 18-21.

Finland. Currency Act, Regulations for the Bank of Finland. Hels., 1952. 23 p.

Junnila, T. "Have the Remedies Adapted in Our Monetary Policy Been Correctly Chosen?" KOPER (1956), 91-99.

Kalliala, Osmo. "Treasury Cash Transactions on Forecasting the Cash Position," KOPER (1959), 67-73.

Larna, Kaarlo. The Money Supply, Money Flows and Domestic Product in Finland, 1910-1956 (Finnish Economic Association Economic Studies, 23). Hels., 1959. 227 p.

Modeen, Gunnar. "The Price Level and the Value of the Currency," Unitas, 13 (1941), 25-27.

"Our Currency: Wartime Inflation and the Present Position," Unitas, 5 (1933), 3-6.

Paunio, J. J. "How Stable is the Finmark?" KOPER (1961), 103-107.

Pipping, Hugo E. "Centenary of the Finnmark," BFMB, 34 (1960, no. 3), 18-22.

———. "The Introduction of the Gold Standard in Finland in 1877" [Review of Swedish book by Heimer Björkqvist], SEHR, 3 (1955), 260-62.

———. "Swedish Paper Currency in Finland After 1809," SEHR, 9 (1961), 68-82.

Stjernschantz, Göran. "Monetary Restriction in Finland," Banker, 106 (1956), 442-47.

Suviranta, Bruno K. "The Economic Consequences of the Devaluation," Unitas, 29 (1957), 159-70.

Tuomioja, Sakari. "The Devaluation of the Mark," BFMB, 23 (1949, no. 7/8), 25-28.

Valvanne, Heikki. "The Monetary Reform of 1963," BFMB, 36 (1962, no. 4), 18-21.

Waris, Klaus. "A Retrospect of Monetary Development in Finland During 1960," BFMB, 35 (1961, no. 1), 18-20.

PUBLIC FINANCE, NATIONAL BUDGET, TAXATION

Elonen, Heikki U. "Public Finances in 1965," BFMB, 40 (1966, no. 9), 18-23.

Junnila, T. "Public Finances in 1946," BFMB, 21 (1947, no. 7-9), 19-23.

———. "State Revenue and Expenditure in 1938-1945," Unitas, 18 (1946), 38-42.

Lassila, Jaako. "Taxation in Finland," BFMB, 33 (1959, no. 12), 18-22.

Leppo, Matti. "Finland's Public Finances Presented According to the International Method," Unitas, 25 (1953), 3-8.

Lindberg, Valter. "The Burden of Taxa-

tion in Finland," KOPER (1951), 14-18.

Meinander, Nils. "The Economic Causes of the Financial Crisis of the State," Unitas, 29 (1957), 113-19.

Nars, Kari. "Public Finance in 1964," BFMB, 39 (1965, no. 8), 18-22.

Oittinen, Osmo. "On Company Taxation," KOPER (1951), 3-10.

———. "A Survey of Fiscal Legislation in Finland Since World War II," BIFD, 6 (1952), 20-30.

———. "A Survey of the Direct Taxes Payable by the Economic Enterprises in Finland," in Enquête sur l'imposition des revenus industriels, commerciaux et professionnels (Archives internationales de finances publiques, 1) (Padova, 1954), 205-26.

———. "The Turnover Tax from the Angle of Production," Unitas, 29 (1957), 61-66.

Ristimäki, Juhani. "Prospects of Budgetary Policy and State Finance," KOPER (1962), 175-85.

Schrey, Eero. "Recent Developments in Finnish Taxation. Taxes on Enterprises in Finland," BIFD, 10 (1956), 277-79.

Suviranta, Bruno K. "The Budget Equalisation Fund," Unitas, 8 (1936), 65-72.

———. "The State Financial Crisis," Unitas, 31 (1959), 13-16.

Takki, Toivo. "The Chain of Events Leading Up to the Treasury Cash Crisis," KOPER (1957), 65-70.

Törnqvist, Erik. "The Finnish National Budget for 1963," Unitas, 35 (1963), 65-71.

———. "Long-Term Budgetary Planning," BFMB, 40 (1966, no. 1), 18-22.

Tudeer, Alf E. "Public Finances in Finland Since the War," PubFin, 7 (1952), 219-32.

Tuomioja, Sakari. "Regarding the Development of State Finances During War-Time," Unitas, 17 (1945), 21-24.

Valvanne, Heikki. "Budgetary Policy and Income Fluctuations," Unitas, 32 (1960), 65-70.

———. "Public Finances in 1948," BFMB, 23 (1949, no. 11), 20-25. A feature also in 1950-1956 in one of the late issues of each year.

———. "Public Finance: the Outlook," KOPER (1953), 117-22.

Vartiainen, Henri J. "Public Finance in 1960," BFMB, 35 (1961, no. 9), 18-23. Articles covering the years 1961, 1962 appear in issues no. 8 or 9 of the next two years, also by Vartiainen.

Viita, Pentti. "Public Finance in 1956,"
BFMB, 31 (1957, no. 8), 18-21.
——. "Public Finance in 1957" [Revenues,
expenditures, debt], BFMB, 32 (1958, no.
8), 18-22.
——. "Public Finance in 1958," BFMB, 33
(1959, no. 8), 18-21.

GOVERNMENT REGULATION OF
ECONOMY

Aminoff, C. G. "The New Pensions Act and
Capital Formation," Unitas, 35 (1963),
121-26.
Finland, Economic Planning Council. Long-
Term Economic Policy: a Basic Pro-
gram Drafted by the Economic Planning
Council; Summary. Hels., 1954. 36 p.
Hämäläinen, Juho. "The Administrative
Concern for Compensation Shares,"
Unitas, 21 (1949), 36-39.
Hetemäki, P. "On the End of Rationing,"
KOPER (1954), 3-9.
Junnila, T. "Public Economy of Finland
During the War and After the Armistice,"
BFMB, 20 (1946, no. 7-9), 19-24.
Mannonen, Aulis. "The State Budget and
Cash Funds," Unitas, 38 (1966), 140-45.
Melin, Ingvar S. "Public Enterprises in
Finland," BFMB, 38 (1964, no. 3), 18-22.
——. "State Enterprise in Finland,"
AnColEc, 34 (1963), 572-76.
Minni, J. W. "State Aid in the Form of
Credits and Guarantees," Unitas, 11
(1939), 2-5.
Pipping, Hugo E. "Welfare and the State,"
Unitas, 25 (1953), 73-79.
Procopé, Victor. "Compensation Policy in
Finland After World War II," Integration,
1 (1955), 38-46.
Ristimäki, Juhani. "The Financing of Capi-
tal Formation by the Public Sector in
Finland," BFMB, 36 (1962, no. 9), 18-22.
Tattari, Veikko. "Local Government Sector
in the Finnish Economy," BFMB, 39
(1965, no. 11), 18-21.
Törnqvist, Erik. "Government Subsidies in
Finland," Unitas, 22 (1950), 85-88.
Valvanne, Heikki. "Three Parliamentary
Bills Providing for Counter-Cyclical
Policies," BFMB, 38 (1964, no. 2), 18-22.
Varjonen, Unto. "The Need for National
Planning in Finland's Economic Life,"
FTR, no. 75 (1953), 76, 96.
Väyrynen, Olavi. "Demobilization of Price
Controls in Finland," BFMB, 28 (1954,
no. 4), 20-23.
Vesanen, Tauno. "State Borrowing and
Lending," KOPER (1963), 114-21.

Viita, Pentti. "Support to Agriculture and
Industry in Finland," KOPER (1959), 178-
88.
Waris, Klaus. "The Future of Controlled
Economy," Unitas, 18 (1946), 3-6.
Waronen, Eino. "The Growth of Municipal
Expenditure in Helsinki," Unitas, 27
(1955), 42-46.

BALANCE OF PAYMENTS, DEBTS,
EXCHANGE CONTROL

Bärlund, Ragni. "Finland's Balance of Payments in 1961," BFMB, 36 (1962, no. 6),
18-21. This article is an annual mid-
year feature, from 1946-1961.
——. "Finland's Long Term Foreign
Credits Since the War," KOPER (1961),
155-63.
"Controlled Imports," Unitas, 19 (1947), 9-
15.
"Finland's Foreign Indebtedness," Unitas
(1934), 62-64; (1935) 16-19, 70-73; (1936)
9-12, 73-74; (1937) 13-15, 77-79; (1938)
3-5, 68-70; (1939) 6-8, 77-79.
"Finland's Short-Term Foreign Indebtedness
and Balances," Unitas, 4 (1932), 3-11,
61-63.
Hendunen, Harry. "The Finnish Balance of
Payments Problem," Unitas, 39 (1967),
75-81.
"Importation of Luxuries, Their Slight Im-
portance at Present for the Balance of
Payments," Unitas, 5 (1933), 65-68.
International Bank for Reconstruction and
Development. Loan Agreement Between
Republic of Finland and International
Bank for Reconstruction and Development.
1949. 22 p.
Järvinen, Kyösti. "Finland's Debt," Unitas,
1 (1929), 25-30.
Kailasvuori, Kalevi. "Finland's Balance of
Payments in 1965," BFMB, 40 (1966, no.
6), 18-23. In issue no. 6 of each of the
three preceding years there is a similar
annual article by Kailasvuori.
Kankkunen, Allan. "The Balance of Payments
After Devaluation," Unitas, 30 (1958),
171-78.
Mäenpää, A. "Finland's Balance of Pay-
ments for 1952," BFMB, 27 (1953, no.
9/10), 23-29.
"Regulations Regarding the Finnish Foreign
Trade," FTR (D 1948), 22+.
A Summary of Prevailing Foreign Exchange
Control Regulations in Finland. Hels.,
1950. 15 p.
Suviranta, Bruno K. "The Foreign Exchange
Reserves," Unitas, 25 (1953), 81-85.

Tudeer, Alf E. "Finland's Foreign Debts
and Balances," Unitas, 4-5 p. Article in
first or second issue each year beginning
1948; continued by Ragni Bärlund beginning 1956.
———. "Finland's Balance of Payments,"
BC, 2 (1936), 47-53.
———. "Finland's Short-Term Foreign Indebtedness," Unitas, 5 (1933), 17, 60-64;
(1934), 8-11.
Waris, Klaus. "The Disturbances in the
Equilibrium of Finland's Trade and Industry," Unitas, 20 (1948), 41-45.
———. "Foreign Exchange Control in Finland," Unitas, 25 (1953), 115-22.
———. "The Foreign Exchange Situation and
Prospects," BFMB, 26 (1952, no. 9/10),
20-22. A feature also of 1953, no. 9/10.

FOREIGN TRADE, FOREIGN ECONOMIC POLICY

Albrecht, Arthur E. Finland, Importer and
Exporter. N.Y., 1956. 32 p. Mimeo-
graphed.
Castren, Erik. "Effects of the Present War
on Finland's Maritime Trade," Nord, 2
(1939), 459-65.
"Exports of Cattle and Poultry Produce,"
Unitas, 6 (1934), 3-7.
Fieandt, R. Von. "Finnish Trade with Swe-
den," Unitas, 13 (1941), 53-56.
Finland. Commercial Convention and Pro-
tocol, Signed at Geneva on March 24th,
1930 (Communication from the Finnish
Government). Note by the Secretary
General. Geneva, 1930. 11 p.
———. Financial Assistance to States Vic-
tims of Aggression: Observations.
Geneva, 1928.
———. Importation System in Finland:
State as of 1 Jan., 1962. Hels., 1962.
17 p.
Finland, Commission on Fairs and Exhibi-
tions. Trade Facts Finland. Hels., 1960.
56 p.
Finland, Ministry of Foreign Affairs. Im-
port Regulations and Customs Procedure
in Finland. Rev. ed., Hels., 1936. 55 p.
"Finland's Foreign Trade at Present,"
Unitas, 12 (1940), 7-12.
"Finland's Foreign Trade in 1952," FTR,
no. 73 (1953), 22-25.
Finnish Foreign Trade Association. Special
issue of FTR published in connection with
British trade fair and exhibition, Hels.,
1957.
Finnish Foreign Trade Directory, 1950-
1951. Hels., 1950. 504 p.

"Finnish Government Policy on Foreign Direct Investments," EFTA Bull, 8 (1967,
no. 3), 13.
Finnish Trade Review, M, 1930—. Preceded
by Finnish Trade, J 31, 1925-D 31, 1927;
Finnish Trade Bulletin, J 31, 1928-D 31,
1929. Published by Finnish Foreign
Trade Commission. [Articles on general
conditions and special topics]
"Government Policy on Foreign Direct In-
vestments," BFMB, 41 (1967, no. 3), 1-2.
Holopainen, Viljo. "The Development of
Finnish Export Trade in Forest Products,
1950-1961," BFMB, 37 (1963, no. 5), 18-
21.
Ilaskivi, Raimo. "Export Credits and Export
Credit Institutions," Unitas, 28 (1956),
151-55.
"Import Duties in Finland," Unitas, 7 (1935),
97-105.
Kahma, Jaakko. "Finland and the Freedom
of International Trade," FTR (N 1948),
10+.
Kaila, Olli. "Finland's Overseas Trade
(General Characteristics, 1948-54),"
KOPER (1959), 3-10.
Kailasvuori, Kalevi. "Finland's Foreign
Trade in 1961," BFMB, 36 (1962, no. 5),
18-23.
———. "Finland's Foreign Trade in 1962,"
BFMB, 37 (1963, no. 4), 18-22.
Kankkunen, Allan. "Our Competitive Ability
on World Markets," KOPER (1952), 16-
20.
Ketola, Erkki. "Finland's Foreign Trade in
1963," BFMB, 38 (1964, no. 5), 18-22.
———. "Finland's Foreign Trade in 1965,"
BFMB, 40 (1966, no. 5), 18-20.
Korpisaari, Paavo. "Our Trade on the
Threshold of a Freemarket Economy,"
Unitas, 21 (1949), 3-6.
Kovero, Martti. "Finnish and Swedish Tim-
ber Exports," BSC, 5 (1939), 126-30.
Laatto, Erkki. "Finland's Foreign Trade in
1959," BFMB, 34 (1960), 18-22.
———. "Terms of Trade and Economic
Growth," Unitas, 31 (1959), 176-81.
Lindgren, Verner. "Foreign Trade During
1947," Unitas, 20 (1948), 7-19.
———. "The Foreign Trade of Finland, Its
Composition and Relation to Local Pro-
duction," Unitas, 2 (1930), 3-12.
———. "Intermediary Trade in Finland's
Imports and Exports," Unitas, 8 (1936),
35-48.
Luukko, Armas. "Finnish Trade in the Early
Seventeenth Century" [Review of Finnish
book by Sylvi Möller], SEHR, 4 (1956),
103-106.

Mäentakanen, Erkki. "Finland's Foreign Trade in 1960," BFMB, 35 (1961, no. 4), 18-22.

Makkonen, Veikko. "The Global Quota Negotiations Between Finland and Western Europe," KOPER (1957), 123-30.

——. "International Capital Movements and Finland," KOPER (1960), 9-22.

——. "The New Prospects for Finland's Foreign Trade," KOPER (1947), 175-81.

Mathelin, T. G. "Finland's Foreign Trade in 1940-1945," BFMB, 21 (1946, no. 4-6), 19-25. A mid-year issue of each of the next eight years contains an annual review article on foreign trade, each by Mathelin.

Mead, William R. A Geographical Consideration of Successive Reorientations in the Fur Trade of Finland, with Special Emphasis on the Post-War Period. Lond., 1939. 406 p.

Meinander, Nils. "Finland's Commercial Policy," FFP, 128-38.

Memorandum on Finnish Commercial Policy (12th International Studies Conference, Bergen, 1939, Memoranda). Paris, 1939. 72 p. Mimeographed.

Nurmela, I. O. "Financing Worries of Trade," KOPER (1956), 57-63.

Nykopp, Johan. "Foreign Trade Prospects," KOPER (1949), 5-9.

Olin, C. E. "The Need of a New Customs Tariff," Unitas, 31 (1959), 169-75.

Paloluoma, Aimo. "Finland's Trade with Asia in 1952," EW (M 1953), 40-42.

——. "Finland's Trade with Asia in 1953," EW (M 1954), 48-51.

Pauli, Ralf. "Finland's Foreign Trade in 1966," BFMB, 41 (1967, no. 5), 18-22.

"Present Foreign Trade Policy of Finland," Unitas, 18 (1946), 34-37.

Ramsay, Henrik. "Current Commercial Treaty Aims," Unitas, 5 (1933), 25-29.

——. "Sea Routes to and from Finland," Unitas, 2 (1930), 56-60.

Rintakoski, Urpo. "Finland's Position in the Sawn Goods Market," Unitas, 29 (1959), 107-12.

Saarnio, Niilo. "The Effect of the New Customs Tariff on the Level of Duties," BFMB, 34 (1960), 18-22.

——. "Finnish Customs Duties in 1919-1954," BFMB, 28 (1954, no. 8), 26-30.

Samuelsson, Kurt. "Finnish Foreign Trade in the Eighteenth Century" [Review of German book by Aulis J. Alanen], SEHR, 7 (1959), 107-109.

Saxen, R. "Pitprops Exports," Unitas, 10 (1938), 6-9.

Sivander, Jouko. "Finland's Foreign Trade in 1964," BFMB, 39 (1965, no. 5), 18-21.

Suviranta, Bruno K. "The Terms of Trade," KOPER (1949), 3-9.

"Tendencies of Finland's Foreign Trade: Some Comparisons Showing the Development during the Period of Depression of Recent Years," Unitas, 4 (1932), 51-60.

Tollet, C. G. "The Exports of Finland," ASR, 50 (1962), 281-85.

Törnqvist, Erik. "The Rates of Exchange and the Price Level," Unitas, 25 (1953), 35-41.

Törnqvist, Leo. "The Effect of a Change in Exchange Rates on Price Indices," KOPER (1949), 9-14.

Trade and Industry of Finland. Hels., 1922. 746 p.

Tudeer, Alf E. "Exports and the Economic Development in Finland," BFMB, 21 (1947, no. 10-12), 19-24.

——. "Finland's Foreign Trade during the Past Half-Year," BFMB, 26 (1952, no. 7/8), 25-28.

——. "Finland's Trade with Different Countries," BFMB, 25 (1951, no. 9/10), 20-26.

——. "Structural Changes in Finland's Foreign Trade," BFMB, 24 (1950, no. 11/12), 20-26.

Vailahti, Olavi. "Finland's Foreign Trade in 1958," BFMB, 33 (1959, no. 3), 18-22.

Varjonen, Unto. "The Possibility of Neutralising the Disturbances Caused by Market Fluctuations for Exports in Finland," Unitas, 24 (1952), 111-14.

Vikman, Olavi. "Finland's Foreign Trade in 1957," BFMB, 32 (1958, no. 3), 18-22.

Virkunen, Matti. "A Fatal Swing in Finland's Foreign Markets," KOPER (1952), 3-6.

Voionmaa, Ilmari. "The Trend Towards Greater Diversity in Finnish Exports," Unitas, 34 (1962), 179-86.

Voionmaa, T. "Export Industries and Home-Market Industries in the Depression," Unitas, 7 (1935), 91-95.

Walden, J. W. "Cost Crisis in the Export Industry," KOPER (1953), 99-103.

Zaba, Norbert. "Finland Between East and West," E&W, 1 (1954), 50-57.

TRADE WITH GREAT BRITAIN AND THE UNITED STATES

Åström, Sven-Erik. "The Transatlantic Tar Trade," SEHR, 12 (1964), 86-90.

Finland-United States, 1938 (Talouselämä and suomen ulkomaankauppa, päätoim; Jaako Kahma no. 21B). Hels., 1938. 147 p.

"Finland's Coal Requirements and Great
   Britain," FTR (Je 1948), 34+.
Gustafsson, Henrik. Market Research Re-
   port Regarding Peat Moss Consumption
   in the United States and Finnish Entrance
   in this Market. Hels., 1962. 37 p.
Lehtinen, Artturi A. "On Trade Relations
   Between Great Britain and Finland,"
   KOPER (1952), 3-10.
——. "The United States as a Source of
   Finland's Imports and a Receiver of Her
   Exports Since World War II," KOPER
   (1951), 3-18.
Mead, William R. "Anglo-Finnish Commer-
   cial Relations since 1918," BSC, 5 (1939),
   117-25.
"Our Trade with Great Britain; a Compari-
   son of Finnish and British Statistics,"
   Unitas, 11 (1939), 9-16.
Runeberg, L. "Trade in Forest Products
   between Finland and the United States of
   America," Acta Forestalia Fennica, 54
   (1946), 166 p.
"Trade with Great Britain in Recent Years,"
   Unitas, 8 (1936), 104-109.

EUROPEAN ECONOMIC INTEGRATION

Bailey, Richard. "Finland Between the
   EFTA and the Eastern Bloc," Westmin-
   ster Bank Review (F 1961), 10-18.
Kirves, Lauri. "Finland and EFTA,"
   KOPER (1961), 57-64.
——. "The Importance of the EEC Market
   to EFTA Countries: Finland," EFTA
   Bull, 6 (1965, no. 7), 13-15.
Korhonen, Gunnar. "Finland's Foreign
   Trade and the Integration Plans," BFMB,
   33 (1959, no. 9), 18-22.
Rossi, Reino. " Finland and the Economic
   Integration of Europe," in EY-1960, 8
   (1961), 58-66.
——. "Finland and the Economic Integra-
   tion of Europe," BFMB, 35 (1961, no. 5),
   18-21.
Stjernschantz, Göran. "European Economic
   Trends and Finland," Unitas, 34 (1962),
   187-95.
——. "Finland and the Plans for Economic
   Integration," Unitas, 30 (1958), 69-75.
Wahlroos, Bror. "Finland's Trade Reacts
   to EFTA Tariff Cuts," EFTA Rep, no.
   106 (1964), 3. Appears also in EFTA
   Bull, 5 (1964, no. 7), 4-5.
Westphalen, Alfred. "Finnish Home-Market
   Industries on the Threshold of EFTA,"
   Unitas, 32 (1960), 178-84.

REPARATIONS AND TRADE WITH
SOVIET UNION

Auer, Jaakko. "Finland's War Reparation
   Deliveries to the Soviet Union," FFP,
   66-83.
"Finland's Reparations" [by JHJ], WT, 8
   (1952), 307-14.
Harki, Ilmari. "A Turning Point in the War
   Reparations Program as From the Beginning of Next Year," Unitas, 21 (1949), 87-
   90.
Jensen, Bartell C. The Impact of Reparations on the Post-war Finnish Economy:
   an Input-Output Study. Homewood, Ill.,
   1966. 179 p. Based on Ph.D. thesis,
   Purdue University, 1965.
Kivinen, Lauri. "Our War Reparations and
   their Fulfillment," Unitas, 17 (1945), 25-
   28.
Lounasmeri, Olavi. "Finnish War Reparations," BFMB, 26 (1952, no. 11/12), 20-
   24.
Mikoyan, Anastas I. "Mikoyan in Finland:
   On New Five-Year Trade Pact," Current
   Digest of the Soviet Press, 11 (1959), 21-
   22.
"The New Finnish-Russian Trade Agreement
   signed July 17, 1954: Provisions and Ef-
   fects" [by Jata], E&W, 3 (1955), 56-63.
Nykopp, Johan. "The New Trade Agreement
   between the Soviet Union and Finland,"
   KOPER (1950), 3-6.
Palmroth, Gunnar. "Trade Between Finland
   and the USSR," BFMB, 28 (1954, no. 9),
   20-24.
Suviranta, Bruno K. "The Completion of
   Finland's War Indemnity," Unitas, 24
   (1952), 77-83. Reprinted, 1952.
——. "Finland's War Indemnity," Integra-
   tion, 1 (1955), 18-25.
——. "Finland's War Indemnity," BFMB,
   21 (1946, no. 10-12), 19-22.
——. "Finland's War Reparations in a New
   Phase," Unitas, 20 (1948), 63-69.
——. "Reparation Payments in Kind,"
   Economica (N 1950), 423-30.
——. "Some Remarks on Indemnity Pay-
   ments in Kind after World War II," in
   Ekonomi-Politik-Samhälle. Published in
   Honor of Prof. Bertil Ohlin's Sixtieth
   Birthday, April 23, 1959.
——. War Indemnities and Capital Levy in
   Finland. SHI Supplement, SHI (1941),
   Stock., 1941. 24 p.
——. "The Way to War Indemnities in
   Kind," Acta Forestalia Fennica, 61.

PERSONAL INCOME, PRICES, INFLATION

Fieandt, R. von. "Inflation," Unitas, 17 (1945), 41-45.

——. "The Price Level in Finland in Recent Years," Unitas, 9 (1937), 97-104.

Fougstedt, Gunnar. "The Development of Prices and the Pressures Against Them," Unitas, 34 (1962), 123-29.

Helelä, Timo. "Prices and Wages in Finland, 1958-62," BFMB, 37 (1963, no. 7), 18-21.

——. "Wages in Finland 1938-1958," BFMB, 33 (1959, no. 4), 18-21.

Laurila, Eino H. "On the Determination of Fluctuation in the Wage and Salary Level," KOPER (1953), 163-72.

——. "On Factors Affecting Wage and Price Changes," KOPER (1955), 128-37.

——. "Factors Responsible for Price-Level Changes in Recent Years," Unitas, 33 (1961), 53-58.

——. "The Recent Development of Wages and Prices," KOPER (1957), 71-77.

Modeen, Gunnar. "The Cost of Living and the Rise in Prices," Unitas, 9 (1937), 69-76.

——. "Focus on the Cost of Living Index," Unitas, 26 (1954), 75-79.

Molander, Ahti. "Wages in Finland in 1958-1965," BFMB, 40 (1966, no. 7), 18-21.

Nykopp, Johan. "The Growth of Social Outlays and Wage Policy," KOPER (1959), 119-23.

——. "Wages and Inflation," Unitas, 31 (1959), 113-19.

"The Recent Adjustment of Prices in Finland," Unitas, 21 (1949), 113-19.

Sahavirta, Aarre. "The Wholesale Price Index, 1949=100," BFMB, 37 (1963, no. 9), 18-21.

Scerey, E. "Inflation and the Depreciation of Fixed Assets in Finland," BIFD, 8 (1954), 71-73.

Suviranta, Bruno K. "A Unique Experiment in Escalated Wages," Banca Nazionale del Lavara Quarterly Review, 54 (1960), 265-81.

"The Threat of Inflation," Unitas, 13 (1941), 79-83.

Varjonen, Unto. "The Future of Controlled Wages," Unitas, 21 (1949), 85-86.

Väyrynen, Olavi. "Demobilization of Price Controls in Finland," BFMB, 28 (1954, no. 4), 20-23.

Waris, Klaus. "Index and Wages," Unitas, 22 (1950), 33-34.

PRIVATE CONSUMPTION

"The Finnish Family Budget Enquiry of 1928," ILR, 30 (1934), 236-42.

Jutikkala, Eino K. "The Great Finnish Famine in 1696-97," SEHR, 3 (1955), 48-63.

Korpelainen, Lauri. "Private Consumption in Finland, 1950-1960," BFMB, 35 (1961, no. 11), 18-21.

——. "Private Consumption in Finland, 1954-1964," BFMB, 39 (1965, no. 12), 18-21.

——. "Trends and Patterns of Private Consumption in Finland," Unitas, 34 (1962), 79-84.

Lehtinen, Artturi A. "The Present Food Supply in Finland," Nord, 3 (1940), 104-11.

BANKING

Alho, K. O. "The Recent Development of the Finnish Money Market," BFMB, 21 (1946, no. 4/6), 25-29.

Fieandt, R. von. "Finnish Joint Stock Banks, 1939-1944," Unitas, 17 (1945), 3-6.

——. "The Index Clause in Bank Deposits and Long-Term Loans," BFMB, 31 (1957, no. 9), 18-21.

"Financial Establishments in Finland, a Review of the Kinds of Business of Different Establishments," Unitas, 2 (1929), 65-71.

Finland. Bank Law: Mortgage Bank Law; Bank Inspection Law. Hels., 1933. 20 p.

Frey, Alexander. "Glimpses from the History of Pohjoismaiden Yhdyspankki-Nordiska Föreningsbanken, 1862-1937," Unitas, 9 (1937), 39-53.

"Funded Credit in Finland; Issues of Bonds, Rates of Interest and Investments in Bonds," Unitas, 6 (1934), 29-38.

Halme, Veikko. "The Structure and Growth of Credits in Recent Years," Unitas, 26 (1954), 83-86.

Ilaskivi, Raimo. "The Finnish Commercial Banks," BFMB, 30 (1956, no. 5), 18-21.

Junnila, T. "Finland Introduces the Index Clause in Deposit and Credit Business," KOPER (1955), 173-79.

——. "The Growing Application of the Index Clause in Deposit and Credit Business in Finland," KOPER (1957), 3-12.

Kansallis-Osake-Pankki. Annual Report, 1955. Hels., 1956. 12 p.

Kastari, Paavo. "The Independence of the Bank of Finland," KOPER (1955), 3-7.

Levämäki, Lauri. "The Finnish Savings

Banks," BFMB, 24 (1950, no. 9/10), 25-30.

——. "The Index Clause in Finnish Banking," BFMB, 30 (1956, no. 3/4), 18-21.

——. "The Index-Clause System in Finnish Banking," World Thrift (1961), 365-67.

Lindgren, Verner. "The Accumulation of Capital in Finland in Recent Years," Unitas, 5 (1933), 85-92.

Linnamo, Jussi. "The Bank of Finland in 1957," BFMB, 32 (1958, no. 1), 18-22.

——. "The Structure and Distribution of Credits to the Private Sector in Finland in 1948-1955," BFMB, 30 (1956, no. 10), 18-23.

Meinander, Nils. "Bank Deposits in Finland Seen in the Lightly Threatening Inflation and the Index System," World Thrift (1959), 331-38. Reprinted from Svensk Sparbankstidskrift, 1 (1959).

"New Base for Index Calculations, a Link in Inter-Northern Collaboration," Unitas, 11 (1939), 54-59.

"New Index Computations," Unitas, 23 (1951), 6-8.

Olin, C. E. "The Finnish Capital Market," EFTA Bull, 7 (1965, no. 3), 10-11.

Puumanen, Kari. "Some Aspects of the Finnish Experience in Index-Tied Deposits," BFMB, 41 (1967, no. 1), 18-22.

Rossi, Reino. "The Bank of Finland in 1955," BFMB, 30 (1956, no. 1), 18-20. Rossi contributed a similar article on the year 1956 in the first issue of 1957.

"The Seventieth Anniversary of the Bank" [the Föreningsbanken], Unitas (1932), 33-36.

Suviranta, Bruno K. "Some Aspects on Banking Policy During Inflation," Unitas, 23 (1951), 89-93.

Toikka, O. "Commercial Banks' Own Funds and the Bank Act," Unitas, 31 (1959), 120-25.

——. "New Sources of Credit," Unitas, 35 (1963), 182-90.

——. "Yhdyspankki/Förenings-banken 100 Years," Unitas, 34 (1962), 67-73.

Tudeer, Alf E. The Bank of Finland, 1912-1936. Hels., 1940. 379 p.

——. "The Bank of Finland in 1939-1945," BFMB, 21 (1946, no. 1/3), 19-23. The first issue of each of the next nine years contains an annual review article on the Bank of Finland, all by Tudeer.

——. "The Commercial Banks During and After the War," BFMB, 21 (1947, no. 4/6), 19-25.

——. "The Finnish Commercial Banks in 1951," BFMB, 26 (1952, no. 5/6), 20-24. A feature of issue no. 5/6 each of the following 3 years.

United States, Bureau of Foreign and Domestic Commerce. Finance and Banking in Finland (Trade Information Bull. no. 43). Prepared in the Eastern European Division from reports by Leslie A. Davis. Wash., 1922. 7 p.

Valvanne, Heikki. "The Bank of Finland in 1961," BFMB, 36 (1962, no. 1/2), 18-23.

——. "Changes in the Balance Sheet of the Bank of Finland in 1960," BFMB, 35 (1961, no. 2), 18-21.

Waris, Klaus, and Heikki Valvanne. "The Bank of Finland in 1958," BFMB, 33 (1959, no. 1), 18-25.

CREDIT AND INTEREST RATES

Knoellinger, Carl Erik. "Supply of Capital and Financial Policy," Unitas, 18 (1946), 29-33.

Pajunen, Valto M. "The Cooperative Credit Society Organization in Finland," BFMB, 29 (1955, no. 11), 20-26.

"Rates of Interest in Finland," Unitas, 6 (1934), 85-89.

Rossi, Reino. "The Expansion of Credit and the Monetary Equilibrium," Unitas, 27 (1955), 120-24.

Toikka, O. "Developments in Monetary Capital During Recent Years," Unitas, 22 (1950), 3-6.

——. "Differentiation of Interest Rates," Unitas, 33 (1961), 107-10.

BUILDING, HOUSING

Aalto, Alvar. Post-war Reconstruction; Re-housing Research in Finland. 1940. 21 p.

Apartment Houses: Post-War Housing Problems in Finland and the ARVA Scheme. Reprinted from Arkkitehti no. 6/7. Hels., 1951.

Gripenberg, O. "The Development of Building Technique and Dwelling Costs," Unitas, 22 (1950), 83-84.

Heikkonen, Eero. "The Building Cost Index, 1964 = 100," BFMB, 41 (1967, no. 2), 18-22.

"Housing Policy," BFMB, 40 (1966, no. 5), 1-2.

Jarle, P. O. "The Housing Question of Population Centres," KOPER (1955), 13-22.

Kulovaara, Esko. "Housing in Finland," BFMB, 31 (1957, no. 6), 18-22.

Lappi-Seppala, Jussi. "Finland Combats a Shortage of Housing," FTR (Aug 1946), 56+.

Laurila, Eino H. "The Trend of Building Activity," Unitas, 30 (1958), 5-10.

Lindblom, Olavi. "Can the Housing Production Programme Be Carried Out?" Unitas, 39 (1967), 67-74.

Linturi, Arvo. "The House Property Crisis," Unitas, 5 (1933), 53-59.

Mantere, Eero. "Arava as the Promoter of Dwelling House Production," Unitas, 21 (1949), 91-94.

Modeen, Gunnar. "Building Development During the 1950's," Unitas, 32 (1960), 71-76.

——. "Building in the Post-War Period," Unitas, 28 (1956), 93-100.

——. "Housing Production in Finnish Towns and Urban Districts Since the War," BFMB, 24 (1950, no. 5/6), 25-28.

Rautkari, Kaarlo. "Building in Finland During and After the War," BFMB, 22 (1948, no. 9/10), 19-26.

Sahavirta, Aarre. "House Building in Finland from 1952 to 1955," BFMB, 30 (1956, no. 11), 18-22.

Siltanen, Pentti. "Post-war Building in Finland," BFMB, 26 (1952, no. 11/12), 24-29.

Tunkelo, Aarre. "Use of Buildings and Electrification," Unitas, 24 (1952), 9-12.

INDUSTRY, BUSINESS

Alanen, Aulis J. "The Finnish Glass Industry" [Review of 2 vol. Finnish study by Prof. Annala], SEHR, 1 (1953), 245-47.

Albrecht, Arthur E. "The Finnish Retailing System," New York Retailer, 11 (1958), 2-5.

Åström, Sven-Erik. "The Way to Industrialization: a Finnish Town History" [Review of Eino Jutikkala's book on history of Turku], SEHR, 6 (1958), 109-12.

Cederberg, Lauri. "The New Provisions of the Joint Stock Company Law for Safeguarding the Rights of Shareholders and Shareholder-minorities," BFMB, 16 (1936, no. 3), 25-30.

"The Course of Finnish Industrial Production," Unitas, 7 (1935), 11-15.

Ekholm, K. E. "Recent Development of Chemical Industry in Finland," Unitas, 18 (1946), 87-91.

Finland, Teollistamiskomitea. The Reports of the Finnish Industrialisation Committee and Metal Industry Committee in 1951: Summary. Hels., 1952. 32 p.

Great Britain, Board of Trade. Hints to Business Men Visiting Finland (Hints to Business Men Series). Lond., 1962. 28 p.

Grönos, Y. "Finnish Asbestos," FTR, no. 74 (1953), 44.

Heikel, Yngvar. "Industry During the War," BFMB, 21 (1946, no. 7/9), 24-29.

"The Industrial Production of Finland Continues to Increase," FTR (Je 1948), 5-6.

Jensen, Waldemar. "Scientific and Industrial Research in Finland," EFTA Bull, 6 (1965, no. 6), 11-13.

Junnila, A. "Insurance in Finland, 1963," BFMB, 39 (1965, no. 9), 18-21.

Jutikkala, Eino K. "The Decline and Fall of an Industry" [Review of Finnish Ph.D. thesis by Kustaa Hautala], SEHR, 4 (1956), 183-85.

——. "History of Finland's Rural Trade and Tradesmen," [Review of Finnish book by Aulis J. Alanen], SEHR, 6 (1958), 101-105.

——. "Industrialization as a Factor in Economic Growth in Finland," in Contributions to the First International Conference of Economic History, Stockholm, 1960 (École pratique des hautes études: 6e section, sciences économiques et sociales. Congrès et colloques, I) (Paris, 1960), 149-63.

——. "Internal Migration and Industrialization in Finland, 1878-1939" [Review of Finnish Ph.D. thesis by Reino Lento], SEHR, 1 (1953), 247-51.

Kairamo, A. Osw. "A Glance at the Industrial Activity of the State of Finland," Unitas, 3 (1931), 3-15; Part II: "The Imatra Power Station." 48-63.

Kaitila, Esa. "Consolidated Balance Sheet and Income Statement of Finnish Industry 1947," BFMB, 22 (1948, no. 11/12), 24-27.

——. "On Interest as a Cost Factor," KOPER (1950), 7-14.

Kauppi, Oskari. "Features of the Development of Wholesale Trade in Finland," Unitas, 2 (1930), 51-56.

"KESKO: Finland's Model Retail Chain," Euromarket, 1 (1959), 18-21.

Kinnunen, Erkki. "Industrialization Plans," Unitas, 31 (1959), 67-70.

Kirves, Lauri. "Last Year's Wholesale Trade," Unitas, 28 (1956), 11-16.

Konttinen, Seppo. "Teollistamisrahasto Oy (Industrialization Fund)," BFMB, 37 (1963, no. 11), 18-21.

Kukkonen, Pertti. "Seasonal Fluctuations in Industrial Production in Finland," BFMB, 35 (1961, no. 8), 18-23.

Larinkari, J. "Some Features of the Finnish Chemical Industry," BFMB, 34 (1960, no. 7), 18-22.

Laurila, Eino H. "Development of Industrial Production in Finland," BFMB, 25 (1951, no. 3/4), 25-28.
——. "On the Development of Production," KOPER (1958), 6-14.
Lehmus, Jaakko. "The Importance of the Nitrogen Industry," Unitas, 28 (1956), 101-105.
Lindgren, S. O. "The Automobile Market in Finland," KOPER (1956), 5-9.
Lindstehl, Sigvard. "A Survey of the Geographical Distribution of Industry in Finland in 1952," Fennia, 79 (1955), 43 p.
Luther, Georg. "The Structure of Distribution in Finland," BFMB, 29 (1955, no. 4), 25-29.
Mannio, Pekka. "The Development of Finland's New Industries," EFTA Bull, 7 (1966, no. 1), 11-14.
——. "Some Notes on Industrial Productivity," Unitas, 22 (1950), 62-64.
Montgomery, Arthur. "Finland and the International Business Trend," Unitas, 10 (1938), 43-47.
Niitamo, O. E. "Productivity in Finnish Industry After the Second World War," Unitas, 30 (1958), 117-22.
Nikula, Oscar. "Industrial History in Finland's Sugar Refining and the Rag-Paper Industry" [Review of Finnish book by Martii Kovero et al], SEHR, 6 (1958), 112-18.
Oittinen, Osmo. "The Home Market Industry and the Removal of Import Restrictions," KOPER (1955), 8-12.
Olin, C.-E. "The Fall in Prices and Industrial Production," Unitas, 2 (1930), 86-94.
——. "Finland's Home Market Industries," ScPP, III, 622-30.
Osara, Niilo A. "Finland's Fuel Problem," Unitas, 17 (1945), 61-65.
Palmén, R. E. "The Relation Between Local and Exporting Industry in Finland," Unitas, 3 (1931), 109-17.
Paukkunen, Leo. "The Consolidated Balance Sheet and Profit and Loss Account of Industry for 1948-1955," BFMB, 31 (1957, no. 5), 18-22.
——. "On Industrial Costs Before and After World War II," KOPER (1953, no. 1), 10-14.
——. "Social Welfare Costs Incurred by Manufacturing in Finland and in Other Selected Countries," BFMB, 38 (1964, no. 12), 18-21.
Pipping, Hugo E. "Commercial Education in Finland," Unitas, 6 (1934), 81-84.
Pohjanpalo, Jorma. "Finnish Plastic Industry," FTR, no. 77 (1953), 130, 134.

Poukka, Pentti. "Financing of Industry in 1947-1952," BFMB, 28 (1954, no. 12), 20-25.
The Reports of the Finnish Industrialisation Committee and Metal Industry Committee in 1951: Summary. Hels., 1952. 32 p.
Salokoski, Aimo. "Hire-Purchase Trade and Its Financing," Unitas, 35 (1963), 11-17.
Salonen, A. M. "Cartel Legislation in Finland: Provisions of the First Finnish Cartel Law," Cartel, 7 (1957), 77-78+.
Schybergson, Per. "Joint Stock Companies in Finland in the Nineteenth Century," SEHR, 12 (1964), 61-78.
"The Share of the Cooperative Movement in the Wholesale and Retail Trade in Finland," RIC, 40 (1947), 227-29.
Strömmer, M. "The Geographical Grouping of Industry in Finland," Unitas, 8 (1936), 91-103.
United States, Office of International Trade, International Reference Service. Living and Office-Operating Costs in Finland. Wash., D 1949, 4 p.
Van Cleef, Eugene. "The Public Markets of Finland," Bulletin of the Geographical Society of Philadelphia, 30 (1924), 37-44.
"The Wärtsilä Combine" [In Karelia], Unitas (1938), 15-21.

TEXTILE INDUSTRY

"The Finnish Cotton Industry, An Historical Review," Unitas, 5 (1933), 30-37.
Olki, Mary, ed. The Handicrafts of Finnish Women. Hels., 1952. 83 p.
Saarto, Martha. Finnish Textiles (Survey of World Textiles, 6). Leigh-on-Sea, Eng., 1954. 20 p.
Sirelius, Uuno T. The Hand-Woven Rugs of Finland. Hels., 1925. 14 p.
——. The Ryijy-Rugs of Finland, a Historical Study. Hels., 1926. 251 p.
Virrankoski, Pentti. "Replacement of Flax by Cotton in the Domestic Textile Industry of South-West Finland," SEHR, 11 (1963), 27-42.
Wasastjerna, Jarl A. "The Textile Situation in Finland," Unitas, 20 (1948), 89-93.

MINING

Helenius, Lauri. "The Growth and Prospects of the Metal Industry," BFMB, 24 (1950, no. 3/4), 25-29.
Huhtamo, O. E. "The Present State of the Finnish Metal Industry," BFMB, 30 (1956, no. 12), 18-21.

"An Industrial Jubilee: 75 Years Since Tam-
merfors Linne-och Jern-Manufaktur Aktie-
Bolag was Founded," Unitas, 3 (1931), 64-
68.
Jutikkala, Eino K. "Iron Ores and Ironworks
in Finland, 1809-1884," SEHR, 1 (1953),
133-36.
Killinen, Ilmari. "The Importance of the
Mining Industry for Finland," Unitas, 7
(1935), 41-49.
Kjellman, I. "Pig Iron Production Increas-
ing," FTR, no. 76 (1953), 102, 113.
Laitakari, Aarne. "Ore Resources in Finland
and the Use of Them," BFMB, 22 (1948,
no. 7/8), 23-27.
———. "Useful Minerals, Rocks and Earth in
Finland and Their Utilization," BFMB, 23
(1949, no. 5/6), 26-31.
Mäkinen, Eino. "Outokumpu Copper Mine and
Smelter in Finland," Mining and Metal-
lurgy (1938), 85-91.
Mikkola, Aimo. "The Vähäjoki Iron Ore in
Tervola, Northern Finland," Bulletin de la
Commission Géologique de Finlande, 140
(1947), 261-80.
Stigzelius, Herman. "The Growing Impor-
tance of Finnish Iron Ore Mining," BFMB,
32 (1958, no. 5), 18-20.
———. "Mining in Finland," BFMB, 29 (1955,
no. 8), 25-28.
Wallenius, Jukka I. "The Metal Industry in
the Finnish Economy," BFMB, 38 (1964,
no. 8), 18-21.

TRANSPORTATION

Castrén, Jalmar. "The Progress of the State
Railways Since the World Depression,"
Unitas, 9 (1937), 2-8.
Grandell, L. "Finnish Air Transport," BFMB,
28 (N 1954), 20-23.
Grönlund, Paavo. "Transport in Finland in
1938-1958," BFMB, 33 (1959, no. 6), 18-21.
Häkkänen, Klaus. "Post-War Road Trans-
port," BFMB, 28 (1954, no. 10), 20-22.
Roos, Harald. "The Finnish Railways in
Post-War Conditions," BFMB, 27 (1953,
no. 7/8), 31-37.
———. "The Part Played by Exports and Im-
ports in the State Railway's Transport
Work," Unitas, 19 (1947), 87-91.
———. "Some Ideas Upon the Economy of the
State Railways," Unitas, 22 (1950), 59-61.
Similä, Yrjö. "Road Conditions in Finland
and the Growth of Motor Traffic," Unitas,
24 (1952), 115-20.
Soivio, Aarno. "Transport in Finland, 1950-
1962," BFMB, 37 (1963, no. 12), 18-
21.

Tolonen, Jorma. "Tourist Traffic in Finland," BFMB, 28 (1954, no. 4), 23-27.
Tolonen, K. J. "Finnish Roads and Motor
Traffic," KOPER (1953), 104-16.
Wallenius, Jukka I. "A Review of the Transportation Survey," BFMB, 40 (1966, no.
2), 18-22.

SHIPPING

Allenius, Harry. "Finland's Merchant
Fleet," BFMB, 23 (1949, no. 3), 24-29.
Ekman, S. V. "The Finnish Shipbuilding In-
dustry," NSN (1960), 150, 153-54.
Hallberg, Hilding. "Finland's Merchant
Tonnage — Its Recent Development and
Future Prospects," Unitas, 32 (1960),
171-77.
———. "Finnish Shipping," ScPP, III, 720-
24.
———. "Finnish Shipping in 1957," NSN
(1958), 283-84.
———. "Our Shipping Connections Abroad,"
Unitas, 18 (1947), 61-67.
———. "Some Views on the Work and Recent
Development of Finland's Merchant Ship-
ping," Unitas, 27 (1955), 35-41.
Osterberg, H. "Finland's Merchant Fleet,"
FTR, no. 82 (1954), 100-102.
Pohjanpalo, Jorma. "Mercantile Shipping of
Finland," KOPER, (1949, no. 4), 1-31.
———. Suomen Kauppamerenkulku ja erityi-
sesti linjaliikenten osuus siina. Summary:
Mercantile Shipping of Finland and the
Role of the Regular Services in It. Hels.,
1949. 314 p.
———. "The Post-War Development of Fin-
land's Merchant Fleet," KOPER (1954),
107-14.
Rahola, Eero. "Finnish Post-War Shipping,"
BFMB, 29 (1955, no. 5), 25-27.
Wright, Gunnar von. "The Finnish Ship-
building Industry; Finnish Shipbuilding
Yards," NSN (1958), 280-82.

HYDROELECTRIC POWER

Aalto, Erkki. "Electric Power in Finland,"
ScPP, III, 619-21.
Christiernin, Georg. Finland's Water-
Power and Electrification. Hels., 1924.
11 p.
Lehtonen, Heikki. "Finnish Power Economy
Today and Its Prospects," KOPER (1954),
57-61.
———. "Our Power Economy During the
1960's," Unitas, 32 (1960), 115-23.
Malaska, Pentti. "Consumption of Electricity
in Finland," BFMB, 40 (1966, no. 3), 18-23.

Nordqvist, Bror. "Future Problems of
Power Supply," Unitas, 28 (1956), 141-50.
——. "The Prospects for Finland's Energy
Supplies," BFMB, 32 (1958, no. 6), 18-22.
——. "Prospects of Power Supply in Fin-
land," BFMB, 22 (1948, no. 5/6), 19-26.
——. "Recent Development in Power Plant
Construction in Finland," BFMB, 26
(1952, no. 5/6), 25-29.
Veijola, V. "Highlights of Electrical Indus-
try in Finland," FTR, no. 79 (F 1954),
10-12.
Wuolle, Bernhard. "Is a Power Crisis Im-
minent?," KOPER (1951, no. 1), 3-13.
——. "Water Power Resources in Fin-
land," Unitas, 2 (1929), 31-34.

LABOR, EMPLOYMENT

"The Conditions of Employment of Finnish
Dockers," ILR, 18 (1928), 423-26.
Elfvengren, Elisabeth. "The Finnish Labour
Force," ILR, 73 (1956), 358-76.
——. "The Finnish Labour Force," BFMB,
32 (1958, no. 10), 18-22.
"Employment Situation in Finland During the
First Half of 1959," I&L, 23 (1960), 88-
90.
Erkko, Eero. "Arbitration in Finland," Ar-
bitration Journal, 3 (1948), 226-27.
Hakkarainen, Jouni. "Employment Policy in
Finland," BFMB, 27 (1953, no. 3/4), 25-
28.
——. "The Averting of Unemployment in
Finland," BFMB, 31 (1957, no. 8), 18-21.
——. "Some Aspects of Unemployment and
Measures to Counter It," KOPER (1952),
7-12.
——. "The State of Employment," Unitas,
24 (1952), 73-76.
——. "The Unemployment Problem in Fin-
land," Unitas, 21 (1949), 31-35.
Hetemäki, P. "Wages in This Year's Col-
lective Agreements," Unitas, 27 (1955),
73-78.
Kahra, Eljas. "Opportunities of Providing
Employment for the Population of Fin-
land," Unitas, 12 (1940), 25-29.
Knoellinger, Carl Erik. Labor in Finland
(Wertheim Publications in Industrial Re-
lations). Cambridge, Mass., 1960. 300 p.
Korpelainen, Lauri. "Trends and Cyclical
Movements in Industrial Employment in
Finland 1885-1952," SEHR, 5 (1957), 26-
48.
Meinander, Nils. "The Economic Situation
After the Strike," Unitas, 28 (1956), 49-
58.
Norrmén, P. H. "Masters and Men on the

Industrial Labour Market," Unitas, 2
(1930), 23-30.
Pipping, K. "Finnish Workers' Participation
in Management," Archives internationales
de Sociologie de la Cooperation, 1 (1957,
no. 1-2), 134-38.
Pulkkinen, Terho. "Employment and Unemployment in 1958," KOPER (1958), 173-81.
——. "Employment in the 1960's," Unitas,
33 (1961), 161-67.
——. "Employment Policy in Finland,"
BFMB, 38 (1964, no. 7), 18-22.
Ranta, Tauno. "Reduction of Working Hours
in Finland," BFMB, 40 (1966, no. 8), 18-
22.
"Unemployment," Unitas, 4 (1932), 90-94.
"Welcome to Finland," Free Labour World,
8 (Aug 1957), 11-16.

COOPERATIVES

Aaltonen, Esko. Consumer Co-operation in
Finland: the Development of the Joint
Finnish Co-operative Movement to 1917
and a Survey of the Progressive Co-
operative Movement After the Separa-
tion. Hels., 1954. 172 p.
Agricultural Co-operation in Finland. Hels.,
1949. 36 p.
The Annual Report of the Cooperative Union
(KK), 1957. Hels., 1958. 57 p.
Bakken, Henry H. Cooperation to the Finn-
ish. Madison, Wisc., 1939. 220 p.
Central Union of Distributive Societies, Hel-
sinki. Finland's Progressive Co-operative
Movement. Hels., 1950, 1952. 28 p.
"Co-operation in Finland," Finland Review,
2 (1920), 22-28.
Finland. The Cooperative Societies Act and
Model Rules for Local Cooperative So-
cieties. Hels., 1955. 126 p.
——. A Quarter of a Century of Co-opera-
tion in Finland. Published for the Twenty-
fifth Anniversary of the Pellervo Society.
Hels., 1924.
"Finland," AnColEc, 14 (1938), 222-24.
Gebhard, Hannes. Co-operation in Finland.
Lond., 1916. 190 p.
Heikkilä, Raimo. Finland, the Land of Co-
operatives. Hels., 1963. 64 p.
Hertzen, Heikki V. "Tapiola Garden Town,"
AnColEc, 30 (1959), 45-50.
Hietanen, Lauri. "The Cooperative Move-
ment in Finland," ASR, 53 (1965), 147-53.
Hyvönen, Valde. "Cooperation in Finland,"
ILR, 8 (1923), 503-20.
——. Finnish Co-operative Credit Organi-
zation. Hels., 1953. 61 p.
Jalava, Jorma. "Cooperative Housing in

Finland: the Work of the Haka Societies," RIC, 46 (1953), 159-62.

——. "Co-operative Restaurants in Finland," RIC, 42 (1949), 328-29+.

——. Finland's Progressive Cooperative Movement. Hels., 1946. 32 p.; 1949, 34 p.; 1950, 34 p.; 1952, 28 p.; 1954, 36 p.

——. "Survey of Finland's Progressive Cooperative Movement," RIC, 46 (1953), 117-19.

Leach, Henry G. "Iwana Rapponen: a Visit to a Finnish Co-operator," ASR, 10 (1922), 481-86.

Linna, E. "SOK Celebrates Its Jubilee," RIC, 47 (1954), 67-70.

Marshall, F. Ray. "The Finnish Cooperative Movement," LandEc, 34 (1958), 227-35.

Odhe, Thorsten. Finland, a Nation of Cooperators. Lond., 1931. 151 p.

Owen, John E. "Cooperative in Finland," S&SR, 37 (M 1953), 230-35.

Panjunen, V. M. "The Co-operative Credit Society Organization in Finland," Bombay Co-operative Quarterly, 39 (1956), 175-85.

Rahola, Ilmari. "Cooperative Activity in Finland," BFMB, 25 (1951, no. 9/10), 26-32.

——. "Co-operation in Finland," ScPP, III, 752-60.

"Three Decades of the Finnish Progressive Cooperative Movement," RIC, 41 (1948), 22-26.

AGRICULTURE

"Agriculture in 1962," BFMB, 36 (1962, no. 10), 1-2.

Ellilä, K. J. "Development of Agricultural Technique and Agricultural Policy," KOPER (1953), 155-62.

European Free Trade Association. "Finland," in Agriculture in EFTA (Geneva, 1965), 43-53.

Finland. Land Reform in Finland, 1922. Hels., 1923. 13 p.

Härmä, Risto. An Appraisal of the Export Subsidy Program on Butter and Cheese in Finland, 1922-39. Thesis (Ph.D.), Cornell University, 1954. 156 p.

Hernberg, Runar. "Crisis in the Wool Industry," Unitas, 32 (1960), 6-14.

Hilden, Nils A., Felix Jonasson, and S. Mattsson, eds. Forestry Illustrated. Porvoo, Hels., 1932. 30 p.

"The Indebtedness of Farmers: the Borrowing of the Last Few Years for Extensions Has Become a Burden

Owing to the Crisis," Unitas, 4 (1932), 85-89.

Jaatinen, Stig A., and William R. Mead. "The Intensification of Finnish Farming," EG, 33 (1957), 31-40.

Jutikkala, Eino K. "Crisis in Finnish Agriculture at the End of the Nineteenth Century" [Review of Finnish Ph.D. thesis by Seppo Simonen], SEHR, 1 (1953), 251-54.

——. "Finnish Agricultural Labour in the Eighteenth and Early Nineteenth Centuries," SEHR, 10 (1962), 203-19.

——. "Origin and Rise of the Crofter Problem in Finland," SEHR, 10 (1962), 78-83.

Jutila, K. T. "Farmers' Earning Economy in Finland and Its Ability to Resist Depression," Unitas, 7 (1935), 2-10.

——. "The Progress of Finnish Agriculture During Recent Years," Unitas, 1 (1929), 53-64.

Kaarlehto, P., and B. F. Stanton. "Productivity in Finnish Agriculture 1956-57 to 1965-66," BFMB, 40 (1966, no. 12), 18-23.

Korpela, E. J. "Grain Growing in Finland," Unitas, 24 (1952), 107-10.

——. "The State of Finnish Agriculture at the End of 1947," BFMB, 22 (1947, no. 10/12), 24-28.

Koskikallio, Onni. "Finnish Agriculture," ScPP, III, 530-36.

Laisaari, Mauno. "The Post-war Land Reform in Finland," BFMB, 22 (1948, no. 3/4), 23-26.

"Land Settlement in Finland," IntRevAg, 30 (1939), 60-67E.

Laurila, Seppo. "Recent Development of the Foodstuffs Industry," BFMB, 25 (1951, no. 11/12), 26-30.

Lehtinen, Artturi A. "Finland's Self Sufficiency in Agriculture and Kindred Branches of Production," Unitas, 10 (1938), 63-67.

Luukko, Armas. "The 'Annual Budget' of North Finnish Farmers at the End of the 17th Century," SEHR, 6 (1958), 132-42.

Mäki, Antti. "The Trend of Agricultural Development in Finland," WorldAg, 6 (Jl 1957), 37-42.

——. "The Trend of Development in Agriculture and the Stabilisation of Agricultural Income," KOPER (1956), 64-70.

Mead, William R. "Agriculture in Finland," EG, 15 (1939), 125-35, 217-34.

——. "The Cold Farm in Finland: Resettlement of Finland's Displaced Farmers," GeoR, 41 (1951), 529-43.

——. Farming in Finland. Lond., 1953. 248 p.

——. Land Use in Early Nineteenth Century Finland (Turun Yliopiston Maantieteellisen Laitoksen Julkaisuja, no. 26). Turku, 1953. 23 p.

——. "The Margin of Transference in Finland's Rural Resettlement," Tijdschrift voor Economische en Sociale Geographie, 48 (1957), 178-83.

——. "The Seasonal Round on Finland's Pioneer Farms: an Experiment in Methodology," IGCong, 17th (Wash., 1952).

Oila, E. "Sugar Beet Growing and the Sugar Beet Industry in Finland," BFMB, 27 (1952, no. 11/12), 25-28.

Perttula, Hans. "The Readjustment of Agricultural Prices," Unitas, 30 (1958), 63-68.

Pihkala, Kaarlo U. "Development of Agriculture During and After War," Unitas, 18 (1946), 61-68.

——. "The Land Settlement Program of Finland," LandEc, 28 (1952), 147-59.

——. "The Land Settlement Program of Finland," in K. H. Parsons, ed., Land Tenure: Proceedings of the International Conference on Land Tenure, 1951 (Madison, Wisc., 1956), 453-65.

——. "The Land Settlement Programme and Its Execution," BFMB, 26 (1952, no. 3/4), 24-31.

Pohjakallia, Onni. "Farming Under the Midnight Sun," CGQ, (D 1950), 42-46.

Puolakka, Niilo O. "The Agricultural Production Campaign in Finland 1941," Nord, 5 (1942), 99-112.

Sauli, Liisa. "The Post-war Development of Finnish Agriculture," BFMB, 28 (1954, no. 6), 20-25.

Sipilä, Martti. "The Mechanization of Farming in Finland," BFMB, 27 (1953, no. 5/6), 25-29.

Smeds, Helmer. "Post-War Land Clearance and Pioneering Activities in Finland," Fennia, 83 (1960), 31 p.

Suomela, Samuli. "Butter as an Agricultural Problem in Finland," KOPER (1958), 117-26.

——. "Finland's Comparative Position in Nordic Agriculture," BFMB, 32 (1958, no. 4), 18-22.

——. "The Problem of the Agricultural Surplus," Unitas, 31 (1959), 59-66.

Tavaila, A. Young Farmers' Club Work [4-H clubwork] Educates Finnish Youth. Hels., 1950. 32 p.

Virtanen, A. I. "The Significance and Future of Agriculture in Finland," KOPER (1950), 5-15.

"Wages in Finnish Agriculture, 1929-1932," ILR, 27 (1933), 810-804.

Westermarck, Nils. Finnish Agriculture. Hels., 1954. 85 p.; 2d ed., 1957. 90 p.

——. "A General Outline of New Farming Policy," BFMB, 36 (1962, no. 7), 18-23.

FORESTRY

The Associations, Education, and Research in the Field of Forestry in Finland. Hels., 1949. 33 p.

Brown, John C. Finland: Its Forests and Forest Management. Lond., 1883. 290 p.

Durrant, Bernard. "Lumbering in Finland," Norseman, 15 (1957), 47-49.

Fieandt, R. von. "The Green Gold of Finland," Progress, 48 (1961), 5-60.

Finnish Paper and Timber. v. 1, Hels., F 1950.

"Forestry in 1966," BFMB, 41 (1967, no. 2), 1-2.

Gripenberg, Henrik. "Stumpage Prices in our Forests and Timber Sales," Unitas, 29 (1957), 171-77.

Gripenberg, Lennart. "The Importance of Forests and Floating Channels in the National Economy of Finland," Unitas, 2 (1930), 79-86.

Helander, Anders B. Finland's Wealth of Wood — Suomen puun tie metsästä maailmalle. Hels., 1948. 222 p.

Hildén, Nils A. The Forrests and Forestry of Suomi, Finland. Hels., 1929.

Hiley, Wilfred E. The Forest Industry of Finland (Oxford Forestry Memoirs, no. 8). Oxford, 1928. 39 p.

Ilvessalo, Yrjö. "Finland's Forests in the Light of Three National Forest Surveys," KOPER (1954), 158-65.

——. "The Forest Resources of Finland in 1936-1938; a Summary of the Main Results of the Second National Survey of the Forests," Fennia, 66 (1940), 48 p.

——. "The Forests of Finland," BFMB, 29 (1955, no. 6), 20-25.

——. The Forests of Present-Day Finland, A Description Based on the National Forest Surveys. Hels., 1949. 56 p.

Jukarainen, N. "Developing the Wood-Working Industry," KOPER (1959), 11-21.

Julin, Jacob von. "Finland's Woodworking Industry after the Armistice," Unitas (1947), 4-8.

Kalkkinen, Ilmari. "This Autumn's Timber Market," Unitas (1955), 113-19.

Kekich, Emil. "Forestry in Finland," JFor, 25 (1927), 27-37.

Koljonen, Juoko. "Productive Capacity of the Finnish Forest Industry," BFMB, 29 (1955, no. 9), 20-22.

Korpelainen, Lauri. "Forestry in the Finnish Economy," KOPER (1959), 74-82.

Koskikallio, Onni. "Stumpage and Forest Earnings Pre-War and Today," KOPER (1951), 19-24.

Kovero, Martti A. The Timber Industry of Finland. Hels., 1924.

———. The Wood Industry of Finland. Hels., 1926.

Kraemer, J. Hugo. "Forest Resources and Lumber Industry of Finland," JFor, 45 (1947), 649-54.

Kuusela, Kullervo. "Cutting Possibilities and Prospective Utilization of Wood in Finland," BFMB, 35 (1961, no. 6), 18-22.

Lappi-Seppälä, M. "Present Market Prospects in the Field of Forestry," KOPER (1956), 168-76.

Osara, Niilo A. "Forestry in Finland," ScPP, III, 542-45.

———. "The Necessity of Developing Finland's Forest Industries," KOPER (1954), 53-56.

———. "Some Current Problems in Finnish Forestry," Unitas (1952), 3-8.

Pipping, Hugo E. "The Early Sawmills Industries" [Review of Finnish Ph.D. thesis by Nils Meinander], SEHR, 1 (1953), 243-45.

Poukka, Pentti. "Features of the Financing of Forest Industry Investments in 1947-1952," KOPER (1954), 62-66.

Savola, U. E. "The Outlook for Finland's Mechanical Woodworking Ability," Unitas, 34 (1962), 130-34.

Schenck, C. A. "Forestry in Finland," JFor, 23 (1925), 968-76.

Söderhjelm, J. O. "Finland's Timber Industry," ScPP, III, 631-35.

———. "The Possibilities of Enlargement of the Finnish Pulp, Paper and Paperboard Industry," BFMB, 32 (1958, no. 12), 18-21.

Solitander, Axel. "The Finnish Woodworking Industries in the Post-War Period," Unitas, 2 (1929), 2-8.

State Forestry. Hels., 1949. 22 p.

Suomen puun miehiä — Finnish Timber Men. Hels., 1954. 337 p.

Valtasaari, Matti. "Aspects of the Finnish Forest Industry," FTR (Jl 1949), 17-19.

———. "Expansion and Renewals within the Forest Industry," FTR, no. 78 (1953), 148, 150.

———. "The Finnish Forest Industry Since the War," BFMB, 25 (1951, no. 11/12), 20-25.

Virkkumen, Matti. "On the Credits Granted to the Timber Industry," KOPER (1954), 99-106.

Vuorimaa, Heikki U. "The Finnish Forest Industry," BFMB, 40 (1966, no. 11), 18-21.

FOREST INDUSTRIES

"The Finnish Cellulose Union, The Joint Export Organization of the Finnish Cellulose Mills," Unitas, 3 (1931), 16-22.

"The Finnish Papermills Association," Unitas, 6 (1934), 39-43.

Gehnich, Karl. "Finland and the Price of Pulp," SRWA, 2 (1952), 10-11.

Hägerström, Sven. "The Development of the Chemical Woodpulp Industry in the 1950's and the Outlook for the Future," Unitas, 34 (1962), 5-9.

Helelä, Timo. "The Paper Industry and Economic Growth in Finland," KOPER (1960), 104-13.

Julin, Jacob von. "The Cellulose Crisis," Unitas, 21 (1949), 59-64.

Kihlman, Åke. "Planning a Cardboard Factory in Heinola," Unitas, 30 (1958), 167-70.

Koljonen, Jouko. "Recent Developments in the Finnish Paper Industry," FTR, no. 81 (1954), 68-69.

"Kymmene Aktiebolag; The Largest Concern in the Finnish Paper Trade," Unitas, 2 (1930), 30-35.

Nystén, Holger. "Development and Future Prospects of Paper and Board Industry," Unitas, 34 (1962), 74-78.

Rinne, V. J. "Difficulties Confronting the Plywood Industry Today," KOPER (1953), 6-9.

Savola, U. E. "The Plywood Industry Since the War," Unitas, 29 (1957), 6-12.

Söderhjelm, J. O. "The Reconstruction of Our Pulp and Paper Industry," Unitas, 23 (1951), 36-39.

ICELAND

Allen, Robert L. "The Vulnerability of Iceland's Economy," Finanzarchiv, 19 (1959), 451-54.

Anderson, S. Axel. "Iceland's Industries," EG, 7 (1931), 284-96.

Chamberlin, William C. The Economic Development of Iceland Through World War II (Studies in History, Economics, and Public Law, no. 531). N.Y., 1947. 141 p.

Clark, Deena. "Iceland Tapestry," NGeogM, 100 (1951), 599-630.

Directory of Iceland, 1950. Official and Commercial Information. 27th ed., 1950. 680 p.; 1954 ed., 734 p.

Eiriksson, Benjamin. "Recent Development of the Icelandic Economy," SBQR, 36 (1955), 76-82.

Gislason, Gylfi P. "Economic Development in Iceland," Socialist World (D 1948), 31-37.

Great Britain, Department of Overseas Trade. Report on Economic and Commercial Conditions in Iceland. Lond., 1937.

Hannesson, Gudmundur. Housing and Town Planning in Iceland. International Federation for Housing and Town Planning Bulletin 37, 1937, S-27.

Hanson, Earl P. "Heating Buildings with Hot Springs, Iceland's Substitute for Coal," Power (1928), 367-69.

Iceland. Statistical Bulletin. Rey., 1932.

Iceland. Treaties, etc., 1952— (Ásgeirsson). Economic Cooperation: Agreement Effected by Exchange of Notes Signed at Reykjavik Oct. 9, 1952, and Oct. 1, 1953. Wash., 1955.

———. Icelandic Report. Rey. Quarterly.

"Iceland's Wartime Prosperity," Banker, 60 (N 1941), 138-41.

International Bank for Reconstruction and Development. Loan Agreement Between Republic of Iceland and International Bank for Reconstruction and Development, dated N 1, 1951. Wash., 1951. 13 p.

Islands Adressebog: Handels-og Industrilalender; Directory of Iceland. Rey., 1907.

Jónsson, Eysteinn. "Progress in Modern Iceland," Nord, 2 (1939), 49-56.

"Labor Conditions in Iceland," MLR, 34 (1932), 805-808.

"Labour Legislation and Social Service in Iceland," Canadian Labour Gazette, 51 (1951), 252-55.

Lotkowski, Wladyslaw M. Economic Activities in Iceland Reflecting the Relationship Between Man and His Environment. Thesis (M.A.), Columbia University, 1953.

MacDonald, H. Malcom. "Iceland in the Post-War World," SSSQ, 25 (1944/45), 1-11.

Mead, William R. "Renaissance of Iceland," EG, 21 (1945), 135-44.

Mutter, J. L. "Inflation and High Cost of Living Serious Problems in Iceland," FT, 7 (May 1950), 845-49.

Nordal, Johannes. "Banking in Iceland," ScPP, III, 840-42.

———. "Finances in Iceland," ScPP, III, 501-502.

Olson, Grant. "Iceland," ForComWk, 4 (1941), 7+.

Organization for Economic Cooperation and Development. Economic Survey by the OECD: Iceland, 1961. Paris, 1961. 33 p.

———. Economic Surveys by the OECD: Iceland. Paris, 1963. 34 p.

Rogalnick, Joseph H. "Iceland's Economy, Yesterday and Now," ForComWk, 20 (1945), 8-12+.

Sorensen, Harry M. Iceland: a Brief Economic Survey (Trade Information Bull. no. 541). Wash., 1928. 17 p.

———. Present-Day Iceland (U.S. Bureau of Foreign and Domestic Commerce, Commerce Reports no. 10). Wash., 1928. 599-602.

United States, Bureau of Foreign Commerce, World Trade Information Service. Basic Data on the Economy of Iceland (Economic Reports, pt. 1, no. 57-67). Wash., 1957. 12 p.

United States, Department of Commerce, Bureau of International Programs, World Trade Information Service. Basic Data on the Economy of Iceland (Economic Reports, pt. 1, no. 61-77). Wash., 1961. 15 p.

Valdirmarsson, Ólafur S. "Icelandic Industry," ScPP, III, 677-82.

Watkins, Ernest. No Depression in Iceland. Lond., 1942. 83 p.

FOREIGN TRADE

Great Britain, Board of Trade. Hints to Business Men Visiting Iceland (Hints to Business Men Series). Lond., 1963. 24 p.

Hughes, G. F. G. "Iceland Forced to Strengthen Her Control Over Foreign Exchange," FT, 2 (1947), 1150-53.

"Iceland's External Trade Problems" BdofTradeJ, 155 (1948), 173-74.

Marcus, G. F. "The Norse Traffic with Iceland," EcHistR, 9 (1957), new series, 408-19.

Mutter, J. L. "Acute Dollar Shortage in Iceland Restricts Imports from Canada," Foreign Trade (Canada), 5 (1949), 1017-20.

Tryggvason, Klemenz. "Icelandic Foreign Trade," ScPP, III, 741-44.

United States. Tariff Commission Trade Agreements Between the United States and Iceland. Wash., 1944. 114 p.

TRANSPORTATION

Kristinsson, Valdimar. "Communications in Iceland," ScPP, III, 369-72.

Leistikow, Gunnar. "The Airminded Icelanders," ASR, 45 (1957), 157-60.

Magnusson, Sigurdur. "Iceland's Air Pioneers: a Saga of Enterprise," Norseman, 15 (1957), 77-81.

Rutherford, Adam. Transport in Iceland. Lond., 1938. 26 p.

Smith, Paul A. "ICAO Conference on Air Navigation Service in Iceland," DeptStateBull (1949), 164-66.

COOPERATIVES

Einarsson, Erlendur. "The Cooperative Movement in Iceland," ASR, 55 (1967), 153-57.

Gröndal, Benedikt. "The Cooperatives in Iceland," ScPP, III, 749-51.

Jónsson, Hannes. Co-operation in Iceland. Rey., 1950.

——. "Cooperation in Iceland," RIC, 45 (1952), 121-24.

——. "A Snapshot of Co-operation in Iceland," RIC, 43 (1950), 16-19.

Olafsson, Ragnar. "Cooperative Iceland," ASR, 27 (1939), 23-31.

Rogalnick, Joseph H. "Iceland's Cooperatives," ForComWk (May 11, 1946), 15+.

AGRICULTURE, FORESTRY

"Agriculture in Iceland," World Crops, 6 (1954), 243-46.

Ashwell, I. Y. "Recent Changes in the Pattern of Farming in Iceland," CG, 7 (1963), 174-81.

Bjørnsson, Gunnar. "Farming and Settlers' Farms in Iceland," Nord, 7 (1944), 184-94.

Eylands, Arni G. A Brief Survey of the Icelandic Farming Industries Today. Rey., 1953. 43 p.; 2d ed., 1955. 63 p.

Leach, Henry G. "Forests for Iceland," ASR, 42 (1954), 319-24.

McWilliams, James P. "Iceland Reforests," American Forests, 61 (1955), 16-53+.

Munro, David A. "The Eider Farms of Iceland," CGJ, 63 (1961), 59-63.

Sigurjónsson, Arnór. "Farming in Iceland," ScPP, III, 537-41.

FISHING

Bárdarson, Hjálmar. "Icelandic Fishing Vessels," IcR, 2 (1964), 29-36.

Close, Albert. The Fishing Grounds and Landmarks of Iceland, Faeroe, the North Sea. Lond., 193?. 100 p.

Elisson, Niar. "The Fishing Fleet and Its Equipment," IcR, 2 (1964), 36-39.

Eydal, Astvaldur. "Some Aspects of the Herring Fishery and Herring Industry of Iceland," IGCong, 17th (Wash., 1957), 612-15.

——. Some Geographical Aspects of the Fisheries of Iceland. Thesis (Ph.D.), University of Washington, 1963.

Frioriksson, Arni. "The Icelandic Fisheries," Nord, 1 (1938), 305-13.

Iceland. Guarantee Agreement, Second Agricultural Project, Between Republic of Iceland and International Bank for Reconstruction and Development, Dated Sept. 4, 1953. Loan Number 79 IC. Wash., 1953. 7 p.

——. The Icelandic Efforts for Fisheries Conservation. Memorandum Submitted to the Council of Europe by the Government of Iceland. 1954. 56 p.

——. The Icelandic Efforts for Fisheries Conservation. Additional Memorandum Submitted to the Council of Europe by the Government of Iceland. 1955. 26 p.

"The Iceland Fresh-Water Fisheries," Bulletin of the United States Fish Commission for 1886 (Wash., 1887), 161-76.

"The Iceland Shark-Fisheries," Bulletin of the United States Fish Commission for 1885 (Wash., 1885), 301-304.

Mangeot, Sylvain. "Iceland's Point of View," GeogM, 31 (1959), 544-48.

Noel, H. S. "The Law of the Sea? No! The Law of Survival," World Fishing, 7 (1958), 30-38.

Olafsson, David. "Iceland and Her Fishing Industry," World Fishing, 3 (1954), 438-42.

——. "Icelandic Fisheries," ScPP, III, 563-66.

——. "New Trends in Herring Fishing," IcR, 1 (1963), 5-6.

NORWAY

Aarflot, Haakon. "The Trend," Norseman (1963, no. 5), 17-19.

Adeler, Arnold. The Principal Norwegian Laws Relating to Commerce Since 1880. Kra., 1915.

Akselsen, Egil. "The Economic Structure," in Ørnulf Vorren, ed., Norway North of 65 (Oslo, 1960), 147-56.

Aukrust, Odd. "On the Theory of Social Accounting," RofES, 16 (1949/1950), 170-88.

——. "Trends and Cycles in Norwegian Income Shares," in International Association for Research in Income and Wealth, Income and Wealth, series vi, 283-305.

Aukrust, Odd, ed. for the Norwegian Central

Bureau of Statistics. Norges økonomi etter krigen; The Norwegian Post-War Economy (Samfunnsøkonomiske Studier 12). Oslo, 1965. 437 p. English summary, 419-34.

Bahr, Henrik. "The Norwegian Gold Clause Case," AJCL, 12 (1963), 1-20.

Bakke, Edward Wight. A Norwegian Contribution to Executive Development. Bergen, 1959. 157 p.

Bengtson, Nels A. "The Economic Geography of Norway," JofGeo, 24 (1925), 243-59.

——. Norway; Commercial and Industrial Handbook (United States, Bureau of Foreign and Domestic Commerce, Special Agents Series, 196). Wash., 1920. 58 p.

Brofoss, Erik. Economic Resources of Norway. Oslo, 1949. 8 p.

——. "Economic Resources of Norway," Norseman, 7 (1949), 230-36.

——. Norway's Economic and Financial Problems: Two Lectures by the Governor of the Bank of Norway, Erik Brofoss, at the University of Oslo Summer School for American Students. Oslo, 1955. Mimeographed.

Christiansen, Herman. "Norway's Economic Life and Post-War Problems," Canadian Banker (1948), 125-36.

"A Comparison of Norway and Sweden," NGeogM, 16 (1905), 429-31.

Coombs, G. M. "The Rehabilitation of Norway," CR, 182 (1952), 280-83.

"Economic and Electoral Reforms in Norway," WT, 9 (1953), 22-29.

The Economic Position of Norway (C.J. Devine Institute of Finance Bull., 11). N.Y., 1960.

Ekblaw, W. Elmer. "Facets of Fjord Economy: a Study in Life on Sogne Fjord, Norway," JofGeo, 36 (1937), 1-16.

Fay, Hans. "Economic Conditions in Norway," ASR, 12 (1924), 19-26.

Great Britain, Department of Overseas Trade. Economic Conditions in Norway. Lond., 1920. An annual report with varying titles 1919-1928, 1949—.

Gylseth, S. "Norway Today," Calcutta Review, 109 (O 1948), 6-17.

Hagerup, Francis. Short Statement of Norwegian Commercial Law. 5th rev. ed., Kra., 1916.

Haight, C. S. "America's Requisition of the Norwegian 'New Buildings'," ASR, 9 (1921), 262-67.

Hammerschlag, Robert. Basic Data on the Economy of Norway. (U.S. Bureau of Foreign Commerce, World Trade Information Service. Economic Reports, pt. I, no. 56-65). Wash., 1956. 8 p.

Holmes, Ann C. Basic Data on the Economy of Norway (U.S. Bureau of International Commerce. Overseas Business Reports, OBR 64-55). Wash., 1964. 13 p.

Jahn, Gunnar. "Short Survey of the Norwegian Economy," ScPP, III, 477-88.

Keilhau, Wilhelm C. "The Importance of Norway's Economic Structure," Appendix I in Frede Castberg, The Norwegian Way of Life (Lond., 1954), 95-102.

Knudsen, Ole F. "Norway's Fifty Years of Economic Development," Norseman, 13 (1955), 173-77.

——. Norway, an Introduction to the Main Branches of the Norwegian Economy. Oslo, 1959. 66 p.

Lester, Richard A. "The Gold-Parity Depression in Norway and Denmark, 1925-8," JPE, 45 (1937), 433-65. See also Christenson, C. Lawrence, "Gold-Parity Depression in Norway and Denmark — A Discussion: a Criticism," JPE, 45 (1937), 808-10. Lester, Richard A., "A Rejoinder," JPE, 45 (1937), 810-13. Christensen, C. Lawrence, "A Reply," JPE, 45 (1937), 813-15.

"Main Trends in Norway's Economy," Lloyds Bank Review (1948), 31.

Mead, William R. "Sogn and Fjordane in the Fjord Economy of Western Norway," EG, 23 (1947), 155-66.

Melander, Johan. "The Financial Aspect of the German Exploitation of Norway," Norseman, 2 (1944), 140-47.

Mutter, J. L. "Norway in 1952: a Six-Months' Review," FT, 12 (O 18, 1952), 9-11.

——. "Norway Looks to the North," FT (Ja 23, 1954), 2-6.

Nilson, Sten S. "Norway — a Country of Immigration?," Norseman, 11 (1953), 319-24.

Norway (Summary of Current Economic Information, International Reference Service, v. 4, no. 16). Jl 1947. 6 p.

"Norway," AnColEc, 14 (1938), 250-52.

Norway, Central Bureau of Statistics. National Accounts, 1900-1929 (Official Statistics of Norway, series 11, 143). Oslo, 1953. 141 p.

——, Norges Bank. Bulletin. 1925—. General survey, with tables. Each issue contains a short article dealing with banking and general finance.

——, Norges Bank. Report and Accounts. 1955—. Includes articles on the economic situation. Oslo, 1956.

"Norway Today: a Survey of Economic Conditions," News of Norway (Je 28, 1941), 1-5.

"The Norwegian Government's Economic Survey for 1949," NorAmCom (May 1949), 7-10

Olsen, Kr. Anker. "Stability is the Keyword of Norway's Economy," Norseman (1960, no. 4), 12-15.

Olson, Grant. Economic Developments in Norway, 1960 (U.S. Bureau of Foreign Commerce, World Trade Information Service. Economic Reports, pt. 1, no. 61-26). Wash., 1961. 5 p.

Organization for European Economic Cooperation. Economic Conditions in Member and Associated Countries of the OEEC: Norway, 1961. Paris, 1961. 33 p.

Organization for Economic Cooperation and Development. Economic Surveys of the OECD: Norway. Paris, 1962. 38 p.

——. Economic Surveys: Norway. Paris, 1966. 47 p.

Palmer, A. M. F. "Norwegian Industry" and "Fishing, Agriculture and Cooperation," in William Warbey et al., Modern Norway: a Study in Social Democracy (Lond., 1950), 82-102, 103-17.

Paulson, Eilif W. The Economy of Western Norway (The Institute of Economics, the Norwegian School of Economics and Business Administration, Bergen. Papers, no. 14). Bergen, 1961. 13 p. Mimeographed.

Paus, C. L. Report on the Industrial and Economic Conditions in Norway, 1925-1926. Lond., 1927.

——. Report on Economic Conditions in Norway, 1927-28. Lond., 1929.

Petersen, Kaare. "Banking and Finance in Norway," ScPP, III, 831-39.

——. "The Capital Market in Norway," EFTA Bull, 5 (1964, no. 8), 11-13.

——. "Commerce and Co-operation in Norway," ScPP, III, 745-48.

——. "Economic Conditions in Norway: Losses Through Occupation and War," OISB, 8 (Ap 1946), 112-16.

——. "The Economic Outlook for 1960," Norseman (1960, no. 1), 22-25.

——. "Norwegian Economy under Pressure," Norseman (1961, no. 6), 24-26.

Prebensen, I. C. "Norway Maintains a High Standard of Living," IntM (S 1953), 14-15+.

Rygg, A. N. "The Economic Situation in Norway," ASR, 20 (1932), 276-83.

Schaty, E. J. The Norwegian Scene: Impressions of a Recent Business Trip to the 'midnight sun'," Export (Jl 1948), 29-32.

Scott, R. D., ed. Preliminary Study of Certain Financial Laws and Institutions: Norway (U.S. Treasury Department). Wash., 1943. 365 p.

"Some Aspects of Norway's Industrial and Economic Life," NSN (1960), 360-62.

Swenson, Harold. "The Banking System of Norway," in H. Parker Willis and B. H. Beckhart, eds., Foreign Banking Systems (N.Y., 1929), 869-92.

Syring, Edward M., Jr. The Demand for Money in Norway: an Econometric Analysis. Thesis (Ph.D.), University of Oregon, 1966.

United States, Department of Commerce, Bureau of Foreign Commerce, World Trade Information Service. Economic Developments in Norway, 1954 (Economic Reports, pt. 1, no. 55-22). Wash., 1955. 6 p.

——. Economic Developments in Norway, 1957 (Economic Reports, pt. 1, no. 58-22). Wash., 1958. 8 p.

United States, Department of Commerce, Bureau of International Programs, World Trade Information Service. Economic Developments in Norway, 1961 (Economic Reports, pt. 1, no. 62-29). Wash., 1962. 5 p.

——. Norway, a Commercial and Industrial Handbook. Wash., 1920. 58 p.

United States, Department of Commerce, Office of International Trade, International Reference Service. Economic Review of Norway, 1948. Wash., Jl 1949, 7 p.

——. Norway: Summary of Current Economic Information. Wash., Jl 1947, 6 p. v. 4, no. 16.

"The Wine Monopoly in Norway," ASR, 11 (1923), 363-64.

ECONOMISTS, SCHOOLS OF ECONOMICS

Aarflot, Haakon. "Ragnar Frisch, Controversial Economist," Norseman (1962, no. 1), 27-29.

Paulson, Eilif W. "The Norwegian School of Economics and Business Administration," Norseman (1961, no. 4), 16-18.

Stanford, Derek. "Thorstein Veblen (1857-1929)," Norseman, 16 (1958), 120-24.

ECONOMIC POLICY, PLANNING, NATIONAL BUDGET

Aarflot, Haakon. "The New Budget Sets

Another Record," Norseman (1963, no. 6), 23-25.

Barton, Allen H. Sociological and Psychological Problems of Economic Planning in Norway. Thesis (Ph.D.), Columbia University, 1957. 593 p.

Bjerve, Petter J. Planning in Norway 1947-1956 (Contributions to Economic Analysis, 16). Amsterdam, 1959. 383 p.

Bourneuf, Alice. Financing the Norwegian Post-War Investment Program and the Elimination of Suppressed Inflation. Thesis (Ph.D.), Radcliffe College, 1955.

———. Norway, the Planned Revival (Harvard Economic Studies, 106). Cambridge, Mass., 1958. 233 p. [Based on thesis above]

Braatoy, Bjarne. "A Norwegian Considers Reconstruction," NewEur, 1 (D 1940), 13-14+.

Due, Eilif. "Norwegian Credit Policy During the Last Two Years," Norwegian Commercial Banks Financial Review (Ja 1957), 1-5.

Galenson, Walter. "Nationalization of Industry in Great Britain and Norway," ASR, 36 (1948), 234-38.

Getz-Wold, Knut. "Norway's Problems of Social and Economic Reconstruction," ILR, 49 (1944), 585-607.

Grønaas, Olaf. "Developing North Norway," Norseman, 12 (1954), 179-82.

Grunwald, Joseph. National Economic Budgeting in Norway. Thesis (Ph.D.), Columbia University, 1951. 337 p.

———. "Planned Economy in Norway: a Reply," AER, 40 (1950), 410-15.

Havens, R. M. "The Norwegian Investment Program," Southern Economic Journal, 17 (1950), 166-75.

Holben, Ralph E. "Planned Economy in Norway: Comment," AER, 39 (1949), 1283-87.

Isachsen, Fridtjof. "Regional Planning in Norway," NGT, 14 (1954), 358-62.

Klein, Lawrence R. "Planned Economy in Norway," AER, 38 (1948), 795-814. Published also as Publication 26, University Institute of Economics, Oslo.

Kleppe, Per. Main Aspects of Economic Policy in Norway. Oslo, 1960. 12 p.

Layton, C. W. "Norway's New Economic Policy," Banker, 105 (1955), 42-47.

Lazarsfeld, Paul F., Allen H. Barton et al. The Psychological and Sociological Implications of Economic Planning in Norway. Oslo, 1950. 120 p. Mimeographed.

Leiserson, Mark W. Wages and Economic Control in Norway, 1945-1957 (Wertheim Publications in Industrial Relations). Cambridge, Mass., Lond., 1959. 174 p.

Lindebraekke, Sjur. "The Post-War Economic Situation in Norway," in Economic Conditions and Banking Problems (Saltsjöbaden, Sweden, 1950), 167-77.

Lloyd, Trevor. The Reconstruction of North Norway, 1945-1955 (Technical Report ONR 438-03-04). Hanover, N.H., 1956. 3 p.

Lund, Diderich H. "Revival of Northern Norway," GeogJ, 109 (1947), 185-97.

MacDonald, S. G. "Reconstruction of Norway Proceeding More Rapidly Than was Expected," FT, 2 (N/D, 1947), 818-20, 906-909, 1153-58. FT, 3 (Ja 1948), 36-37, 83-86, 132-37.

May, Richard, Jr. "Molde, Norway, Rebuilds One-fifth of Its Total Area," American City (D 1952), 92-94.

Norway, Ministry of Finance. National Budget of Norway, 1958 (Storting Report no. 1, 1958) Oslo, 1958. 68 p. Mimeographed.

———. Norwegian Long Term Programme, 1962-1965. Oslo, 1961. 62 p.

Norway, Office of the Prime Minister. The Norwegian Long-Term Program, 1954-1957, Presented by the Prime Minister on April 29, 1953 (Storting Report no. 62). Oslo, 1953. 334 p.

Olsen, Kr. Anker. "Foreign Capital a Key to Long Term Planning," Norseman (1960, no. 5), 21-23.

Pedersen, Sverre. "Methods of Planning for the Expansion of Towns in Norway," in International Housing and Town Planning Congress, Part I (Rome, 1929), 470-77.

Peskin, Henry M. The Norwegian Budget Model. Thesis (Ph.D.), University of California, Berkeley, 1965.

Petersen, E. "Economic Policy and Economic Development in Norway," SBQR (1955), 16-18.

Sedwitz, Walter J. "Inflexible Interest Rates and Economic Policy: the Case of Norway, 1946-1956," PSQ, 71 (1956), 569-96.

Skånland, Hermod. "Current Problems in Norwegian Economic Planning," Weltwirtschaftliches Archiv (1964, no. 1), 94-112.

Soltow, Lee. Toward Income Equality in Norway. Madison, Wisc., 1965. 172 p.

Stolz, Gerhard. Wage Control in Post-War Norway. Oslo, 1950. 35 p. Mimeographed.

Storing, James A. "The State and the Economy," Chap. II in his, Norwegian Democracy (Boston, 1963), 193-205.

Syvrud, Donald E. Post-war Norwegian Financial Problems and Policies: a Study

of the Monetary, Banking and Foreign
Exchange Problem of Norway During the
Post-war Years 1945-1949. Thesis
(Ph.D.), University of Wisconsin, 1956.
273 p.

United States, Economic Cooperation Administration. Norway (Country Data
Book). Wash., 1950. 83 p. Mimeographed.

——. Norway, Country Study, European
Recovery Program. Wash., 1949. 67 p.

Warbey, William. "Economic Planning in
Norway," Chap. III in his, Modern Norway: a Study in Social Democracy (Lond.,
1950), 64-81.

——. "Economic Planning Machinery in
Norway," Changing Epoch Series, 3
(1947), 1-10.

TAXATION

Fagernaes, S. "Profit Taxes Affecting Industrial and Commercial Enterprises,"
BIFD, 11 (1957), 78-85.

Fisher, Janet A. "Taxation of Personal Incomes and Net Worth in Norway," NTJ,
11 (1958), 84-93.

"A Guide to the System of Direct Taxation in
Norway," in Norwegian Chamber of Commerce Yearbook (Lond., 1963), 23-46.

Hauan, Olav. "The Norwegian System of
Taxation: 1958," PubFin, 15 (1960), 62-
70.

Magnus, M. H. "Review of the Norwegian
Taxation System," BIFD, 7 (1953), 39-49.

Norwegian Chamber of Commerce, London.
A Guide to the System of Direct Taxation
in Norway. Lond., 1963. 16 p.

Seip, Helge. "Norwegian Tax Reform,"
BIFD, 6 (1952), 343-48.

——. "Norwegian Taxation: Research and
Reform," Canadian Tax Journal, 1 (1953),
391-98.

Soltow, Lee. "Norwegian and United States
Tax Rates and the Distribution of Income," NTJ, 16 (1963), 200-205.

Strangeby, K. "Legislative Measures to
Fight Tax Fraud in Norway," BIFD, 7
(1953), 257-62.

"Tax Reform and Employment of Married
Women in Norway," I&L, 23 (1960), 68.

"Tax Regulations in Norway," BIFD, 10
(1956), 280-87.

FOREIGN TRADE, FOREIGN
ECONOMIC POLICY

Boquist, Birger. "Trade Development,"
Norseman (1961, no. 1), 24-27.

"Bright Outlook for Norway's Aluminium,"
Euromarket, 1 (1959), 9-11.

Bugge, Alexander. "A Thousand Years of
Norwegian Trade; Present Conditions in
the Light of History," ASR, 14 (1926),
593-99.

Christiansen, Birger. "How the EFTA
Countries Help Exports: Norway," EFTA
Bull, 7 (1966, no. 6), 6-8.

Flaaten, Eivind. "Norway Seeks New Eastern Markets," EW (M 1953), 38-40.

Gade, John A. The Hanseatic Control of
Norwegian Commerce During the Late
Middle Ages. Leiden, 1951. 139 p.

Getz-Wold, Knut. "International Aspects of
Norwegian Economic Reconstruction,"
IA, 20 (1944), 54-67.

Hald, Knut. "The Export Industries of Norway," Norwegian American Consumer
(Ap 1957), 15-16+.

Hambro, Johan. "Export of Know-How,"
Norseman (1960, no. 3), 20-22.

Hiorth, Otto. "The U.S.-Norway Intra-Trade
Development 1915-1955 Surveyed and
Analyzed," NAC (1955), 52-62.

International Studies Conference. Memorandum on External Economic Policy of Norway in Recent Years (International Studies
Conference, 12th. Bergen, Norway, 1939,
Memoranda). Paris, 1939. 127 p.

International Studies Conference. Memorandum on the Repercussions of Modern
Commercial Policies on Economic Conditions in Norway. Paris, 1939. 158 p.

Kent, H. S. K. "The Anglo-Norwegian Timber Trade in the Eighteenth Century,"
EcHistR, new series, 8 (1955), 62-74.

Kjaerheim, Steinar. "Norwegian Timber
Exports in the 18th Century: a Compari-
son of Port Books and Private Accounts,"
SEHR, 5 (1957), 188-201.

Koefod, Holger. "Norway and the American
Loan," ASR, 9 (1921), 42-46.

Lie, Trygve. "Foreign Investments in Norway," Norseman (1960, no. 2), 18-20.

——. Investors' Guide to Norway. Oslo,
1959. 54 p.

——. Why Investors Pick Norway. Oslo,
1959. 14 p.

Malterud, Otto Chr. "New Perspectives for
Norwegian Exports," Norseman (1962, no.
1), 13-16.

Morgenstierne, Wilhelm. "Trade Relations
with Norway," ASR, 7 (1919), 190-93.

New York University Institute of International Finance. Credit Position
of Norway (Bull. 99). N.Y., 1938.
27 p.

Norway, Trade Intelligence Bureau,

Business Information Office. Norway:
Foreign Trade. Kra., 1924. 62 p.
"Norway's Dependence on Foreign Trade,"
BdofTradeJ, 152 (Ap 20, 1946), 467-68.
Norway's Export Trade. Oslo, 1939. 195 p.
"Norway's External Claims and Debts, on
December 31, 1951: Balance of Pay-
ments," NBB, 23 (O 1952), 64-74.
"Norway's Post-War Foreign Trade Policy,"
BdofTradeJ, 155 (Aug 21, 1948), 367-69.
Norwegian Chamber of Commerce in Lon-
don. Yearbook. Lond., 1909. Contains
each year: information about Norway's
government officials in the U. K. and
British offices in Norway, Norwegian
consuls throughout the British common-
wealth, general information on Norway,
statistics of Norwegian economy, and at
least one article on an aspect of Anglo-
Norwegian trade.
———. The Norwegian Chamber of Com-
merce in London, 1906-1931. Lond.,
1931. 30 p.
Norwegian Export Council. Norges Eksport-
kalander (Norway's Directory of Exporters). 1948-49. Oslo, 1948. 448 p.;
1960-61 (20th ed). N.Y., 1961. 246 p.
[Title varies]
———. Norway, Chemical Products Exports.
Ed. by Eivind Flaatten. Oslo, 1952. 64 p.
———. Norway: Machinery and Metal
Products Exports. Ed. by Nils M. Ape-
land. Oslo, 1951.
———. Norway: Survey of Exports. Ed. by
Eivind Flaatten. Oslo, 1955. 120 p.
———. Norway, Survey of Exports and Eco-
nomic Developments. Ed. by Conrad
Hofgaard. Oslo, 1948.
Norwegian Export Review 1948+. Frequently
long articles. A continuation of Norwe-
gian Industry and Export Review.
Norway. Norwegian Trade Review; a Digest
of Commercial Affairs and Current De-
velopments in Norway...new series,
Oslo. Je/Jl 1930—. Continued as Nor-
wegian American Commerce, 1941—;
Preceded by Norwegian Trade Review,
1917—.
Paine, Robert. "The Russian Trade in
Finnmark," Norseman, 16 (1958), 73-80.

EUROPEAN ECONOMIC INTEGRATION

Gjelster, Thor. "Norway and EFTA,"
Norseman (1961, no. 3), 15-17.
Langeland, Arne. "Norway and EEC,"
Norseman (1962, no. 4), 15-17.
Lindebraekke, Sjur. "Economic Coopera-
tion: the Challenge of the New Era of

Free Trade," Norseman (1960, no. 3),
14-16.
Malterud, Otto Chr. "The Importance of the
EEC Market to EFTA Countries: Norway," EFTA Bull, 6 (1965, no. 6), 4-6.
———. "One of Seven: Norway's Place in
the New System of Trade," Norseman
(1960, no. 1), 8-10, 29.

HOUSING

Hoffmann, Johann. Main Features of Norwegian Post-War Housing Policy. Oslo,
1952. Mimeographed.
Norway, State Housing Bank. Housing Needs
and Housing Shortage in Norway, 1939-
1949. Unofficial translation of unpublished report of the statistical department
of the State Housing Bank, May 12, 1950.
Norwegian Joint Committee on International
Social Policy. Building Practices and
Housing Standards in Norway, Statistical
Survey. Oslo, 1951. Supplement to Hous-
ing in Norway.
———. Housing in Norway, A Survey. Oslo,
1951. 143 p.
———. Housing in Norway, 1950-1960. Oslo,
1962. 35 p.
———. Housing Progress in Norway Since
1950. Oslo, 1955. 23 p.
"Norwegian Housing Policy Since the War,"
Norwegian Commercial Banks Financial
Rev, 34 (1960), 25-27.
Royal Norwegian Council for Scientific and
Industrial Research. Building Research
in Norway. Oslo, 1950.
Vatne, Hans. "Norwegian Master Builder
Olav Selvaag," Norseman (1967, no. 2),
37-39.
Wilson, Marie R. "Norway's Postwar Hous-
ing," Journal of Home Economics, 48
(1956), 627-30.

INDUSTRY, BUSINESS

Aars, Ferdinand. Arts and Crafts, Indus-
trial Design in Norway. Oslo, 1953.
32 p.
———. Norwegian Arts and Crafts, Indus-
trial Design. Oslo, 1957. 77 p.
Adamson, Olge J., ed. Industries of Norway,
Technical and Commercial Achievements.
Oslo, Los Angeles, 1952. 392 p.
Aune, Leif. "Industry and Mining," in Ørnulf
Vorren, ed., Norway North of 65 (Oslo,
1960), 216-36.
Barlaup, Asbjørn. "A Globe Girdling Busi-
ness" [Elektrokemisk], Norseman (1962,
no. 4), 22-25.

Brox, Ottar. "Three Types of North Norwegian Entrepreneurship," in Frederik Barth, ed., The Role of the Entrepreneur in Social Change in Northern Norway (Oslo, 1963), 19-32.

Brynildsen, Harald. "'Liquid Gold' in the Arctic: Optimists Predict a Svalbard Oil Boom as Drilling Through the Tundra Begins," Norseman (1965), 141-43.

Ellefsen, Einar S. "A Furniture Boom," Norseman (1966), 84-87.

Eyde, Samuel. "The Industrial Future of Norway," ASR, 1 (1913), 5-13.

Falkberget, Johan. "Röros, the Copper Town of Norway," ASR, 13 (1925), 412-21.

Fischer, Wolfgang. "Record in Tape Recorders: Vebjörn Tandberg," Norseman (1967), 145-48.

Getz-Wold, Knut. "Norwegian Industry," ScPP, III, 636-58.

Gilbo, Ole S. "Aluminum Giants Join Forces," Norseman (1967), 12-16.

——. "Research Develops Resources," Norseman (1967), 91-93.

Great Britain, Board of Trade, Directories and Notices Section. Hints to Business Men Visiting Norway (Hints to Business Men Series). Lond., 1961. 32 p.

Hammerschlag, Robert. "Industrial Developments in Post War Norway," ForCom-Wk (Aug 1951), 3-4.

Haupert, John S. "Recent Developments in the Norwegian Metals Industry," JofGeo, 59 (1960), 76-80.

Holler, Kjell. "Automation — a Norwegian View," Free Labour World, 8 (M 1958), 87-90.

Holmsen, Andreas. "The Mining Industry in Norway," NGT, 7 (1938/39), 420-40.

Jenssen, Harry. "An Outline of Legislative Control in Norway of Restrictive Trade Practices, Prices, and Other Trade Terms," in Norwegian Chamber of Commerce Yearbook (Lond., 1964), 23-39.

Knudsen, Ole F. "Industrial Research in Norway," Norseman, 10 (1952) 242-45.

——. "North Norway's Steel Plant," Norseman, 13 (1955), 95-99.

——. "Norway's Industrial Revolution," Norseman, 9 (1951), 105-108.

Lloyd, Trevor. "Iron Ore Production at Kirkenes, Norway," CG (1955, no. 5), 43-52.

——. "Iron Ore Production at Kirkenes, Norway," EG, 31 (1955), 211-33.

Luckow, Leon. "Norway's First Oil Refinery," Norseman (1961, no. 4), 23-25.

Lyshoel, J. H. "War-Time Business in Norway," ASR, 4 (1916), 218-22.

Major, Robert. "Research and Development in Norway," ASR, 51 (1963), 40-46.

——. "Scientific and Industrial Research in Norway," EFTA Bull, 6 (1965, no. 8), 8-10.

——. "Organization of Scientific Activities in Norway," Science, 129 (1959), 694-700.

"Mustad: Made in Norway," Norseman (1967), 112-15.

Nordby, Ragnar. "Home Arts and Crafts," Norseman (1965, no. 1), 19-24.

Norwegian Export Council. Norway, Arts and Crafts. Ed. by Conrad Hofgaard. Oslo, 1950.

Norwegian Federation of Industry. Industry in Norway. Oslo, 1951. 112 p.

——. Norway's Industry, a Short Review of Its Development and Present Position. Oslo, 1958. 98 p.

"The Norwegian Iron and Steel Industry," British Iron and Steel Federation, Monthly Statistical Bulletin, 24 (1949).

Østenstad, Øistein. "Pulp, Chemicals, Food (Borregaard)," Norseman (1965, no. 1), 16-18.

Paine, Robert. "Entrepreneurial Activity Without Its Profits," in Fredrik Barth, ed., The Role of the Entrepreneur in Social Change in Northern Norway. (Oslo, 1963), 33-55.

Philip, David. "How Norway is Furthering Industrial Rationalisation and Increased Productivity," Norseman, 13 (1955), 392-401.

Randers, Gunnar. "The Dutch-Norwegian Atomic Energy Project," Bulletin of the Atomic Scientists, 9 (1953), 369-71.

"Research a Key to Progress" [Central Institute for Industrial Research], Norseman (1965, no. 3), 87-91.

Roem-Nielsen, Rolf. "'Seven' Alliance Spurs Norway's Industry," EFTA Rep, no. 107 (1964), 4, 7. Appears also in EFTA Bull, 5 (1964, no. 7), 6-7.

Rudie, Ingrid. "Two Entrepreneurial Careers in a Small Local Community," in Fredrik Barth, ed., The Role of the Entrepreneur in Social Change in Northern Norway (Oslo, 1963), 56-69.

Rygh, L. N. "Stavanger and the Norwegian Canning Industry," ASR, 9 (1921), 465-70.

Seip, Helge. "Norway's Post-War Industrialization," Ind, 17 (1949), 476-82.

Semmingsen, Ingrid. "The Machine Age Comes to Norway," ScPP, II, 801-808.

Stenrod, Erling. "The Norwegian Nitrogen Industry and Its Significance for European Agriculture," Triangle, 7 (1949), 11-15.

Stonehill, Arthur I. Foreign-owned Business

Enterprises in Norway. Thesis (Ph.D.),
University of California, Berkeley, 1965.
Published by Norwegian Central Bureau
of Statistics (Samfunnsøkonomiske Studier
14) as: Foreign Ownership in Norwegian
Enterprises. Oslo, 1965. 213 p.

Sundby-Hansen, H. "Norway's Industries,"
nine articles, ASR: I: "The Merchant
Marine," 16 (1928), 675-82. II: "Agri-
culture," 17 (1929), 162-64. III: "The
Fisheries," 17 (1929), 230-36. IV:
"Svalbard Coal," 17 (1929), 427-30. V:
"Nitrate from the Air," 17 (1929), 494-
96. VI: "Aluminum," 17 (1929), 555-56.
VII: "Cod Liver Oil," 17 (1929), 622-23.
VIII: "Forestry, Lumbering, and Wood
Manufacturing," 17 (1929), 677-82. IX:
"Wood Pulp and Paper," 17 (1929), 683-84.

Thomson, Claudia. "Norway's Industrialization," EG, 14 (1938), 372-80.

Ustvedt, Hans J. "National Developments in
Norwegian Research," Norseman, 2
(1944), 320-31.

Vorren, Ørnulf. "The Reindeer Industry," in
his, Norway North of 65 (Oslo, 1960),
172-90.

Wedervang, Fröystein. Development of a
Population of Industrial Firms: the
Structure of Manufacturing Industries in
Norway, 1930-1948 (Skrifter fra Norges
Handelshøyskole, 9), Bergen, Coph., 1965.

LABOR, LABOR RELATIONS, UNEMPLOYMENT

Aarvik, Lars. "Labor Relations and Wage
Policy in Norway," ScPP, III, 812-16.

Berg, Paal. "Now Norway Solves Its Labor
Problem," ASR, 36 (1948), 136-41.

Bull, Edvard. "Industrial Workers and
Their Employers in Norway, Circa 1900,"
SEHR, 3 (1955), 64-84. Reprinted in Val
R. Lorwin, ed., Labor and Working Con-
ditions in Modern Europe (N.Y., 1967),
86-106.

——. The Norwegian Trade Union Movement (International Confederation of Free
Trade Unions' Monographs on National
Trade Union Movements, no. 4). Brussels, N.Y., 1956. 140 p.

Castberg, Johan. "Compulsory Arbitration
in Norway," ILR, 11 (1925), 15-38.

——. "Labor and Industrial Management:
a Norwegian Solution," ASR, 7 (1919),
466-69.

Champion, A. J. "Labour Relations," in
William Warbey et al., Modern Norway:
a Study in Social Democracy (Lond.,
1950), 118-44.

Compulsory Arbitration in Norway. (Trans.
of Norwegian Law). Wash., 1917. 6 p.

Donhowe, G. M. "Economic Analysis in
Norwegian Collective Bargaining," Journal of Business, 33 (1960), 363-72.

Dorfman, Herbert. Labor Relations in Norway. 2d ed. Oslo, 1958. 150 p.

"Employment of the Disabled Under Shel-
tered Conditions in Norway," ILR, 88
(1963), 66-73.

Erlichman, Samuel. The Attitude of Trade
Unions Toward Productivity: the Cases
of Norway, Israel and Ghana. Thesis
(Ph.D.), New School for Social Research,
1966.

"Factory Inspection in Norway in 1924."
ILR, 14 (1926), 574-78.

Finch, Clifford. "Labour Management Cooperation in Norway," IPMJ, 31 (S 1949),
237-43.

Galenson, Walter. Labor in Norway (Harvard University Wertheim Fellowship
Publications). Cambridge, Mass., 1949.
373 p.

——. "Norwegian Labor Regulates Itself,"
Labor and Nation (Jl 1947), 25-27.

Hvidsten, Johan. "Unemployment in Norway," ILR, 7 (1923), 231-39.

Inman, J. "Post-War Wages Policy in Norway," OISB, 12 (Jl/Aug 1950), 195-216.

Keilhau, Wilhelm. "Evolution of Labour
Legislation in Norway," Norseman, 1
(1943), 306-14.

Koht-Norbye, O. D. "Norwegian Trade
Unions," SoCo, 14 (Ap 1950), 93-95.

"Labour-Management Cooperation in Norway," I&L, 22 (1959), 213-14.

Nagell-Erichsen, E. F. Å. Industrial Relations in Norway, with Special Reference
to the Newspaper Industry. Thesis
(M.Sc.), London School of Economics,
1960.

Norway, Directorate of Labor Inspection.
Workers' Protection Act in Norway; a
Survey. Oslo, 1947. 58 p.

Norwegian Federation of Labor (LO). Norwegian Labor Looks at the United States
of America and the Union of Soviet Socialist Republics. Oslo, 1949. 33 p.

——. The Trade Union Movement in Norway. Oslo, 1951. 64 p.

Norwegian Joint Committee on International
Social Policy. Employment Policy in
Norway, a Survey. Oslo, 1950. 47 p.

"The Norwegian Labour Movement," SoCo,
15 (Ap. 1951), 92-95.

Palmström, Henrik. "Labour Conditions in
Occupied Norway," ILR, 48 (1943), 584-
610.

"Recent Wage Changes in Various Countries: Norway," ILR, 18 (1928), 97-101.

Skrindo, Thor. "Manpower Planning in Norway," ILR, 76 (1957), 124-38.

Slaby, Steve M. "Institution for Labour Peace" [The Labour Court in Norway], Norseman, 10 (1952), 145-48.

————. The Labor Court in Norway. Oslo, 1952. 38 p.

————. "The Solution of Labor Disputes in Norway;" ASR, 51 (1963), 255-62.

"Statistics of Occupied Population in Different Countries" [Italy, Norway], ILR, 31 (1935), 903-906.

Trade Union News Bulletin from Norway. Published by the Norwegian Federation of Trade Unions. Oslo, 1946. Mimeographed, monthly.

Ulsaker, Berger. "Local Labour Inspection in Norway," ILR, 96 (1967), 92-99.

"Unemployment Relief and Employment Exchanges in Norway in 1922-1923," ILR, 11 (1925), 252-64.

"Unemployment Relief and Employment Exchanges in Norway in 1925-1926," ILR, 17 (1928), 575-77.

Voss, Fredrik. "Minimum Wage Legislation in Norway," ILR, 12 (1925), 799-819.

HYDROELECTRIC AND ATOMIC POWER

Brochmann, Georg. "Norway, Land of Water Power," ASR, 23 (1935), 129-39.

Eriksen, Viking O. "The Dutch-Norwegian Atomic Energy Center," ASR, 44 (1956), 221-29.

Heggenhougen, Rolv. "Industrial Giant" [Norsk Hydro], Norseman (1962, no. 5), 4-8.

Heiden, Noland R. "Odd and Rjukan: Two Industrialized Areas of Norway," Annals of Association of American Geographers, 42 (1952), 109-28.

Jenssen, Grudbrand. "The Development of Atomic Energy in Norway," Norseman (1962, no. 3), 75-78.

Knudsen, Ole F. "Norwegian Power Export," Norseman, 15 (1956), 24-26.

Leach, Henry G. "Rjukan Revisited," ASR, 39 (1951), 109-14.

Ljone, Oddmund. "The Tokke Project," Norseman (1961, no. 1), 12-15.

Martin, Anthony. "Hydro-Electric Jubilee" [Review of K. Anker Olsen's Norsk Hydro gjennom 50 år], Norseman, 14 (1956), 139-42.

Mutton, A. F. A. "Hydro-electric Power Development in Norway," TIBG, 19 (1953), 123-30.

Planned Utilization of Water Resources. The Norwegian Society of Civil Engineers; Transactions of World Power Conference, 1936, v. 7, 1938. 281-90.

Power Resources, Development, and Utilization. Data Assembled by Norwegian National Committee of World Power Conference; Transactions of World Power Conference, 1936, v. 2, 1938. 301-10.

Pugh, J. C. "The Floating Power Stations of Scandinavia 1959-61," Geog, 47 (1962), 270-77.

Raitt, William L. "The Changing Pattern of Norwegian Hydro-electric Development," EG, 34 (1958), 127-44.

Randers, Gunnar. "Heavy Water Reactor for Industrial Use," Norseman, 11 (1953), 289-96.

————. "New Tricks in an Old Town: the Halden Nuclear Reactor," Norseman (1960, no. 1), 11-15.

Thorne, Christian A. "Norway's White Coal," ASR, 9 (1921), 458-63.

Wasberg, Gunnar. "From Charcoal to Electricity," Norseman (1964, no. 2), 54-57.

TRANSPORTATION

Aase, Asbjørn. "Communications," in Ørnulf Vorren, ed., Norway North of 65 (Oslo, 1960), 237-47.

Knutsen, Fridtjof. "The Road to the Midnight Sun: a New Highway Opening Northern Norway," ASR, 25 (1937), 319-25.

Lloyd, Trevor. Reconstruction of Transportation in North Norway (Technical Report ONR 438-03-06). Hanover, N.H., 1956. 12 p.

Malmström, Vincent H. "The Norwegian State Railways, 1854-1954," ASR, 42 (1954), 221-30.

————. A Study of Land Transport in Norway. Thesis (Ph.D.), University of Michigan, 1954. 205 p.

Norway, Division of Highways. Highways of Norway: a Short Account of Organisation and Development of the Norwegian Highway Service. Tr. by E. Lund Hansen. Oslo, 1925. 37 p.

Paulson, Eilif W. Transport and Communications Problems in Norway (The Institute of Economics, the Norwegian School of Economics and Business Administration, Bergen, Papers, no. 11). Bergen, 1958. 10 p.

SHIPPING

Andersen, Frank. "New Shipping Gains," Norseman (1964), 175-78.

Backen, Kjeld. "The Making of a Sailor,"
Norseman (1964), 13-17.

Boquist, Birger. "'Foreign Minister of
Shipping': Leif Høegh," Norseman,
(1966), 160-62.

Byrde, Godtfred M. "The Revival of Norway's Dominion on the Sea," ASR, 1
(1913, no. 5), 6-12.

Egeland, John O. "Norwegian Shipping After
the World War," Harvard Business Review, 10 (1932), 311-22.

——. "Ships and Shipping in Norway,"
ASR, 12 (1924), 415-22.

Einarsen, Johan. Reinvestment Cycles and
Their Manifestation in the Norwegian
Shipping Industry (Publication 14 of the
University Institute of Economics, Oslo).
Oslo, 1938. 222 p.

Fischer, Alfred J. "Norway's Merchant
Navy," CR, 172 (1947), 364-68.

"Food and Catering in Norwegian Ships,"
ILR, 65 (1952), 636-41.

Gilbo, Ole S. "Bigger and Better Yards:
Norwegian Shipbuilders Meet the Modern
Challenge," Norseman (1966), 110-12.

——. "Shipbuilding on the Increase,"
Norseman (1965), 147-50.

Gjerset, Knut. Norwegian Sailors in American Waters: a Study in the History of
Maritime Activity on the Eastern Sea-
board. Northfield, Minn., 1933. 271 p.

Gogstad, Odd. "New Trends in Norwegian
Shipping," Norseman (1964), 21-24.

Keilhau, Wilhelm. Norway and the Bergen
Line: a Centenary Publication. Bergen,
1953. 369 p.

Kendall, Lane C. "The Norwegian Merchant
Marine Since 1945," USNIP, 82 (1956),
974-97.

Knudsen, Ole F. "Norway and Her Ships,"
Norseman, 5 (1947), 122-26.

Kuhnle, H., Jr. "Post-War Trends in Norwegian Shipping," NCBFR (Ap 1957), 1-4.

——. "Shipping Problems of Today," NSN
(1960), 41-42, 45-46, 49.

Lampe, Stein. "Norway and Her Merchant
Navy," IAF (Jl 1956), 84-89.

Lidemark, Arne, ed. Norwegian Shipbuilding, 1949. Oslo, 1950. 344 p.; 1951 ed.,
339 p.

——. Norwegian Shipbuilding Industry,
1950. [An illustrated propaganda publi-
cation]. Oslo, 1950. 313 p. 1956/57 ed.,
278 p.

Ljone, Oddmund. "Bridge Across the Sea,"
Norseman (1960, no. 4), 8-11.

Lorentzen, Øivind. Norway, Norwegian
Shipping and the War (America in a World
at War, no. 25). N.Y., Toronto, 1942. 32 p.

"Marine Insurance in Norway in 1959," NSN
(1960), 263-64.

Mitsem, Sverre. "Anders Jahre, Leader of
Whaling and Shipping," Norseman (1961,
no. 2), 16-18.

Norway, Information Office. Norway's
Floating Empire. Foreword by Philip
Noel Baker. Montreal, Lond., 1942.
44 p.

"Norway's Shipping Today: Progress and
Prospects," Norseman (1960, no. 6), 21-
23.

"The Norwegian Merchant Fleet: Some Statistical Notes," NSN (1960), 50, 53-54,
57-58, 61-62, 65-66, 69-70, 73.

"Norwegian New Building Contracts," NSN
(1960), 74.

"Norwegian Shipping and Shipping Policy
Since the War," NSN, 25 (1955), 4-21.

"Norwegian Shipping News 1945-1960," NSN
(1960), 5.

"The Norwegian View of the 50 Per Cent
Shipping Clause," NorAmCom (May 1949),
18-20.

Olsen, Kr. Anker. "Shipping Giant 100 Years:
Wilh-Wilhelmsen Celebrating Its Centennial," Norseman (1961, no. 5), 21-25.

Paulson, Eilif W. The Norwegian Shipping
Industry (The Institute of Economics, the
Norwegian School of Economics and Business Administration, Bergen, Papers, no.
15). Bergen, 1961. 8 p.

"Pay and Hours of Seafarers," ILR, 48
(1943), 23-42.

Petersen, Kaare. The Saga of Norwegian
Shipping: an Outline of the History,
Growth and Development of a Modern
Merchant Marine. Oslo, 1955. 238 p.

Rugg, A. N. "Norway's Life Line to the
Sea," ASR, 32 (1944), 121-33.

Seland, Johan. "The Norwegian Shipping Industry," ScPP, III, 691-704.

"Shipping and Shipbuilding During the Last
Five Years," NSN (1960), 10, 13-14, 17-
18, 21-22, 25-26, 29-30, 33-34, 37.

"Tradition and Quality: Norwegian Ship
Building at a New Peak," Norseman
(1962, no. 3), 22-25.

Wilhelmsen, J. "Norwegian Shipbuilding
1955-59," NSN (1960), 93-94, 97.

FISHING, WHALING

Akselsen, Oddvar. "Whaling — Past and Future," Norseman (1961, no. 2), 23-26.

Bailey, P. J. M., and D. G. Symes. "The
Dogfish Processing and Export Industry
of Måløy, Western Norway," Geog, 48
(1963), 73-77.

Dahl, Tor. "Fresh from the Sea," Norseman (1962, no. 2), 17-20.

Danielsen, Rolf. "A Norwegian Fishing Centre" [Review of Norwegian book by Reidar Östensjö], SEHR, 7 (1959), 109-11.

Ellefsen, Einar S. "Leader of Norwegian Fisheries," [Møre og Romsdal], Norseman (1967), 6-9.

Gasmann, J. B. E. "The Great Lofoten Fishery," ASR, 38 (1954), 48-53.

Gerhardsen, Gerhard M. "Fishery Limits from an Economist's Point of View," Norseman (1961, no. 5), 17-20.

——. Fifty Years of Norwegian Fisheries, 1905-1955. (Norwegian School of Economics and Business Administration, Bergen, Papers, no. 1). Bergen, 1955. 20 p.

Gundersen, G. "Co-operation in the Norwegian Fishing Industry," RIC, 43 (M, 1950), 74-75+.

Hofgaard, Conrad, ed. Norway: Fisheries and Fish Processing. Oslo, 1949. 128 p.

Hohman, Elmo P. "American and Norwegian Whaling: a Comparative Study of Labor and Industrial Organization," JPE, 43 (1935), 628-52.

Holtvedt, Reidar. "Guarding the Coast" [Norwegian rescue service], Norseman (1962, no. 4), 26-29.

Isachsen, Fridtjov. "The New Norwegian Dependency in the Antarctic," Nord, 2 (1939), 67-78.

Jahn, Gunnar. "Norway and the Whaling Industry," ScPP, III, 572-74.

Jakobsen, Anton. "Sealing and Whaling," in Ørnulf Vorren, ed., Norway North of 65 (Oslo, 1960), 209-15.

Leach, Henry G. "Antarctic Whaling," ASR, 39 (1951), 198-203.

Lloyd, Trevor, and John Snell. The Fishing Industry of North Norway (Technical Report ONR 438-03-05). Hanover, N.H., 1956. 20 p.

MacDonald, S. G. "Sealing Industry is an Important Factor in Norwegian Economy," FT, 4 (1948), 373-75.

——. "Whaling is of First Importance Among Norwegian Industries," FT, 7 (Ja 1950), 56-59.

Martin, Anthony. "The Lofoten Fisheries," Norseman, 7 (1949), 177-83.

Meyer, Christopher B. V. Norway's Usage and Prescription in the Matter of Coastal Fisheries. Oslo, 1952.

Mutter, J. L. "Norway and the Whaling Industry," FT (Je 20, 1953), 8-10.

——. "Norway's Fishing Industry," FT, 13 (1953), 8-11.

Nilsson, Lennart. "Fishing in the Lofotens," NGeogM, 91 (1947), 377-88.

Nordset, Arne, and Aslak Aasbø. "Cooperation Among Fishermen in Norway," Fiskeridirektoratets Skrifter, 4 (1959, no. 2), Bergen. 71 p.

Norway, Commission for Whaling Statistics. International Whaling Statistics. Oslo, 1950. 71 p. 1951 issue (v. 26), 82 p.

Norway, Ministry of Fishing. "On the Fisheries of Norway," Report of the United States Commissioner of Fish and Fisheries for 1873-74 and 1874-75 (Wash., 1876), 25-30.

——. The Propagation of Our Common Fishes during the Cold Winter 1924: Investigations on the Norwegian Skagerrack Coast (Report on Norwegian Fishery and Marine Investigations, 3, no. 10). By Alf Dannevig. Bergen, 1930.

——. Report on Norwegian Fishery and Marine Investigations. Kra., 1900.

"The Norwegian Fishing Industry," World Fishing, 1 (1952), 43-47.

Østensjø, Reidar. "The Spring Herring Fishing and the Industrial Revolution in Western Norway in the Nineteenth Century," SEHR, 11 (1963), 135-55.

Pontecorvo, Giulio, and Knut Vartdal, Jr. "Optimizing Resource Use: the Norwegian Winter Herring Fishery," Statsøkonomisk tidsskrift, 81 (1967), 65-87.

Risting, Sigurd. "Hunting the Whale," ASR, 14 (1926), 622-27.

Saetersdal, Gunnar. "Fisheries," in Ørnulf Vorren, ed., Norway North of 65 (Oslo, 1960), 191-208.

Sellaeg, Johannes. "Financing of Norway's Fishing Industry," NorAmCom (F 1953), 13-14.

——. "Norwegian Fisheries," ScPP, III, 567-71.

——. "Recent Developments in Norwegian Fisheries," Norseman, 9 (1951), 173-82.

Smith, Hugh M. "King Herring: an Account of the World's Most Valuable Fish, the Industries It Supports and the Part It has Played in History," NGeogM, 20 (1909), 701-35.

Sommers, Lawrence M. "Commercial Fishing in Norway," Tijdschrift voor Economische en Sociale Geografie (1962), 237-42. Reprinted in Howard G. Toepke, ed., Readings in Economic Geography (N.Y., 1967), 71-81.

——. "Fish Processing and Associated Industries of Møre og Romsdal County," NGT, 13 (1951/52), 240-65.

——. The Norwegian Fishing Industry as

Exemplified by Møre Og Romsdal County. Thesis (Ph.D.), Northwestern University, 1951.

———. The Norwegian Slipfish Industry: Nature and Distribution. 1953. Reprinted from Papers of the Michigan Academy of Science Arts and Letters, 38 (1953), 347-55.

Sund, Oscar. "The Lofoten Fisheries," ASR, 10 (1922), 216-24.

Sunnanå, Klaus. "The Norwegian Fisheries and Their Post-War Problems," Norseman, 2 (1944), 263-73.

West, John F. "Fishermen of Lofoten," Norseman, 13 (1955), 252-55.

"The Whaling Industry," Triangle, 3 (1948), 7-10.

COOPERATIVES

Arnesen, Randolf. "Thirty Years of Co-operation in Norway," IO, 2 (1937/38), 148-57.

"The Cooperative Union and Wholesale Society in 1931," AnColEc, 8 (1932). 1931, 255-56; 1932, 356+.

"Fiftieth Anniversary of NKL [Norges Kooperativa Landsforening Wholesale Society]: History and Present Status," RIC, 49 (1956), 131-34.

Grimley, O. B. Agricultural Co-operatives in Norway. Oslo, 1950. 94 p.

———. Cooperatives in Norway. Oslo, 1950. 178 p.

———. The New Norway; a People with the Spirit of Cooperation. Oslo, 1937. 159 p.

Haugen, Reidar. "Consumers' Cooperation in Norway," AnColEc, 34 (1963), 577-84.

Noram, C. C. "The Cooperative Movement in Norway," NorAmCom (O 1947), 18-20.

Norby, J. C. "Consumers' Cooperatives in Norway," JM, 16 (Ap 1952), 423-34.

Söiland, Peder. "Consumer Cooperatives in Norway," RIC, 43 (1950), 102-107.

———. "The Consumer Council in Norway," Cartel, 6 (1953), 210-15.

———. "Problems of the Norwegian Co-operative Movement," Cooperative Productive Review, 28 (Jl 1953), 153-54.

AGRICULTURE

Bjanes, Ole T. Norwegian Agriculture (Landbruksdepartementets småskrifter, 29). Oslo, 1926. 122 p.; 2d ed., 1932. 134 p.

Bjørkvik, Halvard. "Norwegian Seter-Farming," SEHR, 11, (1963), 156-66.

European Free Trade Association. "Nor-

way," in Agriculture in EFTA (Geneva, 1965), 55-67.

Evang, Karl. Norway's Food in Peace and War. Wash., 1942. 77 p.

Evang, Karl and Otto G. Hansen. Inquiry into the Diet of 301 Poorly Situated Families in Norway (Acta Medica Scandinavia, Supplementum 103). Stock., Hels., 1939. 225 p.

Fjelstad, Anders. "Farming in Norway," NorAmCom (Je 1944), 11-14.

Flovik, Karl, and Jonas Tyssø. "Agriculture," in Ørnulf Vorren, ed., Norway North of 65 (Oslo, 1960), 157-71.

Gassaway, Alexander R. Norwegian Government Policy and the Expansion of Cultivated Land in Finnmark Province. Thesis (M.A.), George Washington University, 1957.

Gasser, E. "Present State of the Dairying Industry in the Different Countries: (15) Norway," IntRevAg, 29 (1938), 61T-73T.

"The General Agricultural Census in Norway, 1939," IntRevAg, 31 (1940), 608S-610S.

Gray, Donald. "Farming in Western Norway," Geog, 23 (1938), 24-27.

Holmsen, Andreas. "Desertion of Farms Around Oslo in the Late Middle Ages," SEHR, 10 (1962), 165-202.

———. "Landowners and Tenants in Norway," SEHR, 6 (1958), 121-31.

Hookham, Gloria E. L. Factors Affecting Food Habits in Norway. Thesis (Ed.D.), Columbia University, 1966. 235 p.

International Institute of Agriculture. Norway (The First World Agricultural Census, Bull. 24). Rome, 1936. 35 p.

Løddesøl, Aasulv. "Norway Has Problems, Too," Soil Conservation, 16 (S 1950), 33-37.

Lougee, Clara R. Climate Classification and the Practice of Irrigation in Norway. Thesis (Ph.D.), Clark University, 1956. 192 p.

Mann, E. J. "Dairy Farming in Norway," Agriculture, 5 (1953), 221-29.

Mork, R. "Dairy Farming Conditions in Norway," Food and Agriculture: the FAO European Bulletin, 3 (1947/48), 182-85.

Nordbø, Rasmus. "Aspects of Norwegian Farming," British Agricultural Bulletin, 7 (1954), 198-206.

Norway, Ministry of Agriculture. A Short Review of Agriculture and Forestry in Norway and of Official Efforts for Their Advancement. By Ole T. Bjanes. Kra., 1921. 62 p.

Norway, Royal Agricultural Society. Nor-

wegian Agriculture. Oslo, 1951. 139 p.;
1955 ed. 140 p.

Organization for European Economic Cooperation. Report on Agricultural Price
and Income Policies. Part I: Norway.
Paris, 1957.

Savory, H. J. "Farming in North Trøndelag,"
Geog, 39 (1954), 272-82.

Solbraa, Arne. "Norwegian Agriculture,"
ScPP, III, 522-29.

Sømme, Axel C. Atlas of Norwegian Agriculture. 2 vols. Bergen, 1950.

———. Jordbrukets Geografi Norge: Geography of Norwegian Agriculture (V3B:
Atlas). Coph., 1949. 112 p.

———. "Norwegian Agriculture and Food
Supply," Geog, 35 (1950), 215-27.

———. "The Physical Background of Norwegian Agriculture," Geog, 35 (1950),
141-54.

Teal, John J., Jr. "The Norwegian Musk-Ox
Experiment," ASR, 42 (1954), 33-36.

Thomson, Claudia. "Norway's Agriculture,"
JofGeo, 35 (1936), 165-78.

———. "Norwegian Agriculture," Foreign
Agriculture, 4 (1940), 65-94.

Valen-Sendstad, Fartein. "Two Norwegian
Agricultural Anniversaries," SEHR, 10
(1962), 84-91.

FORESTRY, FOREST PRODUCTS

Aarflot, Haakon. "A Pioneering Concern
(Saugbrugsforeningen)," Norseman (1965),
76-79.

Barth, Agnar. "Reforestation in Norway,"
Nord, 2 (1939), 203-16.

Hare-Scott, Kenneth. "The Forests of Norway," Norseman, 3 (1945), 440-43.

Kraemer, J. Hugo. "Forest Resources and
Lumber Industry of Norway," JFor, 45
(1947), 723-28.

Langsaeter, Alf. Forest Surveys of Norway
(United Nations, Food and Agriculture
Organization, Division of Forestry and
Forest Products, 3) (1949), 106-12.

Larsen, Julius A. "Waste Lands Turned
into Forests," ASR, 12 (1924), 544-48.

Norwegian Export Council. Norway: Paper
and Pulp. Eivind Flaatten, ed. Oslo,
1953. 80 p.

"The Norwegian Forest Industry of Today,"
NorAmCom (S 1953), 23-24.

Nygaard, Julius. "Forest Fire Insurance in
Norway," JFor, 49 (1951), 337-38.

Skinnemoen, Knut. An Outline of Norwegian
Forestry. Oslo, 1957. 103 p.

United States. Office of International Trade.
Pulp and Paper Developments in Norway

(World Trade in Commodities, pt. 10, v.
6, no. 4). Wash., 1948. 7 p.

Wisth, Eyvind. "Forestry in Norway," ScPP,
III, 553-58.

Zionuska, John A. Private Forestry in Norway. Wash., 1959.

SWEDEN

Bachand, B. J. "Economic Situation in Sweden was Favorable in First Half of Year,"
FT, 8 (1950), 302-306.

Björk, Kai. "Sweden's Economic Policy
1947," Norseman, 5 (1947), 346-49.

Bjurling, Oscar, and others. Economy and
History. Lund, 1961. 117 p.

Browaldh, Tore. "Stabilization Policy and
Capital Formation," SHI (M 1957), Supplement 3, 1-7.

Cederwall, Gustav. "An Economic Survey
for Sweden" [1938-1947], OISB, 10 (1948),
245-54.

———. "The Impact of Rearmament on Sweden," PubFin, 7 (1952), 148-63.

Childs, Marquis W. Sweden: the Middle
Way. New Haven, 1936. 171 p.; Rev. ed.,
New Haven, 1947, 1961. 199 p.

Economic Expansion and Structural Change:
Summary of a Report Submitted to the
Swedish TUC (Landsorganisationen Se-
ries). Stock., 1964. 10 p.

"Economic Policy," SHI (1953), 1-9.

"The Economic Situation," SHI, a quarterly
10-25 p. feature.

"The Economic Situation," SBQR, a quarterly 5-20 p. feature.

The Financial Times, London. Sweden; a
Financial Times Survey. Lond., 1956.
32 p.

Fischer, Alfred J. "The Welfare State in
Sweden," CR, no. 1039 (1952), 40-44.

Fleisher, Wilfred. Sweden, the Welfare
State. N.Y., 1956. 255 p.

Gehnich, Karl. "In Sweden: After the Boom,
Recession," SRWA, 3 (1953), 9-10.

Great Britain, Department of Overseas Trade.
Report on Economic and Commercial
Conditions in Sweden. Lond., 1920.

———. Sweden: Review of Commercial
Conditions. Lond., 1945. 32 p.

"Gross National Product and Expenditure in
Sweden," SHI, 14 (1953), 145-47.

Hansen, Alvin H. "Sweden," in his, Economic Policy and Full Employment (N.Y.,
1947), 98-105.

Heckscher, Eli F. An Economic History of
Sweden (Harvard Economic Studies 95).
Cambridge, Mass., 1954. 308 p.

——. "Survey of Sweden's Economic Evolution," in Economic Conditions and Banking Problems (Saltsjöbaden, Sweden, 1950), 44-58.

Hildebrand, Karl-Gustaf. "Sweden" [Economic growth since 1700], in Contributions to the First International Conference of Economic History, Stockholm, 1960. (École pratique des hautes études: 6e section, sciences économiques et sociales. Congrès et colloques, I) (Paris, 1960), 273-85.

Höijer, Ernst. "The Organization of Official Statistics in Sweden," BSC, 3 (1937), 502-505.

Höök, Erik et al. The Economic Life of Sweden. Stock., 1956. 112 p.

Jalakas, R. "Restraining Sweden's Boom," Banker, 110 (1960), 446-51.

Johansson, O. The Gross Domestic Product of Sweden and Its Composition 1861-1955 (Stockholm Economic Studies, new series, v. 8) Stock. 1967. 190 p.

Johnson, Algot F. "Sweden Five Years Ago and Today," ASIB, 7 (1952), 22-24.

Landberg, Erik, and Bengt Senneby. "Views on an Effective Policy," SBQR, 38 (1957), 6-14.

Larson, Cedric. "Sweden: Democracy of the North at Mid Century; an Economic Look into Sweden's Problems and Policies from World War II to the Present," Dun's Review (O 1950), 19-21.

Larsson, Sven. "Economic Information and Production Propaganda in Sweden," Triangle, 8 (1950/51), 5-7.

Lindahl, Erik. "Sweden and Australia — An Economic Comparison," Trade Review of the Swedish Chamber of Commerce for Australia (Sydney), 40 (1953), 16-21.

Lundberg, Erik. "Business Cycle Experience in Sweden," in The Business Cycle in the Post-War World; Proceedings of a Conference held by the International Economic Association (Lond., N.Y., 1955), 366 p.

Montgomery, Arthur. "Current Economic Problems in Sweden," in Economic Conditions and Banking Problems (Saltsjöbaden, Sweden, 1950), 178-87.

——. "The Swedish Economy During Half a Century 1900-1957," ScPP, III, 435-64.

——. "The Swedish Economy in the 1950's," SEHR, 10 (1962), 221-32.

Nieburg, P. E. "Sweden: the 'Wrong' Way," Freeman, 4 (1954), 635-37.

Nilsson, Arne. Sweden's Way to a Balanced Economy. Stock., 1950. 47 p.

Ohlsson, Ingvar. "Balance of the Swedish Community," SBQR, 33 (1952), 90-95.

——. "The National Income," SBQR, 30 (1949), 42-47.

Ohlsson, Ingvar and Gustav Cederwall. "Sweden's Economy, 1946-1949," OISB, 2 (M 1949), 53-58.

Organization for European Economic Cooperation. Economic Conditions in Sweden, 1954. Paris, 1954. 14 p.

——. Economic Conditions in Member and Associated Countries of the OEEC: Sweden, 1961. Paris, 1961. 34 p.

Organization for Economic Cooperation and Development. Review of National Science Policy — Sweden. Paris, 1964. 66 p.

"The Organization of the Swedish Food Control: a Municipal Concern," Swedish Foreign Commerce, 4 (1950), 46-48.

Øste, Alfred. "Sweden After the War," Norseman, 4 (1946), 197-201.

Parks, Richard W. An Econometric Model of Swedish Economic Growth, 1861-1955. Thesis (Ph.D.), University of California, Berkeley, 1966. 349 p.

Smith, George E. K. Sweden Builds: Its Modern Architecture and Land Policy. Lond., N.Y., 1950. 279 p.

"Some Statistical Date Concerning Sweden's Economic Position," SBQR, 34 (1953), 107-108. Continued quarterly.

Stassen, John H. "Sweden's Great Society: Pilot Study of Welfare Capitalism," Modern Age, 10 (1966), 282-92.

Svenska Handelsbanken. Some Basic Figures Relating to Sweden's Economy. Stock., 1957.

——. Sweden's Economy: an Economic Survey. Stock., 1950——. Annual, covers previous year. 60-67 p.

Sweden, National Institute of Economic Research. The Swedish Economy. Quarterly, contains information on trade, labor, prospects, etc.

"Sweden" [An economic survey], International Economic Survey (Ja 1960), 1-10.

Sweden and Finland, Statistical Data. Compiled by W. William-Olsson. Stock., 1964. 227 p.

"Sweden's Economic Crisis (by A. G. S.)," WT, 3 (1947), 537-44.

Sweden's Economy in Figures. Stock., 1963. 45 p.

"Sweden's Uneasy Stability," Banker, 102 (1954), 147-50.

Swedish Banks Association, Public Relations and Research Department. Economic Life in Sweden. Stock., 1950. 59 p.

Swedish Employers' Confederation Public

Relations Department. Facts about Swedish Economy. Stock., 1956. 28 p.

Swedish Institute for Foreign Cultural Exchange. The Outlook in Sweden: Long-Term Economic Survey, 1951-1955. Stock., 1952. 30 p.

United States, Bureau of Foreign Commerce, World Trade Information Service. Economic Developments in Sweden 1954 (Economic Reports, pt. 1, no. 55-32). Wash., 1954. 6. p.; 1957 ed. (Economic Reports, pt. 1, no. 58-28). Wash., 1958. 7 p.; 1960 ed. (Economic Reports, pt. 1, no. 61-45). By Grant Olson. Wash., 1961. 3 p.; 1961 ed. (Economic Reports, pt. 1, no. 62-9). Wash., 1961. 7 p.

——. Basic Data on the Economy of Sweden (Economic Reports, pt. 1, no. 56-55). By Grant Olson. Wash., 1956. 11 p.

United States, Bureau of International Commerce. Basic Data on the Economy of Sweden (Overseas Business Reports, OBR 63-159). By Ann C. Holmes. Wash., 1963. 16 p.

Vinell, Torsten. Sweden: Trade and Industry. Stock., 1945. 296 p.

Westerlind, Erik, and Rune Beckman. The Economy of Sweden: Structure and Tendencies. Stock., 1961. 75 p.

Wilkinson, Maurice. "Evidences of Long Swings in the Growth of Swedish Population and Related Economic Variables," Journal of Economic History, 27 (1967), 17-38.

——. Swedish Economic Growth: a Model of the Long Swing. Thesis (Ph.D.), Harvard University, 1965.

Winch, Donald. "The Keynesian Revolution in Sweden," JPE, 74 (1966), 168-76.

ECONOMIC PLANNING AND PUBLIC ENTERPRISE SINCE WORLD WAR II

Andersson, Henry F. Effects of Swedish Fiscal Policy and Planning on Economic Growth and Stability, 1930-1964. Thesis (Ph.D.), University of Southern California, 1966.

"Economic Conditions and the Marshall Plan," Eastern Economics, 11 (1948), 1065-67.

Hackett, Brian. "Sweden Plans," Landscape Architecture, 41 (1950), 5-12; (1951), 62-70; 110-20; 156-68.

Hamrin, Eva, and Erik Wirén. Town and Country Planning in Sweden Today. Stock., 1962. 15 p.

Höök, Erik. "The Expansion of the Public Sector," SBQR, 47 (1966), 69-72.

Kragh, Börje. Financial Long-term Planning (Occasional Paper 4, National Institute of Economic Research). Stock., 1967. 157 p.

Lindahl, Erik. "Swedish Experiences in Economic Planning," AER, 40 (1950), 11-20.

Mundy, D. B. "Sweden Adopts a Four-Year Plan to Achieve Economic Stability," FT, 5 (1949), 28-32.

"Post-War Planning in Sweden," ILR, 47 (1943), 483-85.

"Post-War Planning in Sweden," ILR, 50 (1944), 751-57.

Svennilson, Ingvar. "Swedish Long-Term Planning — The Fifth Round," SBQR, 47 (1966), 37-42.

Sweden, Commission on Post-War Economic Planning. Coordination of Investment Activities with the General Employment Policy. Stock., 1944. 18 p.

Sweden, Ministry of Finance. The Swedish Economy 1961-1965: Report of the 1959 Long-Term Planning Commission. Stock., 1963.

Sweden. Sweden's Economy; a Long Term Program, Prepared by the Swedish Government and Submitted to the Organization for European Economic Cooperation. Stock., 1948. 48 p.

"Sweden and the Marshall Plan," SHI (1949), 15-24.

Thorelli, Hans B. "The Formation of Economic and Financial Policy; Sweden," ISSB, 8 (1956), 252-73.

United States Congress, Joint Economic Committee. Study of Sweden's Five Year Program of Works Relocation. Wash., 1963.

Verney, Douglas V. Public Enterprise in Sweden. Liverpool, 1959. 132 p.

Wallander, Jan. "Experiences of Long Term Planning in Sweden" [1950-1955], SBQR, 37 (1956), 50-58.

WAGES AND INFLATION SINCE WORLD WAR II

Eskilsson, Sture. "The Wage Drift," SBQR, 47 (1966), 8-15.

Isaac, J. E. "Wages Policy: Recent Swedish Discussions," Economic Record, 28 (1955), 283-90.

Johnston, Thomas L. "Wages Policy in Sweden," Economica, 25 (1958), 213-29.

Rehn, Gösta. "Swedish Wages and Wage Policies," Annals (1957), 99-108.

"Relative Real Wages in Swedish Agriculture and Industry, 1930-1950," OISB, (1953).

Roberts, B. C. "Wage Policy in Sweden," in
his, National Wages Policy in War and
Peace (Lond., 1958), 83-99.

"The Shift in the Distribution of Incomes,
1945-1950," SHI (1952), 27-30.

Thore, Sten A. O. "Household Saving and
the Price Level. Stock., 1961. 291 p.

Thunholm, Lars-Erik. "Sweden's New
Drive Against Inflation," Banker, 97
(1951), 363-68.

———. "Sweden's Steps to Check Inflation,"
Banker, 95 (1950), 163-68.

"The Trends of Wages in Sweden," SHI
(1952), 146-49.

Wage Policy in Sweden, Theory and Prac-
tice: a Trade Union View on Income
Policy (Landsorganisationen Series).
Stock., 1965. 38 p.

DEVELOPMENT PRIOR TO 1930

Bjurling, Oscar. "Price Developments in
the Swedish Realm During the Latter
Part of the 17th Century," EconaHist, 1
(1958), 3-20.

Boëthius, Bertil. "New Light on Eighteenth
Century Sweden," SEHR, 1 (1953), 143-77.

Bolin, Sture. "Mohammed, Charlemagne,
and Ruric," SEHR, 1 (1953), 5-39.

"Cost of Living Among Rural Workers in
Sweden in 1920," ILR, 9 (1924), 403-406.

Fridlizius, Gunnar. "The Crimean War and
the Swedish Economy," EconaHist, 3
(1960), 56-103.

Gasslander, Olle. "The Convoy Affair of
1798," SEHR, 2 (1954), 22-30.

Hammarström, Ingrid. "The Price Revolution of the Sixteenth Century: Some
Swedish Evidence," SEHR, 5 (1957),
118-54.

Heckscher, Eli F. "Natural and Money
Economy as Illustrated from Swedish
History in the Sixteenth Century," Journal of Economic and Business History, 3
(1930/31), 1-29.

Montgomery, Arthur. "Economic Fluctuations in Sweden in 1919-1921," SEHR, 3
(1955), 203-38.

———. "Economic Planning and Cheap
Money 150 Years Ago," SBQR, 35 (1954),
38-44.

Nertorp, H. "Swedish Artisans in the Nineteenth Century" [Review article], SEHR,
5 (1957), 77-82.

"Recent Wage Changes in Various Countries:
Sweden," ILR, 18 (1928), 102-107.

Sundbärg, Axel G. Sweden: Its People and
Its Industry; Historical and Statistical
Handbook. Stock., 1904. 1141 p.

Thomas, Brinley. "Wages, Cost of Living
and National Income in Sweden, 1860-
1930," BSC, 4 (1938), 357-63.

University of Stockholm, Institute of Social
Sciences. Wages, Cost of Living and National Income in Sweden, 1860-1930.
Lond., 1933, 1935, 1937. Vol. I: The
Cost of Living in Sweden, 1830-1930, by
Gunnar Myrdal, assisted by Sven Bouvin.
1933. 263 p. Vol. II: Wages in Sweden,
1860-1930, by Gösta Bagge, Erik Lundberg, Ingvar Svennilson. 1935. 2 pts.,
605 and 413 p. Vol. III: National Income
of Sweden, 1861-1930, by Erik Lindahl,
Einar Dahlgren, Karin Kock. 1937. 2
pts., 319 and 631 p.

"Wages and the Cost of Living in Sweden
from 1860 to 1930," ILR, 29 (1934), 522-
37.

DEVELOPMENT 1930-1945

Apelquist, Seved. "Sweden, a Long Way to
Utopia," Living Age (1937), 506-508.

Bonow, Mauritz. Sweden: Its Economic and
Social Life. Stock., 1937. 70 p.

Braatoy, Bjarne. The New Sweden: a Vindication of Democracy. Lond., N.Y., 1939.
172 p.

Edwards, Daniel J. Processes of Economic
Adaptation in a World War II — Neutral
Country: a Case Study of Sweden. Thesis
(Ph.D.), University of Virginia, 1961.
223 p.

"Features of Sweden's Recovery," Annals,
192 (1937), 161-63.

Glenny, W. J. Economic Conditions in Sweden. Lond., 1932. 170 p.

Holben, Ralph E. Swedish Economic Policy
and Economic Stability, 1927-1938. Thesis (Ph.D.), Columbia University, 1951.

Kjellström, Erik T. H. et al. Price Control, the War Against Inflation. New
Brunswick, 1942. 171 p.

Kock, Karin. Crisis, Depression and Recovery in Sweden, 1929-1937. Stock.,
1938.

———. Swedish Economic Policy During the
War. Manchester, 1943. 12 p.

———. "Swedish Economic Policy During
the War," RofES, 10 (1942), 75-80.

Lorwin, Lewis L. "Stabilization and Planning in Sweden, 1929-1939," in National
Planning in Selected Countries (Wash.,
1941), 173 p.

MacDonald, J. A. "Economic Conditions in
Sweden," Commercial Intelligence Journal (1937), 1110-14.

Montgomery, Arthur. How Sweden Overcame

the Depression, 1930-1933 (New Sweden Tercentenary Publication). Stock., 1938. 91 p.

New Fabian Research Bureau, London. Democratic Sweden: a Volume of Studies Prepared by Members of the New Fabian Research Bureau. Ed. by Margaret Cole and Charles Smith. Lond., 1938. 334 p.

Nylander, Erik. Modern Sweden. Stock., 1937. 470 p.

——. Sweden Today. Stock., 1930. 354 p.

Ohlin, Bertil. "Economic Progress in Sweden," Annals, 197 (1938), 1-6.

Soloveytchik, George. "Sweden's Successful Experiment," New Statesman and Nation (1936), 796-97.

Sterner, Richard. "The Standard of Living in Sweden," Annals, 197 (1938), 7-19.

Sweden, Council for Sweden's Participation in the New York World's Fair, 1939. Sweden's Economic Progress. By Thorsten Streyffert et al., with an introduction by Roy V. Peel. Stock., 1941. 357 p.

Sweden: a Wartime Survey. N.Y., 1946. 250 p.

Thomas, Brinley. "Is Swedish Industrial Prosperity Unstable?," BSC, 3 (1937), 288-95.

——. "Recovery of Sweden," New Statesman and Nation (1935), 237-38.

"Wage Regulation and the Incidence of the Higher Cost of Living in Sweden," ILR, 46 (1942), 79-83.

Wigforss, Ernst. "The Financial Policy During Depression and Boom," Annals, 197 (1938), 25-39.

REGIONAL DEVELOPMENT

Friberg, Nils. "The Growth of Population and Its Economic-Geographical Background in a Mining District in Central Sweden," GeoA, 38 (1956), 395-440.

Jonasson, Olaf G. Economic Geographical Excursion to Middle Sweden. (Gothenburg School of Economics, Publications 1960, no. 1). Gothenburg, 1960. 87 p.

——. The Population and Industry in Middle Sweden Within the Traffic Region of the GDG, 1865-1940, a Railroad Geography Study. Gothenburg, 1950. 247 p.

Nordström, Ludvig. Greater Norrland. 1947.

Svensson, Jörn. "A Case Study in Economic Retardation" [The decline of the province of Östergötland during the period 1870-1913], EconaHist, 3 (1960), 38-55.

MONETARY POLICY

Browaldh, Ernfrid. "Devaluation and Economic Policy," SHI (1950), 1-9.

Cassel, Gustav. The Crisis in the World's Monetary System. 2d ed., Oxford, 1932. 98 p. [Rhodes Memorial Lectures Delivered in Trinity Term, 1932.]

Hallinan, Charles T. "Sweden's Managed Currency," Forum, 90 (1933), 159-63.

Kjellström, Erik T. H. Managed Money: the Experience of Sweden. N.Y., 1934. 109 p.

Kock, Karin. "Paper Currency and Monetary Policy in Sweden," in Economic Essays in Honour of Gustav Cassel (Lond., 1933), 343-56.

Kragh, Börje. "Sweden's Monetary and Fiscal Policy Before and After the Second World War," SHI Supp. (1946), 19 p.

Lindahl, Erik. "Sweden's Monetary Program. The Experiment in Operation, Its Results and Lessons," Economic Forum (N.Y.), 2 (1934), 169-82.

Lundberg, Erik, and Bengt Senneby. "The Dilemma of the New Monetary Policy in Sweden: Views on an Effective Credit Policy," SBQR, 37 (Jl 1956), 79-88; 38 (Ja 1957), 6-14.

Miller, Reuben G. Swedish Monetary Policy in the Postwar Period, 1945-1961. Thesis (Ph.D.), Ohio State University, 1966. 474 p.

"Monetary Policy in Sweden in Recent Years" [1950-1952], SHI (1953), 101-107.

"Sweden's Monetary Muddle," Banker, 104 (1955), 31-34.

Thomas, Brinley. Monetary Policy and Crises: a Study of Swedish Experience. Lond., 1936. 247 p.

——. "Swedish Experience with Managed Currency," Banker's Magazine (1934), 573-75.

Thunholm, Lars-Erik. "Swedish Monetary Policy and the Business Boom," SBQR, 41 (1960), 113-19.

PUBLIC FINANCE, NATIONAL BUDGET, TAXATION

Bille, Sten F. W. The Investment Climate of Sweden: a Short Survey of Swedish Investments Regulations and Corporation and Tax Laws. Stock., 1960. 23 p.

——. "Some Views on the Method of Settling Disputes on Questions of Double Taxation," BIFD, 5 (1951), 201-21.

Ekenberg, Otto. "Alterations in Fiscal
Legislation in Sweden During the Last
War," BIFD, 1 (Je 1946), 21-27.

Geijer, Erland. How Swedish Tax Laws
Affect Persons Removing into or from
Sweden or Residing Abroad. 4th ed.,
Stock., 1959. 122 p.

Greenroyd, J. "Taxation in Sweden," CoR,
23 (1949), 155-56.

Harvard University, International Program
in Taxation. Taxation in Sweden (World
Tax Series, 5). Boston, 1959. 723 p.

Heckscher, Eli F. Swedish State Finances.
Stock., 1915. 17 p. Reprinted from Sweden, Historical and Statistical Handbook.

Hildebrand, Karl-Gustaf. The National Debt
Office, 1789-1939. Stock., 1939. 73 p.

———. "Public Finance and the National
Economy in Early Sixteenth Century
Sweden," SEHR, 7 (1959), 95-106.

A Key to Swedish Taxes. Stock., 1958. 23 p.

Kobb, G. The Swedish National Debt and Its
Administration. Stock., 1932. 17 p.

Myers, Lawrence B. Taxation of Income
and Property in Sweden. Thesis (Ph.D.),
University of Wisconsin, 1954.

Nilsson, Sven A. "The Finances and Financial Administration of Sweden during the
Late Sixteenth Century" [Review of Swedish Ph.D. thesis by Birgitta Odén], SEHR,
4 (1956), 180-82.

Norr, Martin. "The Retail Sales Tax in
Sweden," NTJ, 14 (1961), 174-81.

———. "The Taxation of Corporate Income
in Sweden: Some Special Features," NTJ,
12 (1959), 328-39.

Norr, Martin, and Claes Sandels. The Corporate Income Tax in Sweden. Stock.,
1963. 61 p.

Organization for European Economic Coop-
eration, National Accounts Research Unit.
National Accounts Studies: Sweden.
Paris, 1953. 74 p.

Pavlock, Ernest J. A Comparison of Periodic Income Reporting Among the United
States, West Germany, the Netherlands,
and Sweden. Thesis (Ph.D.), University
of Michigan, 1965.

Rehn, Gösta. "The National Budget and
Economic Policy," SBQR, 43 (1962), 39-
47.

Sandberg, Lars G. "A Value-Added Tax for
Sweden," NTJ, 17 (1964), 292-96.

Sandström, C. O. "The New Swedish Scheme
for Taxation of Dividends," BIFD, 14
(1960), 332-41.

———. "A Review of Some Swedish Tax
Cases in 1950," BIFD, 6 (1952), 31-36.

Sandström, Karl G. A. "The Convention

Between Sweden and Switzerland for the
Avoidance of Double Taxation," BIFD, 3
(1949), 173-81.

———. A Survey of Swedish Taxes on Income
and Capital. Stock., 1954. 76 p.; 2d ed.,
1957. 78 p.

———. "Unrestricted Depreciation. The
Swedish System," Canadian Tax Journal
(1954), 366-70.

Sweden, Ministry of Finance. The Swedish
Budget: a Summary of the Finance Bill.
Stock., annual. Report year ends June 30.

Sweden's Tax Structure. IntM (S 1953), 12-
13+.

"Swedish Government Finances," SHI (1953),
27-32.

The Swedish Taxpayers' Association. Key
to Taxes. Stock., 1948.

"The Tax Convention with Sweden," Taxes,
18 (1940), 30-33.

"Taxation of Business Profits in Sweden,"
SHI (1953), 140-44.

Taxes in Sweden. Stock., 1961.

Västhager, Nils. "Tax Policy and Business
Firms Investment Activities," SBQR, 38
(Jl 1957), 62-73.

Wigforss, Ernst J., and Bertil Ohlin. The
Swedish Budget. N.Y., 1939. 51 p.

Wurzel, H. "A Tax Agreement with Sweden,"
Taxes, 17 (1939), 460-62, 495-97.

ECONOMISTS, SCHOOLS OF ECONOMICS

Amundsen, Arne. A Bibliography of Knut
Wicksell's Published Works (Memorandum fra Universitetets Socialøkonomiske
Institutt, 10). Oslo, 1952. 7 p. Mimeographed.

Caplan, Benjamin. The Wicksellian School:
a Critical Study of the Development of
Swedish Monetary Theory, 1898-1932.
Thesis (Ph.D.), University of Chicago.
1942.

Coats, A. W. "In Defence of Heckscher and
the Idea of Mercantilism," SEHR, 5 (1957),
173-87.

Coleman, D. C. "Eli Heckscher and the Idea
of Mercantilism," SEHR, 5 (1957), 3-25.

"Erik Lindahl: Bibliografi, 1919-1960,"
EkT, 62 (1960), 59-74.

Ford, J. L. The Ohlin-Heckscher Theory of
the Basis and Effects of Commodity
Trade. Thesis (M.A.), University of
Liverpool, 1962.

Frisch, Ragnar A. K. Knut Wicksell: a
Cornerstone in Modern Economic Theory
(Memorandum fra Universitetets Socialø-
konomiske Institutt). Oslo, 1951. 46 p.

Gårdlund, Torsten W. The Life of Knut

Wicksell. (AUS. Stockholm Economic Studies, new series, 2). Stock., 1958. 355 p.

Gerschenkron, Alexander. "Eli F. Heckscher," Preface to Eli F. Heckscher's An Economic History of Sweden (Cambridge, Mass., 1954), xii-xlii.

Hansen, Bent. The Economic Theory of Fiscal Policy. Lond., Cambridge, Mass., 1958. 450 p.

Heckscher, Eli F. "The Place of Sweden in Modern Economic History," EcHistR, 4 (1932), 1-22.

——. "A Plea or Theory in Economic History," Economic History, Supplement to EconJ, 1 (1926-29), 525-34. Reprinted in Frederic C. Lane and Jelle C. Riemersma, eds., Enterprise and Secular Change (Homewood, Ill., 1953), 421-30.

——. "A Survey of Economic Thought in Sweden, 1875-1950," SEHR, 1 (1953), 105-27.

——. "The Teaching of Economic History in Universities: Sweden," EcHistR, 3 (1931), 213-15.

The Industrial Institute for Economic and Social Research in Stockholm. Stock., 1950. 111 p.

Jacobsson, P. "Theory and Practice: Knut Wicksell and Sweden's Monetary Policy 1946-48," Schweizerische Zeitschrift für Volkswirtschaft und Statistik, 88 (1952), 467-85.

Kjellström, Erik T. H. "Gustav Cassel, a World-Famous Teacher, Writer and Thinker on Our Daily Problems," ASR, 25 (1937), 65-67.

Landgren, Karl G. Economics in Modern Sweden. Wash., 1957. 117 p.

Lundberg, Erik. Business Cycles and Economic Policy. Cambridge, Mass., Lond., 1957. 346 p.

——. "The Influence of Gustav Cassel on Economic Doctrine and Policy," SBQR, 48 (1967), 1-6.

——. Studies in the Theory of Economic Expansion (Stockholm Economic Studies, published by writers connected with the Institute for Social Sciences of Stockholm University, no. 6). Lond., 1937. 265 p.

Neuman, Andrzej M. "Swedish Economists and British Economic Theory," BSC, 3 (1937), 82-87.

Ohlin, Bertil. "The Quantity Theory in Swedish Literature," EconaHist, 2 (1959), 3-18.

——. "Some Notes on the Stockholm Theory of Savings and Investment," EconJ (1937), 53-69, 221-40.

——. "Tendencies in Swedish Economics," JPE, 35 (1927), 343-63.

Palander, T. "On the Concepts and Methods of the Stockholm School: Some Methodological Reflections on Myrdal's Monetary Equilibrium," in International Economic Papers No. 3 (Lond., N.Y., 1953), 5-57.

Söderlund, Ernst F. "Eli F. Heckscher, 1879-1952," SEHR, 1 (1953), 137-40.

Stamp, Josiah C. et al. Economic Essays in Honour of Gustav Cassel. Lond., 1933. 720 p.

Turvey, Ralph. "Erik Lindahl," EkT, 62 (1960), 5-8.

Uhr, Carl G. Economic Doctrines of Knut Wicksell (Publications of the Institute of Business and Economic Research, University of California). Berkeley, 1960. 356 p.

——. Knut Wicksell: a Study in Economic Doctrine. Thesis (Ph.D.), University of California, 1956.

——. "Knut Wicksell-Centennial Evaluation," AER, 41 (1951), 829-60.

Wakar, Aleksy. "The Economic Theories of Gustav Cassel," BSC, 3 (1937), 506-509.

Wallander, Jan. "The Industrial Institute for Economic and Social Research," SBQR, 39 (1958), 53-57.

Wicksell, Knut. Selected Papers on Economic Theory. Lond., Cambridge, Mass., 1958. 292 p. With an introduction by Erik Lindahl, "Wicksell's Life and Work." 9-48.

FOREIGN TRADE, FOREIGN ECONOMIC POLICY

Ankarcrona, Conrad. "Swedish Trade with Other Baltic and Scandinavian Countries, 1929-35," BSC, 3 (1937), 450-58.

Boman, Tore. "Where Should Sweden Export?" SBQR, 46 (1965), 71-79.

Brandting, Arne. "Assistance Available to Swedish Exporters," EFTA Bull, 7 (1966, no. 8), 5-6.

Bruhn, Marcus C. Sweden's Balance of Payments 1920-1950. Thesis (Ph.D.), University of Wisconsin, 1955.

Cole, George D. H. "Sweden in World Trade," in his, Democratic Sweden (Lond., 1938), 226-34.

Dahlgren, Einar. "Post-War Production for Export," SBQR, 32 (1951), 14-18.

"The Distribution of Sweden's Foreign Trade by Commodity Groups," SHI (1949), 41-44.

Federation of Swedish Industries, European Tariff Survey. 8 vols. Stock., 1960.

Fleetwood, Erin E. Sweden's Capital Imports

and Exports (Graduate Institute of International Studies, 56). Geneva, Stock., 1947. 223 p.

Fridlizius, Gunnar. Swedish Corn Export in the Free Trade Era, Patterns in the Oats Trade, 1850-1880 (Samhällsvetenskapliga studier, 14). Originally Ph.D. thesis, Lund, 1957. 292 p.

Gorne, Staffan, and Staffan Sohlman. Prospects for Swedish Exports 1970 (Occasional Paper 3, National Institute of Economic Research). Stock., 1967. 116 p.

Hägglöf, M. Gunnar. "Swedish Trade Policy in War Time," Nord, 4 (1941), 93-105.

Hammarskjöld, Dag. "Sweden's International Credit Accommodation in 1944 and 1945," SHI (1945), Supplement B.

Hansen, Bent, and Thora Nilsson. "Foreign Trade Credits," SBQR, 41 (1960), 91-98.

Hildebrand, Karl-Gustaf. "Foreign Markets for Swedish Iron in the 18th Century," SEHR, 6 (1958), 3-52.

"How Sweden Helps Exporters," EFTA Rep (F 6, 1967), 3-4.

Industrial Council for Social and Economic Studies. The Swedish Economy and the Underdeveloped Countries: Report by an SNS Working Group. Stock., 1961. 148 p.

Jäger, Jörg-Johannes. "Sweden's Iron Ore Exports to Germany, 1933-1944: a Reply to Rolf Karlbom's Article on the Same Subject," SEHR, 15 (1967), 139-47. For another reply to Karlbom, see the Milward entry below.

Jensen, F. B. "Sweden's Foreign Trade Position," Export Trade and Shipper (S 21, 1953), 12-13+.

Karlbom, Rolf. "Sweden's Iron Ore Exports to Germany, 1933-1944," SEHR, 13 (1965), 65-93.

Lundberg, Erik, and Jaak Järv. "The Balance of Payments and Economic Growth," SBQR, 47 (1966), 1-7.

Malmberg, Sven G. "Sweden and Latin America: Some Reflections After a Visit," SBQR, 36 (1955), 110-15.

———. What Does Sweden's Foreign Trade Look Like? Stock., 1963.

Milward, Alan S. "Could Sweden Have Stopped the Second World War?" SEHR, 15 (1967), 127-38.

"Mounting Swedish Exports in Nearly All Commodity Fields," Swedish Foreign Commerce, 4 (1950), 31-33.

Mundy, D. B. "External Trade Position of Sweden Continues Unfavorable This Year," FT, 4 (1948), 1315-16; 5 (1949), 12-14.

Myrdal, Gunnar. The Reconstruction of

World Trade and Swedish Trade Policy. Stock., 1947. 29 p.

Nelson, Helge. "Sweden's Trade Relations with the Outer World," BC, 2 (1936), 42-46.

Nilsson, Henry. "Price and Performance in Swedish Trade," AnColEc, 28 (1957), 153-60.

———. "Price and Performance in Swedish Trade," Cartel, 7 (1957), 15-19+.

Odén, Birgitta. "A Netherlands Merchant in Stockholm in the Reign of Erik XIV," SEHR, 10 (1962), 3-37.

"Post-War Development of Sweden's Foreign Trade," OISB, 9 (S 1947), 307-14.

Quigley, J. M. "A Quantitative Discussion of Swedish Foreign Aid and Balance of Payments," Swedish Journal of Economics, 68 (1966), 193-210.

Samuelsson, Kurt. "International Payments and Credit Movements by the Swedish Merchant Houses, 1730-1815," SEHR, 3 (1955), 163-202.

Savosnick, Kurt M. "Capital Imports and Economic Progress in Sweden," SBQR, 37 (1956), 18-26.

Sehlin, Halvor. "Tourism," Ymer, 8 (1960), 96-101.

Simpson, J. L. "The Liquidation of German Assets in Neutral Countries," BYIL, 34 (1958), 374-84. (Sweden, 379-81)

Sjöberg, Åke G. "Swedish Trade in the Mid-Sixteenth Century," SEHR, 8 (1960), 175-79.

Söderberg, Tom. "Swedish Trade," ScPP, III, 725-35.

Söderlund, Ernst F., with Annagreta Hallberg and Jan Sanden. Swedish Timber Exports, 1850-1950. Stock., 1952. 383 p.

Swedberg, Hans. "Some Trends in Swedish Exports," SBQR, 36 (1955), 8-15.

Sweden, Commission on Post-War Economic Planning. Sweden's Trade Policy After the War. Stock., 1945. 19 p.

———. Swedish Trade Policy After the War. Stock., 1946. 39 p.

Sweden, General Export Association. Sweden: Trade and Industry. Stock., 1945. 296 p.

———. Swedish Export Directory. Stock., annual. 1950 ed. (v. 33), 840 p.

Sweden, Ministry of Finance. Swedish Development Assistance. Stock., 1962.

"Sweden's Diminishing International Trade," IntM (S 1953), 10-11+.

Sweden's Most Important Export Markets. Stock., 1962. 6 p.

"Sweden's Post-War Foreign Trade," Archive, 1 (1948), 41-42.

"Sweden's Terms of Trade," SHI (1957), 1-4.

"Sweden's Trade With Germany," SHI (1950), 27-36.

Swedish Chamber of Commerce for Australasia and South Sea Islands. The Swedish-Australasian Trade Journal. Sydney, 1928—.

"Swedish Customs Tariffs Under Revision," SHI (1954), 25-29.

Swedish Union of Exporters. Swedish Foreign Commerce. Stock., 1946—.

Thoman, Richard S. Final Report to the Geog. Branch, Office of Naval Research, on: An Analysis of Selected Foreign-Trade Zones in Germany and Sweden: Their Nature, Their Significance in the Regional Relationships of Their Associated Seaports, and Their Role in the International Trade of Their Host Countries. Chicago, 1955. 10 p. Mimeographed.

Thome, Bo E. "The Swedish Stake in the Developing Countries: Official Aid," SBQR, 46 (1965), 65-70.

Tonndorf, H. G. "The Swedish Tariff," SBQR, 28 (1947), 38-43.

United States, Bureau of Foreign and Domestic Commerce. Sweden: Basic Data on Import Trade and Trade Barriers. Wash., 1953. 162 p. Mimeographed.

———. Leather Industry and Trade of Sweden by Emil Kekich and J. Schnitzer (Trade Information Bull., 450). Wash., 1927. 16 p.

Wallenberg, Marcus, Jr. "Neutral Sweden's Foreign Trade," ASM, 35 (Ja 1941), 8-9+.

Wenner-Gren, Axel L. Call to Reason: an Appeal to Common Sense. N.Y., Toronto, 1938. 152 p.

TRADE WITH GREAT BRITAIN AND THE UNITED STATES

Bachand, B. J. "Swedish Trade with Dollar Area Has Shown Steady Decline," FT, 9 (1951), 90-93.

"Current Trends in Trade with Sweden," BdofTradeJ, 156 (1949), 648-50.

Export Council for Europe. Opportunities for British Ship Components in the Swedish Shipbuilding Market. 1963.

Fleisher, Eric W. "The Beginnings of the Transatlantic Market for Swedish Iron" [1806-1812], SEHR, 1 (1953), 178-92.

Fleisher, Eric W., and Jörgen Weibull. Viking Times to Modern; the Story of Swedish Exploring and Settlement in America and the Development of Trade

and Shipping from the Vikings to Our Time. Minneapolis, 1954. 115 p.

Great Britain, Board of Trade. Hints to Business Men Visiting Sweden (Hints to Business Men Series). Lond., 1961. 28 p.

Hammarström, Ingrid. "Anglo-Swedish Economic Relations and the Crisis of 1857," SEHR, 10 (1962), 141-64.

"Prospects for United Kingdom Trade with Sweden," BdofTradeJ, 160 (1951), 19-20.

Sinclair, George A. "The Scottish Trader in Sweden," Scottish Historical Review, 25 (1928), 289-99.

Stebbing, E. P. "Forestry in Sweden: Its Importance to and Influence on Great Britain," Journal of the Royal Society of Arts, 77 (1928), 78-93.

"Sweden's Trade with the Dollar Area," SHI (1954), 66-92.

Swedish Chamber of Commerce for the United Kingdom, London. Anglo-Swedish Yearbook. 1962 annual, 209 p.

Swedish Chamber of Commerce of the United States. Twenty-fifth Anniversary of the Swedish Chamber of Commerce of the United States of America, 1907-1932. N.Y., 1932. 144 p.

Tilberg, Frederick. The Development of Commerce between the United States and Sweden, 1870-1925 (Augustana Library Publications, no. 12) (1928 University of Iowa Ph.D. thesis). Moline, Ill., 1930 and Rock Island, 1929. 185 p.

United States, Foreign Agricultural Relations Office. The Position of American Cotton in Sweden (Foreign Agriculture Reports, 24). Wash., 1948. 14 p.

EUROPEAN ECONOMIC INTEGRATION

Backman, Hans. The European Economic Community and the Three Neutrals, Austria, Sweden, and Switzerland. Brussels, 1962. 34 p.

Cederwall, Gustav. "Sweden and the Plans for Economic Integration," SBQR, 39 (1958), 1-9.

Erlander, Tage et al. Sweden, Partner in Europe. Stock., 1962. 46 p.

Frankel, Joseph. "Sweden and European Integration," PolS, 8 (1960), 58-59.

Heckscher, Gunnar. "Swedish View on Speeding Up EFTA's Integration," European-Atlantic Review, 9 (1961), 31-32.

Nordenson, Jonas. "The Importance of the EEC Market to EFTA Countries: Sweden," EFTA Bull, 7 (1966, no. 1), 5-8.

Paues, Wilhelm. "'Seven' Partnership Aids Swedish Economy," EFTA Rep, no. 105 (O 2, 1964), 4-5. Appears also in EFTA Bull, 5 (1964, no. 7), 10-11.

Reuterskiöld, Bengt. "EEC Membership or Isolation? The Economic Consequences for Sweden," SBQR, 43 (1962), 19-27.

Sweden. Ministry of Foreign Affairs. Negotiations for a European Free Trade Area, 1956-1958 (Documents Published by the Royal Ministry for Foreign Affairs, II:13). Stock., 1959.

BANKING, STOCK EXCHANGE

Ahrén, F. The Lending Activities of the Swedish Commercial Banks," in Economic Conditions and Banking Problems (Saltsjöbaden, Sweden, 1950), 243-63.

Ames, J. W. "A Swedish System of Buying and Stock Control," RIC, 45 (1952), 108-11.

Browaldh, Ernfrid. "The State and the Private Banking System," SHI Supp (S 1946), 1-16. Also published separately, Stock., 1946. 16 p.

Brundell, P. "In the Service of Foreign Trade" [The role of commercial banks], SBQR, 31 (1950), 57-60.

Carlsson, Torsten. "The Savings Shortage and Credit Policy," SBQR, 47 (1966), 63-68.

"The Commercial Banks and the Interest Policy," SBQR, 30 (1949), 13-17.

"The Credit Restrictions," SBQR, 33 (1952), 86-89.

Elinder, Erik. "Savings Promotion Ideas from Sweden," Burroughs Clearing House (N 1950), 32-34+.

Flux, Alfred W. The Swedish Banking System (U.S. 61st Cong, 2d sess. Senate Doc. 576). Wash., 1910. Also issued in 1911 in Publications of the National Monetary Commission, v. 16, no. 1.

Gasslander, Olle. History of Stockholm's Enskilda Bank to 1914. Stock., 1962. 643 p.

Gavelin, Axel. "The Gold Resources of Sweden," in The Gold Resources of the World. An Inquiry made upon the Initiation of the Organising Committee of the XV International Geological Congress, South Africa, 1929 (Pretoria, 1930), 379-82.

"Government Borrowing and the Surplus Funds of the Bank," SBQR, 30 (1949), 29-32.

Hansen, Bent, and Ursula Wallberg. "Savings and Income Changes," SBQR, 40 (1959), 113-19.

Jacobsson, P. "The Return to a Flexible Credit Policy," SBQR, 36 (1955), 1-7.

Jennison, P. S. "World Economic, Political Problems Shared by Sweden's Bank Trade," Publisher's Weekly, 156 (Jl 2, 1949), 28-32.

Leine, K. H. "The Stock Market in Sweden," SBQR, 34 (1953), 43-44.

Liljefors, Åke O. "The Swedish Capital Market," EFTA Bull, 5 (Jl 1964), 10-12.

Malmberg, Sven G. Commercial Banking in Sweden. Stock., 1963.

Melin, Hilding. "The Banking System of Sweden," in H. Parker Willis and B. H. Beckhart, eds., Foreign Banking Systems (N.Y., 1929), 1011-74.

——. "Some Aspects of Bank Organization," in Economic Conditions and Banking Problems (Saltsjöbaden, Sweden, 1950), 224-42.

Potter, J. "The Role of a Swedish Bank in the Process of Industrialisation," SEHR, 11 (1963), 60-72.

"Promotion of Small Savings in Sweden," AICC Economic Review (N 1, 1956), 11-13.

"The Question of a State Commercial Bank in Sweden," SHI (1949), 57-63.

Samuelsson, Kurt. "The Banks and the Financing of Industry in Sweden, c. 1900-1927," SEHR, 6 (1958), 176-90.

Senneby, Bengt. "Banking in Sweden," ScPP, III, 817-24.

——. "The Development of the Swedish Stock Market," SBQR, 42 (1961), 15-19.

Stén, H. The Post-War Development in Swedish Commercial Banking. Stock., 1936. 14 p.

Svenska Handelsbanken. Annual Report Presented to the General Meeting of Shareholders. Stock., 1951 issue. 28 p.

Swedish Banks Association. Swedish Banking Companies, 1824-1915. Stock., 1915. 27 p.

"The Swedish Bond Market," SBQR, 34 (1953), 65-67.

Thunholm, Lars-Erik. "Sweden," in Benjamin H. Beckhart, ed., Banking Systems (N.Y., 1954), 657-92.

"Tore Browaldh: Chairman, Svenska Handelsbanken" [Interview], Banker, 118 (1968), 8-14.

INDUSTRY, BUSINESS

Akesson, O. A. "Swedish Insurance," ScPP, III, 852-58.

Andersson, Gunnar. Sweden's Natural Resources in Relation to Industry. Upsala,

1927. Reprinted from Industry in Sweden.

Apelqvist, Seved. "Folksam: Sweden's Biggest Insurance Company," RIC, 47 (1954), 75-79.

Beckman, Gunnar. Product of Private Enterprise; Technical Skills Build Sweden's Prosperity — The World Finds Them Useful Too. Stock., 1956. 61 p.

Bergstrom, Irma A., and Ellis I. Folke. "The Uddeholm [Company] Story: a Dynamic Swedish Enterprise," ASM, 52 (Je 1958), 9-16.

Bjurling, Oscar. "The Industry of Sweden," ScPP, III, 598-618.

Carlson, Sune. Executive Behavior, a Study of the Work Load and the Working Methods of Managing Directors. Stock., 1951. 122 p.

Childs, Marquis W. "Company Town," Forum, 100 (1938), 255-60.

Churchill, Allen. The Incredible Ivar Kreuger. N.Y., 1957. 301 p.

Claesson, Göran C.-O. "Sweden's Publicity Weapon," Cartel, 5 (1955), 58-60.

Dahl, Sven. "Travelling Peddlars in Nineteenth Century Sweden," SEHR, 7 (1959), 167-78.

Deck, J. F. "The Match Stick Colossus," FA, 9 (1930), 149-56.

Eberstein, Gösta. "Swedish Law re Limitation of Competition," Trademark Reporter, 50 (1960), 562-63.

Eronn, Lars. "Stronger Measures in Sweden?" Cartel, 6 (1956), 10-13, 36.

Federation of Swedish Industries. Industry in Sweden. Uppsala, 1928.

Hagerstrand, Torsten. The Propagation of Innovation Wares [Showing the development of the motor-car in Scania]. Lund, 1952. 20 p.

Hedin, Naboth. "Sweden's World Industries," series of 10 articles, ASR: "I: The Lappland Ores," 14 (1926), 41-44; "II: Hydroelectric Power," 14 (1926), 112-14; "III: The Green Gold of the Forests," 14 (1926), 168-70; "IV: Telephones," 14 (1926), 233-35; "V: Motor Ships," 14 (1926), 361-63; "VI: Ball Bearings," 14 (1926), 419-21; "VII; Matches," 14 (1926), 489-90; "VIII: Cream Separators," 14 (1926), 554-56; "IX: Vacuum Cleaners and Artificial Refrigerators," 15 (1927), 32-33; "X: Electrical Machinery," 15 (1927), 87-89.

Henriksson, Arne. "A Swedish Approach to Automation," Free Labour World, 8 (Aug 1957), 31-33.

Hildebrand. Karl-Gustaf. "Salt and Cloth in Swedish Economic History," SEHR, 2 (1954), 74-102.

Höglund, B., and L. Werin. The Production System of the Swedish Economy; an Input-Output Study (Stockholm Economic Studies. New Series, 4). Stock., 1964. 231 p.

Höijer, Ernst. "Census of Enterprise in Sweden," BC, 1 (1935), 72-73.

Holmström, Lennart. "Equity Capital in the Family Business," SBQR, 47 (1966), 16-21.

Industria International, 1962. Stock., 1962. 216 p.

"Investments of Insurance Companies in Sweden," SHI (1953), 68-73.

Irsten, Arne. "Voluntary Decartelization in Sweden," Cartel, 6 (1956), 116-18.

"Ivar Kreuger, The Match King," ASR, 18 (1930), 299-300.

Jörberg, Lennart. Growth and Fluctuations of Swedish Industry, 1869-1912; Studies in the Process of Industrialization (Ekonomisk-historiska föreningen, Lund, 3). Stock., 1961. 454 p.

——. "Some Notes on Swedish Entrepreneurs in the 1870's," EEH, 10 (1957-58), 128-33.

Kahlin, Tage. "Developments in the Location of Industry and Government Location Policy," SBQR, 38 (1957), 40-46.

Koefoed, Jean. "Book Investigation in Sweden Into Reading, Selling, Publishing," Publisher's Weekly, 163 (1953), 1140-43.

Leach, Henry G. "The Tobacco Monopoly of Sweden," ASR, 41 (1953), 20-22.

——. "Västerås, a Swedish Industrial Center," ASR, 50 (1962), 261-66.

Leading Companies in Sweden, 1950. Stock., 1950. 90 p.

Ljungberg, Gregory. "Research and Industry in Sweden," EFTA Bull, 5 (1965, no. 5), 4-7.

Lundbergh, Holger. "Sweden's Atomic Energy Program," Bulletin of the Atomic Scientists, 15 (1959), 219-20.

Montgomery, Arthur. The Rise of Modern Industry in Sweden (Stockholm Economic Studies, 8). Lond., 1939. 287 p.

——. "The Rise of Modern Industry in Sweden," AER, 30 (1940), 138-39.

Neumeyer, Fredrik. "Cartels and Publicity in Sweden," RIC, 43 (1950), 179-83.

——. "Swedish Cartel and Monopoly Legislation," AJCL, 3 (1954), 563-67.

Nilsson, Carl-Axel. "Business Incorporations in Sweden: a Study of Enterprise, 1849-1896," EconaHist, 2 (1959), 38-96.

Odhe, Thorsten. "Sweden Proposes New Anti-Monopoly Law," Cartel, 2 (1952), 133-40.

Ohlin, Per Göran. "Entrepreneurial Activities of the Swedish Aristocracy," EEH, 6 (1954), 147-62.

Olivier, Jean-Pierre. "How Sweden Solves Its Housing Problem," Annals of Public and Cooperative Economy, 38 (1967), 191-218.

Palme, Sven U. "Facts and Aspects of the Industrial Revolution," SEHR, 8 (1960), 91-106.

Research Institute for Consumer Affairs Informative Labelling: the Swedish System. Lond., 1964.

Robertsson, Hans. "Some Current Tendencies in Personnel Administration," SBQR, 37 (1956), 89-94.

Scarlat, A. The Development of Shopping Centers in the Stockholm Area. Stock., 1962. 10 p.

Shaplen, Robert. Kreuger: Genius and Swindler. N.Y., 1960. 251 p.

Singer, Kurt D. The Riddle of Sweden's Ballbearings (News Background, Inc. Report 12). N.Y., 1944. 12 p.

Smith, G. Howard. The Development and Present Scope of Industry in Sweden. Stock., 1953. 475 p.

Smith, Susan. Made in Sweden. N.Y., 1934. 15-74.

Stockholm, Chamber of Commerce. Product of Private Enterprise: Technical Skills Build Sweden's Prosperity. Stock., 1956. 64 p.

———. Sweden's Mainspring — Private Enterprise. Stock., 1952.

Strömberg, Håkan. "The Public Corporation in Sweden," in The Public Corporation, A Comparative Symposium (Toronto, 1954), 324-37.

Sweden, Royal Commercial Council. Some Data Illustrating the Development of Swedish Industrial Life. Stock., 1923. 22 p.

Sweden's Industry. Stock., 1961. 13 p.

"Sweden's New Monopoly Law," Cartel, 4 (1954), 29-31.

Swedish Artisans and Small Industry Organization (SHSO) and Swedish Retail Trade Federation. Small Business in Sweden. Stock., 1949. 33 p.

Swedish Employers Confederation. The Swedish Employers Confederation. Stock., 1955. Illustrated.

The Swedish Engineering Industry. Stock., 1962. 7 p.

Swedish Federation of Industries. Industry in Sweden. Stock., 1927. 260 p.

Tengelin, Sten. "Law and Ethics in Marketing," Den svenska marknaden (1960), 9, 87, 89.

Tham, Wilhelm. "Industrialization of Sweden's Rural Areas," ScPP, II, 796-800.

Törnqvist, Gunnar. Transport Costs as a Location Factor for Manufacturing Industry. Lund, 1962. 60 p. (LSG, Series B, 23). Reprinted from Svenskgeografisk årbok, 38 (1962).

Undén, Östen. Survey of Sweden's Patent Laws. Lund, 1915.

AUTOMOTIVE, OIL, CHEMICAL, AND GLASS INDUSTRIES

Carlsson, Arne. "Cooperative Oil in Sweden," RIC, 53 (1960), 19-25.

"Consolidation in Sweden" [Factors in oil consumption and distribution], Petroleum Press Service, 25 (1958), 136-39.

Daugherty, William T. The Chemical Industry and Trade of Sweden (U.S. Bureau of Foreign and Domestic Commerce. Trade Information Bull. 774). Wash., 1931. 29 p.

Linden, H. E. "Sweden's Shale Oil Industry," World Oil, 129 (1949), 213-14+.

"New Phase in Sweden," Petroleum Press Service, 27 (1960), 169-71.

Organization for European Economic Cooperation. Swedish Shale Oil: Production Methods in Sweden. Paris, 1952. 88 p.

Pehrzon, L. E. "Cooperative Oil Trade in Sweden," RIC, 44 (1951), 134-36.

"SAAB of Sweden: the Car and the Planes," ASM, 54 (1960), 11-20.

Sjögren, Erik. "The Volvo Story: People and the Companies Behind the Successful Swedish Car," ASM, 52 (1958), 9-16.

"Some Swedish Automobile Statistics," IFH (1952, no. 2), 72-75.

"The Swedish Glass Industry," SHI (1952), 105-11.

Toundorf, H. G. "Number of Vehicles in Sweden Increasing at a Rapid Rate," Automotive Industry (Je 1, 1953), 51+.

Wettergren, Erik. "An Art Born of Fire" [Glass Industry] ASR, 14 (1926), 33-40.

MONOPOLY CONTROL

Apelqvist, Seved. "Cartels or Competition in Insurance," Cartel, 2 (1952), 116-22.

Bouvin, Sven. "Swedish Anti-Cartel Legislation," RIC, 43 (1950), 26-29.

Irsten, Arne. "Voluntary Decartelization in Sweden," Cartel, 6 (1956), 116-18.

Lundberg, John. "Anti-Monopoly Legislation in Sweden," AnColEc, 26 (1955), 279-83.

Neumeyer, Fredrik. "Cartels and Publicity in Sweden," RIC, 43 (1950), 179-83.

———. "Swedish Cartel and Monopoly Control Legislation," AJCL, 3 (1954), 563-67.

Wetler, J. Gillis. "Swedish Antitrust Law," AJCL, 10 (1961), 19-52.

MINING INDUSTRIES

Åkerman, R. The Present State of Iron Manufacture in Sweden. 1876.

Arpi, Gunnar. "The Supply with Charcoal of the Swedish Iron Industry from 1830-1950," GeoA, 35 (1953), 11-27.

Åselius, Hjalmar. "Investments and Productivity in the Iron and Steel Industry," SHI (1957), 1-13.

———. "The Swedish Ironmasters' Association" [Review of Bertil Boëthius and Åke Kromnow, 'Jernkontorets Historia'], SEHR, 8 (1960), 77-90.

Bergsten, Karl Erik. A Methodical Study of an Ancient Hinterland: the Iron Factory of Finspong, Sweden (LSG, Series B, no. 1). Lund, 1949. 24 p.

Boëthius, Bertil. "A History of Ironmaking" [Review of German book by O. Johannsen], SEHR, 4 (1956), 82-93.

———. "Jernkontoret and the Credit Problems of the Swedish Iron-Works: a Survey," SEHR, 10 (1962), 105-14.

———. "Swedish Iron and Steel, 1600-1955," SEHR, 6 (1958), 143-75.

Brashers, Howard C. "Uppland's Ironworks," ASR, 52 (1964), 299-309.

De Geer, Gerard. "The Importance of Sweden's Iron-Ore in the Present War," Nord, 2 (1939), 466-70.

———. "The Swedish Iron and Steel Industry Today," SBQR, 34 (1953), 58-61.

Donogh, Robert P., and D. B. Stough. "Making Swedish Pig Iron," ForComWk, 19 (1945), 10-13+.

———. "Sweden's Unique Iron-Ore Position," ForComWk, 18 (1945), 4-8+.

Eriksson, Gösta A. "Advance and Retreat of Charcoal Iron Industry and Rural Settlement in Bergslagen," GeoA, 42 (1960), 267-84.

———. "The Decay of Blast Furnaces and Ironworks in Väster Bergslagen in Central Sweden, 1860-1940," GeoA, 35 (1953), 1-10.

———. "The Decline of the Small Blast Furnaces and Forges in Bergslagen after 1850," GeoA, 39 (1957), 257-77.

Friberg, Nils. "Pig-Iron Tithe and Pig-Iron Production; a Critical Study," GeoA, 38 (1956), 441-46.

Furuskog, Jalmar. "Swedish Iron Ages," ASR, 35 (1947), 33-41.

Geijer, P., and N. H. Magnusson. "The Iron Ores of Sweden," in F. Blondel and L. Marvier, eds., Symposium sur les gisements de fer du monde, v. 2 (Algiers, 1952).

Hedin, Naboth. "Sweden's Iron Mountains," ASR, 28 (1940), 129-34.

Horner, M. "Ore Mining in Swedish Lapland," JKCGS, 12 (1960), 14-18.

Iron and Steel in Sweden. Stock., 1920.

Joesten, Joachim. "The Scramble for Swedish Iron Ore," FA, 16 (1938), 347-50.

———. "The Scramble for Swedish Iron Ore," PolQ, 9 (1938), 58-67.

Kastrup, Allan. Expansion of the Swedish Steel Industry. Stock., 1961. 6 p.

Larson, Henrietta. "A Medieval Swedish Mining Company," Journal of Economic & Business History, 2 (1930), 545-59.

"The Lily of Fagersta," ASR, 34 (1946), 227-31.

Litell, Richard J. "Swedish Mining: Mainstay of the Realm," Featuring Sweden (O 1966), 36-43.

Löwengren, Gunnar. Swedish Iron and Steel: an Historical Survey (English version by Nils G. Sahlin). Stock., 1948. 122 p.

Montelius, Sigvard. "Recruitment and Conditions of Life of Swedish Ironworkers During the Eighteenth and Nineteenth Centuries," SEHR, 14 (1966), 1-17.

Nelson, Helge. "The Modern Steel Works of Sweden," BSC, 4 (1938), 47-52.

Nordenson, Jonas. The World's Largest Exporter of Iron Ore. Stock., 1961. 10 p.

Olsson, Gunnar, and B. Anderson. Stora Kopparberg, 600 Years of Industrial Enterprise. Stock., 1951. 82 p.

Rickman, A. F. Swedish Iron Ore. Lond., 1939. 170 p.

Söderlund, Ernst F. "The Swedish Iron Industry During the First World War and the Post-War Depression," SEHR, 6 (1958), 53-94.

———. "The Swedish Iron Industry, 1932-1939," SEHR, 7 (1959), 41-66.

"Sweden Keeps a Front Rank Position Even with Regard to Stainless Steel," Swedish Foreign Commerce, 4 (1950), 39-41.

"Sweden's Mineral Wealth" [by A. H. H.], WT, 15 (1959), 78-88.

"Swedish Iron Ore," SHI (1953), 57-67.

Swedish Iron and Steel Works Association and the Swedish Metal Workers' Union, 1960-1961. Stock., 1960.

"A Visit to Fagersta" [Steel-making combine], ASM, 54 (S 1960), 11-24.

Youngman, E. P. Mining Laws of Sweden (U.S. Bureau of Mines. Information Circular 6703). Wash., 1933. 5 p.

SHIPPING

Anderson, Norman L. "Göteborg Circling the World," ASR, 7 (1919), 208-10.

Eneborg, Helmer. "The Economics of Swedish Shipping," BC, 1 (1935), 198-201.

———. "Swedish Shipping, 1905-1955," ScPP, III, 712-19.

Sidenvall, Gunnar. "Sweden's Merchant Fleet," SBQR, 31 (1950), 10-17.

Sweden, Delegation for International Socio-Political Cooperation. The Seafaring-Trade in Sweden (Published by order of the Swedish Government Delegation for International Sociopolitical Work). Stock., 1920. 48 p.

"The Swedish Merchant Marine," NSN (1960), 133.

"The Swedish Shipbuilding Industry: Production and Employment," SHI (1950), 146-56.

Wollert, W. "The Swedish Shipbuilding Industry," NSN (1960), 134, 137-38.

FISHING

Gerhard, Ingemar. "Cost and Profit in Swedish Fishing Vessels" [1951-1953], FAO Fisheries Bulletin, 10 (1957), 131-41.

Hessle, Chr. The Herring Along the Baltic Coast of Sweden (Conseil permanent international pour l'exploration de la mer. Publications de circonstance, 89). Coph., 1925.

Molander, Arvid R. "The Fisheries of Sweden," ScPP, III, 583-88.

Utterström, Gustaf. "Migratory Labour and the Herring Fisheries of Western Sweden in the 18th Century," SEHR, 7 (1959), 3-40.

LABOR

Åkerman-Johansson, Brita. "Domestic Workers in Sweden," ILR, 67 (1953), 356-66.

Bolin, Bertil. Labour Legislation in Sweden (Landsorganisationen Series). Stock., 1964. 27 p.

"The Conditions of Work of Domestic Servants in Sweden," ILR, 35 (1937), 83-87.

Dahl, Sven. "Duration of Lunch Interval: an Aspect of Urban Social Geography," AcSoc, 4 (1958-59), 16-19.

Dahlander, Gunnar. "Swedish Trade Unions," SoCo, 15 (1951), 15-17.

"Domestic Service and Household Work in Sweden," ILR, 50 (1944), 108-11.

"Enquiries into Conditions of Work in Sweden," ILR, 39 (1939), 54-65.

"Enquiry on Equal Pay in Sweden," ILR, 64 (1951), 90-96.

Fleisher, Frederic. "Manpower Planning for Industry and Individuals," in his, The New Sweden: the Challenge of a Disciplined Democracy (N.Y., 1967), 123-44.

Franklin, D. W. "Industrial Welfare in Sweden," Industrial Welfare, 31 (Ja 1949), 3-6.

Håstad, Elis. "The Importance of Salaried Employees in Sweden," SBQR, 27 (1946), 49ff.

Hansson, Sigfrid. The Trade Union Movement in Sweden (International Trade Union Library, 6). Amsterdam, 1927. 56 p.

———. "The Trade Union Movement in Sweden," ILR, 7 (1923), 481-506.

Hedberg, Magnus. "The Turnover of Labour in Industry, An Actuarial Study," AcSoc, 5 (1960/62), 129-43.

Hedin, Naboth. "The Labor Front in Sweden," ASR, 34 (1946), 16-22.

Hildeman, Nils-Gustav. "Swedish Strikes and Emigration," Swedish Pioneer Historical Quarterly, 8 (1956), 87-93.

Höök, Erik. Salaried Employees and the Industrial Transformation. Stock., 1955. 15 p.

Hydín, Sven. "Accident Prevention in Sweden," ISSAssoc, 13 (1960), 572-74.

"Industrial Accidents in Sweden in 1918 and 1919," ILR, 8 (1923), 437-42.

International Labour Office. The Trade Union Situation in Sweden. Geneva, 1961. 105 p.

Larson, Cedric. "The Swedes are Shaping Up," Occupations, 30 (Ja 1952), 264-70.

Leser, C. E. V. "Trends in Women's Work Participation," PopSt, 12 (1958), 100-10.

Liljedahl, N. A. "Applied Psychology in a Sociatric Approach to the Improvement of Human Relations within Swedish Industry," in J. Elmgren and S. Rubenowitz, eds., Applied Psychology in Industrial and Social Life (Gothenburg, 1952), 144-56.

Lind, Albin. "Sixty Years of Development" [The Swedish Confederation of Trade Unions — LO], Fackfögenings-rörelsen, 38 (Aug 1-8, 1958), 48-96.

Lind, E. Wage Differentiation in Swedish Industry (Publications Issued by the Swedish Employers Confederation, 16). Stock., 1963.

———. Salary Differentiation in Swedish Industry (Publications Issued by the Swedish Employers' Confederation, 17). Stock., 1963.

Lindbom, Tage L. Sweden's Labor Program (League for Industrial Democracy Pamphlet Series). N.Y., 1948. 61 p.

Lokander, Sven. Sick Absence in a Swedish Company: a Sociomedical Study (Acta Medica Scandinavica. Supplementum: 377). Lund, 1962. 172 p.

"The Mobility of Labour in Sweden," ILR, 13 (1926), 897-98.

Nordenskiöld, Otto. "The Organization of Salaried Employees in Sweden," ILR, 52 (1945), 39-46.

Perspective of Labour Conditions in Sweden. Stock., 1954. 52 p.

"Physical Development of Young Workers in Sweden," ILR, 13 (1926), 569-75.

"The Position of Private Employees in Sweden," ILR, 14 (1926), 568-74.

"The Reduction of Hours of Work in Sweden" [by J. R.], ILR, 79 (1959), 325-27.

"The Results of the Eight Hour Day in Sweden," ILR, 7 (1923), 321-27.

Rössel, Agda. "The Employment of Women in Sweden," ILR, 71 (1955), 273-90.

Sjöberg, Sten. "The Swedish Trade Union Movement: Reliance on Democratic Processes," ASM, 52 (Ap 1958), 15-19.

Smith, Gudmund J. W. Stable and Unstable Factory Workers in a Swedish City; A Psychological Investigation by Means of a New Type of Questionnaire (Acta Universitatis Lundensis, 1:53:3). Lund, 1958. 34 p.

"Sweden: Census of 31 December 1930," ILR (1937), 267-70.

Swedish Central Organization of Salaried Employees TCO; The Central Organization of Salaried Employees. Facts and Figures about a New Movement in Sweden. Stock., 1948. 46 p. Subsequent title: The Central Organization of Salaried Employees in Sweden. Stock., 1953. 46 p.; New ed. 1958. 22 p.

Swedish Confederation of Professional Associations. Swedish Professional Associations as Trade Unions. Trelleborg, 1959.

Swedish Confederation of Trade Unions (LO). Economic Expansion and Structural Change: a Trade Union Manifesto; Report submitted to the 16th Cong. Ed. and trans. by Thomas L. Johnston. The Hague, Lond., 1963. 184 p.

——. The Postwar Programme of Swedish Labour: Summary in 27 Points and Comments. Stock., 1946.

——. This Is LO. Stock., 1952. 23 p.

Swedish Employers Confederation. Perspective on Labour Conditions in Sweden. Stock., 1954. 52 p. 1962.

——. A Survey of Social and Labouring Conditions in Sweden. Stock., 1947. 52 p.

The Trade Union Situation in Sweden. Geneva, 1961.

Utterström, Gustaf. "Labour Policy and Population Thought in Eighteenth Century Sweden," SEHR, 10 (1962), 262-79.

Vocational Guidance for Young Persons in Sweden," ILR, 51 (1945), 471-79.

"Vocational Training of Domestic Servants in Sweden," ILR, 36 (1937), 394-98.

LABOR RELATIONS, COLLECTIVE BARGAINING

Adlercreutz, Axel. "Some Features of Swedish Collective Labour Law," Modern Law Review, 10 (1947), 137-58.

Agreement Concerning Time and Motion Studies Concluded by S.A.F. and L.O., 1948. English ed., Stock., 1959.

Agreements Regarding Works Councils Between S.A.F. — T.C.O., 1946 with amendments of 1958. English ed., Stock., 1959.

Bagge, A. "Civil and Commercial Arbitration Law: Arbitration Procedure in Sweden," Arbitration Journal (1937), 271-77.

Basic Agreement Between the Swedish Employers' Confederation and the Confederation of Swedish Trade Unions (As Amended in 1947). Stock., 1950.

Blomkvist, Rune. Collective Bargaining in the Post-War Period (Landsorganisationen Series). Stock., 1966. 18 p.

Bower, R. E. B. "Industrial Relations in Sweden," MLR (1937), 56-64.

Carlson, Sune, and Per Ernmark. A Swedish Case Study on Personnel Relations (Stockholm. Handelshögskolan. Företagsekonomiska Forskningsinstitutet, Meddelande no. 33). Stock., 1951. 66 p.

Carlsson, Thörbjorn. "Labour-Management Relations in Sweden," FLW, 8 (Je 1957), 20-25.

"Collective Agreements in Sweden in 1920," ILR, 6 (1922), 295-99.

"Collective Agreements, Labour Disputes, and the Work of the Official Conciliators in Sweden in 1923," ILR, 10 (1924), 853-58; "...in 1924," 13 (1926), 92-97; "...in 1926," 17 (1928), 714-18.

Collective Wage Negotiations for 1964-1965 and 1966-1968 (Landsorganisationen Series). Stock., 1966. 28 p.

Cooper, Jack. Industrial Relations: Sweden Shows the Way (Fabian Research Series No. 235). Lond., 1963. 32 p.

Crook, Wilfred. "Sweden Tries Anything Once" in his, The General Strike (Chapel Hill, N.C., 1931), 104-44.

Durham, Howard E. "The Place of Mediation in the Swedish Collective Bargaining System," Labour Law Journal (1955), 536-45.

Flaxén, Karl-Olof. "The Collective Agreements System and Wage Determination," SBQR, 42 (1961), 1-7.

Fleisher, Frederic. "Labor-Management Relations and Self-Discipline," in his, The New Sweden: the Challenge of a Disciplined Democracy (N.Y., 1967), 73-96.

Flyboo, Ture, and Rolf Lahnhagen. "The Role of Workers and Employers Organizations in Sweden," Human Relations in Industry (Rome Conf., Ja/F, 1956). Published by the European Productivity Agency of the Organization for European Economic Cooperation (1956), 93 p.

Gustafsson, Stig. Development of Labour Peace in Sweden (Landsorganisationen Series). Stock., 1964. 20 p.

Hansson, Sigfrid. Employers and Workers in Sweden. Stock., N.Y., 1939. 113 p.

"Industrial Relations in Sweden," ILR, 44 (1941), 561-65.

Johnston, Thomas L. Collective Bargaining in Sweden, a Study of the Labour Market and Its Institutions. Cambridge, Mass., Lond., 1962. 358 p. Originally Ph.D. thesis, University of Edinburgh, 1955, The Structure and Functioning of the Swedish Labour Market: a Study of Its Development in the Light of Formative Discussion.

Kugelberg, Bertil. "Centralized or Decentralized Wage Negotiations," SBQR, 32 (1951), 91-98.

——. "Industrial Democracy," SBQR, 34 (1953), 86-91.

——. "Labour Peace in Our Time," Featuring Sweden (O 1966), 33-35, 53.

——. The Saltsjöbaden Agreements Between the Federation of Swedish Employers and the Federation of Swedish Trade Unions. Stock., 1946.

Leach, Henry G. "The Labor Court of Sweden," ASR, 40 (1952), 121-24.

Lester, Richard A. Reflections on Collective Bargaining in Britain and Sweden," ILRR, 10 (1956/57), 375-401.

Lohse, Lennart. "Centralization of Bargaining in Sweden Since 1939," MLR, 81 (1958), 123.

Lundbergh, Holger. "Sweden's Labor Court," American Federationist (1935), 619-21.

Mead, Joseph. "Industrial Relations in Sweden," Economic Forum (1937), 45-51.

Myers, Charles A. Industrial Relations in Sweden: Some Comparisons with American Experience. Cambridge, Mass., 1951. 112 p.

"A New Sliding-Scale Wage Agreement in Sweden," ILR, 47 (1943), 632-34.

Norgren, Paul H. "Collective Wage-Making in Sweden," JPE, 46 (1938), 788-801.

——. The Swedish Collective Bargaining System. Cambridge, Mass., 1941. 339 p. Based on thesis (Ph.D.), Harvard University, 1940.

Østerberg, G. R. "An Empirical Study of Labour Reallocation Gains in Sweden between 1950 and 1960," SJE, 67 (1965), 40-73.

Peterson, Oliver A. "Industrial Conflict – Sweden," in Arthur W. Kornhauser, ed., Industrial Conflict (N.Y., 1954), 487-98.

Robbins, James J. The Government of Labor Relations in Sweden. Chapel Hill, N.C., 1942. 367 p.

——. "Labor Relations: a Successful Swedish Formula," ASR, 31 (1943), 303-12.

Robbins, James J., and Gunnar Heckscher. "Collective Bargaining in Sweden," ABAJ, 24 (1938), 926-27, 933.

Ross, Arthur M., and Donald Irwin. "Strike Experience in Five Countries, 1927-1947: an Interpretation," ILRR, 4 (1950/51), 323-42.

Rydenfelt, Sven. "Comedy at the Bargaining Table," Freeman, 8 (F 1958), 15-24.

"The 'Saltsjöbaden' Agreements Between the Federation of Swedish Employers and the Confederation of Swedish Trade Unions," SBQR, 27 (1946), 103-108.

Schmidt, Carl C. "Mediation in Sweden," in Elmore Jackson, ed., Meeting of Minds: a Way of Peace Through Mediation (Lond., N.Y., 1952).

Schmidt, Folke. The Law of Labour Relations in Sweden. Cambridge, Mass., 1962. 343 p.

Schmidt, Folke, and H. Heineman. Enforcement of Collective Bargaining Agreements in Swedish Law. Stock., 1947. 16 p.

Swedish Employers Confederation, Confederation of Swedish Trade Unions, and Swedish Central Organization of Salaried Employees. Agreement about Enterprise Councils. Stock., 1947.

Underhill, Richard S. Centralization in the Swedish Labor Market. Thesis (Ph.D.), Indiana University, 1965. 280 p.

United States, Department of Labor. Report of the Commission Industrial Relations in Sweden. Wash., 1938. 77 p.

"Wage Negotiations and Wage Policies in Sweden: I, II," ILR, 80 (1959), 319-30, 391-409.

Wagner, Ludwig A. The Wage Policy of the Swedish Trade Unions under Full Employment and Full Unionization. Thesis (Ph.D.), Columbia University, 1955. 340 p.

Wigforss, Ernst. "Industrial Democracy in Sweden," ILR, 9 (1924), 667-79.

Wounsch, John C. The Contribution of the Swedish Labor Movement 1940-1950 to Industrial Relations. Thesis (Ph.D.), University of Southern California, 1953.

LABOR MARKET, EMPLOYMENT SECURITY, UNEMPLOYMENT

Bagge, Gösta. "Wages and Unemployment in Sweden, 1920-1930," in Economic Essays in Honour of Gustav Cassel, October 20, 1933 (Lond., 1933), 691-704.

Clark, Harrison. Swedish Unemployment Policy, 1914 to 1940 (American Council on Public Affairs, Studies in Economics). Wash., 1941. 179 p. Based on thesis (Ph.D.), Harvard University, 1939.

Ekblom, Olle. "The Essence of the Swedish Labor Market Organization," ScPP, III, 787-802.

"Employment and Unemployment in Sweden," ILR, 44 (1941), 322-24.

"Employment Market Organization in Sweden," ILR, 57 (1948), 367-72.

"The Employment Situation in Sweden in 1956," I&L, 19 (1958), 177-83.

"Employment Situation in Sweden in 1958 and 1959," I&L, 23 (1960), 98-103.

"Expenditure on Unemployment Relief in Sweden," ILR, 15 (1927), 593-96.

"The Final Report of the Swedish Unemployment Enquiry," ILR, 32 (1935), 99-104.

Huss, E. G. "The Campaign Against Unemployment in Sweden," ILR, 6 (1922), 721-34.

——. "The Organization of Public Works and Other Measures for the Relief of Unemployment in Sweden," ILR, 26 (1932), 26-50.

Johansson, Alf. "Unemployment in Sweden After the War," ILR, 26 (1932), 617-43.

"Juvenile Employment in Sweden in 1927 and 1928," ILR, 19 (1929), 245-46.

Lagby, Anna-Lisa. The Labour Market Committee for Woman Questions. Stock., 1962. 8 p.

Langway, Walter E. The Employment Security Program in Sweden and Its Possible Applications to the United States.

Thesis (Ph.D.), New York University, 1965. 233 p.

Møller, Gustav. Swedish Unemployment Policy. N.Y., 1939.

——. "The Unemployment Policy," Annals, 197 (1938), 47-71.

Montgomery, Arthur. "Unemployment Policy and Business Revival in Sweden and Finland," BSC, 3 (1937), 280-87.

Ohlin, Bertil. "Economic Recovery and Labour Market Problems in Sweden," ILR, 31 (1935), 498-511, 670-99.

Ohlin, Bertil, ed. The Problem of Employment Stabilization. N.Y., 1959. 173 p.

Olsson, Bertil. "Employment Policy in Sweden," ILR, 87 (1963), 409-34.

Organization for Economic Cooperation and Development, Manpower and Social Affairs Committee. Labour Market Policy in Sweden. Paris, 1963. 72 p.

Rehn, Gösta. "Employment and Welfare: Some Swedish Issues," IndRel, 2 (1963), 1-14.

Skogh, Sven. "The Labor Market and Its Regulation," Annals, 197 (1938), 40-46.

Svenska Handelsbanken. Measures to Combat Unemployment in Sweden Since 1929. Stock., 1938. 20 p.

Swedish Confederation of Trade Unions (LO). Trade Unions and Full Employment. Stock., 1953. 109 p.

Uhr, Carl G. "A National Labor Market Policy: Sweden's Experience," Western Economic Journal, 5 (1967), 141-56.

——. "Sweden's Employment Security Program and Its Impact on the Country's Economy (Benefits and Insurance Research Center Publication No. 11, California Institute of Technology). Pasadena, 1960. 19 p.

"Unemployment Relief in Sweden from 1914 to 1924," ILR, 20 (1929), 713-15.

"The Work of the Employment Exchanges in Sweden in 1925," ILR, 14 (1926), 92-96.

PERSONAL CONSUMPTION
(See also, Cooperatives)

Bentzel, Ragnar. "Consumption in Sweden, 1931-1965," SBQR, 39 (1958), 10-20.

Cederblad, Nils. "The Swedish Family Budget Inquiry of 1923," ILR, 14 (1926), 489-507.

"Recent Family Budget Inquiries: the Swedish Family Budget Inquiry of 1933," ILR, 31 (1935), 869-80.

Tengelin, Sten. "Consumer Protection in Sweden," FBIR (1960), 57-59.

TRANSPORTATION, COMMUNICATIONS

Godlund, Sven. Bus Service in Sweden. Lund, 1963. 72 p.

Greenroyd, J. "Swedish Electric Expresses; New Three-Unit Sets for State Railways," Transport World, 105 (1949), 370-71.

Greville, M. D. "A Century of Railway Development in Sweden," Railway Magazine, 102 (1956), 811-17.

Malmstrom, Vincent H. "The Swedish State Railways, 1856-1956," ASR, 44 (1956), 359-70.

Söderlund, Ernst F. "The Placing of the First Swedish Railway Loan," SEHR, 11 (1963), 42-59.

Sweden, Power Board. Canals and Waterways of Sweden. By F. V. Hansen. Stock., 1915. 14 p.

Sweden, Tele-Communication Directorate. Telephone, Telegraph and Radio Services in Sweden. Stock.

"The Swedish Railway Situation," Foreign Railway News, 16 (1940), 109-13.

Torell, A. "The Swedish Road Plan," Road International, 29 (1958), 35-39, 61.

Viksten, Albert. "A Cultural Achievement, The Swedish Railroads Near Completion," ASR, 20 (1932), 284-91.

HYDROELECTRIC AND ATOMIC POWER

Arpi, Gunnar. The Development of Water Power and the Supply of Energy in Sweden. Stock., 1962. 18 p.

Atomic Energy in Sweden. Stock., 1961. 28 p.

Blomqvist, Erik. "Water Power from the Indalsälven," Ymer, 8 (1960), 127-38.

Borquist, W. "Planned Utilization of Water Resources," in Transactions of the Third World Power Conference, 1936 (1938), v. 7, 291-300.

Ljungberg, Gregory. Sweden, from Natural to Nuclear Resources. Stock., 1959.

MacDonald, I. V. "Sweden Plans Atomic Future," ForTrade (Canada) (Ja 19, 1957), 26-27.

"The Municipal Supply of Water, Gas and Electricity in Sweden," "I: The Municipal Water Supply," by John Bergström; "II: The Municipal Gas and Electric Supply," by H. M. Malmö, AnColEc, 5 (1929), 360-65.

Petri, F. "Forecasts of Power Consumption," SBQR, 35 (1954), 66-72.

Rusck, Åke. "The Swedish Power Supply," ScPP, III, 589-97.

Sweden, Power Board. The Hydraulic Laboratory at Älvkarleby (Blue-white Series, 23). By Stig Angelin. Stock., 1959. 20 p.

———. The Power Team; a Chronicle of the Swedish State Power Board, Its Background and People, Jubilee Year 1959. By Charlie Cederholm, with photos by Lennart Nilsson. Stock., 1960.

———. State Power Plants in Sweden, 1933. Stock., 1933. 121 p.

———. Sweden, Land of Long Transmission Lines (Swedish State Power Board Publication no. 10). 2d rev. ed., Stock., 1953. 54 p.

———. The Swedish State Power Administration's Materials Laboratory in Vasterås (Blue-white Series, 31). By Börje Larsson. Stock., 1961. 16 p.

———. The Swedish 380 kV System. Stock., 1960. 351 p.

———. The Swedish 380 kV Transmission System (Series: Sweden. Vattenfallsstyrels Publications no. 1). 2d rev. ed., Stock., 1952. 15 p.

———. Underground Power Plants in Sweden (Blue-white series, 30). By Tore Nilsson. Stock., 1961. 15 p.

Upmark, Erik. Hydro-Electric Development in Sweden. Stock., 1933. 152 p.

———. "Power Resources, Development and Utilization: Sweden," in Transactions of the Third World Power Conference, 1936 (1938), v. 2, 377-89.

World Power Conference, 1933. Sweden: Power and Industry. Stock., 1933. 319 p.

BUILDING, HOUSING, COOPERATIVE HOUSING

Åkerman, Gustaf. "The Income Elasticity of Demand for Housing," SEHR, 5 (1957), 49-73.

Alm, Ulla. Cooperative Housing in Sweden, N.Y., 1939. 75 p.

Ames, J. W. "Cooperative Housing in Sweden," AnColEc, 26 (1955), 253-68.

Bates, H. C. "The Swedish Way," American Federationist (N 1953), 8-11.

Bogardus, Emory S. "The Cooperative Housing Movement in Sweden," S&SR, 35 (N 1950), 128-35.

"The Building Trade in Sweden," ILR, 6 (1922), 827-28.

Canadian Central Mortgage and Housing Corporation. Housing Progress Abroad. v. 1, nos. 5-6: Sweden. Ottawa, 1948.

Cheetham, J. H. "Housebuilding by Amateurs: Sweden's Successful Experiment," Municipal Journal, 58 (1950), 2567-69.

"Cooperative Housing in Sweden," ILR, 37 (1938), 486-91.

Dickson, Harald. "Sweden Plans Its Housing Policy," LandEc, 23 (1947), 417-27.

Dickson, Harald, and Paul E. Wendt. Housing Characteristics of the United States and Sweden, 1930-1946. Land Ec Supp (Madison, Wisc., 1950). 28 p.

Goodsell, W. "Housing and the Birthrate in Sweden," AmSocR (1937), 850-59.

Hald, Arthur with Per Holm and Gotthard Johansson, eds. Swedish Housing. Stock., 1949. 64 p.

Holm, Per. Swedish Housing. Stock., 1957. 96 p.

"Housing Conditions of Agricultural Workers in Sweden," ILR, 24 (1931), 75-87.

"Housing in Sweden," SHI (1957), 1-3.

Hultén, Bertil. Building Modern Sweden. Harmondsworth, 1951. 64 p.

Hyresgästernas sparkasse och byggnads föreningars riksforbund [Tenants' Savings and Building Society]. Cooperative Housing. Stock., 1948. 35 p.; 1952 ed. 36 p.

Johansson, Alf. "House-Building in the 1950's," SBQR, 41 (1960), 125-32.

———. "Sound Housing Policy in Sweden," Annals, 197 (May 1938), 160-70.

———. "Swedish Housing Policy in Wartime," ILR, 50 (1944), 300-15.

Johansson, Alf, and Waldemar Svensson. Swedish Housing Policy. N.Y., 1939. 47 p.

Lilienberg, A. Housing Conditions in Stockholm: a Summary. Stock., 1930. 16 p.

Markelius, Sven. "Stockholm's First Collective House," ASR, 26 (1938), 243-47.

Michanek, Ernst. Housing Standard and Housing Construction in Sweden. Stock., 1962. 30 p.

Monson, Donald, and Astrid Monson. "Sweden's Housing, Planning Progress is Impressive," Journal of Housing, 6 (1949), 261-66+.

National Association of Swedish Architects. Swedish Housing of the Forties. Stock., 1950.

Oxholm, Axel H. The Small-Housing Scheme of the City of Stockholm. Wash., 1935. 34 p.

"The Production of Prefabricated Wooden Houses in Sweden," SHI (1952), 65-71.

Sandberg, Gösta. "Saving for Home-Ownership in Sweden," World Thrift (1957), 438-45.

Schoenfeldt, Heinz. "House and Home, Stockholm Invites to an Exhibition of Ideal Homes," ASR, 18 (1930), 150-54.

Silk, Leonard S. Sweden Plans for Better Housing. Durham, N.C., 1948. 149 p. Originally thesis (Ph.D.), Duke University.

Smith, George E. K. Sweden Builds. Stock., N.Y., 1950. 279 p. 2d ed., 1957. 270 p.

Stafanson, Ray. Swedish Housing and Community Planning. Thesis (M.A.), University of California, Berkeley, 1959. 353 p.

Svensson, Waldemar. "Home Ownership in Sweden," Annals, 197 (May 1938), 154-59.

Sweden, Agriculture Commission [1935-1939]. Building Research in Sweden, a Brief Survey by Boris Blongren and Sten Rosenström. Stock., 1949. 26 p.

"Sweden's Solution of the Urban Housing Problem," Federal Home Loan Bank Review (1936), 427-36.

Swedish Housing Market. Stock., 1957. 72 p.

Wallander, Sven. "Co-operative Housing in Sweden," AnColEc, 21 (1950), 22-29.

———. "Cooperative Housing in Sweden," RIC, 42 (1949), 129-34.

———. "Cooperative Housing in Sweden: Effects on the Type and Standard of House," RIC, 46 (1953), 143-49.

Wallquist, H. Housing Conditions of the Poorer Classes in Gothenburg. 1891.

COOPERATIVES

Aaltonen, Esko. Consumer Cooperation in Sweden. 1954.

"The Advance of Swedish Cooperation," RIC, 38 (1945), 88-92.

Ames, J. W. Cooperative Sweden Today. Manchester, 1952. 172 p.

———. "Consumer's Cooperation and Quality in Sweden. Quality Service of the Kooperativa Förbundet. Stockholm," AnColEc, 24 (1953), 375-81.

———. "The Price and Dividend Policy of the Swedish Cooperative Movement," AnColEc, 26 (1955), 208-13.

———. "Swedish Consumers' Cooperation," RIC, 45 (1952), 136-40.

———. "The Swedish Movement," SoCo, 14 (1950), 280-83.

Baker, Jacob. Cooperative Enterprise. N.Y., 1937. 266 p.

Baker, Jacob et al. Report of the Inquiry on Cooperative Enterprises in Europe. Wash., 1937. 321 p.

Bergström, Gerta. "Co-operative Housewives' Activity in Sweden," RIC, 38 (1945), 181-83.

Bissonnet, A. P. "How Sweden Buys Consumer Goods: Distributive System There and the Part Played by the Cooperatives," Foreign Trade (Canada), 109 (May 24, 1958), 18-21.

Bogardus, Emory S. "Roles of Consumer Cooperatives in Sweden," S&SR, 35 (Ja 1951), 205-14.

Bonow, Mauritz. "The Consumer Cooperative Movement in Sweden," Annals, 197 (1938), 171-84.

——. "Inflation and Cooperative Policy," RIC, 45 (1952), 220-23+.

Bowen, E. B. "Sweden: Land of Economic Democracy," Consumer Cooperation (1935), 144-50.

Campbell, W. J. "The Consumer's Cooperative Movement," New Frontiers (1937), 21-64.

Co-operative Association. Educational Work at Vår Gård. Stock., 1950.

Dykstra, Waling. "Sweden: a Cooperative Oasis," NFC (N 1942), 12-13+.

Ellidin, H. "Cooperative Employee Education in Sweden," Consumer Cooperation (1935), 193-94.

Eronn, Lars. "The Co-operative Movement, Swedish Experiences," AnColEc, 27 (1956), 271-76.

Fleisher, Frederic. "The Cooperatives: From Penny-Pinching to Consumer Education," in his, The New Sweden: The Challenge of a Disciplined Democracy (N.Y., 1967), 29-39.

Freeburg, Victor O. "Social Welfare at the SKF," ASR, 8 (1920), 363-66.

Gillespie, James E. "Swedish Cooperatives," CH, 18 (1950), 331-36.

Gjöres, Axel. Cooperation in Sweden. Manchester, 1927. 125 p.; 2d ed. 1937. 197 p.

Harris, Thomas. Sweden's Unorthodox Co-operatives. Stock., 1949.

——. "Sweden's Unorthodox Co-ops," Magazine of the Future (May 1948), 87-96+.

Hedberg, Anders. Consumers Cooperation in Sweden. Stock., 1948. 80 p.

——. "Consumer Cooperatives in Sweden," AnColEc, 29 (1958), 375-408.

——. Co-operative Sweden. Stock., 1951.

——. "The ⟨Luma⟩ an International Co-operative Undertaking," AnColEc, 8 (1932), 341-45.

——. Swedish Consumers in Cooperation. Stock., 1939. 94 p.

"K. F. and Consumers' Cooperation in Sweden in 1947," RIC, 41 (1948), 120-24.

Kéler, G. "The Development of Kooperativa Forbundet's Foreign Trade," RIC, 44 (1951), 190-94.

Lamming, N. Sweden's Cooperative Enterprises. Manchester, 1940. 220 p.

Nilsson, Karl. The Co-operative Society of Stockholm and Its Environs. Stock., 1952. 63 p.

Odhe, Thorsten. "Consumer and Housing Co-operatives in Sweden," ScPP, III, 761-75.

——. "Consumer Cooperation in Sweden's Economic Life," Swedish-Australian Trade Journal, 33 (May 1946), 94-97.

——. Consumers' Co-operation in Sweden's Economic Life. Stock., 1949.

——. "Fifty Years K.F. = The Swedish 50 Years Anniversary; Kooperativa Förbundet, 1899-1949," RIC, 42 (1949), 230-33+.

——. "Sweden Wins Women's Support," CoR, 18 (M 1944), 42-43.

Örne, Anders E. Cooperative Ideals and Problems. Manchester, 1937. 157 p.

——. "The Idea and Practice of Co-operation in Sweden," AnColEc, 17 (1941), 192-95.

Schnabel, G. "Youth and the Swedish Cooperative Movement," RIC, 52 (1959), 204-209.

Stolpe, Herman A. Cog or Collaborator: Democracy in Cooperative Education. Stock., 1949.

——. "Co-operation and Monopolies in Sweden," ILR, 18 (1928), 46-57.

——. "Cooperative Book Publishing in Sweden," CPR, 26 (1951), 220-21.

——. "The Co-operative Groups in Sweden," IO, 2 (1937/38), 155-61.

——. A New Family Economy, the Consumers' Cooperative Movement in Sweden. Stock., 1936.

Sweden, Union of Cooperatives. "The Role of the Swedish Consumers' Cooperative Movement in the Constitution and the Safeguarding of Democratic Economy," AnColEc, 24 (1953), 16-22.

"Sweden," AnColEc, 14 (1938), 254-55.

Varshney, N. P. "Swedish Consumers Co-operation," U.P. Cooperative Journal, 29 (1954), 203-14.

Wendel, Harry. "The Last Service" [Funerals], AnColEc, 26 (1955), 276-79.

Whitworth, Daphne. "How Swedish Housewives Help the Cooperative Movement," CPR, 27 (1952), 148-51.

AGRICULTURAL COOPERATIVES

Ames, J. W. "Swedish Agriculture is a Cooperative Enterprise," AnColEc, 24 (1955), 269-75.

Frostenson, Georg. "Agricultural Cooperatives in Sweden," ASR, 34 (1946), 143-49.

Gullander, Åke H. Farmers' Co-operation

in Sweden. Lond., 1948. 152 p.; American ed., Ames, Iowa, 1951. 184 p.

Lindstedt, H. "Agricultural Cooperation in Sweden," IntRevAg, 26 (1935), 330E-339E, 360E-369E, 402E-417E.

"The Malmö Central Dairy Jointly Controlled by Producers' and Consumers Organization," AnColEc, 9 (1933), 377-81.

Myrdal, Alva. "Swedish Agricultural Policy: Joint Control by Cooperatives and Government," AICC Economic Review, 9 (D 1, 1957), 13-18.

United States, Farm Credit Administration. Agricultural Cooperation in Denmark and Sweden (Miscellaneous Reports, 165). Wash., 1952. 42 p.

Ytterborn, G. R. "Agricultural Cooperation in Sweden," Annals (1938), 185-99.

AGRICULTURE

Åberg, Ewert. "How Sweden Feeds Herself," ASR, 30 (1942), 60-62.

——. "Sweden Looks to Its Agriculture," SciM, 57 (1943), 230-39.

Abramson, E. "Food Legislation in Sweden," Food, Drug, Cosmetic Law Journal, 10 (1955), 5-19.

"Agricultural Credit Funds in Sweden," ILR, 12 (1925), 863-68.

"Agricultural Workers on Large-Scale Farms in Sweden," ILR, 12 (1925), 542-54.

Åkerman, Åke et al. Swedish Contributions to the Development of Plant Breeding (New Sweden Tercentenary Publications). Stock., 1938. 111 p.

Allen, G. R. "A Comparison of Real Wages in Swedish Agriculture and Secondary and Tertiary Industries, 1870-1949," SEHR, 3 (1955), 85-107.

——. "Relative Real Wages in Swedish Agriculture and Industry, 1930-1950," OISB, 15 (1953), 436-52.

Åstrand, Halvdan. "The Adjustment of Agriculture," SBQR, 48 (1967), 14-19.

——. "Some Features of Sweden's Agricultural Policy," SBQR, 37 (1956), 115-25.

Dahl, Sven. "Strip Fields and Enclosure in Sweden," SEHR, 9 (1961), 56-67.

DuRietz, Gunnar. "Rising Land Values and the Use of Land," SBQR, 48 (1967), 7-13.

European Free Trade Association. "Sweden," in Agriculture in EFTA (Geneva, 1965), 81-94.

Federation of Swedish Farmers Association. Swedish Farmer's Organizations. Stock., 1950. 55 p.

Freund, Rudolf. "Squandering the Public Domain in Sweden: 1820-1870," LandEc, 22 (1946), 119-30.

Fullerton, B. The Northern Margin of Grain Production in Sweden in the Twentieth Century (Institute of British Geographers Publications, no. 20; Transactions and Papers, 1954), 181-91.

——. The Small Grain Crops in Northern Sweden: a Study of the Balance of Factors Governing Their Contemporary Distribution. Thesis (M.A.), University College, London, 1952.

Gasser, E. "Present State of the Dairying Industry in the Different Countries: (17) Sweden," IntRevAg, 29 (1938), 278T-292T.

Gordon, Max. "Swedish Agriculture Today," World Crops, 7 (1955), 410-13.

Håkansson, Richard, ed. Swedish Agricultural Administration, Education and Research; a Manual for Visitors in Sweden. Stock., 1950. 34 p.

Halmström, Sven. "Investment in Swedish Farming," SBQR, 31 (1949), 33-38.

Hammarskiöld, Sven L. "The Swedish Sugar Company and the New Agricultural Policy," SBQR, 37 (1956), 126-30.

Hävermark, Gunnar. "The Regulation of Hours of Work in Swedish Agriculture," ILR, 39 (1939), 633-47.

Höijer, Ernst. "Swedish Agriculture," BC, 1 (1935), 186-88.

Horne, H. J. "Swedish Agricultural Production has Improved in Recent Years," FT, 7 (1950), 380-82.

"Hours of Work in Swedish Agriculture," ILR, 16 (1927), 841-47.

Huntington, Ellsworth. "Farms and Villages of Sweden," JofGeo, 37 (1938), 85-90.

International Institute of Agriculture (The First World Agricultural Census, Bull. 19). Stock., Rome, 1936. 30 p.

Jonasson, Olaf G. Agricultural Atlas of Sweden. Stock., 1938. 176 p.

"Labour Supply and Unemployment in Swedish Agriculture," ILR, 17 (1928), 571-74.

Lägnert, Folke. Wheat Cultivation in Southern and Central Sweden. Lund, 1949.

Meissner, Frank. "Economics of the Agrarian Reform in Sweden," Norseman, 13 (1955), 177-87.

——. "The Economics of the Swedish Agricultural Act of 1947," Indian Journal of Agricultural Economy, 10 (1955), 35-52.

Montelius, Sigvard. "The Burning of Forest Land for the Cultivation of Crops: 'Svedjebruk' in Central Sweden," GeoA, 35 (1953), 41-54.

Nordström, Ludvig. "North European

Farmers Incorporated," ASR, 20 (1932), 76-79.

Osvald, Hugo, with Lennart Gustafsson et al. Swedish Agriculture. Stock., 1952. 103 p.

Ovesen, Thorild. "Swedish Agricultural Policy and Agricultural Production from 1930 to 1940," EconaHist, 1 (1958), 43-64.

Pettersson, V. I. "Ancient and Modern Swedish Land Tenure Policy," JFE, 30 (1948), 322-31.

Saemund, G. "Swedish Agriculture," ScPP, III, 515-21.

Schmidt, Folke, Leif Gräntze, and Axel Roos. "Legal Working Hours in Swedish Agriculture; a Summary of a Field Study," Theoria, 12 (1946), 181-96.

Sweden, Agricultural Information Office. Swedish Agricultural Education and Research: a Manual for Visitors in Sweden. Richard Håkansson, ed. Stock., 1956. 32 p.

Sweden, Agriculture Commission. Swedish Government Control of Dairy Products and Eggs. Karlskrona, 1959. 23 p.

Sweden, Swedish Legation, London. The Pig Industry and Bacon Cureing in Sweden. Lond., 1927. 48 p.

Utterström, Gustaf. "Population and Agriculture in Sweden, circa 1700-1830," SEHR, 9 (1961), 176-94.

Wolpert, Julian. "A Spatial Behavior Analysis of Decision Making in Middle Sweden's Farming," in Fred E. Dohrs and Lawrence M. Sommers, eds., Introduction to Geography: Selected Readings (N.Y., 1967), 359-69.

———. Decision-Making in Middle Sweden's Farming: a Spatial Behavioral Analysis. Thesis (Ph.D.), University of Wisconsin, 1963.

FORESTRY

Anderson, Sven A. "Forests and Forest Activities in Sweden," ForGeo, 32 (1933), 55-65.

Andersson, Gunnar. "The Forests of Sweden," ASR, 9 (1921), 530-34.

Appleton, John B., and Sybil Mitchell. "The Forests and Lumber Industries of Sweden — a Study in Economic Geography," Bulletin of the Geographic Society of Philadelphia, 30 (1932), 163-81.

Arnborg, Tore. "The Forests from the Tree Limit to the Coast-Line," Ymer, 8 (1960), 139-49.

Arpi, Gunnar. "Swedish Forests — a Survey of Some Current Questions," SBQR, 41 (1960), 1-9.

Baldwin, Henry I. "Forest Colonization in Sweden," JFor, 22 (1924), 241-57.

Eklund, Bo. "The Organization and Work of the Swedish Forest Research Institute," Unasylva, 2 (1948), 243-51.

"The Employment of Forestry Workers in Northern Sweden," ILR, 40 (1939), 700-10.

Forestry and Silviculture in Sweden. Stock., 1962. 7 p.

Forshell, W. Plym. The Swedish Forest. Stock., 1961. 13 p.

———. "Swedish Forestry," ScPP, III, 546-52.

Gerard, Ove. "The Purchase of Agricultural Land by the Timber Industry in Sweden from 1885 to 1906," EconaHist, 1 (1958), 21-33.

Graham, A. "Forestry in Sweden; 1925," JFor, 24 (1926), 764-84.

Löwegren, Gunnar. "The Forest and Forest Industry of Norrland," SHI Supp (S 1945), 63 p.

Lundberg, Gustaf. "The Drainage of Peat for Forest Production," Actes du Ier Congrès international de sylviculture, 4 (1926), 695-700.

———. "Drainage of Swamp Lands for Forestry Purposes," JFor, 24 (1926), 19-37.

Moberg, Vilhelm. "The Men Who Work in Swedish Forests," ASR, 24 (1936), 129-39.

"Notes on Sweden, with Special Reference to the Forests in Relation to Industry and Commerce," SGM, 32 (1916), 227-41.

Perry, George S. Forestry in Sweden and Adjacent Lands from the Viewpoint of an American Forester. Mont Alto, Pa., 1929. 276 p.

Rundblad, Bengt G. "Problems of a Depopulated Rural Community," LSG, Series B, no. 13 (1957), 184-91.

Slosson, Edwin E. "The Land of Timber and Turbines," ASR, 11 (1923), 596-604.

Söderlund, Ernst F. "Short-Term Economic Fluctuation and the Swedish Timber Industry, 1850-1900," JEH, 13 (1953), 388-97.

Streyffert, Thorsten. The Forests of Sweden (New Sweden Tercentenary Publications). Stock., 1938. 72 p.

———. The Forest; Sweden's "Green Gold". N.Y., 1939. 61 p.

Swan, Håkan. "Forestry in the Province of

Västernorrland," Ymer, 8 (1960), 161-70. Reprinted as "A Geographical Excursion through Central Norrland," IGCong, 19th, Stock., 1960.

Sweden, Forest Taxation Commission. Sweden's Forest Resources According to the National Forest Survey Carried Out During the Period 1923-1929. Stock., 1931.

The Swedish Forest Service. Stock., 1956. 44 p.

United States, Bureau of Foreign and Domestic Commerce. Forestry in Sweden. (Trade Promotion Series, 56). By Emil Kekich. Wash., 1927.

FOREST INDUSTRIES

Althin, Torsten K. V. Papyrus, Sweden's Largest Fine Paper and Board Mill. Molndal, Sweden, 1953. 103 + 63 p. Includes paper samples.

Diedrichs, Harry. "A Modern Swedish Forest Industrial Concern," Ymer, 8 (1960), 194-201. Reprinted in Papers, IGCong, 19th, Stock., 1960.

Hägglund, E. "The Early Evolution and Modern Advances within the Cellulose Industry," SBQR, 34 (1953), 15-19.

Johansson, Sven. "Ådalen as a Forest Industrial Centre," Ymer, 8 (1960), 179-93.

Lindberg, Olof. "An Economic-Geographical Study of the Localization of the Swedish Paper Industry," GeoA, 35 (1953), 28-40.

"The Situation and Prospects of the Swedish Pulp Industry," SHI (1949), 45-56.

Swedish Chamber of Commerce of the United States, N.Y. Sweden as Producer of Wood-Goods, Pulp, Paper, Tar and Other Forest Products. 1920. 303 p.

"The Swedish Paper Industry," SHI (1957), 1-3.

"The Swedish Wallboard Industry," SHI (1952), 140-45.

Ullman, Alarik. Softwood Contracts. Stock., 1957. 240 p.

EDUCATION

INTRODUCTION

Scandinavian educational institutions are very much alike and are widely admired for their excellence. Foreigners have been intrigued by the development of folk high schools involving adult education and by the possible causal relationship between the educational system and commitment to democratic values. There are a great many brief descriptive articles, reports in yearbooks on education, and pamphlet-length guides. Most of the guides are publications of the Nordic governments. Scandinavian scholars do not have an English-language journal in the field of education, and the published English-language literature is generally unimpressive, although there are a few works of excellence. Apparently there have been no scholarly monographs in comparative Scandinavian education, and there is a paucity of literature touching upon the development of the universities, the politics of education, the sociology of education, or the recruitment and career patterns of educators. Available to us in relative abundance are curriculum outlines and descriptions of the structure of the primary and secondary education systems. There are remarkably many unpublished American dissertations, but of those completed prior to World War II, many are broadly descriptive and quite out-of-date. All of the postwar dissertations concern either Norway or Sweden.

For overviews of the region as a whole, the best is C. Willis Dixon's *Society, Schools and Progress in Scandinavia* (1965). Alternatively, one may consult Herman Ruge's booklet, *Educational Systems in Scandinavia* (1962), and *Scandinavian Adult Education* (1952), an immense compendium of country studies, edited by Ragnar Lund. For a well-written introduction, read Per Stensland's "Adult Education" in Henning Friis, ed., *Scandinavia Between East and West* (1950). One may obtain a cursory, combined philosophic and descriptive introduction by reading the back-to-back articles by Hal Koch and Stellan Arvidson in J. A. Lauwerys, ed., *Scandinavian Democracy* (1958); these are entitled "Education of Youth" and "Education for Democracy." Additional suggestions are Alina Lindegren's old *Education and Service Conditions of Teachers in Scandinavia, the Netherlands and Finland* (1941), and Howard Southwood's unpublished thesis on *Adult Education in Scandinavia* (1956).

There are excellent works on Denmark's N.F.S. Grundtvig (1783-1872), who was of major significance for the Northern Countries because of his philosophy of education, which inspired the folk schools. Among the Grundtvig studies are two books of recent vintage: Hal Koch's *Grundtvig* (1952), and Johannes Knudsen's *A Danish Rebel: a Study of N.F.S. Grundtvig* (1955). There are also two unpublished theses: Paul Andreasen's *Grundtvig as an Educator* (1936), and David Olson's *The Life and Educational Influence of Nicholai Frederik Severin Grundtvig* (1931). See also the section on Grundtvig under History.

The Danish educational system is best

introduced in C. Willis Dixon's *Education in Denmark* (1958). An older introduction is available, by Andreas Boje et al., entitled *Education in Denmark; the Intellectual Base of a Democratic Commonwealth* (1932). There are two books on the folk high school: Olive Campbell, *The Danish Folk School: Its Influence in the Life of Denmark and the North* (1928), and J. C. Møller's *Education in a Democracy: the Folk High Schools of Denmark* (1944).

For Iceland, there is only one book to recommend: George Trial's *History of Education in Iceland* (1945). For Finland, there is a brief introduction by Niilo Kallio, *The School System of Finland* (1956). Longer treatises are pre-World II and, of these, only one has been published, Thomas Hippaka's *Indomitable Finland; Educational Background* (1940). The most highly commendable theses appear to be Hippaka's *A Survey of Education in Finland, 1800 to 1825* (1938), and Rudolph Seppi's *The Educational System of Finland* (1936).

For Norway the literature is relatively good. There is a commendable introduction by Olav Hove, *An Outline of Norwegian Education* (1958), and there is a longer book on *The Organization and Administration of the Educational System of Norway* (1955) by George Wiley. Also recommended are two brief works: Ingeborg Lyche's *Adult Education in Norway* (1957), and Gunnar Mortensen and Sven Persson, *Vocational Training in Norway: a Survey* (1956). The four descriptive volumes just named were published by the Norwegian government. Helen Huus' *Education of Children and Youth in Norway* (1960) is a fine scholarly work. A published dissertation which still stands as the only major work available to us on its subject is Arne Jensen's *Rural Schools in Norway* (1928). The works just mentioned are nicely complemented by two unpublished American dissertations: Trygve Jansen's *Elementary Teacher Education in Norway: a Descrip-*

tive Historical Study (1957), and Robert Hansen's *The Democratization of Norwegian Education* (1952).

The recent educational reform in Sweden has been treated rather extensively; see particularly the writings of Torsten Husén. Roland Paulston has recently completed a dissertation on the history and politics of educational change: *Swedish Comprehensive School Reform, 1918-1950: the Period of Formulation and Adoption* (1966). Complementary is Madge Lilja's dissertation, *A Study of the Position of Guidance Programs in the Comprehensive Schools in Greater Stockholm and Their Relationship to the Reformed Educational System of Sweden* (1966). Perhaps the best introduction to the Swedish educational system is Stellan Arvidson's *Education in Sweden* (1955), which is brief and now somewhat out-of-date. Technical but of great merit is Nils-Eric Svensson's *Ability Grouping and Scholastic Achievement: Report on a Five Year Follow-up Study in Stockholm* (1962). On sex education, see Birgitta Linner's *Sex and Society in Sweden* (1967). Several of the pre-war American theses would no doubt be helpful to anyone studying the development of Swedish education. Post-war American dissertations examine an impressively wide range of subjects: Emil Johnson, *The Role of Foreign Languages in Swedish Education* (1957); August Hehnstrom, *An Interpretation of the Religious Education in Sweden* (1945); George Broten, *An Exploration of Swedish Physical Education* (1957); Kathleen Fawcett, *A Study of Publicly Supported Summer Educational Services for Children in Sweden* (1954); David Ostergren, *The Folk High Schools of Sweden* (1953); Olaf Tegner, *Adult Education in Sweden: Its Administration and Organization* (1958); and most recently, Robert Calatrello, *The Basic Philosophy of Emanuel Swedenborg, with Implications for Western Education* (1966). Other sources on Swedenborg (1688-1772) are listed under History.

SCANDINAVIA

Arvidson, Stellan. "Education for Democracy," in J. A. Lauwerys, ed., Scandinavian Democracy (Coph., N.Y., 1958), 294-315.

Barry, William R. Schools in Scandinavia.

Thesis, International YMCA College (1952), 109 p.

Brand, Philip. A Comparative Study of the Treatment of the Causes of the World War in Secondary School Textbooks of England, Germany, Neutral Powers, and the United States. Thesis (Ph.D.), College

of the City of New York (1935), 161 p.
[Includes Denmark, Norway, and Sweden]

Buraas, Janette. "Vocational Training in
the Nordic Countries," EFTA Bull, 5
(1964, no. 7), 12-15.

Dixon, C. Willis. Society, Schools and Progress in Scandinavia. Lond., 1965. 206 p.

Hammerich, L. L. "The Scandinavian Universities and Their Place in the Spiritual
Life of Scandinavia," IO, 1 (1936), 40-50.

Highbaugh, I. "School as a Community Center: Some Observations Made in Scandinavia," EdRChina, 25 (1932), 139-44.

Koch, Hal H. "Education of Youth," in J. A.
Lauwerys, ed., Scandinavian Democracy
(Coph., N.Y., 1958), 282-93.

Lathrop, John C. Promotion of International
Understanding Through the Exchange of
High School Students: a Project of the
Metropolitan School Study Council Pro-
viding Exchange Visits between Ameri-
can, Latin-American, and Scandinavian
Students, Thesis (Ph.D.), Columbia Uni-
versity, 1948. 107 p.

Lindegren, Alina M. Education and Service
Conditions of Teachers in Scandinavia,
the Netherlands and Finland (U. S. Office
of Education Bull., 1940, no. 9). Wash.,
1941. 149 p.

Nordlund, Anders. "Scandinavia," in C.
Lynn Vandien and John E. Nixon, eds.,
The World Today in Health, Physical
Education and Recreation (Englewood
Cliffs, New Jersey, 1968), 190-219.

Ruge, Herman. Educational Systems in
Scandinavia. Coph., Oslo, 1962. 86 p.

Sawicki, Stanislaw. "Chairs of Northern
Philology in Scandinavia," BC, 2 (1936),
72-76.

Sewell, William H. "Scandinavian Students'
Image of the United States: a Study in
Cross-Cultural Education," Annals, 295
(1954), 126-35.

Sundet, Olav. "The Scandinavian Countries,"
in The Year Book of Education 1950
(Lond., 1950), 497-506.

Taylor, Kamma. "The Teaching of English
in Scandinavia," BC, 2 (1936), 76-80.

UNESCO. International Guide to Educational
Documentation, 1955-60. Geneva, 1963.
700 p. [A listing, by countries, of reference materials in education, with brief
annotations and explanations in English.
Structure and organization of the countries' schools. All Nordic countries except Finland.]

Vigander, Haakon. Mutual Revision of History Textbooks in the Nordic Countries.
Paris: UNESCO, 1950.

ADULT EDUCATION

"Adult Education in Scandinavia," AdEd, 5
(1954), 16-21.

Arestad, Sverre. "Adult Education in Scandinavia," AmT (D 1946), 5-8; (Ja 1947),
17-20.

Braatoy, Bjarne. "Adult Education in Scandinavia," WAAEB (1937), 8-18.

Bukdahl, Jørgen. "The North and Europe,"
in Elsinor International People's College,
Adult Education in the Struggle for Peace
(Lond., 1949), 180-228.

Coit, Eleanor G. Government Support of
Workers' Education. N.Y., 1940. 72 p.

Conference of Southern Mountain Workers.
Adult Education in Scandinavia and
America. Knoxville, 1925. [Two ad-
dresses given at their Knoxville Conference, A, 1924]

Cook, Eva M. A Survey of Adult Education
in Northern Europe since the World War.
Thesis, College of the Pacific, 1933. 133
p. [Includes Denmark, Norway, and Swe-
den]

Lund, Ragnar, ed. Scandinavian Adult Education. Coph., Hels., 1949; 2d ed., Stock.,
1952. 927 p.

Mottershead, Noel F. A Comparative Study
of World Movements in Adult Education.
Thesis (Ph.D.), University of California,
Berkeley, 1949. 436 p.

Skovmand, Roar. "The Scandinavian Folk
High Schools," ScPP, II, 826-30.

Southwood, Howard D. Adult Education in
Scandinavia: a Study in Democracy and
Its Meaning for Continuing Education in
the United States, Especially as It Per-
tains to the Community College. Thesis
(Ph.D.), University of Florida, 1956. 157
p. [Includes Denmark, Norway, and Swe-
den]

Stensland, Per G. "Adult Education," in
Henning Friis, ed., Scandinavia, Between
East and West (Ithaca, 1950), 225-53.

LIBRARIES, ARCHIVES, MUSEUMS

Ashby, Gwynneth M. "Some Scandinavian
Museums," Norseman, 11 (1953), 45-47.

Harrison, K. C. Libraries in Scandinavia.
Lond., 1961. 240 p.

Jørgensen, Harald. "The Meeting of Scandinavian Archivists in Åbo, 3 Aug. 1954,"
Archivism, 4 (1954), 207-209.

Kent, C. D. et al. "Librarianship, Library
Schools and Library Associations in
Scandinavia," Ontario Library Review,
43 (1959), 210-14.

Kildal, Arne. "Scandinavian Libraries,"
ScPP, III, 268-75.

Kleberg, Tönnes. "Some Notes on the
'Scandia Plan'," Libri, 12 (1962/63),
76-84.

McColvin, L. R. "Scandinavian Visit,"
LibAssnRec, 53 (1951), 392-99.

Smith, R. D. Hilton. Holland and Scandinavia. In Library Association, A Survey
of Libraries, Reports on a Survey Made
by the Library Association during 1936-
1937; Report 15. General Editor, Lionel
R. McColvin (Lond., 1938), 193-223.

Stockholm, Nationalmuseum. The National
Historical Museum: a Brief Guide to the
Collection of Prehistoric and Mediaeval
Antiquities. Stock., 1930. 47 p.

Tudur, Lauri. "Yearly Meetings of the
Heads of the Northern National and University Libraries," Libri, 4 (1953/54),
173-77.

DENMARK

Arvin, G. J. "The Danish School of Tomorrow," PPT, 6 (1946, no. 4), 19-27.

Bailey, Helen L. Hoffding's Theory of Religious Value and Its Relation to Education. Thesis, Boston University, 1922.
63 p.

Benjamin, H. R. W. "Education and National
Recovery in Denmark," Annals, 182
(1935), 173-80.

Bjørneboe, Otto. "Denmark," EdYrbk (1927),
47-64.

Bøje, Andreas et al. Education in Denmark:
the Intellectual Basis of a Democratic
Commonwealth. Lond., N.Y., Coph., 1932.
288 p.

Bokkenheuser, Knud. "Student Life in Denmark," ASR, 12 (1924), 83-88.

Bomholt, Julius. "Danish Schools," ScPP,
III, 225-32.

Burbank, L. B. "Education: Danish Style,"
SocEd, 20 (1956), 156-60.

Burnett, Aminta C. N. Education in the
Virgin Islands under Denmark and the
United States. Thesis, College of the
City of New York, 1940. 130 p.

Cabot, Steven P. "Secondary Education in
Germany, France, England and Den-
mark," Harvard Bulletin in Education,
Part IV (1930), 85-96.

Christensen, A. Højberg. "Denmark," in
EdYrbk (1939), 65-76.

Christensen, Georg. "Danish Schools of Today," PPT, 6 (1946, no. 4), 3-12.

Combs, S. L. "Danish Public Education,"
Ed, 76 (1956), 373-79.

Cox, P. W. L. "Russian and Danish Guide-
posts for American Education," JEdSoc,
2 (1929), 412-18.

Dahlmann-Hansen, J. "Transformation of
Schools in Denmark," PDK, 43 (N 1961),
54-59.

Dam, Poul. "Guidance in Denmark," in
Robert K. Hall and J. A. Lauwerys, eds.,
The Year Book of Education 1955: Guidance and Counselling (Lond., N.Y., 1956),
158-69.

Denmark, Laws, Statutes, etc. The Danish
Gymnasium, the Official Regulations
(1953). Coph., 1959. 66 p.

Denmark, State Educational Library. List
of Books in English on Education in Denmark. 4th ed., Coph., 1960. 6 p.

Denmark, Ministry of Education. Higher
Education in Denmark: a Short Survey of
the Organization and Activities of the
Universities and Other Institutions of
Higher Education in Denmark. Coph.,
1954. 55 p.

———. Survey of Danish Elementary, Secondary, and Further (Non-Vocational)
Education. Coph., 1951. 36 p.

"Denmark," in The Year Book of Education
1948 (Lond., 1948), 275-82.

Dixon, C. Willis. Education in Denmark.
Lond., Coph., 1958. 233 p. Based on
thesis (Ph.D.), Compulsory Education in
Denmark, University of London, 1956.

Donaldson, W. D. E. "Summer Course with
Niels Bukh," School, 26 (1938), 796-99.

Ellgaard, Theodore J. A Comparative Study
of the American Physical Training and
Sir Niels Bukh's "Primitiv Gymnastik."
Thesis, State University of Iowa, 1936.
39 p.

Emborg, S. "Free School Movement in Denmark," New Era, 10 (Ja 1929), 37-39.

Foght, Harold W. Rural Denmark and Its
Schools. N.Y., 1915. 355 p.

Gimsing, T. F. "Educational Developments
in 1951-52: Denmark," IYEd (1952), 95-
101.

———. "Educational Developments in 1949-
50," IYEd (1950), 77-82.

Goodhope, Nanna. Christen Kold — The Little Schoolmaster Who Helped Revive a
Nation. Blair, Nebraska, 1956. 120 p.

Halvorsen, Erik. Primary and Secondary
Education in Denmark (Danish Ministry
of Education, Publication 20). Coph.,
1958.

Haugland, Å. "Educational Research in
Countries Other Than the U.S.A.," RofER,
27 (1957), 119-25.

Haugstrup, Rolf. "Newspapers as School
Material," DFOJ, no. 61 (1968), 19-21.

Hegermann-Lindencrone, C. "Denmark," WAAEB (1930), 1-5.

Higgins, Anna D. "Making the Danish Child Fit," ASR, 5 (1917), 38-44.

India, Ministry of Education. The Educational System of Denmark: a Brief Historical Review (Publication 218). Delhi, 1956. 58 p.

Kålund-Jørgensen, F. C. "Denmark," in Robert K. Hall, N. Hans, and J. A. Lauwerys, eds., The Year Book of Education 1953: Status and Position of Teachers (Lond., N.Y., 1953), 382-403.

———. "The Hadow Schools in England and the 'Practical Middle School' in Denmark," IO, 3 (1937/38), 35-45, 49-54.

Kaper, Ernst. The Traditional Liberty of the Danish School. 1929. 16 p.

Kenworthy, L. S. "Prophet of the North" [Nicola Grundtvig's Contribution to Education in Denmark], NewEur (Ja 1944), 4-7.

King, Edmund J. Other Schools and Ours. N.Y., 1958. 234 p.

Manniche, Peter. "Denmark," EdYrbk (1938), 145-70.

———. "The International Observer" [On the International People's College], IO, 1 (1936), 1-10.

McCormick, P. J. "Education in Denmark," Catholic Education Review, 31 (1933), 321-26.

Mønsted, K. B. "Thoughts About a New Educational System," PPT, 6 (1946, no. 4), 13-18. [Written during the German occupation]

National Union of Danish Students, Danish International Student Committee. How to Study in Denmark. Coph., 1951. 90 p.

Nielsen, M. Julius. "The Danish School System," DFOJ, no. 175 (1935), 107-13.

———. "Denmark," EdYrbk (1935), 133-53.

———. "Denmark," EdYrbk (1936), 249-68.

Novrup, Johannes. "Denmark," EdYrbk (1940), 93-118.

Nursery Schools in Denmark. Coph., 1955. 8 p.

Ohles, J. F. "Danish Education: General or Specialized," Sch&Soc, 85 (F 1957), 41-43.

Olinger, D. "Danish Design for Living," Kansas Teacher, 5 (1936), 6-8.

Olrik, H. G. "A Royal School Democratized," ASR, 20 (1932), 418-27.

Olsen, Albert. "Elementary Schools of Denmark," JofEd, 77 (1945), 234+.

Pihl, M. "Educational Progress in 1955-56," IYEd (1956), 135-38.

Rost, F. E. B. "Education in Denmark," in

The Year Book of Education 1933 (Lond., 1933), 801-21.

Schairer, Reinhold. "Denmark as an Example of the Intensive Education of a People," The Year Book of Education 1937 (Lond., 1937), 728-53.

Stundahl, K. "Fitness of Danish School Children During the Course of One Academic Year," American Association of Health, Physical Education and Recreation Research Quarterly, 34 (M 1963), 34-40. [Bibliography]

Sunesen, Bent. "Recent Developments in Denmark," in George Z. F. Bereday and J. A. Lauwerys, eds., The Year Book of Education 1960: Communication Media and the School (Lond., N.Y., 1960), 357-60.

Thrane, Eigil. Education and Culture in Denmark: a Survey of the Educational, Scientific and Cultural Conditions. Coph., 1958. 90 p.

Torkild-Hansen, E. "Educational Developments in 1950-51," IYEd (1951), 85-89.

———. "Educational Progress in 1952-53," IYEd (1953), 119-25.

United States, Office of Education. Educational Data: Kingdom of Denmark (Information on Education Around the World, 10). Wash., 1960. 10 p.

Wuorinen, John H. "Social Objectives in Danish Education," in R. G. Tugwell, ed., Redirecting Education, 2 (N.Y., 1935), 209-36.

HIGHER EDUCATION AND INSTITUTES

Bodelsen, Carl A. G. The University of Cophenhagen: a Brief Survey of Its Organisation and Activities. Coph., 1938. 64 p.

Copenhagen, Statens institut for blinde og svagsynede. The State Institute for the Blind and Partially Sighted at Copenhagen, Issued on the Occasion of the 100th Anniversary and Its Foundation, 1858-November, 5th-1958. Summary. Coph., 1958. 27 p.

Denmark, Ministry of Education. Higher Education in Denmark: a Short Survey of the Organization and Activities of the Universities and Other Institutions of Higher Education in Denmark. Coph., 1951. 40 p.

Drachmann, Povl. "The Institute of Technology in Copenhagen," ASR, 8 (1920), 189-95.

Esterly, Virginia J. The Higher Education of Women in Denmark. Thesis, Uni-

versity of California, Berkeley, 1930.
228 p.

Geiger, Theodore. "Recruitment of University Students," AcSoc, 1 (1955/56), 39-48.

Hansen, Olaf. "Copenhagen University," ASR, 9 (1921), 127-31.

Knuth-Winterfeldt, E. "A Great New Centre for Danish Engineers" [Denmark's Technical University], DFOJ, no. 61 (1969), 25-28.

Lindegren, Alina M. Institutions of Higher Education in Denmark, U. S. Office of Education Bull. (1934, no. 13). Wash., 1934. 126 p.

Meyer, Raphael. "Where Denmark Teaches Agriculture," ASR, 10 (1922), 98-100.

Normann, Bodie. "The Danish Bibliographical Institute (Dansk Bibliografisk Kontor)," Libri, 6 (1955/56), 239-46.

Opportunities of Young Persons in Higher Education, I. Coph., 1949.

Prince, John D. "University Life in Denmark," ASR, 11 (1923), 106-108.

Spang-Hanssen, E. "The Carlsberg Foundation," BSC, 3 (1937), 490-94.

ADULT EDUCATION

Andreasen, Paul J. Grundtvig as an Educator, with Special Reference to the Folk High School Movement. Thesis (Ph.D.), New York University, 1936. 132 p.

Association of People's High Schools and Agricultural Schools. The Danish People's High-School. 1918. 170 p.

Begtrup, Holger et al. The Folk High Schools of Denmark and the Development of a Farming Community. 4th ed., Lond., Coph., 1948. 163 p.; 1st ed., 1926; 2d ed., 1929; 3d ed., 1936.

Bentwich, Norman. "The Folk High Schools of Denmark," CR, 160 (1941), 299-302.

Bose, Hiralal. "Danish Folk High Schools," CR, 197 (1960), 111-13.

Boyles, James R. A Program of Adult Education for Twante, Burma. Thesis, University of Denver, 1938. 88 p. [Includes Denmark]

Camery, Lura G. The Danish Folk High Schools and Their Significance for American Education. Thesis, Claremont Graduate School, 1940. 117 p.

Campbell, Olive A. The Danish Folk School: Its Influence in the Life of Denmark and the North. N.Y., 1928. 359 p.

——. "Five Weeks at Askov," ASR, 15 (1927), 79-87.

Coolidge, Ruth D. "Vibrations from a Dan-

ish Bell: the John C. Campbell Folk School," ASR, 33 (1945), 104-17.

Cox, P. W. L. "Danish Folk High Schools," School Executive, 56 (1937), 343-45+.

Danish Folk Schools. Newsbackground. N.Y. (Report no. 15).

Danish Information Office in New York. Christen Kold and the Danish Folk Schools, N.Y., 1946. 11 p.

Dorf, A. T. "Danish Folk School," School and Home, 15 (1933), 230-36.

Engberg, P. The Northern Folk High-School. 1956. 32 p.

Engberg-Pedersen, H. "15 pc Take Leisure-time Courses," DFOJ, no. 61 (1968), 14-18.

Fenger, F. "Twenty-five Years — and a Red Castle," WAAEB (1936), 25-29.

Fenger, H. "What Is Denmark?," WAAEB (1939), 23-26.

Filipino, Ralph F. An Examination of the Danish Folk Schools. Thesis, Boston College, 1953. 48 p.

Fletcher, B. A. "County College or Folk High School," JofEd, 82 (1950), 8+, 69-70+.

Fox, G. "Crisis in the Folk High School," Junior College Journal, 23 (N 1952), 125-30.

Grosen, U. The Danish Folk High School. 16 p.

Hansome, Marius. "Effective Enthusiasm of Danish Folk Education," Social Studies, 38 (1947), 159-64, 202-207.

Hart, Joseph K. Light from the North: the Danish Folk High Schools. N.Y., 1927. 159 p.

Hasselriis, Caspar H. W. "The Danish Folk School," AmT (F 1951), 16-18.

Hedebol, F. C. N. "Folk High Schools in Denmark and What They Have Done for Cooperation," Cooperation, 18 (1932), 189-91.

Hegland, Martin. The Danish People's High School, Including a General Account of the Educational System of Denmark N.Y., 1916. 182 p. Thesis (Ph.D.), Columbia University, 1915. Also Wash., 1915 (U. S. Bureau of Education Bull., 1915, no. 45).

Helsingør, Denmark. Internationale Folke Højskole. Adult Education in the Struggle for Peace. Miscellaneous Articles on the Environment and Work of the International People's College, Elsinore, and Other Folk High Schools in Denmark and Elsewhere. Coph., 1949. 400 p.

Hollmann, A. H. The Folk High School (Democracy in Denmark, pt. 2). Wash., 1936. 158 p.

Holm-Jensen, Paul H. People's College, Its Contributions and Its Applications to American Education and Condition. Blair, Neb., 1939. 195 p.

Jones, P. P. "Danish Folk High School," Sch&Soc, 44 (1936), 85-88, 215-17.

Kapasi, A. "Danish Adult Education," JofEd (Lond.) 85 (1953), 178+.

Kavalier, Helena. "The Modern Danish Folk High Schools," ASES, 21 (1962), 393-405.

Kidd, J. Roby. "Word from Abroad: Denmark," AdEdJ, 6 (1947), 11-13.

Koefoed, H. A. "Romanticism and the Danish Folk High Schools," Norseman, 9 (1951), 237-43.

Knudsen, Johannes. A Danish Rebel: a Study of H.N.F.S. Grundtvig. Phila., 1955. 255 p.

Larson, Paul M. A Rhetorical Study of Bishop Frederick Severin Grundtvig. Thesis (Ph.D.), Northwestern University, 1942. 392 p.

Livingston, R. W. "Danish People's High Schools: a Reply to H. Morris," AdEd, 14 (1942), 107-11.

Lund, Hans. "Danish Folk High School of To-Day," NewEur, 10 (Ja 1929), 26-29. [Issue has other articles on Danish Folk High School]

Manniche, Peter. "The Danish Folk High School," ASR, 20 (1932), 167-70.

———. "Danish Folk High School, Its National and International Importance," IntQAdultEd, 1 (1933), 193-212.

———. "Danish Folk Schools," North Central Assn Quarterly, 12 (1938), 430-38.

———. "The International People's College at Elsinore," PPT, 6 (1946, no. 4), 27-30.

Meyer, A. E. "Danish Folk High Schools," in his, Modern European Educators and Their Work (N.Y., 1934), 197-204.

Møller, John Christmas. Education in Democracy: the Folk High Schools of Denmark. Lond., 1944. 160 p.

Nielson, R. "Something About the Danish Folk Schools," Educational Outlook, 26 (N 1951), 17-22.

Novrup, Johannes. Adult Education in Denmark. Coph., 1949. 86 p.

———. "The Danish Folk High Schools, Their History and Present Status," DFOJ (1950, no. 1), 17-21.

Olson, David. The Life and Educational Influence of Nicholai Frederik Severin Grundtvig. Thesis (Ph.D.), Western Reserve University, 1931. 277 p.

Palmer, Mary E. The Development of Characteristic Patterns of Adult Education in the United States, England, Denmark, and Germany. Thesis (Ph.D.), Harvard University, 1946. 216 p.

"People's Schools," Consumers Cooperation, 22 (1936), 133-36.

Petersen, K. Helveg. "The Promotion of International Social Responsibility Within a Nation: The Danish Folk High Schools," in George Z.F. Bereday and J. A. Lauwerys, eds., The Year Book of Education 1964: Education and International Life (Lond., N.Y., 1964), 467-69.

Phimister, Z. S. "Danish Folk High Schools," School, 28 (1939), 313-17.

Rasmussen, C. "Impressions of a Danish Folk-High School," EdRChina, 22 (1930), 301-304.

Schacke, Erik. "The Danish Folk High Schools," IO, 2 (1937/38), 14-24.

Sheats, Paul H. "Report from Denmark," AdEdBull, 14 (1949), 22-24.

Sinha, S. K. "Folk High Schools of Denmark, an Experiment in Co-operative and Social Education," All India Cooperative Review, 21 (1956), 686-88.

Skovmand, Roar. Johannes Novrup and Danish Adult Education, IntRE, 8 (1962), 131-39.

Skrubbeltrang, Fridlev S. The Danish Folk High Schools. 2d ed. rev. by Roar Skovmand (Danish Information Handbook). Coph., 1952. 88 p.

———. The Danish Folk High Schools (Danish Information Handbook). Coph., 1947. 80 p.

Svart, A. Adult Education in Denmark. JofEd, 75 (1943), 512+.

"Technological Instruction in Denmark," DFOJ, no. 190 (1936), 125-28.

Thomson, Marjorie U. The Origin and Development of the Danish Folk High School, with Some Implications for American Education. Thesis, University of Southern California, 1930. 62 p.

"Two Danish Pioneers," WAAEB (1930), 7-15.

Uhrskov, Anders. "The Danish Folk High School," ASR, 11 (1923), 83-93.

Vautrin, M. E. "Folk Schools of Denmark," EdRChina, 29 (1937), 109-14.

Vedel, A. "Glimpses of Danish Folk-School Life," WAAEB (1937), 14-20.

LIBRARIES, ARCHIVES, MUSEUMS

Anker, J. T. H. J. Early Special Public Library, Libri, 4 (1953), 7-13.

Bachmann, Ida. "Public Libraries in Denmark," ASR, 30 (1942), 41-48.

Copenhagen, Nationalmuseet. The National

Museum of Denmark. Aage Roussell, ed., Coph., 1957. 326 p.

"Denmark," Archivum, 5 (1955), 38-39.

Denmark, Rigsarkivet. Denmark's National Record Office. Coph., 1948. 16 p.

Døssing, Th. "Denmark's Public Libraries," DFOJ, no. 204 (1938), 1-8.

Gordon, Max. "Libraries in the Life of a People," LibW, 55 (1954), 207-208.

Holm, Per. "The Old Town: an Outdoor Museum," ASR, 27 (1939), 14-22.

Jespersen, Anders. Nationalmuseets Mølleudvalg, 1953-1960. Danish National Museum Mill Preservation Board, 1953-1960. First Annual Report. Coph., 1960. 50 p. [Text in Danish and English]

Jørgensen, Harald. "Danish Ecclesiastical Archives," Archivum, 4 (1954), 67-70.

Kirkegaard, Preben. The Public Libraries in Denmark (Danish Information Handbook). Coph., 1950. 103 p.

Klem, Knud. "Hamlet's Castle Houses Marine Mementos," ASR, 25 (1937), 122-29.

Larsen, K. "Danish Library System," LibAssnRec, 62 (1960), 275-79.

Mathiassen, Therkel. "Prehistoric Museums in Denmark," BSC, 4 (1938), 376-78.

Matthiessen, Hugo. "A People's Museum," [Prinsens Palace] ASR, 13 (1925), 532-35.

Mollerup, Helga. "Juvenile and School Libraries," DFOJ, no. 204 (1938), 8-12.

Pinholt, H. "Danish Libraries," New Zealand Lib., 17 (1954), 48-50.

Ravn, O. E. A Catalogue of Oriental Cylinder Seals and Seal Impressions in the Danish National Museum (Its, Skrifter, Arkaeol. — hist. raekke, v. 8). Coph., 1960. 136 p.

Thomsen, Thomas. "The Study of Man; Denmark Organized the World's First Ethnographical Museum," ASR, 25 (1937), 309-18.

Westergaard, Waldemar C. "Denmark," in Daniel H. Thomas and Lynn M. Case, Guide to the Diplomatic Archives of Western Europe (Phila., 1959), 43-54.

FINLAND

"Act Concerning Vocational Guidance in Finland," I&L, 23 (1960), 442-43.

Gemmell, J. "Business Education in the Soviet Shadow," Balance Sheet, 39 (1958), 397-98+.

Hippaka, Thomas A. Indomitable Finland; Education Background. Wash., 1940. 199 p.

——. A Survey of Education in Finland, 1800 to 1825. Thesis (Ph.D.), University of Wisconsin, 1938. 175 p.

Hobson, Grace R. A Study of Education in Finland. Thesis, University of Southern California, 1934. 118 p.

Hussong, Herbert L. Physical Measurements of Finnish School Children: a Discussion as to the Relation of Physical Development to Pedagogical Classification. Thesis, University of Oregon, 1918. 35 p.

Kallio, Niilo V. "Finland," in The Year Book of Education 1948 (Lond., 1948), 314-21.

——. The School System of Finland. Hels., 1956. 86 p. 2d ed., 1948. 68 p.; 3d ed., 1952. 66 p.

Kekoni, Karl. "Geography in the Schools of Finland," JofGeo, 25 (1926), 67-71.

Kyöstiö, O. K. "Contemporary Finnish School Legislation," CompEdR, 5 (1961), 130-35.

——. "Trends in Teacher Training in Finland," in George Z.F. Bereday and J. A. Lauwerys, eds., The Year Book of Education 1963: the Education and Training of Teachers (Lond., N.Y., 1963), 235-43.

Larsen, Hanna A. "Rewriting History," ASR, 26 (1938), 162-64.

Lilius, Albert H. "Finland," EdYrbk (1926), 119-41.

Nüni, Aarno. "The National Plan for Vocational Education and Economic Development," KOPER (1960), 63-72.

Oittinen, Reino H. Education in Finland.

——. "The Finnish School System," ScPP, III, 246-50.

"Reforms in Finland," International Bureau of Education Bulletin, 19 (1945), 48.

Sarva, G. "Education and Culture," in Finland Year Book (1936), 120-34.

Seppi, Rudolph H. The Educational System of Finland. Thesis (Ph.D.), Stanford University, 1936. 152 p.

Smith, Donald. "School Life in Medieval Finland," [Mainly in the town of Veborg] (Royal Historical Society, London. Transactions, London, 1871, 4th series, v. 13, 83-116), Lond., 1930. [Illustrated by royal letters and local records]

Takolander, Alfons. "Education in Finland," in The Year Book of Education 1934 (Lond., 1934), 911-26.

Taylor, W. W., and I. W. Taylor. "Education of Physically Handicapped Children in Finland," Exceptional Child, 25 (1959), 358-67.

United States, International Educational Exchange Service. An Investment in

Understanding; Educational Exchange
Program between United States and Finland, 1950-1954 (U. S. Dept. of State
Publication 6366. International Information and Cultural Series, 51). Wash.,
1956. 27 p.

United States, Office of Education. Educational Data: Republic of Finland [With
List of Selected References]. Compiled
by Margaret L. King. Wash., 1963. 11 p.

Vocational Education in Finland Subordi-
nated to the Ministry of Commerce and
Industry. Hels., 1952. 9 p.

Walker, David A. "The Experiences of a
UNESCO Expert in Finland," IntRE, 12
(1966), 280-87.

Zilliacus, Laurin. "Finland," EdYrbk
(1937), 145-68.

——. "School in Finland," New Education
Fellowship Modern Trends in Education,
Proceedings (1937), 166-73.

HIGHER EDUCATION AND INSTITUTES

Åbo, Finland. Akademi: the Swedish University of Åbo-Åbo Akademi — Foundation
and Development. Åbo, 1950. 34 p.

Anderson, C. Arnold. "Social Class as a
Factor in the Assimilation of Women into
Higher Education," AcSoc, 4 (1960), 27-
32.

Finland, Veterinäravdelningen. Veterinary
Institutions in Finland. Hels., 1935. 74 p.

Helsingfors, Statens tekniska forsknings-
anstalt. The State Institute for Technical Research 1/4/1954. Hels., 1954.
13 p. Similar booklet dated 1/10/1956.

Levon, Martti. Teknellenin Korheakonlu,
Finland's Institute of Technology. Hels.,
1949. 44 p.

Saxen, Lauri. "The Academy of Finland,"
ASR, 50 (1962), 42-48.

Taxell, Lars E. "Åbo Academy," ASR, 45
(1957), 151-56.

Tirranen, Hertta. Alma Mater. L'Uni-
versité de Helsinki — University of Helsinki. Porvoo/Helsinki, 1952. 159 p.

ADULT EDUCATION

Adult Education in Finland 1951: a Survey.
Hels., 1951. 20 p.

Castrén, Z. "Finland," WAAEB (1930), 5-9.

Deering, I. E. "Adult Education in Finland,"
New Era, 15 (1934), 105-108.

Kosonen, Vilho. "Finland," in R. Lund, ed.,
Scandinavian Adult Education (Coph.,
1952), 83-160.

Levine, C. "Folk College in Finland.
Viittakivi International Folk College,"
Sch&Soc, 90 (1962), 355-56+.

Railo, Pekka. "Workers' Education in Finland," IO, 2 (1937/38), 158-63.

Workers' Adult Education in Finland. Hels.,
1954. 30 p.

LIBRARIES, ARCHIVES, MUSEUMS

Barstad, A. "Impressions of Libraries in
Finland," District of Columbia Libraries,
19 (1948), 41-43.

Darlington, Ida. "In the Rock: a Brief Account of the National Archives of Finland," Society of Archivists Journal, 2
(Ap 1960), 34-36.

"Finland," Archivim, 5 (1955), 86-87.

Gardberg, Carl-Rudolf. "The New Library
Building of the Åbo Akademi," Libri, 9
(1959), 19-22.

Gardner, Frank M. "Public Libraries in
Finland," UNESCO Bulletin for Libraries,
18 (1964), 114-17.

Lausti, Kaarlo. "The Library of the Student
Union, University of Helsinki," Libri, 9
(1959), 23-27.

McColvin, L. R. "Visit to Finland,"
LibAssnRec, 59 (1957), 291-96.

Neuvonen, Eero K. "Turku University Library (Turun Yliopiston Kirjasto)," Libri,
9 (1959), 14-18.

Nivanka, Eino. Directory of Finnish Research Libraries. Hels., 1962. 52 p.

——. Guide to the Scientific Libraries of
Finland. 2d ed., Hels., 1955. 123 p.

Nopsanen, Aulis. "Luostarinmäki, an Open-
Air Handicraft Museum," ASR, 49 (1961),
56-59.

Nurmio, Yrjö. "Recent Construction Work
on Archive Buildings in Finland,"
Archivim, 7 (1957), 18-20.

Olsoni, K. E. "Some Libraries and Library
Problems in Finland," Special Libraries,
41 (1950), 206-11.

Raittila, Pikha. "Library of the University
College of Jyväskylä (Jyväskylan Kasva-
tusopellesen Korheakoulum Kirjasto),"
Libri, 9 (1959), 28-30.

Randel, W. "Libraries in Finland," Florida
Libraries, 6 (1955), 5+.

Vallinkoski, J. "The Helsinki University
Library," Libri, 9 (1959), 10-13.

——. "The Microfilming of Newspapers in
Finland," Libri, 9 (1959), 38-44.

"The Workers' Institutes and Other Free
Institutes of Finland. Hels., 1924.
18 p.

ICELAND

"Adult Education in Iceland," WAAEB (1931), 13-16.

Beck, Richard. "The University of Iceland," ASR, 24 (1936), 337-38.

Catonis Disticha. Icelandic. The Hólar Cato: An Icelandic Schoolbook of the Seventeenth Century. Ithaca, N.Y., 1958. 125 p.

"Education in Iceland; in Terms of Education in the United States," Education for Victory, 2 (1943), 7-9+.

Eliasson, Helgi. "The Icelandic School System," ScPP, III, 251-54.

Hermannsson, Halldór. "Icelandic Libraries in America," ASR, 3 (1915), 169-73.

"Iceland," Archivim, 5 (1955), 136.

Jóhannesson, Alexander. "The University of Iceland," ASR, 38 (1950), 349-54.

Jonason, J. C. "Iceland Educates for Democracy," ElSchJ, 50 (1949), 212-22.

Jonsdottir, Asa. Secondary Education in Iceland. Thesis, University of North Dakota, 1947. 57 p.

Moran, J. "Schools in Iceland," JofEd, 128 (1945), 238-40.

Trial, George T. History of Education in Iceland. Cambridge, Eng., 1945. 95 p.

United Nations, Committee on Human Rights, Sub-Committee on Prevention of Discrimination and Protection of Minorities. Study of Discrimination in Education: Summary of Information Relating to Iceland. N.Y., 1956. 8 p.

Whatley, E. S. "Iceland's Libraries," LibW, 64 (1963), 260-61.

NORWAY

Andersen, B. H., and G. D. Stevens. "Review of the Education of the Mentally Handicapped in Norway," Exceptional Child, 23 (1957), 251-53+.

Anderson, David A. The School System of Norway. Boston, 1913. 232 p.

——. The School System of Norway: a Preliminary Survey of the Educational Provisions Made for the People of Norway. Thesis, State University of Iowa, 1910. 64 p.

Andresen, Solveig G. "Correspondence Education in Norway," International Journal of Adult and Youth Education, 16 (1964), 15-22.

Arent, Emma. The Relation of the State to Private Education in Norway: a Study of the Historical Development of State Regulations Governing the Various Types of Private Education in Norway. Thesis, Columbia University, 1926. 94 p. Published also as Teachers College, Columbia University, Contributions to Education, no. 235.

Askeland, O., Anna Sethne, and K. Koppang. "Norway," EdYrbk (1935), 383-403.

Barth, S. R. "Democracy with a Difference," American Association of University Women Journal, 25 (1931), 24-26.

Blackburn, Robert. "New Norwegian Elementary School," JofEd, 8 (1954), 178+.

Boyesen, Einar T. "Norway," EdYrbk (1938), 313-46.

Cackerille, C. E. "Teachers and Teaching in Norway and Italy," PennSchJ, 108 (1960), 380-81+.

Clegg, J. M. "The Teaching of Geography in Norwegian Grammar Schools," Geog, 35 (1950), 209-14.

Devik, Olaf M. "Norway," EdYrbk (1944), 247-66.

Eidnes, Asbjørn. "Education, Science, and the Arts," in O. Vorren, ed., Norway North of 65 (Oslo, 1960), 248-70.

Ely, H. B. "The Lapp High School at Karasjok," Norseman, 12 (1954), 86-89.

Fostervoll, Kaare. "Education in Norway," Norseman, 6 (1948), 186-95.

Gallup, George, and Evan Hill. "Is European Education Better than Ours?," Saturday Evening Post (D 24, 1960), 59-76.

Hansen, Robert E. The Democratization of Norwegian Education. Thesis (Ph.D.), Harvard University, 1952. 236 p.

Haug, Arne. A Study of the Education of Administrators in Norway and in Southern California. Thesis, Claremont Graduate School, 1954. 149 p.

Hjelmtveit, Nils. Education in Norway. Lond., 1946. 41 p.

——. "Education under Quisling," AmT, 26 (1941), 10-11+.

——. "The Educational System in Prewar Norway," NorAmCom (S 1944), 3-6.

——. "The Educational System in Pre-War Norway," Norseman, 1 (1943), 47-54.

Hove, Olav. An Outline of Norwegian Education. Prepared for Norwegian Ministry of Foreign Affairs, Office of Cultural Relations. Oslo, 1955. 79 p.; 2d rev. ed., 1958. 189 p.

Huus, Helen. Education of Children and Youth in Norway. Pittsburgh, 1960. 247 p.

——. "Old and New in Norway's Education," University of Pennsylvania Schoolmen's Week Proceedings (1952), 178-91.

Jansen, Trygve D. Elementary Teacher Education in Norway: a Descriptive Historical Study. Thesis (Ph.D.), University of California, Los Angeles, 1957. 147 p.

Jensen, Arne S. Rural Schools of Norway. Boston, 1928. 280 p. Thesis (Ph.D.), University of Washington, 1928. 280 p.

Johnson, P. O. "Norwegian System of Public Secondary Education," SchR, 44 (1936), 608-14.

Kindem, Ingeborg E. A Study of the Practices of Music Teaching in the Secondary Schools of Norway. Thesis, University of Southern California, 1919. 172 p.

Knap, Carl. "Education in Norway," in The Year Book of Education 1935 (Lond., 1935), 876-97.

——. "Norway," EdYrbk (1939), 249-57.

Langeland, Alv St. "Teachers in Norway," in Robert K. Hall and J. A. Lauwerys, eds., The Year Book of Education 1956: Education and Economics (Lond., N.Y., 1956), 478-82.

Loftfield, Gabriel E. Secondary Education in Norway (U. S. Bureau of Education Bull. 17, 1930). Wash., 1930. 112 p.

Norway, Information Office. Norway's Schools in the Battle for Freedom. Lond., 1942. 52 p.

——. Norway's Teachers Stand Firm. Wash., 1942. 32 p.

"Norway," in World Survey of Education, I: Handbook of Educational Organization and Statistics (Paris, 1959), 483-93.

"Norway," in World Survey of Education, II: Primary Education (Paris, 1958), 800-810.

"The Norwegian School System under the Occupation," NorAmCom (Jl 1944), 15-16.

Orbeck, Anders. "The Norwegian Students Association" [Studentersamfund], ASR, 13 (1925), 88-93.

Our Special Schools for Handicapped Children. Oslo. Mimeographed.

Piene, Kay. "The Norwegian School System," ScPP III, 217-24.

Sandven, Johs. Educational Research in Norway in the 20th Century (U.S. Office of Education Bull., 1963, no. 41 [Studies in Comparative Education]). Wash., 1963. 31 p.

——. "Norwegian School System, General Structure and Main Working Principles," New Era, 28 (1947), 92-94.

——. "Problems in Predicting Teacher Attitudes in Norway," in George Z. F. Bereday and J. A. Lauwerys, eds., The Year Book of Education 1963: The Education and Training of Teachers (Lond., N.Y., 1963), 419-24.

Schulstad, Olav. "Norway," EdYrbk (1936), 415-36.

Seip, Didrik A. "School Problems in Norway," ASR, 34 (1946), 120-22.

Sigmund, Einar. "Norway," EdYrbk (1924), 355-83.

——. "Norway," EdYrbk (1932), 369-80.

Sirevaag, Tönnes. "Ten Years of Norwegian School Experimentation," IntRE, 12 (1966), 1-15.

Skår, Dagfinn. "A New School Program," Norseman (1965), 113-16.

Skard, Aase G. "Teachers of a Democracy Fight Nazism," American Association of University Women Journal, 35 (1942), 195-200.

Skard, Sigmund. "Norway Fights On — Morale in Action," in American Association of School Administrators, Official Report (1943), 83-88.

Spiller, M. S. "Child Life in Norway," University of Pennsylvania Schoolmen's Week Proceedings (1951), 51-61.

Stautland, S. A Comparative Study of the Selective Recruitment of Elementary School Teachers in the United States and Norway. Thesis, College of the Pacific, 1956. 98 p.

Stene, Aasta. "English under German Occupation," ASR, 34 (1946), 149-54.

Stene, Helga. "Norway," in The Year Book of Education 1948 (Lond., 1948), 283-98.

Stensland, Per G. "Century of Public Schools," ASM (N 1942), 7-8+.

Studebaker, John W. Education under Enemy Occupation in Belgium, China . . . Norway [etc.]. (U. S. Office of Education Bull., 1945, no. 3). Wash., 1945. 71 p.

Tronvold, Helen L. A Comparative Study of First Grade Reading in Two Communities, One in Minnesota and One in Norway. Thesis, Minnesota State Teachers College, Mankato, 1958. 125 p.

Wiley, George M. The Organization and Administration of the Educational System of Norway. Oslo, 1955. 275 p.

HIGHER EDUCATION AND INSTITUTES

"Academic Emigration," Norseman (1966), 138-40.

Boardman, Philip L. "East Meets West in the North: the International Summer School at the University of Oslo," Norseman (1960, no. 2), 6-8.

——. "5000 Students from 74 Countries," Norseman (1967), 156-58.

——. "Knowledge Plus Good Will Among
the Nations: Norway's International
Summer School," Norseman (1964), 9-12.
——. "A Norwegian Venture in Interna-
tional Education," [The University of
Oslo's Summer School for Foreign Stu-
dents], Norseman, 9 (1951), 28-31.
Devik, Olaf M. "Universities in Norway —
Background and Problems," Universities
Review (Bristol), 22 (1950).
Haines, Ben C. "A University in Rapid
Growth," Norseman (1964), 66-70.
Haugen, Einar. A Study of the Norwegian
Entrance Examination or "Artium" De-
gree with Notes on the University of
Wisconsin Policy for the Foreign Stu-
dents. Oslo, 1954. 28 p.; 3d ed., Madi-
son, Wisc., 1951.
Helland-Hausen, Björn. "The Christian
Michelsen Institute," ASR, 26 (1938),
118-22.
Hustvedt, Sigvard B. "The Norwegian Pro-
fessor," ASR, 12 (1924), 89-94.
"Institutt for Sammenlignende Kulturforsk-
ning," ISSB, 7 (1955), 656-57.
Jenssen, Hans. Building the Book Collection
of the Institute of Economics at the Uni-
versity of Oslo. Thesis, Columbia Uni-
versity, 1937. 55 p.
Kildal, Arne. "Norway's University Expan-
sion," ASR, 53 (1965), 37-43.
Larson, Harold. "Student Life in Oslo,"
ASR, 19 (1931), 682-84.
Lindegren, Alina M. Institutions of Higher
Education in Norway (U.S. Office of Edu-
cation Bull., 1934, no. 2), Wash., 1934.
Loftfield, Gabriel E. "Organization of Stu-
dents and Alumni of Oslo University,"
Sch&Soc, 32 (1930), 456-58.
Mortensen, Gunnar, and Sven Persson. Vo-
cational Training in Norway: a Survey.
Oslo, 1956. 106 p.
Nilson, Sten S. "The Chr. Michelsen Insti-
tute in Bergen," Norseman, 6 (1948),
54-59.
Norway, Information Office. The Norwegian
University Struggle. Intro. by John San-
ness. Lond., 1944. 24 p.
"Oslo University Expands," ASR, 24 (1936),
48-51.
Paasche, Frederik. "Studies and Students at
Christiania," ASR, 10 (1922), 94-98.
Ramberg, Trygve. "A Third University,"
Norseman (1960, no. 4), 2-4.
The Research Councils of Norway. Oslo,
1960. 83 p.
Saeland, Sem. "Trondhjem's Institute,"
ASR, 9 (1921), 123-27.
Simenson, William C., and Gilbert Geiss. "A

Cross-Cultural Study of University Students," JofHEd, 26 (1955), 21-25.
Sivertsen, Helge. "Subsidies to University
Students in Norway," in Robert K. Hall
and J. A. Lauwerys, eds., The Year Book
of Education 1956: Education and Eco-
nomics (Lond., N.Y., 1956), 177-79.
Vogt, Fredrik. "Industry and Technical Edu-
cation in Norway," Norseman, 2 (1944),
197-204.
Vogt, Hans. "The Institute for Comparative
Research in Human Culture," Norseman,
4 (1946), 177-83.
Williams, Alan M. "Oslo Builds for Its Stu-
dents," Norseman (1960, no. 5), 24-25.
Winsnes, Andreas H. "The University in
Oslo," Norseman, 2 (1944), 16-18.
Zavis, William. "Guide for the Wandering
Scholar," Norseman (1961, no. 6), 6-10.

ADULT EDUCATION

Devik, Olaf M. "Adult Education in Norway,"
JofE, 75 (1943), 514+.
Hjelmtveit, Nils. "Folk High Schools,"
Norseman, 3 (1945), 320-27.
Kildal, Arne. "Adult Education in Norway,"
WAAEB (1935), 21-25.
——. "Light Again on the Land: Adult
Education Comes Back on Norway," Adult
Education Journal, 5 (1946), 167-70.
Lyche, Ingeborg. Adult Education in Nor-
way. Oslo, 1957. 65 p.
Naeseth, Henriette C. K. "Early Years of
the Norwegian Folk High School," ScSt,
25 (1953), 87-99.
Richardson, O. D. "Crisis in the Norwegian
Folk High School," Junior College J, 24
(1953), 225-32.
Wilhelmsen, Leif. "The Folk High Schools
in Norway," AdEd, 20 (1948), 182-86.

LIBRARIES

Andreassen, Anders. "New Norwegian Law
Makes Public and School Libraries Com-
pulsory," American Library Association
Bulletin, 43 (1949), 135-36.
Ansteensson, J. "Libraries in Norway,
1935-1936," IFLAP, 8 (1936), 160-62.
Bygstad, Johannes. "Books by Boat and Bus
in Norway," Norseman (1961, no. 3), 8-10.
Danton, J. Periam. "United States Influence
on Norwegian Librarianship, 1890-1940"
(University of California Publications in
Librarianship, v. 2, no. 1), Berkeley, Los
Angeles, 1957.
Fjeld, Kolbjörn. Rural Libraries in Norway.
Thesis, Columbia University, 1930. 98 p.

Hvardal, Maren. "Medical Libraries in Norway, A Short Survey," Libri, 3 (1954), 178-82.

Jacobsen, M. "Libraries and Library Training in Norway," Massachusetts Library Association Bulletin, 43 (1953), 18-19.

Kildal, Arne. "Library Legislation in Norway," Libri, 1 (1950/1951), 261-62.

———. "Popular Libraries of Norway," LJ, 60 (1935), 754-57.

Murrthe, W. "Library Progress in Norway," IFLAP, 10 (1938), 157-59.

Schaanning, H. "Libraries of Norway, 1932-1937," IFLAP, 5 (1933), 120-22.

Skard, Aase G. "Norway's Libraries in the Fight for Freedom," School Library Association of California Bulletin, 14 (1942), 6-7.

Whiteman, P. M. "Libraries of Norway," LibAssnRec, 61 (1959), 241-48.

ARCHIVES, MUSEUMS

Fiskaa, H. "Libraries and Archives," in Norway Year Book 1950 (Oslo, 1950), 165-70.

Haugen, Hellick O. "Hidden Treasures from the Sea," Norseman (1967), 134-37.

Michaelsen, Fin. "Church Registers in Norway," Archivum, 8 (1958), 43-53.

"Norsemen Through the Ages" [Bygdøy Museum], Norseman (1962, no. 4), 4-8.

"Norway," Archivum, 5 (1955), 155-57.

Ödvin, Magnhild. "The Folk Museum at Bygdöy," ASR, 18 (1930), 741-52.

Plant, Ruth. "A Norwegian Folk Museum" [Maihaugen], Norseman, 6 (1948), 233-37.

SWEDEN

Ahlstrom, K. "Educational Research in Countries Other Than the U.S.A.," RofER, 27 (1957), 125-38.

Åkesson, Elof. "Professional Education in Sweden," in George Z. F. Bereday and J. A. Lauwerys, eds., The Year Book of Education 1959: Higher Education (Lond., N.Y., 1959), 176-96.

Arvidson, Stellan. Education in Sweden. Stock., 1955. 105 p.

Berg, Ruben. "History of the Nordisk Familjebok," BSC, 4 (1938), 234-35.

Bergqvist, B. J. "Sweden," EdYrbk (1926), 351-84.

———. "Sweden," EdYrbk (1930), 483-507.

———. "Sweden," EdYrbk (1932), 397-411.

Bogoslovsky, Christina (Staël von Holstein).
The Educational Crisis in Sweden in the Light of American Experience. N.Y., 1932. 301 p.

Borgeson, Frithiof C. The Administration of Elementary and Secondary Education in Sweden (Teachers College, Columbia University, Contributions to Education, no. 278). N.Y., 1927. 231 p.

Brown, Ebba C. J. Educational System of Sweden. Thesis, Stanford University, 1941. 122 p.

Bruun, Ulla-Britta. Nursery Schools in Sweden. Stock., 1962. 14 p.

Calatrello, Robert L. The Basic Philosophy of Emanuel Swedenborg, with Implications for Western Education. Thesis (Ph.D.), University of Southern California, 1966. 210 p.

Coles, P. B. "Education in Sweden," in The Year Book of Education 1932 (Lond., 1932), 903-16.

———. Recent Educational Developments in Sweden (Great Britain, Board of Education Educational Pamphlets, no. 81). Lond., 1930. 198 p.

Coombs, G. M. "Education in Sweden," JofEd, 75 (1943), 26+.

"Co-Operative Education in Sweden," IO, 1 (1936/37), 111-14.

Curtis, H. S. "Sweden Trains for Democracy," EdFor, 10 (1946), 173-77.

Dahllöf, Urban, Sven Zetterlund, and Henning Öberg. Secondary Education in Sweden. Uppsala. 1966. 104 p.

Dobinson, C. H. "Educational Reform in Sweden," Universities Quarterly, 7 (1953), 354-60.

Düring, Ingemar. "Sweden," in The Year Book of Education 1948 (Lond., 1948), 299-313.

Düring, Ingemar, ed. The Swedish School Reform: a Summary of the Government Bill at the Request of the 1946 School Commission. Uppsala, 1951. 171 p.

Edfeldt, A. W. "Education and Related Services in Sweden," Annals, 302 (1955), 114-20.

Education and Scientific Research in Sweden (New Sweden Tercentenary Publication). Stock., N.Y., 1938. 76 p.

Ellidin, H. "Co-operative Education in Sweden," RIC, 43 (1950), 223-25.

Elmgren, John. School and Psychology [A Report on the Research Work of the 1946 School Commission] (Statens offentliga utredningar, 1948: 27). Stock., 1952. 342 p.

Engberg, Greta. A Comparison of Elementary Education in the United States and

Sweden with Suggested Application of Principles and Practices of American Education to Swedish Schools. Thesis, University of California, Los Angeles, 1950. 93 p.

Englund, Amy Jane. "Schooldays in Lapland," ASR, 19 (1931), 426-29.

Erickson, E. J. "Education and Cooperation in Sweden," S&SR, 25 (1941), 226-36.

Fawcett, Kathleen. A Study of Publicly Supported Summer Educational Services for Children in Sweden. (University Microfilms, Ann Arbor, Mich. Publication no. 9305). Ann Arbor, 1954. 2 v. 294 p.

Fleisher, Frederic. "Highway to Equality," in his, The New Sweden: the Challenge of a Disciplined Democracy (N.Y., 1967), 319-32.

Gierow, Arvid. "Sweden," in EdYrbk (1939), 271-80.

Gustafsson, Bruno. "Teachers' Tenure in Sweden," AmT, (1953), 19-21.

Halden, Folke. "Swedish Industry and the School Reforms," Anglo-Swedish Review (N 1963), 9-12.

Hänninger, Nils. "Sweden," EdYrbk (1936), 501-23.

Hären, Y. "Music in the Elementary School in Sweden," in International Conference on the Role and Place of Music in the Education of Youth and Adults. Music in Education, 106-10.

Härnqvist, Kjell. "Recent Educational Research in Connection with the Swedish School Reform," IntRE, 7 (1961), 85-90.

Håstad, M. "Experimental Course in Mathematics for Primary Schools in Sweden," Arithmetic Teacher, 13 (1966), 392-96.

Heden, Greta. "Swedish Educational Problems," Anglo-Swedish Review (1944), 284-87.

Heilborn, Adele. Travel, Study and Research in Sweden, Handbook. Stock., 1957. 243 p.

Henrysson, Sten. "Equalization of School Marks in Sweden," College Board Review, no. 52 (1964), 21-23.

Hermansson, Ester. "Swedish Education During the 1940's," HER, 21 (1951), 233-42.

Hildeman, Nils-Gustav. "Democratic Teamwork or Intellectual Elite," ASM, (Ap 1965), 12-14.

Hok, R. "Coops in Education," ASM (N 1949), 11-13.

Holmbäck, Åke. "Scholarly Freedom in Sweden," Uppsala universitets årsskrift, (1954, no. 7), 20 p.

"How Sweden Educates Herself," SchR, 43 (1935), 405-409.

Hugo, Yngve. "Sweden," in EdYrbk (1940), 301-14.

Huntford, Roland. "Education in the Outback," Industria International (1964), 117+.

Husén, Torsten. "Current Trends in Swedish Teacher-Training," IntRE, 10 (1964), 206-11.

———. "Curriculum Research in Sweden," IntRE, 11 (1965), 189-208.

———. "Detection of Ability and Selection for Educational Purposes in Sweden," in George Z. F. Bereday and J. A. Lauwerys, eds., The Year Book of Education 1962: the Gifted Child (N.Y., 1962), 295-314.

———. "Educational Change in Sweden," Comparative Education, 1 (1965), 181-91.

———. "The Educational Explosion in Sweden," in George Z. F. Bereday and J. A. Lauwerys, eds., The World Year Book in Education 1965: the Educational Explosion (Lond., 1965), 297-301.

———. "Educational Structure and the Development of Ability," in A. H. Halsey, ed., Ability and Educational Opportunity (Paris, 1961), 113-34.

———. "Liberal Democracy Adopts the Comprehensive School System," PDK, 43 (1961), 86-91.

———. "Loss of Talent in Selective School Systems: the Case of Sweden," CompEdR, 4 (O 1960), 70-74.

———. "Pedagogic Milieu and Development of Intellectual Skills," SchR, 68 (1960), 36-51.

———. Problems of Differentiation in Swedish Compulsory Schooling. Stock., 1962. 64 p.

———. School Reform in Sweden (U. S. Office of Education, Division of International Education). Wash., 1961. 45 p.

———. "School Reform in Sweden: a Liberal Democracy Adopts the Comprehensive School System," PDK, 53 (1961), 86-91.

———. "Social Determinants of the Comprehensive School," Comparative Education Research and the Determinants of Educational Policy: Proceedings of the Comparative Education Society in Europe (Amsterdam, 1963), 71-86.

Husén, Torsten, and Urban Dahllöf. Mathematics and Communication Skills in School and Society. Stock., 1960. 35 p.

Husén, Torsten, Urban Dahllöf, and B. Bromsjö. "Curriculum Research in Sweden," EdRes, 7 (1965), 165-85.

Husén, Torsten, and Sten Henrysson, eds. Differentiation and Guidance in the

Comprehensive School, Report on the Sigtuna Course Organized by the Swedish Government under the Auspices of the Council of Europe, August, 1958. Stock., 1959. 195 p.

Husén, Torsten, and Nils-Eric Svensson. "Educational Research in Countries Other than the United States: Sweden," RofER, 32 (1962), 327-31.

The Intellectual Face of Sweden. Special issue of Ergo International. Uppsala, 1964. 150 p.

James, W. "The 'Comprehensive School' in Sweden," Progress, 47 (1959/1960), 173-77.

Johnson, Emil L. The Role of Foreign Languages in Swedish Education. Thesis (Ph.D.), Clark University, 1957. 166 p.

Johnson, Roy A. "'Middle Way' Education," ASR, 52 (1964), 39-48.

Kärre, D. "Educational Developments in 1949-50," IYEd (1950), 182-88.

Ker, Anthony. Schools of Europe (Westminster, 1961), 33-41, 248-50.

Kilander, Holger F. Science Education in the Secondary Schools of Sweden: a Comparative Study of Sweden and the United States (Teachers College, Columbia University, Contributions to Education, no. 463). N.Y., 1931. 166 p.

Landquist, John. "Sweden's Educational System," ScPP, III, 233-45.

Larson, Cedric. "Guidance is Central in Sweden's New School Plan," Personnel and Guidance Journal, 31 (1953), 532-35.

Larsson, Ingemar. "Business Education in Sweden," Business Education Forum, 13 (1959), 9-14.

Lilja, Einar. "Sweden," in Robert K. Hall, N. Hans, and J. A. Lauwerys, eds., The Year Book of Education 1953: Status and Position of Teachers (Lond., N.Y., 1953). 369-81.

Lilja, Madge A. A Study of the Position of Guidance Programs in the Comprehensive Schools in Greater Stockholm and Their Relationship to the Reformed Educational System of Sweden. Thesis (Ph.D.), University of Michigan, 1966.

Lindegren, Alina M. Education in Sweden (U.S. Office of Education Bull., 1952, no. 17), Wash., 1952. 90 p.

Lindqvist, Märta. "Sigtuna," ASR, 22 (1934), 24-32.

Malmborg, Nils M. "Sweden," EdYrbk (1935), 447-67.

Malmsten, Carl. "Sweden: Training in the Form-sense in the Age of Machines," in Robert K. Hall and J. A. Lauwerys, eds.,

The Year Book of Education 1955: Guidance and Counselling (Lond., N.Y., 1956), 323-28.

Marklund, Sixten. "The Attitudes of Intending Teachers to School Reform in Sweden," in George Z. F. Bereday and J. A. Lauwerys, eds., The Yearbook of Education 1963: The Education and Training of Teachers (Lond., N.Y., 1963), 432-42.

McCreary, Anne P. "The Swedish School Reform Observed by a Foreigner," IntRE, 9 (1963-64), 82-89.

Melander, M. Modern Languages in Swedish Schools: a Short Survey (Skoloverstyrelsens skrift serie, 64). Stock., 1963.

Moberg, Sven. "Sweden," The Planning of Education in Relation to Economic Growth: O.E.C.D. Policy Conference on Economic Growth and Investment in Education. Wash., October 16-20, 1961 (1961), 33-40.

Myrdal, Alva R. "Education for Democracy in Sweden," in Congress on Education for Democracy, 1939. 169-80.

National Board of Education. The New School in Sweden: Aims, Organization, Methods. Stock., 1962. 47 p.

Nelson, Lillian M. Modern Trends in Swedish Education. Thesis, University of Southern California, 1928. 130 p.

Norinder, Yngve. "The Evolving Comprehensive School in Sweden," IntRE, 3 (1957), 257-71.

Norman, Ebba A. S. Problems in Training for Leadership in Religious Education in Sweden. Thesis, Boston University, 1924. 57 p.

Øgren, Gustaf. "Mass Media in Swedish Education," in George Z. F. Bereday and J. A. Lauwerys, eds., The Year Book of Education 1960: Communication Media and the School (Lond., N.Y., 1960), 416-27.

Orring, Jonas. Comprehensive School and Continuation Schools in Sweden: a Summary of the Principal Recommendations of the 1957 School Commission. Stock., 1962. 154 p.

————. The School System of General Education in Sweden. Stock., 1964. 14 p.

Ostlund, Leonard A. "Recent Developments in Swedish Education," Sch&Soc, 83 (1956), 149-51.

Paulston, Roland G. Swedish Comprehensive School Reform, 1918-1950: the Period of Formulation and Adoption. Thesis (Ph.D.) Columbia University, 1966. 308 p.

————. "The Swedish Comprehensive School Reform: a Selected Annotated Bibliography," CompEdR, 10 (1966), 87-94.

Rehnstrom, August E. A. An Interpretation of the Religious Education in Sweden. Thesis (Ph.D.), Boston University, 1945. 336 p.

Reith, George. Education in Sweden. Thesis (Ph.D.), University of Edinburgh, 1950.

Rodhe, Sten. "Church and State in Education: Sweden," in George Z. F. Bereday and J. A. Lauwerys, eds., The World Year Book of Education 1966: Church and State in Education (Lond., N.Y., 1966), 351-53.

Sandberg, F., and Börje Knös. Education and Scientific Research in Sweden (New Sweden Tercentenary Publications). Stock., 1938. 76 p.

Sandler, Rickard. "Freedom and Control in Popular Education," ASR, 25 (1937), 26-27.

Sanhueya, G. "Swedish Students Rate Their High School Curriculum," SchR, 70 (1962), 410-14.

"School Reform in Sweden," Foreign Education Digest, 30 (Jl/S 1965), 3-6.

Scott, Franklin D. "The Swedish Students' Image of the United States," Annals, 295 (1954), 136-45.

Sinha, S. K. "Co-Operative Education in Sweden," All India Cooperative Review, 21 (1956), 634-39.

Smith, George E. K. "Stockholm's New Schools," ASR, 30 (1942), 24-31.

Steenberg, Elisa. "Sweden: Functional Aesthetics," in Robert K. Hall and J. A. Lauwerys, eds., The Year Book of Education 1955: Guidance and Counselling (Lond., N.Y., 1956), 329-34.

Stolpe, Herman A. Cog or Collaborator: Democracy in Co-operative Education. Stock., 1946.

Sundbärg, Axel G. Education in Sweden [Extract from: Sweden, Its People and Its Industry]. Stock., 1902. 69 p.

Svensson, Nils-Eric. Ability Grouping and Scholastic Achievement: Report on a Five-Year Followup Study in Stockholm (Stockholm Studies in Educational Psychology, 5). Stock., 1962. 236 p.

Sweden, Skoloverstyrelsen. Survey of the School System in Sweden (The Board of Education Series, no. 31). Stock., 1958. 88 p.

Swedish Institute. A General Survey of the Swedish School System and Higher Education in Sweden. Stock., 1963. 46 p. Mimeographed.

"The Swedish Schools of Social Work and Municipal Administration," ISSB, 2 (1950), 445-46.

Tomasson, R. F. "From Elitism to Egalitarianism in Swedish Education," Sociology of Education, 38 (1965), 203-23.

Ulne, John. The New Primary School Statute. Stock., 1961. 15 p.

Wahlström, Lydia. "Education in Sweden," AmT, 43 (1958), 11-12+.

Westerberg, Ivar S. The School System of Sweden. Thesis (Ph.D.), University of Washington, 1923. 184 p.

HIGHER EDUCATION AND INSTITUTES

Almhult, Artur. "Academies in Sweden," BSC, 3 (1937), 305-19.

Binder, Betty. "Nation Life at Uppsala," ASR, 31 (1943), 142-47.

Björklund, Sven. "The People's University of Stockholm — A University Extension Run by University Students," AdEdJ, 9 (1950), 119-25.

Carlsson, Gösta, and Bengt Gesser. "Universities as Selecting and Socializing Agents: Some Recent Swedish Data," AcSoc, 9 (1966), 25-39.

Carpenter, Nan C. Music in the Medieval and Renaissance Universities. Thesis (Ph.D.), Yale University, 1948. 581 p.

The Central Organisation of Academies in Sweden. Stock., 1953. 20 p.

Dental Education in Sweden. Stock., 1962. 5 p.

Fleisher, Frederic. "The Swedish Academy," ASR, 41 (1953), 303-10.

Foyer, Lars. Higher Education in Sweden. Stock., 63 p.

Holmberg, Arne. "Educational Work at the Swedish Cooperative College," CPR, 24 (1949), 157+.

Johnson, Hallett. "Sweden's 'Fortress of Education'," FSJ, 21 (1944), 236-37+.

Lindegren, Alina M. Institutions of Higher Education in Sweden (U.S. Office of Education Pamphlet no. 32). Wash., 1932. 45 p.

Lundgreen, Karl H. "Ancient Lund," ASR, 10 (1922), 87-93.

Ostergren, Bertil, ed. Higher Education in Sweden: a Handbook for Foreign Students. Stock., 1952. 131 p.

Pålsson, Klas F. Dental Education in Sweden: Its Origin and Development with Due Regard to Its Present Actual Problems. Thesis, Northwestern University Dental School, 1932. 58 p.

Peterson, Axel G. The Training of Elementary and Secondary Teachers in Sweden. Thesis (Ph.D.), Columbia University, 1933; N.Y., 1934. 110 p.

Sjövall, Einar. "The Institute of Pathology and Forensic Medicine at Lund, Sweden," Methods and Problems of Medical Education (N.Y., 1928), 213-25.

Strömbäck, Dag. "The Uppsala Institute for Philology and Folklore," Arv, 8 (1952), 130-39.

Swedish Overseas Institute. Higher Professional Education in Sweden. Stock., 1932. 58 p.

Vestin, Margareta. "Swedish Universities in War Time," ASR, 31 (1943), 148-53.

VOCATIONAL EDUCATION

Engelbrektson, Sune. Sloyd: the Foundation of Industrial Arts Education. Thesis, New York University, 1949. 119 p.

Fredriksson, Nils. "Vocational Education in Stockholm," ILR, 7 (1923), 1-13.

Goddard, Isaac. Gustaf Larsson, and the Sloyd Training School. Thesis, Boston University, 1936. 79 p.

Hessler, Tore. Survey of the Swedish Vocational School System. Stock., 1962. 10 p.

Hutchings, Donald W. Technological Education in Sweden. Stock., 1962. 18 p.

The Municipal Vocational Schools of Stockholm. Stock., 1962. 24 p.

Neymark, Ejnar. "Vocational Guidance in Sweden," ILR, 57 (1948), 438-53.

Schleef, C. "Sweden's Trade-Union College," American Federationist, 37 (1930), 840-43.

Sverige-Amerika Stiftelsen. Vocational and Non-Academic Study in Sweden. Stock., 1951. 103 p.

Sweden, Royal Board of Vocational Education. Vocational Education in Sweden. Stock., 1952.

"Vocational Training of Domestic Servants in Sweden," ILR, 36 (1937), 294-98.

Wiman, Anna. Vocational Training for Adults in Sweden. Stock., 1962. 13 p.

ADULT EDUCATION

Belding, R. E. "Study Circles in Sweden," AdEd, 14 (1964), 146-50.

Bergevin, Paul E. Adult Education in Sweden: an Introduction (Indiana University Monograph Series in Adult Education, no. 1). Bloomington, Ind., 1961. 61 p.

Carlson, Joel S. The People's High School Movement in Sweden. Thesis, Brown University, 1934. 45 p.

Erickson, Herman. "Adult Education and Swedish Political Leadership," IntRE, 12 (1966), 129-43. Reprinted by Institute of

Labor and Industrial Relations, University of Illinois, in University of Illinois Bull., Reprint Series, no. 163.

Evans, F. M. F. "Swedish People's Colleges," JofEd, 75 (1943), 468+.

Forster, F. Margaret. School for Life: a Study of the People's Colleges in Sweden. Lond., 1944. 99 p.

———. "Swedish People's Colleges Revisited," JofEd (London), 79 (1947), 144+, 206+.

———. "Swedish People's High Schools," AdEd, 14 (1942), 137-42.

Hedström, Birgit Magnusdotter. "Studies for Working Men and Women," ASR, 25 (1937), 28-34.

Hirdman, Gunnar. Adult Education in Sweden. Stock.

Johanson, C. H. "Adult Education in Modern Sweden," WAAEB (1939), 25-26.

Lund, Ragnar. "Adult Education in Sweden," Annals, 197 (1938), 232-42.

———. Adult Education in Sweden. 1950, 83 p. [Slightly revised offprint from Scandinavian Adult Education]

Marshall, C. "Sigtuna Foundation: the Realisation of an Ideal," IntQAdultEd, 2 (1935), 148-53.

Marwick, William H. Present Position of Adult Education in Sweden. Lond., 1938. 72 p.

Olsson, O. "Swedish Study-Circle Movement," IntQAdultEd, 1 (1932), 151-59.

Ostergren, David L. The Folk High Schools of Sweden. (University Microfilms, Ann Arbor, Mich., Publication no. 4587). Ann Arbor, 1953. 163 p.

Stensland, Per G. "Adult Education, A Force in Swedish Democracy," ASR, 33 (1945), 118-28.

"The Swedish Folk High School and the Industrial Workers," IO, 1 (1936/37), 125-26.

Tegner, Olaf H. Adult Education in Sweden: Its Administration and Organization, with Implications for Adult Education in California. Thesis (Ph.D.), University of Southern California, 1958. 311 p.

Tynell, K. "Sweden," WAAEB (1930), 26-31.

Vennerström, Ivar. "The Brunnsvik Folk High School," ASR, 19 (1931), 209-17.

"Workers Education in Sweden," ILR, 7 (1923), 780-85.

PHYSICAL EDUCATION

Broten, George A. An Exploration of Swedish Physical Education. Thesis (Ed.D.), University of Southern California, 1957. 156 p.

Halldén, Ola. Physical Education in Sweden. Stock., 1962. 8 p.

Lief, Thomas J. To Show the Comparative Value of the American System of Physical Education and Other Systems, Notably the German and Swedish. Thesis, University of Notre Dame, 1926. 31 p.

Ostman, Karin. Physical Education in the Secondary Schools of Sweden. Thesis, University of Michigan, 1937. 96 p.

Vanderbie, Jan H. An Evaluation of the Principles Underlying European Systems of Physical Education According to Selected American Criteria. Thesis, International YMCA College, 1949. 142 p.

LIBRARIES, ARCHIVES, MUSEUMS

Andersson, Ingvar. Archives in Sweden. Stock., 1954. 38 p.

Björkbom, Carl. "The Learned Libraries of Sweden," BSC, 3 (1937), 485-89.

——. "The Union Catalog Problem with Special Reference to Swedish Catalogs," Libri, 2 (1952/53), 137-49.

Collijn, I.G.A. "Swedish Library and Bibliographical Work, 1932-1933," IFLAP, 5 (1933), 86-89; 8 (1936), 164-66.

Gierow, Krister. "The Rebuilding of Lund University Library," Libri, 8 (1958), 303-309.

Harrison, K. C. "Swedish Library Tour," LibW, 61 (1959), 66-69.

Heintze, Ingeborg. "Cooperation Between Research Libraries and Public Libraries in Sweden," Libri, 12 (1962/63), 272-82.

Holden, K. M. "Libraries in Sweden," N.Y. Library Assn. Bulletin, 9 (1961), 2-3+.

Johnson, Amandus. "The Lessons of the Swedish Archives," in American Historical Association Annual Report for the Year 1909 (Wash., 1911), 365-68.

Kleberg, Tönnes. "Some Uses of Microfilm in the Library of the University of Uppsala," JofDoc, 7 (1951), 244-51.

——. "A Swedish Plan for the Division of Interests in the Acquisition of Books — and a Scandinavian Perspective," Libri, 8 (1958), 97-105.

Kleineberger, H. R. "Some Notes on Librarianship in Sweden," LibW, 57 (1955), 87-92.

Küntzel, Hans. "Folk Libraries in Sweden," BC, 2 (1936), 81-83.

Modén, Arne. "Open Air Museums in Sweden," ASR, 21 (1933), 341-50.

Olson, Alma L. "Historic Documents in the Swedish House of the Knights," ASR, 18 (1930), 543-46.

Munck af Rosenschöld, Kerstin. "Proposals for a New Swedish Public Library Law," Libri, 1 (1950/51), 263-64.

——. "Swedish Libraries and Librarianship," Assistant to the Librarian, 48 (1955), 11-14.

Ottervik, Gösta et al. Libraries and Archives in Sweden. Stock., 1954. 216 p.

——. "Libraries and Archives in Sweden," JofDoc, 11 (1955), 222.

Ottervik, Gösta, ed. "Swedish Libraries," LibJ, 88 (1963), 4299-4331.

"Sweden," Archivism, 5 (1955), 181-85.

GEOGRAPHY

INTRODUCTION

The Geography section is one of the shortest in this bibliography. There are very good introductory textbooks on the region as a whole, and there are some good articles on each of the countries. The most renowned and prolific scholar is an Englishman, William R. Mead, who has specialized on the region generally but on Finland in particular. There has been little American research in Scandinavian geography; few American Ph. D. candidates have pursued dissertation topics in this area. Whereas, British interest is more traditional and persistent.

Many of this section's entries are closely related to those under Economics, particularly the subsections on Agriculture, Forestry, and Industry. Some of Mead's work, for example, has been listed under Economics: Finland: Agriculture. Students of settlement, population, and migration will find numerous relevant articles under Sociology, including all the references to the Lapps. It is the geographer's lament that his works are often listed under other disciplines. Look also under History and under International Relations.

Anyone seeking an introduction to the region has fine choices. The standard text used in Scandinavia is an aesthetically most pleasing volume edited by Axel Sömme, *A Geography of Norden* (1960). No doubt the best introduction, thorough and yet highly readable, it contains chapters by experts from each country. Andrew O'Dell's *The Scandinavian World* (1957) is a competent introduction in reference book tone with tables half a dozen years older than the book itself. Roy Millward's *Scandinavian Lands* (1964) will be more helpful to the general reader. Slanted toward historical geography, the author's specialty at Leicester, its particular emphasis is the history of settlement and economic development. *Geography of the Northlands* (1955), edited for the American Geographical Society by George H. T. Kimble and Dorothy Good, does not serve well as an introduction to Scandinavia because it deals with the region, including the Soviet Union and Canada, as a whole. Most of the chapters are topical. The few relevant country chapters are listed separately in this bibliography. The American geographer Vincent Malmström's inexpensive and easily-read paperback, *Norden: Crossroads of Destiny and Progress* (1965), is very broad in scope, providing discussion of cultural heritage and political history as well as description of the physical setting and an assessment of strategic significance; it is too thin in the geographic sections to be suitable as an introduction to the region's geography. William Mead's *An Economic Geography of the Scandinavian States and Finland* (1958) is thorough and highly commendable but in style rather encyclopedic. Also noteworthy is Mead's *Farming in Finland* (1953), which is listed under Economics. *Finland and Its Geography* (1955), edited by Raye Platt and written with the assistance of Lauri Niemela, is an American Geographical Society Handbook appropriate for the general reader but at the same time sufficiently technical to include a chapter on Finnish cartography. Melvin Aamodt's dissertation, *A Social Geography of Tampere, Finland* (1968), provides a description and causal analysis of post-war urban development patterns. *Norway North of 65* (1960), edited by Ørnulf Vorren, is a splendid interdisciplinary effort.

SCANDINAVIA

Ahlmann, Hans W. "The Present Climatic Fluctuation," GeogJ, 112 (1948), 163-95.

Ajo, Reino. "Fields of Population Change Around the 60th Parallel Capitals and Maritime Cities; Oslo-Stockholm-Helsinki About 1960," Acta Geographica, 17 (1963, no. 5), 1-19.

Branom, Frederick. "The Scandinavian Peninsula," JofGeo, 24 (1925), 52-65.

Church, R. J. H., Peter Hall, G. R. P. Lawrence, William R. Mead, and Alice F. A. Mutton. An Advanced Geography of Northern and Western Europe. Lond., 1967. 480 p. Includes: "Denmark," 133-51; "Finland," 53-71; "Iceland," 115-32; "Norway," 92-114; "Sweden," 72-91.

Conzen, M. R. G. "The Scandinavian Approach to Urban Geography," NGT, 12 (1948/1950), 86-91.

Crone, G. R., and F. George. "Olaus Magnus and His Carta Marina: a Problem in Sixteenth Century Carto-graphy," GeogJ, 114 (1949), 197-99.

Enckell, Carl. "Aegidius Tschudi's Hand-drawn Map of Northern Europe," Imago Mundi, 10 (1953), 61-64.

———. "The Representation of the North of Europe in the Worldmap of Petrus Plancius of 1592," Imago Mundi, 8 (1951), 55-69.

Fawcett, C. B. "The Nordic Region," SGM, 48 (1932), 78-83.

Granlund, John. "The Carta Marina of Olaus Magnus," Imago Mundi, 8 (1951), 35-43.

Hahn, Vernon. "Soil Erosion in Scandinavia," SC, 13 (1948), 260-64.

Homburg, Frederich. "Geographical Influences in the Development of Scandinavia," JofGeo, 12 (1913), 175-78.

Hubbard, George D. The Geography of Europe. 2d ed. (N.Y., 1952): Denmark, 386-98; Finland, 442-62; Norway, 399-417; Sweden, 421-41.

Hustich, Ilmari. "On the Recent Expansion of the Scotch Pine in Northern Europe," Fennia, 82 (1958), 25 p.

Jonasson, Olaf G. "The Relation Between the Distribution of Population and of Cultivated Land in the Scandinavian Countries, Especially in Sweden," EG, 1 (1925), 107-23.

Kimble, George H. T., and Dorothy Good, eds. Geography of the Northlands (American Geographical Society, Special Publication no. 32). N.Y., 1955. 322 p.

Köhlin, Harald. Some 17th-century Swedish and Russian Maps of the Borderland between Russia and the Baltic Countries," Imago Mundi, 9 (1952), 95-96.

Lang, A. Wilhelm. "Traces of Lost North European Sea Charts of the 15th Century," Imago Mundi, 12 (1955), 31-44.

Lynham, Edward. The Carta Marina of Olaus Magnus, Venice 1539 and Rome 1572. Jenkintown, Pa., 1949. 40 p.

———. "The Early Maps of Scandinavia: Review," GeogJ, 70 (1927), 61-67.

Malmström, Vincent H. "Northern Europe," in George W. Hoffman, ed., A Geography of Europe. 2d ed. (N.Y., 1961), 190-261.

Mead, William R. An Economic Geography of the Scandinavian States and Finland. Lond., 1958. 302 p.

———. "Problems of Scandinavia and Finland," in W. Gordon East and A. E. Moodie, eds., The Changing World: Studies in Political Geography (Lond., Toronto, Wellington, Sydney, 1956), 138-61.

———. "Scandinavia and the Scandinavians in the Annals of the Royal Geographical Society," NGT, 18 (1963), 1-45.

Millward, Roy. Scandinavian Lands. Lond., Toronto, N.Y., 1964. 488 p.

Nansen, Fridtjof. In Northern Mists: Arctic Exploration in Early Times. N.Y., 1911. v. I, 384 p.; v. II, 383 p.

"New Link between Denmark and Sweden," EFTA Rep, no. 174 (D 11, 1967), 5.

"A Note on Olaus Magnus' Map," Imago Mundi, 9 (1952), 82.

O'Dell, Andrew C. The Scandinavian World, A Geography (Geographies for Advanced Study). N.Y., 1957. 549 p.

Pearcy, George E. "The Five Fenno-Scandinavian Powers," in his, World Political Geography (N.Y., 1948), 222-37.

Pounds, Norman J. G. "Northern Europe," in his, Europe and the Soviet Union. 2d ed. (N.Y., 1966), 97-133.

Rudberg, Sten, and Erik Bylund. "From the Bothnian Gulf Through Southern and Central Lapland to the Norwegian Fjords," GeoA, 41 (1959), 261-88.

Sansom, William. The Icicle and the Sun. Lond., 1958. 159 p.

Schütte, Gudmund. Ptolemy's Maps of Northern Europe. Coph., 1917. 150 p.

Sømme, Axel C. A Geography of Norden: Denmark, Finland, Iceland, Norway, Sweden. Oslo, 1960. Lond., 1961. 363 p.

Sommers, Lawrence M. "A Subarctic Highway Traverse of the Scandinavian Peninsula," JofGeo, 55 (1956), 14-23.

Spekke, Arnolds. The Baltic Sea in Ancient Maps. Stock., 1961. 75 p.

Teal, John J., Jr. "Northern Scandinavia," in George H. T. Kimble and Dorothy Good, eds., Geography of the Northlands (N.Y., 1955), 415-32.

Von Engeln, O. D. "Scandinavian Cities," JofGeo, 35 (1936), 15-17, 54-59.

Winter, Heinrich. "The Changing Face of Scandinavia and the Baltic in Cartography up to 1532," Imago Mundi, 12 (1955), 45-54.

Woods, Ethel G. The Baltic Region: a Study in Physical and Human Geography. N.Y., 1932. 434 p.

DENMARK

Aagesen, Aage. "Geographical Studies on Esbjerg, the Port of Western Denmark," Papers, IGCong (Lisbonne, 1949), Tome 3. Travaux de la Section IV (1951), 509-18.

———. "A Geographical Study on the Population of the Danish Northfrisian Islands," GT, 52 (1952), 1-10.

———. "The Population of Denmark, 1955-1960," GT, 63 (1964), 191-202.

Aalen, F. H. A. A Geographical Survey of North West Zealand, Denmark. Thesis (M.Sc.), Trinity College, Dublin, 1963.

Bech, Georg. "The Free Port of Copenhagen," ASR, 7 (1919), 184-89.

Bergsmark, Daniel R. "Agricultural Land Utilization in Denmark," EG, 11 (1935), 206-14.

———. "Stages in the Development of the Danish Landscape — Sequent Occupancy," Bulletin of the Geographical Society of Philadelphia, 34 (1936, no. 2), 33-39.

Bjerre, Arne G. Geography of Agricultural Land Resource Use in Denmark. Thesis (M. Sc.), Oregon State College, 1960.

Copenhagen Port Authority. Port of Copenhagen. Coph., 1949. 232 p.; 1958 ed. 160 p.

Denmark: Collected Papers. IGCong, 20th, Lond., 1964.

Great Britain, War Office, Dept. of General Staff, Geographical Section, Directorate of Military Survey. Gazetteer of Denmark (Map series G.S.G.S. 4210 Denmark, 1:100,000). Lond., 1945. 9 p.

Haggard, Henry R. Rural Denmark and Its Lessons. Lond., N.Y., 1911. 335 p.

Hansen, Kaj. "The Sediments and the Transport of Debris in the Graadyb Tidal Area," GT, 52 (1952/1953), 69-82.

Hansen, Viggo. "Linear Settlements in Vendsyssel, Denmark," GT, 63 (1964), 77-81.

Hess, Charles F. "Geographical Aspects of Consumer Behavior in the Retail Service Area of Greater Aalborg," GT, 65 (1966), 1-24.

Illeris, Sven. "The Functions of Danish Towns," GT, 63 (1964), 203-36.

Jakobsen, Børge. "The Tidal Area in South-Western Jutland and the Process of Salt Marsh Foundation," GT, 53 (1954), 49-61.

Jensen, K. M. "A Change in Land-Use in Central Jutland," GT, 63 (1964), 130-45.

Johansen, Anders C. Remarks on the Influence of the Currents in the Waters About Denmark Upon the Climate of Denmark. Coph., 1926.

Jörgensen, A. Holst. "Heligoland," DO, 1 (1948), 61-64.

Kampp, Aa. H. "Agricultural-Geographic Regions in Denmark," Papers, IGCong, 17th, Wash., 1952.

———. "The Agro-geographical Division of Denmark and the Time Factor," GT, 66 (1967), 36-51.

———. "A Method of Dividing Denmark into Agricultural-Geographic Regions," Papers, IGCong, 17th, 1952.

———. "Some Types of Farming in Denmark," Oriental Geographer, 3 (1959), 17-32.

———. "Utilization of Arable Land on Outwash Plain and Moraine Landscape in Denmark," GT, 58 (1959), 103-13.

Kilynack, Theophilus N. Scandinavian Winter Health Resorts. Lond., 1910. 114 p.

Mead, William R. "Esbjerg," EG, 16 (1940), 250-59.

———. "Ribe," EG, 17 (1941), 195-203.

———. "Three City Ports of Denmark," EG, 18 (1942), 41-56.

Nielsen, Niels, ed. Atlas of Denmark. Coph., Vol. I: Landscapes, 1949; Vol. II: Population, 1961.

Nielsen, Niels. "Population Maps of Denmark," Papers, IGCong, 17th (1952).

Reumert, Johannes. The Commercial-Geographic Importance of the Situation of Copenhagen (GT Supplement). Coph., 1929. 132 p.

Richmond, I. A. "Ptolemy's Map of Denmark: a Study of Conflicting Evidence," SGM, 37 (1923), 99-102.

Schacke, Erik. "The Danish Heath Society," SGM, 67 (1951), 45-54.

Schou, Axel. "Educational Wall-Map Systems of the Danish Geodetic Institute," GT, 52 (1952/1953), 255-75.

———. "Educational Wall-Map System of the Danish Geodetic Institute," Papers, IGCong, 17th (1952), 370-73.

Sommers, Lawrence M. "Bornholm, Denmark: Aspects of the Economic Geography of a Baltic Sea Island," Northwestern University Studies in Geography (M 1957), 9-31.

Thomson, M. Pearson. Denmark. Lond., 1924. 91 p.

Thorpe, H. "The Influence of Inclosure on the Form and Pattern of Rural Settlement in Denmark," Institute of British Geographers Publication, 17 (1952), 111-29.

———. "A Special Case of Heath Reclamation in the Alheden District of Jutland, 1700-1955," TIBG, 23 (1957), 87-121.

Vahl, M. "Man's Influence on the Landscape of Denmark," Papers, IGCong (Varsovie, 1934), Tome 3 (1937), 21-24.

———. "Rural Settlement in the Island of Falster," Papers, IGCong (Paris, 1931), Tome 3 (1934), 177-92.

———. "Types of Rural Settlement in Denmark," Papers, IGCong (Paris, 1931), Tome 3 (1934), 165-76.

———. "The Urban Settlement of Denmark," GT, 36 (1933), 5-32.

GREENLAND

Ball, Sydney H. The Mineral Resources of Greenland (Society of Economic Geologists, Publication 15). Coph., 1922. 60 p.

Birket-Smith, Kaj. Knud Rasmussen's Saga. Coph., 1941. 127 p.

Borum, V. "Greenland," DFOJ (1948, no. 1), 14-20; (1948, no. 2), 11-19.

Boyd, Louise A. The Ford Region of East Greenland (American Geographical Society Special Publication no. 18). N.Y., 1935. 369 p.

Denmark, Ministry of Foreign Affairs. The Bear in the Ice Hole, by Knud Rasmussen; Greenland and its People, by P. H. Lundsteen. Coph., 1962. 40 p.

———. Greenland. Ed. by Kristjan Bure; tr. by Reginald Sprink. Ringkøbing, 1954. 166 p. 2d ed., 1956. 168 p.; 3d ed., Coph., 1961. 191 p.

———. A Hundred Pictures from Greenland. Coph., 1932. 47 p.

Fristrup, Børge. "Further Investigations of the Greenland Ice Cap," GT, 63 (1964), 121-29.

———. "Recent Investigations of the Greenland Ice Cap," GT, 58 (1959), 1-29.

Gabel-Jørgensen, Capt. "Dr. Knud Rasmussen's Contribution to the Exploration of the South-East Coast of Greenland, 1931-1933," GeogJ, 86 (1935), 32-53.

Greenland. Published by the Commission for the Direction of the Geological and Geographical Investigations in Greenland. Ed. by M. Vahl. 3 vols. Coph., Lond., 1928-1929.

Hansen, Fredrick C. C. Outlines of the Geography and History of Greenland, for the Use of Anthropologists. Coph., 1915. 34 p.

Hayward, H. O. B. "The Oxford University Greenland Expedition," GeogJ, 88 (1936), 148-62.

Horn, Gunnar. "Recent Norwegian Expeditions to South-East Greenland," NGT, 7 (1938/1939), 452-561.

Hutchison, Isabel W. "In Greenland's Flowery Valleys," GeoM, 15 (1942/1943), 596.

Kent, Rockwell. "Greenland: an Obligation," ASR, 28 (1940), 204-209.

Knuth, E. "Exploring Unknown Greenland: the Danish Pearyland Expedition, 1947-1950," ASR, 40 (1952), 338-50.

Koch, Lauge. "North of Greenland," GeogJ, 64 (1924), 6-21.

———. "North of Seventy, an Explorer's Year in East Greenland," ASR, 16 (1928), 287-95.

———. "Preliminary Report on the Results of the Danish Bicentenary Expedition to North Greenland," GeogJ, 62 (1923), 103-17.

———. "Two Recent Journeys on the Coast of Eastern Greenland," GeogJ, 71 (1928), 1-15.

Kryger, Adolph H. Sondestrom, Greenland
— A Dc Climate. Thesis (M.A.), Ohio
State University, 1965.

Lindsay, Martin. "The British Trans-
Greenland Expedition," GeogJ, 85 (1935),
393-411; 86 (1936), 235-52.

———. Those Greenland Days. Edinburgh,
Lond., 1932. 256 p.

Lloyd, Trevor. "Ivigtut (Oryolite) and Modern Greenland," CG, 13 (1953, no. 3),
39-52.

———. "Progress in West Greenland,"
JofGeo, 49 (1950), 319-29.

———. "Why Greenland?," GeoM, 21 (1948-
1949), 470-80.

Loewe, Fritz. "Central Western Greenland:
the Country and Its Inhabitants," GeogJ,
86 (1935), 263-75.

Longstaff, T. G. "The Oxford University
Expedition to Greenland, 1928," GeogJ,
74 (1929), 61-69.

Moltke, Harald. "Knud Rasmussen," ASR,
17 (1929), 543-53.

Mott, Peter G. "The Oxford University
Greenland Expedition West Greenland,
1936," GeogJ, 90 (1937), 315-34.

"Names in Greenland," GeogJ, 85 (1935),
463-64.

Owen, Ruth B. "Glimpses of Greenland,"
FSJ, 12 (1935), 313-16.

Petersen, Sophie. "Greenland," ASR, 18
(1930), 141-49.

Rasmussen, Knud. "South East Greenland,
the Seventh Thule Expedition, 1932," GT,
36 (1933), 35-41.

———. "South East Greenland, The Sixth
Thule Expedition," GT, 35 (1932), 169-97.

Roberts, Brian. "The Cambridge Expedition
to Scoresby Sound, East Greenland, in
1933," GeogJ, 85 (1935), 234-51.

Spender, Michael. "The Sixth and Seventh
Thule Expeditions of Knud Rasmussen,"
GeogJ, 83 (1934), 140-42.

Straus, Roger W., Jr. "Greenland," CH, 52
(1940-1941), 36.

Sugden, J. C., and Peter G. Mott. "Oxford
University Greenland Expedition, 1938,"
GeogJ, 95 (1940), 43-51.

Symposium on the Physical Geography of
Greenland, Copenhagen, 1960. Physical
Geography of Greenland. IGCong, 19th,
Norden, 1960. Symposium 502 (Folio
Geographica Danica, T. 9). Coph., 1961.
234 p.

Trolle, A. "The Danish North-East Greenland Expedition," SGM, 25 (1909), 57-70.

Uren, P. E. "Greenland," in George H. T.
Kimble and Dorothy Good, eds., Geography of the Northlands (N.Y., 1955), 372-86.

Wager, L. R. "The Kangerdlugssuak Region
of East Greenland," GeogJ (1937), 393-
425.

Whittier, Herbert. Sequence Occupation of
West Greenland: an Historical Geography.
Thesis (M.A.), Florida State University,
1965.

Wordie, J. M. "Cambridge East Greenland
Expedition, 1929; Ascent of Retermann
Peak," GeogJ, 75 (1930), 481-504.

———. "The Cambridge Expedition to East
Greenland in 1926," GeogJ, 70 (1927),
225-65.

———. "An Expedition to North West Greenland and the Canadian Arctic in 1937,"
GeogJ, 92 (1938), 385-421.

———. "Ice in Greenland," GeoM, 27
(1954/1955), 613-20.

FAEROE ISLANDS

Currie, James. "The Faeroe Islands," SGM,
22 (1906), 61-76; 134-47.

———. Mineralogy of the Faeroes. Lond.,
1907. 68 p.

Denmark, Ministry of Foreign Affairs. The
Faroe Islands: Scenery, Culture and
Economy. Coph., 1959. 33 p.

Elkaer-Hansen, Nils. "The Faroe Islands,"
EFTA Bull, 8 (1967, no. 8), 8-12.

———. "The Faroe Islands Today," ASR, 43
(1955), 165-71; also: DFOJ, no. 12
(1954), 13-18.

"The Faroe Islands," DFOJ, no. 196 (1937),
45-57.

Faroe Islanders. The Saga of the Faroe Islanders. Lond., 1934. 113 p.

Hansen, Leo. "Viking Life in the Storm-
Cursed Faeroes," NGeogM, 58 (1930),
602-48.

Harris, George H. The Faroe Islands. Birmingham, 1927. 119 p.

Harshberger, J. W. "The Gardens of the
Faeroes, Iceland and Greenland," GeoR,
14 (1924), 404-15.

Henricksen, Per S. The Faroe Islands: a
Political-Geographic Case Study. Thesis
(M.A.), University of Washington, 1965.

Lockley, R. M. "Faeroe Scene," GeogM, 6
(1938), 215-24.

Matras, Chr. "Oldest History of the Faerøs,"
ScPP, I, 128-29.

Mead, William R. "Glimpses of a Faroese
Village," ASR, 8 (1920), 113-19.

Olrik, H. G. "The Faroe Islands," ASR, 17
(1929), 207-16.

Owen, M. "The Faroe Islands Today,"
JKCGS (1959), 7-13.

Williamson, Kenneth. The Atlantic Islands.

A Study of the Faeroe Life and Scene.
Lond., 1948. 360 p.

FINLAND

Aamot, Melvin H. A Social Geography of
Tampere, Finland. Thesis (Ph.D.), Indiana University, 1968.

Aario, Leo E. Suomen Kartasto (Atlas of
Finland) 1960. Hels., 1961.

Ajo, Reino. Contributions to Social Planning:
a Program-Sketch with Special Regard to
National Planning [Using Finnish data].
LSG, Series B, no. 11 (1953), 27 p.; Reprinted from Svensk Geografisk Årsbok,
29 (1953).

————. "New Aspects of Geographic and Social Patterns of Net Migration Rate: a
Pilot Study Based on Finnish Statistics
for the Year, 1951," LSG, Series B, no.
13 (1957), 170-83; Also: Svensk Geografisk Årsbok, 30 (1954), 153-67.

Finland, Geodetiska Institutet. The Results
of the Base Extension Nets of the Finnish
Primary Triangulation. By Jorma Korhonen, V. R. Olander, and Erkki Hytomen.
Hels., 1959. 57 p.

Finland, Geologinen Tutkimuslaitos. Guide
to the publications of the Geological Survey of Finland, 1879-1960. Compiled by
Marjatta Okko and Marjetta Hannikainen.
Hels., 1960. 104 p.

Finland, Statistiska Centralbyrån. The Population of Finland, 1751-1805. Hels.,
1953. [English summary and table head-
ings]

Finland-USSR Boundary (International
Boundary Study No. 74). Prepared by the
Geographer, Office of Strategic and Func-
tional Research, Bureau of Intelligence
and Research, U. S. Dept. of State.
Wash., 1967. 19 p.

Finnish Geographical Society. Atlas of Finland, 1925. Hels., 1929. 320 p. English
text also contained in Fennia, no. 48.

————. Suomi: a General Handbook on the
Geography of Finland. By J. G. Grano
(Fennia, no. 72 b). Hels., 1952.

Freeman, T. W., and Mary M. MacDonald.
"The Arctic Corridor of Finland," SGM,
54 (1938), 219-30.

Great Britain, War Office, General Staff,
Geographical Section. Short Glossary of
Finnish. Lond., 1943. 10 p.

Hall, Wendy. "Resettlement in Finland,"
GeoM, 24 (1952), 419-28.

Helin, Ronald A. Economic-geographic Reorientation in Western Finnish Karelia

(Publication 909) (Division of Earth Sciences. Foreign Field Research Program.
Report no. 13). Thesis (Ph.D.), University of California, Los Angeles, 1961.
124 p.

Hildén, Kaarlo. "The Geographical Society
of Finland," BC, 1 (1935), 98-99.

Jaatinen, Stig T., and William R. Mead.
"Finland in British Maps: a Review Down
to 1856," Fennia, no. 80 (1956), 27 p.

Jessen, Jørgen. "A Finnish Geographer,"
BC, 2 (1936), 195-200.

Kuchnelt-Leddihn, Erik R. von. "The Petsamo Region," GeoR, 34 (1944), 405-17.

McCallien, W. J., and A. McCallien. "A
Scientific Excursion to Finland," SGM,
48 (1932), 94-98.

Mead, William R. "The Adoption of Other
Lands: Experiences in a Finnish Context," Geog, 47 (1963), 241-54.

————. "The Farmer's Year: a Geographical Record of Seasonal Activities," Indian
Geographical Society Silver Jubilee Sou-
venir (1952), 97-100.

————. "Finland and the Winter Freeze,"
Geog, 24 (1939), 221-29.

————. "Finnish Karelia: an International
Borderland," GeogJ, 118 (1952), 40-57.

————. "Finnish Outlook, East and West,"
GeogJ, 113 (1949), 9-20.

————. "Frontier Themes in Finland," Geog,
44 (1959), 145-56.

————. "The Frontiers of Finland: an Essay
in Political Geography," Norseman, 2
(1944), 389-96.

————. The Geographical Tradition in Finland (Inaugural Lecture, University College, London, 19:XI:1962). Lond., 1963.
19 p.

————. "Land Use in Early Nineteenth Century Finland," Publications of University
of Turku, 26 (1953).

————. "Problems of a Divided Waterway"
[Lake Saimaa], Geog, 47 (1962), 89-92.

————. "Recent Finnish Geographical Publications in English," Geog, 39 (1952),
200-201.

————. "The Seasonal Round: a Study of Ad-
justment on Finland's Pioneer Fringe,"
Tijdschrift voor Economische en Sociale
Geografie, 49 (1958), 157-62.

————. "Viipuri: Its Importance in the Political and Economic Geography of Finland," SGM, 57 (1941), 120-27.

Mead, William R., and Helmer Smeds. Winter in Finland: a Study in Human Geography. N.Y., 1967. 144 p.

"The Nomenclature of Towns and Rural Communes in Finland," Fennia, no. 59 (1934).

Nordenskiöld, Erland. "Finland: the Land and the People," GeoR, 7 (1919), 361-76.

Numelin, Ragnar J. Some Aspects of the Geography of Finland. Hels., 1925. 33 p.

Ohlson, B., V. Okko, and E. Nüranen. Physical and Human Geography of Finnish Lapland. Hels., 1960.

Palmerlee, Albert E. A Finnish-English Glossary of Map Terms. Lawrence, Kansas, 1959. 49 p.

Platt, Raye R. Finland and Its Geography (American Geographical Society Handbook). N.Y., Lond., 1955. 510 p.

Repo, R., V. Varjo, and M. Palomäki. Regional Geography of the Finnish Lake Plateau and of Eastern Finland (Guidebook to excursion E. F. 3): IGCong, 19th, Norden, 1960.

Russell, Wilmot. "Some Aspects of Modern Finland," SGM, 46 (1930), 90-92.

Shaw, Earl B. "The Åland Islands," EG, 15 (1939), 27-42.

Smeds, Helmer. The Distribution of Urban and Rural Population in Southern Finland, 1950 (Helsingin Yliopiston Maantieteen Laitoksen Julkaisuja, Publicationes Instituti Geographici Universitatis Helsingiensis no. 25). Hels., 1957. 21 p. Reprinted from Fennia, no. 81.

——. "A New Population and Settlement Map of Finland," IGCong, 17th (1952), 505-507.

——. "Post-war Land Clearance and Pioneering Activities in Finland," Fennia, no. 83 (1960), 31 p.

——. "The Replot Skerry Guard: Emerging Islands in the Northern Baltic," GeoR, 40 (1950), 103-33.

——. Three Faces of Finland: Guidebooks Prepared for the Three Finnish Excursions at the XIXth International Geographical Congress 1960. Hels., 1960.

Symposium on Man's Influence on Nature in Finland, Helsinki, 1959. Ed. by Ilmari Hustick (Fennia, no. 85). Hels., 1960. 128 p.

United States, Board on Geographic Names. Finland (Cumulative Decision List, no. 5001). Wash., 1950. 14 p.

United States, Dept. of Interior, Office of Geography. Finland: Official Standard Names Approved by the U. S. Board of Geographic Names. Wash., 1962. 556 p.

Van Cleef, Eugene. "Finland-Bridge to the Atlantic," JofGeo, 48 (1949), 99-105.

——. Finland, the Republic Farthest North: the Response of Finnish Life to Its Geographic Environment. Columbus, Ohio, 1929. 220 p.

——. "Finland's Dilemma," JofGeo, 43 (1944), 205-12.

——. "Landscapes in Finland," JofGeo, 35 (1936), 289-300.

PORTS, CITIES

Aario, Leo E. "Helsinki as a Large City," Tijdschrift voor economische en sociale geografie, 44 (1953), 213-29.

Aminoff, Berndt. "The Traffic Problem in Relation to Town Planning in Helsingfors," in Papers of the 13th International Housing and Town Planning Congress (Berlin, 1931), pt. 1, 226-35.

Eiro, Kristian. "The Port of Helsinki: Its Growth and Development as the Chief Port of Finland," Dock and Harbour Authority, 39 (1959), 269-79.

Glassey, Frank P. S. "Helsingfors — A Contrast in Light and Shade," NGeoM, 47 (1925), 597-612.

Hoppu, Haarle W. "Finland's Ports in the Service of Foreign Trade," FTR, 76 (1953), 104, 106, 113.

——. Port of Helsinki. 3d ed., 1952.

Kekoni, Karl. "The Ports of Finland," EG, 8 (1932), 217-44.

Mead, William R. "Turku and Helsinki: Capital Cities of Finland," SGM, 59 (1943), 18-23.

Rosén, Ragnar. "Helsinki-Helsingfors," ScPP, III, 425-34.

Rothery, Agnes. "Helsinki, Gateway to the New Finland," GeoM, 2 (1936), 322-40.

Rydman, Eero. "Helsinki as a Tourist Centre," Unitas (1952), 39-42.

Von Engeln, O. D. "Scandinavian Cities 4: Helsingfors," JofGeo, 35 (1936), 147-50.

Yarham, E. R. "Helsingfors, a Modern Capital," ASR, 20 (1932), 292-98.

ICELAND

Ahlmann, Hans W. Land of Ice and Fire. Lond., 1938. 271 p.

Akselsson, Johannes. "On Geological Investigations in Iceland and Their Bearing on General Geography," Nord, 2 (1939), 177-86.

Barth, Thomas F. W. "Craters and Fissure Eruptions at Myvatn in Iceland," NGT, 9 (1942/1943), 58-81.

——. "Some Unusual Ground-Water Phenomena in Iceland," NGT, 9 (1942/1943), 158-73.

——. Volcanic Geology, Hot Springs and Geysers of Iceland (Carnegie Institution of Wash. Publication 587). Wash., 1950. 174 p.

Beckett, John A. Iceland Adventure: the Double Traverse of Vatnajokull by the Cambridge Expedition. Lond., 1934. 197 p.

Bird, J. Brian. "Iceland," in George H. T. Kimble and Dorothy Good, eds., Geography of the Northlands (N.Y., 1955), 387-400.

Bløndal, Sigfus. Life of Icelander Jon Olafsson, 1661-1679 (Hakluyt Society). Lond., 1932. 290 p.

Bodvarsson, Gunnar. "The Hot Springs in Iceland," IcR (1963), 8-10.

Bruun, Daniel. Iceland, Routes Over the Highlands. Coph., 1907. 118 p.

Dawson, F. L. M. "The Cambridge (Mývatn) Iceland Expedition, 1939," GeogJ, 95 (1940), 439-51.

Eythorsson, J. "On the Present Position of the Glaciers in Iceland," Soc. Scient. Islandica, Pub. 10 (Rey., 1931).

Henderson, Kenneth A. "Some Icelandic Mountains," Alpine J, 10 (1957), 113-20.

Hermannsson, Halldór. "The Cartography of Iceland," Islandica, 21 (Ithaca, 1931), 1-81. Followed by maps.

Ives, John D. Oraefi, South-East Iceland: an Essay in Regional Geomorphology. Thesis (Ph.D.), McGill University, 1956.

Jack, Robert. Arctic Living: the Story of Grimsey. Toronto, 1955. 181 p.

Johannesson, Björn. The Soils of Iceland (Reykjavik University Research Institute; Dept. of Agriculture Reports, Series B, no. 13). Rey., 1960. 140 p.

Keith, D. B., and E. W. Jones. "Grimsey, North Iceland," GeogJ, 86 (1935), 143-52.

Kongelige Danske Geografiske Selskab. Folia Geographia Danica: pt. 1: Reports on the Expeditions to Iceland 1934 and 1936. v. 1-4, 1940-1951; pt. 2: v. 1-3, 1942-1944; pt. 3, Investigations of the Geography and Natural History of the Praesta Fjord, Zealand. v. 1-6, 1944-1953; pt. 4: 1945; pt. 5: 1949; pt. 6: 1955; pt. 8: no. 1-4; pt. 9: (analyzed) 1961. See GT (1964) for full contents.

Lockley, R. M. "The Westmann Islands," GeoM, 4 (1937), 349-56.

McGuiggan, Mary D. "Iceland," Boston Association of Geography Teachers Bulletin, 9 (1941, no. 3), 1-4.

Malmström, Vincent H. A Regional Geography of Iceland (National Research Council Publication 584). Wash., 1958. 255 p.

Muir, T. S. "The Physical Geography of Iceland," SGM, 31 (1915), 254-57.

Nielsen, Jens N. Hydrography of the Waters by the Faroe Islands and Iceland during the Cruises of the Danish Research Steamer "Thor" (Denmark, Kommission for Havundersøgelser Meddelelser Serie: Hydrografi. Bd. 1). 1904. 29 p.

Nielsen, Niels. Contributions to the Physiography of Iceland with Particular Reference to the Highlands West of Vatnajokull (Det Kgl. Danske Videnskabernes Selskabs Skrifter. Naturvidenskabelig og Mathematisk Afdeling, Raekke 9, Bd. 4, no. 5). Coph., 1933. 104 p.

Perkins, Henry A. "The Mountains of Iceland," Alpine J, 6 (1946), 1-13.

Pollitzer-Pollenghi, Andrea de. "The Vatnajukull," Alpine J, 48 (1936), 257-79.

Roberts, Brian. "Vatnajökull, Iceland: the History of Its Exploration," SGM, 50 (1934), 65-76.

Russell, W. S. C. "Askja, a Volcano in the Interior of Iceland," GeoR, 3 (1917), 212-21.

Schell, I. I. "The Ice Off Iceland and the Climates During the Last 1200 Years, Approximately," GeoA, 43 (1961), 354-62.

Stefansson, Jon. "The Land of Fire," NGeogM, 18 (1907), 741-44.

Stefánsson, Unnsteinn. North Icelandic Waters. Rey., 1962. 269 p. Reprinted from Rit Fiskideildar, 3 (1962).

Thorarinsson, Sigurdur. "Population Changes in Iceland," GeoR, 51 (1961), 519-33.

————. The Thousand Years Struggle Against Ice and Fire (Museum of Natural History, Dept. of Geology and Geography, Reykjavik, Miscellaneous papers, no. 14). Rey., 1956. 52 p.

Thorkelsson, Thorkell. The Hot Springs of Iceland (Ac. Copenhagen. Kjobenhavnsk Selskab. Skrifter. Naturvidenskabelig og Mathematisk Afdeling, Raekke 7, Bd. 8). Coph., 1910. 86 p.

Thoroddsen, Th. An Account of the Physical Geography of Iceland. 1914.

Thorsteinsson, Thorsteinn. "The First Census Taken in Iceland in 1703," International Statistical Conferences Proceedings, v. 3, pt. B, 1947 (Wash., 1947), 614-23.

United States, Department of the Interior, Office of Geography. Iceland: Official Standard Names Approved by the United States Board on Geographic Names. Wash., 1961. 231 p.

Wadell, Hakon. "Some Studies and Observations from the Greatest Glacial Area in Iceland," GeoA, 2 (1920), 300-23.

PORT OF REYKJAVIK

"Iceland and Its Port: a Commercial Outpost in Northern Latitudes," Dock and Harbour Authority, 21 (1941), 95-97.

Malmström, Vincent H. "The Rise of Reykjavik: a Study in Historico-Economic Geography," Proceeding of the Minnesota Academy of Science, 25/26 (1957-58), 360-71.

"The Port of Reykjavik, Iceland," ComRep, 30 (1940), 655-56.

NORWAY

Ahlmann, Hans W. "Geomorphological Studies in Norway," GeoA, 1 (1919), 3-148, 193-252.

——. "Glaciers in Jotunheim and the Physiography," GeoA, 4 (1922), 1-57.

Bengtson, Nels A. "The Economic Geography of Norway," JofGeo, 24 (1925), 243-59.

Benneche, Olaf. "The Sörland Comes Into Its Own," ASR, 9 (1921), 179-89.

Berg, Gunnar. "The Wall of Isles" [Lofoten], Norseman (1962, no. 3), 4-7.

Bergsmark, Daniel R. "The Geography of Norway," Bulletin of the Geographical Society of Philadelphia, 27 (1929), 283-99.

Bogen, Hans. "In Sandefjord: Norway's New Bedford," ASR, 25 (1937), 43-46.

Brigham, Albert P. "The Fords of Norway," Bulletin of the American Geographical Society, 38 (1906), 1-12.

Broch, Olaf A., and F. Isachsen. "The Southern Fault-Line Boundary of Nesodden Peninsula, Oslofjord," NGT, 7 (1938/1939), 66-76.

Bukdahl, Jörgen. "Hardanger," ASR, 18 (1930), 598-605.

Bull, Jacob B. "Österdalen," ASR, 14 (1926), 143-55.

Drabble, Mary J. "Bergen and the Northwest Bergenshalvøy," JKCGS, 10 (1958), 8-11.

Ellefsen, Einar S. "Land of Alps and Fjords: Møre og Romsdal," Norseman (1967), 2-5.

Findahl, Theo. "Vestfold, Home of Ancient and Modern Vikings," ASR, 15 (1927), 678-87.

Fönhus, Mikkjel. "Valdres and Hallingdal — Twin Valleys," ASR, 15 (1927), 665-76.

Forström, O. "Östfold," ASR, 17 (1929), 141-49.

Great Britain, Naval Intelligence Division. Norway (Geographical Handbook Series,

20). 2 vols. Lond., 1942. 419, 492 p.

Great Britain, War Office, General Staff, Geographical Section. Gazateer of Norway. Lond., 1944. 16 p. Maps.

——. Norway. Lond., 1940. Maps.

Grønlie, Ole T. "Some Remarks on the Land Area in Nordland Between the Glacier Svartisen and the Frontier," NGT, 7 (1938/1939), 399-406.

Heiden, Noland R. "Odda and Rjukan — Two Industrialized Areas of Norway," AAAG, 42 (1952), 108-28.

Henderson, Bertha. "Man and His Environment in Norway," JofGeo, 10 (1911-12), 46-51.

Holtedahl, H. "On the Norwegian Continental Terrace, Primarily Outside Møre-Romsdal: Its Geomorphology and Sediments," Universitet Bergen Årbok, 1955.

Holtedahl, Olaf. "From the Northern Randsfjord District," NGT, 7 (1938/1939), 441-51.

——. "The Structural History of Norway and Its Relation to Great Britain," Quarterly Journal of the Geological Society, 108 (1952), 65-98.

Hubbard, George D. "The Geography of Residence in Norway Fjord Areas," AAAG, 22 (1932), 109-18.

Isachsen, Fridtjof. "Regional Planning in Norway," NGT, 14 (1953/1954), 358-62.

——. "Rural Settlement in Norway, Excursion E. N. 5, August 14-21, 1960, Oslo-Gudbransdal-Nordfjord-Bergen," NGT, 17 (1959/1960), 187-96.

Jackson, J. N. "Norwegian Colonisation in an Arctic Village," SocR, 44 (1952), 21-38.

Kirk, William, and Francis M. Synge. "Farms of Verdal, Norway," SGM, 70 (1954), 106-23.

Knudsen, Henning. "Norway's New Frontier," Freedom and Union, 13 (Ap 1958), 10-11.

Landmark, K. et al. "Northern Norway: Nature and Livelihood," NGT, 17 (1959/1960), 138-67.

Liestøl, Olav. "Glacier Dammed Lakes in Norway," NGT, 15 (1955/1956), 122-49. Also: Norsk Polarinstitutt Meddelelse, no. 81 (Oslo, 1956), 122-59.

Lloyd, Trevor. "The Norwegian-Soviet Boundary: a Study in Political Geography," NGT, 15 (1955/1956), 187-242.

——. "Norwegian-Soviet Frontier in Lapland," IGCong, 17th (1952), 533-38.

Løddesøl, Aasulv. "Soil Destruction in Norway," NGT, 11 (1946/1947), 238-46.

Lund, Diderich H. "The Revival of Northern Norway," GeogJ, 109 (1947), 185-97.

Mead, William R. "Finmark: an Historico-geographical Study," CGJ, 24 (1942), 204-47.

Molson, Charles R. The Island of Senja in North Norway. Thesis (M.A.), McGill University, 1954.

Nicholson, N. L. "Norway: the Way to the North," CGJ, 45 (Jl 1952), 2-13.

Olsen, Magnus B. Farms and Fanes of Ancient Norway. Oslo, 1928. 349 p.

Ommanney, Francis D. North Cape. Lond., N.Y., 1939. 252 p.

Oxholm, Axel H. "Country Life in Norway: the Beneficent Gulf Stream Enables One-Third of the People in a Far-north, Mountainous Land to Prosper on Farms," NGeogM, 75 (1939), 493-528.

Pickard, J. P. "Manufacturing Regions of Norway," AAAG, 42 (1952), 254.

Rudberg, Sten, and Erik Bylund. "From the Bothnian Gulf through Southern and Central Lapland to the Norwegian Fiords," GeoA, 41 (1959), 261-288. Reprinted in IGCong, 19th (Stock., 1960).

Sansom, William. "Norway: Sea into Land," GeoM, 29 (1956/1957), 575-80. Extracted from his, The Icicle and the Sun (1958).

Scott, Gabriel. "The Sörland, Impressions, Moods, Pictures," ASR, 15 (1927), 653-64.

Smailes, P. J. Mountain Communities in Transition: the Problems of a Modern Marginal Farming District in Southern Norway. Thesis (M.A.), Manchester University, 1962.

Sömme, Axel C. "Sørfjord in Inner Hardanger," NGT, 17 (1959/1960), 168-75.

Sommers, Lawrence M. Grip, A Populated Skerry of Norway. 1953. Reprinted from Papers of the Michigan Academy of Science, Arts and Letters, 37 (1952), 227-32.

——. "Impact of the Common Market Application Revision on Geography of Norway," The East Lakes Geography, 1 (N 1964), 59-64.

Ström, Kaare M. "The Geomorphology of Norway," GeogJ, 112 (1948), 19-27.

——. "The Norwegian Coast," NGT, 17 (1959/1960), 132-37.

Sund, Tore. "Fjord Land and Coast Land of Western Norway," NGT, 17 (1959/1960), 176-86.

Sund, Tore, and Axel C. Sømme. Norway in Maps (Bergen, Norway, Norges handelshøgskole, Skrifter, no. 1). Bergen, 1947.

Symes, D. G. "Changes in the Structure and Role of Farming in the Economy of a West Norwegian Island," EG, 39 (1963), 319-31.

——. The Economic and Social Geography of Selected Areas in the Hordaland Fylke of Western Norway. Thesis (B.Litt.), Oxford University, 1962.

——. "Fruit Farming in Sörfiord, Western Norway," Geog, 50 (1965), 45-57.

Tveteraas, R. "Rogaland, A Province of Fjord and Plain," ASR, 16 (1928), 353-63.

Vorren, Ørnulf, ed. Norway North of 65. Oslo, 1960. 272 p.

Werenskiold, Werner. "Glaciers in Jotunheim," NGT, 7 (1938/1939), 638-47.

PORTS, CITIES

Engelstad, Carl F., ed. Oslo, the Capital of Norway; Art and Intellectual Life at Its 900-Years Jubilee. Oslo, 1950. 190 p.

"The Fjord Harbours and Ports of Northern Norway," Dock and Harbour Authority, 20 (1939), 14-16.

Haugstøl, Henrik. "City of Long Traditions (Bergen)," Norseman (1965), 105-109.

Kinn, Egil. "Capital of Wide Open Spaces (Oslo)," Norseman (1966), 150-54.

Kjelstrup, Y. "The Port of Oslo, Chief Norwegian Shipping Centre," Dock and Harbour Authority, 19 (1939), 281-85, 320-21.

Larson, Laurence M. "Oslo and Christiania," ASR, 13 (1925), 31-39.

"A Nine-Hundredth Anniversary (Oslo)," ASR, 38 (1950), 127-31.

Nordahl-Olsen, Johan. "Bergen, Norway's Window to the Sea," ASR, 16 (1928), 666-74.

"Norway, Ports," in Ports of the World (Lond., 1966), 293-312.

Oslo, Stock Exchange. Report of the Trade, Industry and Shipping of Oslo in 1931. Oslo, 1932. 62 p.

Ouren, Tore H. P. "The Freight Balance Exemplified by the Ports in Trøndelag, Norway," NGT, 13 (1951/52), 111-25.

——. The Port Traffic of the Oslofjord Region (Publications of the Norwegian School of Economics and Business Administration Geographical Series, no. 63). Bergen, 1958. 168 p.

The Ports of Norway. Oslo, 1954. 646 p.

Ring, Barbara. "Oslo," ASR, 16 (1928), 141-49.

Ronold, Jan. "Stavanger Based on Fish and Ships," Norseman (1966), 120-24.

Sommers, Lawrence M. "Distribution and Significance of the Foreign Trade Ports of Norway," EG, 36 (1960), 306-12.

Steen, Tryggve B. "Oslo," ScPP, III, 412-24.

Terry, Beatrice. "Narvik, Norway," JofGeo, 39 (1940), 183-86.

SPITSBERGEN (SVALBARD)

Brown, Robert N. Rudmose. "The Commercial Development of Spitsbergen," SGM, 28 (1912), 561-71.
——. "Mining Development in Spitsbergen," SGM, 38 (1922), 115-17.
——. The Polar Regions: a Physical and Economic Geography of the Arctic and Antarctic. Lond., 1927. 245 p.
——. "Preservation of Wild Life in Spitsbergen," SGM, 43 (1927), 167-70.
——. "Recent Developments in Spitsbergen," SGM, 36 (1920), 111-16.
——. Spitsbergen. An Account of Exploration, Hunting, the Mineral Riches and Future Potentialities of an Arctic Archipelago. Lond., 1920. 319 p.
——. "Svalbard of Today," SGM, 66 (1950), 173-77.
Cadell, H. M. "Coal-Mining in Spitsbergen," Transactions of the Federal Institution of Mining Engineers, 9 (1920), 119-42.
Conway, William M. C. No Man's Land: a History of Spitsbergen from Its Discovery in 1596 to the Beginning of the Scientific Exploration of the Country. Cambridge, Eng., 1906. 377 p.
Floyd, Calvin J. "Svalbard: Crossroads of the Arctic," ASR, 50 (1962), 153-60.
Fraser, R. A. "The Sledge Journey," GeogJ, 64 (1924), 193-204.
Glen, A. R. "The Oxford University Expedition of Spitsbergen, 1933," GeogJ, 84 (1934), 104-35.
Haverfield, F. "The Coal and Iron Ores of Spitsbergen," Nature, 102 (1919), 310.
Hoel, Adolf. The Norwegian Svalbard Expeditions, 1906-1926 (Skrifter om Svalbard og Ishavet). Oslo, 1929. 104 p.
Howe, Fisher. "Black Coal in a White Land," FSJ, 38 (1961, no. 9), 51-52.
Illingworth, Frank. "Spitzbergen," CR, 177 (1950), 108-11.
Iversen, Thor. "The Coal and Who Owns It," ASR, 12 (1924), 230-37.
Longyear, John M. "Spitsbergen — the World's Most Northerly Coal Bin," ASR, 5 (1917), 206-11.
Mathiesen, Trygve. Svalbard in the Changing Arctic. Oslo, 1954.
"Mining in Norway and at Spitzbergen and Metal Production," NorAmCom (Je 1949), 36-39+.
Norway, Norges Svalbard og Ishavsundersøkelser. The Place-Names of Svalbard (Skrifter om Svalbard og Ishavet, no. 80). Oslo, 539 p. Supplement, new names 1935-55 (Norsk

Polarinstitutt, Skrifter, no. 112). By Anders K. Orvin. Oslo, 1958.
——. Report on the Activities of Norges Svalbard og Ishavs-undersøkelser, 1927-1936. Oslo, 1937.
——. The Survey of Bjørnøya (Bear Island) 1922-1931. Oslo, 1944. 82 p.
Omberg, Asbjørn. "White Land of Black Coal," Norseman (1961, no. 1), 16-20.
Orvig, Svenn. "Svalbard, and Jan Mayen," in George H. T. Kimble and Dorothy Good, eds., Geography of the Northlands (N.Y., 1955), 401-14.
Orvin, Anders K. "The Settlements and Huts of Svalbard," NGT, 7 (1938/1939), 571-84.
Owen, Russell D. "The Norge at Svalbard," ASR, 14 (1926), 408-11.
Rabot, Charles. "The Norwegians in Spitsbergen," GeogR (1919), 209-26.
Relf, E. R. "The Cruise of the Terningen," GeogJ, 64 (1924), 204-13.
Siedlecki, Stanislaw. "Crossing West Spitsbergen from South to North," NGT, 7 (1938/1939), 79-91.
"Spitsbergen Mines Coal Again," NGeogM, 94 (1948), 113-20.
United States, Office of Geography. Norway: Svalbard, and Jan Mayen; Official Standard Names Approved by the United States Board on Geographic Names (U. S. Board on Geographic Names, Gazetteer no. 77). Wash., 1963. 1029 p.
Werenskiold, Werner. "The Strand Flat of Spitsbergen," GT, 52 (1952/1953), 302-309.
Wieder, Frederik C. The Dutch Discovery and Mapping of Spitsbergen, 1596-1829. Amsterdam, 1919. 124 p.
Wordie, J. M. "Present-Day Conditions in Spitsbergen," GeogJ, 58 (1921), 25-49.

SWEDEN

"Agricultural Atlas of Sweden," Stock., 1952.
Ahlberg, Gösta. "Population Trends and Urbanization in Sweden, 1911-1950," LSG, Series B, 16 (1956), 31 p.
Ahlmann, Hans W. "The Economic Geography of Swedish Norrland," GeoA, 3 (1921), 97-164.
——. Norrland, the Land of Forests, Waterfalls, and Iron Mountains. Stock., 1921.
——. "Some Working Hypotheses as Regards the Geomorphology of South Sweden," GeoA, 2 (1920), 131-45.
Åkerhielm, Erik. "Småland," ASR, 16 (1928), 333-44.

Aldskogius, H. "Changing Land Use and Settlement Development in the Siljan Region," GeoA, 42 (1960), 250-61.

Arnborg, Lennart. "The Delta of Ångermanälven," GeoA, 30 (1948), 673-90.

Bagrow, Leo. Maps of the Neva River and Adjacent Areas in Swedish Archives. Malmö, 1953.

Behren, S., Karl E. Bergsten, O. Nordström, and L. Ameen. Regional Geography of Southern Sweden (Guidebook to excursion E. Sw-5 A-B). IGCong, 19th, Norden. Lund, 1960.

Bergsten, F. "The Land Uplift in Sweden from the Evidence of the Old Water Marks," GeoA, 36 (1954), 81-111.

Bergsten, Karl E. "Some Characteristics of the Dispersion of the Annual Precipitation in Sweden during the Period, 1881-1940," LSG, Series A, 1 (1950), 10 p.

——. "Variability in Intensity of Urban Fields as Illustrated by Urban Fields as Illustrated by Birth-Places" [in Southern Sweden], LSG, Series B, 3 (1951), 25-32.

Bodvall, G. "Expansion of the Permanently Settled Area in Northern Hälsingland," GeoA, 42 (1960), 244-49.

——. "Periodic Settlement, Landclearing and Cultivation, with Special Reference to the Boothlands of North Hälsingland," GeoA, 39 (1957), 213-56.

Boheman, Ezaline. "Dalarna," ASR, 18 (1930), 77-85.

Bruno, William. "The Storsjö District from a Geographico-cultural Viewpoint," Ymer, 8 (1960), 81-95. Reprinted in IGCong, 19th, as: A Geographical Excursion through Central Norrland. Stock., 1960. 128 p.

Cornish, R. T. "The Influence of Physical Features on Rural Settlement in East-Central Sweden," TIBG, 16 (1950), 125-35.

Dahl, Sven. "The Contacts of Västeras with the Rest of Sweden," LSG, Series B, 13 (1957), 206-43.

——. "New Aspects on the Economic Geography of Sweden," IGCong, 17th (1952).

Davies, D. H. A Regional Study of the Geography of Sweden. Thesis (M.A.), University of Wales, 1951.

De Geer, Sten. "A Map of the Distribution of Population in Sweden: Method of Preparation and General Results," GeoR, 12 (1922), 72-83.

Edwards, K. C. "Notes on Transhumance: Sweden," Geog, 27 (1942), 67-68.

Edwards, K. C., ed. Sweden: Dalarna Studies. Lond., 1942. 55 p.

Enequist, Gerd. Geographical Changes of Rural Settlement in Northwestern Sweden since 1523 (Uppsala Universitet, Geografiska Institution. Meddelanden. Series A, No. 143). Uppsala, 1959. 43 p.

——. "The Habitation of Sweden," IGCong, 17th (1952), 737-41.

——. "Regional Planning in Sweden: a Survey," IGCong, 17th (1952), 233-35.

Enequist, Gerd, and Gunnar Norling, eds. "Advance and Retreat of Rural Settlement. Papers of the Siljan Symposium at the XIXth International Geographical Congress," GeoA, 42 (1960), 210-93.

Erixon, Sigurd. "Villages and Common Lands in Sweden," WestSocTrans, 3 (1956), 122-34.

Friberg, Nils. "The Growth of Population and Its Economic-Geographical Background in a Mining District in Central Sweden, 1650-1750," GeoA, 38 (1956), 395-440.

——. "A Province-map of Dalecarlia by Andreas Bureus (?)," Imago Mundi, 15 (1960), 73-83.

Godlund, Sven. "Bus Services, Hinterlands, and the Location of Urban Settlements in Sweden, Specially [sic] in Scania," LSG, Series B, 3 (1951), 14-24.

——. The Function and Growth of Bus Traffic Within the Sphere of Urban Influence. LSG, Series B, 18 (1956), 80 p.

Great Britain, Admiralty Naval Intelligence Department. Handbook of Norway and Sweden. Lond., 1920. 476 p.

"Gripsholm," ASR, 31 (1943), 214-19.

Grytzell, Karl G. "The Demarcation of Comparable City Areas by Means of Population Density," LSG, Series B, 25 (1963), 111 p.

Hackett, Brian. "Towards an Urban Landscape: an Appreciation of the Swedish Urban Scene in Its Landscape Setting," Planning Outlook, 1 (1948), 25-35.

Hägerstrand, Torsten. "Migration and the Growth of Culture Regions in Sweden," LSG, Series B, 3 (1951), 33-36.

Hannerberg, David, ed. [et al.] "Migration in Sweden: a Symposium," LSG, Series B, 13 (1957), 336 p. [All papers analyzed]

Haupert, J. S. "The Impact of Geographic Location Upon Sweden as a Baltic Power," JofGeo, 58 (1959), 5-14.

Haywood, Terence. Background to Sweden. Lond., 1950. 332 p.

Hedenstierna, Bertil. "Ambrosius Thoms' South-Sweden, 1564," Imago Mundi, 9 (1952), 65-68.

Hedström, Birgit M. "Jämtland: the Province and the People," ASR, 19 (1931), 329-39.

International Geographical Congress, 19th, Stock., 1960. Economic Geographical Excursion to Middle Sweden. Ed. by Olof Jonasson with Bo Carlsund. Gothenburg, 1960. 87 p.

Kant, Edgar. "Suburbanization, Urban Sprawl and Commutation, Examples from Sweden," LSG, Series B, 13 (1957), 244-309.

Klein, Ernst. "Runö, an Old Swedish Community," ASR, 31 (1933), 407-16.

——. "Uppland," ASR, 18 (1930), 86-96.

Kulldorff, Gunnar. "Migration Possibilities," LSG, Series B, 14 (1955), 44 p.

Larsson, Ingemar. "Structure and Landscape in Western Blekinge, Southeast Sweden," LSG, Series A, 7 (1954), 176 p.

Leighly, John B. "Population and Settlement: Some Recent Swedish Studies," GeoR, 42 (1952), 134-37.

——. "The Towns of Malardalen in Sweden; a Study in Urban Morphology," University of California Publications in Geography, 3 (1928, no. 1).

Lindberg, E. "Seasonal Migration of Labour from the Siljan Area and Its Economic Background," GeoA, 42 (1960), 262-66.

Lönborg, Sven. Swedish Maps. Gothenburg, 1906.

Lundgren, Svante. Off the Beaten Track: Sweden, North of the River Dal. Stock., 1952. 160 p.

Mannerfelt, C. M. A Geographical Excursion Through Central Norrland (International Geographical Congress). Stock., 1960.

Merrild, Else. "Visby Soil Yields New Treasures," ASR, 24 (1936), 339-42.

Modin, Karl. "Boliden, the Swedish Klondyke," ASR, 22 (1934), 236-42.

Mogensen, Patrik. "A Short Résumé of Swedish Cadastral Conditions," Proceedings of the Fifth Congress of the International Federation of Surveyors (Lond., 1934), 225-27.

Montelius, Sigvard. "The Burning of Forest Land for the Cultivation of Crops — 'Svedjebruk' in Central Sweden," GeoA, 35 (1953), 41-54.

——. "Finn Settlement in Central Sweden," GeoA, 42 (1960), 285-93.

Nihlen, John. "Visby: Capital of the Baltic Crete," Art and Archaeology, 23 (1927), 175-86.

Nordell, P. O., and Harald Rydberg. "From the Plains of Middle Sweden to

the High Mountains," GeoA, 41 (1959), 170-92.

Norling, G. "Abandonment of Rural Settlement in Västerbotten Lappmark, North Sweden, 1930-1960," GeoA, 42 (1960), 232-43.

Nuttonson, M. Y. Agricultural Climatology of Sweden and Its Agroclimatic Aralogues in North America (American Institute of Crop Ecology International Agro-climatological Series, Study no. 11). Wash., 1950. 27 p.

Pålsson, Elis. "Gymnasiums and Communications in Southern Götaland," LSG, Series B, 7 (1953), 19 p.

Parenius, P. "Comments on the Development of Rural Regions in Norrland," GeoA, 42 (1960), 221-24.

Prince Wilhelm, Duke of Sörmland. "Sörmland from the Clouds," ASR, 15 (1927), 726-39.

Rosenius, Paul. "Skåne," ASR, 15 (1927), 269-82.

Spong, Berit. "Östergötland," ASR, 16 (1928), 150-64.

Steckzen, B. "Storage and Preservation of Maps in Swedish Military Archives," Indian Archives (New Delhi), 4 (1950), 14-19.

"Studies in Rural-Urban Interaction" [in Sweden], LSG, Series B, 3 (1951), 26 p.

Svedelius, Julia. "Norrbotten," ASR, 16 (1928), 77-90.

Sveriges Geologiska Undersökning. The Exhibition of the Geological Survey of Sweden at the Exhibition in Philadelphia 1876. Stock., 1876. 55 p.

——. A General Earth Magnetic Investigation of Sweden Carried Out during the Period 1928-1934 by the Geological Survey of Sweden... Part I. Stock., 1936.

——. Maps and Memoirs on Swedish Geology: a Catalogue Published by the Geological Survey of Sweden. Stock., 1910. 132 p.

Sweden, Fiskeristyrelsen med Statens Fiskeriförsök (Hydrography Series Report). 1-Gothenburg, 1952—.

Sweden, Sjöfartsstyrelsen. Charts of Average Geomagnetic Elements D, H and Z 1955 for Denmark, Finland, Norway, Sweden (Its Jordmagnetiska Publikationer, No. 18). Stock., 1958.

Sweden, Kungl. Vattenfallsstyrelse; Waterfalls of Sweden. By F. V. Hansen. Stock., 1915. 15 p.

Swedish Geographical Society. Atlas of Sweden, 1953—.

Thomas, Dorothy S. Social and Economic

Aspects of Swedish Population Movements, 1750-1933. N.Y., 1941. 487 p.

Thordeman, Bror. "The Swedish General
Staff Lithographic Institute," BC, 2 (1936),
260-64.

United States, Office of Geography. Sweden;
Official Standard Names Approved by the
United States Board on Geographic Names
(U. S. Board on Geographic Names Gaz-
etteer no. 72). Wash., 1963. 1033 p.

Vetterlund, Fredrik. "Halland," ASR, 17
(1929), 150-56.

——. "Vastergötland and Göteborg," ASR,
17 (1929), 333-43.

Wallén, Axel. Climate of Sweden (Statens
Meteorologiskhydrografiska Anstalt, No.
279). Stock., 1930.

Watts, Noel. "Kiruna; Sweden's Northernmost Mining Town," GeogM, 28 (1955),
231-41.

Wendel, Bertil. A Migration Schema; Theories and Observations. LSG, Series B,
9 (1953), 38 p.

Widén, L. "A Population Forecast for 1960-
1975," Statistical Review, 6 (1960), 357-
60.

Wirde, Gottlieb. "Blekinge," ASR, 18 (1930),
333-44.

PORTS, CITIES

Artle, Roland. The Structure of the Stockholm Economy: Toward a Framework
for Projecting Metropolitan Community
Development. Ithaca, N.Y., 1965. 197 p.

Brilioth, Börje H. "Three Hundred Years of
History in Göteborg," ASR, 11 (1923), 219-
23.

Carlson, Lucile. "Luleå and Narvik: Swedish Ore Ports," JofGeo, 52 (1953), 1-13.

De Geer, Sten. "Greater Stockholm: a Geographical Interpretation," GeoR, 13
(1923), 497-506.

Edlund, G. "The Port of Malmö, a Thriving
Swedish Seaport," Dock and Harbour Authority, 17 (1938), 157-61.

Eneborg, Helmer. "Swedish Ports," Swedish Foreign Commerce, 2 (1957), 92-94.

Freeburg, Victor O. "The Harbor of Göteborg," ASR, 8 (1920), 183-88.

Graves, Ralph A. "Granite City of the
North: Austere Stockholm, Sweden's
Prosperous Capital, Presents a Smiling
Aspect in Summer," NGeogM, 54 (1928),
403-24.

Hedvall, Yngve. "Among the Skerries of
Stockholm," ASR, 15 (1927), 160-66.

Jansson, Herman. "Swedish Ports and Harbours: Trends of Modern Development,"
Dock and Harbour Authority, 35 (May
1954), 9-14.

Jungen, E. "The Influence on the Swedish
Cities of a Situation Characterized as
Economic Expansion, Raising of Stan-
dards of Living and Full Employment,"
AnColEc, 27 (1956), 276-79.

Landgren, Gunvor. "The Imports of
Malmö," BSC, 4 (1938), 204-208.

Larsson, Yngve. "Stockholm," ScPP, III,
403-11.

Laurin, Carl G. "Stockholm," ASR, 10
(1922), 211-15.

Leche, Carl, ed. Swedish Harbours; Nautical Information and Plans of Principal
Ports and Loading Places. Stock., 1928.

Lindgren, Ivan. "Stockholm — A Brief History of Its Development," Town Planning
Review, 12 (1927), 260-66.

Møller, Anna. Stockholm, the Capital of
Sweden. Stock., 1923. 70 p.

Munthe, Gustaf L. Gothenburg: Sweden's
Gateway to the West. Stock., 1948. 92 p.

Nordin, Sven E. "The Distribution of Swedish Foreign Trade via Swedish Ports and
Frontier Railways," GeoA, 19 (1937), 84-
95.

The Port of Gothenburg. Yearbook. 1927—.
Gothenburg.

Scarlat, Sacha S. Key to Stockholm. Stock.,
1960. 117 p.

Swedish Ports: Harbours and Trade Condi-
tions of 50 Important Staple Towns and
Customs-Places, Canals and Railways.
Stock., 1923.

Vinberg, Sal. The Port of Stockholm.
Stock., 1929. 1935.

William-Olsson, W. "Stockholm: Its Structure and Development," GeoR, 30 (1940),
420-38.

——. Stockholm: Structure and Development. Stock., 1960. 90 p.

HISTORY

INTRODUCTION

Historians have contributed an excellent body of writings on Scandinavia. There has been noteworthy emphasis on the age of the Vikings, on World War II, and on the great Swedish monarchs, particularly Gustavus Adolphus, Charles XII, and Bernadotte. The extensive sources on economic history are listed under Economics; particularly good is Eli Heckscher's *An Economic History of Sweden* (1954). International Relations is a separate section of this bibliography and follows History. For the history of law, see Law; see particularly: Lester Orfield, *The Growth of Scandinavian Law* (1953). For sources on internal migration, see both Geography and Sociology. For articles on political leaders, look also under Political Science. Most of the sources on religion will be found under Sociology. This bibliography does not cover the history of literature. However, four excellent surveys sponsored by the American-Scandinavian Foundation have been included: P. M. Mitchell, *A History of Danish Literature* (1957); Stefan Einarsson, *A History of Icelandic Literature* (1957); Harald Beyer, *A History of Norwegian Literature* (1956); Alrik Gustafson, *A History of Swedish Literature* (1961). With the exception of the *Scandinavian Economic History Review*, there is no English-language journal of Scandinavian history. Historical articles appear frequently, however, in *The American-Scandinavian Review*, which contains a section on "The Quarter's History" in each issue.

For a highly readable twentieth-century history of the five countries, see John Wuorinen's *Scandinavia* (1965), available in paperback format. There is only one general history of Scandinavia, Stanley Toyne's *The Scandinavians in History* (1948). Both scholar and layman will appreciate the three magnificent, richly illustrated volumes of *Scandinavia Past and Present* (1959), a compendium on the development of Scandinavian civilization. Among the books on Scandinavia as a whole, several merit mention. A scholarly landmark and basic book for students of the sixteenth century is Oskar Garstein's *Rome and the Counter-Reformation in Scandinavia, 1539-1583* (1963), which is the first volume in a two-volume study. Brynjolf Hovde's two-volume work, *The Scandinavian Countries 1720-1865; The Rise of the Middle Classes* (1943) is essential for those wishing to examine the early development of modern democracy. The basic book on Scandinavian unionism is Theodore Jorgenson's *Norway's Relations to Scandinavian Unionism, 1815-1871* (1935). Two very good books on Scandinavia in the world wars are *Sweden, Norway, Denmark, and Iceland in the World War* (1930), by Eli Heckscher et al.; and *The Northern Tangle; Scandinavia and the Post-War World* (1946), by Rowland Kenney. Many of the books on the world wars are listed under International Relations.

On the pre-Viking period, the most readable presentations are Ole Klindt-Jensen's *Denmark before the Vikings* (1957), and Marten Stenberger's *Sweden* (1962), which likewise covers only the pre-Viking

period. *Scandinavian Archeology* (1937) by
Haakon Shetelig and Hjalmar Folk is well
known. The literature on the Viking age is
based principally upon sagas and artifacts.
There are many excellent introductions,
among them the Penguin Books paperback
by Danish archeologist Johannes Brøndsted,
The Vikings; P. H. Sawyer's very good *The
Age of the Vikings* (1962); and Eric Oxenstierna's enthusiastic *The Norsemen* (1965).
Holger Arbman's *The Vikings* (1961) is particularly strong with regard to art, archeology, and economic factors; Axel Olrik's
Viking Civilization (1930) is a broad survey.
Mary Williams' *Social Scandinavia in the
Viking Age* (1920) remains a basic book on
the social system. On religion, see Gabriel
Turville-Petre's *Myth and Religion of the
North: The Religion of Ancient Scandinavia*
(1964). Haakon Melberg's two-volume *Origin of the Scandinavian Nations and Lan-
guages* (1949-1952) is a history of linguistic
development suited mainly for the philolo-
gist. Thomas Kendrick, in *A History of the
Vikings* (1930), places great emphasis on the
Vikings abroad. Thamar Dufwa's *The Viking
Laws and the Magna Carta* (1963) is a capti-
vating and provocative little book. Laurence
Larson's *Canute the Great and the Rise of
Danish Imperialism During the Viking Age*
(1912) likewise ties into English history.

On the discoveries of America, which
are of course covered in the surveys cited
above, there is an extensive but highly repetitive specialized literature. One might
well begin with Gwyn Jones' fine treatment,
The Norse Atlantic Saga (1964), available
from Oxford University Press. Penguin
Books recently published, in paperback, *The
Vinland Sagas — The Norse Discovery of
America* (1965). It includes new translations. For an entertaining yet scholarly effort, one may recommend Farley Mowat's
*West-viking: The Ancient Norse in Greenland
and North America* (1965); it includes saga
translations and presents fresh and controversial interpretations. Very readable is
the work of explorer Helge Ingstad, *Land
Under the Pole Star* (1966), which has been a
best-seller in Scandinavia. A scholarly
landmark is *The Vinland Map and the Tartar
Relation* (1965) by R. A. Skelton, Thomas
Marston, and George Painter; it is significant for its cartographical evidence of the
existence of Vinland.

The various sagas recorded by the
great Icelandic historian Snorri Sturluson
(1179-1241) have been published in numerous
translations and editions. They are very

significant for Norwegian, as well as Icelandic, history. Some translations are pain-
fully archaic. The sagas are numerous, and
many of them have not been included in this
bibliography. Listed here, with the help of
Professor Lee Hollander of the University
of Texas, are some leading recent editions.
For an anthology, see H. G. Leach's fine *A
Pageant of Old Scandinavia* (1946). Histori-
ographers will be interested in Theodore
Andersson's *The Problem of Icelandic Saga
Origins* (1964), and the book by Halvdan
Koht, *The Old Norse Sagas* (1931), which includes a chapter on "Historical Value of the
Sagas." *The Icelandic Sagas* (1962) by Peter
Hallberg and Paul Schach, contains reliable
information on the saga literature, editions,
translations, and commentaries.

On Iceland there are only a few histories, but they complement one another
nicely. Knut Gjerset, widely esteemed for
his two-volume history of Norway, also
wrote a *History of Iceland* (1925), which remains the basic work. The Sturlung Age, in
which the historian Sturluson lived, is presented in Einar Sveinsson's *The Age of the
Sturlungs: Icelandic Civilization in the 13th
Century* (1954). William Chamberlin has
provided an economic history which is the
only scholarly book on the Icelandic economy: *Economic Development of Iceland
through World War II* (1947). In addition, it
is appropriate again to mention Stefan
Einarsson's *A History of Icelandic Literature* (1957).

There are several general histories of
Denmark. Most detailed is *Denmark in History* (1938) by J. H. S. Birch. The most recent history, a brief, popular, and much
more easily read presentation, is Palle
Lauring's *A History of the Kingdom of Denmark* (1960). Commendable also is John
Danstrup's *A History of Denmark* (1949,
1952). The confines of Viggo Starcke's *Denmark in World History* are indicated by the
subtitle, "The External History of Denmark
from the Stone Age to the Middle Ages with
Special Reference to the Danish Influence on
the English-Speaking Nations." Fletcher
Pratt, known to many as an historian of the
American military, has written a biography
of a 14th-century king, *Valdemar IV: The
Third King* (1950). John Gade has provided
two biographies, *Christian IV, King of Denmark and Norway: a Picture of the Seventeenth Century* (1928), and *The Life and
Times of Tycho Brahe* (1947). Tycho Brahe
was a versatile astronomer of the sixteenth
century. Between 1430 and 1660 Denmark

controlled the gateway to the Baltic, and until 1857 Denmark continued to levy sound
dues. The basic book on these four centuries of activity is Charles Hill's *The Danish
Sound Dues and the Command of the Baltic:
a Study of International Relations* (1926);
this is a fine book. Oliver Warner's *The
Sea and the Sword: the Baltic 1630-1945*
(1965) is a broad history, focused in part on
Poland. As one might expect, there are both
books and dissertations on N. F. S. Grundtvig (1783-1872); see Education. For the
Schleswig-Holstein conflict, look under the
next section, International Relations. For
Danish rule in the West Indies, the basic
book is Waldemar Westergaard's *The Danish
West Indies Under Company Rule* (1917).
Charles Tansill, an American diplomatic
historian, wrote his *The Purchase of the
Danish West Indies* (1932) from primarily
American sources and only very fleetingly
from the viewpoint of Danish politics.

For none of the Northern Countries is
there a better introductory literature than
for Finland. John Wuorinen's *A History of
Finland* (1965) is an excellent presentation
of twentieth-century domestic politics, economic development, and foreign affairs.
Eino Jutikkala, in his *A History of Finland*
(1962), very ably traces Finnish history up
to the twentieth century. Those wishing a
more general introduction to Finland might
look at J. Hampden Jackson's *Finland* (1938).
For those who enjoy biography, *The Memoirs of Marshal Mannerheim* (1953) is en-
thusiastically recommended. On the growth
of Finnish nationalism, John Wuorinen's *Nationalism in Modern Finland* (1931) is basic
and very good, but attention should also be
attracted to two other studies: Anders
Myhrman's *The Swedish Nationality Movement in Finland* (1939), and Pekka Hamalainen's dissertation, *The Nationality Struggle
Between the Finns and the Swedish-Speaking
Minority in Finland, 1917-1939* (1966). Many
of the best books on the last forty years of
Finnish history are listed under International Relations. For a guide to these books,
see the introduction to that section.

The standard history of Norway is
Karen Larsen's *A History of Norway* (1948).
For a shorter work, half of which treats the
period since 1814, see T. K. Derry's *A
Short History of Norway* (1957). The two-
volume set by Knut Gjerset, *History of the
Norwegian People* (1915, 1932), which prior
to Larsen's book was the basic history in
English, is still highly commendable. *The
Voice of Norway* (1944) by Halvdan Koht and

Sigmund Skard, is very readable general
history. The first half is by Koht, "Free
Men Build Their Society;" the second half is
a parallel history of literature by Skard,
"Life Unfolds in Literature." There are
five regional histories by Frank Stagg, all
published between 1952 and 1958: *East Norway and Its Frontier; The Heart of Norway;
North Norway; South Norway; West Norway
and Its Fjords.* On Norwegian historians,
see Leslie Smith's *Modern Norwegian Historiography* (1962).

Among the writings on the various centuries are several landmarks. One of these
is a biography by G. M. Gathorne-Hardy of
a late twelfth-century king: *A Royal Imposter: King Sverre of Norway* (1956). *Kristin
Lavransdatter* (1920-1922), the three-volume
novel for which Sigrid Undset was awarded
the Nobel Prize for Literature, deals with
fourteenth-century rural life. On the Hanseatic League, see John Gade's *The Hanseatic Control of Norwegian Commerce
During the Late Middle Ages* (1951). The
leading works on the nineteenth century are:
Oscar Falnes, *National Romanticism in Norway* (1933); Theodore Jorgenson, *Norway's
Relations to Scandinavian Unionism, 1815-
1871* (1935); Raymond Lindgren, *Norway-
Sweden; Union, Disunion and Scandinavian
Integration* (1959).

Unfortunately, there is not yet a history
of twentieth-century Norway. The best
works on the world wars are noted in the
next section, International Relations. There
is a book on Haakon VII, king from 1905 to
1957, who was widely acclaimed for his
leadership in World War II: Maurice Michael, *Haakon, King of Norway* (1958). For
the opening of World War II in Norway, see
Carl Hambro's *I Saw It Happen in Norway*
(1940). For the campaigns in detail, there
are excellent volumes by T. K. Derry, *The
Campaign in Norway* (1952), and by J. L.
Moulton, *The Norwegian Campaign of 1940*
(1966); Derry's is the more detailed. Ralph
Hewins' *Quisling; Prophet Without Honour*
(1965) is not a generally accepted interpretation. The best broad survey is *Norway and
the Second World War* (1966) by Johs. Andenaes, Olav Riste, and Magne Skodvin. Amanda
Johnson's *Norway, Her Invasion and Occupation* (1948) is good, and one may wish also to
consult William Warbey's *Look to Norway*
(1945). One unpublished dissertation merits
mention: George Williams, *Blitzkrieg and
Conquest: Policy Analysis of Military and
Political Decisions Preparatory to the German Attack upon Norway, April 9, 1940* (1966).

There are several biographies of Fridtjof Nansen. As most of them stress his life and accomplishments as explorer and scientist, it may be helpful to point out those biographies which focus at least in part on his life as diplomat and humanitarian and on his role in politics. Very good are Jon Sörenson's *The Saga of Fridtjof Nansen* (1932) and Ernest Reynold's *Nansen* (revised edition, 1949). *Fridtjof Nansen* (1961), edited by Per Vogt, is a centennial collection of very good articles about the various facets of Nansen's life. For Nansen's writings on the union crisis of 1905, look in this section under Sweden.

The present standard history of Sweden is Ingvar Andersson's *A History of Sweden* (1956), but this reviewer regards Andrew Stomberg's *A History of Sweden* (1931) as being in many ways the best history available in English. Most recent is Stewart Oakley's *A Short History of Sweden* (1966), which is very worthwhile but weighted toward the periods prior to the nineteenth century; it contains a good, up-to-date annotated bibliography. The *History of Sweden* (1938) by Carl Hallendorf and Adolf Schück, and *A History of Sweden* (1935) by Carl Grimberg are also good general histories. The most significant of Michael Roberts' articles on the sixteenth, seventeenth, and eighteenth centuries have been gathered in one volume, *Essays in Swedish History* (1967). There is an extensive literature on the lives and times of the various Swedish monarchs who either achieved greatness or were peculiarly interesting. To this reviewer's surprise, there seem to be no scholarly books published in this century in English on Gustav Vasa, Charles X, or Oscar II. On Gustav Vasa, one can point only to Paul Watson's *The Swedish Revolution under Gustavus Vasa* (1889). On Gustavus Adolphus, the definitive work is Michael Roberts' two-volume study entitled *Gustavus Adolphus, A History of Sweden, 1611-1632* (1953, 1958). Nils Ahnlund's *Gustav Adolph, the Great* (1940) is very fine. Conveniently re-issued in paperback is Charles Fletcher's *Gustavus Adolphus and the Thirty Years War* (1966 ed.).

Queen Christina has been the subject of numerous biographies; while this reviewer is not familiar with all of them, he does want to recommend two: Paul Lewis, *Queen of Caprice: a Biography of Kristina of Sweden* (1962), and Margaret Goldsmith, *Christina of Sweden: a Psychological Biography* (1933).

On Charles XII, the best recent book is Frans Bengtsson's *The Sword Does Not Jest: the Heroic Life of King Charles XII of Sweden* (1960). Wonderfully readable, of course, is Voltaire's account, *History of Charles XII, King of Sweden*, of which there have been many editions. Nisbet Bain, an eminent historian of Sweden, also provides an account: *Charles XII and the Collapse of the Swedish Empire, 1682-1719* (1895). An unpublished dissertation on the Charles XII era is *The Maritime Powers and Sweden, 1698-1702* (1959) by Edward Natharius. Nisbet Bain wrote our only major account of Gustavus III: *Gustavus III and His Contemporaries, 1747-1792* (1894). On Gustavus IV there is a two-volume biography by Sophie Elkan, *An Exiled King, Gustaf Adolf IV of Sweden* (1913).

The life of Bernadotte (Charles XIV or Karl XIV Johan) has been the subject of four volumes by Sir Dunbar Barton, who first completed a three-volume study and thereafter wrote a single-volume biography entitled *The Amazing Career of Bernadotte, 1763-1844* (1929). The volumes in the original set bear the titles *Bernadotte, the First Phase, 1763-1799* (1914); *Bernadotte and Napoleon, 1763-1810* (1921); *Bernadotte, Prince and King, 1810-1844* (1925). Solid works also are Franklin Scott's *Bernadotte and the Fall of Napoleon* (1935), and Friedrich Wencher's *Bernadotte* (1936). On the Norwegian-Swedish union and its disintegration, one should read Raymond Lindgren's excellent *Norway-Sweden; Union, Disunion and Scandinavian Integration* (1959). There is a commendable history of Sweden focusing exclusively on the first half of the twentieth century: Fritiof Ander's *The Building of Modern Sweden: the Reign of Gustav V, 1907-1950* (1958). For the numerous studies in Swedish economic history, see Economics.

SCANDINAVIA

American-Scandinavian Review. "The Quarter's History." A section in each issue summarizing current events, beginning Winter, 1932. [Prior to 1932 this section was entitled "Current Events"]

Ekman, Ernst. "The Teaching of Scandinavian History in the United States," ScSt, 37 (1965), 259-70.

Hertzberg, Sidney. "Nations of Northern Europe," CH, 39 (1933/34), 239-42; 368-71.

Malmström, Vincent H. Norden: Crossroads of Destiny and Progress. Princeton, N.J., 1965. 128 p.

Scandinavian Council for Applied Research. Scandinavian Research Guide. 2 vols. Blindern, Norway, 1960.

Toyne, Stanley M. The Scandinavians in History. Lond., N.Y., 1948. 352 p.

Wuorinen, John H. "Nations of Northern Europe," CH, 34 (1931), 626-30; 783-86; 469-71.

——. Scandinavia. Englewood Cliffs, N.J., 1965. 146 p.

PRE-HISTORY

Abercromby, John. The Pre- and Proto-Historic Finns; Both Eastern and Western with the Magic Songs of the West Finns. 2 vols. Lond., 1898.

Althin, Carl A. G. The Chronology of the Stone Age Settlement of Scania, Sweden (Acta Archaelogia Lundensis). Lond., 1954.

——. "New Finds of Mesolithic Art in Scania (Sweden)," AcAr, 21 (1950), 253-60.

"Archaeological Investigations and Finds in the Scandinavian Countries in the Year 1934-[1937], A Summary," AcAr, 6 (1935) 261-82; 7 (1936), 308-339; 8 (1937), 301-36; 9 (1938), 231-53.

Arwidsson, Greta. "Armour of the Vendel Period," AcAr, 10 (1939), 31-69.

——. "A New Scandinavian Form of Helmet from the Vendel Time," AcAr, 5 (1934), 243-57.

Baeksted, Anders. "The Runic Inscriptions from the Lindholm Cemetery," AcAr, 24 (1953), 196-99.

Becker, C. J. "An Arctic-Type Arrow Head from North Jutland," AcAr, 29 (1958), 157-61.

——. "Arrow or Spear Heads? Observations on Some Tanged Flint Points Belonging to the Pitted Ware Culture in Scandinavia." AcAr, 27 (1956), 137-48.

——. "The Date of the Neolithic Settlement at Trelleborg," AcAr, 27 (1956), 91-108.

——. "Flint Mining in Neolithic Denmark," Antiquity, 33 (1959), 87-92.

——. "The Introduction of Farming into Northern Europe," Journal of World History 2 (1955), 749-66.

——. "An Irish Bronze Cauldron Found in Jutland," AcAr, 20 (1949), 265-70.

——. "Late-Neolithic Flint Mines at Aalborg," AcAr, 22 (1951), 135-52.

——. "A Neolithic Antler Weapon from Rye Aa, North Jutland," AcAr, 27 (1956), 148-53.

——. "The Pitted-Ware Culture in Denmark," Aarbøger for Nordisk Oldkyndighed og Historie (1950), 265-74.

——. "The Second Flint Arrow-Head from Snejstrup, North Jutland," AcAr, 28 (1957), 201-203.

——. "A Segmented Faience Bead from Jutland; With Notes on Amber Beads from Bronze Age Denmark," AcAr, 25 (1954), 241-52.

Brøgger, Anton W. The Prehistoric Settlement of Northern Norway (Bergens Museums Årbok, v. 3, Historiskantikvarisk Rekke, no. 2, 1933), 15 p.

Broholm, Hans C. "Anthropomorphic Bronze Age Figures in Denmark," AcAr, 18 (1947), 196-202.

——. "The Bronze Age People in Denmark," AcAr, 13 (1942), 100-49.

——. Costumes of the Bronze Age in Denmark: Contributions to the Archaeology and Textile-History of the Bronze Age. Coph., 1940. 172 p.

——. "Danish Records of the Past Now Housed in Their New Home," ASR, 24 (1936), 116-28.

——. "The Inhabitants of Denmark in the Bronze Age: Corrections and Supplements," AcAr, 15 (1944), 201-209.

——. Yngre Bronzealder; Late Bronze Age [Text in Danish and English]. Coph., 1953. 104 p.

Broholm, Hans C., William P. Larsen, and Godtfred Skjerne. The Lures of the Bronze Age: an Archaeological Technical and Musicological Investigation. Coph., 1949. 129 p.

Brøndsted, Johannes. "Bronze Age Clothing," ASR, 43 (1955), 376-82.

——. "Danish Arm-and-Hand Carvings," AcAr, 12 (1941), 119-25.

——. "The Danish Lurs, Aspects of the Religious Life of the Bronze Age in Denmark," ASR, 18 (1930), 416-22.

——. "An Early Bronze Age Hoard in the

Danish National Museum," AcAr, 2 (1931), 111-16.

------. "Human Figures on a Danish Mesolithic Urus Bone," AcAr, 11 (1940), 207-12.

------. "News from Ancient Denmark," ASR, 36 (1948), 330-41.

------. "Out of the Dim Past," ASR, 17 (1929), 24-29.

Bröste, Kurt. Prehistoric Man in Denmark: a Study in Physical Anthropology. Vol. 1, Stone and Bronze Ages. Coph., 1956. 598 p.

Brown, John C. People of Finland in Archaic Times. Lond., 1892. 290 p.

Burnham, Robert E. Who Are the Finns: a Study in Prehistory. Lond., 1946. 90 p.

Chamberlain, A. F. "Prehistoric Finland," American Antiquarian, 23 (1903), 42-44.

Christiansen, Reidar T. The Migratory Legends: a Proposed List of Types with a Systematic Catalogue of the Norwegian Variants (FF Communications, no. 175). Hels., 1958. 221 p.

Clark, John G. D. The Mesolithic Settlement of Northern Europe. A Study of the Food Gathering Peoples of Northern Europe During the Early Post-Glacine Period. Cambridge, 1936. 283 p.

Copenhagen, Nationalmuseet. The Danish Collections; Antiquity (Guides to the National Museum). Coph., 1938. 116 p.; 2d ed., Coph., 1952.

Curtin, L. S. M. "Archaeological Finds in the Peat Bogs of Finland and Other Countries," El Palacio, 66 (1959), 53-58.

Curwen, E. C. "Early Agriculture in Denmark," Antiquity, 12 (1938), 135-53.

Dreyer, W. "The Main Features of the Advance in the Study of Danish Archeology," AmAnthro, 10 (1908), 505-30.

Eldjárn, Kristján. "Carved Panels from Flatatunga, Iceland," AcAr, 24 (1953), 81-101.

------. "Romans in Iceland," ASR, 39 (1951), 123-26.

Erä-Esko, Aarni. "Sutton Hoo and Finland," Speculum, 28 (1953), 514-15.

Erixon, Sigurd. "The North-European Technique of Corner Timbering," Folkliv, 1 (1937), 13-60.

Fett, Per. "Arms in Norway Between 400-600 A.D.," in Bergens Museum Årsbok, 1938, no. 2; 1939, no. 1.

"Flint Mining in Neolithic Denmark," Antiquity, 33 (1959), 87-92.

Flom, George T. "A Recently Discovered Stone Sculpture in Öland, Sweden," AmAnthro, 24 (1922), 441-47.

Freundt, E. A. "Komsa-Fosna-Sandarna. Problems of the Scandinavian Mesolithicum," AcAr, 19 (1948), 1-68.

Gjessing, Gutorm. Yngre Steinalder; Nord-Norge; With a Summary in English. Cambridge, Mass., 1942. 525 p.

Glob, P. V. "Lifelike Man Preserved 2,000 Years in Peat: a Danish Bog Yields Remains of Human Sacrifice That Helps Reconstruct the Life of Europe's Ancient Tribes," NGeogM, 105 (1954), 419-30.

------. "Ploughs of the Døstrup Type Found in Denmark," AcAr, 16 (1945), 93-111.

Grieg, Sigurd. "The House in Norwegian Archaeology," AcAr, 13 (1942), 169-78.

Grinsell, L. V. "The Kivik Cairn, Scania," Antiquity, 16 (1942), 160-74.

Hagen, Anders. "The Excavations at Hunn," ASR, 42 (1954), 135-44.

Hald, Margrethe. "Ancient Textile Techniques in Egypt and Scandinavia, A Comparative Study," AcAr, 17 (1946), 49-98.

Hallström, Gustav. Monumental Art of Northern Sweden from the Stone Age: Nämforsen and Other Localities. Stock., 1960. 401 p.

Hatt, Gudmund. "A Dwelling Site of Early Migration Period at Oxbøl, Southwest Jutland," AcAr, 29 (1958), 142-54.

------. "An Early Roman Iron Age Dwelling Site in Holmsland, West Jutland," AcAr, 24 (1953), 1-25.

------. "Iron Age Cellars at Baekmoien, North Jutland," AcAr, 30 (1959), 201-16.

------. Nørre Fjand, An Early Iron Age Village Site in West Jutland (Det kgl. danske Vidensk. Selsk. Arkaeologisk-kunsthistoriske Skrifter, Bd. 2, no. 2). 382 p.

------. "Prehistoric Fields in Jylland," AcAr, 2 (1931), 117-58.

Hatting, Jørgen. "The North Friesians: the Seventh Nordic People," DO, 1 (1948), 106-10.

Helbaek, Hans. "Preserved Apples and Panicum in the Prehistoric Site at Nørre Sandegaard in Bornholm," AcAr, 23 (1952), 107-15.

------. "Spelt (Tritisum spelta L.) in Bronze Age Denmark," AcAr, 23 (1952), 97-107.

Hermannsson, Halldór. Icelandic Manuscripts. Ithaca, N.Y., 1929. 80 p.

Hildebrand, Hans. The Industrial Arts of Scandinavia in the Pagan Time. Lond., 1883. 150 p.

Holst, Hans. "Numismatica; I, Remarks Concerning Some of the Ptolemaic Coins in the Numismatic Cabinet of the University; II, The Roman-Byzantine Coins of the Hoenfind; III, Roman and Byzantine

Gold Coins, Found in Norway; IV, Three Unpublished Roman and Byzantine Silver Coins, Found in Norway; V, Roman Bronze Coins, Found in Norway, Charon's Obulus," Symbolae Osloenses, 6 (1929), 69-76; 7 (1928), 83-91; 8 (1929), 114-19; 9 (1930), 106-14.

——. "Numismatica VII, Roman and Byzantine Gold and Silver Coins Found in Norway" Symbolae Osloenses, fasc. 14 (1935), 115-18.

Hougen, Björn. The Migration Style of Ornament in Norway. Catalogue of the Exhibition of Norwegian Jewellery from the Migration Period. Oslo, 1936. 43 p. [34 plates]

Janson, Sverker, and Olaf Vessberg. Swedish Archaeological Bibliography, 1939-1948. Uppsala, 1951. 360 p.

Jansson, Sven B. F. "On Nordic Runes," ScPP, I, 73-98.

——. The Runes of Sweden. Stock., N.Y., 1962. 165 p.

Jessen, Knud. "Archaeological Dating in the History of North Jutland's Vegetation," AcAr, 5 (1934), 185-214.

——. "The Environment and Dating of the Vebbestrup Plough. With Observations on the Age of the Walle Plough," AcAr, 16 (1945), 67-91.

Kivikoski, Ella. "New Light on Finland's Past," Archaeology, 12 (1959), 251-57.

Klindt-Jensen, Ole. Denmark before the Vikings (Ancient Peoples and Places). Lond., N.Y., 1957. 212 p.

——. Foreign Influences in Denmark's Early Iron Age. Coph., 1950. 248 p. Also in AcAr, 20 (1949), 1-229.

Larsen, Henning. An Old Icelandic Miscellany. Mo. Royal Irish Academy 23 D. 43. With a Supplement from Mo. Trinity College (Dublin), L. 2. 27. Oslo, 1931. 328 p.

Lauring, Palle. Land of the Tollund Man: the Prehistory and Archaeology of Denmark. Lond., 1957. 160 p.

——. "Preserved for Two Thousand Years," ASR, 41 (1953), 343-50.

Lethbridge, Thomas C. Herdsmen and Hermits: Celtic Seafarers in the Northern Seas. Lond., 1950. 146 p.

Lid, Nils. "Scandinavian Heathen Cult Places," Folkliv, 21 (1957), 79-84.

Lindqvist, Sune. "Wendel-time Finds from Valsgärde in the Neighbourhood of Old Uppsala," AcAr, 2 (1932), 21+.

Marstrander, Sverre. "New Rock Carvings of Bronze Age Type in the District of Trøndelag, Norway," in Acts of the 3d

Session of the International Congress of Pre- and Protohistoric Sciences (Zurich, 1953).

Mathiassen, Therkel. "Blubber Lamps in the Ertebølle Culture?" AcAr, 6 (1935), 139-51.

——. "Norse Ruins in Labrador?" AmAnthro, 30 (1928), 569-79.

——. "Prehistory in Denmark, 1939-1945," Proceedings of the Prehistory Society, 11 (1945), 61-65.

——. "Some Recently Found Reindeer Antler Implements in Denmark," AcAr, 9 (1938), 173-75.

——. "Some Unusual Danish Harpoons," AcAr, 9 (1938), 224-28.

——. "Two New Danish Implements of Reindeer Antler," AcAr, 12 (1941), 125-34.

Melberg, Håkon. Origin of the Scandinavian Nations and Languages (his Scandinavian and Celtic Series, Book 1, pt. 1-2). 2 vols. Oslo, Coph., 1949-1952. 952 p.

Molte, Erik. "The Asmild Rune Stone," ASR, 41 (1953), 222-27.

Monge, Alf, and O. G. Landsverk. Norse Medieval Cryptograms in Runic Carvings. Glendale, Calif., 1967. 228 p.

Montelius, Oscar. Remains From the Iron Age in Scandinavia. Stock., 1869. 66 p.

Munksgaard, Elisabeth. "Collared Gold Necklets and Armlets. A Remarkable Danish Fifth Century Group," AcAr, 24 (1953), 67-80.

——. "Late Antique Scrap Silver Found in Denmark: the Hardenberg, Høstentorp and Simmersted Hoards," AcAr, 26 (1955), 31-67.

Nerman, Birger. The Poetic Edda in the Light of Archaeology (Viking Society for Northern Research. Extra Series, v. 14). Lond., 1931. 94 p.

Nielsen, Viggo. "Another Blade Handle of Reindeer Antler," AcAr, 17 (1946), 135-39.

Nordman, C. A. "The Archaeological Literature of Finland in 1932," Man, 23 (1923), 192-94.

——. "The Cultures and Peoples of Prehistoric Finland," Journal of the Royal Anthropological Institute of Great Britain and Ireland, 63 (1933), 111-22.

Norling-Christensen, H. "The Haraldsted Burial Ground and the Early Migration Period," Aarbøger for Nordisk Oldkyndighed og Historie (1956), 76-143.

——. "The Viksø Helmets: a Bronze Age Votive Find from Zealand," AcAr, 17 (1946), 99-115.

Norn, Otto. "Serlio and Denmark," Analecta Romana, (1960), 105-21.

Oldeberg, A. "A Contribution to the History of the Scandinavian Bronze Lur in the Bronze and Iron Ages," AcAr, 18 (1947), 1-91.

Osborn, H. F. Our Ancestors Arrive in Scandinavia. 1924.

Paulli, Richard. "Dyrehavsbakken, an Ancient Playground of Copenhagen," ASR, 15 (1927), 717-25.

"Primeval Scandinavia." Eleven articles by Roar Skovmand and four by Niels Th. Mortensen, ScPP, I, 31-72.

Ramskou, Thorkild. "Lindholm: Preliminary Report of the 1952-1953 Excavation of a Late Iron Age Cemetery and an Early Mediaeval Settlement," AcAr, 24 (1953), 186-96.

———. "Lindholm Høje: Second Preliminary Report for the Years 1954-55 on the Excavation of a Late Iron Age Cemetery and an Early Mediaeval Settlement," AcAr, 26 (1955), 177-85.

———. "Lindholm Høje: Third Preliminary Report for the Years 1956-1957 on the Excavation of a Late Iron Age Cemetery and an Early Mediaeval Settlement," AcAr, 28 (1957), 193-201.

———. "Some Scandinavian Iron Age Bronze Brooches," AcAr, 17 (1946), 126-35.

Rasmussen, Holger. Prehistoric Dane. Coph., 1956. 36 p.

Riis, P. J. "The Danish Bronze Vessels of Greek Early Campanian and Etruscan Manufactures," AcAr, 20 (1959), 1-50.

Rydbeck, Otto. "The Earliest Settling of Man in Scandinavia," AcAr, 1 (1930), 55-86.

Sandklef, Albert. "Are Scandinavian Flint Saws to be Considered as Leaf Knives?" AcAr, 5 (1934), 284-90.

Scargill, M. H. "Evidence of Totemism in Edda and Saga," ASR, 40 (1952), 146-49.

Shetelig, Haakon. Classical Impulses in Scandinavian Art from the Migration Period to the Viking Age (Instituttet for Sammenlignende Kulturforskning, Series A: Forelesninger, 19). Lond., Oslo, 1949. 151 p.

———. "Roman Coins Found in Iceland," Antiquity, 23 (1949), 161-63.

Shetelig, Haakon, and Hjalmar Falk. Scandinavian Archeology. Oxford, 1937. 435 p.

Simonsen, Povl. "An Animal-Headed Dagger from Karlebotn in East Finnmark," AcAr, 25 (1954), 304-309.

———. "Recent Research on East Finn-

mark's Stone Age," Rivista di Scienze Prehistoriche, 13 (1958), 131-50.

Sjövold, Thorleif. Iron Settlement of Arctic Norway: a Study in the Expansion of European Iron Age Culture within the Arctic Circle: 1, Early Iron Age (Roman and Migration Periods). Oslo, 1962. 253 p.

Skjelsvik, Elizabeth. The Stave Circles and Related Monuments of Norway. Congreso Internacional de Ciencias Prehistóricas y Protohistóricas. Actas de la IV Session. Madrid, 1954.

Skovmand, Roar. "Southern Scandinavian Bronze Age," ScPP, I, 49-54.

Steensberg, Axel. "North West European Plough-types of Prehistoric Times and the Middle Ages," AcAr, 7 (1936), 244-80.

———. "Primitive Black Pottery in Jutland," Folkliv, 3 (1939), 113-45.

———. "The Vebbestrup Plough: an Iron Age Plough of the Crook-ard Type from a Jutland Bog," AcAr, 16 (1945), 57-66.

Stenberger, Gustav, and Ole Klindt-Jensen. Vallhager: a Migration Period Settlement in Gotland, Sweden. 2 vols. in 4 pts. Coph., 1955.

Stenberger, Mårten K. H. "Remnants of Iron Age Houses on Öland," AcAr, 2 (1931), 93-104.

———. Sweden (Ancient Peoples and Places, v. 30). Lond., N.Y., 1962. 229 p.

———. Tuna in Badelunda: a Grave in Central Sweden with Roman Vessels," AcAr, 27 (1956), 1-33.

Stephens, George. Handbook of the Old-Northern Runic Monuments of Scandinavia and England. Lond., 1884.

———. The Old-Northern Runic Monuments of Scandinavia and England, Now First Collected and Deciphered. 4 vols. Coph., Lond., 1866-1901.

———. The Runes, Whence Came They. Coph., Lond., 1894. 95 p.

Troels-Smith, J. "Geological Dating of a Reindeer Antler Hammer from Vedbaek," AcAr, 12 (1941), 135-44.

Vebaek, Christen L. "New Finds of Mesolithic Ornamented Bone and Antler Artifacts in Denmark," AcAr, 9 (1938), 205-23.

———. "Smederup, An Early Iron Age Sacrificial Bog in East Jutland," AcAr, 16 (1945), 195-211.

———. "Ten Years of Topographical and Archaeological Investigations in the Mediaeval Norse Settlements in Greenland," International Congress of Americanists Proceedings, 32 (Coph., Aug 8-14, 1956), 732-43.

Vigfússon, Gudbrander, and F. Y. Powell.
Origines Islandicae. Collections of the
more important Sagas and other writings
relating to the settlement and early history of Iceland. 2 vols. Oxford, 1905.

Voss, Olfert. "The Høstentorp Silver Hoard
and Its Period: a Study of a Danish Find
of Scrap Silver from About 500 A.D.,"
AcAr, 25 (1954), 171-219.

Wåhlin, Hans. Visby and the Ancient Civilisation of Gothland. Stock., 1938. 82 p.

Wessén, Elias. "Swedish Rune Stones,"
ASR, 21 (1933), 208-17.

Williams, Carl O. Thraldom in Ancient Iceland. Chicago, 1937. 168 p.

Worsaae, Jens J. A. The Pre-History of the
North, Based on Contemporary Memo-
rials. Lond., 1886. 206 p.

THE VIKINGS

Abeel, Neilson. "The Vikings in Ireland,"
ASR, 23 (1935), 140-47.

Almedingen, Edith M. "Vikings and
'Christ's Men'," ASR, 14 (1926), 525-31.

Anderson, Sven A. Viking Enterprise. N.Y.,
1936. 165 p.

Andersson, Theodore M. The Problem of
Icelandic Saga Origins. New Haven, 1964.
190 p.

Arbman, Holger. The Vikings (Ancient Peoples and Places, v. 21). Lond., N.Y.,
1961. 212 p.

Arngart, O. "Some Aspects of the Relation
between the English and the Danish Element in the Danelaw," Studia Neophilo-
logica, 20 (1947/48), 73-87.

Ashdown, Margaret. English and Norse
Documents Relating to the Reign of
Ethelred the Unready. Lond., 1930.
311 p.

Babcock, W. H. Early Norse Visits to North
America. Wash., 1913. 213 p.

Baerlein, Henry. "The Coming of the
Danes," Norseman, 15 (1957), 307-309.

Bengtsson, Frans G. The Long Ships: a
Saga of the Viking Age. N.Y., 1954.
503 p.; 1957 ed., 414 p. [Historical novel]

Bezemer, K. W. L. "The Fate of the Medieval Norse Colonists in Greenland," T.
Nederland. Aardrijksk. Gen., 70 (1953),
507-10.

Bibliography of Old Norse-Icelandic Studies,
1965. Coph., 1966. 77 p.

Blair, Peter H. "The Cultural Life of Cnut's
Empire," Norseman, 6 (1948), 105-108.

——. "Olaf the White and the Three Frag-
ments of Irish Annals," Viking, 3 (1939),
1-35.

Blindheim, Charlotte. "The Market Place in
Skiringssal," AcAr, 31 (1960), 83-100.

——. "New Light on Viking Trade in Norway," Archaeology, 13 (1960), 275-78.

Bremner, Robert L. The Norsemen in Alban.
Glasgow, 1923. 286 p.

Brøgger, Anton W. Ancient Emigrants: a
History of the Norse Settlements of Scotland. Oxford, 1929. 208 p.

——. "The Oseberg Ship," ASR, 9 (1921),
439-47.

——. "The Vikings of the Mediterranean
and the Vikings of the North," Annual of
the British School at Athens, 37 (Lond.,
1939), 13-20.

——. "The Vinland Voyages," ASR, 24
(1936), 197-215.

Brøgger, Anton W., and Haakon Shetelig.
The Viking Ships, Their Ancestry and
Evolution. Oslo, Los Angeles, 1953.
248 p.

Brøndsted, Johannes. "A Frog as a Viking
Age Burial Gift," AcAr, 13 (1942), 315-18.

——. "Danish Inhumation Graves of the
Viking Age: a Survey," AcAr, 7 (1936),
81-228.

——. The Vikings; An Illustrated History
of the Vikings: Their Voyages, Battles,
Customs, and Decorative Arts. Harmondsworth, 1960. 320 p.

Bruun, Daniel. The Icelandic Colonization
of Greenland and the Finding of Vineland.
Coph., 1918. 228 p.

Bugge, Alexander. Contributions to the History of the Norsemen in Ireland (Viden-
skabsselskabets skrifter; II, Historisk-
filosofisk klasse, 1900, nos. 4-6). 3 pts.
Kra., 1900.

——. "The Earliest Guilds of Northmen in
England, Norway and Denmark," in
Sproglige og historiske Afhandlinger
viede Sophus Bugges Minde (Kra., 1908),
197-209.

——. "The Norse Settlements in the British Islands," Transactions of the Royal
Historical Society, London. 4th series, 4
(1921), 173-210.

——. "The Origin and Credibility of the
Icelandic Saga," AHR, 14 (1909), 249-61.

Bugge, Anders. "The Golden Vanes of Viking Ships," AcAr, 2 (1931), 159-84.

——. "The Origin, Development and Decline of the Norwegian Stave Church,"
AcAr, 6 (1935), 152-65.

Campbell, A. "Two Notes on the Norse
Kingdoms in Northumbria," EHR, 57
(1942), 85-97.

Candlin, E. Frank. "The Last of the Vikings," Norseman, 4 (1946), 163-68.

Christiansen, Reidar T. The Vikings and
the Viking Wars in Irish and Gaelic Tradition (Skrifter utgitt av det Norske
Videnskaps-Akademi; II, Hist.-filos,
Klasse, 1930, no. 1). Oslo, 1931. 429 p.

Churchill, Winston S. "The Vikings," in his,
The Birth of Britain (Vol. I of his, A His-
tory of the English-Speaking Peoples)
(N.Y., 1956), 88-103.

Coffey, George, and E. C. R. Armstrong.
Scandinavian Objects Found at Island-
Budge and Kilmainhavn (Royal Irish
Academy Proceedings. v. 28. Sect. C.
no. 5). Dublin, 1910.

Cohen, Sidney L. Viking Fortresses of the
Trelleborg Type. Coph., 1965. 99 p.
plus 22 plates.

Coke, Dorothea. "The Coming of the Vikings to the Lea Valley," Norseman, 11
(1953), 257-58.

Connor, Franklin G. "On the Trail of the
Vikings," Bulletin of the Geographical
Society of Philadelphia, 31 (1933), 49-60.

Crone, G. R. "The Vinland Map Carto-
graphically Considered," GeogJ, 132
(1966), 75-80.

Cross, Samuel H. "Scandinavian-Polish
Relations in the Late Tenth Century," in
Studies in Honor of Hermann Collitz
(Baltimore, 1930), 114-40.

——. "Yaroslav the Wise in Norse Tradition," Speculum, 4 (1929), 177-97.

Dufwa, Thamar E. The Viking Laws and the
Magna Carta: a Study of the Northmen's
Cultural Influence in England and France.
N.Y., 1963. 92 p.

Dunlap, Maurice P. "Leidra, the Early Viking Capital of Denmark," ASR, 11 (1923),
147-52.

Dyggve, Ejnar. "Gorm's Temple and Harald's Stave-Church at Jelling," AcAr, 25
(1954), 221-39.

Egils Saga. Sigurdur Nordal Edition. Tr.
by Gwyn Jones. Syracuse, N.Y., 1960.
259 p.

Eiriks Saga Rauda. Einar Ol. Sveinsson and
Matthias Thordarson Edition (Eirik the
Red and Other Icelandic Sagas). Tr. by
Gwyn Jones. N.Y., 1961. 318 p.

Eyrbyggja Saga. Einar Ol. Sveinsson and
Matthias Thordarson Edition. Tr. by
Paul Schach and Lee M. Hollander. Lin-
coln, Nebraska, 1959. 140 p.

Fischer, Joseph. The Discoveries of the
Norsemen in America. Lond., 1903. 130 p.

Fossum, Andrew. The Norse Discovery of
America. Minneapolis, 1918. 160 p.

Franklyn, Julian. "Archaeology and the
Vikings," CR, 157 (1940), 469-75.

Gathorne-Hardy, Geoffrey M. The Norse
Discoveries of America: the Wineland
Sagas. Oxford, 1921. 304 p.

Gjessing, Gutorm. "Viking Ships in a New
Home," ASR, 22 (1934), 218-26.

Godfrey, William S. "Vikings in America:
Theories and Evidence," AmAnthro, 57
(1955), 35-43.

Goodwin, William B. The Truth about Leif
Ericsson and the Greenland Voyages.
Boston, 1941. 445 p.

Gray, Edward F. Leif Eriksson, Discoverer
of America, A.D. 1003. N.Y., 1930.
188 p.

Green, Charles. Sutton Hoo: the Excavation
of a Royal Ship Burial. N.Y., 1963.
168 p.

Grimble, Ian. "The Norsemen in Ireland,"
ASR, 40 (1952), 125-31.

Haglund, Donn K. "Brattahlid: an Ancient
Greenland Sagastead," ASR, 45 (1957),
236-46.

Hallberg, Peter, and Paul Schach. The Icelandic Saga. Lincoln, Nebraska, 1962.
179 p.

Hambro, Johan. "Norsemen Before Columbus," Norseman (1964), 166-69.

Haskins, Charles H. The Normans in European History. Boston, N.Y., 1915.
258 p.

Haugen, Einar. "Snorri Sturluson and Norway," ASR, 41 (1953), 119-27.

——. Voyages to Vinland. Chicago, 1941.
127 p.

Hencken, H. O'Neill. "A Gaming Board of
the Viking Age," AcAr, 4 (1933), 85-104.

Hermannsson, Halldor. The Problem of
Wineland. Ithaca, 1936. 84 p.

——. "The Vinland Voyages," Nord, 3
(1940), 129-37.

——. The Wineland Sagas. Ithaca, 1944.
75 p.

Hildburgh, W. L. "A Twelfth Century Cross
from Scania," Antiquity Journal, 23
(1943), 48-51.

Hobbs, W. H. "Zeno and the Cartography of
Greenland," Imago Mundi, 6 (1949), 15-19.

Holand, Hjalmar R. Explorations in America
before Columbus. N.Y., 1956. 381 p.

Hollander, Lee M. The Saga of the Jóms-
víkings. Austin, Texas, 1955. 116 p.

Homquist, Wilhelm. "Viking Art in the
Eleventh Century," AcAr, 22 (1951),
1-56.

Hovgaard, William. The Voyages of the
Norsemen to America (Scandinavian
Monographs, v. I) N.Y., 1914. 304 p.

Howorth, Henry H. "The Conquest of Norway
by the Ynglings," in Transactions of the

Royal Historical Society, London (1884), 309-63.

———. "Harald Fairhair" and His Ancestors. Two papers read before the Viking Society in London in 1918 (Sage Book of the Viking Society, v. 9, pt. 1). Lond., 1920. 252 p.

Ingstad, Helge. "Discovery of Vinland," Arctic Circular, 15 (1963), 2-5.

———. "Erik the Red," Norseman, 14 (1956), 387-91.

———. Land Under the Pole Star. Lond., N.Y., 1966.

———. "Vinland Ruins Prove Vikings Found the New World," NGeogM, 126 (1964), 708-34.

Jamieson, Peter. "The Viking Congress," Norseman, 8 (1950), 408-10.

Jones, Gwyn. The Norse Atlantic Saga, Being the Norse Voyages of Discovery and Settlement to Iceland, Greenland, America. Lond., N.Y., 1964. 246 p.

Keary, Charles F. The Vikings in Western Christendom; A.D. 789 to A.D. 888. Lond., N.Y., 1891. 571 p.

Kejlbo, Ib Rønne. "Claudius Clavus and the Vinland Map," ASR, 54 (1966), 126-31.

Kendrick, Thomas D. A History of the Vikings. N.Y., 1930, 1968. 412 p.

———. "Vikings in Great Britain" [Review of several books], Norseman, 5 (1947), 222-25.

Klindt-Jensen, Ole. The Vikings in England. Coph., 1948. 38 p.

Koch, Hal H. "Canute the Great and the Descendants of Sven Estridsøn," ScPP, I, 175-78.

Kristjansson, Jonas. "Eddaic and Skaldic Poetry," ScPP, II, 145-51.

Landsverk, O. G. The Kensington Rune Stone. Glendale, Calif., 1961. 77 p.

———. "Norse Medieval Cryptography in American Runic Inscriptions," ASR, 55 (1967), 252-63.

Larson, Laurence M. Canute the Great, 955 (circa)-1035 and the Rise of Danish Imperialism During the Viking Age. Lond., N.Y., 1912. 375 p.

———. "The Effort of the Danish Kings to Recover the English Crown After the Death of Harthacnut," in American Historical Association, Annual Report, 1910 (Wash., 1912), 69-81.

———. "Problems of the Norwegian Church in the Eleventh Century," ChHist, 4 (1935), 159-72.

Laxdoela Saga. Einar Ol. Sveinsson Edition. Tr. by A. Margaret Arent. Lincoln, Nebraska, 1964.

Leach, Henry G., ed. A Pageant of Old Scandinavia. Princeton, 1946. 350 p.

Lewis, Archibald R. The Northern Seas: Shipping and Commerce in Northern Europe A.D. 300-1100. Princeton, 1958. 498 p.

Liestøl, Knut. The Origin of the Icelandic Family Sagas (Instituttet for Sammenlignede Kulturforskning, Series A, no. 10). Oslo, 1930. 261 p.

Linklater, Eric R. "The Battle of Cloutarf," Viking, 15 (1951), 1-14.

———. The Ultimate Viking. Lond., 1955; N.Y., 1956. 295 p.

Lukman, N. "The Catalaunian Battle (A.D. 451) in Medieval Epics. Hjadningavig-Kudrun-Saxo," Classica et Mediaevalia, 10 (1949), 60-130.

———. "The Viking Nations and King Arthur in Geoffrey of Monmouth (1138)," Classica et Mediaevalia, 20 (1959), 170-212.

Magnússon, Eiríkr. Notes on Ship Building and Nautical Terms of Old in the North. Lond., 1906. 56 p.

Marcus, G. J. "The Early Norse Traffic to Iceland," Mariner's Mirror, 46 (1960), 174-81.

———. "Hafvilla: a Note on Norse Navigation," Speculum, 30 (1955), 610-15.

———. "The Navigation of the Norsemen," Mariner's Mirror, 39 (1953), 112-31.

———. "The Norse Traffic with Iceland," EHR, 9 (1957), 408-19.

Marshall, Edison. West with the Vikings. Garden City, N.Y., 1961. 444 p. [Historical novel]

Marstrander, Sverre. Problems of Scandinavian Hoards from the Viking Age. Congresso International de Ciencias Prehistóricas y Protohistóricas, Actas de la IV Sesion, Madrid, 1954. Zaragoza, 1956.

Mawer, Allen. "The Scandinavian Kingdom of Northumbria," in Essays and Studies Presented to William Ridgeway on his Sixtieth Birthday (Lond., 1914), 306-14.

———. The Vikings (The Cambridge Manuals of Science and Literature). Cambridge, N.Y., 1913. 150 p.

Meinberg, Carl H. "The Norse Church in Medieval America," CHistR, 5 new series (1925), 179-216.

Mercer, A. C. "The Last Norwegian Invasion of England" [King Harald Hardrada], Norseman, 7 (1949), 155-62.

———. "The Norse Settlement in Cumberland," Norseman, 11 (1953), 85-92.

———. "Norsemen on Merseyside," Norseman, 6 (1948), 303-306.

———. "Norway in Man," Norseman, 8 (1950), 19-26.

———. "Vikings in Ireland," Norseman, 10 (1952), 6-13.

Merrild, Else. "A Viking Ship Found in Denmark," ASR, 25 (1937), 51-57.

Mitford, R. B. "The Sutton Hoo Ship Burial," ASR, 29 (1951), 27-32.

Montelius, Oscar. The Civilization of Sweden in Heathen Times. Lond., N.Y., 1888. 214 p.

Mowat, Farley. Westviking: the Ancient Norse in Greenland and North America. Boston, 1965. 494 p.

Nansen, Fridtjof. "The Norsemen in America," SGM, 27 (1911), 617-32.

Nemos, W. Swedish Viking Claims in Europe. Malmö, 1928.

Nerman, Birger. "The Grobin Finds Evidence of the First Incorporation of Gotland under the Svea Kingdom," AcAr, 3 (1932), 157-67.

Nicolaysen, N. Guide to the Vikingship from Gokstad in the Christiania Museum. Kra., 1881. 53 p.

Njals Saga. Einar Ol. Sveinsson Edition. Tr. by Carl F. Bayerschmidt and Lee M. Hollander. N.Y., 1954. 390 p.

Nordal, Sigurdur. The Historical Element in the Icelandic Family Sagas (Ker Memorial Lecture, 1954). Glasgow, 1957. 35 p.

Nørlund, Poul. "Trelleborg, a Fortified Viking Camp Near the Great Belt," BSC, 3 (1937), 325-28.

———. Viking Settlers in Greenland and Their Descendents during Five Hundred Years. Lond., Coph., 1936. 160 p.

Oftedal, Magne. "Norse Cultural Remains in the Hebrides," Norseman, 12 (1954), 73-77.

Oleson, Tryggvi J. Early Voyages and Northern Approaches 1000-1632 (The Canadian Centenary Series, v. 1). Toronto, 1963. 211 p.

Olrik, Axel. Viking Civilization. Revised by H. Ellekilde (Scandinavian Classics, v. 34). N.Y., 1930. 246 p.

Olsen, Olaf F. "Fyrkat: a Viking Camp in Jutland," ASR, 48 (1960), 47-52.

———. The Viking Camp Near Hobro. Coph., 1949. 16 p.

Olson, Alma L. "A Visit to a Viking City," ASR, 20 (1932), 80-85.

Olson, Julius E., ed. "Original Narratives of the Voyages of the Northmen" [Includes: The Saga of Eric the Red; The Vinland History of the Flat Island Book; selections from Adam of Bremen, The Icelandic Annals, and Papal Letters Concerning Greenland), in Julius E. Olson and Edward G. Bourne, eds., The Northmen, Columbus and Cabot 985-1503 (N.Y., 1906, 1934, 1959), 1-74.

Oman, Charles C. "The Danish Kingdom of York," Archaeological Journal, 91 (1934), 1-21.

Oxenstierna, Eric. The Norsemen. Greenwich, Conn., 1965. 320 p.

Pohl, Frederick J. Atlantic Crossings before Columbus. N.Y., 1961. 315 p.

———. "Leif Erikson's Campsite in Vinland," ASR, 54 (1966), 25-29.

———. The Viking Explorers. N.Y., 1966. 246 p.

Pratt, Fletcher. "Sports of the Vikings," ASR, 16 (1928), 726-31.

Ramskou, Thorkild. Everyday Viking-Life. Coph., 1967. 176 p.

———. "Viking Age Cremation Graves in Denmark: a Survey," AcAr, 21 (1950), 137-82.

———. "The Viking Town of Lindholm Høje," ASR, 48 (1960), 369-77.

Ravndal, Gabriel B. Stories of the East-Vikings. Minneapolis, 1938. 383 p.

Reeves, A. M. The Finding of Wineland the Good. Lond., 1895. 205 p.

Reman, Edward. The Norse Discoveries and Explorations in America. Ed. by Arthur G. Brodeur. Berkeley, 1949. 201 p.

———. "The Norse Discoveries and Explorations in America," Antiquity, 25 (1951), 42-43.

Roos, William. "The Swedish Part in the Viking Expeditions," EHR, 7 (1892), 209-23.

Sawyer, P. H. The Age of the Vikings. Lond., N.Y., 1962. 254 p.

———. "The Density of the Danish Settlement in England," University of Birmingham Historical Journal, 6 (1957), 1-17.

Saxo Grammaticus. The First Nine Books of the Danish History of Saxo Grammaticus. Tr. by O. Elton (Folk-lore Society Publications, 33, 1893). Lond., 1894; N.Y., 1905. 435 p.

———. The Swords of the Vikings; Stories from the Works of Saxo Grammaticus. Retold by Julia Davis Adams. Lond., N.Y., 1928. 225 p.

Seaver, Esther I. "Some Examples of Viking Figure Representation in Scandinavia and the British Isles," in Medieval Studies in Memory of A. Kingsley Porter (Cambridge, Mass., 1939), v. 1, 589-610.

Shetelig, Haakon. "Normandy and the

Vikings," Norseman, 4 (1946), 371-73.

——. "The Norse Style of Ornamentation in the Viking Settlements," AcAr, 19 (1948), 69-113.

——. "The Viking Graves in Great Britain and Ireland," AcAr, 16 (1945), 1-55.

Simpson, Jacqueline. Everyday Life in the Viking Age. Lond., 1967. 208 p.

Sinding-Larsen, Henning. "Helge Ingstad: a Roaming Norseman," Norseman (1961, no. 4), 12-15.

Skelton, R. A., Thomas E. Marston, and George D. Painter. The Vinland Map and the Tartar Relation. New Haven, Lond., 1965. 291 p. Excerpts and commentary in "Vinland the Good Emerges from the Mists," American Heritage, 16 (O 1965), 4-11, 99-106.

Skovmand, Roar. "The Excursions of Ottar and Ulvstein," ScPP, I, 104-105.

——. "Hedeby: a Viking Metropolis," ASR, 39 (1951), 280-89.

——. "Hedeby and Birka," ScPP, I, 111-14.

——. "A Viking Fort Unearthed in Denmark," ASR, 25 (1937), 208-16.

——. "The Vikings," ScPP, I, 99-103.

Smith, Charles M. Northmen of Adventure: a Survey of the Exploits of Dominant Northmen from the Earliest Times to the Norman Conquest. Lond., 1932. 389 p.

Snorri Sturluson. Heimskringla. Cambridge, 1932. 770 p.

——. Heimskringla; History of the Kings of Norway. Tr. and intro. by Lee M. Hollander. Austin, Texas, 1964. 854 p.

——. The Heimskringla: a History of the Norse Kings. 3 vols. Lond., N.Y., 1906.

——. Heimskringla: the Norse King Sagas. Lond., Toronto, N.Y., 1930. 441 p.

——. Heimskringla: the Olaf Sagas. Lond., Toronto, N.Y., 1915. 420 p.

——. The Saga of Sigurd the Crusader, A.D. 1107-1111 [From the Heimskringla, or Chronicle of the Kings of Norway], in Thomas Wright, Early Travels in Palestine (Lond., 1948), 50-62.

——. The Sagas of Olaf Tryggvason and of Harald the Tyrant [Harald Haardraade]. Lond., 1911. 219 p.

——. The Stories of the Kings of Norway Called the Round World [Heimskringla]. 4 vols. Lond., 1893-1905.

Solver, Carl V. "The Ladby Ship Anchor," AcAr, 17 (1946), 117-26.

Spekke, Arnolds. "Arabian Geographers and the Early Baltic Peoples," BSC, 4 (1938), 155-59.

Stang, Ragna. "The Norwegian Stave Churches," ScPP, I, 169-74.

——. "The Viking Ships," ScPP, I, 106-10.

Steensby, Hans P. The Norsemen's Route from Greenland to Wineland. Coph., 1918. 109 p.

Stenton, F. M. The Danes in England (Proceedings of the British Academy, v. 13). Lond., 1928. 46 p.

——. "The Free Peasantry of the Northern Danelaw," in Kungliga humanistiska Vetenskapssamfundet i Lund. Årsberättelse (1926), 73-185.

Storm, Gustav. Studies on the Vinland Voyages. Coph., 1889. 64 p.

Sveinsson, Einar Ol. Dating the Icelandic Sagas: an Essay in Method. Lond., 1958. 126 p.

Sverri's Saga. The Saga of King Sverri of Norway. Tr. by John Sephton. Lond., 1899. 288 p.

Thomsen, Vilhelm L. P. The Relations between Ancient Russia and Scandinavia, and the Origin of the Russian State. Lond., Oxford, 1877. 150 p.

Thordarson, Matthias. The Vinland Voyages. N.Y., 1930. 76 p.

Turville-Petre, E. O. Gabriel. Heroic Age of Scandinavia. Lond., N.Y., 1951. 196 p.

——. Myth and Religion of the North: the Religion of Ancient Scandinavia. N.Y., 1964. 340 p.

Uppvall, Axel J. The Truth about Leif Ericsson and the Greenland Voyages. Boston, 1941. 445 p.

Videnskapelige forskningsfond av 1919. Viking Antiquities in Great Britain and Ireland. Ed. by Haakon Shetelig. 6 vols. Oslo, 1940-54.

Viking Congress, Lerwick, July, 1950. Ed. by W. Douglas Simpson (Aberdeen University Studies, no. 132). Lond., 1954. 294 p.

Viking Society for Northern Research, London. Ruins of the Sage Time: Travels and Explorations in Iceland in the Summer of 1895. Lond., 1899.

Vilmundarson, Thorhallur. "Reflections on the Vinland Map," ASR, 54 (1966), 20-24.

The Vinland Sagas — The Norse Discovery of America. Lond., 1965. 124 p.

Wahlgren, Erik. "The Case of the Kensington Rune Stone," American Heritage, 10 (Apr 1959), 34-35. For bibliography on the Kensington Stone, see Harvard Guide to American History (1955), 252.

——. The Kensington Stone — A Mystery Solved. Madison, Wisc., 1958. 228 p.

Walsh, Annie. Scandinavian Relations with

Ireland during the Viking Period. Dublin, 1922. 82 p.

Ward, A. W. "The Lower-Saxon and Danish War," in The Cambridge Modern History (Cambridge, 1906), v. 4, 85-109.

Wax, Rosalie, and Murray Wax. "The Vikings and the Rise of Capitalism," AJS, 61 (1955-56), 1-10.

Werenskiold, Werner. "New Theories About Vineland," NGT, 12 (1948/50), 4-8.

"What Did the Norsemen Discover?" Saturday Review (N 6, 1965), 49-52.

Williams, Mary W. Social Scandinavia in the Viking Age. N.Y., 1920. 451 p.

Yarham, E. R. "The Ancient Stave Churches of Norway," ASR, 38 (1950), 322-33.

——. "Shetland's Viking Fire Festival," ASR, 44 (1956), 319-24.

TO WORLD WAR I

Ahnlund, Nils. "The Historical Frontiers of the Northern Nations," Le Nord, 5 (1942), 243-55.

Andersen, N. K. "The Reformation in Scandinavia and the Baltic," in The New Cambridge Modern History (Cambridge, 1958), v. 2, 134-60.

Andersson, A. English Influence in Norwegian and Swedish Figure Sculpture in Wood, 1220-1270. Lond., 1950. 318 p.

Bain, R. Nisbet. "The Hats and Caps and Gustavus III," in The Cambridge Modern History (Cambridge, 1909), v. 6, 758-84.

——. Scandinavia: a Political History of Denmark, Norway and Sweden from 1513 to 1900 (Cambridge Historical Series, no. 15). Cambridge, 1905. 460 p.

Brown, John. Memoirs of the Courts of Sweden and Denmark during the Reigns of Christian VII of Denmark and Gustavus III and IV of Sweden (Secret Court Memoirs, no. 18-19). 2 vols. Boston, 1900; Lond., 1904.

Bukdahl, Jørgen. "Folk Songs and Visionary Poetry," ScPP, I, 307-24.

Chance, James F. George I and the Northern War: a Study of British-Hanoverian Policy in the North of Europe in the Years 1709 to 1721. Lond., 1909. 516 p.

Christensen, Aksel E. "Scandinavia and the Advance of the Hanseatics," SEHR, 5 (1957), 89-117.

Collins, W. E. "The Scandinavian North," in The Cambridge Modern History (Cambridge, 1903), v. 2, 599-633.

Falnes, Oscar J. "Paul Christian Sinding: an Early Scandinavian-American Historian," ASR, 48 (1960), 53-58.

Futrell, Michael. Northern Underground; Episodes of Russian Revolutionary Transport and Communications Through Scandinavia and Finland. 1863-1917. Lond., N.Y., 1963. 240 p.

Garstein, Oskar. Rome and the Counter-Reformation in Scandinavia. Vol. I, 1539-1583. Oslo, 1963. 412 p.

Hatton, Ragnhild M. "Scandinavian Unity: J. R. Crowe's Report From Christiania 1856," Historisk Tidsskrift (Oslo), 46 (1967), 130-54.

Hovde, Brynjolf J. "Notes on the Effects of Emigration upon Scandinavia," JMH, 6 (1934), 253-79.

——. The Scandinavian Countries, 1720-1865; the Rise of the Middle Classes. 2 vols. Boston, Ithaca, N.Y., 1943. 811 p.

Jorgenson, Theodore. Norway's Relation to Scandinavian Unionism, 1815-1871. Northfield, Minn., 1935. 530 p.

Koht, Halvdan. "The Scandinavian Kingdoms During the Fourteenth and Fifteenth Centuries," Cambridge Medieval History, v. 8 (Lond., 1936), 533-55.

Leach, Henry G. Angevin Britain and Scandinavia (Harvard Studies in Comparative Literature, v. 6). Cambridge, Mass., 1921. 432 p.

——. "Tynwald Day on the Isle of Man," ASR, 43 (1955), 125-36.

Lindroth, Sten. "Science in Scandinavia," ScPP, III, 276-90.

Litzenberg, K. The Victorians and the Vikings: a Bibliographical Essay on Anglo-Norse Literary Relations. Ann Arbor, 1947. 27 p.

Lyng, Jens S. The Scandinavians in Australia, New Zealand and the Western Pacific. Melbourne, 1939. 207 p.

Marcus, G. J. Ocean Navigation of the Middle Ages: Northern Waters. Thesis (Ph.D.), Oxford University, 1955.

Marwick, Hugh. The Orkney. Lond., 1951. 232 p.

Moritzen, Julius. "Scandinavian Renaissance," CH, 8 (1945), 330-35.

Nash, E. Gee. The Hansa: Its History and Romance. Lond., N.Y., 1929. 279 p.

Otte, Elise C. Norway, Sweden, and Denmark. N.Y., 1939. 351 p. [Many different editions]

Reddaway, William F. "Scandinavia," in The Cambridge Modern History (Cambridge, 1909), v. 11, 677-96.

——. "The Scandinavian Kingdoms," in The Cambridge Modern History (Cambridge, 1908) v. 5, 558-83.

——. "The Scandinavian North," in The

Cambridge Modern History (Cambridge, 1906) v. 4, 560-91.

Scandinavia Past and Present. Ed. by Jørgen Bukdahl and Aage Heinberg. Vol. 1, From Viking Age to Absolute Monarchy; 441 p.; Vol. 2, Through Revolutions to Liberty; 655 p.; Vol. 3, Five Modern Democracies; 888 p. Odense, Denmark, 1959.

Seaton, Ethel. Literary Relations of England and Scandinavia in the Seventeenth Century (Oxford Studies in Modern Languages and Literature). Oxford, 1935. 384 p.

Semmingsen, Ingrid. "The Black Death," ScPP, I, 332-36.

——. "Emigration," ScPP, II, 814-19.

——. "Scandinavia during the Napoleonic Wars," ScPP, II, 674-82.

——. "The Scandinavian Seven Years' War," ScPP, I, 441-45.

Skovmand, Roar. "The Hanseatic Towns and Scandinavia," ScPP, I, 325-31.

——. "Kingdoms and People," ScPP, I, 115-20.

Stavenow, Ludwig V. A. "Scandinavia," in The Cambridge Modern History (Cambridge, 1910), v. 12, 273-93.

Stefansson, Jóre. Denmark and Sweden with Iceland and Finland (The Story of Nations, v. 66). Lond., 1916. 384 p.

Stomberg, Andrew A., ed. "Letters of an Early Emigrant Agent in the Scandinavian Countries Who Visited Scandinavia in 1854-1861 to Stimulate Emigration," Swedish-American Historical Bulletin, 3 (1930), 7-52.

Tennant, Peter F. D., ed. The Scandinavian Book. Lond., 1951. 314 p.

Tham, Wilhelm. "Power Politics and Union Conflicts," ScPP, I, 346-52.

——. "Period of the Kalmar Union," ScPP, I, 341-45.

——. "Scandinavianism," ScPP, II, 728-31.

Tissot, L. "The Events of 1848 in Scandinavia," in François Fetö, ed., The Opening of an Era — 1848; an Historical Symposium (Lond., 1948), 167-79.

Utterström, Gustaf. "Climatic Fluctuations and Population Problems in Early Modern History," SEHR, 3 (1955), 3-47.

Vigander, Haakon. Mutual Revision of History Text Books in the Nordic Countries. Paris, 1950.

Westergaard, Waldemar, C. "The Hansa Towns and Scandinavia on the Eve of Swedish Independence," JMH, 4 (1932), 349-60.

Wuorinen, John H. "Scandinavia and the Rise of Modern National Consciousness," in Edward Mead Earle, ed., Nationalism and Internationalism: Essays Inscribed to Carlton H. Hayes (N.Y., 1950), 455-81.

SCANDINAVIA AND THE BALTIC REGION (mainly seventeenth century)

Anderson, Roger C. Naval Wars in the Baltic during the Sailing Ship Epoch, 1522-1850. Lond., 1910. 443 p.

Åström, Sven-Erik. "The English Navigation Laws and the Baltic Trade, 1660-1700," SEHR, 8 (1960), 3-18.

Bamford, Paul W. "French Shipping in Northern European Trade, 1660-1789," JMH, 26 (1954), 207-19.

Bilmanis, Alfred. "The Struggle for Domination of the Baltic: an Historical Aspect of the Baltic Problem," JCEA, 5 (1945), 119-42.

Bjork, David J. "Piracy in the Baltic, 1375-1398," Speculum, 18 (1943), 39-68.

Bowman, Francis J. "The Baltic in the Thirty Years War," University of Iowa Studies, Abstracts in History II, v. 10 (1934, no. 3), 7-16.

——. "Dutch Diplomacy and the Baltic Grain Trade, 1600-1660," Pacific Historical Review (1936), 337-48.

——. "Seventeenth Century Colonization by Baltic and Scandinavian Countries," BSC, 5 (1939), 103-106.

Cross, Samuel H. "The Scandinavian Infiltration into Early Russia," Speculum, 21 (1946), 505-14.

Malowist, Marian. "Baltic Affairs in the Sixteenth and Seventeenth Centuries in the Light of Historical Literature," BSC, 3 (1937), 417-27.

Murray, John J. Baltic Diplomacy, 1715-1716. Thesis (Ph.D.), University of California, Los Angeles, 1942.

Piwarski, Kazimierz. "The Baltic Policy of King John Sobieski," BC, 2 (1936), 24-29.

Reddaway, William F. "Canning and the Baltic in 1807," BC, 2 (1936), 13-23.

Urban, William L. The Baltic Crusade of the Thirteenth Century. Thesis (Ph.D.), University of Texas, 1967. 435 p.

Warner, Oliver. The Sea and the Sword: the Baltic, 1630-1945. N.Y., 1965. 305 p.

WORLD WAR I

Björkman, Edwin A. Scandinavia and the War (Oxford Pamphlets, 1914-1915, no. 56). Lond., N.Y., 1914. 21 p.

Guichard, L. "The Three Scandinavian

Countries," in his, The Naval Blockade, 1914-1918 (Lond., 1930), 133-72.

Heckscher, Eli F. et al. Sweden, Norway, Denmark and Iceland in the World War [Translated and abridged edition]. New Haven, Lond., 1930. 593 p.

Joesten, Joachim. "North Europe's War Rehearsal," CH, 46 (1937), 51-54.

Laursen, Aage. "Scandinavia During the First World War," ScPP, II, 975-81.

Moritzen, Julius. "The War and a Greater Scandinavia," NoAmRev, 201 (1915), 372-79.

Murray, Gilbert. Impressions of Scandinavia in War Time. Lond., 1916. 32 p.

Nansen, Fridtjof. "The Mission of the Small States," ASR, 6 (1918), 9-13.

Siney, Marian C. The Allied Blockade of Germany, 1914-1916 (University of Michigan Publications, History and Political Science, v. 23). Ann Arbor, 1957. 339 p.

Strangeland, Charles E. "The Scandinavian Countries Since the War," Atlantic Monthly, 133 (1924), 844-55.

Wuorinen, John H. "Nations of Northern Europe," CH, 34 (1931), 147-49.

WORLD WAR II AND AFTER

Cole, Hugh M. "Hitler Invades Scandinavia," CH, 51 (1940, no. 9), 15-17.

Divine, Arthur D. Navies in Exile. Lond., 1944. 194 p. Pp. 46-85 also published separately as Norwegian Navy in Action. Lond., 1944. 47 p.

Eliott, A. Randle. "The Oslo States and the European War," FPR, 15 (Ja 15, 1940), 257-72.

Gillis, James M. "Scandinavian Invasion: Crime or Blunder?" Catholic World, 151 (Ja-Je 1940), 129.

Glascow, George. "Hitler's Scandinavian Blunder," CR, 157 (1940), 543-54.

Gran, Bjarne. "Five Nations — Three Standpoints," ScPP, II, 1241-44.

Hambro, Carl J. "The Forgotten Nations," ASR, 31 (1943), 22-25.

Hambro, Edvard. "The Northern Countries After This War," Annals, 228 (1943), 60-64.

Höjer, Torvald. "The Scandinavian Heads of State," ScPP, III, 17-24.

Joesten, Joachim. "Scandinavia in the New Order," FA, 19 (1941), 818-27.

Jones, S. Shepard. "War Comes to Scandinavia," ASR, 28 (1940), 105-17.

Kenney, Rowland. The Northern Tangle: Scandinavia and the Post-War World. Lond., 1946. 255 p.

Linklater, Eric R. The Northern Garrisons. Lond., 1941. 72 p.

Norman, Albert. The Allied Invasion of Northwestern Europe: Design and Reality, 1940-1944. Thesis (Ph.D.), Clark University, 1957.

Olson, Alma L. Scandinavia: the Background for Neutrality. Phila., N.Y., 1940. 358 p.

Segerstedt, Torgny T. "The Future of Scandinavia," Norseman, 3 (1945), 11-13.

Shirer, William L. The Challenge of Scandinavia: Norway, Sweden, Denmark, and Finland in Our Time. Boston, 1955. 437 p.

——. "The Conquest of Denmark and Norway," in his, The Rise and Fall of the Third Reich (Lond., N.Y., 1960), 673-712.

Singer, Kurt D. Arctic Invasion, the Battle of Iceland, Greenland, Spitzbergen and Northern Finland (News Background, Inc. Report no. 13). N.Y., 1944. 12 p.

——. Duel for the Northland: the War of Enemy Agents in Scandinavia. N.Y., 1943. 212 p.

Skodvin, Magne. "German and British-French Plans for Operations in Scandinavia, 1940," Norseman, 9 (1951), 361-76.

Soloveytchik, George. "Europe's Quiet Corner: the Scandinavian Countries Today," Harper's Magazine, 206 (1953), 57-65.

——. "Scandinavia and the War," CR, 159 (1941), 169-78.

——. "Scandinavia Revisited," CR, 169 (1946), 143-47.

——. "Scandinavia Revisited," CR, 172 (1947), 198-204.

——. "Scandinavia Revisited," CR, 179 (1951), 330-37.

——. "The Scandinavian Debacle," CR, 157 (1940), 659-69.

——. "Some Scandinavian Impressions," Norseman, 14 (1956), 150-61.

Spencer, Arthur. Scandinavia (Current Affairs, no. 93). Lond., 1949. 19 p.

"Summer, 1939 in Scandinavia," ASR, 27 (1939), 152-55.

Worm-Müller, Jacob S. "The Northern States and the Turning Point in the War," Norseman, 1 (1943), 323-28.

Ziemke, Earl F. The German Northern Theater of Operations, 1940-1945 (Dept. of the Army Pamphlet no. 20-271). Wash., 1960. 342 p.

DENMARK

Anderson, Robert T. "The Danish and Dutch

Settlements on Amager Island: Four Hundred Years of Socio-Cultural Interaction," AmAnthro, 60 (1958), 683-701.

Andrup, O. Bonds of Kinship Between the Royal Houses of Great Britain and Denmark. Coph., 1948, 31 p.

Birch, J. H. S. Denmark in History. Lond., 1938. 444 p.

Bjork, David J. "The Peace of Stralsund, 1370," Speculum, 7 (1932), 447-76.

Buhl, M. L. "Some Islamic Objects in the Danish National Museum," Berytus, 11, facsimile 1, 61-65.

Candlin, E. Frank. "Oslo Wedding" [Wedding of Anna of Denmark-Norway and James VI of Scotland], Norseman, 8 (1950), 161-66.

Christensen, Carlo. "H. C. Hansen, in Memoriam," ASR, 48 (1960), 142-44.

Copenhagen, Danske Kongers Kronologiske Samling. A Guide to the Chronological Collection of the Danish Kings. Coph., 1946. 80 p.

Copenhagen, Nationalmuseet. The Danish Collections; Middle Ages and Thereafter to 1750 (Guides to the National Museum). Coph., 1940. 70 p.

Copenhagen, Tøjhusmuseet. The Armory Hall; Guide to the Royal Danish Arsenal Museum. Coph., 1953. 124 p.

Copenhagen, Universitet, Bibliotek. Prominent Danish Scientists through the Ages, with Facsimiles from Their Works. V. Meisen, ed. Coph., 1932. 193 p.

Danstrup, John. A History of Denmark. 2d ed., Coph., 1949. 190 p.; Lond., 1952. 200 p.

Denmark, Haeren, Hjemmevaernet. A Survey of the Danish Home Guard, Its History and Organization. Coph., Lyngby, 1954. 45 p.

Denmark, Ministry of Foreign Affairs. A Short History of Denmark. Coph., 1957. 63 p.

Desmond, Shaw. "The Republic of Denmark," Weekly Review, 3 (1920), 126-27.

Falnes, Oscar J. "Denmark and Norway: When They Were European Powers," ASR, 28 (1940), 118-26.

Fischer, Alfred J. "Medieval Nordic Culture on Ice; the Faroe Islanders and Their Problems," Norseman, 14 (1956), 89-94.

Great Britain, Foreign Office, Historical Section. Greenland (Handbooks, no. 132). Lond., 1920.

———. Schleswig-Holstein. (Handbooks, no. 35). Lond., 1920.

Haeberling, Carl. "The Frisians of Föhr," ASR, 39 (1951), 189-97.

Hannover, H. I. "Ellenhammer, A Danish Inventor," ASR, 17 (1929), 277-86.

Jacobsen, Ole. "The Faerøe Islands from the Middle Ages to the Present Day," ScPP, II, 996-1003.

Koch, Hal H. "King and Archbishop," ScPP, I, 179-87.

Lauring, Palle. A History of Denmark in Pictures. Coph., 1963. 299 p.

———. A History of the Kingdom of Denmark. Coph., 1960. 265 p.

Liisberg, Bering. "The Diaries of Leonora Christine," ASR, 9 (1921), 386-93.

———. "Vitus Bering and the Discovery of the Bering Strait, A Hundredth Anniversary," ASR, 16 (1928), 345-52.

Lomholt, Svend. "Niels Finsen: In Memorium," ASR, 21 (1933), 163-71.

Lukman, N. "British and Danish Traditions: Some Contacts and Relations," Classica, 6 (1944), 72-109.

Mitchell, Philip M. A History of Danish Literature. Coph., 1957; N.Y., 1958. 322 p.

Mygdal, Elna. "Danish Kinsmen of Father Knickerbocker: the Amager Colony at Copenhagen," ASR, 18 (1930), 728-40.

Nørregård, Georg. Danish Settlements in West Africa, 1658-1850. Boston, 1966. 287 p.

Olrik, Axel. The Heroic Legends of Denmark (Scandinavian Monographs, v. 4). Tr. by Lee M. Hollander. N.Y., 1919. 530 p.

Olrik, Hans. "Tisvilde and Helene's Spring," ASR, 2 (1914), 7-11.

Palsbo, Susanne, ed. The Daily Life of the King of Denmark. Coph., 1957. [56 p. of illustrations]

Pratt, Fletcher. The Third King [Valdemar IV]. N.Y., 1950. 313 p.

Rambusch, Frode C. W. "Dannevirke," ASR, 7 (1919), 34-41.

Rose, Stuart. "Prince Aage of Denmark," ASR, 14 (1926), 350-54.

Shetelig, Haakon. "The False Queen Gunhild from Jutland," Norseman, 9 (1951), 255-58.

Sick, Ingeborg M. "Karen Jeppe of Denmark and America," ASR, 25 (1937), 18-25.

Skovmand, Roar. "Christian II — the Tyrant," ScPP, I, 379-81.

———. "Danish Absolute Monarchy," ScPP, I, 505-11.

———. "The Danish Community under the Valdemars," ScPP, I, 257-62.

———. "The Great Period of the Valdemars," ScPP, I, 253-56.

———. "Nobles and Commoners in Denmark," ScPP, I, 436-39.

Starcke, Viggo. Denmark in World History.
Phila., 1963. 381 p.

Stejneger, Leonhard. "Witus Jonassen
Bering," ASR, 29 (1941), 295-307.

Tham, Wilhelm. "Denmark-Norway Lamed,"
ScPP, I, 466-68.

——. "Monarchy and Aristocracy in Denmark," ScPP, I, 463-65.

Toksvig, Signe. "Troels Frederik Troels-
Lund," ASR, 15 (1927), 607-11.

Ward, Gordon R. Hengest: an Historical
Study of His Danish Origins and of His
Campaigns in Frisia and South-East Eng-
land. Lond., 1949. 58 p.

Winther, Oscar O. "One More Day; Denmark's Sorest Trial Six Centuries Ago,"
ASR, 30 (1942), 112-22.

LOCAL HISTORY

Barfoed, Per. "Historical Pageants at Elsinore," ASR, 15 (1927), 37-41.

Bokkenheuser, Knud. "Öresund," ASR, 13
(1925), 151-59.

Christensen, Carl. "Frederikvaerk, the
Oldest Industrial Town in Denmark," ASR,
17 (1929), 31-35.

Copenhagen, Danske Kongers Kronologiske
Sammling. Royal Arms at Rosenberg.
By Arne Hoff. 2 vols. Coph., 1956. (v.
2: plates).

Diemer, Asmus. "Historic Corners of Sön-
derjylland," ASR, 9 (1921), 190-99.

Hendriksen, K. "Fredensborg Castle Park,"
ASR, 41 (1953), 23-29.

"Historic Towns of Denmark." I, Fang,
Arthur. "Roskilde, the Cathedral City,"
ASR, 14 (1926), 156-60. II, Olrik, Henrik
G. "Helsingör, The City of Hamlet,"
ASR, 14 (1926), 341-49. III, Vejlö, A.
"Kalundborg, the City of Five Towers,"
ASR, 14 (1926), 491-94. IV, "Odense, the
City of Hans Christian Andersen," ASR,
14 (1926), 663-70. IV [sic], Paulli, Rich-
ard. "Ribe, Famous in Ballad and Story,"
ASR, 15 (1927), 154-59. V [sic], Møller,
J. E., "Christianshaven, Roccoco and
Classicism," ASR, 15 (1927), 549-57.

"Historic Towns of Denmark: Kjöge," ASR,
17 (1929), 157-61.

Holck, A. "Maribo," ASR, 19 (1931), 154-58.

Janssen, Börge. "The Romance of the Clois-
ters" [at Vallö in Sjaelland], ASR, 9
(1921), 802-10.

Leach, Henry G. "The Private Castles of
Denmark," ASR, 47 (1959), 319-27.

Lebech, Mogens. "The Citadel of Copenhagen," ASR, 51 (1963), 270-79.

Leistikow, Gunnar. "Christiansø: Tiny

Eden in the Baltic," ASR, 55 (1967), 143-
52.

Linvald, Axel. "Kristiansborg: the Castle
of the Kingdom," ASR, 13 (1925), 212-21.

Linvald, Steffen. "Eight Centuries of Copenhagen," ASR, 55 (1967), 239-45.

Olrik, Henrik G. "Kronborg," ASR, 15
(1927), 13-22.

Olsen, Albert. "Aarhus — A Modern City,"
ASR, 24 (1939), 39-47.

Paulli, Richard. "Fredensborg, Castle of
Peace," ASR, 21 (1933), 71-80.

——. "Historic Towns of Denmark:
Nakskov — City of Red Roofs," ASR, 17
(1929), 467-73.

Pedersen, Laurits. Elsinore: A Guide and
a Historical Account with Special Regard
to its English Memories. Hel., 1937.
56 p.

Pratt, Fletcher. "The Curious Castles of
Denmark," Military Engineer, 25 (1933),
392-94.

Rosenkrantz, Palle. "Danish Castles and
Manor Houses," ASR, 16 (1928), 165-74.

Sørensen, H. P. "Copenhagen," ScPP, III,
397-402.

Stub-Jörgensen, Christian. "Denmark's
Outpost in the Baltic," ASR, 19, (1931),
137-47.

Sutherland, Mason. "Bornholm-Denmark in
a Nutshell," NGeogM, 87 (1945), 239-56.

"Tordenskjold," ASR, 10 (1922), 19-22.

Von Der Recke, Karin. "Bornholm, the
Pearl of the Baltic," ASR, 26 (1938),
230-38.

Wanscher, Vilhelm. "The History of Kronborg Castle," I (ca. 1423-1576), Artes, 6
(1938), 167-216; II (1577-1777), Artes, 7
(1939), 95-190.

Weilbach, Frederick. Kronborg Castle
[Completed by Charles Christensen]. The
Section Dealing with the Commercial and
Naval Museum by Knud Klem. Elsinore,
1953. 32 p.

GREENLAND

"Agreement Regarding Greenland," ASR, 29
(1941), 155-58.

Bech, Georg. "The East Greenland Question," ASR, 19 (1931), 665-69.

Bobé, Louis. "Greenland — A Two Hundredth
Anniversary," ASR, 9 (1921), 659-65.

Bornemann, Claus. "Greenland Faces a
New Age," ASR, 53 (1965), 277-83.

Breckinridge, Henry. "Nazis in Greenland,"
CH, 51 (1939/1940), 13-14.

Brun, Eske. "Greenland during the War,"
Norseman, 5 (1947), 91-93.

——. "Greenland Today, ScPP, III, 38-42.
——. "Greenland Weathers the Crisis,"
ASR, 28 (1940), 321-25.
Fischer, Alfred J. "Greenland's Silent
Revolution," Norseman, 8 (1950), 189-92.
——. "Modern Greenland," Norseman, 7
(1949), 318-22.
Greenland Administration. Report on Green-
land [To the United Nations], 1949. 82 p.
Mimeographed.
Holtved, Erik. Archaeological Investiga-
tions in the Thule District. (Meddelelser
om Grønland, Bd. 141, no. 1). 2 vols.
Coph., 1944.
Krabbe, Thomas N. Greenland: Its Nature,
Inhabitants, and History. Coph., 1930.
129 p.
Malaurie, Jean. The Last Kings of Thule.
Lond., 1956. 295 p.
Marstrander, Sverre. "Farms and Churches
in the Mediaeval Norse Settlements of
Greenland," NGT, 12 (1943), 355-58.
Mathiassen, Therkel. "The Archaeology of
the Thule District," GT, 47 (1944/1945),
43-57.
Mehlem, Max. "Denmark's Greenland —
From Colony to Province," SRWA, 11
(1962, no. 12), 7-8.
Porsild, A. E. "Greenland at the Cross-
roads," Arctic, 1 (1948), 53-57.
Roussell, Aage. Farms and Churches in the
Mediaeval Norse Settlements of Green-
land. Coph., 1941. Reprint from Med-
delelser om Grønland, Bd. 89.
Stauning, T. "The New Greenland," ASR, 19
(1931), 524-34.
Stefansson, Vilhjalmur. Greenland. N.Y.,
1942. 338 p.
Williamson, Geoffrey. Changing Greenland.
Lond., 1953. 280 p.

GREENLAND: VIKINGS, COLONIZATION

Bobé, Louis. Hans Egede: Colonizer and
Missionary of Greenland. Coph., 1952.
207 p.
Bruun, Daniel. The Icelandic Colonization
of Greenland and the Finding of Vineland.
Coph., 1918. 228 p.
Hansen, Fredrick C. C. "Homo Gardaren-
sis," ASR, 19 (1931), 412-20.
Marcus, G. J. "The Earliest Voyages
to Greenland," ASR, 48 (1960), 65-
70.
Mikkelsen, Ejnar. "The Colonization of
Eastern Greenland," GeogR, 17 (1927),
207-25.
Nørlund, Poul. "The First Scandinavian
Settlers in Greenland, Medieval Paris

Fashions in the Far North," ASR, 11
(1923), 547-53.
——. Viking Settlers in Greenland, and
Their Descendants during Five Hundred
Years. Lond., Coph., 1936. 160 p.
Wolfe, Michael. "Norse Archeology in
Greenland since World War II," ASR, 49
(1961), 380-92.

THE SIXTEENTH AND SEVENTEENTH
CENTURIES

Ady, Julia M. Cartwright. Christina of Den-
mark, Duchess of Milan and Lorraine,
1522-1590. N.Y., 1913. 562 p.
Ainsley, Harold. Denmark, England, and the
Balance of Power in the North, 1672-1678;
Based Primarily on the Reports of Mar-
cus Gjöe, Danish Envoy Extraordinary in
London. Thesis (Ph.D.), University of
California, Los Angeles, 1950.
Askgaard, Finn. "The Siege of Copenhagen:
a Tercentenary," ASR, 47 (1959), 347-56.
Bowman, Francis J. "The Creation and Dis-
solution of the Danish-Swedish Alliance
of 1628," Research Studies of the State
University of Washington, 5 (1937), 131-
44.
Bridges, J. H. "Tycho Brahe," CR, 81
(1902), 196-213.
Cant, R. "The Embassy of the Earl of
Leicester to Denmark in 1632," EHR, 54
(1939), 252-62.
Cheyney, Edward P. "England and Denmark
in the Latter Days of Queen Elizabeth,"
JMH, 1 (1929), 8-39.
Christensen, Aksel E. Dutch Trade to the
Baltic about 1600. Studies in the Sound
Toll Register and Dutch Shipping. Coph.,
1941.
Clissold, Stephen. "Tycho Brahe," CR, 185
(1954), 39-43.
Commager, Henry S. "Anders Sorensen
Vedel: the Hamlet of Lilliebjerget," in
his, The Search for a Usable Past and
Other Essays in Historiography (N.Y.,
1967), 335-48. Appears also in Carl F.
Bayerschmidt and Eric J. Friis, eds.,
Scandinavian Studies: Essays Presented
to Henry Goddard Leach (Seattle, 1965),
385-95.
Ekman, Ernst. "The Danish Royal Law of
1665," JMH, 29 (1957), 102-107.
Faaborg, Theodor. "Christian IV of Denmark," ASR, 18 (1930), 13-22.
Gade, John A. Christian IV, King of Denmark and Norway; a Picture of the Seventeenth Century. Boston, N.Y., 1928.
319 p.

———. The Life and Times of Tycho Brahe. N.Y., 1947. 209 p.

Harthan, John P. "James VI of Scotland and Anna of Denmark: a Scandinavian Honeymoon in the Sixteenth Century," Norseman, 6 (1948), 158-64.

Holck, Preben A. C. J. von. List of the Danish-Norwegian Fleet, 1650-1700 (Society for Nautical Research Occasional Publications, no. 5). Lond., 1936.

Lane, Margery. "Heligoland in 1689," EHR, 30 (1915), 704-705.

Lindenov, Christopher. The First Triple Alliance: the Letters of the Danish Envoy to London, 1668-1672. Tr. and ed., with an historical introduction by Waldemar Westergaard. New Haven, Lond., 1947. 528 p.

Mortensen, Harald. "Tycho Brahe, Ruins of His Castle to be Restored after 350 Years," ASR, 14 (1926), 77-83.

———. "Tycho Brahe," ASR, 35 (1947), 42-47.

Mortensen, Niels Th. "The Baroque in Copenhagen and Jutland," ScPP, I, 565-70.

———. "Construction under Christian IV," ScPP, I, 501-504.

Polisenský, J. "Denmark-Norway and the Bohemian Cause in the Early Part of the Thirty Years' War," in Festgabe für L. L. Hammerich, aus Anlass seines siebzigsten Geburtstag. (Coph., 1962), 215-27.

Schoolcraft, Henry L. "England and Denmark, 1660-1667," EHR, 25 (1910), 457-79.

Skovmand, Roar. "The Danish Reformation," ScPP, I, 382-85.

———. "Denmark's Unfree Peasantry," ScPP, I, 546-49.

———. "Emancipation of the Peasants," ScPP, II, 643-46.

———. "Estates Assemblies and June Constitution in Denmark," ScPP, II, 702-709.

———. "Strife between King and Nobles in Denmark, ScPP, I, 263-66.

Ulfeldt, Leonora Christina. Memoirs of Leonora Christina, Daughter of Christian IV of Denmark. N.Y., 1929. 342 p. Originally published Lond., 1872. 330 p.

1715-1914

Arnheim, Arthur. "German Court Jews and Denmark During the Great Northern War," SEHR, 14 (1966), 117-33.

Baker, Elizabeth F. Henry Wheaton, 1785-1848 [American Representative in Denmark in 1827]. (Phila., 1937), 81-137.

Bukdahl, Jørgen. "Danish Folk Revivals after 1864." ScPP, II, 820-25.

Chance, James F. "The Baltic Expedition and Northern Treaties of 1715," EHR, 17 (1902), 443-65.

Commager, Henry S. "Struensee and the Enlightenment: a Study in Historiography," in his, The Search for a Usable Past and Other Essays in Historiography (N.Y., 1967), 349-63.

"Dagmar of Denmark and Bohemia," ASR, 17 (1929), 29-30.

Downs, Brian W. "Anglo-Danish Literary Relations, 1867-1900," Modern Language Review, 43 (1948), 145-74.

Floyd, Calvin J. "The Sound Dues," ASR, 50 (1962), 386-96.

Hansen, Thorkild. Arabia Felix, the Danish Expedition of 1761-1767. N.Y., 1964. 381 p.

Hill, Charles E. The Danish Sound Dues and the Command of the Baltic: a Study of International Relations. Durham, N.C., 1926. 305 p.

Hill, Mary. Margaret of Denmark. Lond., 1898. 156 p.

Jones, W. Glyn. "The End of a System," Norseman, 14 (1956), 230-38.

———. "Denmark in the Nineteenth Century — through British Eyes," Norseman, 16 (1958), 24-34.

Kjølsen, F. H. "A Danish Pioneer in Egypt," ASR, 55 (1967), 163-69.

Kulsrud, Carl J. "Seizure of the Danish Fleet, 1807," AJIL, 32 (1938), 280-311.

Larsen, Hanna A. "Johanne Luise Heiberg," ASR, 34 (1946), 103-12.

———. "Pontoppidan of Denmark," ASR, 31 (1943), 231-39.

Madol, Hans R. Christian IX. Compiled from Unpublished Documents and Memoirs. Lond., 1939. 301 p.

Møller, K. F. "Holberg — A Great European," ASR, 42 (1954), 145-52.

Nors, P. The Court of Christian VII of Denmark. Lond., 1928. 287 p.

Randall, Alec. "The Ambassador and the 'Tragic' Queen," [Sir Robert Murray Keith and Caroline Mathilda, Queen of Denmark], Norseman, 11 (1953), 297-98.

Reddaway, William F. "Denmark Under the Bernstorffs and Struensee," in The Cambridge Modern History (Cambridge, 1909), v. 6, 735-57.

———. "King Christian VII," EHR, 31 (1916), 59-84.

———. "Struensee and the Fall of Bernstorff," EHR, 27 (1912), 274-86.

Rose, John H. "A British Agent at Tilsit," EHR, 16 (1901), 712-18.

———. "Canning and Denmark in 1807," EHR, 11 (1896), 82-92.

———. "Canning and the Secret Intelligence from Tilsit," Transactions of the Royal Historical Society, 20 (1906), 61-77.

Ruppenthal, Roland G. "Denmark and the Continental System," JMH, 15 (1943), 7-23. Thesis (Ph.D.), same title, University of Wisconsin, 1939.

Ryan, A. N. "The Causes of the British Attack upon Copenhagen in 1807," EHR, 68 (1953), 37-55.

Schulerud, Mentz. "Ludvig Holberg and His Times," ScPP, I, 550-64.

Taylor, Alfred H. "The Battle of Copenhagen, April 2nd, 1801," Tidsskrift for Søvaesen, 122 (1951), 162-88.

Thomsen, Frede. "Mathilde Fibiger, a Fifty Year Memorial," ASR, 10 (1922), 487-91.

Wilkins, William H. A Queen of Tears: Caroline Matilda, Queen of Denmark and Norway, and Princess of Great Britain and Ireland. 2 vols. Lond., N.Y., 1904.

Wraxall, Frederick C. L. Life and Times of H. M. Caroline Matilda, Queen of Denmark and Norway. 3 vols. Lond., 1864.

N.F.S. GRUNDTVIG

Allen, Edgar L. Bishop Grundtvig: a Prophet of the North (Modern Christian Revolutionaries, no. 8). Lond., 1949. 94 p.

Bredsdorff, Elias. "Grundtvig in Cambridge," Norseman, 10 (1952), 114-23.

Koch, Hal H. Grundtvig. Tr. by L. Jones. Yellow Springs, Ohio, 1952. 231 p.

MacKaye, David L. "Grundtvig and Kold," ASR, 30 (1942), 228-39.

Mitchell, P. M. "Grundtvig," in his, A History of Danish Literature (N.Y., 1958), 126-34.

Rosenberg, P. A. "Grundtvig," ASR, 21 (1933), 482-91.

"Some Paragraphs on Grundtvig," ASR, 21 (1933), 492-93.

THE WEST INDIES

"Convention Providing for the Cession of the West Indies, August 4, 1916," AJIL, 11 (1917), Supplement, 53-61.

Finch, George A. "The Danish West Indies," AJIL, 11 (1917), 413-16.

Koht, Halvdan. "The Origin of Seward's Plan to Purchase the Danish West Indies," AHR, 50 (1945), 762-67.

Larsen, Jens P. M. Virgin Islands Story. Phila., 1950. 250 p.

Raphael, Robert. "Denmark's Caribbean Venture," ASR, 55 (1967), 5-17.

Scott, James B. "The Purchase of the Danish West Indies by the United States of America," AJIL, 10 (1916), 853-59.

Spingarn, Lawrence P. "Slavery in the Danish West Indies," ASR, 45 (1957), 35-43.

Tansill, Charles C. The Purchase of the Danish West Indies. Baltimore, Lond., 1932. 548 p.

Westergaard, Waldemar C. The Danish West Indies Under Company Rule (1671-1754), with a Supplementary Chapter, 1755-1917. N.Y., 1917. 359 p.

WORLD WAR I

Falnes, Oscar J. "Denmark and Norway, 1914-40," in War as a Social Institution. Ed. by J. D. Clarkson and T. C. Cochran (N.Y., 1941), 144-53.

Glad, L. C. The United States and England in Their Relation with Denmark During the War. Coph., 1917. 26 p.

Grön, Alfred H. "Denmark during the War," ASR, 3 (1915), 362-67.

Hassö, Arthur G. "King Christian X of Denmark and Iceland, 1912-1937," ASR, 25 (1937), 103-105.

Jørgensen, Johannes. The War Pilgrim. Lond., 1917. 120 p.

Poulsen, Svenn. "King Christian's Sixtieth Birthday," ASR, 18 (1930), 535-42.

The War Through Danish Eyes (Oxford Pamphlets). Lond., 1915. 19 p.

WORLD WAR II AND THEREAFTER

Anderson, Nils. "Denmark Since Liberation," SoCo, 12 (1948), 323-25.

Anglo-Danish Society, London. Mr. Eden's Salute to Denmark. Lond., 1944. 19 p.

Baerlein, Henry. "Danish Problems," CR, 174 (1948), 303-306.

Bang, Carol K. "Kaj Munk's Autobiography," ASR, 33 (1945), 45-50.

Bertelsen, Aage. October '43. N.Y., 1954. 246 p.

Bredsdorff, Elias. "Danish Literature During the Occupation," Norseman, 4 (1946), 184-90.

Bruel, Erik. "The Danish-German Non-Aggression Pact," Acta scandinavica juris gentium, 10 (1939), 157-63.

Chilston, Viscount. "Denmark," in Part V

of Arnold and Veronica Toynbee, eds.,
Hitler's Europe, in the series Survey of
International Affairs, 1936-1946. (Lond.,
1954), 519-34.

Dancy, Eric. Danes Stand for Zero: the
First-hand Story of the Danish Resistance. Lond., 1943. 35 p.

"The Danish Scene, Summer 1957" [by
A.H.H.], WT, 13 (1957), 401-10.

Denmark, Statens Filmcentral. Documen-
tary in Denmark: One Hundred Films of
Fact in War, Occupation, Liberation,
Peace, 1940-48. Ed. by Ebbe Neergård.
Coph., 1948. 89 p. [Catalogue, with
synopses]

"Denmark under German Occupation" [by
C.M.C.], BIN, 20 (1943), 811-19.

"Denmark under Nazi Rule," Free Europe,
2 (Je 1940), 75-76.

Fabritius, Albert. "Gleams of Free Thought;
Danish Underground Publications," ASR,
33 (1945), 337-39.

Flender, Harold. Rescue in Denmark.
Lond., N.Y., 1963. 281 p.

Gluckstadt, Hans. "The Eclipse of Democracy in Denmark," New Eur, 2 (1942),
131-34.

Great Britain, Association of Free Danes in
Great Britain and Northern Ireland. The
Free Danes. Lond., 1944.

Great Britain, Foreign Office, Historical
Section. Denmark (Handbooks). Lond.,
1943-44.

Gudme, Sten. Denmark: Hitler's "Model
Protectorate." Lond., 1942. 165 p.

——. "Denmark Resists," ASR, 30 (1942),
5-13.

——. "Denmark without a Government,"
ASR, 32 (1944), 113-20.

Haestrup, Jørgen. From Occupied to Ally:
Denmark's Fight for Freedom, 1940-45.
Coph., 1963. 40 p.

Hansen, Christian U. Last Letters of a
Young Danish Patriot Who Was Executed
by the Gestapo, June 23, 1944. Lond.,
1945. 27 p.

Hansen, H. H. Danish Council in London;
Triumph in Disaster. Lond., 1945. 65 p.

Hasselriis, Caspar H. W. Denmark Fights
On. N.Y., 1945. 36 p. Rev. and enl. reprint of Denmark in Revolt. N.Y., 1943.
21 p.

Hicks, Agnes H. "Denmark," in Part III of
Arnold and Veronica Toynbee, eds., The
Initial Triumph of the Axis, in the series
Survey of International Affairs 1939-1946
(Oxford, 1958), 102-109.

Hurwitz, Stephan. "Denmark's New Year,"
Norseman, 3 (1945), 14-15.

——. "Was Denmark at War?" Acta
scandinavica juris gentium, 16 (1945),
49-60.

Joesten, Joachim. Denmark under the
Jackboot. N.Y., 1942. 24 p. Mimeographed.

——. Denmark's Day of Doom. Lond.,
1939. 288 p. American edition, Rats in
the Larder: the Story of Nazi Influence
in Denmark. N.Y., 1939. 270 p.

——. "North Schleswig Next?" PolQ, 10
(1939), 69-82.

Johnson, Harold E. "An American Student
in Denmark," ASR 28 (1940), 257-59.

Jonassen, Hagbard. "Resistance in Denmark," War Resisters International (S
1945), 8 p.

Kauffmann, Henrik. "A Dane Looks at the
Post-War World," ASR, 31 (1943), 103-
108.

Lampe, David. The Savage Canary: the
Story of Resistance in Denmark. Lond.,
1957. 236 p.

Leistikow, Gunnar. "Denmark Under the
Nazi Heel," FA, 21 (1943), 340-53.

——. "Ruining Denmark," Free World, 3
(Je 1942), 70-73.

Madsen, Kai Berg, and Knud Rasmussen.
"Fighting Denmark: a Résumé," ASR, 33
(1945), 328-36.

Mentze, Ernst. Five Years: the Occupation
of Denmark in Pictures. Malmö, 1946.
203 p.

Møller, John Christmas. "The Causes of
Denmark's April 9th," Norseman, 1
(1943), 373-80.

——. Denmark, the War and the Future.
Lond., 1944. 8 p.

——. Denmark, To-day and To-morrow.
Lond., 1944. 11 p.

——. "What Is Happening in Denmark,"
ASR, 31 (1943), 8-15.

——. When Denmark Is Free Again.
Lond., 1944. 12 p.

"Must We Hate?" ASR, 28 (1940), 231-35.

Neiiendam, R. "A Theatre Under Occupation," ASR, 35 (1947), 122-34.

Outze, Børge, ed. Denmark During the German Occupation. Chicago, Coph., 1946.
155 p.

Palmer, Paul. Denmark. Lond., 1945.
171 p.

——. Denmark in Nazi Chains. Lond.,
1942. 128 p.

Palsgaard, Aage. "The Admiral's Wife,"
ASR, 34 (1946), 334-41.

Ringsted, Henrik V. "The Danish Merchant
Fleet in the Second World War," DFOJ
(1946, no. 1), 6-8.

———. "Nazi Terror in Denmark, as Exposed at the Nuremberg Trial," DFOJ (1946, no. 2), 11-15.

Ross, Alf. "Denmark's Legal Status During the Occupation," Nordisk Tidsskrift for Folkerett og international Privatrett, 1 (1949), 3-21.

Satz, Margot. "Enemy Legislation and Judgements in Denmark," Journal of Comparative Legislation and International Law, 31 (1949), 1-3.

Simon, Joseph T. "Nothing Rotten in Denmark," CH, 11 (1946), 25-30.

"Sir William Beveridge's Article in The Times on German 'Refugees' in Denmark," DFOJ (1946, no. 2), 22-23.

Skovmand, Roar. "Denmark During the Occupation," ScPP, III, 1229-36.

"Some Problems Facing Denmark" [by A.H.H.], WT, 8 (1952), 420-29.

Sprenghest, Margrete. "Spring in Denmark 1940, A Personal Narrative," ASR, 28 (1940), 342-49.

Stephasius, Ludwig. "National Socialist Propaganda on the Danish Frontier," CR, 150 (1936), 577-84.

Terkelsen, Terkel M. Denmark: Fight Follows Surrender. Lond., 1st ed., 1941; 2d ed., 1942; 3d ed., 1943; 4th ed., 1947. 28 p.

———. Front Line in Denmark. Lond., 1944. 48 p.

Thaulow, T. "King Christian X of Denmark," ASR, 35 (1947), 234-39.

Vestbirk, Anthon. "Trends in Post-War Developments in Denmark," Norseman, 11 (1953), 21-26.

Wulff, Cecily. "Freedom Returns to Denmark," WAQ, 12 (1946), 41-47.

HISTORIOGRAPHY

Higgs, J. W. Y. "Local History Studies in Denmark," Amateur Historian, 5 (1963), 221-24.

Jørgensen, Harald. "The Study of History in Denmark During the Last Five Years," BSC, 5 (1939), 52-54.

Linvald, Axel. "Danish Historical Research in Recent Times," ScSt, 8 (1924/25), 185-90.

Mathiassen, Therkel. "Prehistory in Denmark, 1939-1944," in Proceedings of the Prehistoric Society (1945), 61-65.

Westergaard, Waldemar C. "Danish History and Danish Historians," JMH, 24 (1952), 167-80.

FINLAND

Anthoni, Eric. "Finland in the Conflict between Sigismund, King of Sweden and Poland, and Carl, Duke of Södermanland," BC, 2 (1936), 181-86.

Brody, Alter. "Finland and Its Rulers: Who Are the Swedo-Finns; Their Role in Finland's History," Soviet Russia Today (Ja 1940), 21-22.

Finland's Progress As an Independent State. Hels., 1939. 39 p.

Fischer, Alfred J. "The Thoughts of a Statesman; Helsinki Meeting with the Finnish President, M. Juho Paasikivi," Norseman, 6 (1948), 21-25.

———. "A Visit to Juho Paasikivi," Norseman, 12 (1954), 386-90.

Forster, Kent. "Fifty Years of Finnish Independence," ASR, 55 (1967), 341-44.

Gleichen, Edward. The Baltic and Caucasian States. Boston, N.Y., 1923. 269 p.

Hamalainen, Pekka K. The Nationality Struggle Between the Finns and the Swedish-Speaking Minority in Finland, 1917-1939. Thesis (Ph.D.), Indiana University, 1966. 384 p.

Heinrichs, Erik, and K. J. Mikola. "The Defense of Finland through the Ages," ScPP, III, 139-46.

Hornborg, Eirik. "Finland and Scandinavia," ScPP, III, 32-37.

Jackson, J. Hampden. Finland. Lond., 1938; N.Y., 1940. 243 p.

Jenness, Eileen. "A Background to Finnish Renaissance," CGJ, 20 (1940), 113-25.

Jutikkala, Eino K., ed. Atlas of Finnish History — Suomen Historian Kartasto (Suomen tisdettä, no. 2). Hels., 1949. 82 p.

———. "The Great Finnish Famine in 1696-1697," SEHR, 3 (1955), 48-63.

———. A History of Finland. N.Y., Lond., 1962. 291 p.

Kaila, Eino. "Finland and Scandinavia," ScPP, I, 24-27.

Kalijarvi, Thorsten V. "Finland," in Joseph S. Roucek, ed., Contemporary Europe (N.Y., 1941), 591-602; 2d ed., N.Y., 1947. 478-89.

King, Alexander. "Finland Yesterday," GeoM, 11 (1940), 1-11.

Lindström, Aune. "Finnish Art in the Last Century," ScPP, II, 1131-48.

———. "The National Awakening of Finnish Art," ScPP, II, 775-82.

Luukko, Armas. "The Birkarlians in the Melting Pot," SEHR, 15 (1967), 148-57.

Mead, William R. "The Conquest of Finland," Norseman, 9 (1951), 14-22, 98-104.

——. "The Discovery of Finland by the British," Norseman, 7 (1949), 249-62.

——. "Finland in the 16th Century," GeoR, 30 (1940), 400-11.

The Memoirs of Marshal Mannerheim. Lond., 1953. 540 p.

Myhrman, Anders M. The Swedish Nationality Movement in Finland. Chicago, 1939. 198 p. Based on thesis (Ph.D.), University of Chicago, 1938.

Nikula, Oscar. "Åbo (Turku) — The Economic Centre of Finland in the Eighteenth Century" [Review of Aimo Wuorinen, Turku kauppakaupunkina Ruotsin vallan loppukautena], SEHR, 14 (1966), 188-93.

Norris, H. T. "Life in Mediaeval Finland," GeoM, 25 (1952), 35-44.

Oppermann, Charles J. A. The English Missionaries in Sweden and Finland. N.Y., Lond., 1937. 221 p.

Pohjakallio, Jussi. Tunnettuja Suomalaisia; Well-known Finns. Hämeenlinna, 1962.

Puramo, Eino, and P. Sjöblom. The Epic of Finland. Hels., 1952. 105 p.

Rosvall, Toivo D. Finland: Land of Heroes. N.Y., 1940. 272 p.

Rothery, Agnes. Finland: the New Nation. Lond., 1936. 258 p.

Ryohomäki, Ilma. "Modern Finland," ASR, 28 (1940), 8-21.

Sergeyev, I. The Saga of the Kavelo-Finnish Republic. N.Y., 1941. 47 p.

Shearman, Hugh. Finland: the Adventures of a Small Power (The Library of World Affairs, no. 13). Lond., 1950. 114 p.

Simons, Roger L. "Sturdy Finland," CH, 65 (1936-37), 81-86.

Soloveytchik, George. "Finland in Perspective," Norseman, 11 (1953), 78-84.

——. "Finland Revisited," CR, 148 (1935), 570-76.

Stevensson, Lilian. Mathilde Wrede of Finland, Friend of Prisoners. Lond., 1925. 159 p.

Stormbom, Nils-Børje. "Twentieth Century Swedish Literature in Finland," ScPP, II, 1107-20.

Tallqvist, J. O. "Finland's Swedish-Language Literature before Runeberg," ScPP, II, 630-42.

——. "Mikael Agricola," ScPP, I, 428-35.

Tigerstedt, Örnulf. "President Svinhufvud of Finland," ASR, 24 (1936), 327-36.

Tuthill, Richard L. "An Analysis of Post-war Finland," JofGeo, 39 (1940), 356-61.

Ullmann, Stephen I. The Epic of the Finnish Nation. Lond., 1940. 128 p.

Virrankoski, Pentti. "Local History in Finland," SEHR, 14 (1966), 179-87.

Wahlroos, Helmer J. "Finland — The Borderland," ScPP, I, 230-34.

——. "Finland by Sweden's Side," ScPP, I, 426-27.

——. "Finland's Struggle to Preserve Her Lawful Order," ScPP, II, 737-41.

——. "Swedish and Finnish Finland," ScPP, II, 732-36.

Wanklyn, Harriet G. "Finland," in her, The Eastern Marchlands of Europe (N.Y., 1941), 41-74.

Wickberg, Nils Erik. "Plan for a Capital: Neo-classical Architecture in Helsinki," ASR, 50 (1962), 58-64.

Wolf, Simon. "Finland Today," CR, 191 (1957), 220-23.

Wuorinen, John H. "Democracy Gains in Finland," CH, 21 (1951), 208-11.

——. "Finland Stands Guard," FA, 32 (1954), 65-70.

——. "Finland," in Stephen Kertesz, ed., The Fate of East Central Europe (South Bend, 1956), 321-37.

——. A History of Finland. N.Y., 1965. 548 p.

——. Nationalism in Modern Finland. N.Y., 1931. 302 p.

Yarham, E. R. "Historic Finland," ASR, 19 (1931), 485-89.

KALEVALA

Haavio, Martti. "Kanteletar," ScPP, I, 243-52.

Haavio, Martti, and Jørgen Bukdahl. "Kalevala," ScPP, I, 235-42.

The Kalevala, or, Poems of the Kaleva District. Compiled by Elias Lönnrot. Cambridge, Mass., 1963. 410 p.

Mead, William R. "Kalevala and the Rise of Finnish Nationality," Folklore, 73 (1962), 217-29.

Shetelig, Haakon. "Finland's National Saga," Norseman, 5 (1947), 179-84.

Turunen, Aimo. "The Kalevala: Finland's National Epic," ASR, 50 (1962), 133-36.

Väisänen, A. O. "The Origin of 'Kalevala'," Norseman, 7 (1949), 132-34.

1815 THROUGH THE 1910 CRISIS

Berendts, E. N. The Rights of Finland According to European Scholars. Lond., 1910. 29 p.

Borodkin, M. M. Finland, Its Place in the Russian State. Lond., 1911. 110 p.

Churberg, W. The Situation of Finland. Lond., 1911. 27 p.

Evreinov, G. A. Russia's Policy in Finland. Lond., 1912. 44 p.

Facts Relating to the Recent Affairs in Finland. Coventry, 1899. 16 p.

Federov, Eugenii. The Finnish Revolution in Preparation 1899-1905 as Disclosed by Secret Documents. St. Petersburg, 1911. 82 p.

Finland. Lantdagen (Reports of committees, etc. in reply to a message from the throne); The Reply of the Finnish Estates Adopted at the Extraordinary Diet of 1899 to the Proposals of His Imperial Majesty, Nicholas II, Grand Duke of Finland, for a New Military Service Law in Finland. Lond., 1900. 256 p.

Fisher, Joseph R. Finland and the Tsars, 1809-1899. Lond., 1899. 272 p. 2d ed. with supplementary chapter relating to the events of 1900. Lond., 1901. 304 p.

Ginsburg, Michael. "From a Family Archive, 1824-1834; Aleksandr Muxanov's Tour of Duty in Finland," Scando-Slavica, 7 (1961), 5-19.

Great Britain, Parliament. A Memorial to the Russian Duma from British and Irish Members of Parliament (An Appeal for the Maintenance of the Finnish Constitution). Lond., 1910. 13 p.

Hodgson, John H., III. "Finland's Position in the Russian Empire, 1905-1910," JCEA, 20 (1960), 158-73.

Korevo, Nikolai N. The Finnish Question: a lecture read before the United Nobility of the Russian Empire at St. Petersburg, 17/30 March, 1910. Lond., 1911. 36 p.

London, Parliamentary Russian Committee. The Crisis in Finland. Lond., 1910. 16 p.

Mechelin, Leopold H. S., ed. Finland in the Nineteenth Century. Hels., Lond., 1894. 367 p.

Minzès, Boris. Russia's Treatment of Finland and Its Bearing on Present World Politics. Brooklyn, 1900. 36 p.

Osten-Sacken, Wolf. The Legal Position of the Grand Duchy of Finland in the Russian Empire. Lond., 1912. 192 p.

Russia. The Russo-Finnish Conflict: the Russian Case. Lond., 1910. 101 p.

Stead, William T. "The Resurrection of Finland," CR, 88 (1905), 761-68.

Suvorov, P. The Finnish Question, Equal Rights: the Position of the Russian in Finland of the Finns. Lond., St. Petersburg, 1910. 60 p.

Wahlroos, Helmer J. "Finland as a Nordic Legal State Under Russia," ScPP, II, 688-91.

———. "The Independence Movement in Finland," ScPP, II, 628-29.

———. "Russia's War Against Finland," ScPP, II, 1205-11.

Waliszewski, Kazimierz. The Finnish Question; The Ostrich and the Sparrow: a Letter from Paris to the "Novae Vremya." Lond., 1910. 10 p.

WORLD WAR I

Anderson, Edgar. "An Undeclared Naval War: the British-Soviet Naval Struggle in the Baltic, 1918-1920," JCEA, 22 (1962), 43-78.

Bennett, Geoffrey M. Cowan's War: the Story of British Naval Operations in the Baltic, 1918-1920. N.Y., 1964. 254 p.

Donner, Herman M. "Finland Crushed or Finland Free?" ASR, 4 (1916), 135-41.

Elviken, Andreas. "Sweden and Finland, 1914-18," in Jesse D. Clarkson and Thomas C. Cochran, eds., War as a Social Institution: the Historian's Perspective. (N.Y., 1941), 134-43.

Harmaja, Leo. Effects of the War on Economic and Social Life in Finland (Carnegie Endowment for International Peace, Division of Economics and History. Economic and Social History of the World War, Translated and Abridged Series). New Haven, Lond., 1933. 125 p.

Hedengren, Torsten. Save Finland from Germany and Starvation. N.Y., 1918. 4 p.

Kalijarvi, Thorsten V. "Finland between World War I and World War II" and "Finland up to 1918," in Joseph S. Roucek, ed., Central Eastern Europe (N.Y., 1946), 160-73, 455-73.

Knoellinger, Carl Erik. "Finland: Twenty Years of Freedom," ASR, 26 (1938), 222-29.

Larson, Laurence M. "The Boundaries of Finland," ASR, 6 (1918), 315-25.

League of Nations. Claim made by the Finnish Government with Regard to Finnish Vessels used during the War by the Government of the United Kingdom. Geneva, 1931-35. 5 pts.

INDEPENDENCE AND THE RED REVOLT

Great Britain, Foreign Office, Historical Section. Finland. Lond., 1920. 130 p.

Halter, Heinz. Finland Breaks the Russian Chains. Lond., 1940. 232 p.

Hannula, Joose O. Finland's War of Independence. Toronto, Lond., 1939. 229 p.

Hyndman, Rosalind T. "The Emancipation of Finland," NewEur 3 (1917), 97-106.

Long, Robert C. "Finland's Independence: a Letter from Helsingfors," Fortnightly Review, 611 (N 1917), 646-63.

"The New Republic in Finland" [Interview with E. Rudolf Holsti], NewEur, 6 (1918), 62-64.

Saastamoinen, Armas H. "Free Finland," ASR, 7 (1919), 362-69.

Smith, Clarence Jay, Jr. Finland and the Russian Revolution, 1917-1922. Athens, Ga., 1958. 251 p.

Söderhjelm, Henning. The Red Insurrection in Finland in 1918: a Study Based on Documentary Evidence. Lond., 1919. 159 p.

"The Struggle for Independence and the Red Insurrection in Finland," Finland Review, 2 (D 1919), 17-34.

Texts of the Finland "Peace." Wash., 1918. 55 p.

Wahlroos, Helmer J. "Finland Wins Her Independence," ScPP, II, 982-88.

Watson, H. G. An Account of a Mission to the Baltic States in the Year 1919. Lond., 1957. 64 p.

"White Terror" in Finland. Hels., 1919. 27 p.

Wuorinen, John H. "Finland's War of Independence, 1918," ASR, 51 (1963), 389-95.

WORLD WAR II AND THEREAFTER

Alenius, Sigyn. Finland Between the Armistice and the Peace. Hels., 1947. 55 p.

Borenius, Tancred. Field-marshal Mannerheim. Lond., Melbourne, 1940. 288 p.

Cartwright, Reginald. Mercy and Murder: an American Ambulance Driver's Experiences in Finland, Norway, and France. Lond., 1941. 86 p.

Citrine, Walter M. My Finnish Diary. Harmondsworth, N.Y., 1940. 192 p.

Coates, William P. Russia, Finland and the Baltic. Lond., 1940. 144 p.

———. The Soviet-Finnish Campaign, Military and Political, 1939-1940. Lond., 1941. 172 p.

Council of Foreign Ministers...Draft Peace Treaty with Finland. Prepared by the Council of Foreign Ministers for Consideration by the Peace Conference of Twenty-One Nations Meeting in Paris on 29th July, 1946. Lond., 1946. 19 p.

Cox, Geoffrey. The Red Army Moves. Lond., 1941. 278 p.

Dancy, Eric. "Finland Takes Stock," FA, 24 (1946), 513-25.

Elliston, Herbert B. Finland Fights. Lond., 1940. 397 p.; Boston, 1940. 443 p.

"Finland in Recent Swedish Books," ASR, 29 (1941), 144-46.

"Finland Today," WT, 13 (1957), 118-27.

"Finnish Outlook," WT, 8 (1950), 165-75.

Fischer, Alfred J. "Finland Revisited," CR, 173 (1948), 165-70.

Fox, Annette Baker. "Finland: Fighting Neutral," in her, The Power of Small States: Diplomacy in World War II (Chicago, 1959), 43-77.

Hinshaw, David. An Experiment in Friendship. Quaker Relief in Finland. Lond., N.Y., 1947. 147 p.

———. Heroic Finland. N.Y., 1952. 306 p.

Iloniemi, Jaakko. "Finland and the Second World War" [review article], C&C (1965, no. 2), 92-94.

Jakobson, Max. The Diplomacy of the Winter War: an Account of the Russo-Finnish War, 1939-1940. Cambridge, Mass., 1961. 281 p.

Jackson, J. Hampden. "Finland Since the Armistice," IA, 24 (1948), 505-14.

———. "Russian Control in Finland," CR, 170 (1946), 69-72.

Kalijarvi, Thorsten V. "Finland Since 1939," RevPol, 10 (1948), 212-25.

Krosby, H. Peter. Petsamo in the Spotlight: a Case Study in Finnish-German Relations 1940-1941. Thesis (Ph.D.), Columbia University, 1965.

Langdon-Davies, John. Finland, The First Total War. Lond., 1940. 202 p.

Lowery, Sidney. "Finland," in Part VI of Arnold and Veronica Toynbee, eds., Hitler's Europe in the series Survey of International Affairs, 1939-1946 (Lond., 1954), 576-84.

Lundin, C. Leonard. Finland in the Second World War (Indiana University Publications, Slavic and East European Series, no. 6). Bloomington, Ind., 1957. 303 p.

Luukkanen, Eino A. Fighter over Finland: the Memoirs of a Fighter Pilot. Ed. by William Green. Lond., 1963. 254 p.

Matson, Alexander. "Finland's Army of Women," ASR, 28 (1940), 39-44.

Mazour, Anatole G. Finland Between East and West. Princeton, 1956. 298 p.

Montagu, Ivor. "The Truth About Finland," Labour Monthly, 22 (Ja 1940), 15-28.

Owen, John E. "Finland Today," Norseman, 11 (1953), 16-20.

Pallo, A. "Post-War Finland," BRI, 1 (1945-47), 105-109.

Pritt, Denis N. Light on Moscow: Soviet Policy Analysed with a New Chapter

on Finland.   Harmondsworth, 1940.
223 p.

——.   Must the War Spread? Harmondsworth, 1940. 256 p.

Rodzianko, Paul. Mannerheim: an Intimate
Picture of a Great Soldier and Statesman.
Lond., 1940. 223 p.

Saari, John. "Finnish Nationalism, Justify-
ing Independence," Annals, 232 (1944),
33-38.

Soloviev, Mikhail. My Nine Lives in the
Red Army. N.Y., 1955. 308 p.

Stowe, Leland. No Other Road to Freedom.
N.Y., 1941. 432 p.; Lond., 1942. 340 p.

Suviranta, Bruno K. Finland's War Indemnity. Stock., 1947. 43 p. Supplement to
SHI (M 1947).

——. War Indemnities and Capital Levy in
Finland. Stock., 1941. 24 p.

Tanner, Väinö A. The Winter War: Finland
Against Russia, 1939-1940. Stanford,
Calif., 1957. 274 p.

Upton, Anthony F. Finland in Crisis, 1940-
41. A Study in Small Power Politics.
Lond., 1964; Ithaca, 1965. 318 p.

Voipio, Anni. "Marshal Mannerheim," ASR,
52 (1964), 389-402.

Ward, Edward H. H. Despatches from Finland, January-April, 1940. Lond., 1940.
160 p.

Waris, Heikki, and J. Siipi. Resettlement of
Displaced Persons in Finland. Hels.,
1954. 35 p.

Wickman, Johannes. "The Finnish Problem," Norseman, 1 (1943), 380-86.

Wuorinen, John H., ed. Finland and the
World War, 1939-1944. N.Y., 1948.
228 p.

ICELAND

Andersson, Theodore M. The Icelandic
Family Saga: an Analytic Reading.
Cambridge, Mass., 1967. 315 p.

Beck, Richard. "Sveinn Björnsson, 1881-
1952," ASR, 40 (1952), 109-11.

——. "Sveinn Björnsson, Regent of Iceland," ASR, 30 (1942), 321-23.

Benediktsson, Pétur. "Independent Iceland,"
Norseman, 1 (1943), 409-16.

Björnsson, Björn Th. "Icelandic Art of the
Middle Ages," ASR, 55 (1967), 345-59.

——. "Icelandic Gothic," ScPP, I,
293-95.

——. "Recent Art in Iceland," ScPP, II,
1195-97.

——. "Romanesque Art in Iceland," ScPP,
I, 218-19.

——. "Visual Arts of Iceland," ScPP, I,
152-54.

Björnsson, Sveinn. "Recollections of an Icelandic Statesman" [Autobiography],
Norseman, 16 (1958), 217-25.

Bløndal, Sigfus, "Iceland a Treasure Trove
of Manuscripts," ASR, 18 (1930), 275-82.

——. "Iceland in the North," Nord, 4
(1941), 153-65.

Briem, Helgi P. "King Jorgen Jorgenson,
An Episode in Iceland's History," ASR,
31 (1943), 120-31.

Bryce, James B. Primitive Iceland (Studies
in History and Jurisprudence). N.Y.,
1901. 926 p.

Butcher, Harold. "In Iceland Today," ASR,
30 (1942), 342-47.

Clark, E. V. "Impressions of Iceland," CR,
181 (Ja 1952), 30-34.

Conybeare, Charles A. V. The Place of Iceland in the History of European Institutions. Oxford, 1877. 160 p.

Davies, Rhys. Sea Urchin: Adventures of
Jorgen Jorgensen [Ruler of Iceland in
1809]. Lond., 1940. 288 p.

Einarsson, Stefan. A History of Icelandic
Literature. N.Y., 1957. 409 p.

Friters, Gerard M. "Iceland and Greenland," CR, 160 (1941), 294-98.

Gjerset, Knut. History of Iceland. N.Y.,
1925. 482 p.

Guthmundsson, Barthi. The Origin of the
Icelanders. Tr. by Lee M. Hollander.
Lincoln, Nebraska, 1967. 173 p.

Hermannson, Halldór. "Jon Gudmundson
and his Natural History of Iceland,"
Islandica, 15 (1924), 56 p.

——. "Willard Fiske and Icelandic Bibliography," Papers of the Bibliographic
Society of America (Chicago), 12 (1918,
no. 3/4), 97-106.

Hood, John C. Icelandic Church Saga.
Lond., 1946. 241 p.

Icelandic Institutions. Coph., 1903. 80 p.

Islandica: an Annual Relating to Iceland and
the Fiske Icelandic Collection in Cornell
University Library. Ithaca, N.Y. v. 1——.
1908——.

Johannesson, Thorkell. "The Colonization
of Iceland and the Old Althing," ScPP, I,
121-24.

——. "Greenland and Vinland (Wineland),"
ScPP, I, 125-27.

——. "Iceland and Enlightened Absolutism,"
ScPP, II, 671-73.

——. "Iceland – From Home Rule to Independent Republic," ScPP, II, 989-95.

——. "The Icelandic Church in the Period
of Independence," ScPP, I, 214-17.

——. "The Icelandic Reformation," ScPP, I, 417-20.

——. "National Rebirth in Iceland," ScPP, II, 699-701.

——. "Youthful Iceland," ScPP, I, 16-19.

Johnson, Skuli, ed. Iceland's Thousand Years: a Series of Popular Lectures on the History and Literature of Iceland. Winnipeg, 1945. 169 p.

Johnson, Sveinbjorn. Pioneers of Freedom: an Account of the Icelanders and the Icelandic Free State, 874-1262. Boston, 1930. 361 p.

Jónsson, Hannes. Iceland's Unique History and Culture. Lond., 1961.

Magoun, F. P. "The Pilgrim-Diary of Nikulas Munkathvera: the Road to Rome," Medieval Studies, 6 (1944), 314-54.

Marcus, G. J. "The First English Voyages to Iceland," Mariner's Mirror, 42 (1956), 313-18.

Morris, Franklyn K. "Icelanders Celebrate 900 Years of Christianity," Norseman, 15 (1957), 117-19.

Oleson, Tryggvi J. "Bishop Jón Arason, 1484-1550" [Last Roman Catholic Bishop in Iceland until the twentieth century], Speculum, 28 (1953), 245-78.

——. "Book Collections of Mediaeval Icelandic Churches," Speculum, 32 (1957), 502-10.

Perkins, Mekkin S. "Piracy in Iceland," ASR, 49 (1961), 259-65.

——. "Three Career Women of Iceland" [20th century], ASR, 42 (1954), 239-42.

Rutherford, Adam. The Origin and Development of the Icelandic Nation. Lond., 1938. 29 p.

Schlauch, Margaret. "The Women of the Icelandic Sagas," ASR, 31 (1943), 333-40.

Skúlason, Thorlákur, Bishop of Hólar. Two Treaties on Iceland from the 17th Century. Thorlákur Skúlason: Responsia subitanea. Brynjólfur Sveinsson: Historica de rebus islandicis relation (Bibliotheca arnamagnaeana, v. 3). Coph., 1943. 59 p.

Stefánsson, Jón. "Iceland; Its History and Inhabitants," Smithsonian Institution Annual Report, 1906 (Wash., 1907), 275-94. Reprinted from the Journal of Transactions of the Victoria Institute of Philosophical Society of Great Britain, 34 (1902), 167-78; 38 (1906), 54-63.

Stefansson, Vilhjalmur. "Icelandic Independence," FA, 7 (1929), 270-81.

Storek, Martha H. Women in the Time of the Icelandic Family Saga. Thesis (Ph.D.), Bryn Mawr College, 1946. 305 p.

Sveinsson, Einar Ol. The Age of the Sturlungs, Icelandic Civilization in the 13th Century (Islandica, v. 36). Lond., 1954. 198 p.

Tennant, Peter F. D. "The Struggle for Iceland's Independence," BSC, 5 (1939), 107-12.

Thomas, Richard G. Aspects of the Sturlung Age, with Special Reference to "Sturlunga Saga": a Study in the Life and Literature of Iceland during the Twelfth and Thirteenth Centuries. Thesis (Ph.D.), Wales, 1944.

——. The Position of Women in Icelandic Life and Social Economy as Shown in the Icelandic Sagas. Thesis (M.A.), Cardiff, 1940.

Thorarinsson, Sigurdur. The Thousand Years Struggle Against Ice and Fire (Museum of Natural History, Dept. of Geology and Geography, Miscellaneous Papers, no. 14). Rey., 1956. 52 p.

Thórdarson, Björn. Iceland, Past and Present. Lond., 1941. 46 p.; 2d ed., Lond., 1945. 48 p.

Thorgilsson. Ari. The Book of the Icelanders (Íslendingabók). Ithaca; Lond., 1930. 89 p.

Thorlakson, Edward J. "Jon Sigurdsson, Icelandic Statesman," ASR, 32 (1944), 17-25.

Turville-Petre, E. O. Gabriel. "Notes on the Intellectual History of the Icelanders," History, 27 (1942), 111-23.

WORLD WAR II

"The American Occupation of Iceland," ASR, 29 (1941), 255-59.

Bjornson, Hjalmar. "The Point of No Return," ASR, 32 (1944), 304-14.

Chamberlin, William C. Economic Development of Iceland through World War II (Columbia University, Faculty of Political Science, Studies in History, Economics and Public Law, no. 531) N.Y., 1947. 141 p.

Dreyfus, L. G., Jr. "Independence of the Republic of Iceland," DeptStateBul, 10 (1944), 557-64.

Gröndal, Benedikt. "President Asgúrsson of Iceland," ASR, 42 (1954), 109-15.

Gunnarson, Olafur. "Iceland and the War," Norseman, 1 (1943), 205-11.

Johannesson, Thorkell. "Iceland's Struggle for Independence," ScPP, II, 742-47.

Jónsson, Snaebjörn. Iceland and the War; Ísland og ófridurinn. Rey., 1940. 16 p.

——. "The Occupation of Iceland," Norseman, 7 (1949), 225-29.

Kroyer, Haraldur. The Union of Denmark and Iceland, 1918-1944. Thesis (M.A.), University of California, 1945.

Simmons, Stephen. "Iceland and the Post-War World," Norseman, 5 (1947), 426-31.

Thors, Thor. "Iceland," ASR, 32 (1944), 197-201.

——. "Independent Iceland," ASR, 28 (1940), 325-27.

Weigert, Hans W. "Iceland, Greenland and the United States," FA, 23 (1944), 112-22.

Whittaker, James. "Iceland and Her Post-War Problems," Norseman, 6 (1948), 91-95.

NORWAY

Aagaard, Bjarne. "Norwegians in the Antarctic," ASR, 22 (1934), 33-45.

Anderson, Rasmus B. "Restaurationen — the Norse Mayflower," ASR, 13 (1925), 348-60.

Beyer, Harald. A History of Norwegian Literature. N.Y., 1956. 370 p.

Bløndal, Sigfús, "The Last Exploits of Harald Sigurdsson in Greek Service," Classica, 2 (1939), 1-26.

Boyesen, Hjalmar H. A History of Norway from the Earliest Times (The Story of the Nations). N.Y., Lond., 1900. 572 p.

Brøgger, Anton W. "From the Stone Age to the Motor Age: a Sketch of Norwegian Cultural History," NGT, 7 (1938/39), 77-97.

Bull, Francis. "Norway and Scandinavia — and the World," ScPP, I, 12-15.

Candlin, E. Frank. "North Sea Traffic," Norseman, 11 (1953), 156-60.

Christensen, Christian A. R. "Fifty Years of History," Norseman, 15 (1957), 361-65.

——. Norway, a Democratic Kingdom: 1905-1955; Fifty Years of Progress. Oslo, 1955. 47 p.

Derry, Thomas K. A Short History of Norway. Lond., 1957. 281 p.

Elviken, Andreas. "Genesis of Norwegian Nationalism," JMH, 3 (1931), 365-91.

Falnes, Oscar J. National Romanticism in Norway. N.Y., 1933. 398 p.

Gathorne-Hardy, Geoffrey M. Norway. Lond., N.Y., 1925. 324 p.

Gjerset, Knut. History of the Norwegian People. 2 vols. N.Y., 1915; 2d ed. 1932. 1 v.; new ed. Lond., 1927. 2 v. in 1 (644 p.).

Gulbrandsen, Leif T. "Bishop Eivind Berggrav," ASR, 30 (1942), 127-30.

Johnson, Alex. Eivind Berggrav: God's Man of Suspense, Minneapolis, 1960. 222 p.

Keilhau, Wilhelm C. Norway in World History. Lond., 1944. 206 p.

Koht, Halvdan. Education of an Historian. N.Y., 1957. 237 p.

Koht, Halvdan, and Sigmund Skard. The Voice of Norway. Lond., 1944. 176 p.; N.Y., 1944. 313 p. Part I: Koht, "Free Men Build Their Society," 1-116; Part II: Skard, "Life Unfolds in Literature," 117-296.

Larsen, Karen. A History of Norway. Princeton, N. J., 1948. 591 p.

Lund, Diderich H. "The Revival of Northern Norway," GeogJ, 109 (1947), 185-97.

Major, Harlan. Norway, Home of the Norseman. N.Y., 1957. 195 p.

Manus, Max. "In the Trap and Out Again," Norseman, 11 (1953), 325-33.

Martin, Anthony H., and Fredrik Wulfsberg, eds. Across the North Sea. Oslo, 1955. 152 p.

Midgaard, John. A Brief History of Norway. Oslo, 1963. 149 p.

Mohn, Einar K. "A Fortnight in Western Norway," ASR, 3 (1915), 142-50.

Mortensen, Sverre, ed., and Per Vogt. One Hundred Norwegians: an Introduction to Norwegian Culture and Achievement. Oslo, 1955. 206 p.

Norman, Carl. "The Seventeenth of May," ASR, 49 (1961), 20-29.

The Norseman. Each issue since 1942 contains a brief review of recent events.

Oleson, John Y. History of Norway and the Norsemen. Storm Lake, Iowa, 1952. 46 p.

Popperwell, R. G. "A Split Tradition," Norseman, 13 (1955), 241-45.

Q[vamme], B[ørre]. "English Monks in Norway," Norseman, 9 (1951), 326-32.

Ramn, Frederik. "The Flight of the Norge," ASR, 14 (1926), 399-407.

Scott, Franklin D. "Søren Jaabaek, Americanizer in Norway," Norwegian-American Studies and Records, 17 (1952), 84-107.

Semmingsen, Ingrid. "Norway's Flight," ScPP, II, 1219-28.

Sherriff, Florence Janson. "Norway," in Daniel H. Thomas and Lynn M. Case, eds., Guide to the Diplomatic Archives of Western Europe (Phila., 1959), 179-92.

Smith, Leslie F. Modern Norwegian Historiography. Oslo, 1962. 116 p.

Stagg, Frank N. East Norway and Its Frontier: a History of Oslo and Its Uplands. Lond., N.Y., 1956. 285 p.

——. The Heart of Norway: a History of

the Central Provinces. Lond., N.Y.,
1953. 194 p.
——. North Norway: a History. Lond.,
1952. 205 p.
——. South Norway. Lond., N.Y., 1958.
232 p.
——. West Norway and Its Fjords: a His-
tory of Bergen and Its Provinces. Lond.,
1954. 245 p.
Stiansen, Peder. History of the Baptists in
Norway. Chicago, 1933. 176 p.
Teal, John J., Jr. "The Rebirth of North
Norway," FA, 32 (1953), 123-34.
Undset, Sigrid. Kristin Lavransdatter.
N.Y. Several editions, including 1928,
1961.
Wergeland, Agnes M. Leaders in Norway,
and Other Essays. Menasha, Wisc., 1916.
193 p.

LOCAL HISTORY

Bagöien, Anders. "Trondheim — A Blend of
Tradition and Drive," Norseman (1966),
94-99.
Bartlett, Kenneth E. "Maihaugen: a Thou-
sand Years of Norwegian History," ASR,
55 (1967), 26-33.
Blessum, Ben. "Maihaugen and Its Maker,"
ASR, 26 (1938), 248-58.
——. "Gudbrandsdalen," ASR, 14 (1926),
600-11.
——. "Möre and Nordfjord," ASR, 16
(1928), 269-80.
——. "Nordland," ASR, 15 (1927), 536-48.
——. "Trondhjem Cathedral," ASR, 18
(1930), 285-92.
Bøjer, Johan. "Trondhjem and Tröndelagen,"
ASR, 14 (1926), 16-25.
Dehlin, Stene. "Utstein Abbey," Norseman
(1965), 2-6.
Egge, Peter. "Trondhjem," ASR, 15 (1927),
331-40.
Fett, Harry. "From Norwegian Impres-
sionism to Oslo City Hall," ScPP, II,
1047-63.
Fischer, Gerhard. "Nidaros Cathedral in
Trondheim," Norseman, 11 (1953), 178-
86.
——. "The Norwegian Capital 900 Years,"
Norseman, 8 (1950), 170-75.
Fjellbu, Arne. "The Church Anniversary in
Trondheim," Norseman, 11 (1953), 187-90.
Freding, Thyra. "In Historic Ringerike, On
the Shores of the Tryifjord," ASR, 20
(1932), 10-15.
Gjessing, Gutorm. "The Skjomen Carving:
an Arctic Rock Carving in Northern Nor-
way," AcAr, 2 (1931), 278+.

Hambro, Johan. "A Beloved Museum" [Col-
lections at Maihaugen], Norseman (1963,
no. 6), 4-7.
Henriksen, Ragnar. "Fredrikstad 400 Years
Old," Norseman (1967), 32-36.
Hopstock, Carsten. "Castle with Viking
Traditions: Austråt by the Trondheims-
fjord," Norseman (1967), 104-108.
——. "Kragerø Tricentenary," Norseman
(1966), 68-73.
——. "Proud Period Piece, Bogstad Gård,"
Norseman (1967), 80-84.
——. "Rosendal on the Hardangerfjord,"
Norseman (1965), 64-68.
Lund, Kjell. "Churches Old and New: Tra-
ditions and Innovations in Norwegian Ar-
chitecture," Norseman (1961, no. 2), 2-7.
Ødvin, Magnhild. "Skaugum" [the Royal
Residence], ASR, 18 (1930), 423-27.
Olsen, Magnus B. Farms and Fanes of An-
cient Norway: the Place-Names of a
Country Discussed in their Bearings on
Social and Religious History. Oslo, Cam-
bridge, Mass., 1926. 349 p.
Polak, Ada. "A National Shrine: the Cathe-
dral of Trondheim," Norseman (1966),
100-104.
Semmingsen, Ingrid. "The Folk Revivals:
Hans Nielsen Hauge and the Rising of
Norwegian Farmers," ScPP, II, 710-15.
Shetelig, Haakon. Cruciform Brooches of
Norway (Bergens Museums Aarsberetning
for 1906, 2). Bergen, 1906. 106 p.
Simonsen, Povl. "The History of Settle-
ment," in Ørnulf Vorren, ed., Norway
North of 65 (Oslo, 1960), 100-21.
Sjøvold, Thorlief. The Iron Age Settlement
of Arctic Norway (Tromsø Museum,
Skrifter, v. 10). Tromsø, 1963. 253 p.
Sogner, Björn. "A Contribution to Norwe-
gian Urban History" [Trondheim; Review
article], SEHR, 5 (1957), 74-77.
Stang, Ragna. "The Norwegian Cathedrals,"
ScPP, I, 276-81.
——. "Norwegian Folk Art," ScPP, I,
580-85.
Svare, Richard. "Oriental Touch in Norway,"
Norseman (1961, no. 4), 4-7.
Tveteraas, R. "The See of Stavanger," ASR,
13 (1925), 222-27.

NORWEGIAN HISTORY TO 1715

Blindheim, Martin. Main Trends of East-
Norwegian Wooden Sculpture in the Second
Half of the Thirteenth Century (Skr. utg.
av det Norske Videnskaps-Akademi, Oslo.
2. Hist.-Filos. kl., 1952, no. 3). Oslo,
1952. 128 p.

———. "Norwegian Church Art in the Middle Ages," ASR, 51 (1963), 355-77.

Borgarthings, Kristinirettr. The Borgarthing Law of the Codex Tunsbergensis, An Old Norwegian Manuscript of 1320-1330 (University of Illinois Studies in Language and Literature, v. 10, no. 4). Ed. by George T. Flom. Urbana, Ill., 1925. 202 p.

Brown, Keith. "A Wedding in Oslo: Princess Anna of Denmark-Norway Married James I and Became the First Queen of a United Britain," Norseman (1967), 141-44.

Bugge, Alexander. "An Empire of the Sea, A Fourteenth Century Journey Through the Realm of Norway," ASR, 14 (1926), 724-38.

Bukdahl, Jörgen. "St. Olav and Norway," ASR, 18 (1930), 405-13.

Candlin, E. Frank. "Saint Olaf of Norway," Norseman, 10 (1952), 221-24.

———. "William the Norseman," Norseman, 13 (1955), 361-67.

Dickins, Bruce. "St. Olav and the British Isles," Norseman, 2 (1944), 370-74.

Ellis, Ruth. "In the Hanseatic Days" [in Bergen], Norseman, 14 (1956), 242-49.

Findahl, Theo. "Norway's Eternal King: the Death of St. Olav Commemorated," ASR, 17 (1929), 537-39.

Gade, John A. The Hanseatic Control of Norwegian Commerce During the Late Middle Ages. Leiden, 1951. 139 p. Based on Ph.D. thesis, Columbia University, 1950.

Gathorne-Hardy, Geoffrey M. "A Medieval 'Whodunit'," Norseman, 12 (1954), 321-24.

———. A Royal Imposter: King Sverre of Norway. Lond., 1956. 305 p.

Grieg, Sigurd. "Cologne and Bergen. Imports of German Glasses into Norway in the Middle Ages," AcAr, 1 (1930), 283-92.

Grimble, Ian. "The King of Norway in Gaelic Folk Lore," Norseman, 8 (1950), 225-30.

Gulathingslög hin eldre. The Earliest Norwegian Laws, being the Gulathing Law and the Frostathing Law. Tr. by Laurence M. Larson (Records of Civilization. Sources and Studies, no. 20; ed. under the auspices of the Dept. of History, Columbia University), N.Y., 1935. 451 p.

Haco, King of Norway. Norwegian Account of Haco's Expedition Against Scotland; A.D. 1263. Edinburgh, 1882. 74 p.

Hermannsson, Halldór. The Ancient Laws of Norway and Iceland (Islandica: an Annual Relating to Iceland and the Fiske Icelandic Collection in Cornell University Library, v. 4). Ithaca, 1911. 83 p.

Herteig, Asbjørn E. "Excavating Bergen's Hanseatic Wharf," ASR, 48 (1960), 171-78.

Johnsen, Arne O. "Nicolaus Brekespear and the Norwegian Church Province, 1153," Norseman, 11 (1953), 244-51.

Larson, Laurence M. "The Beginnings of the Norwegian Church," ASR, 12 (1924), 726-35.

———. "The Household of the Norwegian Kings in the Thirteenth Century," AHR, 13 (1908), 459-79.

Leach, Henry G. Relations of the Norwegian with the English Church, 1066-1399. N.Y., 1909.

Lödrup, Hans P. "Saint Olav," ASR, 18 (1930), 397-404.

Michell, Thomas. History of the Scottish Expedition to Norway in 1612. Lond., 1886. 189 p.

Muir, J. W. "'The Battle of Largs' or the Autumn Gale That Saved Scotland," Norseman, 14 (1956), 167-76.

Nilson, Sten S. "A Medieval Dictator," Norseman, 6 (1948), 387-94.

Sandberg, Rei. "Battle at Midtskogen," Norseman, 4 (1946), 212-17.

Semmingsen, Ingrid. "Norway During the Kalmar Union," ScPP, I, 369-77.

———. "The King's Mirror," ScPP, I, 288-92.

———. "The Norwegian Peasant Community," ScPP, I, 571-79.

———. "The Norwegian Viceregency," ScPP, I, 479-85.

———. "The Norwegians and the Union with Sweden," ScPP, II, 748-58.

———. "The Reformation in Norway," ScPP, II, 401-402.

———. "St. Olav," ScPP, I, 165-68.

———. "A Strong Monarchy in Norway," ScPP, I, 271-75.

———. "Sverre and the 'Birch-legs'," ScPP, I, 220-25.

———. "Town Patricians in Norway," ScPP, II, 655-60.

Simonsen, Povl. "Block Houses in North Norway in the Middle Ages," Universitets Årsbok, Bergen, 1955.

Solheim, Svale. The Horse-Fight and Horse-Race in Norse Tradition (Studia Norvegica; Ethnologica and folkloristica, v. 3, no. 8), Oslo, 1956. 173 p.

Undset, Sigrid. Saga of Saints. N.Y., 1934. 321 p.

Vreim, Halvor. "The Ancient Settlements in Finnmark, Norway," Folkliv, 1 (1937), 169-203.

Willson, Thomas B. History of the Church and State in Norway from the Tenth to the Sixteenth Century. Westminster, 1903. 382 p.

1715-1914

"The Career of Roald Amundsen," ASR, 16 (1928), 651-55.

Delmé-Radcliffe, Charles. A Territorial Army in Being: a Practical Study of the Swiss Militia by Lt. Col. C. Delmé-Radcliffe ... and the Norwegian militia by James W. Lewis, late 19th century Hussars. Lond., 1908. 132 p.

Ellsworth, Lincoln. "Roald Amundsen; a Tribute," ASR, 16 (1928), 656-58.

Gathorne-Hardy, Geoffrey M. Bodö-Saken; British Diplomatic Correspondence Relating to the Bodö Affair [1819-35] Extracted from the Public Foreign Office Records. Oslo, 1926, 103 p.

Great Britain, War Office, Intelligence Division. Handbook of the Armies of Sweden and Norway. By T. H. V. Crowe. Lond., 1901. 122 p.

Jorgenson, Theodore. Norway's Relation to Scandinavian Unionism 1815-1871. Northfield, Minn., 1935. 530 p.

Koht, Halvdan. "Björnstjerne Björnson," ASR, 20 (1932), 551-64.

Langeland, Alv S. "Our Dear Foes: Anglo-Norwegian Sentiments in 1814," Norseman, 8 (1950), 84-86.

Larson, Harold. Björnstjerne Björnson: a Study in Norwegian Nationalism. N.Y., 1944. 172 p.

Lescoffier, Jean. "Bjørnstjerne Bjørnson (1832-1910)," Norseman, 3 (1945), 258-64.

Lewis, James W. Norwegian Militia System. Lond., 1908. 132 p.

Neserius, Philip G. "Ibsen's Political and Social Ideas," APSR, 19 (1925), 25-37.

Østvedt, Einar. "Great Britain and the Norwegian Fight for Freedom in 1814," Norseman, 6 (1948), 368-72.

Schulerud, Mentz. "Ludvig Holberg and His Times," ScPP, I, 550-64.

Semmingsen, Ingrid. "The Norwegian Constitution of May 17, 1814," ScPP, II, 692-97.

MIGRATION

Blegen, Theodore C. "The Norwegian Government and the Early Norwegian Emigration," Minnesota History, 6 (1925), 115-40.

————. Norwegian Migration to America, 1825-1860. Northfield, Minn., 1931. 413 p.

Flom, George T. A History of Norwegian Immigration to the United States from the Earliest Beginnings Down to the Year 1848. Iowa City, 1909. 407 p.

Hovde, Brynjolf J. "Norwegian Migrations to the United States before the Civil War," Norwegian-American Historical Association Studies, 6 (1931), 162-67.

FRIDTJOF NANSEN

Christensen, Christian A. R. Fridtjof Nansen: a Life in the Service of Science and Humanity. 1961. 32 p.

Hall, Anna G. Nansen. N.Y., 1940. 165 p.

Hambro, Johan. "He Belongs to the World: Fridtjof Nansen, 1861-1961," Norseman (1961, no. 5), 8-11.

Høyer, Liv Nansen. Nansen, A Family Portrait, by his daughter. Lond., N.Y., 1957. 269 p.

Leach, Henry G. "Fridtjof Nansen," ASR, 49 (1961), 360-67.

Lodge, Thomas. "Fridtjof Nansen," Norseman, 1 (1943), 30-34.

Nansen, Fridtjof, ed. The Norwegian North Polar Expedition, 1893-1896. 6 vols. N.Y., Lond., 1900-1906.

Noel-Baker, Francis E. Fridtjof Nansen, Arctic Explorer. Lond., N.Y., 1958. 126 p.

————. "I Knew a Man — Nansen," Norseman, 1 (1943), 93-98.

Reynolds, Ernest E. Nansen. Lond., 1932. 274 p.; 2d ed., Lond., 1949. 283 p.

Rygg, A. N. "Fridtjof Nansen," ASR, 19 (1931), 265-83.

Saunders, Hilary S. G. "Nansen as I Knew Him," Norseman, 3 (1945), 86-93.

Sélincourt, Aubrey de. Nansen. Lond., 1957. 166 p.

Smith, Bertie W. Fridtjof Nansen. Lond., 1939. 208 p.

Sörenson, Jon. The Saga of Fridtjof Nansen. N.Y., Lond., 1932. 372 p.

Starritt, S. Stuart. The Life of Nansen. Lond., 1931. 142 p.

"Tributes to Fridtjof Nansen from the Public Prints," ASR, 18 (1930), 547-51.

Turley, Charles. Nansen of Norway. 3d ed., Lond., 1934. 210 p.

Vogt, Per, ed. Fridtjof Nansen. Explorer — Scientist — Humanitarian. Oslo, 1961. 197 p.

Whitehouse, John H., ed. Nansen: a Book of Homage. Lond., 1930. 189 p.

Worm-Müller, Jacob S. "Fridtjof Nansen," Impact of Science on Society, 11 (1961), 223-56.

———. "Homage to Fridtjof Nansen," Norseman, 1 (1943), 90-92.

SPITSBERGEN (SVALBARD)

Brown, Robert N. Rudmose. "British Work in Spitsbergen; Some Historical Notes," SGM, 27 (1911), 180-87.

———. "The Present State of Spitsbergen," SGM, 35 (1919), 201-12.

Bruce, William S. "Spitsbergen, 1898 and 1899: Voyages with H.S.H. the Prince of Monaco," SGM, 16 (1900), 534-50.

Conway, Martin. "The Political Status of Spitsbergen," GeogJ 53 (1919), 83-90.

Great Britain, Foreign Office, Historical Section. Spitsbergen (Handbooks, no. 36). Lond., 1920.

Isachsen, Gunnar. "Green Harbour, Spitsbergen," SGM, 31 (1915), 1-22.

THE TWENTIETH CENTURY

Blackburn, Robert. "Norway and the Norwegians," CR, 190 (1956), 227-32.

Boveri, Margaret. "Knut Hamsun — the Deaf Poet," in her, Treason in the Twentieth Century (Lond., 1961; N.Y., 1963), 173-84.

Candlin, E. Frank. "The Maid of Norway" [Princess Margaret], Norseman, 4 (1946), 406-12.

Collier, Laurence, "Haakon VII; A Foreigner's Tribute," Norseman, 10 (1952), 217-20.

"Crown Prince Harald," Norseman (1960, no. 4), 5-7.

Friis, Erik J. "Trygve Lie," ASR, 36 (1948), 11-16.

Geiss, Gilbert L. "Knut Hamsun, 1859-1952," Norseman, 10 (1952), 160-66.

Hambro, Carl J. "Haakon the Seventh of Norway," ASR, 30 (1942), 197-201.

———. "Norway Today," ASR, 24 (1936), 7-18.

Hauge, Hans N. Autobiographical Writings. Minneapolis, 1954. 159 p.

Keilhau, Wilhelm C. King Haakon VII in the History of Norway. Lond., 1942. 72 p.

Knaplund, Paul. "Finnmark in British Diplomacy," AHR, 30 (1925), 478-501.

Lindgren, Raymond E. "Norway's Golden Jubilee, 1905-1955," ASR, 43 (1955), 237-45.

Michael, Maurice. Haakon, King of Norway. Lond., N.Y., 1958. 207 p.

Mjelde, M. "Norway in War and Peace," NewEur, 14 (1920), 110-14, 206-209, 234-38.

Paneth, Philip. Haakon VII; Norway's Fighting King. Lond., 1944. 107 p.

Ring, Barbara. "Crown Prince Olav and Crown Princess Märtha," ASR, 19 (1931), 98-102.

"The Royal Family of Norway," ASR, 27 (1939), 7-10.

Rygg, Andrew N. "Andrew Furuseth," ASR, 26 (1938), 123-33.

Semmingsen, Ingrid. "Norway 1905-1940," ScPP, II, 1009-18.

Thompson, C. Patrick. "Old Man Norway" [Johan Nygaardsvold], Norseman, 2 (1944), 93-99.

Tvedt, Knut. "'Until the Dovre Mountains Fall' — 150th Anniversary of the Norwegian Constitution," Norseman, (1964, no. 2), 34-37.

Worm-Müller, Jacob S. "Professor Wilhelm Keilhau," Norseman, 12 (1954), 239-41.

Wulfsberg, Fredrik. "Arne Garborg 1851-1951," Norseman, 9 (1951), 37-41.

Zusman, Sybil. "Bjørnstjerne Bjørnson," Norseman, 13 (1955), 302-10.

WORLD WAR I

Keilhau, Wilhelm C. "Norway and the World War," in Sweden, Norway, Denmark, and Iceland in the World War (Carnegie Endowment for International Peace, Economic and Social History of the World War, Scandinavian Series) (New Haven, 1930), 279-407.

"Norway and the War," NewEur, 1 (1916), 111-15.

Norway's Shipping Losses During the War to the End of June, 1917. Lond., 1918. 28 p.

Riste, Olav. The Neutral Ally: Norway's Relations with Belligerent Powers in the First World War. Oslo, 1965. 295 p.

Vigness, Paul G. The Neutrality of Norway in the World War (Stanford University Publications, University Series: History, Economics and Political Science, v. 4, no. 1). Stanford, 1932. 188 p.

WORLD WAR II

Adamson, Hans Chr., and Per Klem. Blood on the Midnight Sun. N.Y., 1964. 282 p.

Ash, Bernard. Norway, 1940. Lond., 1964. 340 p.

Assmann, Kurt. "The Invasion of Norway," USNIP, 78 (Ap 1952), 400-13.

"At Pooks Hill," ASR, 32 (1944), 239-44.

Barker, Ernest. "Norsemen in Britain," Norseman, 2 (1944), 183-86.

Bean, Robert W. "An American Student in Norway," ASR, 28 (1940), 243-57.

Berg, Paal. "Rebirth of a Nation: The Extraordinary Story of Norway's Underground," Free World (O 1945), 64-69.

Berggrav, Eivind J. With God in the Darkness. Lond., 1943. 108 p.

Black, C. E. "Quisling's Norway," CH, 2 (1942), 128-30.

Boardman, Philip L. "The Lights Go Out in Lillehammer: The Story of the Nansen School," ASR, 29 (1941), 21-24.

"Books and Pamphlets on Norway in English Published in England between April 9, 1940 and May 7, 1945," Norseman, 3 (1945), 299-302.

"Books in English on Norway and the War," Norseman, 1 (1943), 232-36.

Boveri, Margaret. "The Quisling Riddle," in her, Treason in the Twentieth Century (Lond., 1961; N.Y., 1963), 64-79.

Broch, Theodor. "The Lofoten Fishermen and the War," ASR, 29 (1941), 151-54.

——. The Mountains Wait. Saint Paul, 1942. 325 p.; Issued with an introduction by the Prime Minister of Norway. Lond., 1943. 192 p.

[Brøgger, Waldemar]. "The Battle for the Home Fronts," by Carsten Frogner [pseud.], Norseman, 1 (1943), 336-44.

Bronner, Hedin. "War Poems: a Norwegian Secret Weapon," ASR, 36 (1948), 225-33.

Buckley, Christopher. Norway, the Commandos, Dieppe (The Second World War, 1939-1945: a Popular Military History). Lond., 1951. 276 p.

Chilston, Viscount. "Norway," in Part V of Arnold and Veronica Toynbee, eds., Hitler's Europe, in the series Survey of International Affairs, 1939-1946. (Oxford, 1954). 534-48.

Christensen, Synnöve. Norway Is My Country. Lond., 1943. 160 p.

Churchill, Winston S. "Scandinavia" in his, The Second World War. Vol. 1: The Gathering Storm. (Lond., 1948), 420-519.

Colban, Erik. "Liberty in Liberated Norway," Norseman, 3 (1945), 193-98.

Cook, Raymond A. Last Boat from Bergen; or 'Norway as It Was, and Is Today.' Newcastle upon Tyne, 1943. 72 p.

Curtis, Monica, ed. Norway and the War, September 1939 - December 1940 (Documents on International Affairs). Lond., N.Y., 1941. 154 p.

Derry, Thomas K. The Campaign in Norway (History of the Second World War; United Kingdom Military Series). Lond., 1952. 289 p.

"Documents in the Case: Aggression on Norway," Norseman, 1 (1943), 122-28.

Dybwad, E. I Saw the Invader; the Destiny of Norway. Lond., 1940. 95 p.

Edwards, Kenneth. "Norway and the Sea War," Norseman, 2 (1944), 100-11; Reply by Reginald Winster, 204-10.

Falls, Cyril. "The British Expedition to Norway, 1940," Norseman, 4 (1946), 255-58.

——. "The Narvik Episode, 1940," Norseman, 5 (1947), 309-14.

Falnes, Oscar J. "Medieval Hansa and Modern Nazi; Two Periods of German Domination in Norway," ASR, 29 (1941), 101-109.

Fen, Aake. Nazis in Norway. Harmondsworth, 1943. 160 p.

Fischer, Alfred J. "Liberated Norway," CR, 168 (1945), 86-90.

Fjellbu, Arne. "The Church and Nazism," Norseman, 3 (1945), 181-85.

Fridtjof [pseud.]. Why Norway? A Contribution to the History of Germany's Aggression against the North. Lond., N.Y., 1942. 76 p.

Gade, John A. "The Question of Norwegian Relief," ASR, 31 (1943), 207-13.

Gathorne-Hardy, Geoffrey M. Norway and the War (Oxford Pamphlets on World Affairs, no. 51). Lond., 1941. 32 p.

Germany, Auswärtiges Amt. Britain's Designs on Norway; Documents Concerning the Anglo-French Policy of Extending the War; Full text of White Book no. 4. N.Y., 1940. 68 p.

"The Gestapo and Its Helpmates in Norway," Norseman, 2 (1944), 222-26.

Great Britain, Foreign Office. Norway No. 1, 1941: Secret German Documents Seized during the Raid on the Lofoten Islands (Parliamentary Papers. Session, 1940-41, v. 8). Lond., 1941. 28 p.

Gregson, Harry. "Inside a Nazi Slave Camp; Norway," Free Europe, 3 (N 1940), 42-43.

Hambro, Carl J. I Saw It Happen in Norway. Lond., N.Y., 1940. 219 p.; Lond., N.Y., 1941. 238 p.

Hambro, Edvard. "Fact and Fiction in the Norwegian War," ASR, 28 (1940), 328-38.

——. "Norwegians in Great Britain Today," ASR, 32 (1944), 55-60.

Hansen, Otto G. "The Food Situation in Norway during the War," Norseman, 2 (1944), 428-35.

Harriman, Florence J. [Hurst]. Mission to

the North. Lond., 1941. 235 p.; Phila.,
N.Y., 1941. 331 p.

Hauge, E. Odds Against Norway. Lond.,
1941. 218 p.

Hayes, Paul M. "Quisling's Political Ideas,"
JCH, 1 (1966, no. 1), 145-57.

Henry, Thomas R. "White War in Norway,"
NGeogM, 88 (1945), 617-40.

Hewins, Ralph. Quisling; Prophet without
Honour. Lond., 1965. 384 p.

Heyst, Axel. "Crosses in Narvik," Norseman, 9 (1951), 11-13.

Hicks, Agnes H. "Norway: Political Ante-
cedents to the German Invasion," in Part
III of Arnold and Veronica Toynbee, eds.,
The Initial Triumph of the Axis, in the
series Survey of International Affairs,
1939-1946 (Oxford, 1958), 109-22.

"Hitler Attacks Norway; Documented from
the 'Fuehrer Conferences'," Norseman,
5 (1947), 437-47.

Holst, Johan J. "Surprise, Signals and Reaction: the Attack on Norway April 9th
1940 — Some Observations," C&C (1966,
no. 1), 31-45.

Holtermann, Reidar. "The Defence of Hegra
Fortress," Norseman, 1 (1943), 112-22.

Höye, Bjarne, and Trygve M. Ager. The
Fight of the Norwegian Church against
Nazism. N.Y., 1943. 180 p.

Jameson, Alexander K. Unarmed against
Fascism: How the Norwegians Resisted
the German Occupation During World
War II. Lond., 1963. 16 p. Previously
published as New Way in Norway? Lond.,
1948.

Joesten, Joachim. "A Front in Norway?"
FA, 20 (1942), 564-67.

——. "Hitler's Nordic Empire: Norway,"
CR, 160 (1941), 171-74.

Johansen, Dagfinn. "The Norwegians under
the Nazi Regime," Norseman, 2 (1944),
291-99.

Johnson, Amanda. Norway, Her Invasion
and Occupation. Lond., Decatur, Ga.,
1948. 372 p.

Juve, Jørgen. "The Clothes from Wisconsin," Norseman (1964), 172-74.

——. "Norwegian Homecoming," Norseman, 3 (1945), 4-10.

——. "Norwegian Refugees in Sweden,"
ASR, 31 (1943), 160-62.

Kenney, Rowland. "Backwaters of War; Impressions of Then and Now," Norseman,
6 (1948), 149-57.

Keyes, Roger. "Combined Operations in
Norway," Norseman, 1 (1943), 358-65.

Kielland, Eugenia. "Norwegian War Fiction," ASR, 34 (1946), 51-55.

Koht, Halvdan. "German Reports from Norway, 1939-1940," Norseman, 13 (1955),
73-77.

——. "Mr. Winston Churchill and the Norwegian Question," Norseman, 8 (1950),
73-84.

——. Norway, Neutral and Invaded. Lond.,
Melbourne, 1941. 224 p.

——. "Norwegian Archives in the War,"
AA, 8 (1945), 19-25.

Lang, Arnold. "Cooperation and the War in
Norway," CoopR, 17 (1943), 108-109.

Lapie, Pierre O. With the Foreign Legion
at Narvik. Lond., 1941. 138 p.

"Legislation in Exile: Norway," JCL, 24
(1942), 125-30.

Lehmkuhl, Herman K. Hitler Attacks Norway. Lond., 1943. 99 p.

——. The Invasion of Norway. Lond.,
1940. 62 p.

——. Journey to London: the Story of the
Norwegian Government at War. Lond.,
N.Y., 1946. 152 p.

——. "The Ninth of April, 1940," Norseman, 1 (1943), 99-109.

Liddell Hart, B. H. "Ten Years After:
How — and Why — Hitler Pounced on Norway," U.S. Marine Corps Gazette, (Jl
1958), 20-27.

Lorentzen, Øivind. Norway, Norwegian
Shipping and the War (America in a
World at War, no. 25). N.Y., 1942. 32 p.

Lund, Diderich H. Resistance in Norway.
Enfield, 1945. 7 p.

Lyon, Katherine. "Norway's Secret Weapon,"
Free World, 3 (Je 1942), 49-53.

MacClure, Victor. Gladiators Over Norway.
Lond., 1942. 46 p.

Macintyre, Donald G. Narvik. Lond., 1959;
N.Y., 1960. 224 p.

Manus, Max. Nine Lives Before 30. Garden
City, N.Y., 1947. 328 p.

Marshall-Cornwall, General Sir James.
"The Campaign in Norway, 9 April to 10
June, 1940," in Part I of Arnold and Veronica Toynbee, eds., The Initial Triumph
of the Axis, in the series Survey of International Affairs, 1939-1946. (Oxford,
1958), 5-6.

"The Martyrdom of the Norwegian Teachers,
By One of Them," Norseman, 1 (1943),
285-94.

Moe, Finn. "Norway after the War," ASR,
29 (1941), 318-23.

Mohr, Otto L. "Winston Churchill and Norway," Norseman, 6 (1948), 220-25.

Morgenstierne, Wilhelm. "Norway, an
Active Ally," NGeogM, 83 (1943), 333-
57.

———. "Norway, Three Years of Achievement," ASR, 31 (1943), 197-206.

Moulton, J. L. The Norwegian Campaign of 1940. Lond., 1966. 328 p.

Myklebost, Tor. They Came as Friends. Lond., 1943. 204 p.; N.Y., 1943. 297 p.

Nansen, Odd. From Day to Day [Diary of a Norwegian Hostage]. Lond., 1949. 600 p.; N.Y., 1949. 485 p.

———. "Grini Prisoner No. 480," ASR, 34 (1946), 8-15.

"The Nazi Heel in Norway: How the Germans Deal with Local Government," Municipal Journal, 50 (1942), 1561.

Norland, Realph. "Elder Statesman: When Norway Was Attacked 20 Years Ago This April C. J. Hambro Was the Man of the Hour," Norseman (1960, no. 2), 9-12.

Norman, Carl. "The Seventeenth of May," ASR, 49 (1961), 20-29.

Norway, Royal Norwegian Government Information Office. All for Norway! Lond., 1942. 150 p.

———. Arctic War; Norway's Role on the Northern Front. Lond., 1945. 64 p.

———. Before We Go Back: a Pictorial Record of Norway's Fight Against Nazism. Lond., 1944. 63 p.

———. The Gestapo at Work in Norway. Lond., 1943. 38 p.

———. Norway — A Fighting Ally! Wash., 1944. 96 p.

———. Norway: A Handbook. Rev. ed., Lond., 1944. 95 p.

———. The Norwegian Church Struggle. Lond., 1943. 68 p.

Norway Does Not Yield: The Story of the First Year. N.Y., 1941. 64 p.

"Norway's Ace in the Hole: the Strategy of the North Cape in Any Arctic Conflict," U.N. World, (M 1949), 18-23.

"Norwegian Flyers in Canada," ASR, 29 (1941), 51-53.

Nyquist, Roi B. Fighting Norsemen. Lond., 1944. 80 p.

———. "Germany's Problem in Norway," Central European Observer, 20 (F 5, 1943), 40-41.

———. Sons of the Vikings. Lond., 1943. 128 p.

"Occupied Norway during 1943," Norseman, 2 (1944), 73-74.

Øksnevad, Toralv. "Norway and B.B.C.," Norseman, 2 (1944), 136-39.

Olav, Hans, ed. He Who Laughs... Lasts, Anecdotes from Norway's Home Front. Brooklyn, 1942. 48 p.

———. Norway. Brooklyn, 1941. 72 p.

———. Norway Fights! Brooklyn, 1943? 31 p.

Oliver, R. W. R., "Operation 'Doomsday'," Norseman, 3 (1945), 274-77.

Ording, Arne. "Norway's Foreign Policy in the War and the Future," News of Norway, 2 (Jl 17, 1942), 103-106.

"Paal Berg, Underground Leader," ASR, 33 (1945), 199-202.

Paasche, Fredrik. "The Development of Freedom in Norway," Norseman, 1 (1943), 212-16.

Palmström, Finn, and Rolf N. Torgerson. Preliminary Report on Germany's Crimes Against Norway. Oslo, 1945. 67 p.

Petersen, Kaare. "Under the Norwegian Flag: the Merchant Marine of Norway in the Battle of the Atlantic," ASR, 29 (1941), 209-17.

Poland, Ministerstwo Informacjii i Dokumentacji. Polish Troops in Norway: a Photographic Record of the Campaign at Narvik. Lond., 1943. 3 p. [155 p. illustrations]

Richmond, Sir Herbert, and Sir Charles Gwynn. "The Norwegian Campaign," Fortnightly, 153 (1940), 596-604.

Royal Institute of International Affairs, London. Documents on International Affairs: Norway and the War, September, 1939-December, 1940. Lond., 1941. 154 p.

Rygg, Andrew N. American Relief for Norway During and After the Second World War. Chicago, 1947. 320 p.

Scarfe, Ronald. In the Norwegian Trap: the Battle for and in Norwegian Waters. Lond., 1940. 157 p.

Schwitters, Ernst, and Roi B. Nyquist. This Norway. Lond., 1944. 123 p.

Semmingsen, Ingrid. "April 9, 1940," ScPP, II, 1212-18.

Simpson, Evan J. Lofoten Letter, by Evan John [pseud.]. Lond., 1941. 67 p.

Singer, Kurt D. "Hitler's Northern Legions," WAI, 14 (1943), 277-88.

———. White Book of the Church of Norway on Its Persecution by the German Occupation Forces and the Quisling Regime in Norway. N.Y., 1941. 32 p.

Skard, Aase G. "Why Norwegian Teachers Fight Nazism," ASR, 30 (1942), 314-20.

Skodvin, Magne. "German and British-French Plans for Operations in Scandinavia after 13 March, 1940," Norseman, 9 (1951), 361-76.

———. "Norway in the Second World War," Humaniora Norvegica, 1 (1950), 178-88.

Sommerfelt, Alf. "Norway and the Western World," Free Europe, 3 (D 1940), 57-58.

Sonsteby, Gunnar. Report from No. 24. Lond., 1965. 192 p.

Sparrow, Catherine G. "Lieutenant Colonel
    Ole Reistad," ASR, 33 (1945), 141-46.
———. "Little Norway — Muskola — Vesle
    Skaugum; Training Centers of the Royal
    Norwegian Air Force in Canada," ASR,
    30 (1942), 203-15.
———. "Norway Needs Food," ASR, 31
    (1943), 26-31.
Stand, Nicolay. "Cultural Life in Norway
    since the Liberation," Norseman, 5
    (1947), 55-64.
Steinnes, Asgant. "The Official Archives of
    Norway During the War," Indian Archives,
    2 (1948), 19-21.
Stelzle, Hope. "Seamen's Churches in War-
    time," ASR, 31 (1943) 349-51.
Stiernstedt, Marika. "They Have Not Died
    in Vain," Norseman, 2 (1944), 29-31.
"Story of the Attack on German 'Heavy
    Water' Supplies for Atomic Energy Ex-
    periments," Norseman, 3 (1945), 414-24.
Strabolgi, Joseph M. K. Narvik and After:
    a Study of the Scandinavian Campaign.
    Lond., 1940. 216 p.
A Teacher. "Can Former Nazis Be Recon-
    verted?" Norseman, 3 (1945), 248-52.
Tevnan, James, and Terence Horsley. Nor-
    way Invaded. Lond., 1940. 143 p.
Torgersen, Rolf N. "Compensation for War
    Damage," Norseman, 5 (1947), 355-59.
Torgesen, Nils. Norwegian Adventure.
    N.Y., 1945.
———. Seven Lives. N.Y., 1945.
Tschuppik, Walter. The Quislings: Hitler's
    Trojan Horses. Lond., 1940. 128 p.
Tunak, F. "With the Foreign Legion to
    Narvik," Norseman, 5 (1947), 315-21.
"Under Nazi Occupation: a Brief Chroni-
    cle," Norseman, 1 (1943), 74-78.
"Under Nazi Occupation — Documents of the
    Struggle [I: The Church Front; II: The
    School Front]," Norseman, 1 (1943), 236-
    38.
Undset, Sigrid. "Fredrik Paasche; In Me-
    moriam," ASR, 31 (1943), 326-31.
———. "Norway, Fighting and Invaded,"
    Norseman, 1 (1943), 227-32.
———. "Spring-day in Norway, April, 1940,"
    Norseman, 1 (1943), 60-67.
Vogt, Benjamin. "Quisling, the Man and the
    Criminal," ASR, 35 (1947), 201-209; 36
    (1948), 37-46.
Waage, Johan. The Narvik Campaign.
    Lond., 1964. 211 p.
Walker, Roy. A People Who Loved Peace:
    the Norwegian Struggle Against Nazism.
    Lond., 1946. 111 p.
Warbey, William. Look to Norway. Lond.,
    1945. 242 p.

Wigan, Anthony. "Quisling on Trial," Norse-
    man, 3 (1945), 394-404.
Williams, George B. Blitzkrieg and Con-
    quest: Policy Analysis of Military and
    Political Decisions Preparatory to the
    German Attack upon Norway, April 9,
    1940. Thesis (Ph.D.), Yale University,
    1966.
Winsnes, Andreas H. "Norwegian Literature
    in the Years of Crisis," Norseman, 1
    (1943), 266-73.
———. "The Resistance of the Norwegian
    People to Nazi Germany," Norseman, 1
    (1943), 140-50.
Wold, Terje. "The Plight of Norway,"
    Norseman, 3 (1945), 1-3.
Woods, William H. The Edge of Darkness.
    Phila., N.Y., 1942. 334 p.
Worm-Müller, Jacob. "Norway Looks to the
    Future," ASR, 29 (1941), 14-17.
———. Norway Revolts Against the Nazis.
    Lond., 1941. 152 p.
———. "Norway's Path," Norseman, 1,
    (1943), 167-71.
Wright, Myrtle A. Nothing Can Hinder a
    Star from Shining: Some Tales about
    Norway under Occupation. Lond., 1946.
    16 p.
Zbyszewski, Karol. The Fight for Narvik:
    Impressions of the Polish Campaign in
    Norway. Lond., 1940. 30 p.
Zinovieff, Kyril. "Norway: The Church and
    the 'New Order'," CR, 161 (1942), 342-46.

SWEDEN

Andersson, Ingvar. A History of Sweden.
    Lond., N.Y., 1956. 461 p.
Benson, Adolph B. "Cultural Relations be-
    tween Sweden and America to 1830,"
    Germanic Review, 13 (1938), 83-101.
———. The Old Norse Element in Swedish
    Romanticism (Columbia University Ger-
    manic Studies). N.Y., 1914. 192 p.
Block, Marguerite B. "A Prophet in His
    Own Country," ASR, 24 (1936), 24-38.
Creese, James. "John Ericsson, Civil En-
    gineer," ASR, 14 (1926), 286-301.
Cronholm, Neander N. A History of Sweden
    from the Earliest Times to the Present
    Day. 2 vols. Chicago, N.Y., 1902.
Edmundson, George. "The Swedish Legend
    of Guiana," EHR, 14 (1899), 71-92.
Ekman, Ernst. "Gothic Patriotism and Olof
    Rudbeck," JMH, 34 (1962), 52-63.
Elkan, Sophie. An Exiled King, Gustaf Adolf
    IV of Sweden. 2 vols. Lond., 1913.
    711 p.

Fischer, Thomas A. The Scots in Sweden; Being a Contribution Towards the History of the Scot Abroad. Ed. by John Kirkpatrick. Edinburgh, 1907. 278 p.

Fleetwood, Gustav. "The Conservation of Medieval Seals in the Swedish Riksarkiv," AA, 12 (1949), 166-74.

Fleisher, Eric W., and Jörgen Weibull. Viking Times to Modern. Minneapolis, 1954. 115 p.

Gade, John A. "Autograph Letters of Swedish Kings," ASR, 3 (1915), 16-26.

Great Britain, War Office. Handbook of the Armies of Sweden and Norway. By J.H.V. Crowe. Lond., 1901. 122 p.

Grimberg, Carl. A History of Sweden. Rock Island, Ill., 1935. 428 p.

——. "Karin Månsdotter," ASR, 15 (1927), 341-46.

——. "Louisa Ulrika of Prussia," ASR, 16 (1928), 91-97.

——. "Ulrika Eleonora, the Gentle," ASR, 15 (1927), 612-17.

A Guide to the Materials for Swedish Historical Research in Great Britain (Meddelanden från Kungl. Krigsarkivet, V). Stock., 1958. 264 p.

Guinchard, Axel J. J., ed. Sweden: Historical and Statistical Handbook. 2 vols. Stock., 1914. 759 p.

Gustafson, Alrik. A History of Swedish Literature. Minneapolis, 1961. 708 p.

Hallendorf, Carl J. H., and Adolf Schück. History of Sweden. Stock., 1929. 466 p.

——. History of Sweden [Delaware Edition]. With a Supplement: Crisis, Depression and Recovery in Sweden, 1929-1937, by Karin Kock. Stock., 1938. 484 p.

Hatton, Ragnhild M. "John Robinson and the Account of Sweden," Bulletin of the Institute of Historical Research, 28 (1955), 128-59.

——. "Some Notes on Swedish Historiography," History, 37 (1952), 97-113.

Heckscher, Eli F. An Economic History of Sweden. Cambridge, Mass., 1954. 308 p.

Heidenstam, Verner Von. The Swedes and Their Chieftains. N.Y., 1925. 351 p.

Heldtander, Tore. "Church and State in Sweden," ASR, 50 (1962), 15-24.

Hernmarck, Carl. "Swedish Furniture, 1700-1800," Burlington Magazine, 83 (1943), 305-308.

Hertzman-Ericson, Gurli. "Fabian Månsson," ASR, 20 (1932), 212-15.

Hirsch, Felix E. "The Decline of Empires, IV: Sweden," CH, 17 (1949), 144.

Izikowitz, K. G., Carl-Axel Moberg, and Albert Eskerod. "Trends in Anthropology: Sweden," AmAnthro, 61 (1959), 669-76.

Johnson, E. "Prince Eugen, Painter and Patron, ASR, 37 (1949), 343-51.

Jung, Helge. "Sweden's Armed Forces Through the Ages," ScPP, III, 126-38.

Kastrup, Allan. The Making of Sweden. N.Y., 1953. 128 p.

Landquist, John. "Erik Gustaf Geijer, Swedish Poet and Historian," ASR, 16 (1928), 489-501.

Lannoy, Charles de. A History of Swedish Colonial Expansion [1638-1938]. Newark, Del., 1938. 46 p.

Liljedahl, Ragnar. "Swedish Historical Research in 1926-1929," Bulletin of the International Committee of the Historical Sciences, 10 (1938), 797-864.

Liljencrants, Johan. "A Swedish-American Inventor" [E.F.W. Alexanderson], ASR, 14 (1926), 229-32.

Lindroth, Sten, ed. Swedish Men of Science, 1650-1950. Stock., 1952. 295 p.

Lundh-Eriksson, Nanna. Hedvig Eleonora: a Biography of the Queen Consort of Charles X Gustavus, King of Sweden. Stock., 1947. 281 p.

Lundström, N. S. "A Repatriation Epic; The Return to Their Homeland of the Swedish Villagers of Gammalsvenskby in Russia," ASR, 17 (1929), 728-40.

Luthin, Reinhard H. "St. Bartholomew: Sweden's Colonial and Diplomatic Adventure in the Caribbean," Hispanic-American Historical Review, 14 (1934), 307-24.

Murray, Robert, ed. The Church of Sweden, Past and Present. Malmö, 1960. 286 p.

Nilsson, Victor A. Sweden. N.Y., 1899. 463 p.

North, George. Description of Swedland, Gotland, and Finland. Facsimile of 1561 ed. Ed. by Marshall W. S. Swan. N.Y., 1946. 78 p.

Oakley, Stewart. A Short History of Sweden. N.Y., 1966. 292 p. London ed. entitled The Story of Sweden.

Oppermann, Charles J. A. The English Missionaries in Sweden and Finland. N.Y., 1937. 221 p.

Piekarczyk, Stanislaw. "Some Notes on the Social and Economic Situation of the Swedish Tenants in the XIIIth Century," Scandia, 27 (1961), 192-216.

Rasmusson, N. L. "Foreign Coins in Swedish Coin-Finds," in Transactions of the International Numismatic Congress, Lond., 1936 (Lond., 1938), 324-33.

Roberts, Michael. Essays in Swedish History. Lond., 1967. 358 p.

——. "On Swedish History in General," in his, Essays in Swedish History (Lond., 1967), 1-13.

Roddis, Louis H. "Linnaeus, King of Flowers," ASR, 32 (1944), 32-47.

Ross, Stanley. Axel Wenner-Gren: the Sphinx of Sweden. N.Y., 1947. 60 p.

Sandberg, Arnold. "The Archives of the Church and the Religious Movements in Sweden," Archivum, 4 (1954), 123-34.

Scott, Franklin D. "Jacob Letterstedt and Nordic Cooperation," in The Immigration of Ideas [Augustana Historical Society Publication] (Rock Island, Illinois, 1968), 15-28.

Sherriff, Florence Janson. "Sweden," in Daniel H. Thomas and Lynn M. Case, eds., Guide to the Diplomatic Archives of Western Europe (Phila., 1959), 263-78.

Stomberg, Andrew A. A History of Sweden. N.Y., 1931. 823 p.

Svanström, Ragnar, and C. F. Palmstierna. A Short History of Sweden. N.Y., 1934. 443 p.

"The Swedish-Norwegian Arctic Expedition, 1931," GeogJ, 83 (1934), 420-25.

Tennant, Peter F. D. "August Strindberg's Politics," BSC, 4 (1938), 368-75.

"The Tercentenary in Retrospect," ASR, 26 (1938), 197-208.

Thermaenius, Edvard. "Geopolitics and Political Geography," BSC, 4 (1938), 165-77.

Thompson, Ralph. "Northern Europe," CH, 41 (1934/35), 629-30.

Toksvig, Signe. Emanuel Swedenborg, Scientist and Mystic. New Haven, 1948. 389 p.

——. "Emanuel Swedenborg, Stockholmer," ASR, 36 (1948), 31-36.

Trobridge, George. Swedenborg; Life and Teaching. 4th ed., N.Y., 1935. 298 p.

Wägner, Elin. "Kerstin Hesselgren," ASR, 31 (1943), 242-44.

Wahlbäck, Krister. "Sweden: Secrecy and Neutrality," JCH [Issue on historiography], 2 (1967), 183-91.

Wahlström, Lydia. "A Queen's Cavalier" [Count Axel von Fersen], ASR, 19 (1931), 748-55.

Ward, A. W. "Wallenstein and Bernard of Weimar" in The Cambridge Modern History (Cambridge, 1906), v. 4, 223-55.

Westergaard, Waldemar C. "The Study of History in Sweden," ASR, 12 (1924), 95-98.

White, Ruth. Yankee from Sweden: the Dream and the Reality in the Days of John Ericsson. N.Y., 1960. 299 p.

Worcester, Benjamin. The Life and Mission of Emanuel Swedenborg. Boston, 1883; N.Y., 1901. 473 p.

Yarham, E. R. "Baltic's Tale of Ancient Glory," ASR, 46 (1958), 127-34.

LOCAL HISTORY

Allwood, Martin S. "Jewel in the Wilderness," ASR, 42 (1954), 131-34.

Blohmé, Esbjörn. The Study of Swedish Place-Names. Groningen, 1950. 19 p.

Fahlström, Jan M. The History of a Gothenburg House of Merchants. Gothenburg, 1952. 70 p.

Floderus, Erik. "Sigtuna. A Summary of Recent Research Concerning Sweden's Oldest Mediaeval City," AcAr, 1 (1930), 97-110.

Hasselberg, Gösta. "The King's Eriksgata," ASR, 48 (1960), 271-76.

Hedström, Birgit Magnusdotter. "Old Uppsala," ASR, 20 (1932), 492-500.

Hertzman-Ericson, Gurli. "Summer Pasturing in Dalarna," ASR, 19 (1931), 546-51.

Heywood, Terence. "Øland," ASR, 40 (1952), 44-48.

Hofrén, Manne. "Kalmar Castle, the Key to Sweden," ASR, 21 (1933), 137-48.

Holdsworth, Robert P. "The Crown Park at Garpenberg," ASR, 17 (1929), 601-608.

Liljegren, Mårten. "Castles of the Vasa Period," ScPP, I, 394-98.

Lundbergh, Holger. "Stockholm Seven Centuries Old," ASR, 40 (1952), 221-27.

Nyblom, Knut. "Uppsala, the City of Eternal Youth," ASR, 13 (1925), 77-86.

Stockholm, Stadsarkiv. The City Archive of Stockholm (Stockholms Stadsarkiv). By Arne Forssell. Stock., 1948? 26 p.

"Visby, the City of Roses and Ruins," ASR, 4 (1916), 94-97.

Wåhlin, Theodor. "The Astronomical Clock in Lund Cathedral, A Minute Copy of the Universe," ASR, 15 (1927), 25-31.

SWEDISH HISTORY TO 1600

Bukdahl, Jørgen, and Wilhelm Tham. "St. Birgitta of Vadstena," ScPP, I, 337-40.

Cnattingius, Hans J. Studies in the Order of St. Bridget of Sweden. Vol. 1: The Crisis of the 1420's (Stockholm Studies in History, 7). Stock., 1963. 198 p.

Cross, J. E. King Eric the Saint of Sweden. Thesis (M.A.), University of Bristol., 1951.

Gábriel, Astrik L. Skara House at the Mediaeval University of Paris; History,
Topography, and Chartulary (Texts and
Studies in the History of Mediaeval Education, no. 9). South Bend, Ind., 1960.
195 p.

Heywood, Terence. "Erik of the Bloody
Fist," Norseman, 7 (1949), 162-65.

Howorth, Henry H. "The Early History of
Sweden," Transactions of the Royal Historical Society, 9 (1881), 174-215.

Kephart, Calvin. The Swedes and Swedish
Goths; Their Origin and Migration; A
Contribution to Fundamental Swedish
History. Wash., 1938. 19 p.

Modén, Arne. "Medieval Boat Dug up in
Stockholm," ASR, 20 (1932), 481-86.

Montelius, Oscar. The Civilisation of Sweden in Heathen Times. Lond., N.Y., 1888.
214 p.

Murray, John J. "The Peasant Revolt of
Engelbrekt Engelbrektsson and the Birth
of Modern Sweden," JMH, 19 (1947), 193-
209.

Oppermann, C. J. A. Sweden and the Papacy,
822-1248. Thesis (Ph.D.), University of
London, 1931.

Reddaway, William F. "The Vasa in Sweden
and Poland," in The Cambridge Modern
History (Cambridge, 1906) v. 4, 158-89.

Redpath, Helen M.D. "God's Ambassadress
— St. Bridget of Sweden. Milwaukee,
1947. 216 p.

Scott, Franklin D. "On Law Shall the Land
Be Built," Swedish Pioneer Historical
Quarterly (1967), 209-20.

"St. Birgitta of Sweden," ASR, 5 (1917),
362-64.

Tham, Wilhelm. "The Age of the Folkungs,"
ScPP, I, 296-301.

———. "Conservative Autocracy and Liberal Reform Policies," ScPP, II, 716-21.

———. "Early Middle Ages in Sweden,"
ScPP, I, 226-29.

———. "Gustavus Vasa," ScPP, I, 386-93.

———. "The Later Vasa Period," ScPP, I,
455-62.

———. "Reconstruction in Sweden," ScPP,
II, 683-87.

———. "The Swedish Era of Freedom,"
ScPP, I, 523-31.

———. "The Union of Nobles and the Stures,"
ScPP, I, 353-59.

———. "The Vasa Sons," ScPP, I, 446-50.

Thordeman, Bengt J. N. Medieval Wooden
Sculpture in Sweden. Stock., 1964.

Thordeman, Bengt J.N., with P. Nörlund and
B. E. Ingelmark. Armour from the Battle
of Visby, 1361. 2 vols. Stock., 1939-40.

Tunberg, Sven. "Sigismund III and Sweden,
1597-98," BSC, 3 (1937), 215-18.

Watson, Paul B. The Swedish Revolution
under Gustavus Vasa. London, 1889.
301 p.

Westergaard, Waldemar C. "Denmark, Russia and the Swedish Revolution, 1480-
1503," Slavonic Review, 16 (1937), 129-40.

———. "Gustavus Vasa's Russian Diplomacy:
the Swedish Mission of 1537," in Communications of the International Congress of
Historical Sciences, 8th, Zurich, 1938
(Paris, 1938), 152-53. Also in Runer og
Rids, Festskrift til Lis Jacobsen (Coph.,
1952), 175-84.

GUSTAVUS ADOLPHUS AND
SEVENTEENTH CENTURY PROBLEMS

Ahnlund, Nils. Gustav Adolph, the Great.
Princeton; N.Y., 1940. 314 p.

Anderson, Albin T. Sweden in the Baltic
1612-1630: a Study in the Politics of Expansion under King Gustav Adolphus and
Chancellor Axel Oxenstierna. Thesis
(Ph.D.), University of California, 1947.

Börjeson, D. H. T. Lists of the Swedish
Fleet, 1650-99 (Society for Nautical Re-
search, Occasional Publications, no. 5).
Lond., 1936.

Bowman, Francis J. "Gustavus II Adolphus
and the Protestant Reformation," BSC, 3
(1937), 410-16.

———. "Sweden's Wars, 1611-1632," Review article of Sveriges krig, 1611-1632
(Stock., 1936, 2 v.), BSC, 4 (1938), 255-
58.

———. "Sweden's Wars, 1611-32," JMH, 14
(1942), 357-69.

Bukdahl, Jørgen, and Wilhelm Tham. "Gustavian Literature," ScPP, II, 626-27.

Campbell, Colin. Colin Campbell, 1686-
1757, Merchant, Gothenburg, Sweden:
His Will, Annotated; A Scoto-Swedish
Study. Peterculter, 1960.

Dallmann, William. The Midnight Lion:
Gustav Adolf, the Greatest Lutheran Layman. St. Louis, 1930. 128 p.

Dodge, Theodore A. Gustavus Adolphus. 2
vols. Boston, N.Y., 1895.

Ekman, Ernst. "Three Decades of Research
on Gustavus Adolphus," JMH, 38 (1966),
243-55.

Fletcher, Charles R. L. Gustavus Adolphus
and the Struggle of Protestantism for Existence. N.Y., 1890; Lond., 1892. 316 p.

———. Gustavus Adolphus and the Thirty
Years War. Paperback ed. N.Y., 1966.
336 p.

Floyd, Calvin J. "The Sound Dues," ASR, 50 (1962), 386-96.

Franzén, Anders. "The Warship 'Vasa'," ASR, 51 (1963), 13-26.

Gardiner, Samuel R., ed. Letters Relating to the Mission of Sir Thomas Roe to Gustavus Adolphus 1629-1630. Westminster, 1875. 98 p.

Heckscher, Eli F. "Economic Aspects of the European Policy of Gustavus Adolphus," BC, 2 (1936), 178-80.

Krey-Lange, Elisabeth. "A Gustavus Adolphus Exhibition," ASR, 20 (1932), 579-83.

MacMunn, George F. Gustavus Adolphus: the Northern Hurricane. Lond., 1930. 318 p. Also Published as Gustavus Adolphus, the Lion of the North. N.Y., 1931. 318 p.

Mellander, K., and Edgar Prestage. The Diplomatic and Commercial Relations of Sweden and Portugal from 1641 to 1670. Lond., 1930. 123 p.

Monroe, Harriet [Earhart]. History of the Life of Gustavus Adolphus II, the Hero-General of the Reformation. Phila., 1910. 139 p.

Nixon, C. L. "Gustavus Adolphus and England: a Study of His Relations with the English Monarchy," Thesis (M.A.), University of California, 1954.

Noel, E. Gustaf Adolf, King of Sweden, The Father of Modern War. Lond., 1905. 113 p.

Roberts, Michael. "Charles XI," History, 50 (1965), 160-92. Reprinted in his, Essays in Swedish History (Lond., 1967), 226-68.

——. "The Constitutional Development of Sweden in the Reign of Gustav Adolf," History, 24 (1940), 328-41.

——. "Gustav Adolf and the Art of War," in his, Essays in Swedish History (Lond., 1967), 56-81.

——. Gustavus Adolphus: a History of Sweden, 1611-1632. Vol. 1: 1611-1626. Lond., N.Y., 1953. 585 p. Vol. 2: 1626-1632. Lond., N.Y., 1958. 848 p.

——. The Military Revolution, 1560-1660," in his, Essays in Swedish History (Lond., 1967), 195-225.

——. "On Aristocratic Constitutionalism in Swedish History, 1520-1720," in his, Essays in Swedish History (Lond., 1967), 14-55. Expansion of his Creighton Lecture in History, same title, 1965. Lond., 1966. 45 p.

——. "The Political Objectives of Gustav Adolf in Germany, 1630-2," in his, Essays in Swedish History (Lond., 1967), 82-110.

Tham, Wilhelm. "The Gustavian Period," ScPP, II, 613-20.

——. "Swedish Baltic Policy," ScPP, I, 451-54.

Trevor-Roper, H. R. "Gustavus Adolphus and the Swedish Empire," in his, Historical Essays (N.Y., 1957, 1966), 167-72.

Tyszkowski, K. "Gustavus Adolphus in Present-Day German Historiography," BC, 1 (1935), 118-20.

Wahlström, Lydia. "Gustavus Adolphus, a Tercentenary," ASR, 20 (1932), 537-45; 571-78.

Ward, A. W. "Gustavus Adolphus" in The Cambridge Modern History (Cambridge, 1906) v. 4, 190-222.

Westin, Gunnar. John Durie in Sweden, 1636-1638. Documents and Letters. Uppsala, 1936. 172 p.

Whitelock, Bulstrode. A Journal of the Swedish Embassy in the Years 1653 and 1654. 2 vols. Lond., 1855.

Zeeh, Erik. "The Struggle for Poland's Prussian Ports during the Reign of Gustavus Adolphus," BSC, 4 (1938), 315-20.

CHRISTINA

Bain, Francis W. Christina, Queen of Sweden. Lond., 1890. 383 p.

Bjurström, Per. Feast and Theatre in Queen Christina's Rome. Stock., 1966. 154 p.

Cartland, Barbara. The Outrageous Queen: a Biography of Christina of Sweden. Lond., 1956. 256 p.

Elliott, J. H. "Queen Christina," Horizon, 9 (1967, no. 3), 66-79.

Glass, Dudley. "Christina, Queen of Sweden," ASR, 54 (1966), 385-91.

Goldsmith, Margaret L. Christina of Sweden: a Psychological Biography. Lond., 1933. 324 p.; Garden City, N.Y., 1933. 308 p.

Gribble, Francis H. The Court of Christina of Sweden and the Later Adventures of the Queen in Exile. Lond., N.Y., 1913. 355 p.

Grimberg, Carl. "Kristina, Daughter of Gustavus Adolphus," ASR, 15 (1927), 525-35.

Harrison, Ada M. Christina of Sweden. Lond., 1929. 95 p.

Lewis, Paul. Queen of Caprice: a Biography of Kristina of Sweden. N.Y., 1962. 307 p.

Mackenzie, Faith C. The Sibyl of the North:

the Tale of Christina, Queen of Sweden. Boston, N.Y., Lond., 1931. 262 p.

Neumann, Alfred. The Life of Christina of Sweden. Lond., 1935. 287 p.

Roberts, Michael. "Queen Christina and the General Crisis of the Seventeenth Century," in his, Essays in Swedish History (Lond., 1967), 111-37.

Stolpe, Sven. Christina of Sweden. Lond., N.Y., 1966. 360 p.

Strandh, Sigvard. "Queen Christina and the Men of Learning," Featuring Sweden (O 1966), 10, 13-14.

Taylor, Ida A. Christina of Sweden. Lond., 1909. 336 p.

Wiebull, Curt. Christina of Sweden. Stock., 1966. 186 p.

Woodhead, Henry. Memoirs of Christina, Queen of Sweden. 2 vols. Lond., 1863.

CHARLES XII AND THE BALTIC: 1682-1719

Almédingen, Edith M. The Lion of the North: Charles XII, King of Sweden. Lond., 1938. 424 p.

Åström, Sven-Erik. From Stockholm to St. Petersburg: Commercial Factors in the Political Relations between England and Sweden, 1675-1700 (Studia Historica, no. 2). Hels., 1962.

Bain, Robert Nisbet. Charles XII and the Collapse of the Swedish Empire, 1682-1719. Lond., N.Y., 1895. 320 p.

———. "Charles XII and the Great Northern War" in The Cambridge Modern History (Cambridge, 1908), v. 5, 584-615.

Bengtsson, Frans G. The Life of Charles XII, King of Sweden, 1697-1718. Stock., Lond. 1960. 495 p. Also published as The Sword Does Not Jest: the Heroic Life of King Charles XII of Sweden. N.Y., 1960. 495 p.

Borenius, Tancred. "Sweden and the Jacobites," SHR, 23 (1926), 238-40.

British Diplomatic Instructions 1689-1789: Sweden. Ed. by J. F. Chance. Lond., 1922-28. Vol. 1: 1689-1727. 250 p. Vol. 2: 1727-1789. 268 p.

Chance, James F. "England and Sweden in the Time of William III and Anne," EHR, 16 (1901), 676-711.

———. "George I in His Relations with Sweden Before His Accession and to May, 1715," EHR, 17 (1902), 50-75.

———. "The Mission of Fabrice to Sweden, 1717-1718," EHR 21 (1906), 57-77.

———. "Northern Affairs in 1724," EHR, 27 (1912), 483-511.

———. "The Northern Pacification of 1719-1720," EHR, 22 (1907), 478-507; 694-725; EHR, 23 (1908), 35-64.

———. "The Northern Question in 1716," EHR, 18 (1903), 676-704; EHR, 19 (1904), 55-79.

———. "The Northern Question in 1717," EHR, 20 (1905), 33-60; 251-74.

———. "The Northern Question in 1718," EHR, 21 (1906), 460-92.

———. "The 'Swedish Plot' of 1716-1717," EHR, 18 (1903), 81-106.

———. "William Duncombe's 'Summary Report' of His Mission to Sweden, 1689-92," EHR, 39 (1924), 571-87.

Dahl, Folke. "King Charles Gustavus of Sweden and the English Astrologers William Lilly and John Gadbury," Lychnos, 2 (Uppsala, 1937), 161-86.

Erskine, S. J. R. The Great Baltic Bubble [On Jacobite Attempts to Enlist Swedish Aid, 1715-1718]. Lond., 1940. 122 p.

Gade, John A. Charles the Twelfth, King of Sweden. Trans. from the manuscript of Carl Gustav Klingspor. Boston, 1916. 370 p.

Gill, Conrad. "The Affair of Porto Novo: an Incident in Anglo-Swedish Relations," EHR, 73 (1958), 47-65.

Godley, Eveline C. Charles XII of Sweden: a Study in Kingship. Lond., 1928. 254 p.

Jefferyes, James. Captain James Jefferyes' Letters from the Swedish Army, 1707-1709. Ed. by Ragnhild M. Hatton. Stock., 1954. 93 p.

Kurat, Akdes N. "The Political Activity of Charles XII, King of Sweden, in Turkey," BSC, 3 (1937), 428-31.

Murray, John J. "Robert Jackson's Mission to Sweden (1709-1717)," JMH, 21 (1949), 1-16.

———. "Scania and the End of the Northern Alliance (1716)," JMH, 16 (1944), 81-92.

———. "Sweden and the Jacobites," Huntington Library Quarterly, 7 (1944/45), 259-76.

Natharius, Edward W. The Maritime Powers and Sweden, 1698-1702. Thesis (Ph.D.), Indiana University, 1959. 370 p.

Sheppard, E. W. "A Former Invader of Russia: Charles XII of Sweden," Army Quarterly, 45 (1942), 86-94.

Stenart, A. Francis. "Sweden and the Jacobites, 1719-1720," SHR, 23 (1926), 109-27.

Tham, Wilhelm. "Charles XII and the Great Northern War," ScPP, I, 517-22.

Voltaire, François M. A. de. History of
Charles XII, King of Sweden. Boston,
1883. 352 p. Many editions.

THE EIGHTEENTH CENTURY

Bain, Robert Nisbet. Gustavus III and His
Contemporaries, 1747-1792: an Over-
looked Chapter of Eighteenth Century
History. 2 vols. Lond., 1894.

Bertoni, Karol. "Eighteenth Century Swedish Diplomats in Poland," BSC, 3 (1937),
108-16.

Boëthius, Bertil. "New Light on Eighteenth
Century Sweden," SEHR, 1 (1953), 143-77.

Johnson, William A. Christopher Polhem,
The Father of Swedish Technology. Lond.,
1963. 249 p.; Hartford, Conn., 1963.
288 p.

Kuylenstierna, J. "Badin, the Queen's
Blackamoor," ASR, 41 (1953), 128-33.

Liljegren, Mårten. "Late Baroque and Ro-
cocco in Sweden," ScPP, I, 532-37.

Lodge, Richard. "The Treaty of Abo and the
Swedish Succession," EHR, 43 (1928),
540-71.

Lönnroth, Erik. "Gustavus III of Sweden:
the Final Years — a Political Portrait,"
Sc, 6 (1967), 16-25.

Roberts, Michael. "Great Britain and the
Swedish Revolution, 1772-3," in his,
Essays in Swedish History (Lond., 1967),
286-347.

——. "The Swedish Aristocracy in the
Eighteenth Century," in his, Essays in
Swedish History (Lond., 1967), 269-85.

Tham, Wilhelm. "Absolute Monarchy and
'Reduktion' in Sweden," ScPP, I, 512-16.

BERNADOTTE AND NAPOLEONIC TIMES

Achorn, Erik. "Bernadotte or Bonaparte,"
JMH, 1 (1929), 378-99.

Barton, Sir Dunbar P. Bernadotte, the First
Phase, 1763-1799. Lond., 1914. 532 p.

——. Bernadotte and Napoleon. 1763-
1810. Lond., 1921. 343 p.

——. Bernadotte, Prince and King, 1810-
1844. Lond., 1925. 248 p.

——. The Amazing Career of Bernadotte,
1763-1844. Lond., 1929. 396 p.

Bearne, C. M. A Queen of Napoleon's Court:
Desirée Bernadotte. Lond., 1905. 498 p.

Carr, Raymond. "Gustavus IV and the British Government, 1804-9," EHR, 60 (1945),
36-66.

Kukiel, Marian. "Baltic Problems of
the War of 1812," BSC, 4 (1938),
10-16.

Mercer, A. C. "The First Bernadotte,"
Norseman, 7 (1949), 12-22.

Muriel, John St. C. Sergeant Belle-Jambe;
The Life of Marshall Bernadotte, by
Simon Dewes [pseud.]. Lond., 1943.
168 p.

Scott, Franklin D. Bernadotte and the Fall
of Napoleon (Harvard Historical Monographs, 7). Cambridge, Mass., 1935.
190 p.

——. "Bernadotte and the Throne of
France, 1814," JMH, 5 (1933, 465-78.

——. "Propaganda Activities of Bernadotte, 1813-1814," in Donald C. McKay,
ed., Essays in the History of Modern
Europe (N.Y., 1936), 16-30.

Wencker, Friedrich. Bernadotte. Lond.,
1936. 317 p.

MIGRATION

Ander, Oscar Fritiof. "A Bibliography on
Swedish Immigration and Immigrant Con-
tributions," Swedish Pioneer Historical
Quarterly, 3 (1952), 35-44.

Janson, Florence E. [Sherriff] The Background of Swedish Immigration, 1840-
1930 (Social Service Monographs, no. 5).
Chicago, 1931. 517 p.

Lindberg, John S. The Background of Swedish Emigration to the United States: an
Economic and Sociological Study in the
Dynamics of Migration. Minneapolis,
1930. 272 p.

Stephenson, George M. "The Background of
the Beginnings of Swedish Immigration,
1850-1875," AHR, 31 (1926), 708-23.

——. The Religious Aspects of Swedish
Immigrations. Minneapolis, 1932. 542 p.

THE 1905 UNION CRISIS

Braekstad, Hans L. Political Pamphlets:
Articles on the Political Relations of
Norway and Sweden. Lond., 1883-1907.
5 pts.

"Decision of the Permanent Court of Arbi-
tration in the Matter of the Maritime
Boundary Dispute Between Norway and
Sweden," AJIL, 4 (1910), 226-36.

"The Dissolution of the Union of Norway and
Sweden," AJIL, 1 (1907), 440-44.

Edén, N. Sweden for Peace: the Programme
of Sweden in the Union Crisis. Stock.,
Uppsala, 1905. 40 p.

Gathorne-Hardy, Geoffrey M., "Nansen in
1905," Norseman, 14 (1956), 1-5.

Lindgren, Raymond E. Norway-Sweden;
Union, Disunion and Scandinavian

Integration (Publication of the Center for Research on World Political Institutions, Princeton University). Princeton, N.J., 1959. 298 p.

Moritzen, Julius. "The Rupture Between Norway and Sweden," Forum, 37 (1905/6), 141-52.

Nansen, Fridtjof. Supplementary Chapter to Dr. Fridtjof Nansen's Norway and the Union with Sweden [The Dissolution of the Union]. Lond., N.Y., 1905. 155 p.

———. Norway and the Union with Sweden. Lond., N.Y., 1905. 96 p.

Nordlund, Karl. The Swedish — Norwegian Union Crisis: a History with Documents. Stock., Uppsala, 1905. 107 p.

———. Norwegian National Council of Women. Norway: a Few Facts from Norwegian History and Politics. 2d ed., Kra., 1905. 26 p.

Rinman, Erik B. Fiction and Fact about the Scandinavian Crisis. Stock., 1905. 19 p.

Sears, J.E.W. "Norway and Sweden: the Case for Norwegian Liberalism," Fortune, 64 (Aug 1895), 269-81.

Staaf, K. "The Grounds of Sweden's Protest," NoAmRev, 181 (1905), 288-95.

Steveni, James W. B. The Scandinavian Question. Lond., 1905. 152 p.

Sweden, Riksdagen. The Union Between Sweden and Norway; the Address Presented to the King by the Swedish Parliament. Stock., 1905. 16 p.

Thomas, C. "Karlstad Convention," Nation, 81 (1905), 295-96.

———. "Plebiscite of the Norseman," Nation, 81 (1905), 161-63.

Wallenberg, Anna E. C. Sweden's Rights and Her Present Political Position, by Anders Svenske [pseud.]. Lond., 1907. 118 p.

THE TWENTIETH CENTURY

Andenberg, R. Recruitment of the Royal Swedish Navy with the Aid of Intelligence Tests. Uppsala, 1935. 77 p.

Ander, Oscar Fritiof. The Building of Modern Sweden: the Reign of Gustav V, 1907-1950. Rock Island, Ill., 1958. 271 p.

Anderson, Ruth C. Sweden during the World War. Thesis (M.A.), University of California, 1932.

Arne, T. J. "The Swedish Archaeological Expedition to Iran, 1932-1933," AcAr, 6 (1935), 1-48.

Benedikt, Ernst. "The Grand Old Man of Sweden" [King Gustav V], CR, 173 (1948), 333-36.

Bernadotte af Wisborg, Folke. Instead of Arms; Autobiographical Notes. Stock., N.Y., 1948. 227 p.

Bernholm, Bernt. "Tage Erlander," ASR, 35 (1947), 30-32.

Björkman, Edwin. "Sweden's Position in the War," Scribners Magazine, 63 (1918), 213-18.

Childs, Marquis. "Sweden Revisited," Yale Review (S 1937), 30-44.

Dannfelt, Brita J. "Swedish Women Do Their Part," ASR, 29 (1941), 120-24.

Elviken, Andreas. "Sweden and Finland, 1914-1918," in Jesse D. Clarkson and Thomas C. Cochran, eds., War as a Social Institution: the Historian's Perspective (N.Y., 1941), 134-43.

Fischer, Alfred J. "The Welfare State in Sweden," CR, 182 (Jl 1952), 40-44.

Hedin, Sven. "Sweden's Crown Prince [Gustav Adolf] as an Archaeologist," ASR, 14 (1926), 273-80.

Herbert, Basil. King Gustave of Sweden. Lond., 1938. 288 p.

Hewins, Ralph. Count Folke Bernadotte; His Life and Work. Lond., 1950. 264 p.; Minneapolis, 1950. 279 p.

Heyst, Axel. "Sweden To-day," CR, 177 (1950), 149-54.

Lind, Inez. "Dag Hammarskjöld," ASR, 41 (1953), 205-12.

Mjöberg, Jöran. "Swedish Post-War Literature," Norseman, 8 (1950), 132-40.

"The Present Position in Sweden" [by D. P. E.], BIN, 20 (1943), 145-51.

"A Royal Anniversary: King Gustaf VI Adolf Celebrates His Eightieth Birthday," ASR, 50 (1962), 359-61.

"A Royal Democrat" [Prince Gustav Adolf], ASR, 14 (1926), 281-85.

Sandler, Åke. "The Truth about Swedish Concessions," ASR, 30 (1942), 136-38.

Soloveytchik, George. "Democracy in Sweden," CR, 147 (1935), 46-54.

———. "Europe's Not So Quiet Corner: Postwar Sweden," Survey Graphic, 35 (1946), 282-87.

"Some Trends in Post-War Sweden" [by E.J.L.], WT, 2 (1946), 313-30.

Spångberg, Valfried. "Hjalmar Branting," ASR, 13 (1925), 283-84.

Stolpe, Sven. Dag Hammarskjöld, A Spiritual Portrait. N.Y., 1966. 127 p.

Sweden: a Wartime Survey. N.Y., 1943. 250 p.

Warne, Colston E. "Sweden in 1947," CH, 13 (1947), 330-34.

INTERNATIONAL RELATIONS

INTRODUCTION

The Northern Countries have much in common in their international relations and have extraordinarily cooperative relations with one another. They are known for their strategies of peace and neutrality and for their contributions to humanitarian causes and international organizations. Finland is different from the others in that she has been repeatedly and tragically affected by her most powerful neighbor, the Soviet Union. This bibliography contains references to some excellent articles in the fields of world politics, international organization, and diplomatic history. Many related entries will be found under History and under Political Science. Entries concerning foreign trade and European economic integration, including references pertaining to the participation of these countries in the European Free Trade Association, appear under Economics. Most of the works mentioned here are either case studies or overviews in diplomatic history, or descriptions of institutions. Few are social science studies in the sense of relating data and theory.

In 1965 Scandinavian scholars began publishing a journal which will be central for research on the region: *Cooperation and Conflict: Nordic Studies in International Politics*. Relevant articles also appear frequently in *The American Scandinavian Review*, *The Danish Foreign Office Journal*, *The Norseman*, and the publications of the European Free Trade Association. Since 1952 the Swedish Ministry for Foreign Af-

fairs has been publishing an annual, *Documents on Swedish Foreign Policy*. The Norwegian Foreign Ministry planned to publish, in 1967, three huge volumes entitled *Norway's International Agreements 1661-1966*, a compendium of treaties. There is one bibliography, which is admirable but brief and out-of-date: *The Scandinavian Countries in International Affairs* (1953) by Folke Lindberg and John Kolehmainen.

In the English language there is no volume providing an overview of Scandinavia's present place in world politics. Neither is there any analytical work on comparative Nordic foreign policy, nor is there yet a volume on Scandinavia's relationship to the European Economic Community or the European Free Trade Association. There are many fine articles on the Nordic Council, but one probably ought to begin with Frantz Wendt's *The Nordic Council and Co-operation in Scandinavia* (1959), or Stanley Anderson's *The Nordic Council: a Study of Scandinavian Regionalism* (1967). A highly commendable unpublished Ph.D. dissertation is Otto Leroy Karlström's *The "Scandinavian" Approach to Political Integration* (1952).

Particularly noteworthy books treating more than one of the Northern Countries can conveniently be mentioned in chronological order of their coverage: Folke Lindberg, *Scandinavia in Great Power Politics 1905-1908* (1958); Nils Ørvik, *The Decline of Neutrality 1914-1941* (1953); Annette Baker Fox's *The Power of Small States: Diplomacy in World War II* (1959), which contains country chapters; Rowland Kenney's *The*

Northern Tangle: Scandinavia and the Post-War World (1946). The volume edited by Henning Friis, Scandinavia Between East and West (1950), treats foreign policy only in small part. To these volumes one may add Samuel S. Jones' The Scandinavian States and the League of Nations (1939), and Franklin Scott's The United States and Scandinavia (1950).

There is only one book on twentieth-century Danish foreign affairs: Denmark and the United Nations (1956) by Max Sörensen and Niels Haagerup. There is a parallel volume, Sweden and the United Nations (1956), by the Swedish Institute of International Affairs. Each of these was prepared for the Carnegie Endowment for International Peace. There is one recently completed dissertation on Danish foreign policy options, Gunnar Nielssen's Denmark and European Integration: a Small Country at the Crossroads (1966). For Iceland there are two very fine books: Iceland Extends Its Fisheries Limits: a Political Analysis (1963) by Morris Davis, and Iceland: Reluctant Ally (1961), by Donald Nuechterlein. These books are complemented by a recent dissertation, John Hunt's The United States Occupation of Iceland 1941-1946 (1966).

Those interested in the Slesvig (or Schleswig-Holstein) controversy in Dano-German relations should be aware that the two leading books were inspired by interest in the growth of German nationalism and do not cover material subsequent to the era of Bismarck: William Carr, Schleswig-Holstein, 1815-48: a Study in National Conflict (1963), and Lawrence Steefel, The Schleswig-Holstein Question (1932). For twentieth-century relationships, one must consult articles.

For Finland, there are numerous excellent articles on the Paasikivi Line and post World War II relations with the Soviet Union. The Aaland Islands controversy is well covered by articles, and a book by James Barros is now in press. The Finnish Political Science Association has published a volume of articles constituting a fine introduction: Finnish Foreign Policy: Studies in Foreign Politics (1963); each article is entered separately in this bibliography. There are few book-length studies of the period prior to 1939. The most notable have been C. Jay Smith's Finland and the Russian Revolution 1917-1922 (1958), which has received mixed reviews, and Kal Holsti's dissertation, The Origins of Finnish Foreign Policy 1918-22: Rudolf

Holsti's Role in the Formulation of Policy (1961), which has been published in Finnish. The main thrust of Anatole Mazour's Finland Between East and West (1956) is twentieth-century Finnish-Russian relations; it serves well as an introduction. The literature on the Winter War and on World War II is extensive, including many articles in this section and in the History section, as well as several books. Three of the books are by men directly involved with Finnish foreign policy. Väino Tanner, Socialist leader and former Foreign Minister, provides a highly readable personal account in his The Winter War: Finland Against Russia 1939-40 (1957). Finnish Foreign Service Officer Max Jacobsen has written a more scholarly work, The Diplomacy of the Winter War: an Account of the Russo-Finnish Conflict, 1939-1940 (1961). Illuminating are the memoirs of Finland's envoy to London and Stockholm during World War II, Georg Gripenberg: Finland and the Great Powers: Memoirs of a Diplomat (1965). Virtually anyone would enjoy reading the fascinating Memoirs of Marshal Mannerheim (1953), which spans his entire life. Covering mainly the period immediately following the Winter War is Anthony Upton's Finland in Crisis 1940-1941: a Study in Small-Power Politics (1965). Two books review the position of the United States with regard to the Winter War: America and the Russo-Finnish War (1960) by Andrew Schwartz, and Robert Sobel's The Origins of Interventionism: the United States and the Russo-Finnish War (1960). On Finland in World War II see Leonard Lundin's Finland in the Second World War (1957) and the volume edited by John Wuorinen, Finland and World War II: 1939-1944 (1948).

On Norway, the most challenging recent publication is a short one concerning questions of strategies and responses in the era of nuclear stalemate: Nils Ørvik's Europe's Northern Cap and the Soviet Union (1963). On the last century there is a lengthy work on inter-Scandinavian relations by Theodore Jorgenson: Norway's Relation to Scandinavian Unionism, 1815-1871 (1935). Highly commendable are Trygve Mathisen's Svalbard in the Changing Arctic (1954), and Olav Riste's The Neutral Ally: Norway's Relations with Belligerent Powers in the First World War (1965); the latter supercedes The Neutrality of Norway in the World War (1932) by Paul Vigness. The literature includes five unpublished dissertations presented to American universities: Haakon Lindjord's The Foundations of Norway's Role in

International Politics (1954); Doris Linder's *The Reaction of Norway to American Foreign Policy, 1918-1939* (1961); Sylvester Choffy's *The Diplomacy of Norway 1939-1945* (1960); Kai Lie's *An Analysis of the Changing Role of Norway in the Struggle for Power and Peace in the North Since the Second World War* (1967); and Philip Burgess' *Norway, the North and NATO: a Study of Authoritative Elite Perceptions as Related to Foreign Policy* (1966), which emphasizes the period of the Scandinavian defense negotiations, January 1948 through April 1949. A revised version of this dissertation has been published under the title *Elite Images and Foreign Policy Outcomes: a Study of Norway* (1968). Although Alfred Nobel was a Swede, one of his prizes, the Nobel Peace Prize, is awarded by a committee named by the Norwegian parliament. Entries on the Nobel Peace Prize are therefore here under Norway; other entries on Nobel are listed under Sweden.

On Sweden, the articles by Karl Birnbaum and by Herbert Tingsten are first-rate. Samuel Abrahamsen presents a brief overview of policy since World War I in his *Sweden's Foreign Policy* (1957). In *Power Balance and Non-Alignment* (1967), Nils Andrén provides an analysis of Swedish foreign policy since World War II. Highly recommended are Eric Bellquist, *Some Aspects of the Recent Foreign Policy of Sweden* (1929), and Herbert Tingsten, *The Debate on the Foreign Policy of Sweden, 1918-1939* (1949). Unpublished American doctoral dissertations include: Hans Gunther, *German-Swedish Relations 1933-39: the Background for Swedish Neutrality* (1955); John Haupert, *The Critical Era of Swedish Neutrality 1939-1945* (1955); Åke Sandler, *Political Aspects of Swedish Diplomacy During World War II* (1950); and E. Luther Johnson, *Freedom from Alliances: Contemporary Swedish Views Toward International Relations* (1966).

SCANDINAVIA

Åhman, Brita S. "Scandinavian Foreign Policy, Past and Present, in Henning Friis, ed., Scandinavia Between East and West (Ithaca, N.Y., 1950), 255-305.

Ahnlund, Nils. "The Historical Frontiers of the Northern Nations," Nord, 5 (1942), 243-55.

Alexander, Lewis M. A Comparative Study of Offshore Claims in Northwestern Europe. Wash., 1960. 239 p.

Anderson, Stanley V. "Supranational Delegation Clauses in Scandinavian Constitutions," WPQ, 18 (1965), 840-47.

Barclay, G. St. J. "Alliance Against Nobody: the Scandinavian Experiment in Neutrality, 1936-48," Australian Outlook, 19 (1965), 192-206.

Bellquist, Eric C. "As We Look at Northern Europe," American Swedish Handbook, II (1945), 139-50.

Birnbaum, Karl E. "The Nordic Countries and European Security," C&C (1968), 1-17.

Branston, Ursula. "How Neutral Is the North: Impressions of Finland and Scandinavia," Soundings (O 1948), 46-52.

Branting, Hjalmar. "The Peace Movement After the War," ASR, 10 (1922), 532-36.

Brodin, Katarina, Kjell Goldmann, and Christian Lange. "The Policy of Neutrality: Official Doctrines of Finland and Sweden," C&C (1968), 18-51.

Brundtland, Arne O. "The Nordic Balance," C&C (1966, no. 2), 30-63.

Bukdahl, Jørgen. The North and Europe. Coph., 1949. 53 p.

Burbank, Lyman B. "The East-West Struggle for the Baltic," Social Education, 17 (1953), 364-66+.

Christophersen, Jens A. "The Nordic Countries and the European Balance of Power," C&C (1965, no. 1), 39-52.

Cohn, Georg. Neo-Neutrality. Thesis (Ph.D.), University of Copenhagen, 1937. N.Y., 1939. 398 p.

Cowie, Donald. "Scandinavia and the Dominions," Norseman, I (1943), 386-92.

"Declaration by Norway, Denmark and Sweden Relative to the Establishment of Uniform Rules of Neutrality," AJIL: Supplement, 7 (1913), 187-91.

Engen, Hans. "Disagreement in the North," Norseman, 7 (1949), 213-16.

Fischer, Alfred J. "Northern Europe Today," WA, 2 (1948), 49-61.

——. "The Scandinavian Scene," CR, 166 (1944), 359-63.

Fox, Annette Baker. The Power of Small

States: Diplomacy in World War II. Chicago, 1959. 211 p.

Friis, Henning K., ed. Scandinavia Between East and West. Ithaca, N.Y., 1950. 398 p.

Glenn, Gene W. "The Troubled Baltic," ASR, 44 (1956), 137-41.

Grossman, Vladimir. "Scandinavia's Strategic Position," IntJ, 1 (1947), 71-75.

Hambro, Carl J. How to Win the Peace. N.Y., 1942. 384 p.

———. "The Role of the Smaller Powers in International Affairs Today," IA, 15 (1936), 167-82.

Hambro, Edvard. "The Northern Countries After This War," Annals (Jl 1943), 60-64.

Haskel, Barbara. The Attempt to Create a Scandinavian Defence Pact, as Reflected in the Public Statements of the Swedish, Norwegian and Danish Members of Government during 1948-1949. University of Stockholm, 1963. Mimeographed.

Hatton, Ragnhild M. "Scandinavia and the Baltic," in The New Cambridge Modern History (Cambridge, 1958), v. 7, 339-64.

Heckscher, Eli F., and Kurt Bergendal. Sweden, Norway, Denmark and Iceland in the World War. New Haven, Conn., 1930. 593 p.

Hinterhoff, Eugene. "Problems Along NATO's Flanks," Orbis, 8 (1964), 607-23.

Hula, Erich. "The European Neutrals," SocRes, 7 (1940), 151-68.

Hutchison, Keith. "Scandinavia Between the Blocs," Nation, 167 (Jl 17, 1948), 67-69.

India, Information Services. Nehru in Scandinavia. Stock., 1958. 156 p.

Kalijarvi, Thorsten V. "Scandinavian Claims to Jurisdiction over Territorial Waters," AJIL, 26 (1932), 57-69.

Kenney, Rowland. The Northern Tangle: Scandinavia and the Post-War World. Lond., 1946. 255 p.

Kent, H. S. K. "The Historical Origins of the Three-Mile Limit," AJIL, 48 (1954), 537-53.

Koht, Halvdan. "The Oslo Convention and After," Nord, 1 (1938), 37-47.

Lakhtine, W. "Rights Over the Arctic," AJIL, 24 (1930), 703-17.

Lange, Christian, and Kjell Goldmann. "A Nordic Defense Alliance 1949-1965-197?" C&C (1966, no. 1), 46-63.

Lange, Christian L. "Past and Future Policies in Scandinavia," Living Age (1919), 762-68.

———. "Scandinavian Cross-Currents," Atlantic Monthly, 121 (Ja 1918), 128-37.

Lange, Halvard M. "Scandinavian Co-

operation in International Affairs," IA, 30 (1954), 285-93.

Lehmkuhl, Herman K. "Northern States and the Crisis," [Events in Hungary and Egypt, 1956], Norseman, 14 (1956), 361-63.

Lindberg, Folke. "Power Politics in the Baltic," ASR, 54 (1966), 158-68.

———. Scandinavia in Great Power Politics, 1905-1908. Stock., 1958. 329 p.

Lindberg, Folke, and John I. Kolehmainen. The Scandinavian Countries in International Affairs: a Selected Bibliography on the Foreign Affairs of Denmark, Finland, Norway, and Sweden 1800-1952. University of Minnesota Program in Scandinavian Area Studies. Minneapolis, 1953. 17 p.

Luchsinger, Fred. "The Role of the Small States in Europe," SRWA, 17 (Jl 1967), 10-13.

Magnus, R. "Neutrality of the Scandinavian Powers is Aid to the Aggressor," Communist International, 15 (1938), 830-38.

Mead, William R. "Canada and the 'Northern Countries;' The Challenge of Common Interests," Norseman, 4 (1946), 85-91.

———. "The Northern Countries in the World Policy," Norseman, 4 (1946), 449-53.

Mehlem, Max. "Present Status of Scandinavia's Defense," SRWA, 5 (Jl 1955), 11-13.

Nansen, Fridtjof. "The Mission of the Small States," ASR, 6 (1918), 9-13.

Neutral War Aims; Essays by Representative Writers of Leading Neutral Countries. Lond., 1940. 192 p.

"Northern Solidarity," DFOJ, no. 226 (N 1939), 181-84.

"Not Feeding Germany," ASR, 5 (1917), 201-205.

Olson, Alma L. Scandinavia: the Background for Neutrality. Phila., 1940. 358 p.

Ording, Arne. "Problems of Nordic Foreign Policy," Free Europe, 5 (May 22, 1942), 168-69.

Ørvik, Nils. The Decline of Neutrality, 1914-1941; With Special Reference to the United States and the Northern Neutrals. Oslo, 1953. 294 p.

Osborne, Lithgow. "Scandinavia Speaks," United Nations World, 5 (Aug 1951), 36-39.

———. "Scandinavian Balance Sheet," Foreign Policy Bulletin, 21 (1952, no. 24), 4-8.

Padelford, Norman J. "New Scandinavian
    Neutrality Rules," AJIL, 32 (1938), 789-
    93.
Ryder, Wilfred. "The End of Nordic Neu-
    trality," Soundings (M 1949), 15-21.
Sandler, Åke. "The Strategic Importance of
    Scandinavia in Case of War," WAI, 22
    (1951), 320-27.
"Scandinavia Faces the Future: Neutrality
    or Alliance," WT, 4 (1948), 191-97.
Scandinavia in a Divided World; Papers read
    at an Institute held under the Auspices of
    the University of Minnesota Program in
    Scandinavian Area Studies. Minneapolis,
    1950. 64 p. Mimeographed.
"Scandinavia's Efforts for Peace," CR, 156
    (1939), 676-83.
"The Scandinavian States," Bulletin of Inter-
    national News, 17 (1940), 461-68.
Schou, August. "Scandinavia and the World,"
    in J. A. Lauwerys, ed., Scandinavian De-
    mocracy (Coph., N.Y., 1958), 388-99.
Scott, Richard. "Trouble in Northern Waters:
    the Background to the Fishing Disputes,"
    GeoM, 25 (1952-53), 483-88.
Seidenfaden, Erik. "Scandinavia Charts a
    Course," FA, 26 (1948), 653-64.
Sherrill, Charles H. "Scandinavia's Prob-
    lem," Forum, 66 (1921), 338-47, 442-52.
Soloveytchik, George. "Europe's Quiet
    Corner," Harper's (F 1953), 57-65.
Teal, John J., Jr. "Europe's Northernmost
    Frontier," FA, 29 (1951), 263-75.
White, Alice H. Scandinavia and the Prob-
    lem of Security Since the End of World
    War II. Thesis (M.A.), University of
    Chicago, 1950.
Wight, Martin. "Neutrality Without Guaran-
    tees: the Netherlands and Scandinavia,"
    in Part I (C) of Arnold Toynbee and Frank
    T. Ashton-Gwatkin, eds., The World in
    March 1939, in the series Survey of In-
    ternational Affairs 1939-1946. Oxford
    University Press, for the Royal Institute
    of International Affairs (Lond., 1954),
    151-65.
Wolfe, Henry C. "Scandinavia: Pace Setter
    in Peace," CH, 49 (1938-39), 27-29.
Wuorinen, John H. "Neutralism in Scandi-
    navia," CH, 31 (1956), 276-80.
——. "Russia, Scandinavia and the Baltic
    States," CH, 28 (1955), 70-74.
——. "Scandinavian Foreign Policy Prob-
    lems: Recent Trends and Emerging Pros-
    pects," ASR, 48 (1960), 161-65.
Wyndham, E. H. "The Military Situation in
    Europe" [Scandinavia], Army Quarterly,
    58 (Ap 1949), 17-20.
Zartman, I. William. "Neutralism and Neu-
trality in Scandinavia," WPQ, 7 (1954),
    125-60.

NORDIC COUNCIL AND SCANDINAVIAN
COOPERATION

Anderson, Stanley V. "Negotiations for the
    Nordic Council," Nord. Tids. for Int. Ret,
    33 (1963), 23-33.
——. The Nordic Council: a Study of Scan-
    dinavian Regionalism. Seattle, Lond., N.Y.,
    1967. 194 p.
——. The Nordic Council: an Institutional
    Analysis. Thesis (Ph.D.), University of
    California, Berkeley, 1961. 490 p.
——. "The Nordic Council and the 1962
    Helsinki Agreement," Nord. Tids. for Int.
    Ret, 34 (1964), 278-300.
Andrén, Nils. "The Nordic Cultural Commis-
    sion 1947-1957," Norseman, 15 (1957),
    375-82.
——. "Nordic Integration," C&C (1967), 1-25.
Arestad, Sverre. "Regional Collaboration in
    Scandinavia," North Europe (1943), 10-17.
Bellquist, Eric C. "Inter-Scandinavian Co-
    operation," Annals (1933), 183-96.
Burbank, Lyman B. "Scandinavian Integra-
    tion and Western Defense," FA, 35 (1956),
    144-50.
Dahl, Paul. "Scandinavian Integration," Yale
    Review, 45 (1956), 634-36.
de Sydow, Gunnar. "The Scandinavian Coop-
    eration in the Field of Legislation after
    the Second World War," Unification of Law,
    3 (1954), 486-95.
Dolan, Paul. "The Nordic Council," WPQ, 12
    (1959), 511-26.
Ekeberg, Birger. "The Scandinavian Coop-
    eration in the Field of Legislation," Uni-
    fication of Law, (1948), 320-39.
Embree, George. "Cooperation a Habit With
    Northern Countries," EFTA Rep, no. 90
    (1964), 1-2.
Eriksen, Erik. "The Nordic Council's Fourth
    Session," Inter-Parliamentary Bulletin,
    36 (1956), 56-63.
Etzioni, Amitai. "A Stable Union: the Nordic
    Associational Web, 1953-1964," Chap. 6 in
    his, Political Unification: a Comparative
    Study of Leaders and Forces (N.Y., 1965),
    184-228.
Franzen, Gösta. "Will There be a United
    States of Scandinavia?" WAI, 15 (1944),
    147-58.
Gregson, Harry. "Northern Cooperation,"
    Norseman, 4 (1946), 171-73.
Hammerich, Borghild. "Lysebu: Norway's
    Gift to the Danish People," ASR, 54 (1966),
    169-73.

Haekkerup, Per. "Nordic Cooperation and the World Around Us." Coph., Danish Secretariat of the Nordic Council, 1964. 18 p. Mimeographed.

Haskel, Barbara G. "Is There an Unseen Spider? a Note on Nordic Integration," C&C (1967), 229-34.

Heckscher, Kay. "A Scandinavian Federation," Free Europe, 10 (1944), 57-58.

Hedtoft, Hans. "The Nordic Council," ASR, 42 (1954), 13-21.

Herlitz, Nils. "The Nordic Council," ScPP, III, 43-48.

Holly, Norman E. "Legal and Legislative Cooperation in the Scandinavian States," ABAJ, 49 (1963), 1089-91.

Hønsvald, Nils. "The Second Session of the Nordic Council," Inter-Parliamentary Bulletin, 34 (1954), 166-77.

"Inter-Scandinavian Co-operation," External Affairs (Ottawa), 7 (1955), 246-52.

Karlström, Otto Leroy. The "Scandinavian" Approach to Political Integration. Thesis (Ph.D.), University of Chicago, 1952.

Lange, Halvard M. "Scandinavian Cooperation in International Affairs," IA, 30 (1954), 285-93.

Leistikow, Gunnar. "Co-operation Between the Scandinavian Countries," in Henning Friis, ed., Scandinavia Between East and West (Ithaca, N.Y., 1950), 307-24.

———. "How Scandinavia Cooperates," Forum (1948), 332-36.

———. "Scandinavian Collaboration — What It Was, What It May Be," ASR, 30 (1942), 15-23.

Lindgren, Raymond E. "International Cooperation in Scandinavia," The Yearbook of World Affairs, 1959 (Lond., 1959), 95-114.

Lindsay, Kenneth. European Assemblies: the Experimental Period, 1949-1959. Lond., N.Y., 1960. 267 p.

Løchen, Einar. "A Comparative Study of Certain European Parliamentary Assemblies," EY, 4 (1958), 150-73.

———. "The Nordic Council," in Kenneth Lindsay, ed., European Assemblies: the Experimental Period 1949-1959 (Lond., N.Y., 1960), 252-59.

Matteucci, Mario. "The Scandinavian Legislative Cooperation as a Model for European Cooperation," in Liber Amicorum of Congratulations to Algot Bagge (Stock., 1956), 136-45.

Mead, William R. "Scandinavianism and the Future of Scandinavia," Norseman, 1 (1943), 438-43.

Meinander, Ragnar, and Sven-Olof Hultin.

"Fifth Session of the Nordic Council and the Recommendation Concerning Nuclear Energy," Inter-Parliamentary Bulletin, 37 (1957), 20-26.

Moritzen, Julius. "Scandinavian Renaissance: Is A Scandinavian Federation a Post-War Possibility?" CH, 8 (1945), 330-35.

———. "The War and a Greater Scandinavia," NoAmRev, 101 (1915), 372-79.

Nagel, Heinrich. "The Nordic Council: Its Organs, Functions and Juridical Nature," Annuaire Revue de l'A.A.A./Annual Journal of the A.A.A., 26 (1956), 51-67.

Nordic Committee on Social Policy. Nordic Co-operation in the Social and Labour Field. Oslo, 1965. 47 p.

Nordic Council. Nordic Cooperation: Conference Organized by the Nordic Council for International Organisations in Europe, Hässelby 2-4 June 1965. Stock., 1965. 127 p.

Nordic Economic Co-operation. Report by the Nordic Economic Co-operation Committee. Coph., 1958. 143 p.; Supplement. Coph., 1959. 43 p.

"The Nordic Council," in EY, 2 (1956), 575-79.

"The Nordic Council," in EY, 3 (1957), 397-401.

"The Nordic Council," in EY, 4 (1958), 369-73.

"Nordic Council," in EY, 5 (1959), 597-609.

"The Nordic Council," in EY-1962, 10 (1963), 937-54.

"The Nordic Council," in Ivan Sipkov and Johannes Klesment, "Political Organizations," LCQJ, 21 (1964), 305-13.

"Northern Council," in EY, 1 (1955), 463-67.

"Northern Council," in Amos J. Peaslee, ed., International Government Organizations: Constitutional Documents (The Hague, 1956), 526-28.

Orfield, Lester B. "Uniform Scandinavian Laws," ABAJ, 38 (1952), 773-75.

Padelford, Norman J. "Regional Cooperation in Scandinavia," IOrg, 11 (1957), 597-614.

Pakstas, K. Baltoscandian Confederation. N.Y., 1942. 27 p.

Pedersen, Poul T. "Four Nations Break Down the Barriers," DFOJ, no. 14 (1954), 18-19.

Petrén, Gustaf. "Memorandum on the Problem of Method in Nordic Legislative Co-operation," Unification of Law, 9 (1960), 209-18.

———. The Nordic Council. Stock., 1961. 7 p.

———. "The Nordic Council: a Unique Factor in International Law," Nord. Tids. for Int. Ret, 29 (1960), 346-62.

———. "Scandinavian Co-operation," in EY, 2 (1956), 60-74. Also printed separately.

Pontoppidan, Neils. "A Mature Experiment:

the Scandinavian Experience," AJCL, 9
(1960), 344-49.

Riis, R. W. "Friendship Towns," ASR, 38
(1950), 24-29.

Salvesen, Kaare. "Cooperation in Social Affairs between the Northern Countries of
Europe," ILR, 73 (1956), 334-57.

Sawicki, Stanislaw. "The Norden Association," BC, 1 (Aug 1935), 101-104.

"Scandinavian Cooperation" [in Political,
Economic, and Social Matters], ACNIA,
26 (1955); 156-63.

Scandinavian Cooperation; A Report to the
Council of Europe by the Delegates from
Denmark, Iceland, Norway, and Sweden to
the Consultative Assembly to the Council.
Stock., 1951. 25 p.

"Scandinavian Cooperation in Social Affairs,"
in George R. Nelson, ed., Freedom and
Welfare: Social Patterns in the Northern
Countries of Europe (Coph., 1953), 485-96.

"Scandinavianism as an Idea and as a Reality,"
IO, 2 (1937/38), 59-67.

Scott, Franklin D. "Cultural Interchange in
Scandinavia," Institute of International Education News Bulletin (Ja 1951), 13-14+.

Seidenfaden, Erik. "Scandinavian Renaissance: Federation," CH, 8 (1945), 330-35.

Seip, Helge. "The Pursuit of the Possible in
Scandinavian Cooperation," Norseman, 14
(1956), 145-50.

Sletten, Vegard. Five Northern Countries
Pull Together. Oslo, 1967. 92 p.

Strahl, Ivar. "Scandinavian Cooperation in
the Field of Legislation," ScPP, III, 113-
17.

——. "The Scandinavian Jurists' Congresses," ScPP, III, 118-21.

Tenhaeff, F. "Scandinavian Co-operation:
an Example of Regionalistic Integration,"
in International Sociological Association,
Lieges Congress, 1953, Papers. Section
II, "Intergroup Conflicts and Their Mediation." Oslo, 1953. 5 p. Mimeographed.

Tybjerg, Oluf. "Scandinavian Co-operation,"
ASR, 5 (1917), 106-10.

von Bonsdorff, Göran. "Regional Cooperation
of the Nordic Countries," C&C, (1965, no.
1), 32-38.

von Eyben, William E. "Inter-Nordic Legislative Cooperation," 6 (1962), 62-93.

Wasberg, Gunnar C. "The Nordic Cultural
Commission," ASR, 49 (1961), 169-73.

Wendt, Frantz W. "The Norden Association,"
ASR, 44 (1956), 245-49.

——. "The Norden Association," in ScPP,
III, 49-54.

——. The Nordic Council and Co-operation
in Scandinavia. Coph., 1959. 247 p.

——. "Nordic Cooperation – Past and Present," in J. A. Lauwerys, ed., Scandinavian
Democracy (Coph., N.Y., 1958), 370-87.

——. The Nordic Council, Its Background,
Structure and First Session. Coph., 1953.
Reprint from Travaux de l'Institut International de Finances Publique, 9 (1953),
199-210.

Wuorinen, John H. "Problems of a Scandinavian Bloc," CH, 16 (1949), 12-15.

——. "Scandinavian Unity: Problems and
Prospects," ASR, 45 (1957), 264-68.

Ybarra, T. R. "United States of Scandinavia,"
Outlook, 155 (1930), 585.

INTERNATIONAL ORGANIZATIONS

Burbank, Lionel B. "Scandinavia and
N.A.T.O.," CH, 23 (1952), 20-23.

Eek, Hilding. "Attitude of the Scandinavian
Countries to the Revision of the Charter,"
in Revision of the United Nations Charter:
a Symposium (New Delhi, 1956), 93-101.

Falnes, Oscar J. "Organizing for Security;
Scandinavian Leadership in Regional Internationalism," ASR, 25 (1937), 299-308.

——. "The Scandinavian Peoples in the
League of Nations," ASR, 22 (1934), 201-
17.

Friis, Erik J. "Scandinavians on Guard in
the Middle East," ASR, 45 (1957), 125-32.

Haas, Ernst B. Consensus Formation in the
Council of Europe. Lond., Berkeley,
1960. 70 p.

Hambro, Carl J. "The Northern Countries
at the League," Nord, 1 (1938), 351-56.

Hansen, Johs. "The Scandinavian Countries
and the Atlantic Pact," DO, 2 (1949), 1-5.

Haekkerup, Per. "Scandinavia's Peace-
Keeping Forces for U.N.," FA, 42 (1964),
675-81.

Jacobsen, Kurt. "Voting Behaviour of the
Nordic Countries in the General Assembly," C&C (1967), 139-57.

Jones, S. Shepard. The Scandinavian States
and the League of Nations. Princeton,
N.J., 1939. 298 p.

Kalela, Jaakko. "The Nordic Group in the
General Assembly," C&C (1967), 158-70.

Karup Pedersen, Ole. "Scandinavia and the
'UN Stand-by Forces'," C&C (1967), 37-
46.

Kildal, Arne. "Scandinavian Aid to the Developing Countries," ASR, 51 (1963), 378-88.

——. "Scandinavian Aid to Refugees," ASR,
51 (1963), 135-44.

L., E. "The Scandinavian Countries in the
Council of Europe," Norseman, 7 (1949),
383-87.

Leysen, P. Scandinavia and the North Atlantic Treaty Organisation. Thesis (M.S.), London School of Economics, 1962.

Lidstrom, Jan-Erik, and Claes Wiklund. "The Nordic Countries in the General Assembly and Its Two Political Committees," C&C (1967), 171-88.

Ørvik, Nils. "NATO – the Role of the Small Members," Atlantic Community Quarterly, 4 (1966), 92-103; IntJ, 21 (1966), 173-85.

Ørvik, Nils, and Niels J. Haagerup. The Scandinavian Members of NATO. Adelphi Paper No. 23, Institute for Strategic Studies. Lond., 1965. 14 p.

Schöpflin, George. "NATO and the Nordic Balance," WT, 22 (1966), 114-22.

Sommerseth, Leif. Scandinavia in the United Nations. Thesis (M.A.), University of California, 1951.

Svennevig, Tormod P. "The Scandinavian Bloc in the United Nations and its New Outlook," Norseman, 13 (1955), 145-53.

——. "The Scandinavian Bloc in the United Nations," SocRes, 22 (1955), 39-56.

"The Three New Members," UNB, 1, no. 17 (1946), 17-21.

Trytten, Martha. The Scandinavian Countries and the United Nations. Thesis (M.A.), University of Wisconsin, 1953.

EUROPE

Borowik, Józef. "The Equilibrium in the Baltic," BSC, 5 (1939), 95-100.

Cole, Hugh M. "Hitler Invades Scandinavia," CH, 51 (1939/40), 15-17+.

Deutelmoser, Arno. Misadventure in Scandinavia. Scotch Plains, N.J., 1940. 94 p.

Ellinger, Tage U. H. "The Anglo-American-Scandinavian Situation," ASR, 29 (1941), 313-18.

Firth, Charles H., ed. Notes on the Diplomatic Relations of England with the North of Europe; List of English Diplomatic Representatives and Agents in Denmark, Sweden and Russia and of those Countries in England, 1689-1762. Oxford, 1913. 52 p.

Gathorne-Hardy, Geoffrey M. "Department of Scandinavian Studies" [University College, London], Norseman, 4 (1946), 140-43.

Joesten, Joachim. "Scandinavia in the 'New Order'," FA, 19 (1941), 818-27.

——. "Storm Over Northern Europe" [Soviet and German Surveillance in Scandinavia], CR, 151 (1937), 454-60.

Jones, W. Glyn. "British and Scandinavians Meet" [Scandinavian Conference at Cambridge, 1956], Norseman, 15 (1957), 29-31.

Kent, H. S. K. Anglo-Scandinavian Economic and Diplomatic Relations, 1755-1763. Thesis (Ph.D.), Cambridge, 1956.

Koczy, Leon. "Scandinavian Things in Polish Literature," BSC, 3 (1937), 517-26.

Lane, Margery. "The Relations Between England and the Northern Powers, 1689-1697," Transactions of the Royal Historical Society, 5 (1911), 157-93.

Marwick, William H. "Scandinavia and Britain," IO, 2 (1937/38), 151-55.

Olberg, Paul. "Scandinavia and the Nazis," CR, 156 (1939), 27-34.

Patterson, Eric J. "Scandinavia and the German Aims," Empire Review 71 (May 1940), 280-83.

Roberts, Michael. "Cromwell and the Baltic," EHR, 76 (1961), 402-46.

Ryan, A. N. "The Defense of British Trade With the Baltic, 1808-1813," EHR, 74 (1959), 443-66.

Siney, Marian C. Allied Negotiations with the Netherlands, Denmark, Norway, and Sweden to Make Effective the Blockade of Germany, 1914-1916. Thesis (Ph.D.), University of Michigan, 1938.

Smout, T. C. The Overseas Trade of Scotland, with Particular Reference to the Baltic and Scandinavian Trades, 1660-1707. Thesis (Ph.D.), Cambridge, 1959.

Soloveytchik, George. "Fears and Realities in Scandinavia," IA, 16 (1937), 894-919.

——. "The Scandinavian Debacle," CR, 157 (1940), 659-69.

——. "Who Threatens Scandinavia," CR, 155 (1939), 169-78.

Whitehead, R. "Cultural Relations," [Norway, Sweden – Great Britain] Norseman, 5 (1947), 288-98.

"Yugoslavia and the Scandinavian Countries," Yugoslav Survey, 2 (1961), 545-58.

UNITED STATES

"The American-Scandinavian Foundation, 1911-1946; Thirty-fifth Anniversary," ASR, 34 (1946), 297-326.

Anderson, Arlow W. The Scandinavian Immigrants and American Public Affairs, 1840 to 1872. Thesis (Ph.D.), Northwestern University, 1943.

Babcock, Kendric C. The Scandinavian Element in the United States (University of Illinois Studies in the Social Sciences, v. 3, no. 8). Urbana, Ill., 1914. 223 p.

Bronner, Hedin. "The Promotion of

Scandinavian Studies in the United States," in Carl Bayerschmidt and Erik Friis, eds., Scandinavian Studies: Essays Presented to Henry Goddard Leach (Seattle, 1965), 141-49.

Bronner, Hedin, and Gösta Franzen. "Scandinavian Studies in Institutions of Learning in the United States," ScSt, 39 (1967), 345-67.

Evjen, John O. Scandinavian Immigrants in New York, 1630-1674. Minneapolis, 1916. 438 p.

Fonkalsrud, Alfred O. Scandinavians as a Social Force in America. Brooklyn, 1914. 88 p. Based on Ph.D. Thesis, New York University, 1913.

Friis, Erik J. The American-Scandinavian Foundation 1910-1960: a Brief History. N.Y., 1961. 135 p.

———. "Pioneer in Cultural Exchange: Golden Jubilee of the American-Scandinavian Foundation," Norseman, 5 (1960), 4-7.

Hovde, Brynjolf J. Diplomatic Relations of the U.S. with Sweden and Norway, 1814-1905. Iowa City, 1920. 70 p.

———. "We Americans and Scandinavia," in Henning Friis, ed., Scandinavia Between East and West (Ithaca, N.Y., 1950), 325-50.

Hovgaard, William. "The American-Scandinavian Movement," ASR, 3 (1915), 290-95.

———. "The Mission of the American-Scandinavian Foundation," ASR, 5 (1917), 220-25.

Johnson, Lyndon B. "Friendly Flight to Northern Europe," NGeogM, 125 (1964), 268-93.

Kelman, H. C., and L. Bailyn. "Effects of Cross-Cultural Experience on National Images: a Study of Scandinavian Students in America," Journal of Conflict Resolution, 6 (1962), 319-34.

Koht, Halvdan. American Spirit in Europe: a Survey of Trans-Atlantic Influences. Oslo, Phila., 1949. 289 p.

Peterson, C. Stewart. American-Scandinavian Diplomatic Relations, 1776-1876. Baltimore, 1948. 92 p. Multigraphed.

Schou, Marie. "Scandinavian Homes of Uncle Sam;" I: "The Legation at Copenhagen," ASR, 13 (1925), 612-15; II: Richards, Edith. "The Legation in Stockholm," ASR, 13 (1925), 666-71; III: "The Legation in Oslo," ASR, 14 (1926), 218-21.

Scott, Franklin D. "American Influences in Norway and Sweden," JMH, 18 (1946), 37-

47. Revised from a paper read at the 8th International Congress of Historical Sciences, Zurich, 1938.

———. The United States and Scandinavia. Cambridge, Mass., 1950. 359 p.

United States, House of Representatives, Committee on Foreign Affairs, Subcommittee on Europe Special Study Mission Report. "Scandinavia," in The Soviet Union and Scandinavia (Wash., N 30, 1967), 10-13.

Vice President Johnson Visits Northern Europe: Text of One of the Speeches Made by Veep...with a Press Statement...by Johnson and Kekkonen on Sept. 10, 1963," DeptStateBul, 49 (1963), 583-94.

Wolfston, Patricia S. "The ASR International Exchange Programs," ASR, 48 (1960), 343-48.

Woodhouse, C. M. "Attitudes of NATO Countries toward the U.S.," WP, 10 (1958), 202-19.

Wuorinen, John H. "Scandinavian Studies at Columbia University," ASR, 49 (1961), 289-92.

RUSSIA

Anderson, Albin T. "The Soviets and Northern Europe," WP, 4 (1952), 468-87.

Coombs, G. M. "Russo-Scandinavian Problems," CR, 181 (1952), 14-17.

Dörfer, Ingemar. Soviet Policy in the North — Finland, Sweden, Norway 1948-1949. Thesis (M.A.), Harvard University, 1963.

Futrell, Michael. Northern Underground: Episode of Russian Revolutionary Transport and Communications Through Scandinavia and Finland, 1863-1917. Lond., 1963. 240 p.

Hessler, William H. "The Baltic: Russian Bottle with a Swedish Cork," Reporter, 7 (Aug 19, 1952), 21-24.

"The Kremlin Looks at Scandinavia Through the Eyes of the Baltic States," BR, 2 (S 7-21, 1956), 71-75.

Mehlem, Max. "Scandinavia and Strategy in the Baltic," SRWA, 2 (Ap 1952), 7-9.

———. "Scandinavia Skeptical of Russian Peace Moves," SRWA, 3 (Je 1953), 18-19.

"Norway, Denmark and Soviet" [Letters of Marshal Bulganin of March 27 and 28, 1957, to Prime Ministers Einar Gerhardsen and H. C. Hansen and their answers], Norseman, 15 (1957), 145-59.

Ørvik, Nils. Europe's Northern Cap and the Soviet Union. Cambridge, Mass., 1963. 64 p.

Pick, O., and A. Wiseman. "The U.S.S.R.

and Her Northern Neighbours," WT, 15 (1959), 387-94.

Pochljobkin, W. W. "The Development of Scandinavian Studies in Russia up to 1917," Scandinavica, 1 (1962), 89-113.

Schapiro, L. B. "The Limits of Russian Territorial Waters in the Baltic," BYIL, 27 (1950), 439-48.

Spencer, Arthur. "Soviet Pressure on Scandinavia," FA, 30 (1952), 651-59.

DENMARK

Bellquist, Eric C. "Possible Effects of Danish Disarmament," ASR, 19 (1937), 299-300.

Bjøl, Erling. "Foreign Policy-making in Denmark," C&C (1966, no. 2), 1-17.

Bruel, Erik. "The Little Belt Bridge and International Law," Acta scandinavica juris gentium, 6 (1935), 142-56.

——. "The Danish Straits," Acta scandinavica juris gentium, 11 (1940), 3-107.

Cagle, M. W. "The Strategic Danish Straits," USNIP, 86 (O 1960), 36-41.

Chilston, Viscount. "Denmark," in Part V of Arnold and Veronica Toynbee, eds., The Realignment of Europe, in the series Survey of International Affairs 1939-1946. Oxford Univ. Press, for the Royal Institute of International Affairs (Lond., 1955), 565-78.

Christian, John L. "Denmark's Interest in Burma and the Nicobar Islands," Journal of the Burma Research Society, 29 (1939), 215-32.

Council on Foreign Relations. Danish Peace Aims. N.Y., 1942. 12 p.

"Danish Rules of Neutrality," DFOJ, no. 228 (Ja 1940), 4-5.

Dauphin, Guy. "Some Danish Problems," MidwestJ (Winter, 1952-53), 60-64.

Denmark, Civilforsvarsstyrelsen. Danish Civil Defence. Coph., 1953. 29 p.

——. Danish CD Mobile Columns. Coph., 1957. 17 p.

Denmark, Ministry of Foreign Affairs. Consular Congress in Copenhagen, 1955. Coph., 1955. 48 p.

——. Danish Consular Instructions of January 18th, 1912. Coph., 1912. 187 p.

——. Danish Foreign Office Journal: Special Issue for the United States. Coph., 1955. 56 p.

——. Instructions for the Danish Foreign Service of September 21, 1932. Coph., 1933. 428 p.

Haekkerup, Per. "A Danish View of Europe and the Atlantic," Atlantic Community Quarterly, 3 (1965), 217-23. Same as "Europe: Basic Problems and Perspectives – A Danish View," IA, 41 (1965), 1-10.

——. "The Foreign Policy of Denmark," ASR, 54 (1966), 341-50.

——. "The Four Planks in Danish Foreign Policy: the UN, NATO, the Economic and Political Association of Europe, and Northern Cooperation," DFOJ, no. 46 (1963), 8-16.

Hansen, G. Nasselund. "Current Problems in Danish Foreign Policy," Norseman, 6 (1948), 216-20.

Hecksher, Kay. "Denmark in World Politics," CR, 182 (1952), 206-10.

Helwig, Hjalmar. "Denmark," in George W. Kisker, ed., World Tension: The Psychopathology of International Relations (N.Y., 1951), 40-51.

Henningsen, Sven. "Denmark," in Joseph E. Black and Kenneth W. Thompson, eds., Foreign Policies in a World of Change (N.Y., 1963), 89-114.

Hill, Charles E. The Danish Sound Dues and the Command of the Baltic. A Study of International Relations. Durham, N.C., 1926. 305 p.

Jakobsen, Frode. "Home Guard," DO, 1 (1948), 157-67.

Karup Pedersen, Ole. "The Teaching and Study of International Politics in Denmark 1960-1966," C&C (1966, no. 2), 102-106.

Kirchner, Walther. "A Milestone in European History, the Danish-Russian Treaty of 1567," SEER, 22 (1944), 39-48.

Konradsen, Henrik B. "Denmark: Key to the Baltic Gate," Military Review, 46 (Je 1966), 47-54.

Leistikow, Gunnar. "Denmark's Precarious Neutrality," FA, 17 (1939), 611-17.

Lund, Erik. "Khrushchev in Denmark: a Study of the Soviet and East European Press Reactions," C&C (1967), 26-36.

Mehlem, Max. "Denmark's Preparedness," SRWA, 1 (O 1951), 19-20.

Munch, Peter. "Co-operation Between the Northern Countries," DFOJ, no. 216 (Ja 1939), 2-3.

——. "The Neutrality Policy of Denmark," Nord, 2 (1939), 276-83.

Norlund, Niels. "The Danes' Dilemma," Reporter, 24 (1961, no. 5), 28-30.

Petersen, Henrik M. "Maritime Denmark" [Royal Danish Navy], USNIP, 94 (1968), 37-49.

Qvistgaard, E. J. C. Danish Defense: Postwar Progress and Future Plans. Coph., 1951. 16 p.

Seidenfaden, Erik. "The Foreign Policy of Denmark," ASR, 42 (1954), 205-10.

"Some Problems Facing Denmark," WT, 8 (1952), 420-29.

Sorenson, V. "Danish Civil Defense is a Skeleton of a Call-Up Scheme," Municipal Journal, 59 (1951), 1221.

Stauning, M. Th. "Denmark and the War," DFOJ, no. 228 (Ja 1940), 1-3.

Street, John C. "Free Danes," GeoM, 15 (1942-43), 592-95.

The War Through Danish Eyes. Oxford, 1915. 19 p.

Westengard, Jens I. "Danes in Siam," ASR, 5 (1917), 14-19.

Zaslovsky, David. "Hamlet's Home Today: 'Little Denmark is Afraid of Finding Herself a Pawn in the Imperialist Game of Certain Strong Powers'," New Masses (O 15, 1946), 6-8+.

INTERNATIONAL ORGANIZATION

Bjøl, Erling. "NATO and Denmark," C&C, 3 (1968), 93-107.

Canada, Department of National Defence, Bureau of Current Affairs. Denmark, a Member of the North Atlantic Treaty Organization. Ottawa, 1953. 48 p.

Denmark, FAO Delegation. Report to the Food and Agriculture Organization of the UN (FAO) May 1947, Coph. 59 p.

Denmark, Ministry of Foreign Affairs. Danish Report on the Operation and Progress under the European Recovery Program April/Sept. 1948-1952. Coph.

——. Denmark in NATO: an Outline. Coph., 1953. 11 p.

——. Denmark and the Marshall Plan. April/Sept. 1948-1952. Coph.

Denmark, Udvalget for de Forende Nationers udvidede program for teknisk bistant til underudviklede lande. Denmark's Participation in International Technical Assistance Activities; Report on Danish Participation in International Technical Co-operation. Coph., 1961. 84 p.

Fischer, Alfred J. "Denmark's Defence and NATO," Norseman, 13 (1955), 89-90.

Frisch, Hartvig. "Denmark and the League of Nations," IO, 2 (1937/38), 92-106.

Hansen, H. C. "Speech at the NATO Meeting of Ministers in Paris, Dec. 16, 1957," Norseman, 16 (1958), 3-5.

Hecksher, Kay. "Denmark and NATO," CR, 184 (1953), 278-83.

Kragh, Erik. "Danish Defense Within NATO," ScPP, III, 153-57.

Mehlem, Max. "NATO Bases and Elec-

tions in Denmark," SRWA, 3 (Aug 1953), 15-16.

Nielssen, Gunnar P. Denmark and European Integration: a Small Country at the Crossroads. Thesis (Ph.D.), University of California, Los Angeles, 1966. 665 p.

Sørensen, Max, and Niels J. Haagerup. Denmark and the United Nations (Prepared for the Carnegie Endowment for International Peace). N.Y., 1956. 154 p.

Wilkinson, Joe R. "Denmark and NATO: the Problems of a Small State in a Collective Security System," IOrg, 10 (1956), 390-401.

GREAT BRITAIN AND THE UNITED STATES

Bladt, Holger J. "Rebild," ScPP, III, 872-73.

Brønsted, Georg K. "Anglo-Danish Relations," DO, 1 (1948), 144-48.

Cheyney, Edward P. "England and Denmark in the Later Days of Queen Elizabeth," JMH, I, (1929), 9-39.

Dahlerup, Joost. "Early Danish-American Diplomacy," ASR, 30 (1942), 308-13.

Denmark, Treaties, etc., 1947-(Frederick IX). Convention... for the avoidance of double taxation and the prevention of fiscal evasion with respect to taxes on income. Lond., 1950. 23 p.

——. Convention on payment of compensation or benefit in respect of industrial injuries (including occupational diseases) as relating to Denmark and Northern Ireland; London, July 9, 1956. Lond., 1956. 9 p.

——. Convention on payment of compensation or benefit in respect of industrial injuries. London, July 9, 1956. Lond., 1957. 9 p.

——. Convention regarding payment of compensation or benefit in respect of industrial injuries, including occupational diseases. London, Dec. 15, 1953. Lond., 1954. 7 p.

Egan, Maurice F. [Former Ambassador to Denmark]. Recollections of a Happy Life. N.Y., 1924. 374 p.

Fogdall, Soren J. M. P. Danish-American Diplomacy, 1776-1920 (University of Iowa Studies in the Social Sciences, v. 8, no. 2), Iowa City, 1922. 171 p.

Kirchner, Walther. "England and Denmark, 1558-1588," JMH, 17 (1945), 1-15.

Kulsrud, Carl J. "The Seizure of the Danish Fleet, 1807," AJIL, 32 (1938), 280-311.

Lane, Margery. "The Relations Between England and the Northern Powers,

1689-1697; Part I: Denmark," Transactions of the Royal Historical Society, 3rd
series, v. V, Lond., 1911. 183 p. B. of
T., Journals 3/8, 27/11/1696, C.O. 391/9.

Lorenzen, Poul. "The Rebild Festival, a
Fourth of July Celebration on Danish
Ground," ASR, 18 (1930), 345-52.

Manniche, Peter. "England and Denmark,"
IO, 2 (1937-38), 110-21.

Sonne, Hans Christian. "Ambassador Henrik
Kauffman," ASR, 51 (1963), 251-54.

Swan, Marshall W. S. "The United States
and Denmark, a Diplomatic Anniversary,"
FSJ, 2 (1951), 36-37+.

GREENLAND

Anker, E. The Right of Norway to Eirik
Rande's Land. Oslo, 1931. 15 p.

Berlin, Knud D. Denmark's Right to Green-
land: a Survey of the Past and Present
Status of Greenland, Iceland and the
Faroe Islands in Relation to Norway and
Denmark. Oxford, Coph., 1932. 185 p.

Breckinridge, Henry. "Nazis in Greenland,"
CH, 51 (May 1940), 13-14.

Briggs, Herbert W. "The Validity of the
Greenland Agreement," AJIL, 35 (1941),
506-13.

Castberg, Frede. Greenland. Oslo, 1925.
27 p.

Denmark, Treaties, etc..., 1947— (Frederik IX). Defense of Greenland. Agreement...signed at Copenhagen April 27,
1951. Wash., 1951. 14 p.

Dunbar, M. J. "Common Cause in the
North," IntJ, 1 (1946), 358-64.

Federspiel, Per T. "The Disputed Sovereignty over East Greenland," IA, 11
(1932), 784-811.

Friis, Erik J. "Standing Guard in Greenland," ASR, 48 (1960), 241-49.

Hanson, Earl P. "Should We Buy Greenland?" Harper's, 180 (May 1940), 570-77.

Hudson, Manley O. "An Important Judgment
of the World Court," ABAJ, 19 (1933),
423-25.

Hyde, Charles C. "The Case Concerning the
Legal Status of Eastern Greenland," AJIL,
27 (1933), 732-38.

Knaplund, Paul. "The Dano-Norwegian Conflict Over Greenland," AJIL, 19 (1925),
374-77.

"Legal Status of Certain Parts of Greenland," AJIL, 27 (1933), 27-30.

"The Legal Status of East Greenland,"
GeogJ, 82 (1933), 151-56.

"Legal Status on Eastern Greenland," AJIL,
28 (1934), 4-8.

Mikkelsen, Ejnar. "A Summer Voyage to
Scoresby Sound," ASR, 13 (1925), 21-28.

Mogens, Victor. Greenland: the Norwegian-
Danish Conflict — the Greenland Question
in the Light of History and International
Law. Oslo, 1932. 46 p.

Morgenstierne, Wilhelm. "Greenland and
Norway Through a Thousand Years," ASR,
19 (1931), 535-45.

Mosely, Philip E. "Iceland and Greenland:
an American Problem," FA, 18 (1940),
742-46.

Norway and East Greenland: a Short Survey.
Oslo, 1931. 23 p.

Preuss, L. "Disputes between Denmark and
Norway on the Sovereignty of East Greenland," AJIL, 26 (1932), 469-87.

Raymond, Allen. "Greenland, Northern Sen-
try Post," Reporter (Jl 10, 1951), 21-24.

Skeie, Jon. Greenland: the Dispute Between
Norway and Denmark. Lond., 1932. 94 p.

Stefansson, Vilhjalmur. "The American Far
North," FA, 17 (1939), 508-23.

Teal, John J., Jr. "Greenland and the World
Around," FA, 31 (1952), 128-41.

Thalbitzer, William. "Denmark and the
Greenlanders," ASR, 9 (1921), 680-84.

"U.S.-Denmark Sign Defense Agreement for
Greenland," DeptStateBul, 24 (1951), 943-
45.

SLESVIG CONTROVERSY

Andersen, Holger. "Slesvig Again," ASR, 15
(1927), 407-11.

Andersen, J. South-Jutland under Prussian
Rule; a Brief Description. Coph., 1914.
16 p.; 1917. 25 p.; 1918. 32 p.

Baerlein, Henry. "The Problem of South
Slesvig," Norseman, 6 (1948), 228-33.

Bodholdt, K. C. "Slesvig Before 1864," ASR,
6 (1918), 259-67.

"The British Policy in South Slesvig," DO, 1
(1948), 52-60.

Bury, J. P. T. "The Schleswig-Holstein
Problem," in the New Cambridge Modern
History (Cambridge, 1958), v. 10, 219-20.

Carr, William. Schleswig-Holstein, 1815-
48: a Study in National Conflict. Manchester, 1963. 341 p.

Coussange, Jacques de. "Slesvig Since the
Armistice," NewEur, 10 (1919), 132-36.

Damm, Christian. "South Slesvig as a
Nordic Problem," Norseman, 4 (1946),
235-37.

Danes in South-Slesvig. Edited by the Joint
Committee of the Danish South-Slesvigers.
Flensborg, 1945. 36 p.

Danish Outlook. A Periodical which started

in 1948 dealing with the post-war Slesvig problem.

Denmark, Ministry for Foreign Affairs. The German Minority in South Jutland; a Summary of the Danish Legislation, Coph., 1924. 12 p.; 2d ed., 1929; 3d ed., 1936.

Diemer, Asmus. "Historic Corners of Sönderylland," ASR, 9 (1921), 190-99.

——. "With the King Through South Jutland," ASR, 8 (1920), 721-49.

Egan, Maurice F. Ten Years Near the German Frontier, a Retrospect and a Warning. N.Y., 1919. 364 p.

Erichsen, Erich. Forced to Fight: the Tale of a Schleswig Dane. Lond., 1917. 184 p.

Eskildsen, Claus H. The South Slesvig Question. Coph., 1946. 22 p.

Fabricius, Knud. "The South Slesvig Problem," ASR, 36 (1948), 207-18.

Fabricius, L. P. "Notes on a Journey to South Slesvig, December 1947," DO, 1 (1948), 130-35.

Fuglsang-Damgaard, Hans. The Problem of South Slesvig and the Christian Church. Coph., 1946. 24 p.

Gjessing, Erland. "Slesvig," ASR, 33 (1945), 212-17.

Hansen, Jesper P. Sleswig under the Prussian Rule: an Exposition Regarding the Fluctuations of the Population of Sleswig Mainly During the Period 1864-1910. Prepared from official German sources. Coph., 1919. 24 p.

Hanssen, H. P. "How North Slesvig Has Come Back," ASR, 14 (1926), 109-12.

——. "The Present Situation in South Jutland," ASR, 23 (1935), 103-12.

Haugsted, Mogens. "Return of the Lion," ASR, 34 (1946), 39-47.

Hayman, Eric. Danish-German Relations in Schleswig. Lond., 1940. 44 p.

Heberle, Rudolf. "The Political Movements Among the Rural People in Schleswig-Holstein, 1918 to 1932," JP, 5 (1943), 3-26; 115-41.

Jensen, Jens. "Are the Slesvigers Danes or Germans?" ASR, 6 (1918), 268-72.

Johansen, Jens. "Denmark's Struggle for Slesvig in the 19th Century," DO, 1 (1948), 5-15; 34-40.

Jones, Karen M. "Commentary on Denmark," ASR, 33 (1945), 203-11.

Jørgensen, Adolf D. The Dano-German Question. Lond., 1900. 19 p.

Kirkegaard, Ivor. "The Fall of Dannevirke and Dybböl," ASR, 6 (1918), 17-23.

——. "Fifty Years Under German Rule," ASR, 6 (1918), 252-58.

Kristensen, Thorkil. "Speech Relative to the London Round Table Conference on South Slesvig," DO, 1 (1948), 173-76.

Kruse, Frederik V. The Fate of Southern Slesvig. Coph., 1954. 45 p.

Larsen, Karen. "Danes in the German Reichstag," ASR, 6 (1918), 274-76.

——. "The Settlement of the Slesvig Question," PSQ, 34 (1919), 568-90.

Larson, Laurence M. "Prussianism in North Sleswick," AHR, 24 (1919), 227-52.

Leach, Henry G. "On the Eve of Reunion," ASR, 8 (1920), 684-88.

Linvald, Axel. "H. P. Hanssen of North Slesvig," ASR, 24 (1936), 216-26.

Meyer, Poul. Topical Guide to the South-Slesvig Question. Coph., 1945. 22 p.

Møller, Erik. "Danish Aspirations," NewEur, 10 (1919), 226-31.

Mortensen, Tage. "The Election in South Slesvig: Votes Contra Smoke Bombs," DO, 1 (1948), 149-53.

——. "Prior to the Round Table: Conference on South Slesvig in London," DO, 1 (1948), 99-103.

Mosse, W. E. "Queen Victoria and Her Ministers in the Schleswig-Holstein Crisis 1863-1864," EHR, 78 (1963), 263-83.

Nygaard, Georg. "Beating Cannon Into Church Bells," ASR, 15 (1927), 231-34.

Prior, W. R. North Sleswick Under Prussian Rule, 1864-1914 (Oxford Pamphlets, no. 40). Lond., N.Y., 1914. 15 p.

"Prussian Rule in North Slesvig," NewEur, 3 (1917), 140-47.

Savory, Douglas. "South Slesvig in 1960," CR, 198 (1960), 374-76; 674-76.

Schütte, Gudmund. "German Mendacity Concerning Slesvig and Denmark," DO, 1 (1948), 110-11.

——. Pan-Germanism and Denmark: a Danish Reply to Unjustifiable Accusation. Coph., 1913. 80 p.

——. Pan-Germanism and Denmark II: a Pictorial and Carto-graphical Supplement. Coph., 1914. 16 p.

Skovgaard, Jes. "South Slesvig," DO, 1 (1948), 15-21.

Skovmand, Roar. "The Awakening of North Slesvig," ScPP, II, 722-27.

——. "North Slesvig under Prussian Dominion," ScPP, II, 759-63.

——. "The Reunion of North Slesvig," ScPP, II, 1004-1008.

"Slesvig Pictures" [Illustrations], ASR, 8 (1920), 352-55.

"The Slesvig Plebiscite and the Danish-German Boundary" [by A. R. H.], GeogJ, 56 (1920), 484-91.

Stauning, T. "Neutral Denmark," ASR, 23 (1935), 295-301.

Steefel, Lawrence D. The Schleswig-Holstein Question. (Harvard Historical Studies, v. 32). Cambridge, Mass., 1932. 400 p.

Vander Veer, J. C. "Slesvig: the Legacy of 1864," NewEur, 4 (1917), 142-50.

Vinding, M. The Federal State of South-Slesvig. Coph., 1948. 23 p.

Westergaard, Waldemar C. Denmark and Slesvig (1848-1864); With a Collection of Illustrative Letters by Daniel Bruhn, including his Letters from California and Nevada (1864-1872). N.Y., 1946. 144 p.

FINLAND

Aaltio, Tauri. Finland and Inter-Scandinavian Cooperation. Thesis (M.A.), University of California, Berkeley, 1957. 152 p.

Aho, I. R. A Record of the Activities of the Finnish Missionary Society in Northwest Hunan, China, 1902-1952. Thesis (M.A.), University of California, Berkeley, 1953.

Bilmanis, Alfreds. The Baltic States and the Problem of the Freedom of the Baltic Sea. Wash., 1943. 71 p.

"The Boundaries of Finland," ASR, 6 (N/D 1918). Entire issue devoted to the topic.

Broms, Bengt. "'American Days' in Finland," ASR, 50 (1962), 417-22.

———. "Scholarship Programs Linking the United States and Finland," ASR, 49 (1961), 15-19.

Castrén, Erik. "Peace Treaties and Other Agreements Made by Finland," FFP, 50-65.

Chanter, Llewellyn. "Finland, Between East and West," Norseman, 5 (1947), 236-38.

Elovainio, Mauri K., and Jukka Huopaniemi. "Finland and the Study of International Relations 1960-1964," C&C (1965, no. 2), 60-67.

Fachiri, Alexander P. "The Local Remedies Rule in the Light of the Finnish Ship Arbitration," BYIL, 17 (1936), 19-36.

Finland. National Supervision of the Manufacture of and Trade in Arms. Geneva, 1939.

Finnish Political Science Association. Finnish Foreign Policy; Studies in Foreign Politics. Hels., 1963. 232 p.

Finnish Trade Association. Finland-United States, 1938. Hels., 1938. 147 p.

Hoglund, Arthur W. Finnish Immigrants in America 1880-1920. Madison, Wisc., 1960. 213 p.

Huopaniemi, Jukka. "A Council for Peace Research Established in Finland," C&C (1966, No. 2), 116-17.

Hyvämäki, Lauri. "Finland in the Mainstream of European Thought," FFP, 139-56.

Hyvärinen, Risto. "Foreign Policy Decision-Making and the Administration of Foreign Affairs," FFP, 99-112.

Jackson, J. Hampden. The Baltic. Oxford, 1940. 32 p.

———. "Russia, Finland and Estonia," CR (1952), 334-37.

Jakobson, Max. "Finland's Foreign Policy," IA, 38 (1962), 196-202.

———. "The Foreign Policy of Independent Finland," FFP, 34-49.

Killinen, K. "The Press and Foreign Policy," FFP, 196-217.

Kolehmainen, John I. "Antti Jalana and Hungarian-Finnish Rapproachement," SEER, 21 (1942-43), 167-74.

Kuusinen, Otto. Finland Unmasked. Lond., 1944. 32 p.

Larson, Laurence M. "The Boundaries of Finland," ASR, 6 (1918), 315-25.

Mazour, Anatole G. Finland Between East and West. Princeton, N.J., 1956. 298 p.

Mead, William R. "Anglo-Finnish Cultural Relations," Norseman, 6 (1948), 376-87.

———. "The Birth of the British Consular System in Finland," Norseman, 15 (1957), 101-11.

———. "Finland and the Landfall of British Authority," Norseman, 16 (1958), 51-59.

———. "Finland and the U.S.S.R.," Geog, 41 (1956), 189-91.

———. "The Rise of the British Consular System in Finland," Norseman, 15 (1957), 1-13.

Meiksins, Gregory. The Baltic Riddle: Finland, Estonia, Latvia, Lithuania-Key-Points of European Peace. N.Y., 1943. 271 p.

Mourin, Maxime. "Finland and Coexistence," Military R, 42 (1962), 58-66.

Moyne, Ernest J. Studies in Cultural Relations Between Finland and America, 1638-1938. Thesis (Ph.D.), Harvard University. 1948.

Mustanoja, Tauno F. "Some Aspects of the American Impact upon Finland," in Lars Åhnebrink, ed., Amerika och Norden (Stock., 1964), 54-58.

Newman, E. W. P. "Finland: Democracy and Foreign Policy," CR, 153 (1938), 692-98.

———. Britain and the Baltic. Lond., 1930. 275 p.

Nousiainen, Jaakko. "The Parties and Foreign Policy," FFP, 177-95.

Pajunen, Aimo. "Finland's Security Policy,"
C&C (1968), 75-92.

Pesonen, Pertti. "Finnish Societies for International Contacts," FFP, 157-76.

Pijp, Antonius. "The Baltic States as a Regional Unity," Annals, 168 (1933), 171-82.

Puntila, Lauri A. "Finland's Neutrality,"
FFP, 218-28.

Reddaway, William F. Problems of the
Baltic. Cambridge, 1940. 120 p.

Renvall, Pentti. "The Foreign Policy Attitudes of the Finns During the Swedish
Rule," FFP, 3-22.

Shearman, Hugh. Finland: the Adventures
of a Small Power. Lond., 1950. 114 p.

Soloveytchik, George. "'The Vicissitudes of
Finland'," Norseman, 14 (1956), 304-10.

Soviet Russia Today: the U.S.S.R. and Finland; Historical, Economic, Political;
Facts and Documents. N.Y., 1939. 64 p.

Strode, Hudson. Finland Forever. N.Y.,
1941. 443 p.

Swenson, S. H. The Finnish Paradox: an
Analysis of a Peripheral State's Struggle
Against Soviet Integration. Wash., 1954.
219 p.

Wuorinen, John H. "Finland," in Stephen D.
Kertesz, ed., The Fate of East Central
Europe: Hopes and Failures of American
Foreign Policy (South Bend, Ind., 1956),
321-37.

THROUGH THE WAR OF INDEPENDENCE

Anderson, Edgar. "An Undeclared Moral
War: the British-Soviet Moral Struggle
in the Baltic, 1918-1920," JCEA (1962),
43-78.

Bain, Robert Nisbet. "Finland and the
Tsar," Fortnightly Review, 65 (1899),
735-44.

Birrell, Augustine. "Finland and Russia,"
CR, 78 (1900), 16-27.

Donner, Herman M. "Finland Crushed or
Finland Free?," ASR, 4 (1916), 135-41.

Elviken, Andreas. "Sweden and Finland,
1914-18," in Jessie D. Clarkson and
Thomas C. Cochran, eds., War as a Social Institution: the Historian's Perspective (N.Y., 1941), 134-43.

Finland. Treaties; Treaty of Peace Between
Finland and the Russian Soviet Republic.
Hels., 1921. 34 p.

Finland and Russia. International Conference in London, Feb. 25-Mar. 1, 1910.
Lond., 1911. 87 p.

The Finnish Question in 1911: a Survey of

the Present Position of the Finnish Constitutional Struggle. Lond., 1911. 79 p.

Germany. Treaties; Treaty of Peace, Signed
at Berlin Between Germany and Finland,
Together with the Commercial and Shipping Agreement. Lond., 1918. 30 p.

Holmes, Arthur S. "Finland and Russia,"
Calcutta Review, 112 (1901), 1-14.

Kuusinen, Otto. "The Finnish Revolution,"
Labour Monthly, 22 (F/M 1940), 115-24;
173-84.

Leiss, Amelia C., ed. European Peace
Treaties after World War II: Negotiations
and Texts of Treaties with Italy, Bulgaria,
Hungary, Rumania and Finland (Supplementary to Documents on American Foreign Relations, 8, 1945-46 and 9, 1947).
Boston, 1954. 341 p.

Limedorfer, Eugene. "Finland's Plight,"
Forum, 32 (1901/02), 85-93.

Numminen, Jaakko. "Finland's Foreign
Policy as an Autonomous Grand Duchy
and the Winning of Independence," FFP,
23-33.

Reinikainen, Veikko. "Finland and Russia
and the Initial Period of Finland's Political Independence" [Bibliography], in
English, French and German Literature
on Finnish Law in 1860-1956 (Library of
the Parliament Publications 2) (Hels.,
1957), 96-110.

Reuter, J. N. "Finland's Independence and
Its Recognition," CR, 115 (1919), 511-16.

——. "Russia in Finland," NiCen (1899),
699-715.

——. "The Rights of Finland at Stake,"
English Review (1909), 138-45.

Ruhl, Arthur B. New Masters of the Baltic.
N.Y., 1921. 239 p.

The Russo-Finnish Conflict: the Russian
Case, as Stated by Representatives of the
Russian Government with Introduction,
Appendices, and Notes in Criticism and
Reply. Lond., 1910. 101 p.

Schenck, Frederic. "A Nation Without a
Flag," ASR, 6 (1918), 338-39.

Smith, Clarence J., Jr. Finland and the Russian Revolution 1917-1922. Athens,
Georgia, 1958. 251 p.

——. "Russia and the Origins of the Finnish Civil War of 1918," ASEER, 14 (1955),
481-502.

Söderhjelm, Henning. The Red Insurrection
in Finland: a Study Based on Documentary
Evidence. Lond., 1919. 159 p.

Söderhjelm, Werner. "Finland and Germany
During the War," CH, 10 (Jl 1919), 94-98.

Stead, William T. "The Resurrection of
Finland," CR, 88 (1905), 761-68.

Stenberg, Herman. The Greater Finland: a Union Between the Fennobaltic Lands (Carelian Citizens League Publication, no. 1). Hels., 1919. 30 p.

"The Treaty Between Germany and Finland" [Text], NewEur, 6 (1918), 381-83.

United States, Department of State. Texts of the Finland "Peace." Wash., 1918. 55 p.

Westermarck, Edvard. "Finland and the Czar," CR, 75 (1899), 652-59.

Westlake, J. "The Case of Finland," National Review, 35 (1900), 111-21.

Whitford, V. (Rudolf Holsti). "Russia, Finland and Scandinavia," CR, 102 (A 1912), 212-20.

Wuorinen, John H. "Finland's War of Independence, 1918," ASR, 51 (1963), 389-95.

INTER-WAR PERIOD

Bellquist, Eric C. "Finland's Treaties for the Peaceful Settlement of International Law," AJIL, 26 (1932), 70-86.

Borchard, Edwin M. "The Local Remedy Rule," AJIL, 28 (1934), 729-33.

Broms, Bengt. "Finland and the League of Nations," FFP, 84-98.

Finland, Ministry of Foreign Affairs. Claim of the Finnish Government with Regard to Finnish Ships Used During the War by the Government of the United Kingdom. Rapporteur: the Representative of Spain. Geneva, 1932. 3 p.

Finland. Treaties; Extract from Convention Between the Republic of Finland and the Republic of Poland, Regarding Public Relief, Signed at Helsinki, December 19th, 1931. Geneva, 1933. 5 p.

Finland and Norway. "Convention Regarding Measures to be Taken in Order to Prevent Reindeer from Crossing the Frontier," League of Nations Treaty Series, v. 169, nos. 3911-3925 (1936-1937), 33-77.

Graham, Malbone W. The Diplomatic Recognition of the Border States; Part I: Finland. Berkeley, Calif., 1935. 230 p.

Holsti, Kalevi J. The Origins of Finnish Foreign Policy 1918-22: Rudolf Holsti's Role in the Formulation of Policy. Thesis (Ph.D.), Stanford University, 1961. 440 p.

Holsti, Rudolf. "Finland and the Baltic Region," Proceedings of the Institute of World Affairs, 19 (1941), 134-43.

"International Relations in the Gulf of Finland and Ladoga Lake," Morskoi sborni, no. 10 (1929), 55-87.

Kelley, Robert F. "Soviet Policy on the European Border," FA, 3 (1924/25), 91-98.

Rutenberg, Gregory. "The Baltic States and the Soviet Union," AJIL, 29 (1935), 598-615.

WINTER WAR AND WORLD WAR II

Aaronson, L. "Russia Invades Finland," NiCen, 127 (Ja 1940), 1-3.

Alenius, Sigyn. Finland Between the Armistice and the Peace. Hels., 1947. 55 p.

Anderson, Albin T. "Origins of the Winter War: a Study of Russo-Finnish Diplomacy," WP, 6 (1954), 169-89.

The Appeal of the Finnish Government to the League of Nations (Monthly Summary of the League of Nations. Special Supplement December 1939). Geneva, 1939. 71 p.

——. "Armistice Terms Granted to Finland," CH, 7 (1944), 407-12.

"Armistice with Finland," DeptStateBul, 12, no. 295 (1945), 261-68.

Arnold-Forster, W. "After Finland," PolQ, 11 (1940), 209-22.

Bilmanis, Alfreds. Baltic States and World Peace and Security Organization; Facts in Review. Wash., 1945. 67 p.

——. Baltic States in Post-War Europe. Wash., 1943. 86 p.; 1944. 45 p.

Borenius, Tancred. "Finland, Russia, and the World," Empire Review, 71 (Ja 1940), 13-15.

Broad, Walter. "Washington Helps the Berlin-Helsinki Axis," New Masses (May 13, 1941), 16-17.

Brody, Alter. War and Peace in Finland: a Documented Survey. N.Y., 1940. 128 p.

Crotch, W. Walter. "The Reversal in Finland's Foreign Policy" [Away from Neutrality and Towards a German Alliance], CR, 151 (1937), 185-90.

Dreiser, Theodore et al. "The Soviet-Finnish Treaty and World Peace," Soviet Russia Today (Ap 1940), 8-9.

Elliston, Herbert B. "On the Finnish Front," Atlantic Monthly, 165 (Feb 1940), 243-49.

Fay, Sidney B. "Russo-Finnish Relations," CH, 6 (1944), 385-90.

"A Few Lessons of the Finnish Events," Communist International, 4 (Ap 1940), 234-40.

Finland. Attitude of the USSR to Finland: After the Peace of Moscow, Finland Reveals Her Secret Documents on Soviet Policy, March 1940-June 1941. N.Y., 1941. 109 p. [Documents]

——. Communications Relating to the

Present State of War. Communication from the Finnish Government Concerning the Neutrality of Finland. Geneva, 1939. 8 p.

———. Documents Concerning the Relations Between Finland, Great Britain and the United States of America During the Autumn of 1941. Hels., 1942. 42 p.

Finland, Ministry of Foreign Affairs. Development of Finnish-Soviet Relations During the Autumn of 1939 in the Light of Official Documents. Hels., Lond., 1940. 114 p.

———. The Finnish Blue Book. The Development of Finnish--Soviet Relations During the Autumn of 1939; Including the Official Documents and the Peace Treaty of March 12, 1940. Phila., N.Y., 1940. 120 p. [Same as preceding entry].

———. Documents, Concerning Finnish-Soviet Relations II; The Attitude of the USSR and Finland After the Peace of Moscow. Hels., 1941. 42 p.

———. The Evolution of Fenno-Soviet Relations in the Course of the Autumn of 1939. Lond., 1940. 114 p.

———. Finland Reveals Her Secret Documents on Soviet Policy, March 1940-June 1941; the Attitude of the USSR to Finland After the Peace of Moscow. N.Y., 1941. 109 p.

———. Statement Concerning Finnish-Russian Relations and the Circumstances Leading to the Invasion of Finland. Lond., 1940. 19 p.

"Finland Between War and Peace" [by H. W.], WT, 2 (1946), 384-91.

"Finland Since the Moscow Treaty" [by D. P. E.], BIN, 21 (1944), 507-12; 543-49.

"Finnish Draft Treaty of Peace of Paris 1946," CH, 11 (1946), 170-77.

"The Finnish Peace Settlement With the U.S.S.R.," BIN, 17 (1940), 339-42.

"Finnish Peace Treaty signed at Peace of Paris, 10 Feb. 1947," CH, 12 (1947), 283-94.

"The Finnish-Russian Conflict of 1939," in Joel Larus, ed., From Collective Security to Preventive Diplomacy (N.Y., 1965), 155-75.

Fox, Annette Baker. "Finland: Fighting Neutral," in her, The Power of Small States: Diplomacy in World War II (Chicago, 1959), 43-77.

Friends of Finland for Dewey. Let the American People Know; the Story of Finland's Tragic Struggle for Survival and Its Significance for American Foreign Policy. N.Y., 1944. 30 p.

Glascow, George. "Russia, Finland, and Eastern Europe," CR, 157 (1940), 9-21.

Gottlieb, Wolfram. "Baltic Neutrality," Fortnightly Review, 146 (1939), 74-78.

———. "Triple Pact and the Baltic States," NiCen, 126 (1939), 34-39.

Great Britain. Treaties; Draft Peace Treaty with Finland. Prepared by the Council of Foreign Ministers, for consideration by the Peace Conference of twenty-one nations meeting in Paris on July 29, 1946. Lond., 1946. 19 p.

Gripenberg, Georg A. Finland and the Great Powers: Memoirs of a Diplomat. Tr. by Albin T. Anderson. Lincoln, Neb., 1965. 380 p.

Haataja, Kyösti. Finland and Russia: Historical and Social Background of the War. Hels., 1940. 32 p.

Heideman, Bert M. A Study in the Causes of Finland's Involvement in World War II at Three Separate Times: Nov. 1939; June 1941; Sept. 1944. Thesis (Ph.D.), University of Michigan, 1953. 396 p.

Hooper, Arthur S. The Soviet-Finnish Campaign, Dec. 1, 1939 to March 13, 1940. Lond., 1940. 24 p.

———. Through the Soviet Russian and Finnish Campaign, 1940. Lond., 1944. 140 p.

Hyde, Charles C. "International Law for Finland," AJIL, 34 (1940), 285-88.

Jackson, J. Hampden. "Britain and the Finnish Treaty," Norseman, 5 (1947), 175-78.

———. "Finland and the Soviet Union," WAQ, 2 (1948), 305-10.

———. "German Intervention in Finland," Slavonic Review, 18 (1939), 93-101.

Jakobson, Max. The Diplomacy of the Winter War: an Account of the Russo-Finnish War, 1939-40. Cambridge, Mass., 1961. 281 p.

Krosby, H. Peter. "The Diplomacy of the Petsamo Question and Finnish-German Relations, January-June 1941," Scandia, 32 (1966), 169-211.

Kuusinen, Otto. Finland Unmasked. Lond., 1944. 31 p.

Langdon-Davies, John. Invasion in the Snow: a Study of Mechanized War. Boston, 1941. 202 p.; Lond. ed. 1940 has title: Finland: the First Total War.

League of Nations, 20th Assembly, 1939. Appeal by the Finnish Government. Geneva, 1939. 12 p.

Lowery, Sidney. "Finland," in Part II of Arnold and Veronica Toynbee, eds., The Realignment of Europe, in the series Survey of International Affairs 1939-1946. Oxford University Press, for the Royal

Institute of International Affairs (Lond., 1955), 261-85.

Lundin, C. Leonard. Finland in the Second World War. Bloomington, Ind., 1957. 303 p.

Marshall-Cornwall, General Sir James. "The Russian Conquest of Finland, 30 November 1939 to 12 March 1940," in Part I of Arnold and Veronica Toynbee, eds., The Initial Triumph of the Axis, in the series Survey of International Affairs 1939-1946 (Lond., 1958), 4-5.

Molotov, Vracheslav M. Soviet Foreign Policy: the Meaning of the War in Finland. N.Y., 1940. 22 p.

New World Review. The U.S.S.R. and Finland. N.Y., 1939. 64 p.

Procopé, Hjalmar J. F. Stalin Over Finland (News Background Report no. 31). N.Y., 1948. 11 p.

——. War Criminal Trials in Finland. 1947.

Round Table War Pamphlets: no. 3. The Facts About Finland. Lond., 1940. 22 p.

Russia, Embassy. The Criminal Mannerheim Gang Will not Escape Its Responsibilities. Lond., 1943. 24 p.

"Russo-Finnish Peace," CH, 51 (1939/40), 8-12.

Ruutu, Y. "The Relations Between Finland and the U.S.S.R.," Nord, 2 (1939), 481-86.

Schwartz, Andrew J. America and the Russo-Finnish War. Wash., 1960. 103 p.

Sobel, Robert. The Origins of Interventionism: the United States and the Russo-Finnish War. N.Y., 1960. 204 p.

Soloveytchik, George. "Finland's Struggle," CR, 157 (1940), 151-59.

Soviet Information Bureau of the Russian Foreign Commissariat. "Moscow's Peace Offers to the Finns," CH, 6 (1944), 351-52.

Toivola, Urho. "The Peace Treaties Concluded by Finland in 1940 and 1947," The Finland Year Book 1947 (Hels., 1947), 74-81.

Treaty of Peace Between the Union of Soviet Socialist Republics and Finland, and Protocol," DeptStateBul, 2 (1940), 453-56.

Voigt, F. A. "The Baltic States," NiCen, 131 (1942), 193-97.

Ward, Edward H. H. Despatches from Finland, January-April, 1940. Lond., 1940. 160 p.

Wuorinen, John H. ed. Finland and World War II: 1939-1944. N.Y., 1948. 228 p.

——. "The Finnish Treaty," Annals, 257 (1948), 87-96.

POST WORLD WAR II

Ambartsumov, E. "Soviet-Finnish Relations — Relations of Peace and Friendship," IAF (O 1955), 44-53.

Baüde, E. J. "The Finnish Armed Forces," MilitaryR, 42 (Aug 1962), 67-70.

Brophy, John. "Those Plucky Finns Are Sticking with the Free," American Federationist, 63 (N 1956), 24-27.

Crankshaw, Edward. "Finland and Russia," National and English Review, 140 (F 1953), 87-91.

Dancy, Eric. "Finland Takes Stock," FA, 24 (1946), 513-25.

"Did Finland Outsmart Stalin?," U.S. News (Aug 15, 1962), 30-33.

Doras, Peter. "Finland: Third Force in the Soviet Orbit," AmPers, 2 (1948), 289-300.

"Finland Under Pressure" [by A. G. S.], WT, 4 (1948), 144-51.

Fischer, Alfred J. "Finland and the Kremlin," CR, 177 (1950), 283-88.

——. "Finland and the Soviet Union," Norseman, 13 (1955), 230-35.

Forster, Kent. "Finland's Policy in the United Nations and the Paasikivi Line," JCEA, 21 (1962), 465-76.

——. "The Finnish-Soviet Crisis of 1958-1959," IntJ, 15 (1960), 147-50.

Gervasi, Frank. "Next Door to the Soviets," Reporter (O 25, 1949), 22-24.

Greer, Deon C. Russo-Finnish Relations in the Post War Era, 1945-1959. Thesis (M.A.), Brigham Young University, 1960. 186 p.

Heiskanen, Piltti. "The Eleventh Wave-Baltic Shores and the Russian Tide," SocRes, 17 (1950), 492-97.

Hodgson, John H., III. "The Paasikivi Line," ASEER, 18 (1959), 145-73.

——. "Postwar Finnish Foreign Policy: Institutions and Personalities," WPQ, 15 (1962), 80-90.

Holsti, Kalevi J. "Strategy and Techniques of Influence in Soviet-Finnish Relations," WPQ, 17 (1964), 63-82.

Hudson, George E. The Influence of the Soviet Union on the Finnish Political System in the Postwar Years. Thesis (M.A.), University of Colorado, 1967. 169 p.

Huizinga, J. H. "Finland: Freedom under the Guns," Reporter (S 22, 1955), 20-22.

Ilvessalo, Jaakko. "Finland and the Great Problems of the United Nations," FFP, 113-27.

Jackson, J. Hampden. "Finland and the Soviet Union," WAQ, 2 (Jl 1948), 305-10.

Kalb, Madeleine, and Marvin Kalb. "The
Finns Buy Time and Hope for Better
Days," Reporter (Ja 4, 1962), 19-22.

Karjalainen, Ahti. "The Foreign Policy of
Finland," ASR, 54 (1966), 5-10.

Kuusisto, Allan A. "The Paasikivi Line in
Finland's Foreign Policy," WPQ, 12
(1954), 37-49.

Lenoy, Ursula. "Divided Finland," EEur &
SovRussia, (D 3, 1953), 9-11.

Meyers, Albert J. "A Small Country Finds
Out What It's Like to Coexist; Report
from Finland," U.S. News, 47 (N 9, 1959),
84-86.

Mikoyan, Anastas I. "Mikoyan in Finland;
New Five-Year Trade Pact," Current Digest of the Soviet Press, 11 (N 25, 1959),
21-22.

Mourin, Maxine. "Finland and Coexistence,"
MilitaryR, 42 (1962), 58-66.

Owen, John E. "Ten-Year Tightrope: Post-
War Finland," WAQ, 29 (1958), 278-90.

Pakarinen, Erik. "News Communication in
Crisis: a Study of the New Coverage of
Scandinavian Newspapers during the
Russo-Finnish Note Crisis in the Autumn
of 1961," C&C (1967), 224-28.

Shepherd, Gordon. "Finland's Mortgaged
Democracy," Reporter (N 26, 1959), 30-
32.

"The Soviet Union and Finland, As Seen by a
Norwegian" [by H. G.], WT, 9 (1953),
952-60.

"Stalin's Letter to Finnish President" [Feb.
27, 1948], CH, 14 (1948), 304-305.

Törngren, Ralf. "The Neutrality of Finland,"
FA, 39 (1961), 601-609.

von Bonsdorff, Göran. "Soviet-Finnish Relations and Peace in Northern Europe,"
IAF (Je 1957), 39-43.

Wuorinen, John H. "Continuing Finnish
Neutrality," CH, 36 (1959), 224-28.

——. "Finland and the USSR, 1945-1961,"
JIA, 16 (1962), 38-46.

——. "Finland Stands Guard," FA, 32
(1954), 651-60.

AALAND ISLANDS

"Aaland Islands," Report by M. Harmsworth
and resolution adopted by the Council on
January 11, 1922. League of Nations Official Journal, 3 (1922), 124-25.

"The Aaland Islands Question," Minutes of
the sixth meeting of the Council on August
30, 1921. League of Nations Official
Journal, 2 (1921), 691-705.

"The Aaland Islands Question," Report presented by the British representative, Mr.

H. A. L. Fisher, and adopted by the Council of the League of Nations. League of
Nations Official Journal, 1 (1920), 394-96.

The Aaland Question; Representation in the
Matter of the Aaland Question to the
Council of the League of Nations and to
the Commission of Jurists by the Delegates of the Population of the Aaland Islands. Stock., 1920. 31 p.

"The Åland Islands," NewEur, 15 (1920),
226-31.

The Åland Question and the Rights of Finland: a Memorandum by a Number of
Finnish Jurists and Historians. Hels.,
1920. 37 p.

Brown, Philip Marshall. "The Aaland Islands Question," AJIL, 15 (1921), 268-72.

"Convention for the Non-Fortification and
Neutralization of the Aaland Islands,"
League of Nations Official Journal, 3
(1922), 90-91.

Correspondence Relating to the Question of
the Aaland Islands — the Finnish Case;
the Swedish Case (League of Nations Official Journal, Special Supplement 1).
Geneva, 1920. 67 p.

Ekengren, W. A. F. "The Aaland Question;
a Statement from the Minister of Sweden
to the U.S.," ASR, 8 (1920), 919-20.

Finland, The Aaland Islands. Guarantees to
be Given to the Population and to be Inserted in the Finnish Law of Autonomy of
the Aaland Islands of May 7, 1920; Adopted
by the Council, June 27th, 1921. Geneva,
1921.

Finland, Ministry of Foreign Affairs. Aaland
Islands. Letter from Mr. Enchell [Enckell]
Dated October 7th, 1920. Lond., 1920.
[Refers to League Document du Conseil
J 3]

——. The Aaland Islands Question; Memorandum, Dated 23/6/20, by the Secretary
General Giving Record of Conversation
with the Finnish Minister on 23/6/20.
Lond., 1920.

——. The Aaland Islands Question; Letter,
Dated 5th July 1920, from the Finnish
Minister in London. Lond., 1920.

——. Aaland Islands. Statements Made by
the Finnish Minister in Paris Before the
Council of the League of Nations on 16
and 18 Sept. 1920. 1920. 7 p.

——. Convention of 1921 for the Non-
Fortification and Neutralisation of the
Aaland Islands: Measures Proposed by
the Finnish and Swedish Governments.
Geneva, 1939. 12 p.

Fischer, Alfred J. "The Aaland Islands,"
Norseman, 9 (1951), 145-48.

"The Fortification of the Åland Islands," AJIL, 2 (1908), 397-98.

Gregory, Charles N. "The Neutralisation of the Aaland Islands," AJIL, 17 (1923), 63-76.

Hedvall, Yngve. "Sweden, Finland, and Åland," ASR, 8 (1920), 101-104.

Jaatinen, Stig. "Åland — A Border Province of Finland," Norseman, 13 (1955), 246-51.

Johnsson, Alex J. The Åland Question Before the Peace Conference. Chicago, 1919. 18 p.

League of Nations. The Aaland Islands Question; Report Submitted to the Council of the League of Nations by the Commission of Rapporteurs. Geneva, 1921. 53 p.

League of Nations Official Journal. Special Supplement nos. 1, 3 (Aug, 1920). Geneva; no. 1 (Aug 1920), The Åland Islands Question. Lond., 1920. 87 p.; no. 3 (O 1920), The Åland Islands Question. Lond., 1920. 19 p.

Leiyiskä, Ilvari. "Finland, Sweden and the Åland Islands," BSC, 5 (1939), 113-16.

Padelford, Norman J., and K. Gösta A. Andersson. "The Aaland Islands Question," AJIL, 33 (1939), 465-87.

"The Question of the Aaland Islands," Seventh Session of the Council of the League of Nations 12th July 1920. League of Nations Official Journal, 1 (1920), 246-50.

Reinikainen, Veikko. "The Aaland Question," in his, Bibliography of English, French and German Literature on Finnish Law, 1860-1956 (Library of Parliament Publications, 2) (Hels., 1957), 81-96.

Schybergson, Magnus G. The Position of Aaland in Historical Times. Hels., 1919. 13 p.

Sederholm, J. J., The Åland Question from a Swedish Finlander's Point of View. Hels., 1920. 58 p.

Sjöstedt, Erik. The Åland Question: a Baltic Problem. Paris, 1919. 64 p.

Sweden, Ministry of Foreign Affairs. The Aaland Islands; Guarantees to be Given to the Population and to be Inserted in the Finnish Law of Autonomy of the Aaland Islands of May 7, 1920. Adopted by the Council, June 17th, 1921. Geneva, 1921.

——. Convention of 1921 for the Non-Fortification and Neutralisation of the Aaland Islands: Measures Proposed by the Finnish and Swedish Governments. Geneva, 1939.

——. The Questions of the Aaland Islands; Letter, Dated 25th June 1920, from the Swedish Minister in London. Lond., 1920.

[Concerns Sweden's compliance with Council mediation in the Aaland Islands question]

"Sweden and Finland: a Swedish Protest," NewEur, 7 (1918), 35-38.

Thesloff, Georg H. "A Finnish View of the Aaland Problem," ASR, 8 (1920), 767-69.

Vallentin, Hugo. "Sweden and the Åland Islands," NewEur, 6 (1918), 184-88.

Westermarck, Edvard. "The Aaland Question," CR, 118 (1920), 790-94.

EASTERN CARELIA

East-Carelia: a Survey of the Country and Its Population, and a Review of the Carelian Question. Hels., 1934. 216 p.

Eastern Carelia: Acts and Documents Relating to Judgments and Advisory Opinions Given by the Court (Publications of the Permanent Court of International Justice, series C3). 2 vols. Leiden, 1923. v. I, 62-67, 122-36; v. II, 1-213.

"The Eastern Carelia Question," AJIL, 18 (1924), 7-10.

Enckell, Carl. "Statement Concerning Eastern Carelia," League of Nations Official Journal, 3 (1922), 165-69.

"Finland and the Claim to Eastern Karelia" [by M. B.], BIN, 18, pt. 2 (Jl-D 1941), 1958-60.

Gadolin, Carl A. J. The Solution of the Carelian Refugee Problem in Finland (Publications of the Research Group for European Migration Problems, 5). The Hague, 1952. 47 p.

Hudson, Manley O. "Advisory Opinions of National and International Courts," Harvard Law Review, 37 (1923/1924), 970-1001. Eastern Carelia Question, 995-96.

——. "The Second Year of the Permanent Court of International Justice," AJIL, 18 (1924), 1-37. Eastern Carelia Question, 7-10.

Jaakkola, Jalmari. The Finnish Eastern Question. Hels., 1942. 90 p.

Kalijarvi, Thorsten V. "The Question of East Carelia," AJIL, 18 (1924), 93-97.

Keynäs, W. "Soviet Russia and Eastern Carelia," SEER, 6 (1928), 520-28.

Mead, William R. "Finnish Karelia: International Borderland," GeogJ, 118 (1952), 40-57.

An Outline of the East Carelia Question. Hels., 1935. 31 p.

The Question of East Karelia and Pechenga. Hels., 1920.

"Resettlement of Karelian Refugees," WT, 9 (1953), 249-55.

Ruuth, Y. O. "The East Carelian Question," in Kaarlo Blomstedt, ed., Finland: Its Country and People, A Short Survey (Hels.), 84-86.

"Situation of Eastern Carelia," League of Nations Official Journal, 3 (1922), 104-105; 107-108.

The Status of Eastern Carelia; Collection of Advisory Opinions (Publications of the Permanent Court of International Justice, series B5). Leiden, 1923. 29 p.

ICELAND

"Ancient Iceland, New Pawn of War," NGeogM, 80 (1941), 75-90.

Astraudo, Amidie E. Iceland, the Island in the Limelight. Los Angeles, 1941. 47 p.

Burbank, Lyman B. "Problems of NATO Diplomacy: Fish and an Air Base in Iceland," SAQ, 58 (1939), 237-47.

Clark, Austin H. Iceland and Greenland (Smithsonian Institution War Background Studies, no. 15). Wash., 1943. 103 p.

Gudmundsson, Gudmundur I. "The Foreign Policy of Iceland," ASR, 53 (1965), 125-29.

Hanson, Earl P. "Iceland Plays a New Role," Travel, 75 (1940, no. 3), 10-14.

Iceland. Guarantee Agreement Second Agricultural Project, Between Republic of Iceland and International Bank for Reconstruction and Development, Dated Sept. 4, 1953; Loan Number 79 IC. Wash., 1953. 7 p.

———. Guarantee Agreement, Transmitter Project, Between Republic of Iceland and International Bank for Reconstruction and Development, Dated Sept. 4, 1953; Loan number 80 IC. Wash., 1953. 7 p.

———. Treaties, etc., 1941— (Björnsson); Agreement...Relating to Certain Air Transport Services, with Annex and Schedules. London, 26th May, 1950. Lond., 1951. 15 p.

———. Exchange of Notes...in Regard to the Mutual Abolition of Visas, London, May 19th-20th, 1949. Dublin, 1949. 3 p.

———. Exchange of Notes...Extending the Visa Abolition Agreement of 20th June 1947 to Certain British Overseas Territories, with Annex, London, 26th October 1948. Lond., 1948. 3 p.

———. Trade Agreement...Concluded by an Exchange of Notes, Paris 2nd December, 1950. Dublin, 1951. 4 p.

Iceland, Ministry of Foreign Affairs. Diplo-matic List, Including Consuls of Career Accredited at Reykjavik...and List of Honorary Consuls in Iceland. Reykjavik.

"Iceland: Its Importance in an Air Age" [by J. W.], WT, 4 (1948), 297-307.

"Iceland: Reluctant Ally," WT, 12 (1956), 321-29.

"Iceland's Place in the World," NATO Letter, 14 (1966, no. 1), 10-15.

Jónsson, Agnar K. "Iceland's Foreign Service: an Outline of Its Development," IcR, 2 (1964, no. 3), 8-9.

Leistikow, Gunnar. "Iceland Between West and East," ASR, 43 (1955), 347-51.

Lindal, Walter J. The Saskatchewan Icelanders: a Strand of the Canadian Fabric. Winnipeg, 1955. 363 p.

Nuechterlein, Donald E. Iceland: Reluctant Ally. Ithaca, N.Y., 1961. 240 p.

Roucek, J. S. "The Geopolitics of Iceland," Social Studies, 41 (1950), 339-43.

"A Solution for Iceland," Freedom and Union, 13 (O 1958), 3-4.

Thors, Thor. "Iceland in the United Nations," ICR, 2 (1964, no. 3), 12-15.

———. "Strategic Iceland," FSJ, 18 (1941), 545-49+.

Tomasson, Helgi. "Iceland," in George W. Kisker, ed., World Tension: the Psychopathology of International Relations (N.Y., 1951), 122-32.

FISHERIES DISPUTE

"Atlantic Council Statement on Iceland," CH, 31 (1956), 361-63.

Chanter, Llewellyn. "The Anglo-Icelandic Fishery Dispute," Norseman, 13 (1955), 85-88.

Davis, Morris. Iceland Extends Its Fisheries Limits: a Political Analysis. Lond., Oslo, 1963. 136 p.

Green, L. C. "The Territorial Sea and the Anglo-Icelandic Dispute," Journal of Public Law, 9 (Spring 1960), 53-72.

Iceland, Ministry of Foreign Affairs. British Aggression in Icelandic Waters. Rey., 1959. 43 p.

"Iceland; Note Verbale Dated 6 April 1956 from the Ministry for Foreign Affairs of Iceland," AJIL, 50 (1956), 1045-49.

"Iceland; Note Verbale Dated 26 March 1955 from the Ministry of Foreign Affairs of Iceland," AJIL, 50 (1956), 247-51.

Jónsson, Jon. "Cod Fishing off Iceland," ICR, 2 (1964), 7-10.

Leistikow, Gunnar. "The Fisheries Dispute in the North Atlantic," ASR, 47 (1959), 15-24.

Mettler, E. "Fisheries and Territorial Waters — Britain's Dispute with Iceland," SRWA, 8 (N 1958), 6-9.

"The Territorial Sea and the Anglo-Icelandic Fisheries Dispute," WT, 14 (1958), 415-17.

UNITED STATES

Grimson, Gudmundur. "Iceland and Its Relation to the North American Continent," Lawyer, 5 (F 1952), 15-18.

Grimson, Gudmundur, and Sveinbjorn Johnson. "Iceland and the Americas," ABAJ, 26 (1940), 505-509.

Hannesson, Johann S. "The American Impact in Iceland," in Lars Åhnebrink, ed., Amerika och Norden (Stock., 1964), 59-64.

Hunt, John J. The United States Occupation of Iceland, 1941-1946. Thesis (Ph.D.), Georgetown University, 1966.

Iceland. Treaties, etc., 1941-1952 (Björnsson); Defense of Iceland Pursuant to North Atlantic Treaty... Signed at Reykjavik May, 1951. Wash., 1952. 21 p.

———. Defense of Iceland Pursuant to North Atlantic Treaty. Agreement... Signed at Reykjavik May 5, 1951, Entered into Force May 5, 1951. Wash., 1952. 7 p.

———. Economic Cooperation with Iceland Under Public Law 472, 80th Congress, as Amended; Agreement... Effected by Exchange of Notes Signed at Washington Feb. 7, 1950. Wash., 1950. 9 p.

Iceland. Treaties, etc., 1941-1952 (Björnsson); Economic Cooperation with Iceland Under Public Law 472, 80th Congress, as Amended; Agreement... Amending Agreement of July 3, 1948, as Amended, Effected by Exchange of Notes Dated at Reykjavik February 23, 1951. Wash., 1951. 2 p.

———. Economic Cooperation with Iceland Under Public Law 472, 80th Congress; Agreement... Signed at Reykjavik July 3, 1948. Wash., 1948. 69 p.

———. Passport Visas; Agreement... Effected by Exchange of Notes Signed at Reykjavik October 1 and December 9, 1947. Wash., 1950. 2 p.

———. Trade Application of Most Favored-Nation Treatment to Areas Under Occupation or Control; Agreement... Effected by Exchange of Notes Signed at Reykjavik July 3, 1948. Wash., 1948. 7 p.

———. Treaties, etc., 1952— (Ásgeirsson); Defense of Iceland Pursuant to North Atlantic Treaty; Agreement Effected by Exchanges of Notes Signed at Reykjavik December 6, 1956. Wash., 1957. 5 p.

———. Mutual Security, Purchase by Iceland of Military Equipment, Materials, and Services; Agreement Effected by Exchange of Notes Signed at Reykjavik October 4, and December 10, 1954. Wash., 1955. 3 p.

———. Reciprocal Trade; Agreement Amending Agreement of August 27, 1943, Effected by Exchange of Notes Signed at Reykjavik March 5 and 6, 1956 and Proclamation by the President of the U.S.A., Issued March 16, 1956. Wash., 1956. 8 p.

———. Settlement of Claims of Icelandic Insurance Companies; Agreement Signed at Washington November 23, 1956. Wash., 1956. 3 p.

———. Surplus Agricultural Commodities; Agreement Signed at Washington April 11, 1957. Wash., 1957. 5 p.

———. Treaties, etc., 1952— (Ásgeirsson). Tele-communications; Registration of Frequencies Used in Iceland by U. S. Authorities; Agreement Effected by Exchange of Notes Signed at Reykjavik July 11 and 20, 1955. Wash., 1956. 3 p.

———. U. S. Educational Foundation in Iceland; Agreement Signed at Reykjavik February 23, 1957. Wash., 1957. 13 p.

Jónsson, Agnar K. "Iceland Looks at the United States," FSJ, 17 (1940), 5-7.

McKeever, Porter. "How to Throw Away an Airbase," Harper's (O 1956), 39-44.

Mosely, Philip E. "Iceland and Greenland: an American Problem," FA, 18 (1940), 742-46.

"U. S.-Icelandic Defense Negotiations," DeptStateBul, 36 (Ja 21, 1957), 100.

United States, Tariff Commission. Trade Agreement Between the U.S. and Iceland; Analysis of the Agreement and Digests of Trade Data with Respect to Products on Which Concessions were Granted by the U.S. Wash., 1944. 114 p. Mimeographed.

Weigert, Hans W. "Iceland, Greenland and the United States," FA, 23 (1944), 112-22.

Zimmerman, J. L. "A Note on the Occupation of Iceland by American Forces," PSQ, 62 (1947), 103-106.

NORWAY

Amundsen, Hans. "Halvdan Koht, Norway's Foreign Minister," ASR, 23 (1935), 341-45.

Aubert, Vilhelm, with Burton Fisher and Stein Rokkan. "A Comparative Study of Teachers' Attitudes to International Problems and Policies," Journal of Social Issues, 10 (1954), 25-39.

Brown, Robert N. Rudmose. "Political Claims in the Antarctic," WA, 1 (1947), 393-401.

Burgess, Philip M. Norwegian Leadership and Foreign Policy: a Norwegian Survey. Oslo; Columbus, Ohio, 1967. 29 p. Mimeographed.

"Case of Certain Norwegian Loans" [France v. Norway], AJIL, 51 (1947), 777-83; 52 (1948), 1-4.

Castberg, Frede. "The Norwegian People and Their Place in the Community of Nations," in his, The Norwegian Way of Life (Lond., 1954), 84-94.

Christensen, Christian A. R. "A Record Breaker: Halvard Lange Has Been Norwegian Foreign Minister Longer Than Any Other Man," Norseman, 1 (1960), 16-18, 29.

Christophersen, Jens A. "The Making of Foreign Policy in Norway," C&C (1968), 52-74.

"Civil Defense in Norway," Norseman (1967). 149-51.

Coolidge, Calvin. "Children of Freedom," ASR, 13 (1925), 483-90.

Drolsum, Axel C. Sovereign Norway and Her State Rights. Kra., 1905. 75 p. Reprinted from Farmand.

Evensen, Jens. "Norway and the Antarctic," ASR, 45 (1957), 13-21.

Galtung, Johan. "Popular Inspection of Disarmament Processes: the Reaction of a Norwegian Population Sample," C&C (1967), 121-38.

Giverholt, Helge. "North Norway in International Politics," Norseman, 12 (1954), 1-6.

Gran, Bjarne. "Norway and Northern Co-operation," Norseman, 12 (1954), 230-33.

Greve, Tim. A Key to Norwegian Foreign Policy. Oslo, 1959. 29 p.

Groth, E. "Some Aspects of Norwegian Foreign Policy After the War," International Spectator, 6 (Apr, 1952), 1-6.

Halle, Nils H. "Social Position and Foreign Policy Attitudes," Journal of Peace Research (1966), 46-74.

Hambro, Edvard. "The Legal Position of Aliens in Norway," IRAS, 24 (1958), 142-47.

———. "Where Do We Stand? — Norway Between East and West Politically and Economically," Norseman, (1964, no. 2), 41-44.

———. "The World League of Norsemen," ScPP, III, 867-70.

Hambro, Johan. "The World League of Norsemen (Nordmanns-Forbundet)," Norseman, 14 (1956), 43-46.

Hayton, Robert D. National Interests in Antarctica: an Annotated Bibliography. Wash., 1960. 137 p.

Holst, Johan J. "Norwegian Security Policy," C&C (1966, no. 2), 64-79.

Independent Norwegian Group (Uavhengig Norsk Gruppe; Carl Bonnevie). A Norwegian Initiative: the Oslo Peace Meeting 1958 and Its Program. Oslo, 1959. 19 p.

"Integrity of Norway Guaranteed," AJIL, 2 (1908), 176-78; 646-48.

Jorgenson, Theodore. Norway's Relation to Scandinavian Unionism, 1815-1871. Northfield, Minn., 1935. 530 p.

Karlström, Otto Leroy. "Beginning and End of Norwegian Neutrality," Norseman, 9 (1951), 217-31; 289-98.

———. A Survey of Norwegian Foreign Policy: 1905-1950. Oslo, 1951. 43 p. Mimeographed.

Koht, Halvdan. "Law and Freedom: Norway's Contribution to the Cause of International Justice," ASR, 31 (1943), 113-19.

———. "Neutrality and Peace, the View of a Small Power," FA, 15 (1937), 280-89.

———. "Problems of Neutrality," Nord, 2 (1939), 129-37.

Lange, Christian. "Germany and Geneva II: a Norwegian View," PolQ, 5 (1934), 7-12.

Lange, Halvard M. "The Foreign Policy of Norway," ASR, 52 (1964), 15-23.

———. "The Northern Countries and Europe: Some Norwegian Viewpoints," Norseman, 8 (1950), 1-9.

———. "Norway's Foreign Policy and the International Situation," Norseman, 6 (1948), 132-45.

Lie, Kai O. An Analysis of the Changing Role of Norway in the Struggle for Power and Peace in the North Since the Second World War. Thesis (Ph.D.), American University, 1967.

Lindjord, Haakon. The Foundations of Norway's Role in International Politics. Thesis (Ph.D.), Princeton University, 1954. 398 p.

Lloyd, Trevor. "The Norwegian-Soviet Boundary in Lapland," in IGCong 17th (1957), 533-38.

———. "The Norwegian-Soviet Boundary: a Study in Political Geography," NGT, 15 (1956), 187-242. Also published Hanover, N.H., 1954. 32 p.

Løchen, Einar. Norway in European and Atlantic Co-operation. Oslo, 1965. 88 p.

Løchen, Einar, and Rolf N. Torgersen. Norway's Views on Sovereignty: a Report Prepared for UNESCO. Bergen, 1955. 102 p.

Moe, Finn. "Norwegian Foreign Policy Today," Norseman, 16 (1958), 367-73.

Morgenstierne, Bredo. "Norway's Integrity
and Neutrality," Law Quarterly Review,
31 (1915), 389-96.

Nygaard, Gunnar. "The Voice of Norway:
the Short Wave Service of the Norwegian
Broadcasting Corporation Covers the
Globe," Norseman (1960, no. 2), 28-30.

Omang, Reidar. "Fifty Years of Norwegian
Foreign Policy," Norseman, 13 (1955),
154-60.

Ording, Arne. "Norway and International
Co-operation," Norseman, 1 (1943), 12-
16.

———. "Norway in World Affairs," ASR, 43
(1955), 141-50.

———. "Norwegian Foreign Policy" [Review
of Halvard M. Lange, Norsk utenrikspoli-
tikk siden 1945], Norseman, 11 (1953),
73-76.

Ørvik, Nils. "Base Policy — Theory and
Practice: the Norwegian Case," C&C
(1967), 188-204.

———. "Norwegian Activities in the Study of
International Relations 1960-1964," C&C
(1965, no. 1), 79-84.

———. Sikkerhetspolitikken, 1920-1939.
Oslo, 1961. English summary, v. 2, 455-
60.

———. Trends in Norwegian Foreign Policy.
Oslo, 1962. 36 p.

Quisling, Vidkun. Russia and Ourselves.
Lond., 1931. 284 p.

Raestad, Arnold. Europe and the Atlantic
World. Oslo, 1958. 114 p.

Riste, Olav. The Neutral Ally: Norway's
Relations with Belligerent Powers in the
First World War. Oslo, 1965. 295 p.

"Sixty Years of Bridge-Building" [The
Norsemen's Federation], Norseman
(1967), 63-66.

Smedal, Gustav. Acquisition of Sovereignty
Over Polar Areas. Oslo, 1931. 143 p.

Smith-Kielland, Ingvald. "Norwegian Treaty
Policy," Norwegian Trade Review, 1
(1926), 1-5.

Sommerfelt, Alf. "Norway's Progress and
Atlantic Destiny," GeogM, 15 (1942/43),
250.

Storing, James A. "Norway in the World
Community," in his, Norwegian Democracy (Boston, 1963), 206-21.

Villard, Henry S. "Flight to Finnmark,"
FSJ, 28 (1951), 18-20.

Warbey, William. "Norway's Foreign Relations," in his, Modern Norway: a Study
in Social Democracy (Lond., 1950), 14-
35.

Whyte, Anne. "Norway and the West," SoCo,
13 (F 1949), 34-37.

Worm-Müller, Jacob S. "Norway's Foreign
Relations and Policy," Norseman, 2
(1944), 77-85; 153-61.

NOBEL PEACE PRIZE

Falnes, Oscar J. "Norway Administers Nobel's Peace Prize," ASR, 24 (1936), 295-
304.

———. Norway and the Nobel Peace Prize.
N.Y., 1938. 332 p.

Hambro, Johan. "From Dynamite to Peace:
the Nobel Peace Prize," Norseman (1960,
no. 5), 11-14.

Knudsen, Ole F. "The Nobel Peace Prize
Through Fifty Years," Norseman, 8
(1950), 371-74.

Kraft, Tone. "Forty-seven Were Unworthy,"
Norseman (1967), 138-40.

Lipsky, Mortimer. The Quest for Peace:
the Story of the Nobel Award. N.Y., 1966.
281 p.

Schou, August. "The Nobel Peace Prize,"
ASR, 46 (1958), 221-28.

INTERNATIONAL ORGANIZATION

Castberg, Frede. "Norway and the League
of Nations," Woodbrooke International
Journal, 1 (1929).

Chelwood, Cecil Viscount of. "Nansen and
the League of Nations," Nord, 1 (1938),
191-200.

Christensen, Dag. "General of Peace: Odd
Bull, UN Commander in Trouble Spots,"
Norseman (1966), 129-32.

Hambro, Edvard. "Small States and a New
League — From the Viewpoint of Norway,"
APSR, 37 (1943), 903-909.

Jensen, Björn. Norway in the United Nations. Norwegian Universities Press,
1963. 36 p.

———. "Norway in the United Nations,"
Norseman, (1961, no. 5), 4-7.

Kildal, Arne. "Fridtjof Nansen," ASR, 11
(1923), 94-97.

Kinn, Egil, "Norway's Spokesman in the World
Organization: Dr. Edvard Hambro New UN
Ambassador," Norseman (1966), 77-79.

La Guardia, Fiorello H. "Norway and
UNRRA," Norseman, 4 (1946), 313-14.

Moe, Finn. "Norway and the United Nations,"
Norseman, 4 (1946), 107-10.

"Norway; Transmitted by a Note Verbale
Dated 2 May, 1955 from the Permanent
Delegation of Norway to the United Na-
tions," AJIL, 50 (1956), 262-65.

Stoneman, William H. "The Secretary General" [Trygve Lie], Norseman, 4 (1946), 95-99.

Valand, Gustav. "Modern Crusaders: the Norwegian UN Forces in the Middle East," Norseman, 4 (1961), 19-22.

FOREIGN AID

Bøe, Wilhelm S. "The Spirit of Nansen: Norwegian Aid to Refugees Around the World," Norseman (1962, no. 2), 4-8.

Haines, Ben C. "Experiment Abroad: Norway's Peace Corps in Action," Norseman (1966), 80-83.

——. "First Norse Peace Corps," Norseman (1964, no. 1), 18-20.

Lid, Halvard, and Astri Baasen. The Norwegian Indian Project in Travancore — Cochin. Oslo, 1957. 80 p.

Norway, Ministry of Foreign Affairs. International Assistance to Refugees. Geneva, 1935. 3 p.

Pettersen, Kåre. "Norwegian Development Aid," Norseman (1962, no. 2), 22-25.

Sandven, Per. The Indo-Norwegian Project in Kerala. Oslo, 1959. 151 p.

Sverdrup, Harald U. "Norway's Aid to India," ASR, 44 (1956), 19-26.

——. "Norway's Assistance to India," Norseman, 11 (1953), 27-30.

NATO

Araldsen, O. P. "Norwegian Defence Problems," USNIP, 84 (1958), 38-47.

Burgess, Philip M. Elite Images and Foreign Policy Outcomes: a Study of Norway. Columbus, Ohio, 1968. 179 p.

——. Norway, the North, and NATO: a Study of Authoritative Elite Perceptions as Related to Foreign Policy. Thesis (Ph.D.), American University, 1966. 266 p.

Canada, Department of National Defence, Bureau of Current Affairs. Norway, a Member of the North Atlantic Treaty Organization. Ottawa, 1956. 43 p.

The Defence of Norway. Oslo, Ja 1952. 40 p. Mimeographed.

Gerhardsen, Einar. "Speech at the NATO Meeting of Ministers in Paris, Dec. 16, 1957," Norseman, 16 (1958), 1-3.

Greve, Tim. Norway and NATO. Oslo, 1959, 1963. 31 p.

Hambro, Johan. "Norway and the Atlantic Pact," AmPers, 2 (1949), 431-39.

Hansteen, W. "Norwegian Defense Within NATO," ScPP, III, 147-52.

Holthe, Tore. "Norway and NATO," Norseman (1961, no. 1), 4-7.

Keilhau, Wilhelm C. "Norway and the Atlantic Pact," Norseman, 7 (1949), 80-85.

Kerry, Richard J. "Norway and Collective Defense Organization," IOrg, 17 (1963), 860-71.

Krosby, H. Peter. "Norway in NATO: a Partial Commitment?," IntJ, 20 (1964/1965), 68-78.

Lange, Halvard M. "NATO — a Partnership for Peace" [Speech Delivered in Glasgow, M 15, 1954], Norseman, 12 (1954), 145-55.

Martin, Anthony H. "NATO's Arctic Flank," Norseman, 12 (1954), 7-10.

Mehlem, Max. "The Defense of Norway," SRWA, 1 (1951, no. 3), 17-19.

——. "Norway in NATO," SRWA, 2 (1952/53, no. 8), 9-11.

Moon, Victor B. "Soviet-Norwegian Relations Since 1945," WPQ, 17 (1964), 659-70.

Morgenstierne, Wilhelm M. "The Atlantic Pact: a Norwegian Point of View," Academy of Political Science, 23 (1949), 325-30.

——. "Norway Never Pressured into North Atlantic Negotiations," NAC (Ap 1949), 23-25.

Norway, ABC-Sekretariatet. Defense Against Biological Warfare, Norway. Wash., JPRS, 1962. 29 p.

"Norway and the Atlantic Pact," WT, 5 (1949), 154-60.

"Norway's Reply to Moscow" [February 1, 1949], CH, 66 (1949), 170-71.

Ørvik, Nils. Europe's Northern Cap and the Soviet Union. Cambridge, Mass., 1963. 64 p.

Refsnes, Finn. "Guarding the Iron Curtain," Norseman (1962, no. 2), 26-29.

Sington, Anne. "NATO Defensive Installations in Norway," NATO Letter, 14 (1966, no. 1), 2-9.

Vogt, Benjamin. "Norway Faces West," Norseman, 6 (1948), 16-19.

Wold, Terje. "Europe and the Atlantic Alliance — a Norwegian Point of View," Norseman, 8 (1950), 289-92.

GREAT BRITAIN

"Anglo-Norwegian Fisheries Case," AJIL, 46 (1952), 23-30.

Candlin, E. Frank. "Saint Olaf in London," Norseman, 12 (1954), 313-20.

Christiansen, Reidar Th. "The Scotsmen and Norsemen, Cultural Relations in the North Sea Area," Scottish Studies, 1 (1957), 15-38.

Evensen, Jens. "The Anglo-Norwegian Fisheries Case and Its Legal Consequences," AJIL, 46 (1952), 609-30.

"Fisheries Case" [United Kingdom v. Norway], AJIL, 46 (1952), 348-70.

Friis, Erik J. "Anglo-Norwegian Relations 1939-1940," Norseman, 16 (1958), 161-64, 231-44, 311-31.

Gathorne-Hardy, Geoffrey M., ed. British Diplomatic Correspondance Relating to the Bodö Affair. Extracted from the Public Foreign Office Records. Oslo, 1926. 103 p.

Great Britain, Foreign Office. Survey of Anglo-Norwegian Cultural Relations. Lond., 1954. 29 p.

Hambro, Carl J. "British-Norwegian Academic Cooperation," Norseman, 16 (1958), 91-94.

Jessup, Philip C. "Norwegian Maritime Courts in England," AJIL, 36 (1942), 653-57.

Johnson, D. H. N. "The Anglo-Norwegian Fisheries Case," International and Comparative Law Quarterly, 1 (1952), 145-80.

Keilhau, Wilhelm C. "Britain and Norway: a Survey of Mutual Relations," Norseman, 11 (1953), 1-9.

Kent, H. S. K. "The Background to Anglo-Norwegian Relations," Norseman, 11 (1953), 150-55.

Knaplund, Paul. "Finmark in British Diplomacy, 1836-1855," AHR, 30 (1925), 478-502.

———. British Views on Norwegian-Swedish Problems, 1880-1895; Selections from Diplomatic Correspondence. Oslo, 1952. 269 p.

Koht, Halvdan. "Mr. Winston Churchill and the Norwegian Question," Norseman, 8 (1950), 73-84.

Martin, Anthony H. "The Anglo-Norwegian Fisheries Dispute," Norseman, 10 (1952), 73-76.

Mixed Commission on Cultural Relations [Great Britain and Norway]. Survey of Anglo-Norwegian Cultural Relations, July 1, 1954. Lond., 1954. 29 p.

Murray, Gilbert. "England and Norway: the View of an Onlooker," Norseman, 1 (1943), 86-89.

"Norway and England," NewEur, 3 (1917), 345-49.

Ørvik, Nils. "The Anglo-Norwegian Shipping Agreement and German Invasion," Norseman, 12 (1954), 289-94.

Plant, Ruth. "Norway's Contribution to Britain and the Post-War World," Norseman, 2 (1944), 256-62.

Robinson, Nora I. A. "Modern England and the Norseman," Norseman, 14 (1956), 394-95.

Ross, W. D. "Relations Between British and Norwegian Universities," Norseman, 3 (1945), 53-56.

Smith, H. A. "The Anglo-Norwegian Fisheries Case," in Yearbook of World Affairs 1953 (Lond., 1953), 283-307.

Thesen, Rolv. "England in Norwegian Eyes 1830-1870," Norseman, 10 (1952), 96-103.

Waldock, C. H. M. "The Anglo-Norwegian Fisheries Case," BYIL, 28 (1951), 114-71.

Young, Richard. "The Anglo-Norwegian Fisheries Case," ABAJ, 38 (1952), 243-45.

UNITED STATES

"Aviation Arrangements Between the United States and Norway," Journal of Air Law, 5 (1934), 134-40.

"Award of the Tribunal of Arbitration Between the United States of America and the Kingdom of Norway Under the Special Agreement of June 30, 1921," AJIL, 17 (1923), 362-99.

Blegen, Theodore C. "The Norwegian Government and Early Norwegian Emigration," Minnesota History, 6 (1925), 115-40.

Cleven, N. A. N. "Some Phases of United States-Norwegian Relations in World War I: a Study in Diplomacy," Historian, 7 (1944-45), 5-19.

Cowles, Willard B. "The Hannevig Case," AJIL, 32 (1938), 142-48.

Davis, Richard B. "American Studies in Norway," ASR, 44 (1956), 348-53.

Flom, George T. "The Coming of the Norwegians to Iowa," Iowa Journal of History and Politics, (1905), 347-83.

Gade, Gerhard. "General Grant in Norway," ASR, 21 (1933), 283-90.

Garner, James W. "An Arbitration Case Between Norway and the United States," BYIL, 4 (1923/24), 159-62.

Guterman, Stanley S. "The Americanization of Norwegian Immigrants: a Study in Historical Sociology," S&SR, 52 (1968), 252-70.

Harriman, Florence J. Mission to the North. Lond., 1941. 235 p.; Phila., N.Y., 1941. 331 p.

Hessler, William H. "Norway's Role in U.S. Defense," USNIP, 86 (Jl 1960), 31-37.

Hovde, Brynjolf J. Diplomatic Relations of the United States with Sweden and Norway, 1814-1905. Iowa City, 1920. 70 p.

Hudson, Manley O. "American-Norwegian

Postal Arbitration," AJIL, 20 (1926),
534-36.

Kildal, Arne. "American Studies in Norway:
a Progress Report," ASR, 50 (1962), 397-
401.

Larson, Laurence M. "A Century of
Achievement, 1825-1925: the New Norway in the New World," ASR, 13 (1925),
333-47.

Linder, Doris H. The Reaction of Norway to
American Foreign Policy, 1918-1939.
Thesis (Ph.D.), University of Minnesota,
1961. 337 p.

Lysgaard, S. A Study of Intercultural Contact: Norwegian Fulbright Grantees Visiting the United States. Oslo, 1954.
236 p.

Norway. Treaties, etc., 1905— (Haakon
VII); Claims: Hannevig against the U.S.,
Jones Against Norway. Convention...
Signed at Washington March 28, 1940.
Wash., 1949. 8 p.

———. Treaties, etc., 1905— (Haakon VII);
Conflicting Claims to Enemy Property.
Understanding Signed at Washington June
21, 1952. Wash., 1955. 7 p.

———. Norway-United States Arbitration;
Agreement of June 30, 1921: the Counter
Case of the Kingdom of Norway Against
the U.S.A., With an Appendix of Documents...1922. 102 p.

———. United States-Norway Arbitration;
Agreement of June 30, 1921: the Case
and Documentary Evidence of the Kingdom of Norway Against the U.S.A....
1922. 2 vols.

Norwegian-American Studies and Records.
Northfield, Minn.: Norwegian-American
Historical Association series in emigrant
history. v. 20, 1959.

Permanent Court of Arbitration. Norway-
United States Arbitration; Agreement of
June 30, 1921: the Argument of the King-
dom of Norway. The Hague, 1922. 218 p.
Also published by Norwegian Government,
1922. 218 p.

———. Norway-United States Arbitration;
Agreement of June 30, 1921: the Counter
Case of the Kingdom of Norway Against
the United States of America. The Hague,
1922. 250 p.

Rygg, Andrew N. American Relief for Norway. Chicago, 1947. 320 p.

Scott, Franklin D. "American Influences in
Norway and Sweden," JMH, 18 (1946),
37-47.

Scott, James B. "United States-Norway
Arbitration Award," AJIL, 17 (1923),
287-90; 362-99. [With text of award]

Smith, Stanley P. "An Arbitration with Norway," AJIL, 16 (1922), 81-84.

Swanson, H. Fred. "The Attitude of the
United States Toward Norway in the Crises of 1905," Nor-Am, 4 (1929), 43-53.

SPITSBERGEN (SVALBARD)

Fischer, Alfred J. "Spitsbergen," CR, 188
(D 1955), 399-401.

Floyd, Calvin J. "Svalbard: Crossroads of
the Arctic," ASR, 50 (1962), 153-60.

Iversen, Thor. "Spitsbergen. The Happy
Hunting Ground of Nations," ASR, 11
(1923), 611-19.

Mathisen, Trygve. Svalbard in the Changing
Arctic. Oslo, 1954. 112 p.

Orvin, Anders K. "Svalbard," ASR, 43
(1955), 260-69.

Spitsbergen. Lond., 1920. 50 p.

Treaty Regulating the Status of Spitsbergen
and Conferring the Sovereignty on Norway; Signed at Paris, February 9, 1920.
Lond., 1924. 17 p.

WORLD WAR II

Aas, Oddvar. "Between Neighbours" [White
Paper regarding relations between Sweden and Norway in 1940], Norseman, 5
(1947), 114-21.

Bone, Stephen. "The End of the War in
Northern Norway," GeoM, 18 (1945-46),
265-73.

Borchard, Edwin M. "Was Norway Delin-
quent in the Case of the Altmark," AJIL,
34 (1940), 289-94.

Chilston, Viscount. "Norway," in Part V of
Arnold and Veronica Toynbee, eds., The
Realignment of Europe, in the series
Survey of International Affairs 1939-1946
(Lond., 1955), 578-90.

Choffy, Sylvester C. The Diplomacy of Norway, 1939-1945. Thesis (Ph.D.), American University, 1960. 292 p.

Curtis, Monica, ed. Norway and the War,
September, 1939-December, 1940 (Documents on International Affairs). N.Y.,
1941. 154 p.

Fox, Annette Baker. "Norway: Maritime
Neutral," in her, The Power of Small
States: Diplomacy in World War II (Chi-
cago, 1959), 78-107.

Norway Does Not Yield: the Story of the
First Year; With an Introduction by Mrs.
J. Borden Harriman. Wash., N.Y., 1941.
64 p.

Norway, Komitéen for internasjonale sosial-
politiske saker. War Victims in Norway;

Measures of Compensation and Relief. Oslo, 1949. 60 p.

Norway, Norske informasjonstjeneste i Amerika. After Three Years. Wash., 1943. 48 p.

——. Norway at War! Wash., 1942. 29 p.

——. Norway's Role in the "New Order." Wash., 1942. 11 p.

——. Norway's Teachers Stand Firm. Wash., 1942. 32 p.

Norway, Ministry of Foreign Affairs. Authorized English Translation of the White Paper Issued by the Norwegian Government on April 14th 1940: the German Aggression on Norway. Lond., 1940. 7 p.

——. Correspondence Respecting the German Steamer "Altmark." London, F 17, M 15, 1940. 15 p.

——. Preliminary Survey of Pre-War German Assets and Holdings in Norway. Oslo, 1945. 7 p.

——. Preliminary Statement of the Royal Norwegian Government's Reparation Claim Against Germany. Oslo, 1945. 53 p.

Norway, Norske regjerings informasjonskontor. Arctic War; Norway's Role on the Northern Front. Lond., 1945. 64 p.

——. Before We Go Back: a Pictorial Record of Norway's Fight Against Nazism, Both Inside and Outside the Country, with a Postscript by Philip Noel-Baker. Lond., 1944. 63 p.

——. The Gestapo at Work in Norway: Extracts from Judicially Attested Witness Reports of Terror and Torture in German Prisons in Norway. Foreword by Lord Chancellor Viscount Simon. Lond., 1942. 38 p.

——. Norway, a Fighting Ally! Wash., 1944. 96 p.

Norwegian Peace Aims (Council on Foreign Relations Studies of the Peace Aims of the European Nations, no. A-3). N.Y., 1941. Various pagings.

"Norwegian Views on the German Problem," IA, 21 (1945), 74-78.

Palmström, Finn. Preliminary Report on Germany's Crimes Against Norway; Prepared by the Royal Norwegian Government for Use at the International Military Tribunal in Trials Against the Major War Criminals of the European Axis. By Major Finn Palmstrøm, Deputy Norwegian Representative on the U.N.'s War Crimes Commission, and Rolf N. Torgersen. Oslo, 1945. 67 p.

Stabell, P. P. "Enemy Legislation and Judgments in Norway," JCL (N 1949), 3-8.

United Kingdom, Foreign Office. Secret Documents Seized During the Raid on the Lofoten Islands on March 4, 1941. Lond., 1941. 28 p.

Walker, Basil C. "Norway; Fortunate Disaster," CH, 51 (1940), 15-19.

War Crimes Trials, Vol. VI: The Trial of Von Falkenhorst. Lond., 1949.

SWEDEN

Abrahamsen, Samuel. Sweden's Foreign Policy. Wash., 1957. 99 p.

Andrén, Nils. Power-Balance and Non-Alignment. Stock., 1967. 212 p.

——. "The Study of International Relations 1960-1965: Sweden," C&C (1966, no. 1), 82-89.

Bilainkin, George. "A Swedish Diplomat" [Gunnar Hagglof], CR, 196 (1959), 103-105.

Birnbaum, Karl E. "The Formation of Swedish Foreign Policy," C&C (1965, no. 1), 6-31.

——. "Sweden's Nuclear Policy," IntJ, 20 (1965), 297-311.

——. "The Swedish Experience," in Alastair Buchan, ed., A World of Nuclear Powers? (N.Y., 1966), 68-75.

——. Swedish Foreign Policy. Stock., 1962. 16 p.

Brodin, Katarina. "The Undén Proposal," C&C (1966, no. 2), 18-29.

"Case Concerning the Application of the Convention of 1902 Governing the Guardianship of Infants" [Netherlands v. Sweden], IOrg, 13 (1959), 146-51.

Clausen, Oliver. "Operation Granite: Sweden Goes Underground," New York Times Magazine (May 22, 1966), 23-25, 110-12.

Dahlman, Sven. Speech Delivered by Mr. Sven Dahlman, Head of Political Division, Ministry of Foreign Affairs, at the Annual Meeting of the Swedish Society for World Federation, Stockholm, May 21, 1950. Stock., 1950. 16 p. Mimeographed.

Danielson, John I. Sweden and the European Recovery Program. Thesis (M.A.), University of California, Berkeley, 1953.

Ehrenburg, Ilya. "Seek Peace First," LM, 32 (1950), 219-24.

Elmer, Åke. "The Norden Society in Sweden," ASR, 33 (1945), 159-61.

Enander, Bo. "Current Problems in Swedish Foreign Policy," Norseman, 6 (1948), 77-82.

——. "Sweden and the Atlantic Pact," Norseman, 7 (1949), 85-88.

Fischer, Alfred J. "Swedish Red Cross

Brings Home Greek Children from Yugoslavia," Norseman, 10 (1952), 157-59.

Gihl, Torsten. "The Limits of Swedish Territorial Waters," AJIL, 50 (1956), 120-22.

Goldmann, Kjell. "An 'Isolated' Attack Against Sweden and Its World Political Preconditions," C&C (1965, no. 2), 16-38.

Grafström, Anders. The Swedish Army. Stock., 1954. 158 p.

Heckscher, Gunnar. Sweden and the East-West Conflicts. Stock., 1960. 9 p.

———. "Sweden and the East-West Conflict," in The Fifteen Nations (Amsterdam, 1961).

———. Sweden in International Affairs; Comments Before the International Graduate School at the University of Stockholm. Stock., 1954. 13 p. Mimeographed.

Herz, Ulrich. "How Can We Help the Under-Developed Countries?" SBQR, 42 (1961), 109-18.

Hessler, William H. "An A-Bomb for Sweden," Report (N 12, 1959), 29-30.

———. "Sweden, the Cautious Old Man on the Quivering Tightrope," Reporter (D 9, 1952), 23-26.

Hinshaw, David. Sweden: Champion of Peace. N.Y., 1949. 309 p.

Hirschfeldt, Lennart. Swedish Foreign Policy After the Second World War. Stock., 1952. 14 p.

Johnson, E. Luther. Freedom from Alliances: Contemporary Swedish Views Toward International Relations. Thesis (Ph.D.), American University, 1966.

Kastrup, Allan. "Outpost on the Baltic," ASM (Ap 1949), 8-9.

———. Rock Excavations for Total Defense and Peaceful Uses in Sweden. Stock., 1962. 20 p.

Lang, William W. "Can Sweden Defend Herself?" USNIP, 93 (1967), 47-57.

Lerche, Charles O. "Sweden Faces the Nuclear Dilemma," WA, 123 (1960), 14-16.

Lichten, Joseph L. "The Mystery of a War Hero," ASR, 44 (1956), 241-44.

Lodge, Richard. "The Treaty of Åbo and the Swedish Succession," EHR, 43 (1928), 540-71.

Mehlem, Max. "Sweden's Foreign Policy," SRWA, 1 (May 1951), 8-10.

Mellander, Karl, and Edgar Prestage. The Diplomatic and Commercial Relations of Sweden and Portugal from 1641 to 1670. Lond., 1930. 123 p.

Moberg, Erik. "The Effect of Security Policy Measures: a Discussion Related to Sweden's Security Policy," C&C (1967), 67-81.

Myhrman, Sam. "Swedish Total Defense," MilitaryR, 41 (1961), 53-63.

Nilsson, Torsten. "The Foreign Policy of Sweden," ASR, 53 (1965), 15-19.

Ohlström, Bo. "Information and Propaganda: a Content Analysis of Editorials in Four Swedish Daily Newspapers," Journal of Peace Research (1966), 75-87.

Öste, Alfred. "International Position of Sweden," ASR, 36 (1948), 132-35.

Peace and Security After the Second World War: a Swedish Contribution to the Subject. Uppsala, 1945. 191 p.

Robbins, James J. Recent Military Thought in Sweden on Western Defense (Rand Corporation Research Memorandum, RM-1407). Santa Monica, Calif., 1955. 255 p.

Sandler, Åke. "Sweden's Postwar Diplomacy: Some Problems, Views, and Issues," WPQ, 13 (1960), 924-33.

Simons, Roger L. "Sweden's Defense Problem," USNIP, 84 (1958), 62-70.

"Sweden; Letter Dated 12 April 1955 from the Ministry of Foreign Affairs of Sweden," AJIL, 50 (1956), 266-71.

Sweden, Ministry for Foreign Affairs. Documents on Swedish Foreign Policy, 1950-51; 1952; 1953; 1954; 1955; 1956; 1957; 1958; 1959; 1960; 1961; 1962. Stock., 1952—.

Sweden, Riksarkivet. Sweden and the World. Documents from the Swedish National Archives. Stock., 1960. 94 p.

"Sweden and the Marshall Plan," Economist, 154 (F 7, 1948), 230-31.

"Sweden Today, Some Problems of Internal and Foreign Policy" [by A. H. H.], WT, 5 (1949), 438-45.

Tingsten, Herbert L. G. "The Debate on Sweden's Foreign Policy," ASR, 43 (1955), 13-19.

———. "Issues in Swedish Foreign Policy," FA, 37 (1959), 474-85.

———. "Swedish Foreign Policy After the Second World War," ASR, 33 (1945), 307-12.

Undén, Östen. Our Foreign Policy. Stock., 1953.

———. "Sweden Won't Choose Sides," United Nations World (May 1948), 16-17.

Whiteside, Thomas. An Agent in Place: the Wennerström Affair. N.Y., 1966. 150 p.

Wigforss, Harald. "Sweden and the Atlantic Pact," IOrg, 3 (1949), 434-43.

Young, Gordon. Outposts of Peace. Lond., 1945. 192 p.

INTERNATIONAL ORGANIZATION

Hewins, Ralph. Count Folke Bernadotte,

His Life and Work. Minneapolis, 1950. 279 p.

Lash, Joseph P. Dag Hammarskjöld. A Biography. Lond., 1962. 304 p.

Osborne, Lithgow. "Dag Hammarskjöld: In Memoriam," ASR, 49 (1961), 357-59.

Stolpe, Herman A. "Sweden and the League of Nations," IO, 2 (1937/38), 107-10.

Stolpe, Sven. Dag Hammarskjöld: a Spiritual Portrait. N.Y., 1966. 127 p.

Sweden, Armén, Generalstaben. Covenant of the League of Nations from Point of View of Swedish Military Policy; Despatch Dated 31.10.19 from British Representative, Stockholm, to Foreign Office, London. Lond., 1919.

Sweden, Ministry for Foreign Affairs, Press Department. Extracts from Documents Concerning Sweden's Application for Membership in the United Nations. Stock., 1946.

Sweden and the United Nations. Report by a Special Study Group of the Swedish Institute of International Affairs (Prepared for the Carnegie Endowment for International Peace). N.Y., 1956. 315 p.

Van Dusen, Henry P. Dag Hammarskjold: the Statesman and His Faith. N.Y., 1967. 240 p.

Zacher, Mark W. Dag Hammarskjold's Conception of the Political Role of the United Nations. Thesis (Ph.D.), Columbia University, 1966.

PRE-WORLD WAR I

Johnson, Amandus B. Swedish-German Relations in the Seventeenth Century. Thesis (Ph.D.), University of Pennsylvania, 1914.

Murray, John J. "British Public Opinion and the Rupture of Anglo-Swedish Relations in 1717," Indiana Magazine of History, 44 (1948), 125-42.

——. "The Görtz-Gyllenborg Arrests — a Problem in Diplomatic Immunity," JMH, 28 (1956), 325-37.

——. "Robert Jackson's Mission to Sweden" [1709-1717], JMH, 21 (1949), 1-16.

——. "Sweden and the Jacobites in 1716," Huntington Library Quarterly, 8 (1945), 259-76.

Natharius, Edward W. Anglo-Dutch Relations with Sweden, 1696-1702. Thesis (Ph.D.), Indiana University, 1965.

Roberts, Michael. "Cromwell and the Baltic," in his, Essays in Swedish History (Lond., 1967), 138-94.

——. "Great Britain and the Swedish Revolution, 1772-3," in his, Essays in Swedish History (Lond., 1967), 286-347.

"Swedish Politics by a Neutral," NewEur, 4 (1917), 294-301.

WORLD WAR I

Henschen, Henry S. "Count Ehrensvärd" [Minister of Foreign Affairs], ASR, 1 (1913), 5-6.

Meynell, Hildamarie. "The Stockholm Conference of 1917," International Review of Social History, 5 (1960), 1-25, 202-225.

Morris, Ira N. From an American Legation: Sweden, 1914-1922. N.Y., 1923. 287 p.

Scott, Franklin D. "Gustaf V and Swedish Attitudes Toward Germany, 1915," JMH, 39 (1967), 113-18.

Stowe, Leland. "The High Cost of Neutrality," in No Other Road to Freedom (Lond., N.Y., 1941), 120-34.

"Sweden and Neutrality," NewEur, 4 (1917), 280-82.

Tham, Wilhelm. "Neutral Sweden," ScPP, II, 1237-40.

Thompson, Elizabeth M. "Sweden: Armed Neutral," Editorial Research Reports (1952), 563-79.

Villehardouin. "Stockholm: a French View," NewEur, 4 (1917), 257-66.

"What Sweden Thinks Today," NewEur, 10 (1919), 251-55.

INTER-WAR PERIOD

Bellquist, Eric C. Some Aspects of the Recent Foreign Policy of Sweden. Berkeley, 1929. 378 p.

Böhm, Franciszek. "Pioneers of Polish-Swedish Collaboration," BC, 2 (1936), 67-71.

Boström, Wollmar F. "Treaty of Arbitration Between Sweden and Belgium," ASR, 15 (1927), 283-85.

Gunther, Hans K. German-Swedish Relations 1933-39: the Background for Swedish Neutrality. Thesis (Ph.D.), Stanford University, 1955. 216 p.

Konopszynski, Wtalyslaw. Poland and Sweden Baltic Institute. 1935. 60 p.

——. "Poland and Sweden," BC, 1 (1935), 19-32.

Mingos, Howard. "Sweden Again Looks to the East," ASR, 12 (1924), 216-20.

Tingsten, Herbert L. G. The Debate on the Foreign Policy of Sweden, 1918-1939. N.Y., Lond., 1949. 324 p.

WORLD WAR II

Aas, Oddvar. "Between Neighbours" [White Paper on relations between Sweden and Norway in 1940], Norseman, 5 (1947), 114-21.

Ashby, Corbett. "Four Weeks in Neutral Sweden," CR, 162 (1942), 7-11.

Bellquist, Eric C. "Sweden's Position in the War," American Swedish Handbook 1943, 109-12.

Benedikt, Ernst. "Sweden and the War," CR, 167 (1945), 265-67.

——. "Swedish Neutrality," CR, 175 (1949), 198-201.

Boström, Wollmar F. "Sweden Looks to the Post-War World," ASR, 31 (1943), 293-302.

Brook-Shephard, Gordon. "Does Europe Need Its Neutrals?" Reporter (May 24, 1962), 29-32.

Childs, Marquis W. "Sweden: Her Tragic Dilemma," CH, 51 (1939/40), 16-18.

Dahlman, Sven. "How a Democracy Survived: Sweden's Course of Neutrality in World War II," ASIB, new series, 1 (Ap/S, 1945), 6-16.

Ehrlich, Blake. "Sweden's Muscular Neutrality," Reporter, (May 19, 1955), 31-34.

Fagrell, Gunnar. "With the Swedish Army," ASR, 29 (1941), 238-45.

Fox, Annette Baker. "Sweden: Armed Neutral," in her, The Power of Small States: Diplomacy in World War II (Chicago, 1959), 108-46.

Gade, John A. "Great-Hearted Sweden," ASR, 32 (1944), 103-12.

Hägglöf, M. Gunnar. "A Test of Neutrality: Sweden in the Second World War," IA, 36 (1960), 153-67.

Hammarskjöld, Dag. Sweden's International Credit Accommodation in 1944 and 1945. Stock., 1946. 23 p.

Haupert, John S. The Critical Era of Swedish Neutrality, 1939-1945. Thesis (D.S.S.), Syracuse University, 1955. 223 p.

Hedin, Naboth. "The Allies Planned to Invade Sweden," ASM, 47 (1953), 6+.

——. "Relations Between Sweden and Finland," ASM (N 1941), 4-5+.

——. "Sweden and the War," ASM, 35 (1941, no. 3), 4-7.

——. "Sweden: the Dilemma of a Neutral," FPR, 19 (May 15, 1943), 50-63.

Hessler, William H. "Sweden's Armed Neutrality," USNIP, 81 (1955), 39-49.

Hicks, Agnes H. "Sweden," in Part III of Arnold and Veronica Toynbee, eds., The War and the Neutrals, in the series Survey of International Affairs 1939-1946 (Lond., 1956), 171-99.

Hopper, Bruce. "Sweden: a Case Study of Neutrality," FA, 23 (1945), 435-49.

Jägerskiöld, Stig. "The Immunity of State-Owned Vessels in Swedish Judicial Practice During World War II," AJIL, 42 (1948), 601-607.

Joesten, Joachim. "Phases in Swedish Neutrality," FA, 23 (1945), 324-29; Norseman, 3 (1945), 186-92.

——. Stalwart Sweden. N.Y., 1943. 215 p.

Kahn, H. L. On Postwar Neutrality. Stock., 1953. Mimeographed.

Lambert, C. A. "Sweden and the Finnish War," NiCen, 27 (1940), 274-87.

Larsen, Hanna A. "The Neutrality Alliance of Sweden and Norway," ASR, 2 (1914), 8-14.

Lerche, Charles O. "Sweden: Neutralism or Neutrality?," USNIP, 87 (1961), 68-76.

Lindberger, Örjan. "Swedish Literature During the Second World War," Norseman, 5 (1947), 123-37.

Milward, Alan S. "Could Sweden Have Stopped the Second World War?" SEHR, 15 (1967), 127-38.

Myrdal, Gunnar. "With Dictators as Neighbors: What About Sweden," Survey Graphic, 28 (May/Je 1939), 309-11+; 385-88+.

——. "The Defenses of Democracy," Survey Graphic, 28 (Je 1939), 385.

Öste, Alfred. "Sweden After the War," Norseman, 4 (1946), 197-201.

"Recent Aspects of Sweden's Foreign Policy" [by C. M. C.], BIN, 21 (1944), 423-31.

Sandler, Åke. Political Aspects of Swedish Diplomacy During World War II. Thesis (Ph.D.), University of California, Los Angeles, 1950.

Singer, Kurt D. The Riddle of Sweden's Ballbearings (News Background, Inc., Report no. 12). N.Y., 1944. 12 p.

Soloveytchik, G. "Whither Sweden and Finland," CR, 160 (1941), 99-102.

"Sweden: a Case Study in Neutrality," FA, 23 (1945), 435-49.

Sweden, a Wartime Survey. Ed. and pub. in Sweden with the assistance of public authorities. N.Y., 1943. 250 p. Same as: Sweden, a Wartime survey. Ed. and pub. by the Press Bureau of the Royal Ministry for Foreign Affairs. Stock., 1942. 250 p.

"Sweden Between the Fronts," CR, 164 (1943), 213-17.

"Sweden's Dilemma," CR, 157 (1940), 410-17.

Toksvig, Signe. "How Neutral is Sweden," Atlantic Monthly, 170 (N 1942), 91-96.

Towers, Charles. "Sweden's Defence," Empire Review, 71 (F 1940), 86-87.

Undén, Östen. "Sweden and the New Order," ASR, 29 (1941), 5-8.

Vowles, Richard B. "An American Student in Sweden," ASR, 28 (1940), 259-61.

Willemson, Vaino. Some Problems of Sweden's Foreign Policy 1939-1945. Thesis (M.A.), University of California, 1961. 142 p.

Witting, Gustave, ed. Sweden Speaks. Lond., 1942. 212 p.

Young, George G. Outposts of Peace [Newspaper Correspondent in Stockholm]. Lond., 1945. 192 p.

UNITED STATES

"Air Navigation Agreements Between the United States and Sweden," Journal of Air Law, 5 (1934), 140-42.

Aldrich, Winthrop W. Sweden and the United States: an Address. N.Y., 1938. 17 p.

"Arbitral Decision; Rendered in Conformity with the Special Agreement Concluded on December 17, 1930, Between the Kingdom of Sweden and the United States of America Relating to the Arbitration of a Difference Concerning the Swedish Motor Ships 'Kronprins Gustaf Adolf' and 'Pacific'," AJIL, 26 (1932), 834-903.

Attman, Artur. Swedish-American Economic Relations. 1954.

Benson, Adolph B. "Our First Unsolicited Treaty," ASR, 7 (1919), 43-49.

———. Sweden and the American Revolution. New Haven, Conn., 1926. 216 p.

Capps, Finis H. From Isolationism to Involvement: the Swedish Immigrant Press in America 1914-1945. Chicago, 1966. 238 p.

Carlson, Knute E. Relations of the United States with Sweden. Thesis (Ph.D.), University of Pennsylvania, 1919. Published: Allentown, Pa., 1921. 94 p.

Fleisher, Eric W., and Jörgen Weibull. Viking Times to Modern. Stock., 1953; Minneapolis, 1954. 115 p.

Hovde, Brynjolf J. Diplomatic Relations of the United States with Sweden and Norway, 1814-1905. Iowa City, 1920. 70 p.

Koht, Halvdan. "Bernadotte and Swedish-American Relations, 1810-1814," JMH, 16 (1944), 265-85.

Lerche, Charles O. "Swedish Attitude To-

ward American Foreign Policy," Free World Forum (Spring 1960).

Mergen, Bernard. "American Studies in Swedish Universities," ASR, 53 (1965), 399-402.

Morris, Ira N. From an American Legation. N.Y., 1923. 287 p.

O'Neill, Anna A. "United States-Sweden Arbitration," AJIL, 26 (1932), 720-34.

Osborne, John Ball. "The Personal Side of Swedish-American Relations," ASR, 19 (1931), 91-97.

Scott, Franklin D. The American Experience of Swedish Students: Retrospect and Aftermath. Minneapolis, 1956. 129 p.

———. "Swedish Trade With America in 1820: a Letter of Advice from Baron Axel Klinkowström," JMH, 25 (1953), 407-14.

RUSSIA

Andreyeva, M., and K. Dimitrieva. "The Soviet Union and Swedish Neutrality in the Second World War," IAF (S 1960), 66-71.

Benedikt, Ernst. "Sweden Between the Fronts" [Russia and the West], CR, 170 (1946), 141-45.

du Guerny, Yves. "Sweden Between East and West," IntJ, 7 (1951/52), 48-54.

Glenn, Gene W. "The Swedish-Soviet Territorial Sea Controversy in the Baltic," AJIL, 50 (1956), 942-49.

Hallström, Björn. I Believed in Moscow. Lond., 1953. 300 p.

"A Note on the Swedish-Russian Dispute. Repercussions in Sweden," WT, 8 (1952), 388-92.

Nylander, L. "Russia and Sweden To-Day," ASR, 35 (1947), 110-15.

Sweden, Ministry of Foreign Affairs. Attacks Upon Two Swedish Aircraft Over the Baltic in June 1952; Notes Exchanged Between Sweden and the Soviet Union, Press Releases, etc. (Its Documents. New series II:2). Stock., 1952. 47 p.

NOBEL PRIZES

Almhult, Artur. "The Nobel Prizes," BSC, 4 (1938), 228-33.

Bergengren, Erik. Alfred Nobel: the Man and His Work. Lond., N.Y., 1962. 222 p.

Falnes, Oscar J. Norway and the Nobel Peace Prize. N.Y., 1938. 332 p.

Gross, Fritz. "Holders of the Nobel Prize," CR, 163 (1943), 306-10.

Halasz, Nicholas. Nobel: a Biography of
    Alfred Nobel. N.Y., 1959. 281 p.

Hedvall, Yngve. "Alfred Nobel: Inventor of
    Dynamite and Patron of Peace," ASR, 14
    (1926), 91-96.

Landquist, John. "Alfred Nobel, Founder of
    the Nobel Prizes," ASR, 21 (1933), 472-
    81.

MacCallum, Thomas W., and Stephen Taylor,
    eds. The Nobel Prize Winners and the
    Nobel Foundation 1901-1937. Zurich,
    1938. 599 p.

Nobel Foundation. Nobel: the Man and His
    Prizes. Stock.; Norman, Okla., 1950.
    620 p.

Pauli, Hertha E. Alfred Nobel: Dynamite
    King, Architect of Peace. N.Y., 1942.
    325 p.; Lond., 1947. 323 p.

Schück, Johan Henrik E., and Ragnar Sohl-
    man. The Life of Alfred Nobel. Lond.,
    1929. 353 p.

Sohlman, Ragnar, and Johan Henrick E.
    Schück. Nobel, Dynamite and Peace.
    N.Y., 1929. 353 p.

Ståhle, Nils. "Alfred Nobel and the Nobel
    Prizes," ScPP, III, 291-97.

LAW

INTRODUCTION

In law, as in other fields, there is a tendency for Scandinavians to publish in English in order to make Scandinavian developments and scholarship known to the rest of the world. Indeed, the overwhelming majority of the entries listed here are by Scandinavian scholars. There are two excellent English-language annuals published in Scandinavia: *Scandinavian Studies in Law* (1957—) and *Scandinavian Studies in Criminology* (1965—); entries from the latter appear under Sociology. Much of the published work is comparative or examines the region as a whole. The Northern Countries have a common legal heritage which they maintain through consultations of lawmakers, of scholars, and of jurists. Laws and procedures throughout the region are very much alike.

Some of the articles on jurisprudence and legal history are good introductions to the Scandinavian systems; one might begin by reading articles by Frede Castberg, Torstein Eckhoff, Bernhard Gomard, Nils Herlitz, and William von Eyben. One of the best introductory books available is an American study in history: Lester Orfield's *The Growth of Scandinavian Law* (1953); it contains chapters on each of the countries. Highly commendable are *Legal Values in Modern Sweden* (1964) by Folke Schmidt and Stig Stromholm, and *Civil Procedure in Sweden* (1965), by Ruth Ginsburg and Anders Bruzelius. Folke Schmidt's *The Law of Labour Relations in Sweden* (1962) is also excellent. *Danish and Norwegian Law, A General Survey* (1963), edited by Nils Boeg for the Danish Committee on Comparative Law, is intended as an introduction. Covering some points of philosophy, legislation, the courts, the main fields of law, and civil and criminal procedure, it is the only broad introduction to Scandinavian law to date; the layman would probably find it quite technical, but it is well organized and interestingly presented. A very good introduction to a Scandinavian judicial system is *Administration of Justice in Norway* (1957), edited by the Royal Norwegian Ministry of Justice. This bibliography contains references to numerous translations of texts of statutes. There is a *Compilation of Norwegian Laws* (1956) by Hjalmar Willett. *The Danish Criminal Code* was published by the Danish Committee on Comparative Law with an introduction by Knud Waaben in 1958.

Those interested in the institution of the ombudsman will find some fifty entries on it under Political Science. Most of the articles on crime appear under Sociology. Some treaties and writings on international legal relations are listed under International Relations. Sources on anti-trust and on taxation will be found under Economics.

Other bibliographies may be helpful to the scholar. One compilation, by Stig Iuul, Åke Malmström, and Jens Søndergaard, is *Scandinavian Legal Bibliography* (1961). For Finland alone there is Veikko Reinikainen's *English, French and German Literature on Finnish Law in 1860-1956* (1957). Two parallel bibliographies have appeared in the annual *Scandinavian Studies in Law:* Jens Søndergaard, "Danish Legal Publications in English, French and German" (1963), and Lars Frykholm, "Swedish Legal Publications in English, French and German 1935-60" (1961).

SCANDINAVIA

Adlercreutz, Axel. "The Rise and Development of the Collective Agreement," ScStL, 2 (1958), 9-53.

Arnholm, Carl J. "Some Basic Problems of Jurisprudence," ScStL, 1 (1957), 9-50.

Bengtsson, Bertil. "Contractual Liability and Liability Insurance: a Comparative Study," ScStL, 6 (1962), 33-62.

Birnbaum, Henrik. "On Old Russian and Old Scandinavian Legal Language; Some Comparative Notes on Style and Syntax," Scando-Slavica, 8 (1962), 115-40.

Blix, Hans. "The Rights of Diplomatic Missions and Consulates to Communicate with Authorities of the Host Country," ScStL, 8 (1964), 9-43.

Borum, O. A. "The Scandinavian Countries and the Hague Conventions on Private International Law 1951-64," ScStL, 11 (1967), 37-62.

———. "Scandinavian Views on the Notion of Recognition of Foreign Companies," Nederlands Tijdschrift voor Internationaal Recht, 9 (1962), 82-88.

Braekhus, Sjur. "Competing Salvors," ScStL, 11 (1967), 63-118.

Castberg, Frede. "Philosophy of Law in the Scandinavian Countries," AJCL, 4 (1955), 388-400.

Eckhoff, Torstein. "Sociology of Law in Scandinavia," ScStL, 4 (1960), 29-58.

Ekelöf, Per Olof. "Free Evaluation of Evidence," ScStL, 8 (1964), 44-66.

Falk, Magne. "The Nordic Patent Offices," NIR, 27 (1958), 11-17.

Gihl, Torsten. "The Baseline of the Territorial Sea," ScStL, 11 (1967), 119-74.

Glindemann, Poul. Scandinavian Banking Laws. N.Y., 1926. 122 p.

Gomard, Bernhard. "Civil Law, Common Law and Scandinavian Law," ScStL, 5 (1961), 27-38.

Haekkerup, Hans. Nordic Co-operation in the Legal Field. Coph., 1963. 11 p.

Hambro, Edvard. "Autonomy in the International Contract Law of the Nordic States," International and Comparative Law Quarterly, 6 (1957), 689-97.

———. "Recognition and Enforcement of Foreign Judgement in the Nordic Countries," Journal du droit international, 84 (1957), 908-47.

Hart, H. L. A. "Scandinavian Realism," Cambridge Law Journal (1959), 233-40.

Herlitz, Nils. "Critical Points of the Rule of Law as Understood in the Nordic Countries," in Civibus et Rei Publicae; Festskrift till Georg Andrén (Stock., 1960), 162-75.

Hjerner, Lars A. E. "The General Approach to Foreign Confiscations," ScStL, 2 (1958), 177-218.

Holm-Nielsen, Henning. "The Scandinavian Convention on Bankruptcy and Arrangements Outside Bankruptcy," Journal of Comparative Legislation and International Law, 3d series, 18 (1936), 262-65.

Iuul, Stig, Åke Malmström, and Jens Søndergaard. Scandinavian Legal Bibliography. Stock., 1961. 196 p.

Kruse, A. Vinding. "The Foreseeability Test in Relation to Negligence, Strict Liability, Remoteness of Damage, and Insurance Law," ScStL, 9 (1965), 93-129.

Kruse, Frederick V. A Nordic Draft Code. Coph., 1963. 412 p.

Kutschinsky, Berl. "Law and Education: Some Aspects of Scandinavian Studies into 'The General Sense of Justice'," AcSoc, 10 (1966), 21-41.

Lando, Ole. "The Proper Law of Contract," ScStL, 8 (1964), 105-201.

———. "Scandinavian Conflict of Law Rules Respecting Contracts," AJCL, 6 (1957), 1-26.

Lögdberg, Åke. "The Right in a Person's Own Likeness," ScStL, 11 (1967), 211-39.

Ljungman, Seve. "Brief Comments on Industrial Property in Scandinavian Education and Research," NIR, 27 (1958), 18-19.

Lüning, Nils. "Police Systems in the Scandinavian Countries," ScPP, III, 122-25.

Marshall, Geoffrey. "Law in a Cold Climate: the Scandinavian Realism," Judicial Review (1956), 259-67.

Munch-Petersen, Hans. "Main Features of Scandinavian Law," Law Quarterly Review, 43 (1927), 366-77.

———. "The Social Aspect of Procedure from a European Point of View," Minnesota Law Review, 11 (1927), 624-34.

Nylen, Torsten. "Scandinavian Co-operation in the Field of Air Legislation," Journal of Air Law and Commerce, 24 (1957), 36-46.

Olsson, Curt. "General Clauses for the Protection of Minority Shareholders in the Scandinavian Companies Acts," ScStL, 11 (1967), 269-95.

Orfield, Lester B. The Growth of Scandinavian Law. Phila., 1953. 363 p.

———. "Scandinavian Health Insurance Legislation," South Carolina Law Quarterly, 12 (1960), 202-344.

———. "A Survey of Scandinavian Legal Philosophy," Wisconsin Law Review (1956), 448-80, 585-624.

Orfield, Lester B. "Uniform Scandinavian Laws," ABAJ, 38 (1952), 773-75.
——. "A Visit to the Scandinavian University Law Schools," Journal of Legal Education, 11 (1959), 534-42.
Philip, Allan. "The Scandinavian Conventions on Private International Law," (Recueil des cours 1958, v. 96) Académie du droit international (Leiden, 1959), 247-348.
Portin, Göran. "The Doctrine of Non-Acceptance (Mora Accipiendi)," ScStL, 8 (1964), 203-19.
Ross, Alf. "On the Concepts of 'State' and 'State Organs' in Constitutional Law," ScStL, 5 (1961), 111-29.
Sandart, Kaj. "Nordic Associations of Independent Patent Agents and Their International Relations," NIR, 27 (1958), 33-35.
"Scandinavia Legislation," ABAJ, 12 (1926), 268-72.
"Scandinavia Legislation 1914," ABAJ, 2 (1916), 265-75.
"Scandinavia Legislation 1915," ABAJ, 3 (1917), 248-61.
"Scandinavia Legislation 1916," ABAJ, 4 (1918), 193-207.
"Scandinavia-1917," ABAJ, 7 (1921), 198-200.
Schmidt, Folke. "The 'Leniency' of Scandinavian Divorce Laws," ScStL, 7 (1963), 107-21.
——. "Model, Intention, Fault: Three Canons for Interpretation of Contracts," ScStL, 4 (1960), 177-208.
Skavang, Nils B. "History and Development of Scandinavian Law – Some Salient Traits," Seminar, 6 (1948), 60-71.
Strahl, Ivar. "Scandinavian Cooperation in the Field of Legislation," ScPP, III, 113-17.
——. "The Scandinavian Jurists' Congresses," ScPP, III, 118-21.
Strömberg, Håkan. "On the Idea of Legislation,"ScStL, 8 (1964), 221-42.
Sundberg, Jacob. "The Law of Contracts: Jurisprudential Writing in Search of Principles," ScStL, 7 (1963), 123-49.
Teisen, Axel. Bibliography for Scandinavia (American Foreign Law Association publication). 1926.
——. "Scandinavia Bibliography of Comparative Law," ABAJ, 1 (1915), 160-62; 2 (1916), 270-75.
Tengelin, Sten. "Associations in the Field of Industrial Property in the Scandinavian Countries, Denmark, Finland, Norway and Sweden," NIR, 27 (1958), 31-33.
Tiberg, Hugo. Time for Loading and Unloading of Ships: a Comparative Study of English and Scandinavian Law. Oslo, 1957. 111 p.
Uggla, Claes. "The Scandinavian Trademark Law Reform, a Preview," Trademark Reporter, 46 (1956), 759-61.
Ussing, Henry. "The Scandinavian Law of Torts – Impact of Insurance on Tort Law," AJCL, 1 (1952), 359-72.
von Eyben, William E. "Inter-Nordic Legislative Co-operation," ScStL, 6 (1962), 63-93.
——. "Judicial Law in the Making in Scandinavia," AJCL, 5 (1956), 112-15.
von Zweigbergk, Åke. "Legislation on Industrial Property in the Scandinavian Countries," NIR, 27 (1958), 5-10.
Walton, F. P. "Scandinavian Law of Husband and Wife," Journal of Comparative Legislation and International Law, 3d series, 9 (1927), 263-64.

DENMARK

Andreasen, Hardy. "Legal Advertising in Danish Law," Ugeskrift for Retvaesen (1961), 166-69.
Bentzon, Agnete W. "The Structure of the Judicial System and Its Function in a Developing Society" (Greenland), AcSoc, 10 (1966), 121-46.
Boeg, Nils V., ed. Danish and Norwegian Law: a General Survey. Coph., 1963. 251 p.
Carlsen, Bent. Danish Patent, Design and Trade Mark Law: a Brief Manual. 2d ed., Coph., 1933. 26 p.
"Copyright in Denmark," DFOJ, no. 204 (Ja 1938), 12-14.
Dahl, Frantz. Anders Sandøe Ørsted as a Jurist. Coph., 1932. 48 p.
The Danish Criminal Code. Coph., 1958. 119 p.
DeMontmorency, J. E. G. "Danish Influence on English Law and Character," Law Quarterly Review, 40 (1950), 324-43.
"Denmark," in "Law: Annual Reports on Recent Acquisition," LCQJ, 9 (1952), 205-206; 14 (1957), 217-19.
Denmark, Constitution. The Constitution of the Kingdom of Denmark Act 5th June, 1953, and the Succession to the Throne Act 27th March, 1953. Coph., 1953. 12 p.
Denmark, Laws, Statutes, etc. The Danish Criminal Code. With an Introduction by Knud Waaben. Coph., 1958. 118 p.
——. The Danish Gymnasium: the Official Regulations (1953). Published by the Danish Ministry of Education. Coph., 1959. 66 p.

Denmark, Laws, Statutes, etc. The Danish
    Public Libraries Act of May 27, 1950
    (Statens bibliotekstilsyns publikationer,
    22). Coph., 1953. 14 p.
——. Public Libraries Act of May 27, 1950
    with Amendments of May 25, 1956 and
    March 21, 1959. Coph., 1961. 9 p.
Denmark, Laws, Statutes, etc., 1670-1699
    (Christian V). The Danish Laws: or, the
    Code of Christian the Fifth; Faithfully
    translated for the use of the English in-
    habitants of the Danish settlements in
    America. Lond., 1756. 476 p.
Denmark, Laws, Statutes, etc., 1766-1808
    (Christian VII); Translation of the Law
    for the Government of Privateers and
    Prize-Courts in the Dominions of Den-
    mark. Rendsburg, 1808. 8 p.
Denmark, Laws, Statutes, etc., 1863-1906
    (Christian IX). Law Relating to the Mea-
    surement of Ships in Denmark. Coph.,
    1867. 13 p.
——. Law Relating to the Registration of
    Danish Ships. Coph., 1867. 16 p.
——. Maritime Law, Sanctioned by H. M.
    Christian IX on the 1st of April 1802.
    Coph., 1893. 131 p.
Denmark, Laws, Statutes, etc., 1912-1947
    (Christian X). Law (no. 64 — 1914) Con-
    cerning Custom House and Ship Dues in
    St. Thomas and St. Jan, 1st April, 1914.
    St. Thomas, 1914. 8 p.
——. Law no. 131 Regarding Children Born
    Out of Wedlock in Denmark. Geneva,
    1937. 25 p.
——. Law no. 133 on Measures for Obtain-
    ing and Ensuring the Payment of Mainte-
    nance Contributions in Denmark. Geneva,
    1937. 13 p.
"Denmark; Legislation, 1917," ABAJ, 6
    (1920), 327-37.
Ekman, Ernst. "The Danish Royal Law of
    1665," JMH, 29 (1957), 102-107.
Givskov, Carl G. "The Danish 'Purge
    Laws'," Journal of Criminal Law and
    Criminology, 39 (1948), 447-60.
Goas, C. The Danish Law of Crimes. Coph.,
    1916.
Goldschmidt, Verner. "The Greenland Crim-
    inal Code and Its Sociological Background,"
    AcSoc, 1 (1955/56), 217-65.
——. "From Unwritten Law to Modern
    Practice," DFOJ, no. 28 (1958), 16-19.
——. "New Trends in Studies on Greenland
    Social Life: Codification of Criminal Law
    in Changing Greenland," Folk, 5 (1963),
    113-21.
Gomard, Bernhard. "Legal Problems of
    Compensation Involved in the Use of
    Nuclear Energy," ScStL, 4 (1960), 59-100.

Groes, Ebbe. "Danish Monopoly Legislation,
    the Next Stage," Cartel, 4 (1954), 2-9.
Hoffman, Willy. "The Danish Law Against
    Disturbances of Radio Broadcasting," Air
    Law Review, 3 (1932), 44-47.
Holm-Nielsen, Henning. "Functional Juris-
    prudence and the Law of Torts with Spe-
    cial Reference to Danish Law," in Studi in
    Memoria di Aldo Albertini (Padua, 1938),
    225-32.
——. "Law of Torts in Denmark," Journal
    of Comparative Legislation and Interna-
    tional Law, 3d series, 15 (1933), 176-79.
Iuul, Stig. "The Danish Supreme Court
    Through 300 Years," ScStL, 6 (1962),
    163-83.
Jessel, Albert H. "Poor Man's Lawyer in
    Denmark," Law Quarterly Review, 7 (1891),
    176-83.
Jörgensen, Stig. "Towards Strict Liability
    in Tort," ScStL, 7 (1963), 25-59.
Kean, A. W. G. "Early Danish Criminal Law,"
    Journal of Comparative Legislation and In-
    ternational Law, 3d series, 19 (1937), 253-
    59.
Kemp, F. "Danish Law Rules Relating to
    Bankruptcy and Composition." Journal of
    the National Association of Referees in
    Bankruptcy, 5 (1931), 103-106.
Korst, Mogens. "Restrictions in Denmark,"
    Cartel, 8 (1958), 38-39.
Kruse, Frederick V. The Right of Property.
    Oxford; v. I, 1939. 495 p.; v. II, 1953.
    348 p.
Lando, Ole. "Methods and Policies Under-
    lying Decisions on International Conflict-
    of-Law Cases," AJCL, 15 (1966/67), 230-50
Lehmann, Julius, and H. Ree. Patent and
    Trade Mark Rights in Denmark: a Com-
    pendium of the Legal Regulations and
    Patent Office Practice in Force from
    1 Oct. 1936. 2d ed., Coph., 1936. 68 p.
Lundberg, K. The Danish Contracts of In-
    surance Act 1930. Coph., 1931. 54 p.
Møller, Heinrich A., and Harry Wolff. "Den-
    mark," in Handbook of Foreign Legal
    Procedure: Legal Relations in Europe.
    4th Year (Lond., 1924), 99-162.
Møller, J. Kiesby. "Greenland's New Judi-
    cial System," DO, 7 (1954), 733-38.
Munch-Petersen, Hans. The Danish Law of
    Settlement of Estates (Decedents and
    Bankrupts). Coph., 1915.
——. "The Social Aspects of Procedure
    from a European Point of View," Minne-
    sota Law Review, 11 (1927), 624-34.
——. "The System of Legal Education in
    Denmark," Journal of Public Teachers of
    Law, (1928), 31-32.
Nielsen, Thøger. "Working Expenses and

Working Losses: a Study of Taxation Law,"
ScStL, 4 (1960), 151-76.

Nørgaard, Carl A. "The Principle of Equality
in Danish Administrative Law," ScStL, 11
(1967), 241-68.

Orfield, Lester B. "Danish Law," in his, The
Growth of Scandinavian Law (Phila., 1953),
1-79.

——. "Danish Law," Miami Law Quarterly,
5 (1950/51), 1-39, 197-237.

Ostenfeld, George H. "Danish Courts of
Conciliation," ABAJ, 9 (1923), 747-48.

Ostenfeld, Th. "Prosecution of Infringers in
Denmark," Patent Office Society Journal,
35 (1953), 378-80.

Pedersen, Inger M. "Matrimonial Property
Law in Denmark," Modern Law Review,
28 (1965), 137-53.

Philip, Allan. American-Danish Private International Law. (Bilateral Studies in
Private International Law, no. 7). N.Y.,
1959. 125 p.

——. "The Application of Foreign Law in
Denmark," American Bar Association,
Section on International and Comparative
Law, Proceedings, 1960 (Chicago, 1961),
151-57.

——. "Commercial Arbitration in Denmark," Arbitration Journal, 13 (1958),
16-22.

——. "Danish Law," ScPP, III, 108-109.

——. "Denmark," in W. G. Friedmann, ed.
Legal Aspects of Foreign Investment (Boston, 1959), 200-208.

——. "Notes on Danish Judicial Decisions
(1939-1952)," Journal du droit international, 81 (1954), 480-505.

——. "Survey of Danish Judicial Decisions,"
Journal du droit international, 87 (1960),
462-69.

Rørdam, Kjeld. Treatises on the Baltcon-
charterparty. Coph., Lond., 1954. 198 p.

Sandström, Jan. "The Limitation of the
Stevedore's Liability," Journal of Business
Law (1962), 34-50.

Satz, Margot. "Enemy Legislation and Judgments in Denmark," Journal of Comparative Legislation and International Law, 31
(1949), 1-3.

Sindball, Kristian. History of the Danish
Law of Will. Coph., 1915.

Søndergaard, Jens. "Danish Legal Publications in English, French and German,"
ScStL, 7 (1963), 167-260.

Teisen, Axel. "Danish Judicial Code," University of Pennsylvania Law Review, 65
(1917), 543-70.

——. "Power to Declare Legislation Un-
constitutional in Denmark," ABAJ, 10
(1924), 792-94.

——. "Seisin Gewere," ABAJ, 1 (1915), 76-91.

Torfing, H. B. "The New Danish Trade Mark
Act 1960." Trademark Reporter, 52 (1962),
378-89.

van der Hude, Harry. "Short Survey of the
Provisions of the Danish Trade Mark Act,"
Trademark Reporter, 41 (1953), 151-55.

Von Eyben, William E. "The Attitude Towards Judicial Precedent in Danish and
Norwegian Courts," ScStL, 3 (1959), 53-86.

Waaben, Knud. "Criminal Responsibility and
the Quantum of Proof," ScStL, 9 (1965),
243-79.

Wheaton, Henry. "Public Law of Denmark,"
NoAmRev, 27 (1928), 285-99.

FINLAND

Beckman, Rudolf K. "Some Remarks on the
Handling of Maritime Law Suits and Ex-
tended Protests in Finland," in Liber
Amicorum of Congratulations to Algot
Bagge (Stock., 1956), 1-9.

Bellquist, Eric C. "Finland's Treaties for
the Peaceful Settlement of International
Disputes," AJIL, 26 (1932), 70-86.

Chydenius, Wilhelm. "Jurisprudence," in
Finland: the Country, Its People and Institutions (Hels., 1926), 476-78.

Ellilä, Tauno. "Summary Procedure of Dis-
tress According to Finnish Law," Rap-
ports Relatifs à la Finlande (Annales
academiae scientiarum fennicae B 69)
(Hels., 1950), 77-83.

Fachiri, Alexander P. "The Local Remedies
Rule in the Light of the Finnish Ships Arbitration," BYIL, 17 (1936), 19-31.

Finland, Laws, Statutes, etc. Currency Act;
Regulations for the Bank of Finland. Hels.,
1952. 23 p.; 1959. 24 p.

——. Local Self-Government in Finland,
and the Finnish Municipal Law. Ed. by
Suomen Maalaiskuntien Liitto, the Union
of Finnish Rural Municipalities, and Suomen Kaupunkiliitto, the Union of Finnish
Towns. Hels., 1954. 73 p.

——. Patent-Law of Finland. Hels., 1899.
31 p.

Franfeldt, George. The Finnish Law of Notes
and Drafts. Hels., 1916.

Godenhielm, Berndt. "The Legal Effects of
Patents as a Legislative Problem," ScStL,
2 (1958), 119-48.

Gripenberg, Alexandra. The Legal Position
of the Finnish Women. Hels., 1913. 18 p.

Helsingfors, Riksdagsbiblioteket. Yheisluettela
Suomen [Union list of foreign juridical
journals and serial publication in the research libraries of Finland. Prefatory

matter in Finnish, Swedish and English].
(Library of the Parliament Publications
1). Hels., 1956. 215 p.

Ignatius, Kaarlo. "Law and the Administration of Justice," in Finland: The Country,
Its People and Institutions (Hels., 1926),
270-85.

Jokela, Heikki. "Finnish Choice of Law Problems of East-West Trade," ScStL, 6 (1962),
185-200.

Kastari, Paavo. "The Constitutional Protection of Fundamental Rights in Finland,"
Tulane Law Review, 34 (1959/1960), 58-73.
——. "Guarantees of Fundamental Rights
and the Constitutional Principle," Jahr-
buch des Offentlichen Rechts der Gegen-
wart (1964), 438-52.

Kruse, Frederick V. "On the Rights to the
Sea and Its Subsoil: a Decision by the
Supreme Court of Finland," in Legal Essays: a Tribute to Frede Castberg (Oslo,
1963), 570-87.

Lang, J. N. Maritime Law of Finland. Hels.,
1915.

Mäkelä, Klaus. "Public Sense of Justice and
Judicial Practice," AcSoc, 10 (1966), 42-
67.

Mäkinen-Ollinen, Aune. "Juvenile Law in
Finland," the summary pp. 281-92 in
Huoriso-oikeus. Hels., 1954. 298 p.
Reprinted.

Mechelin, Leopold H. S. A Précis of the Public Law of Finland. Lond., 1889. 168 p.

Merikoski, V. "Legality in Administrative
Law: Some Trends in Evolution and Practical Experiences," ScStL, 4 (1960), 125-
49.

Muukkonen, P. J. "Formal Provisions and
the Elimination of Their Detrimental Consequences," ScStL, 5 (1961), 79-94.

Pulkkinen, A. "Law and the Administration
of Justice," in Atlas of Finland, 1925
(Hels., 1929), 296-98.

Reinikainen, Veikko. English, French and
German Literature on Finnish Law in
1860-1956 (Library of the Parliament
Publications, 2). Hels., 1957. 179 p.

Rowat, Donald C. "Finland's Defenders of
the Law: the Chancellor of Justice and
the Parliamentary Ombudsman," Canadian
Public Administration, 4 (1961), 316-25.

Saario, Voitto. "Control of the Constitution-
ality of Laws in Finland," AJCL, 12 (1963),
194-205.

Soukka, Paavo. "Criminal Justice in Finland,"
Justice of the Peace and Local Government
Review (1938), 682-83.

Suviranti, Antti. "Allocation of Taxable Income and Net Wealth Between Spouses,"
ScStL, 7 (1963), 151-66.

——. "Invisible Clauses in Collective Agreements," ScStL, 9 (1965), 177-215.

Zitting, Simo. "An Attempt to Analyze the
Owner's Legal Position," ScStL, 3 (1959),
227-47.

ICELAND

Clinton, George, Jr. "Icelandic Lawsuit of
the Eleventh Century," Lincoln Law Review, 2 (O 1928), 6-13.

Hermannsson, Halldór. The Ancient Laws of
Norway and Iceland (Islandica v. 4), Ithaca,
N.Y., 1911. 83 p.

Iceland. The Constitution of the Republic of
Iceland. Lond., Rey., 1948. 19 p.

Iceland, Laws, Statutes, etc. Act on the Iceland Bank of Development, Framkvaemda-
banki Islands, Passed by the Althing on
February 2, 1953; Translation. Rey.,
1953. 11 p.

Orfield, Lester B. "Icelandic Law," in his,
The Growth of Scandinavian Law (Phila.,
1953), 80-127. Also: Dickinson Law Review, 56 (1951), 42-87.

Repp, Thorleifr G. A Historical Treatise on
Trial by Jury, Wager of Law and Other Co-
ordinate Forensic Institutions, Formerly
in Use in Scandinavia and in Iceland. Edinburgh, 1832.

NORWAY

Andenaes, Johannes. "Choice of Punishment,"
ScStL, 2 (1958), 54-74.

Arnholm, Carl J. "The New Norwegian Legislation Relating to Parents and Children,"
ScStL, 3 (1959), 9-20.

Aubert, Vilhelm. "Conscientious Objectors
Before Norwegian Military Courts," in
Glendon Schubert, ed., Judicial Decision-
Making (Glencoe, Ill., 1963), 201-19.
——. "Price Control and Rationing: A
Pilot Study in the Sociology of Law," AJS,
58 (1953), 263-71.

Bahr, Henrik. "The Norwegian Gold Clause
Case," AJCL, 12 (1963), 1-20.

Boeg, Nils V., ed. Danish and Norwegian
Law: a General Survey. Coph., 1963.
251 p.

Castberg, Frede. Norway and the Western
Powers: a Study of Comparative Consti-
tutional Law. Oslo, 1957. 24 p.
——. "State and Individual in Norwegian
Public Law," Nord, 2 (1939), 284-304.

Eckhoff, Torstein. "Impartiality, Separation
of Powers, and Judicial Independence,"
ScStL, 9 (1965), 9-48.

Eckhoff, Torstein. "Norway," in W. Fried-
man, ed., Anti-Trust Laws: a Comparative Symposium (University of Toronto
Faculty of Law, Comparative Law Series,
v. 3) (Toronto, 1956), 281-307.

Flom, George T., ed. The Old Norwegian
General Law of the Gulathing According
to Codex Gl. k. S. 1154 folio. Urbana,
Ill., 1937. 204 p.

Gisvold, Sven S. "Norwegian Law," in ScPP,
III, 110-12.

Grevstad, Nicolay. "Norway's Conciliation
Tribunals," Journal of the American Judicial Society, 2 (1918), 5-8.

Haavind, T. "Bankruptcy Act of Norway,"
Journal of the National Association of
Referees in Bankruptcy, 5 (1931), 100-
101, 115.

Hallager, G. The Supreme Court of Norway,
1815-1915. v. 1, 1815-1863; v. 2, 1864-
1915. Kra., 1916.

Hambro, Edvard. "Some Remarks about the
Relation between Municipal Law and International Law in Norway," Nord. Tids.
for Int. Ret., 19 (1949), 3-22.

———. "The Theory of the Transformation
of International Law into National Law in
Norwegian Law," in Salo Engel, ed., Law,
State, and International Legal Order
(Knoxville, Tennessee, 1964), 97-106.

Hermannsson, Halldór. The Ancient Laws of
Norway and Iceland (Islandica, v. 4).
Ithaca, 1911. 83 p.

Larson, Laurence M. The Earliest Norwegian Laws, Being the Gulathing Law and
the Frostathing Law (Records of Civilization). N.Y., 1935. 451 p.

———. "Witnesses and Oath Helpers in Old
Norwegian Law," in C. H. Taylor and J.
L. LaMonte, eds., Anniversary Essays in
Medieval History by Students of Charles
Homer Haskins (Boston, 1929), 133-56.

Lassen, Birger S. "Collectivism and Individual Rights in Norwegian Copyright
Law," ScStL, 7 (1963), 79-106.

Leivestad, Trygve. "Custom as a Type of
Law in Norway," Law Quarterly Review,
58 (1938), 95-115, 266-86.

Meyer, P. Norman. "Norwegian Marine
Law," NSN (Ja 1960), 224, 227-28, 231.

Nieuwejaar, Otto. "Norwegian Laws Concerning Protection of Forests and the
Prevention of Forest Destruction," JFor,
29 (1931), 87-91.

Norway. The Constitution of Norway and
other Documents of National Importance.
Ed. by Tønnes Andenaes. Oslo, 1951.
71 p.; 2d rev. ed., Oslo, 1960. 62 p.

Norway, Laws, Statutes, etc. Compulsory

Arbitration in Norway; Translation of the
Norwegian Law Relating to Compulsory
Arbitration in Labor Disputes; Approved
June 9, 1916. Wash., 1917. 6 p.

———. The Game and Salmon Fishery of
Norway. Lond., 1877. 73 p.

———. Laws and Regulations of the Kingdom
of Norway Relative to Life-Saving Appli-
ances and Their Use on Ships. Wash., 1912.
15 p.

———. Laws Concerning the Diplomatic and
Consular Service of June 12, 1906; General
Norwegian Consular Instructions of July
24, 1906, with Commentary. Kra., 1906.
254 p.

———. Norway Income Tax Service. (Foreign
Tax Law Association, Income tax service,
N8). Deerpark, N.Y., 1955—.

———. Norwegian Laws Concerning Illegitimate Children. Intro. and tr. by Leifur
Magnusson. Wash., 1918. 37 p.

———. Norwegian Social and Labour Legislation; a Collection of Laws and Regulations. 2d ed., Oslo, 1953—; 3d ed., Oslo,
1954—.

———. Norwegian Social Insurance Laws.
Oslo, 1949. [Pagination varies].

———. Workers' Protection Act in Norway,
a Survey. Oslo, 1947. 58 p.

Norway, Ministry of Justice. Administration
of Justice in Norway: a Brief Summary.
Oslo, 1957. 145 p.

Norway, Sjøfartstraadet. Legal Status of
Seamen... Involuntary Service: a Review
of the Development of the Ancient Maritime Laws upon which are Based Existing
Maritime Law. Prepared and pub. by the
Maritime Commission of Norway. Wash.,
1910. 20 p.

Norwegian Law of Civil Procedure of August
13, 1915. Kra., 1915.

"OSA: Administrative Procedure in Norway,"
IRAS, 25 (1959), 67-78.

Orfield, Lester B. "Norwegian Law," in his,
The Growth of Scandinavian Law (Phila.,
1953), 128-226.

Oyen, E. "Commercial Arbitration in Norway," Arbitration Journal, 3 (1948), 164-
68.

Paasche, Fredrik. "A Recent Event in Norway and Some Points of International Law"
[The Act of Aug 14, 1943, promulgated by
the Quisling government], Norseman, 1
(1943), 329-30.

Selmer, Knut S. "Limitation of Damages According to the Circumstances of the 'Average Citizen'," ScStL, 5 (1961), 131-53.

Slaby, Steve M. The Labor Court in Norway.
Oslo, 1952. 38 p.

Smith, Reginald H. "Conciliation Procedure in the Administration of Justice in Norway," Monthly Labor Review, 22 (1926), 1199-1207.

Sollie, Finn. Courts and Constitutions: a Comparative Study of Judicial Review in Norway and the United States. Thesis (Ph.D.), Johns Hopkins University, 1957.

Storing, James A. "The Courts," in his, Norwegian Democracy (Boston, 1963), 144-62.

Taranger, Absalon. "The Meaning of the Words 'Odal' and 'Skeyting' in the Old Laws of Norway," in Paul Vinogrador, ed., Essays in Legal History (Lond., 1913).

Torgersen, Ulf. "The Role of the Supreme Court in the Norwegian Political System," in Glendon Schubert, ed., Judicial Decision-Making (Glencoe, Ill., 1963), 221-44.

von Eyben, William E. "The Attitude Towards Judicial Precedent in Danish and Norwegian Courts," ScStL, 3 (1959), 53-86.

Warbey, William. "The Land Shall Be Built on Law," in his, Look to Norway (Lond., 1945), 1-38.

Willett, Hjalmar, ed. Compilation of Norwegian Laws, etc. for the Use of Foreign Service Representatives, 1814-1953. Oslo, 1956. 1225 p.

Wold, Terje. "Legislation Promulgated by the Norwegian Government," Norseman, 1 (1943), 430-38.

SWEDEN

Adlercreutz, Axel. "Some Features of Swedish Collective Labor Law," Modern Law Review, 10 (1947), 137-58.

Agell, Anders. "Gaming Winnings, Debts of Honour, and Acts of Friendship," ScStL, 11 (1967), 9-35.

Amilon, Clas. Survey of the Swedish Penal System. Stock., 1961. 25 p.

——. The Youth Prison — a Method of Treating Young Offenders in Sweden. Stock., 1961. 34 p.

Anderman, Steven D. "The Swedish Justitieombudsman," AJCL, 11 (1962), 225-38.

Anrep, Edith. Some Features of Women's Status in Swedish Family Law. Stock., 1962. 7 p.

Arnholm, Carl J. "Olivecrona on Legal Rights: Reflections on the Concept of Rights," ScStL, 6 (1962), 9-31.

Bagge, A. "Civil and Commercial Arbitration Law; Arbitration Procedure in Sweden," ArbLJ, 1 (1937), 271-77.

Beckman, Nils. "Precedents and the Construction of Statutes," ScStL, 7 (1963), 9-24.

Bexelius, Alfred. "The Swedish Institution of the Justitieombudsman," IRAS, 27 (1961), 243-56.

Bolding, Per Olof. "Aspects of the Burden of Proof," ScStL, 4 (1960), 9-28.

Bolin, Bertil. "Sweden," in Wolfgang Friedmann, ed., Anti-Trust Laws: a Comparative Symposium (University of Toronto Faculty of Law, Comparative Law Series, v. 3) (Lond., 1956), 319-39.

Chydenius, Wilhelm. "The Swedish Lawbook of 1734: an Early Germanic Codification," Law Quarterly Review, 20 (1904), 377-91.

Eek, Hilding. "The Administration of Justice in Conflict Cases Involving Refugees," ScStL, 3 (1959), 21-52.

——. "Protection of News Sources by the Constitution," ScStL, 5 (1961), 9-26.

"The Effects of Swedish Legislation on Hours of Work," ILR, 13 (1926), 875-84.

Ekelöf, Per Olof. "Teleological Construction of Statutes," ScStL, 2 (1958), 75-118.

Fahlkrantz, Gustof E. "The Naemnd; or the Remnant of the Jury in Sweden," American Law Review, 22 (1888), 837-52.

Fehr, M. N. "Bankruptcy Law and Practice in Sweden," Journal of the National Association of Referees in Bankruptcy, 5 (1931), 102-103.

"A Few Points on the New Civil Procedure in Sweden," Irish Law Times, 82 (1948), 159-61.

Frykholm, Lars. "Swedish Legal Publications in English, French and German 1935-60," ScStL, 5 (1961), 153-217.

Garrison, L. K. "Legal Service for Low Income Groups in Sweden," ABAJ, 26 (1940), 215-20; 293-97.

Gellhorn, Walter. "The Swedish Justitieombudsman," Yale Law Journal, 75 (1965), 1-58.

Ginsburg, Ruth B. "Civil Procedure — Basic Features of the Swedish System," AJCL, 14 (1965), 336-45.

Ginsburg, Ruth B., and Anders Bruzelius. Civil Procedure in Sweden. The Hague, 1965. 491 p.

Grönfors, Kurt. "Apportionment of Damages in the Swedish Law of Torts," ScStL, 1 (1957), 93-122.

——. "Powers of Position in the Swedish Law of Agency," ScStL, 6 (1962), 95-128.

Hagander, J. "The Swedish Labor Court," ArbLJ, 1 (1937), 411-14.

Hellner, Jan. Exclusions of Risks and Duties Imposed on the Insured. A Study of Insurance Law. Stock., 1955. 67 p.

Hellner, Jan. "Legal Philosophy in the Handling of Tort Problems," ScStL, 2 (1958), 149-76.

———. "Tort Liability and Liability Insurance," ScStL, 6 (1962), 129-62.

Herlitz, Nils. "Swedish Administrative Law: Some Characteristic Features," ScStL, 3 (1959), 87-124.

Hjerner, Lars A. E. "The General Approach to Foreign Confiscations," ScStL, 2 (1958), 177-218.

Jackson, Robert H. "Swedish Contributions to Our Law," Pennsylvania Bar Association Quarterly, 15 (1944), 122-27.

Jägerskiöld, Stig. "The Immunity of State-Owned Vessels in Swedish Judicial Practice during World War II," AJIL, 42 (1948), 601-607.

———. "Roman Influence on Swedish Case Law in the 17th Century," ScStL, 11 (1967), 175-209.

———. "A Swedish Case on the Jurisdiction of States over Foreigners," AJIL, 41 (1947), 909-11.

———. "Swedish State Officials and Their Position under Public Law and Labour Law," ScStL, 4 (1960), 101-24.

———. "Tyrannicide and the Right of Resistance, 1792-1809," ScStL, 8 (1964), 67-103.

Karlgren, Hjalmar. "Usage and Statute Law," ScStL, 5 (1961), 39-77.

Kinberg, Olov. "Obligatory Psychiatric Examination of Certain Classes of Accused Persons," Journal of Criminal Law and Criminology, 2 (1912), 858-67.

Lagergren, Gunnar. Delivery of the Goods and Transfer of Property and Risk in the Law of Sale. Stock., 1954. 151 p.

———. "The Preparatory Proceeding and the Hearing-in-Chief in Sweden," Irish Law Times, 82 (1948), 165-67.

Ljungman, Seve. "Swedish Law," ScPP, III, 95-107.

Lundstedt, Vilhelm. "Law and Justice: a Criticism of the Method of Justice," in Interpretations of Modern Legal Philosophies: Essays in Honor of Roscoe Pound (N.Y., 1947), 450-83.

———. Legal Thinking Revised: My Views on Law. Stock., 1956. 420 p.

———. "The Relation Between Law and Equity," Tulane Law Review, 25 (1950), 59-69.

Maktos, J. "Arbitration Between the United States and Sweden relating to the Swedish Motor Ships 'Kronprins Gustaf Adolf' and 'Pacific'," George Washington Law Review, 1 (1932), 105-108.

Malström, Åke. "Children's Welfare in Family Law," ScStL, 1 (1957), 123-36.

———. "The Legal Status of International Non-Governmental Organizations in Sweden," International Associations, 8 (1956), 501-502, 505.

———. "Matrimonial Property Law in Sweden," in Matrimonial Property Law (Lond., 1955), 410-29.

"New Swedish Legislation Concerning Illegitimate Children," Journal of Criminal Law and Criminology, 11 (1920/21), 284-88.

Nial, Håkon. American-Swedish Private International Law. N.Y., 1965. 111 p.

———. "Arbitration Law and Practice in Sweden," ArbLJ, 1 (1946), 320-27.

Olivecrona, Karl H. K. "Is a Sociological Explanation of Law Possible?" Theoria, 14 (1948), 167-207.

———. Law as Fact. Coph., Lond., 1939. 222 p.

———. "Law as Fact," in Interpretations of Modern Legal Philosophies: Essays in Honor of Roscoe Pound (N.Y., 1947), 542-57.

———. "The Legal Theories of Axel Hägerström and Vilhelm Lundstedt," ScStL, 3 (1959), 58-62.

———. "Realism and Idealism: Some Reflections on the Cardinal Point in Legal Philosophy," New York University Law Review, 26 (1951), 120-31.

O'Neill, Anna A. "United States-Sweden Arbitration, Relating to Motorships 'Kronprins Gustav Adolf' and 'Pacific'," AJIL, 26 (1932), 720-34.

Orfield, Lester B. "Swedish Law," in his, The Growth of Scandinavian Law (Phila., 1953), 227-326.

Palmgren, Bo. "The Rule Against Retroactive Criminal Legislation: Reflections Based on an Early Swedish Case," ScStL, 5 (1961), 95-110.

Pineus, Kaj. "From an Average Adjuster's Practice," Arkiv for Sjørett, 1 (1953), 445-64. Addendum in v. 2 (1955), 160-62.

———. "Sources of Maritime Law Seen from a Swedish Point of View," Tulane Law Review, 30 (1955), 85-98.

———. "To the Question of Competency of the Average Adjuster," in Liber Amoricum of Congratulations to Algot Bagge (Stock., 1956), 173-79.

Pontoppidan, Nils. "A Mature Experiment: the Scandinavian Experience," AJCL, 9 (1960), 344-49.

Robbins, James J. "The Jurisdiction of the Labor Court in Sweden," Illinois Law Review, 35 (1940), 396-408.

Rodhe, Knut. "Adjustment of Contracts on Account of Changed Conditions," ScStL, 3 (1959), 151-98.

Sandberg, Lars G. "Antitrust Policy in Sweden," Antitrust Bulletin, 9 (1964), 535-58.

Schlesinger, Rudolf B. "Note on the Swedish Code of Civil Procedure," in Comparative Law: Cases and Materials (Brooklyn, 1950), 552 p.

Schmidt, Folke. "Construction of Statutes," ScStL, 1 (1957), 155-98.

——. The Law of Labour Relations in Sweden. Cambridge, Mass.; Stock., 1962. 344 p.

——. "Nationality and Domicile in Swedish Private International Law," International Law Quarterly, 4 (1951), 39-52.

Schmidt, Folke, and Henry Heineman. "Enforcement of Collective Bargaining Agreements in Swedish Law," University of Chicago Law Review, 14 (1947), 184-99.

Schmidt, Folke, and Stig Strömholm. Legal Values in Modern Sweden. Stock., 1964; Totowa, N.J., 1965. 87 p.

Sellin, J. Thorsten. Recent Penal Legislation in Sweden. Stock., 1947. 70 p.

Strahl, Ivar. Probation and Conditional Sentence in Sweden. Stock., 1961. 28 p.

——. "Tort Liability and Insurance," ScStL, 3 (1959), 199-226.

Strömholm, Stig. "Bona Fides in the Swedish Law of Property," AJCL, 12 (1963), 41-60.

Sussman, Howard A. "Spouses and Their Property under Swedish Law," AJCL, 12 (1963), 553-89.

"Sweden" [Law acquisitions], LCQJ, 14 (1957), 234-36.

Sweden. The Law of the Westgoths according to the Manuscript of Aeskil. Rock Island, 1906. 90 p.

Sweden. The Constitution of Sweden (Documents Published by the Royal Ministry for Foreign Affairs, new series II:4). Stock., 1954. 100 p.

Sweden, Laws, Statutes, etc. Corporation Laws of Sweden. St. Petersburg, 1962. [Loose-leaf]

——. Draft Law on Copyright in Literary and Artistic Works Proposed by the Swedish Government from the Official Swedish Text. Wash., 1960. 22 p.

——. Draft Law on Rights in Photographic Pictures Proposed by the Swedish Government, from the Official Swedish Text. Wash., 1960. 6 p.

——. Inheritance and Gift Tax Laws of Sweden. Prepared in the Office of the General Councel for the Dept. of the Treasury. Wash., 1938. 23 p.

——. The Principal Swedish Laws, Ordinances, Decrees and Official Instructions Relating to the Protection of the Industrial Property. Stock., 1945. 48 p.

——. Royal Decree Containing Certain Regulations Promulgated under the Law Regarding an Alien's Right to Reside in the Kingdom. Stock., November 11, 1927. 13 p.

——. Royal Ordinance Concerning the Consular Service of Sweden Given at the Palace of Stockholm Sept., 24, 1906 and General Instructions for the Performance of the Consular Office. Stock., 1909. 388 p.

——. Ship's Command Ordinance; Ordinance of June 12, 1936 (no. 315) Concerning the Command of Swedish Merchant Vessels, etc., with Amendments; Additional Provision and Exceptions in Force on Sept. 1, 1958 (Documents Published by the Royal Ministry for Foreign Affairs, new series II:12). Stock., 1958. 48 p.

——. Statute Book for Legations and Consulates. Stock., 1931. 369 p.; 1937, 396 p.

——. The Stock Corporation Act of 1944. Stock., 1949. 183 p.

——. The Swedish Banking Companies Act, 1955. Stock., 1958. 71 p.

——. Swedish Merchant Seamen Act, 1952 (Documents Published by the Royal Ministry for Foreign Affairs, new series II:3). Stock., 1953. 37 p.

——. Swedish Seamen's Hours of Work Act 1948 (Documents Published by the Royal Ministry for Foreign Affairs, new series II:6). Stock., 1954 [1955], 121 p.

——. Swedish Seamen's Unemployment Relief Ordinance 1950. Royal Ordinance of June 29th, 1950 (SFS Nr 473) Concerning Relief to Swedish Seamen During Unemployment in Foreign Ports (Documents Published by the Royal Ministry for Foreign Affairs, new series II:7). Stock., 1955. 8 p.

——. Translation from Swedish of the Law of June 20, 1918, re Measures against the Spreading of Venereal Diseases. Hels., 1938.

——. Translation of the New Swedish Customs Tariff Law, to Come into Force from 1st December, 1911; with a Comparison of the New and Existing Rates of Duty. Presented to both houses of Parliament by command of His Majesty. Lond., 1911. 86 p.

——. Laws, Statutes, etc., 1907— (Gustavus V). Law, Dated June 18th, 1937, Concerning Advance Payments of Maintenance Contributions for Children in Sweden (League of Nations, Secretariat, Child Welfare Information Center, Legislative and Administrative Series, no. 36). Geneva, 1938.

——. Royal Decree of April 8th, 1938, Governing the Care and Treatment of Persons

Sentenced to Detention in a Prison for
Youthful Offenders (League of Nations,
Secretariat, Child Welfare Information
Center, Legislative and Administrative
series, no. 72). Geneva, 1938. 1 p.
——. Royal Decree of June 4th, 1937,
Concerning Government Contributions to
the Operating Expenses of Establishments
for Children Suffering from Psychopathic
and Nervous Disturbances in Sweden
(League of Nations, Secretariat, Child
Welfare Information Center, Legislative
and Administrative series, no. 62). Ge-
neva, 1938. 1 p.
——. Royal Ordinance, Dated June 11th,
1937, Concerning Maternity Allowances in
Sweden (League of Nations, Secretariat,
Child Welfare Information Center, Legis-
lative and Administrative series, no. 31).
Geneva, 1937. 1 p.
——. Law on Child Welfare Contributions

in Sweden, Dated June 18th, 1937 (League
of Nations, Secretariat, Child Welfare Information Center, Legislative and Administrative series, no. 35). Geneva, 1937. 1 p.
Sweden, Tulltaxekommitten, 1952. Revision
of the Swedish Customs Tariff, as Proposed by the Swedish Customs Tariff Commission. Stock., 1957. 67 p.
Thompson, Seymour. "Swedish Law Reform,"
American Law Review, 38 (1904), 388-401.
Thornstedt, Hans. "The Principle of Legality
and Teleological Construction of Statutes
on Criminal Law," ScStL, 4 (1960), 211-46.
Tiberg, Hugo. "Bailees' and Lessees' Protection Against Third Parties Under Swedish Law," ScStL, 9 (1965), 217-42.
Uggla, Claes. "Report of the Swedish Trademark Law Committee, A Summary,"
Trademark Reporter, 48 (1958), 1167-72.
Wetter, J. Gillis. "Swedish Anti-Trust Law,"
AJCL, 10 (1961), 19-52.

POLITICAL SCIENCE

INTRODUCTION

Political studies were generally slow to develop in Scandinavia. Only in Sweden was noteworthy literature developed prior to the 1950's, and that literature was fundamentally historical. Nothing of lasting merit was produced in Denmark, and the standard work on Norwegian politics was a political history by a Swede from the University of Uppsala. The Northern Countries are record-keeping societies, and the data available for analysis are relatively plentiful. Thorough election statistics maintained throughout this century have made possible fine recent ecological analysis of voting behavior, and the existence of a party press has permitted interesting work in content analysis. Major projects have been undertaken on the basis of survey research. Many of the most obvious gaps in the literature of these countries are now being filled either by well-trained professionals, by research teams, or by means of M.A. theses. Moreover, in recent years three of the parliaments have sponsored commemorative series in the form of solid, multi-authored histories of political development (in Denmark, six volumes in 1949; in Norway, four volumes in 1964; in Sweden, five volumes in 1966). However, despite the recent surge, the literature available in the native languages remains weak.

The political behavior research now being conducted in Finland, Norway, and Sweden is widely acclaimed, and much of the new publication is in English. Some of the work in political sociology has appeared in *Acta Sociologica*. Scandinavian political scientists recently decided to begin a series of English-language annuals containing both research articles and accounts of political developments. The series is entitled *Scandinavian Political Studies;* volume I was published in 1966. The only good annotated bibliography, Åke Sandler and Ernst Ekman's *Government, Politics, and Law in the Scandinavian Countries* (1954) is brief and badly out-of-date. For a superb overview of recent research, see Stein Rokkan and Henry Valen, "Parties, Elections and Political Behaviour in the Northern Countries: a Review of Recent Research (1960),"

There is a very good, textbook-like introduction to Scandinavian government, Nils Andrén's *Government and Politics in the Nordic Countries* (1964). For a general background, see *The Scandinavian States and Finland: a Political and Economic Survey* (1951), published by the Royal Institute of International Affairs. There is no English-language volume which surveys the twentieth-century domestic political history of any of the five countries. Furthermore, little has been written in English on the generally dominant socialist parties: there is no book on any of them. Nor is there any good description of the conduct of an election campaign in the style of Britain's Nuffield Studies. There are to date very few comparative studies in Scandinavia, but one might predict that first-class comparative work will appear in the next few years, most likely on parties, recruitment, and voting behavior. For a comparative treatment of party systems, see Dankwart Rustow's article, "Scandinavia: Working Multiparty Systems" (1956). If interested in political leadership, one should consult the biographies listed in this bibliography under History. Entries on organized labor will be found under Economics.

With the exception of articles on the ombudsman, curiously little has been published on Denmark in English. There is a good, recent, textbook-like coverage by Kenneth Miller, *Government and Politics in Denmark* (1968). Noteworthy are two long, unpublished Ph.D. dissertations: Gerald McDaniel's *The Danish Unicameral Parliament* (1963) and William Laux's *Interest Groups in Danish Politics* (1963). On Iceland, there is one book to recommend: Donald Nuechterlein's *Iceland, Reluctant Ally* (1961). It provides considerable information on Icelandic party politics.

There is no English-language survey volume on the government and politics of Finland, but those able to read Swedish will be pleased by Jaakko Nousiainen's very substantial *Finlands politiska system* (1966). There are, however, numerous worthwhile journal articles. One may recommend with enthusiasm the work of Erik Allardt, Göran von Bonsdorff, Jan-Magnus Jansson, Sven Lindman, Lolo Krusius-Ahrenberg, Jaakko Nousiainen, Pertti Pesonen, and the American scholar Marvin Rintala, and there are also some fine articles by other scholars. The Finnish Political Science Association published a brief collection of articles under the title *Democracy in Finland* (1960), probably the best introduction to Finnish political life available. Those seeking historical background may prefer to begin by reading the political sections of John Wuorinen's excellent *A History of Finland* (1965). Some may wish to consult Raymond Kaaret's dissertation, *The Government of Finland Since 1947* (1958). One of the very interesting and distinguishing factors in Finnish politics is the existence of a large Communist Party. Most of the articles on this party are commendable and complementary; one might well begin with the recent chapter by Bengt Matti (1966). In addition to the articles, note John Hodgson's fine book, *Communism in Finland* (1967). There is material relevant to politics to be found under History and under International Relations. Subsequent to the completion of this bibliography, Martti Julkunen and Anja Lehikoinen published their compilation for the Institute of Political

History of the University of Turku, *A Select List of Books and Articles in English, French and German on Finnish Politics in the 19th and 20th Century* (1967). Organized largely around major events and periods, it is a particularly useful compendium.

For Norway, there is a very good paperback introduction: James Storing's *Norwegian Democracy* (1963). There is also a superb volume based on survey research in the Stavanger area, *Political Parties in Norway* (1964) by Henry Valen, and Ulf Torgersen is of the highest quality. An interesting theoretical book is Harry Eckstein's *Division and Cohesion in Democracy: a Study of Norway* (1966). There are five American dissertations on political movements and parties, three of which are based on post-World War II data. Gaylon Greenhill's *The Norwegian Agrarian Party: a Case Study of a Single Interest Party* (1962); Sven Groennings' *Cooperation Among Norway's Non-Socialist Political Parties* (1962), which is being developed into an updated book to be entitled *Coalition Politics in Norway;* and the sociologist Sverre Monsen's *Social Structure and Political Change in a Multi-party System* (1967). A fine dissertation focusing in large part on voter attitudes is Allen Barton's *Sociological and Psychological Problems of Economic Planning in Norway* (1957). It is no mistake that linguist Einar Haugen's *Language Conflict and Language Planning: the Case of Modern Norwegian* (1966) is listed here. Language controversy has been of great importance in Norwegian politics, and Haugen's treatment of the political aspects of the controversy is excellent.

For Sweden, there are two good introductions: Nils Andren's *Modern Swedish Government* (1961), and Dankwart Rustow's *The Politics of Compromise.* On Parliament there are also two books: Elis Haastad's *The Parliament of Sweden* (1957), and Douglas Verney's *Parliamentary Reform in Sweden 1866-1921* (1957). Herbert Tingsten's publications, beginning with his now classic *Policial Behavior* (1937), have been of major significance, and the writings of Eric Bellquist, Neil Elder, Gunnar Heckscher, and Nils Stjernquist are also very good. Noteworthy too is the Jörgen Westerståhl and C. G. Janson study of *The Political Press* (1958). There is only one unpublished American dissertation on post-World War II political parties, Donald Hancock's *Opposition Parties in Post-War Sweden: Dilemma and Prospects* (1966), but Robert Eckelberry's *The Swedish System of Proportional Representation* (1965) also bears closely on this subject. Only for Sweden is there much literature on local government, and only in Sweden have American dissertations been produced on the subject, for example, most recently: Bertil Hanson, *Stockholm Municipal Politics* (1959) and Donald Niemi, *Sweden's Municipal Consolidation Reforms* (1966). Those interested in this topic should also see Roland Artle's *The Structure of the Stockholm Economy: Toward a Framework for Projecting Metropolitan Community Development* (1965).

In the last few years there has been world-wide interest in the institution of the ombudsman, the official who serves as a check against abuse of administrative power. Originally Swedish, the position has been created in Denmark, Finland, Norway, and other countries. There are already approximately fifty articles, pamphlets, and books on Scandinavia's ombudsmen. Those seeking an introduction to this office will find chapters on the ombudsman in each of these countries in *The Ombudsman* (1965), edited by Donald Rowat. Walter Gellhorn's *Ombudsmen and Others* (1966), which also contains country chapters, complements the Rowat volume. So do the five articles on the Scandinavian ombudsman in the May, 1968, issue of *The Annals of the American Academy of Political and Social Science*. This issue bears the title: *The Ombudsman or Citizen's Defender: a Modern Institution*.

Materials relevant to Government and Politics appear under every other heading in this bibliography, particularly under Economics, History, International Relations, Law, and Sociology. The user is hereby reminded that entries in this bibliography are normally listed only once.

SCANDINAVIA

Abrahamsen, Samuel. "Democratic Government in Scandinavia," Social Studies, 43 (1952), 335-38.

Andenaes, Johannes. "The Development of Political Democracy in Scandinavia," in J. A. Lauwerys, ed., Scandinavian Democracy (Coph., N.Y., 1958), 93-106.

Andersson, Ingvar. "Early Democratic Traditions in Scandinavia," in J. A. Lauwerys, ed., Scandinavian Democracy (Coph., N.Y., 1958), 69-92.

Andrén, Nils. Government and Politics in the Nordic Countries. Stock., 1964. 241 p.

——. Modern Nordic Government: a Brief Survey of the Governments of Denmark, Finland, Iceland, Norway and Sweden. Stock., 1960. 105 p. Mimeographed.

Arneson, Ben A. The Democratic Monarchies of Scandinavia. 2d ed., N.Y., 1949. 294 p.; 1st ed., 1939. 244 p.

Bellquist, Eric C. "Government and Politics in Northern Europe," in David Fellman, ed., Post-war Governments of Europe (Gainesville, Fla., 1946), 241-404.

——. "Government and Politics in Northern Europe: an Account of Recent Developments," JP, 8 (1946), 362-91.

——. "Political and Economic Conditions in the Scandinavian Countries," FPR, 24 (1948), 50-63.

Birke, Wolfgang. European Elections by Direct Suffrage (European Aspects: a Collection of Studies Relating to European Integration; series C: Studies on Politics, no. 5) Leiden, 1961. 124 p.

Bull, Edvard. "The Labor Movement in Scandinavia," ScPP, II, 853-63.

Castles, Francis G. "Scandinavia," in his, Pressure Groups and Political Culture (Lond., N.Y., 1967), 60-72.

Cole, George D. H. "Scandinavia and Finland," in his, Socialism and Fascism, 1931-1939 (A History of Socialist Thought, v. 5) (Lond., N.Y., 1960), 170-86.

Dahl, Robert A., and Charles E. Lindblom. Politics, Economics and Welfare; Planning and Politico-Economic Systems Resolved into Basic Social Processes. N.Y., 1953. 557 p.

Dasgupta, Ramaprasad. "Scandinavia: Denmark, Sweden and Norway," in his, A Study in Hindu and European Political Systems (Calcutta, 1958), 102-23.

de Lespinasse, Paul F. The Monarchical Institution in Constitutional Democracy. Thesis (Ph.D.), Johns Hopkins University, 1966. 309 p.

Dernby, Karl G. "The Scandinavian Bolsheviki," ASR, 6 (1918), 277-82.

Devlin, Kevin. The Prospects for West European Communism (Columbia University Research Institute on Communist Affairs Pamphlet). N.Y., 1967. 36 p.

Elder, Neil C. M. "Parliamentary Government in Scandinavia," ParAf, 13 (1959), 363-73. Partially reprinted as "Party Systems in Scandinavia," in Roy C. Macridis and Bernard E. Brown, eds., Comparative Politics: Notes and Readings (Homewood, Ill., 1961), 210-16.

Fischer, Alfred J. "Reform Socialism in Scandinavia," CR, 185 (1954), 223-27.

Friis, Henning K. "Scandinavian Democracy," in Henning Friis, ed., Scandinavia Between East and West (Ithaca, 1950), 1-22.

Herlitz, Nils, and John H. Wuorinen. "The Government and Politics of the Scandinavian Countries," in James T. Shotwell, ed., Governments of Continental Europe (N.Y., 1940), 939-75.

Hermens, Ferdinand A. "Population Representation in the Scandinavian Countries," in his, Democracy or Anarchy? A Study of Proportional Representation (Modern Politics, a Series of Studies in Politics and Political Philosophy, v. 1). (South Bend, Ind., 1941), 348-55.

Hovde, Brynjolf J. "Democracy in Scandinavian Life," AJES, 10 (1950/51), 85-86.

Jacobs, Walter D., and Harold Zink. "The Governments of Norway and Sweden," in their, Modern Governments, 3d ed. (Princeton, N.J., 1966), 471-97. Previous editions by Harold Zink alone, 1958 and 1962.

Joesten, Joachim. "The Nazis in Scandinavia," FA, 15 (1937), 720-28.

Kalijarvi, Thorsten V. "Scandinavian Nations and Finland," in Joseph S. Roucek, ed., Governments and Politics Abroad (N.Y., 1947), 319-41.

Krosby, H. Peter. "Is Social Democracy Dying in Scandinavia?" Progressive (Ap 1968), 27-30.

Laidler, Harry W. Labor Governments at Work, British, Scandinavian, Australasian. N.Y., 1948. 23 p.

Lauwerys, Joseph A., ed. Scandinavian Democracy: Development of Democratic Thought and Institutions in Denmark, Norway, and Sweden. N.Y., Coph., 1958. 437 p.

Lehtinen, Rauno. "Bibliography of Scandinavian Political Science, 1960-1964," ScPolSt, 1 (1966), 288-336.

Mason, John Brown. "Constitutional Government: the Scandinavian Tradition," in Fritz Morstein-Marx, ed., Foreign Governments (N.Y., 1949), 278-306.

Nilson, Sten S. "The Political Parties," in J. A. Lauwerys, ed., Scandina-

vian Democracy (Coph., N.Y., 1958), 107-25.

Ogg, Frederic A., and Harold Zink. "The Governments of Norway and Sweden," in Fritz Morstein-Marx, ed., Foreign Governments (N.Y., 1949), 762-90.

Ronhovde, A. G. "The Effects of the War on the Governments of Norway and Sweden," in Harold Zink and Taylor Cole, eds., Government in Wartime Europe (Lond., 1941), 205-19.

Royal Institute of International Affairs. The Scandinavian States and Finland: a Political and Economic Survey. Lond., 1951. 312 p.

Rustow, Dankwart A. "Scandinavia: Working Multiparty Systems," in Sigmund Neumann, ed., Modern Political Parties (Chicago, 1956), 169-93.

Simon, Sir Ernest D. The Smaller Democracies. Lond., 1939. 191 p.

Spencer, Richard C. "Unified Representative Authority in the Scandinavian Governments," JP, 4 (1942), 361-82.

Stewart, Michael. "Scandinavia," in his, Modern Forms of Government: a Comparative Study (Lond., 1959), 171-84.

Teisen, Axel. "Law Making Bodies of Denmark, Sweden and Norway," Case and Comment, 23 (1917), 635-38.

Tuominen, Arro. "The Northern Countries and Communism," Norseman, 12 (1954), 217-29.

"The Underground Press of France, Belgium, Norway, Denmark and the Netherlands," LCQJ, 34 (1945, no. 2), 3-29.

Verney, Douglas V. The Analysis of Political Systems. Lond., 1959; Glencoe, Ill., 1960. 239 p.

von Bonsdorff, Göran. Studier Rörande den Moderna Liberalismen i de Nordiska Länderna. English Summary (Lund, 1954), 237-52.

Westerståhl, Jörgen. "Some General Observations on Scandinavian Democracy," in J. A. Lauwerys, ed., Scandinavian Democracy (Coph., N.Y., 1958), 400-10.

POLITICAL BEHAVIOR

Allardt, Erik, and Richard F. Tomasson. "Stability and Strains in Scandinavian Student Politics," Daedalus, 97 (Winter 1968), 156-65.

Rokkan, Stein. Approaches to the Study of Political Participation (Christian Michelsen Institute Reprint no. 210). Bergen, 1962. 172 p. Reprint from Acta Sociologica, 6 (1962).

Rokkan, Stein. Ideological Consistency and
    Party Preference: a Note on Findings
    from a Seven-Country Survey of Teach-
    ers' Attitudes. Bergen, N.Y., 1956. 11
    p. Mimeographed.
——. Party Identification and Opinions on
    Domestic and International Policy. Cam-
    bridge, Mass., 1955. 51 p. Mimeo-
    graphed.
——. "Party Preferences and Opinion
    Patterns in Western Europe: a Com-
    parative Analysis," ISSB, 7 (1955), 575-
    95. Includes Norway and Sweden.
——. "Research on Elections and the So-
    ciology of Politics in the Northern Coun-
    tries," Sociological Inquiry, 31 (1961),
    3-22.
Rokkan, Stein, and Henry Valen. "Parties,
    Elections and Political Behaviour in the
    Northern Countries: a Review of Recent
    Research," Politische Forschung, v. 17
    in Schriften des Instituts für politische
    wissenschaft an der Freien Universität
    Berlin (Köln, 1960), 103-36, 237-49.
    Christian Michelsen Institute Reprint no.
    202.

PUBLIC ADMINISTRATION

Anderson, Stanley V. "The Ombudsman:
    Public Defender Against Maladministra-
    tion," Public Affairs Report (1965), 4 p.
——. "The Scandinavian Ombudsman,"
    ASR, 52 (1964), 403-409.
Asher, Charles S. "The Grievance Man or
    Ombudsmania," Public Administration
    Review, 27 (1967), 174-78.
Gellhorn, Walter. Ombudsmen and Others:
    Citizens' Protectors in Nine Countries.
    Cambridge, Mass., 1966. 448 p. In-
    cludes: "Denmark," 5-47; "Finland,"
    48-90; "Norway," 154-93; "Sweden," 194-
    255.
Hurwitz, Stephan. "The Experience of Par-
    liamentary Commissioners in Certain
    Scandinavian Countries," background pa-
    per for UN Seminar on Judicial and Other
    Remedies Against the Illegal Exercise or
    Abuse of Administrative Authority (UNDoc
    TE 326/1 [40-47]). N.Y., 1959. 28 p.
    Mimeographed.
——. "The Scandinavian Ombudsman,"
    Political Science (Wellington, New Zea-
    land), 12 (1960), 121-42. Reprint of 1959
    UN background paper.
Meyer, Poul. "The Administrative Aspects
    of the Constitutions of the Northern Coun-
    tries," Nordisk Administrativt Tidskrift,
    41 (1960), 254-65.

——. Administrative Organization: a
    Comparative Study of the Organization of
    Public Administration. Lond., Coph.,
    1957. 322 p.
——. "The Development of Public Admin-
    istration in the Scandinavian Countries
    Since 1945," IRAS, 26 (1960), 135-46.
Moss, John. "Public Assistance Administra-
    tion in Scandinavia," Justice of the Peace,
    95 (1931), 151, 168.
Murray, C. H. "The Grievance Man: In
    Scandinavia," Administration, 8 (1960),
    231-37.
Rowat, Donald C., ed. The Ombudsman:
    Citizen's Defender. Lond., Toronto,
    Stock., 1965. 348 p.
——. "The Parliamentary Ombudsman,"
    in Roy C. Macridis and Bernard E. Brown,
    eds., Comparative Politics: Notes and
    Readings (rev. ed., Homewood, Ill., 1964),
    470-80.
——. "The Parliamentary Ombudsman:
    Should the Scandinavian Scheme Be Trans-
    planted?" IRAS (1962), 399-405. Re-
    printed in Nimrod Raphaeli, ed., Read-
    ings in Comparative Public Administration
    (Boston, 1967), 135-48.
Sawyer, Geoffrey. Ombudsmen. Melbourne,
    1964. 42 p.
United Nations. Remedies Against the Abuse
    of Administrative Authority — Selected
    Studies (UNDoc ST/TAO/HR/19). 1964.
    Reprint of papers on the Ombudsman in
    Denmark and Sweden by Alfred Bexelius,
    E. Holmberg, Björn Kjellin, Stephan Hur-
    witz. N.Y., 1964.
Utley, Thomas E. Occasion for Ombudsman.
    Lond., 1961. 160 p.

LOCAL GOVERNMENT

Dahlgaard, Bertel. "Local Government," in
    J. A. Lauwerys, ed., Scandinavian De-
    mocracy (Coph., N.Y., 1958), 174-84.
Marshall, A. H. "Local Government in Swe-
    den and Denmark," Journal of African
    Administration, 9 (1957), 37-41.
Peel, Roy V. "Home Rule in Scandinavian
    Local Government," Minnesota Munici-
    palities (1940), 155-57.
——. "Lessons from Scandinavian Cities,"
    Public Management (1936), 102-106.
——. "Local Government in Scandinavia,"
    National Municipal Review, 25 (1936),
    528-34.
Williams, John I. "Coordinated Urban
    Transport Planning in Scandinavia,"
    Traffic Engineering, 29 (1959, no. 5),
    14-16+.

Andersen, K. B. "Political and Cultural Development in 19th Century Denmark," in J. A. Lauwerys, ed., Scandinavian Democracy (Coph., N.Y., 1958), 150-59.

Andersen, Niels. "Denmark Since Liberation," SoCo, 12 (1948), 323-25.

Börde, Ketil. The Conservative Thought of Kirkegaard. Thesis (M.A.), University of California, Berkeley, 1957, 99 p.

Campion, Gilbert F. M. C., and D. W. S. Lidderdale. "Denmark," in European Parliamentary Procedure: a Comparative Handbook (Lond., 1953), 54-70.

Christensen, Arthur E. Politics and Crowd-Morality: a Study in the Philosophy of Politics. Lond., 1915. 270 p.

Colby, R. "Denmark's Dilemma," Quarterly Review (1957), 417-29.

"A Democratic Election in Denmark," National Municipal Review, 32 (1943), 345-46.

"Denmark Today: Political and Economic Problems" [by A. H. H.], WT, 3 (1947), 477-85.

"Denmark's Antipolitical Union," Canadian Bar Review, 6 (1928), 296-97.

Engelstoft, Poul. "The Return of the Peasant," ASR, 17 (1929), 15-23.

Fischer, Alfred J. "Interim Solution in Denmark," CR, 168 (1945), 348-53.

Glans, Ingemar. "Denmark: the 1964 Folketing Election," ScPolSt, 1 (1966), 231-36.

Glascow, George. "The Easter Crisis in Denmark," NewEur, 15 (1920), 11-16.

Goldmark, Josephine. "Democracy in Action," Part I of Democracy in Denmark (Wash., 1936), 187 p.

Goslin, Ryllis C. A. Changing Governments Amid New Social Problems: a Survey of the Governments of France, Germany, Italy, Russia, and Denmark (Headline Books, no. 11). 2d ed., N.Y., 1939. 64 p.

Gudme, Sten. Denmark: Hitler's "Model Protectorate." N.Y., Lond., 1942. 165 p.

Henningsen, Sven, and Erik Rasmussen. "Political Research in Scandinavia, 1960-65: Denmark," ScPolSt, 1 (1966), 254-57.

Hoover, G. E. "Learning from the Danes," Freeman, 2 (1952), 841-42.

"Internal Politics in Denmark," DFOJ (1946, no. 1), 10-11.

Johnson, Howard A. "Kierkegaard and Politics," ASR, 43 (1955), 246-54.

Larsen, Elkjaer. "How Denmark is Governed," ScPP, III, 67-76.

Lavesen, Holger. "Where Every Vote is Open" [Functions of the Supreme Court], DFOJ, no. 61 (1968), 9-11.

Lewis, Harold O. "Danish Social Democracy," AmPers, 1 (1947), 567-74.

McDaniel, Gerald R. The Danish Unicameral Parliament. Thesis (Ph.D.), University of California, Berkeley, 1963.

——. "No One Misses the Landsting, but ..." ASR, 49 (1961), 266-71.

Manniche, Peter. Living Democracy in Denmark. Coph., 1952. 237 p.

Miller, Kenneth E. "The Danish Electoral System," ParAf, 18 (1964/1965), 71-81.

——. Government and Politics in Denmark. Boston, 1968. 308 p.

Moritzen, Julius. "Denmark's Frontier and Minority Problem," CH, 10 (1946), 43-47.

Pedersen, Kenneth S. "The First Socialist Majority: Denmark's 1966 Election," ParAf, 20 (1967), 144-57.

Pedersen, Mogens N. "Preferential Voting in Denmark: the Voters' Influence on the Election of Folketing Candidates," ScPolSt, 1 (1966), 167-87.

Philip, Kjeld. "The Social Politics of Denmark," ScPP, III, 190-200.

Rasmussen, Knud. The Political Philosophy of Sören Kierkegaard. Thesis (Ph.D.), Rutgers University, 1965.

Renard, Gilbert. "Denmark: a Swing to the Left," International Socialist Journal, 3 (1966), 692-99.

Saby, Rasmus S. "Danish Parliamentary Elections of 1918," APSR, 13 (1919), 656-62.

——. "A New Election Method in Denmark," ASR, 8 (1920), 132-34.

Wendt, Frantz W. "Denmark," in Kenneth Lindsay, ed., European Assemblies: the Experimental Period, 1949-1959 (Lond., N.Y.), 209-14.

CONSTITUTION

Adrian, C. R. "Danes Pick Middle Way: Constitution Follows League Model With One-House Parliament Elected by Proportional Representation," NMR, 44 (1955), 238-41.

Anderson, Stanley V. "Article Twenty of Denmark's New Constitution," AJIL, 50 (1956), 654-59.

"The Constitution of the Kingdom of Denmark Act, 5th June 1953, and the Succession to the Throne Act, 27th March 1953," in Amos J. Peaslee, ed., Constitutions of Nations. 2d ed. (The Hague, 1956), v. 1, 733-46.

Danstrup, John. "The Danish Monarchy," DFOJ (1950, no. 2), 4-7.

Denmark. The Constitution of the Kingdom

of Denmark, Act 5th June, 1953 and Succession to the Throne Act, 27th March 1953. Coph., 1953. 12 p.

Eriksen, Erik. "Denmark's Constitution," ASR, 41 (1953), 213-16.

Goodman, Ray. "The New Danish Constitution," Politica, 4 (1939), 124-38.

Hansen, H. C. "King and Constitution," DFOJ, no. 30 (1959), 17-19.

Hedtoft, Hans. "Centenary of the Danish Constitution," DFOJ (1949, no. 1), 1-4.

Thorsen, Svend. "How Denmark Has Placed the People Above Parliament," ParAf, 11 (1957), 57-60.

POLITICAL BIOGRAPHY

Christensen, Carlo. "Hans Hedtoft," ASR, 43 (1955), 137-40.

Hansen, Poul. Contemporary Danish Politicians: 45 Portraits with a Brief Look at the Development of Danish Parliamentary Democracy. Coph., 1949. 179 p.

Leistikow, Gunnar. "Jens Otto Krag: the Prime Minister of Denmark," ASR, 51 (1963), 130-34.

——. "Viggo Kampmann, The Prime Minister of Denmark," ASR, 50 (1962), 25-28.

Moritzen, Julius. "Thorvald Stauning, Premier of Denmark," ASR, 23 (1935), 240-41.

PARTIES AND PRESSURE GROUPS

Laux, William E. Interest Groups in Danish Politics. Thesis (Ph.D.), University of Nebraska, 1963. 426 p.

Raffaele, Joseph A. Labor Leadership in Italy and Denmark. Madison, Wisc., 1962. 436 p.

Schiöler, A. K. "Danish Women in Politics," ASR, 14 (1926), 532-38.

Skovmand, Roar. "The Struggle of the Danish 'Venstre' Party," ScPP, II, 831-35.

"Social Democratic Party of Denmark," Yearbook of the International Socialist Labour Movement 1956-1959 (Lond., 1956), 185-91.

Stauning, Theodore. "The Work of the Danish Social Democratic Party," IO, 1 (1936), 37-40.

PUBLIC ADMINISTRATION AND LOCAL GOVERNMENT

Abraham, Henry J. "The Danish Ombudsman," Annals, 377 (1968) 55-61.

Blumenfeld, Hans. "A Hundred Year Plan:

the Example of Copenhagen," in his, The Modern Metropolis: Its Origins, Growth, Characteristics, and Planning (Cambridge, Mass., 1967), 93-110.

Bomholt, Julius. "The Danish State Radio," DFOJ (1949, no. 1), 15-19.

Brun, A. A. "The Civil Servant in Denmark," Personnel Administration, 14 (1951), 18-25.

Christensen, B. "The Danish Ombudsman," University of Pennsylvania Law Review, 109 (1961), 1100-26.

Glahn, Borge. "Copenhagen's Finger Plan, and Denmark's Urban Development Act," American City (S 1952), 118-19+.

Holm, Axel. "Danish Local Government," APSR, 50 (1956), 117-18.

Hurwitz, Stephan. "Control of the Administration in Denmark: the Danish Parliamentary Commissioner for Civil and Military Government Administration," Journal of the International Commission of Jurists, 1 (1958), 224-243. Also in Public Law (1958), 236-45.

——. "The Danish Ombudsman and his Office," The Listener, 63 (1960), 835-38.

——. "Denmark's Ombudsman: the Parliamentary Commissioner for Civil and Military Government Administration," Wisconsin Law Review (1961), 170-99.

——. "The Folketingets Ombudsmand," ParAf, 12 (1958), 199-208.

——. The Ombudsman. Coph., 1961. 63 p.

——. "Public Trust in Government Services," DFOJ, no. 20 (1956), 11-15.

Kemble, H. S. "The Danish State Police School," Police Journal (1948), 151-56.

Koch, Ejler. "Development of Public Administration in Denmark since 1960," IRAS, 33 (1967), 1-8.

Koch, Hal H. "Democracy by Town Hall," ASR, 34 (1946), 155-58.

Krarup, Ole. "Judicial Review of Administrative Action in Denmark," IRAS, 33 (1967), 9-16.

Lindgren, Erik. "State Administration and Civil Service in Denmark," in J. A. Lauwerys, ed., Scandinavian Democracy (Coph., N.Y., 1958), 166-73.

National Planning Committee, Secretariat. Danish Planning Legislation — A Survey (Publication No. 8). Coph., 1965. 21 p.

Pedersen, Inger M. "The Danish Parliamentary Commissioner in Action," Public Law (1959), 115-27.

——. "Denmark's Ombudsmand," in Donald Rowat, ed., The Ombudsman: Citizen's Defender (Lond., Toronto, Stock., 1965), 75-94.

Sington, Anne. "Bureaucrats and Citizens, an Interview with Denmark's Ombudsmand, Professor Stephan Hurwitz," NATO Letter, 14 (1966, no. 2), 16-21.

GREENLAND

Koch, Hans H. "A New Era for Greenland: Important Reforms Planned," DFOJ (1950, no. 3), 1-10.
Stefansson, Vilhjalmur. "The Republic of Greenland," Forum, 80 (1928), 250-66.

FINLAND

Ahava, Teini. "The Government of Finland," in The Finland Year Book 1936 (Hels., 1936), 87-92. 2d ed., 1936/1937 (1937), 87-92.
Bellquist, Eric C. "Finland: Democracy in Travail," WPQ, 2 (1949), 217-27.
Bruce, Neil. "The Finnish Political Scene," Norseman, 13 (1955), 6-8.
Democracy in Finland: Studies in Politics and Government (Finnish Political Science Association). Hels., 1960. 104 p.
Enckell, Arvid. Democratic Finland. Lond., 1948. 151 p.
"Finland Since the Moscow Treaty," BIN, 21 (Je 24, Jl 8, 1944), 507-12, 543-49.
"Finland Today," WT, 13 (1957), 118-27.
Fischer, Alfred J. "The Finnish Scene," WAQ, 1 (1947), 286-301.
Graham, Malbone W. "Finland," FPR, 7 (1931, no. 6), 119-24.
——. "Finland," in his, New Governments of Eastern Europe (N.Y., 1927), 169-245.
——. "Stability in the Baltic States: Finland," in Raymond L. Buell et al., New Governments in Europe: the Trend Toward Dictatorship (Lond., N.Y., 1934), 261-79.
Heinberg, Aage. "Finland in the Red Shadow," Plain Talk (D 1947), 34-37.
Hiitonen, Ensio. "The Republic of Finland: Its Political and Administrative Structure," in Urho Toivola, ed., The Finland Year Book 1947 (Hels., 1947), 35-62.
Hyndman, Rosalind T. "Politics in Finland," NewEur, 8 (1918), 31-34, 60-63.
Jackson, J. Hampden. "Finland Since the Armistice," IA, 24 (1948), 505.
Jansson, Jan-Magnus. Recent Trends in Scandinavian Political Science: Finland. Communication to the Seventh Round Table of the International Political Science Association Held in Opatija (S 1959), 19 p. Mimeographed.

Kaaret, Raymond H. The Government of Finland Since 1947. Thesis (Ph.D.), American University, 1958, 368 p.
Kalijarvi, Thorsten V. "Finland Since 1939," JP, 10 (1948), 289-300.
Kastari, Paavo. "How Finland is Governed," ScPP, III, 86-90.
Killinen, K. "The Relation Between the Political and the Military Direction in Finland," DF, 74-80.
Kivimäki, T. M. "The Insurrection in Finland," Finnish Trade Review, 3 (1932).
Kolehmainen, John I. "When Finland's Tolstoy Met His Russian Master," SlR, 16 (1957), 534-41.
Korft, Alletta. "Where Women Vote," NGeogM, 21 (1910), 487-93.
Kuusisto, Allan A. "Parliamentary Crises and Presidential Governments in Finland," ParAf, 11 (1957), 341-49.
Lemberg, Magnus. "Finland: Domestic Politics During 1962-65," ScPolSt, 1 (1966), 246-53.
Lewis, Harold O. "Finland: Trends and Pressures," AmPers, 1 (1947), 356-67.
Marshall, F. Ray. "Labor, Politics, and Economics in Finland," SSSQ, 40 (Je 1959), 5-15.
Mead, William R. "The Finnish Outlook, East and West," GeoJ, 113 (1949), 9-20.
Merikoski, V. "The Realization of the Equality of the National Languages in Finland," DF, 81-92.
Nousiainen, Jaakko. "Political Research in Scandinavia, 1960-65: Finland," ScPolSt, 1 (1966), 257-65.
"Political Developments in Finland Since 1950," Current Notes on International Affairs, 25 (1954), 403-409.
"The Political Scene in Finland," WT, 11 (1955), 210-16.
"Protection of Minorities in Finland," League of Nations Official Journal, 2 (1921), 1165-66.
Puntila, Lauri A. "The Historical Basis of Political Life in Finland," DF, 3-17.
Rintala, Marvin. "Short List of English-Language Studies of Finnish Politics," JCEA, 23 (1963), 77-80.
Selleck, Roberta G. The Language Issue in Finnish Political Discussion 1809-1863. Thesis (Ph.D.), Radcliffe College, Harvard University, 1961.
Shearman, Hugh. Finland: the Adventures of a Small Power. Lond., N.Y., 1950. 114 p.
Shepherd, Gordon. "Finland's Mortgaged Democracy," Reporter, 21 (N 26, 1959), 30-32.

Simon, Ernest D. "Finland: a Democ-
racy in the Making," in his, The
Smaller Democracies (Lond., 1939),
155-66.
Spencer, Arthur. "Finland Maintains De-
mocracy," FA, 31 (1953), 301-309.
Ståhlberg, K. J. "The Finnish Government,"
in Suomi: a General Handbook on the
Geography of Finland (Hels., 1952), 608-
20.
——. "The Organization of the State," in
Atlas of Finland 1925 (Hels., 1929), 1-17.
Tarkiainen, Tuttu. "The Stability of Demo-
cratic Institutions in Post-War Finland,"
ParAf, 19 (1966), 241-50.
Törnudd, Klaus. The Electoral System of
Finland. Hels., 1967. 202 p.
Valros, Fredrik. Finland 1946-1952. Hels.,
1953. 63 p.
Verney, Douglas V. "The Political and Eco-
nomic State of Finland," Norseman, 9
(1951), 380-86; 10 (1952), 14-22.
Voionmaa, Väinö. "The Birth of a Nation,"
Nord, 1 (1938), 163-72.
Wuorinen, John H. "Democracy Gains in
Finland," CH, 21 (1951), 208-11, 327-30.
——. Nationalism in Modern Finland.
N.Y., 1931. 302 p.
Zilliacus, K. "Parliamentary Democracy in
Finland," ParAf, 9 (1956), 427-38.

CONSTITUTION

Finland. Constitution Act and Parliament
Act of Finland. Hels., 1959. 56 p.
——. Form of Government Act of Finland,
Promulgated at Helsinki (Helsingfors)
July 14, 1919 and Diet Act, Adopted Jan.
13, 1928 as Amended Through 1955.
Hels., 1955. 15, 21 p.
——. Form of Government Act and Diet
Act of Finland. Hels., 1947. 47 p. Ad-
denda and Corrigenda. Hels., 1948. 2 p.
——. Form of Government of Finland.
Given at Helsingfors, July 17, 1919.
Hels., 1924. 31 p.
——. Laws, Statutes on the Validity of the
Fundamental Laws of Finland. Stock.,
1892. 62 p.
"Finland Constitution," in Amos J. Peaslee,
ed., Constitutions of Nations. 2d ed.
(The Hague, 1956), v. 1, 860-96.
The Finnish Reform Bill of 1906. Hels.,
1906. 23 p.
Kaila, Erkki. Legislation Concerning Lib-
erty of Faith in Finland. Hels., 1923.
10 p.
Kaira, Kurt. "The Budget and the Constitu-

tion," Economic Review (Hels.), 4 (1956),
162-67.
Kastari, Paavo. "Constitutional Protection
of Civil Rights in Finland," DF, 58-73.
——. "The Historical Background of Finn-
ish Constitutional Ideas," ScStL, 7 (1963),
61-77.
McBain, Howard Lee, and Lindsay Rogers.
"Finland," in The New Constitutions of
Europe (N.Y., 1923), 465-95.
Mirkine-Guetzévitch, B. "Finland: Recent
Developments in Laws, Constitution and
Administration," PolQ, 3 (1932), 416-21.
Ruutu, Y. "The Finnish Constitution," in
The Finnish Yearbook 1936 (Hels., 1936),
81-86; (2d ed., 1936/1937), 81-86.
Saario, Voitto. "Control of the Constitu-
tionality of Laws in Finland," AJCL, 12
(1963), 194-205.

PARLIAMENT

Campion, Gilbert F. M. C., and D. W. S.
Lidderdale. "Finland," in European Par-
liamentary Procedure: a Comparative
Handbook (Lond., 1953), 88-103.
Erich, Rafael. "Parliament," in Finland:
the Country, Its People and Institutions
(Hels., 1926), 272-79.
Finland, Riksdagen. The Finnish Parlia-
ment: Sketch of the National Assembly
and the Parliament Building. Hels., 1952.
32 p.
——. The Finnish Parliament. Ed. by
Eino Mäkinen. Hels., 1957. 70 p.
Jansson, Jan-Magnus. "Some Remarks on
Parliamentary Procedure in Finland,"
DF, 50-57.
Lindman, Sven. "The 'Dualistic' Conception
of Parliamentary Government in the Finn-
ish Constitution," DF, 44-49.
——. "The Parliamentary System in Fin-
land," in Urho Toivola, ed., The Finland
Year Book 1947 (Hels., 1947), 63-67.
Noponen, Martti, and Pertti Pesonen. "The
Legislative Career in Finland," in Erik
Allardt and Yrjö Littunen, eds., Cleav-
ages, Ideologies and Party Systems,
WestSocTrans, 10 (1964), 441-63.
Nyholm, P. G. "Some Aspects on the Cohe-
sion of the Finnish Diet in 1948-51,"
Politiika (1959, no. 1/2), 42-52.
Sipponen, Kauko. "Some Aspects of the Del-
egation of Legislative Power in Finland,"
ScStL, 9 (1965), 159-76.
Wahlroos, Helmer J. "Finnish Diet of Es-
tates Becomes Single — Chamber Assem-
bly," ScPP, II, 842-43.

POLITICAL BIOGRAPHY

Friis, Erik J. "President Kekkonen of Finland," ASR, 49 (1961), 239-45.

Gummerus, Herman G. P. E. Svinhufud, 1861-1935. Hels., 1936. 30 p.

Mannerheim, Carl G. E. Memoirs. Lond., N.Y., 1954. 540 p.

Pedersen, A. E., Jr. "Kekkonen and the Finnish Press," Journalism Review (1962, no. 5), 16-18.

Pollock, John. "Silhouettes in Finland," NewEur, 11 (1919), 177-180, 206-10.

Räikkönen, Erkki. Svinhufud, the Builder of Finland: an Adventure in Statecraft. Lond., 1938. 252 p.

Rintala, Marvin. "The Politics of Gustaf Mannerheim," JCEA, 21 (1961), 67-83.

———. "Väinö Tanner in Finnish Politics," ASEER, 20 (1961), 84-98.

Salonen, K. D. J. "J. V. Snellmann, the Great 19th Century Statesman and Political Philosopher of the North," Nord, 2 (1939), 351-63.

Tokoi, Oskari. Sisu, "Even Through a Stone Wall": Autobiography of the First Premier of Finland. N.Y., 1957. 252 p.

PARTIES AND PRESSURE GROUPS

Allardt, Erik. "Social Sources of Finnish Communism: Traditional and Emerging Radicalism," International Journal of Comparative Sociology, 5 (1964), 49-72.

Allardt, Erik, and Pertti Pesonen. "Cleavages in Finnish Politics," in Seymour M. Lipset and Stein Rokkan, eds., Party Systems and Voter Alignments: Cross-National Perspectives. (Lond., N.Y., 1967), 325-66.

Billington, James H. "Finland," in Cyril E. Black and Thomas P. Thornton, eds., Communism and Revolution (N.Y., 1964), 125-44.

Birnbaum, Immanuel. "The Communist Course in Finland," PC (S/O 1959), 42-47; (Ja/F 1960), 63-64.

Borg, Olavi. "Basic Dimensions of Finnish Party Ideologies: a Factor Analytical Study," ScPolSt, 1 (1966), 94-117.

Fifty Years of Social Democracy in Finland. Short Summary of the History of the Social Democratic Party, 1899-1949. Hels., 1949. 12 p.

Finland — Suomalainen Puolue. The Finnish Party in Finland and Their Present Program. Hels., 1907. 47 p.

"From the Experience of the Work of the Communist Party of Finland," World Marxist Review (F 1962), 57-64.

Hodgson, John H., III. Communism in Finland: a History and Interpretation. Princeton, N.J., 1967. 240 p. Based on 1964 thesis (Ph.D.), Harvard University.

Krosby, H. Peter. "The Communist Power Bid in Finland in 1948," PSQ, 75 (1960), 229-43.

Krusius-Ahrenberg, Lolo. "The Political Power of Economic and Labor Market Organizations: a Dilemma of Finnish Democracy," in Henry W. Ehrmann, ed., Interest Groups on Four Continents (Pittsburgh, 1958), 33-59.

Marshall, F. Ray. "Communism in Finland," JCEA, 19 (1960), 375-88.

Matti, Bengt. "Finland," in William E. Griffith, ed., Communism in Europe (Cambridge, Mass.; Lond., 1966), 371-410.

Mehlem, Max. "Communism in Finland," SRWA, 11 (1961/62, no. 2), 13-16.

Nopsanen, Aulis. "Communism in Finland," Norseman, 16 (1958), 20-23.

———. "Finland's Non-Communist Parties," Norseman, 16 (1958), 289-95.

Nousiainen, Jaakko. "The Structure of the Finnish Political Parties," DF, 28-43.

Puntila, Lauri A. The Evolution of the Political Parties in Finland. Hels., 1953.

———. "Finland's Multi-Party System," Finlandia Review (1959), 24-26.

Rintala, Marvin. "Finland," in Hans Rogger and Eugen Weber, eds., The European Right: a Historical Profile (Berkeley, 1965), 408-42.

———. "An Image of European Politics: the People's Patriotic Movement," JCEA, 22 (1962), 308-16.

———. "The Problem of Generations in Finnish Communism," ASEER, 17 (1958), 190-202. Comment by C. Jay Smith, Jr., ASEER, 19 (1960), 623-27.

———. Three Generations: the Extreme Right Wing in Finnish Politics. Bloomington, Ind., 1962. 281 p. Based on Thesis (Ph.D.), Fletcher School of Law and Diplomacy, 1959.

Saarinen, Aarne. "Finland: Cooperation Among the Democratic Forces," World Marxist Review, 9 (1966), 62-64.

Snell, W. "The Communist Movement and the Youth," World Marxist Review, 5 (1962), 74-75.

"Social Democratic Party of Finland," Yearbook of the International Socialist Labour Movement 1956-1957 (Lond., 1956), 194-201.

von Bonsdorff, Göran. "The Party Situation in Finland," DF, 18-27.

ELECTIONS

Bellquist, Eric C. "Presidential Elections
in Finland," BSC, 4 (1938), 186-97.
Fischer, Alfred J. "Finland's New Way"
[1945 election], CR, 167 (1945), 267-71.
Forster, Kent. "The Silent Soviet Vote in
Finnish Politics," IntJ, 18 (1963), 341-52.
Holsti, Kalevi J. "The U.S.S.R. and Finnish
Electoral Politics," Canadian Forum
(May 1962), 31-32.
Jansson, Jan-Magnus. "Post-war Elections
in Finland," BFMB, 36 (1962, no. 4), 22-
27.
Lindman, Sven. "Notes on the Presidential
Elections in Finland," Acta Academiae
Aboensis Humaniora (Åbo), 19 (1951, no.
2), 1-17.
Wuorinen, John H. "Democratic Gains in
Finland," CH, 21 (1951), 208-11, 327-30.

POLITICAL BEHAVIOR

Allardt, Erik. Factors Explaining Variation
in Strength and Changes of Strength of
Political Radicalism. Hels., 1962.
———. "Implications of Within-Nation Vari-
ations and Regional Imbalances for
Cross-National Research," in Richard
L. Merritt and Stein Rokkan, eds., Com-
paring Nations: the Use of Quantitative
Data in Cross-National Research (New
Haven, Lond., 1966), 337-48.
———. "Institutionalized versus Diffuse
Support of Radical Political Movements,"
in Transactions of the Fifth World Con-
gress of Sociology (International Socio-
logical Association), 4 (1964), 369-80.
———. "Patterns of Class Conflict and
Working Class Consciousness in Finnish
Politics," in Erik Allardt and Yrjö Lit-
tunen, eds., Cleavages, Ideologies and
Party Systems, WestSocTrans, 10 (1964),
97-131.
Allardt, Erik and Ketil Bruun. "Character-
istics of the Finnish Non-Voter" [1951
Election], WestSocTrans, 3 (1956), 55-76.
Allardt, Erik, and Pertti Pesonen. "Citizen
Participation in Political Life: Finland,"
ISSJ, 12 (1960; no. 1), 27-39.
Pesonen, Pertti. Citizen Participation in
Finnish Politics. Paper for the 5th
World Congress of the International Po-
litical Science Association. Paris, 1961.
30 p. Mimeographed.
———. Studies on Finnish Electorate Be-
havior. Ann Arbor, Mich., 1960. 17 p.
———. "Studies on Finnish Political Be-
havior," in Austin Ranney, ed., Essays

on the Behavioral Study of Politics (Ur-
bana, Ill., 1962), 217-34.
———. "The Voting Behaviour of Finnish
Students," DF, 93-104.

PUBLIC ADMINISTRATION AND
LOCAL GOVERNMENT

Bruun, Otto. The Administration of the City
of Helsinki. Hels., 1950. 66 p.
[Carlson, D. C.] "The Supreme Power and
the Administration," in Finland: Its
Country and People, a Short Survey
(Hels., 1919), 45-53.
Eskola, Aarne. "The Council-Manager Plan
in Finland," Public Management, 42 (F
1960), 33-35.
———. "Local Government in Finland,"
Quarterly Journal of the Local Self-
Government Institute (Bombay), 29 (1958),
278-80. Reprinted from Municipal Review, 29 (1958), 409-11.
Finland, Office of the Ombudsman. The Po-
sition and Functions of the Finnish Par-
liamentary Ombudsman. Hels., 1965.
Finland, Suomen Maalaeskuntien Lütto. Lo-
cal Self-Government in Finland, and the
Finnish Municipal Law. 2d ed., Hels.,
1960.
Hidén, Mikael J. V. "Finland's Defenders
of the Law," Annals, 377 (1968), 31-40.
Kastari, Paavo. "The Chancellor of Justice
and the Ombudsman," in Donald Rowat,
ed., The Ombudsman: Citizen's Defender
(Lond., Toronto, Stock., 1965), 58-74.
———. "The Constitutional Protection of
Fundamental Rights in Finland," Tulane
Law Review, 34 (1960), 695-710.
———. "The Parliamentary Ombudsman:
His Functions, Position, and Relation to
the Chancellor of Justice in Finland,"
IRAS, 28 (1962), 391-98.
Knapp, David C., and Abraham Yeselson.
"Finland's Manager Plan: Mixed Admin-
istration on Collective Leadership Bear
Little Relationship to American Concept,"
National Civic Review, 50 (1961), 76-79+.
Malinen, Torsten. "Local Government," in
Finland: the Country, Its People and In-
stitutions (Hels., 1926), 262-69.
———. "Local Government in the Finnish
Towns," BFMB, 6 (1926, no. 3), 27-31.
Rowat, Donald C. "Finland's Defenders of
the Law," Canadian Public Administration,
4 (1961), 316-25, 412-15.
Sipponen, Kauko. Working Paper No. 5 (on
Finland) for the United Nations Seminar
on Judicial and Other Remedies Against
the Abuse of Administrative Authority

(UNDoc. SO 216/3 (3) EUR 1962). N.Y., 1962. Mimeographed.

Uotila, Jaakko. "Improving Public Administration in Finland," IRAS, 27 (1961), 65-70.

ICELAND

Bløndal, Sigfús. "Iceland in the North," Nord, 4 (1941), 153 p.

Fischer, Alfred J. "The Iceland Problem," CR, 195 (1959), 233-36.

Gröndal, Benedikt. "Elections and Coalitions in Iceland," New Leader (Aug 3/10, 1959), 10-11.

Hliodal, Guomundur. Postal Service in Iceland, May 13, 1776-1951. Rey., 1951. 52 p.

"Iceland: a Political and Geographical Note" [by M.C.], BIN, 19 (1942), 742-46.

Johnson, Jakobina. "An Icelandic Statesman and Skald," ASR, 11 (1923), 346-49.

Johnson, Sveinbjorn. An Account of the Icelanders and the Icelandic Free State. Boston, 1930. 361 p.

MacGill, Alexander. The Independence of Iceland: a Parallel for Ireland. Glasgow, 1921. 32 p.

Malone, Kemp. "Political and Social Tendencies in Iceland," ASR, 10 (1922), 226-31.

Mould, Pochin. "An Impression of Modern Iceland" [political, social, and economic conditions], Table Studies (Ireland), 53 (Spring 1964), 61-71.

Nuechterlein, Donald E. Iceland, Reluctant Ally. Ithaca, N.Y., 1961. 213 p. Based on thesis (Ph.D.), University of Michigan: The Icelandic Defense Problem, 1940-1956.

Olmsted, Mary S. "Communism in Iceland," FA, 36 (1958), 340-47.

Yershova, Tamara. "Iceland Today," New Times (Moscow), (O 3, 1957), 22-25.

CONSTITUTION AND PARLIAMENT

Beck, Richard. "Iceland's Thousand Year Old Parliament," ScSt, 10 (1928-29), 149-53.

Benediktsson, Bjarni. "The Two Chambers of the Icelandic Althing," in, Legal Essays: a Tribute to Frede Castberg (Oslo, 1963), 394-410.

Björnsson, Sveinn. "The Kingdom of Iceland, Some Remarks on Its Constitutional and International Status," Nord, 1 (1938), 75-81.

Hermannson, Halldór. "A Thousand-Year-Old Parliament," ASR, 16 (1928), 397-400.

"Iceland: Constitution," in Amos J. Peaslee, ed., Constitutions of Nations (2d ed., The Hague, 1956), v. 2, 198-217.

Johannesson, Olafur. "The Icelandic Form of Government," in ScPP, III, 91-94.

"The Millenium of Iceland's Althing," ASR, 18 (1930), 554-58.

Thordarson, Matthias. The Althing, Iceland's Thousand Year Old Parliament, 930-1930. Rey., 1930.

Williams, Mary W. "Iceland's Millenial," ASR, 18 (1930), 268-74.

NORWAY

Arneson, Ben A. "Democratized Socialism Makes Gains in Norway," APSR, 28 (1934), 109-12.

———. "Norway Moves Toward the Right," APSR, 25 (1931), 152-57.

Barton, Allen H. Sociological and Psychological Problems of Economic Planning in Norway. Thesis (Ph.D.), Columbia University, 1957. 593 p. Chap. 5: "The Rise of the Labor Party," 242-306; Chap. 6: "The Structure of the Electorate, 1945-1949," 307-49; Chap. 7: "The Voter Looks at the Economy," 350-87; Chap. 8: "Class Attitudes Toward the Government's Economic Policies," 388-450.

Bellquist, Eric C. "Political and Economic Conditions in the Scandinavian Countries: Norway, Bibliography," FPR, 24 (May 15, 1948), 56-59.

Berggrav, Eivind J. Man and State. Phila., 1951. 319 p.

———. State and Church – The Lutheran View (Speech Presented at Lutheran World Federation Assembly, Hanover, Germany). 1952. Mimeographed.

Boyeson, H. H. "Norway's Political Crisis," NoAmRev, 157 (Jl 1893), 68-74.

Castberg, Frede. "Economic and Social Controversies in Norwegian Political Life," in his, The Norwegian Way of Life (Lond., 1954), 66-83.

Duffy, Frank J. The Political Institutions and Government of Norway: a Survey. Oslo, 1956. 120 p. Mimeographed. First printing, Oslo, 1953.

Eckstein, Harry. Division and Cohesion in Democracy: a Study of Norway. Princeton, N.J., 1966. 306 p.

"Economic and Electoral Reforms in Norway" [by A.G.S.], WT, 9 (1953), 22-30.

Eidheim, Harald. "Entrepreneurship in

Politics," in Fredrik Barth, ed., The
Role of the Entrepreneur in Social Change
in Northern Norway (Oslo, 1963), 70-82.

Fischer, Alfred J. Norway After the Elections," CR, 176 (1949), 338-43.

Gehnich, Karl. "Norway: Socialism Tries
to Get in by the Backdoor," SRWA, 2 (N
1952), 12-15.

Granerad, Charles. "National and Local
Government in Norway," ScPP, III, 77-
86.

Grinin, P. "Changes in Norway," SPT, 3
(May 15, 1948), 304-307.

Hambro, Johan. "Election of Paradoxes: a
Precarious Balance Between the Parties
in the New Norwegian Parliament,"
Norseman (1961, no. 5), 26-29.

———. "A New Political Era: the Socialist
Rule Comes to an End After 30 Years as
the Norwegian Coalition Parties Form a
New Government," Norseman (1965),
138-40.

Hauge, Jens C. "Defence and Democracy in
Norway," in J. A. Lauwerys, ed., Scandinavian Democracy (Coph., N.Y., 1958),
355-65.

Haugen, Einar. Language Conflict and Language Planning: the Case of Modern
Norwegian. Cambridge, Mass., 1966.
393 p.

Knaplund, Paul. "The Norwegian Elections
of 1927 and the Labor Government,"
APSR, 22 (1928), 413-16.

Larsen, Hanna A. "Social Reform Legislation in Norway," ASR, 3 (1915), 27-31.

Lewis, Harold O. "Norwegian Social Democracy," AmPers, 1 (1947), 479-94.

Norway. Compilation of Norwegian Laws,
etc., for the use of Foreign Service Representatives: 1814-1953. Ed. and comp.
by Hjalmar Willett. Oslo, 1956. 1225 p.

———. Government and Political Institutions. Wash., 1957. 16 p.

Øisang, Per. "Elections Coming Up,"
Norseman (1961, no. 1), 21-23.

Osborne, Lithgow. "The Task of Norwegian
Democracy," Norseman, 4 (1946), 319-
21.

"Political Development in Norway," World
Affairs (Jl 1947).

"Political Developments in Norway" [by
J.L.], WT, 3 (1947), 306-16.

"Political Interlude: First Defeat of a Socialist Cabinet in Norway Since 1935,"
Norseman (1963, no. 5), 4-6.

Rodnick, David. "Political Trends," in his,
The Norwegians: a Study in National
Culture (Wash., 1955), 122-44.

Rokkan, Stein. "Norway: Numerical De-

mocracy and Corporate Pluralism," in
Robert A. Dahl, ed., Political Oppositions
in Western Democracies (New Haven,
Lond., 1966), 70-115.

———. "Political Research in Scandinavia,
1960-65: Norway," ScPolSt, 1 (1966),
266-80.

Rokkan, Stein, and Torstein Hjellum. "Norway: the Storting Election of September
1965," ScPolSt, 1 (1966), 237-46.

Saby, Rasmus S. "Absent Voting in Norway,"
APSR, 12 (1918), 296-300.

Semmingsen, Ingrid. "Parliamentarianism
Wins Through in Norway," ScPP, II, 844-
52.

Stanton, T. "Why Norway is Not a Republic,"
Independent, 160 (1906), 1538-42.

Steen, Sverre. "The Democratic Spirit in
Norway," in J. A. Lauwerys, ed., Scandinavian Democracy (Coph., N.Y., 1958),
139-49.

Storing, James A. Constitutional Government in Norway. Thesis (Ph.D.), University of Iowa, 1938.

———. Norwegian Democracy. Boston,
1963. 246 p.

Strong, D. F. "Labor Leads a United Norway," Progressive (Ja 1953), 30-31.

Teal, John J., Jr. "The Rebirth of North
Norway," FA (1953), 123-34.

Torgersen, Ulf. "The Role of the Supreme
Court in the Norwegian Political System,"
in Glendon Schubert, ed., Judicial Decision-
Making (Glencoe, Ill., 1963), 221-44.

Ulmer, S. Sidney. "Stable Democracy in
Norway: a Review" [Review of Harry
Eckstein's Division and Cohesion in De-
mocracy: a Study of Norway], Journal of
Conflict Resolution, 12 (1968), 242-48.

Warbey, William et al. Modern Norway:
a Study in Social Democracy. Lond.,
1950. 181 p.

Whyte, Anne. "The Form of Government,"
in William Warbey et al., Modern Norway:
a Study in Social Democracy (Lond., 1950),
36-63.

Wilberg, Ingeborg. "Some Aspects of the
Principle of Ministerial Responsibility in
Norway," ScStL, 8 (1964), 243-64.

CONSTITUTION

Abrahamsen, Samuel. "Wergeland and Article 2 of the Norwegian Constitution," ScSt,
38 (1966), 102-23.

Braekstad, Hans L. The Constitution of
Norway: an Historical and Political Survey. Lond., 1905. 75 p.

Castberg, Frede. "Constitution and Consti-

tutional Life," in his, The Norwegian Way
of Life (Lond., 1954), 44-65.

Castberg, Frede. Norway and the Western
Powers: a Study in Comparative Constitutional Law. Lond., Oslo, 1958. 24 p.

Hoel, G. Astrup. "The Constitution of Norway," ASR, 52 (1964), 383-88.

"Norway: Constitution," in Amos J. Peaslee,
ed., Constitutions of Nations (2d ed., The
Hague, 1956), v. 2, 47-64.

Norway. The Constitution of Norway and
Other Documents of National Importance.
Ed. by Tönnes Andenaes. Oslo, 1951.
71 p.

——. The Constitution of Norway. Foreword by Wilhelm Keilhau. Montreal,
Lond., 1943. 25 p.

——. The Constitution of Norway; Translation Published by the Ministry of Justice. Oslo, 1937. 24 p.

——. The Constitution of the Kingdom of
Norway; Given by the Constituent Assembly at Eidsvold, May 17th, 1814, and...
Decreed by the Storthing in Extra Session
at Christiania, Revised and Affirmed on
Nov. 4th, 1814; With Amendments. Tr.
by Knute Nelson. Chicago, 1895. 27 p.

Wold, Terje. "The 1942 Enactment for the
Defence of the Norwegian State," Canadian Bar Review, 20 (1942), 505-509.

PARLIAMENT

Bowring, Nona, and Johan Stang. "On Ask-
ing Questions in the Norwegian Parliament," PolS, 10 (1962), 284.

Campion, Gilbert F. M. C., and D. W. S.
Lidderdale. "Norway," in European Par-
liamentary Procedure: a Comparative
Handbook (Lond., 1953), 192-207.

Hoff, Gunnar. "Norway's Three 'Tings',"
ParAf, 5 (1951), 445-48.

Lees-Smith, H. B. Second Chambers in
Theory and Practice. Lond., 1923.

——. "The Parliamentary System in Norway," Journal of Comparative Legislation
and International Law, 3d series, 5 (1923),
35.

Løchen, Einar. "Norway," in Kenneth Lindsay, ed., European Assemblies: the Experimental Period 1948-1959 (Lond.,
N.Y., 1960), 204-208.

Øisang, Per. "The House on the Lion's Hill"
[Parliament], Norseman (1962, no. 5), 9-12.

——. Norway's Parliament: the Storting.
Oslo, 1962. 39 p.

Rossvoll, Frank. "The History of the Norwegian Parliament" (Review Article),
SEHR, 14 (1966), 60-70.

Storing, James A. "Unique Features of the
Norwegian Storting," WPQ, 16 (1963),
161-66.

GOVERNMENT-IN-EXILE

Friis, Erik J. "The Norwegian Government-
in-Exile, 1940-1945," in Carl Bayerschmidt and Erik Friis, eds., Scandinavian Studies: Essays Presented to Henry
Goddard Leach (Seattle, 1965), 422-44.

Hambro, Carl J. "Norway's Government
Still Valid," ASR, 28 (1940), 236-37.

Myrdal, Alva. "Norway's Government-in-
Exile," ASR, 30 (1942), 160-62.

"Norway: Legislation in Exile," Journal of
Comparative Legislation and International
Law, 3d series, 24 (1942), 125-30.

POLITICAL BIOGRAPHY

Hambro, Johan. "Per Borten: Norway's
Coalition Premier," ASR, 55 (1967), 246-
51.

——. "Einar Gerhardsen, Prime Minister
of Norway," ASR, 38 (1950), 14-19.

Helle, Egil. "President of the Storting: Nils
Langhelle," Norseman (1964), 38-40.

Lokvam, Kjell. "A New Prime Minister"
[Per Borten], Norseman (1965), 166-68.

Olav, Hans. "Johan Ludwig Mowinckel,"
ASR, 19 (1931), 618-19.

Rønning, Åge. "Opposition Leader John
Lyng: Prime Minister in Short-Lived
Coalition Cabinet," Norseman (1963, no.
5), 7-9.

Skog, Jon. "He Turns Up Everywhere"
[Kaare Willoch], Norseman (1967), 60-62.

——. "The Profile: Bent Røiseland,"
Norseman (1965), 110-12.

Vatne, Hans. "The Prime Minister" [Einar
Gerhardsen], Norseman (1965), 7-10.

PARTIES AND PRESSURE GROUPS

Anker, E. How Women Got the Vote in Norway. Lond., 1910. 11 p.

Apeland, Nils M. "Public Relations in Norway," Public Relations Journal (Jl 1958),
20-24.

Broch, Lisbeth. Political Interests and Activity of Women in Norway. Report to the
International Political Science Association,
Hague Congress, 1953. 49-56. Tables,
35-45.

Christensen, H. C. "The Influence of Major
Functional Groups and the Relationship
Between These Groups and the State in
Scandinavia with Particular Respect to

Norway," Les Cahiers de Bruges (Autumn 1958), 114-38.

Christophersen, Jens A. "'Mot Dag' and the Norwegian Left," JCH, 1 (1966, no. 2), 135-48.

Fischer, Alfred J. "Communism in Norway," CR, 178 (1950), 32-37.

Galenson, Walter. "The Political Labor Movement," in his, Labor in Norway (Cambridge, Mass., 1949), 56-77.

Greenhill, H. Gaylon. The Norwegian Agrarian Party: a Case Study of a Single Interest Party. Thesis (Ph.D.), University of Illinois, 1962. 176 p.

——. "The Norwegian Agrarian Party: a Class Party?" Social Science, 40 (1965), 214-19.

Groennings, Sven. Cooperation Among Norway's Non-Socialist Political Parties. Thesis (Ph.D.), Stanford University, 1962. 382 p.

Gronseth, Erik. "The Political Role of Women in Norway," Appendix 4 to Maurice Duverger, The Political Role of Women (Paris, 1955), 194-221.

Hølaas, Odd. "The Problem of De-Nazification," and "The Political Picture," in The World of the Norseman (Lond., 1949), 25-34, 72-82.

Johansen, Jahn Otto. "Norway," in William E. Griffith, ed., Communism in Europe (Cambridge, Mass.; London, 1966), 321-69.

Kjekshus, Helge I. Notes on the Political Parties in Norway: a Study of the Norwegian Multi-Party System. Thesis (M.A.), Syracuse University, 1960. 178 p.

Moe, Finn. Does Norwegian Labor Seek the Middle Way? N.Y., 1937. 40 p.

Monsen, Sverre H. Social Structure and Political Change in a Multi-party System. Thesis (Ph.D.), University of Texas, 1967. 222 p.

Nissen, Bernt A. Political Parties in Norway: an Introduction to Their History and Ideology. Oslo, 1949. 54 p. Mimeographed.

"The Norwegian Labour Party," in Yearbook of the International Socialist Labour Movement 1956-1957 (Lond., 1956), 395-413.

Rokkan, Stein. "Geography, Religion, and Social Class: Crosscutting Cleavages in Norwegian Politics," in Seymour M. Lipset and Stein Rokkan, eds., Party Systems and Voter Alignments: Cross-National Perspectives. (Lond., N.Y., 1967), 367-444.

Scheldrup, Sverre I. The Farmer-Labor

Movement in Norway. Thesis (Ph.D.), University of Wisconsin, 1953.

Shannon, Jasper B. "The Norwegian Experience," in Money and Politics (N.Y., Toronto, 1959), 64-82.

Storing, James A. "Norway's Conservative Socialists," New Leader, 38 (S 4/11, 1961), 10-11.

Tollefson, Roy M. Political Thought Inside the Norwegian Labor Party, 1917-1928. Thesis (Ph.D.), University of Chicago, 1957. 334 p.

Torgersen, Ulf. The Anti-Party Ideology: Elitist Liberalism in Norwegian Social and Political Structure. Oslo, 1966. 52 p. Mimeographed.

——. The Formation of Parties in Norway: the Problem of Right-Left Differences. Oslo, 1966. 81 p. Mimeographed.

——. The Political Participation of Norwegian Professionals 1870-1940: Minister and Lawyer. Oslo, 1966. 45 p. Mimeographed.

——. "The Structure of Urban Parties in Norway during the First Period of Extended Suffrage 1884-1898," in Erik Allardt and Yrjö Littunen, eds., Cleavages, Ideologies and Party Systems, WestSoc Trans, 10 (1964), 377-99.

——. "The Trend Towards Political Consensus: the Case of Norway," AcSoc, 6 (1962), 159-72.

Valen, Henry. "Factional Activities and Nominations in Political Parties," AcSoc, 3 (1958/59), 183-99.

——. "The Recruitment of Parliamentary Nominees in Norway," ScPolSt, 1 (1966), 121-66.

Valen, Henry, and Daniel Katz. "An Electoral Contest in a Norwegian Province," in Morris Janowitz, ed., Community Political Systems (Glencoe, Ill., 1961), 207-36.

——. Political Parties in Norway. Oslo, 1964. 383 p.

Vidnes, Jacob. "Bolshevism on the Wane in Norway," ASR, 7 (1919), 114-17.

Warbey, William, et al. "Summary of Joint Programme Agreed Upon by the Labour, Conservative, Farmers' and Liberal Parties, June 1945," and "Norwegian Labour Party's Election Manifesto, 1945," Appendix 2 and 3 in Modern Norway: a Study in Social Democracy (Lond., 1950), 173-79.

Wyller, Thomas Chr. "National Socialism and the German Occupation of Norway" [Review of Arild Haaland, Nazismen i Tyskland; and of Magne Skodvin, Striden

om okkupasjonsstyret i Norge fram til
25 September 1940], Norseman, 14 (1956),
423-28.

Wyller, Thomas Chr. Nyordning og Motstand
[The New Order and Resistance]. Oslo,
1958. English Summary, 311-19.

POLITICAL BEHAVIOR

Campbell, Angus, and Henry Valen. "Party
Identification in Norway and the United
States," POQ, 25 (1961), 505-25. Reprinted in Angus Campbell, Philip Con-
verse, Warren Miller and Donald Stokes,
eds., Elections and the Political Order
(N.Y., 1966), Chap. 13, 245-68. Also reprinted as Bobbs-Merrill Reprint PS-368.

Jonassen, Christen T. "A Comparison of
Political Beliefs of College Students in
Norway and the United States," AcSoc, 9
(1966), 201-208.

Park, George K., and Lee Soltow. "Politics
and Social Structure in a Norwegian Village," AJS, 27 (1961), 152-64.

Rokkan, Stein. "The Comparative Study of
Political Participation: Notes Toward a
Perspective on Current Research," in
Austin Ranney, ed., Essays on the Be-
havioral Study of Politics (Urbana, Ill.,
1962), 47-90.

——. "Electoral Activity, Party Membership and Organizational Influence: an
Initial Analysis of Data from the Norwegian Election Studies 1957," AcSoc, 4
(1959), 25-37.

——. Ideological Consistency and Party
Preference: a Note on Findings from a
Cross-Country Survey of Teachers' Atti-
tudes. Paper for WAPOR Conference,
May, 1956. 11 p. Mimeographed.

——. "Mass Suffrage, Secret Voting and
Political Participation," European Journal of Sociology, 2 (1961), 132-52.

——. National Consensus and Political
Participation: Problems in the Current
Studies of Elections in Norway. Stanford,
Calif., 1960. 27 p. Mimeographed.

——. "Party Preferences and Opinion Patterns in Western Europe: a Comparative
Analysis," ISSB, 7 (1955), 575-96.

——. The 1956-59 Programme of Research on Political Process and Electoral Behavior in Norway. Oslo, 1956.
17 p. Mimeographed.

Rokkan, Stein, and Angus Campbell. "Citizen Participation in Political Life; Norway and the United States," ISSB, 12
(1960), 69-99. Also, Christian Michelsen
Institute, Reprint no. 194.

Rokkan, Stein, and Per Torsvik. "The Voter,
the Reader and the Party Press," Gazette,
6 (1960), 311-28.

Rokkan, Stein, and Henry Valen. "Archives
for Statistical Studies of Within-Nation
Differences," in Richard L. Merritt and
Stein Rokkan, eds., Comparing Nations:
the Use of Quantitative Data in Cross-
National Research (New Haven, Conn.;
Lond., 1966), 411-18.

——. "The Mobilization of the Periphery:
Data on Turnout, Party Membership and
Candidate Recruitment in Norway," AcSoc,
6 (1962), 111-58.

——. "Regional Contrasts in Norwegian
Politics: a Review of Data from Official
Statistics and from Sample Surveys," in
Erik Allardt and Yrjö Littunen, eds.,
Cleavages, Ideologies and Party Systems,
WestSocTrans, 10 (1964), 162-238.

Valen, Henry. "The Motivation and Recruitment of Political Personnel," Paper for
UNESCO Seminar, Bergen, 1961. Mimeographed.

PUBLIC ADMINISTRATION

Breie, Lars. The Auditing and Control of
Government Accounts in Norway. Oslo,
1960. 8 p.

Castberg, Frede. "The Civil Service of
Norway," in Leonard D. White, ed., The
Civil Service in the Modern State (Chi-
cago, 1930), 507-12.

Evers, Kjell T. "Municipal Government in
Norway," Public Management, 41 (1959),
250-52.

Galenson, Walter. "Nationalization of Industry in Great Britain and Norway,"
ASR, 36 (1948), 234-38.

Jacobsen, Knut Dahl. "Public Administration under Pressure: the Role of the Expert in the Modernization of Traditional
Agriculture," ScPolSt, 1 (1966), 59-93.

Moss, John. "Public Assistance Administration in Norway," Justice of the Peace,
95 (1931), 256-58.

Norman, Carl. "The Norwegian State Radio,"
ASR, 45 (1957), 173-76.

Norway, Justice and Police Department. Ad-
ministration of Justice in Norway; a Brief
Summary. English version prepared by J.
Aars Rynning. Oslo, 1957. 145 p.

Os, Audvar. "Administrative Procedure in
Norway," IRAS, 25 (1959), 67-78.

——. "The Ombudsman for Civil Affairs,"
in Donald Rowat, ed., The Ombudsman:
Citizen's Defender (Lond., Toronto,
Stock., 1965), 95-110.

Os, Audvar. Working Paper on Norway
Prepared for UN Seminar on Judicial and
Other Remedies Against the Abuse of Ad-
ministrative Authority (UNDoc. SO 216/3
(3) EUR 1962). N.Y., 1962. 19 p. Mim-
eographed.
Ruud, Arthur. "The Military Ombudsman
and His Board," in Donald Rowat, ed.,
The Ombudsman: Citizen's Defender
(Lond., Toronto, Stock., 1965), 111-18.
Sollie, Finn. "Control over Public Adminis-
tration in Norway," Journal of Public
Law, 5 (1956), 174-96.
Storing, James A. "The Norwegian Om-
budsmann," Norseman (1965), 121-25.
———. "The Norwegian Ombudsman for
Civil Affairs: the First Three Years,
1963-66," WPQ, 21 (1968), 302-24.
Thune, Sverre. "The Norwegian Ombudsmen
for Civil and Military Affairs," Annals,
377 (1968), 41-54.
Wold, Terje. "The Norwegian Parliament's
Commissioner for the Civil Administra-
tion," Journal of the International Com-
mission of Jurists, 2 (1960), 23-29.
Wymann, S. M. Municipal Government in
Norway and the Norwegian Municipal Law
of 1954. 1963.

SWEDEN

Anderson, Perry. "Sweden: Mr. Crosland's
Dreamland: a Study of the Swedish
Model," New Left Review (Ja/F, 1961),
4-12; (May/Je, 1961), 34-45.
Andrén, Nils. Modern Swedish Government.
Stock., 1961. 252 p.
———. "National and Local Government in
Sweden," ScPP, III, 55-66.
———. The Government of Sweden. Tr. by
Sarah Thorelli and Milton Williams.
Stock., Lond., 1955. 119 p.
Austensen, A. "Sweden: a Scandinavian De-
mocracy," Current Affairs (Jl 1, 1953),
4-31.
Benedikt, Ernst. "The Grand Old Man of
Sweden," CR (1948), 333-36.
Braatoy, Bjarne. The New Sweden: a Vin-
dication of Democracy. Lond., N.Y.,
1939. 172 p.
Brilioth, Börje H. "Sweden's Crown
Prince," Forum, 75 (1926), 870-76.
Brogan, Denis W., and Douglas V. Verney.
Political Patterns in Today's World.
N.Y., 1963. 274 p. 2d ed., 1968. 278 p.
Erickson, Herman. "Adult Education and
Swedish Political Leadership," IntRE, 12
(1966), 129-43.

Fischer, Alfred J. "The Welfare State in
Sweden," CR (Jl 1952), 40-44.
Fleisher, Frederic. The New Sweden: the
Challenge of a Disciplined Democracy.
N.Y., 1967. 365 p. Includes: "From
Class Conflict to Disciplined Democracy,"
40-72; "Government Planning and Indus-
try," 97-122; "Government by Discipline,"
145-60; "Officialdom on Display and the
Scrutinizing Ombudsman," 161-67.
Halsey, A. H. "Science and Government in
Sweden: Impressions from an OECD
Conference," Minerva, 2 (Autumn 1963),
54-60.
Hartman, R. S. "Sweden Re-Visited: Po-
litical and Social Impressions of the
Country of the Middle Way," Free World
(N 1946), 32-34.
Håstad, Elis W. "The Political System,"
Chap. 2 in Sweden, A Wartime Survey
(N.Y.).
———. "Swedish Political Science," in
UNESCO, Contemporary Political Science
(Paris, 1950), 150-64.
Heckscher, Gunnar. The Development of
Political Science in Sweden. Stock., 1961.
11 p.
Hedin, Naboth. "The King's Role in Sweden's
Government," ASM (Jl 1943), 14-15ff.
Herlitz, Nils. Sweden: a Modern Democracy
on Ancient Foundations. Minneapolis,
1939. 127 p.
———. "Publicity of Official Documents in
Sweden," Public Law, 50 (1958), 50-69.
Jansson, Jan-Magnus. Recent Trends in
Scandinavian Political Science: Sweden.
Communication to the Seventh Round Ta-
ble of the International Political Science
Association. Opatija, 1959. Mimeo-
graphed.
Johanssen, Otto. "The Triumph of Democ-
racy in Sweden," ASR, 7 (1919), 117-19.
Juridiska Fakulteten i Uppsala. Festskrift
tillägnad Halvar Sundberg [Papers dedi-
cated to Halvar Sundberg]. Uppsala, 1959.
English Summary, 413-25.
Lager, Fritjof. "The Working Class and the
Fight for Democracy at the Enterprises,"
World Marxist Review, 9 (1966), 28-31.
Lewis, Harold O. "Swedish Social Democ-
racy," AmPers, 2 (1948-49), 358-69.
Michanek, Ernst. Swedish Government in
Action. Stock., 1962. 21 p.
Molin, Björn. "Political Research in Scan-
dinavia, 1960-65: Sweden," ScPolSt, 1
(1966), 281-87.
Olberg, Paul. "Sweden's Middle Way
Continues," New Leader (O 22, 1956),
6-8.

"Political and Social Trends in Sweden" [by
A.H.H.], WT, 12 (1956), 503-11.

"Political Situation in Sweden" [by M.B.],
BIN, 18, pt. 2 (Je/D, 1941), 1917-19.

"Politics and Industry in Sweden" [by
A.H.H.], WT, 7 (1951), 529-37.

Rustow, Dankwart A. The Politics of Compromise: a Study of Parties and Cabinet
Government in Sweden. Princeton, N.J.,
1955. 257 p.

Schaaf, Carl H. Parties and Elections in
Sweden. Thesis (Ph.D.), University of
Michigan, 1940.

"Socialism in Sweden," Economist (Ja 17,
1948), 102.

Soloveytchik, George. "Sweden, Socialism
Without Tears," Reporter, 7 (S 30, 1952),
21-23.

Spencer, Henry R. "Democratic Monarchies:
Sweden," in Government and Politics
Abroad (N.Y., 1936), 434-48.

Spencer, Richard C. "The Swedish Pattern
of Responsible Government," SSSQ, 21
(1940/41), 53-65.

Spiro, Herbert J. "Sweden," in his, Government by Constitution: the Political Systems of Democracy (N.Y., 1959), 45-54.

Stjernquist, Nils. "Sweden: Stability or
Deadlock?" in Robert A. Dahl, ed., Political Oppositions in Western Democracies (New Haven, 1966), 116-46.

"Sweden: Political Developments During the
War; Post-War Developments," ACNIA,
22 (F/Ap 1951), 86-97, 193-208.

"The Swedish Outlook: Local Elections and
Foreign Affairs" [by EJL], WT, 8 (1950),
480-89.

Thorelli, Hans B. "The Formation of Economic and Financial Policy: Sweden,"
ISSB, 7 (1956), 252-73.

Thorelli, Sarah S. "Political Science in
Sweden," APSR, 44 (1950), 977-90.

Tingsten, Herbert L. G. "Stability and Vi-
tality in Swedish Democracy," PolQ, 26
(1955), 140-51.

CONSTITUTION

Bellquist, Eric C. "Constitutional Monarchy
in Sweden," BSC, 4 (1938), 297-300.

———. The Development of Parliamentary
Government in Sweden. Thesis (Ph.D.),
University of California, 1932. 753 p.

Elder, Neil C. M. "Swedish Constitutional
Reform Proposals, 1963," ParAf, 16
(1962), 302-307.

Heckscher, Gunnar. The Swedish Constitution, 1809-1959: Tradition and Practice
in Constitutional Development. Stock.,
1959. 24 p.

Stjernquist, Nils. "The Swedish Constitution
and the Budgetary Principles," ScStL, 6
(1962), 201-28.

Sweden, Ministry for Foreign Affairs. The
Constitution of Sweden. Tr. by Sarah
Thorelli. Stock., 1954. 110 p.

"Sweden," in Amos J. Peaslee, ed., Constitutions of Nations (2d ed., The Hague,
1956), v. 3, 298-324.

PARLIAMENT

Ahnlund, Nils. "Five Hundred Years of Parliamentary Government in Sweden," ASR,
23 (1935), 199-206.

Andrén, Nils. "The Riksdag and Foreign
Policy," ASM (M. 1958), 9-12.

Bellquist, Eric C. "Five Hundredth Anniversary of the Swedish Riksdag," APSR,
39 (1935), 857-65.

Campion, Gilbert F. M. C., and D. W. S.
Lidderdale. "Sweden," in European Par-
liamentary Procedure: a Comparative
Handbook (Lond., 1953), 208-23.

Elder, Neil C. M. "Parliament and Foreign
Policy in Sweden," PolS, 1 (1953), 193-
206.

———. "The Parliamentary Role of Joint
Standing Committees in Sweden," APSR,
45 (1951), 464-73.

———. "The Swedish Riksdag," ParAf, 10
(1956), 288-95.

———. The System of Standing Committees
of the Swedish Riksdag. Thesis (B.Litt.),
Oxford University, 1954.

Fahlbeck, Erik. "500 Years of the Swedish
Riksdag," Anglo-Swedish Review (F
1935), 43-48.

Foster, William C. "Legislative Research
in Sweden," WPQ, 9 (1956), 56-69.

Håstad, Elis W. The Parliament of Sweden.
Lond., 1957. 165 p.

Petrén, Gustaf. "Sweden," in Kenneth Lindsay, ed., European Assemblies: the Experimental Period 1949-1959 (Lond.,
N.Y., 1960), 196-203.

Sandelius, Walter E. "Dictatorship and Ir-
responsible Parliamentarism — A Study
in the Government of Sweden," PSQ, 49
(1934), 347-71.

Spencer, Richard C. "Separation of Control
and Lawmaking in Sweden," PSQ, 55
(1940), 217-30.

Tham, Wilhelm. "Sweden's Road to Democracy and Parliamentarism," ScPP, II,
836-41.

Verney, Douglas V. Parliamentary Reform
in Sweden, 1866-1921. Oxford, 1957. 295
p. Based on thesis (Ph.D.), Liverpool
University, 1954.

CABINETS

Björkman, Edwin. "The New Swedish Cabinet," ASR, 6 (1918), 25-27.
——. "Sweden Under Socialist Government," ASR, 7 (1920), 341-44.
Gerdner, Gunnar. Parlamentarismens Kris
i Sverige vid 1920 — Talets Början [The
crisis in Swedish parliamentarism at the
beginning of the 1920's]. Uppsala, 1954.
English Summary, 441-64.
Janson, Florence E. "Minority Governments
in Sweden," APSR, 22 (1938), 407.
Spencer, Richard C. "Party Government
and the Swedish Riksdag," APSR, 39
(1945), 437-58.
Thulstrup, Åke. "Swedish Parliamentarism,"
Journal of Comparative Legislation and
International Law, 3d series, 10 (1928),
314-17.

ELECTIONS, ELECTORAL SYSTEM

Arneson, Ben A. "The Recent Parliamentary
Elections in Sweden," APSR, 35 (1941),
107-108.
——. "Swedish Parliamentary Elections,
1919," APSR, 14 (1920), 123-25.
——. "Workers' Parties Show Gains in
Sweden and Norway," APSR, 31 (1937),
96-99.
Eckelberry, Robert L. The Swedish System
of Proportional Representation. Thesis
(Ph.D.), University of Nebraska, 1965.
Elder, Neil C. M. "The Swedish Election of
1956," PolS, 5 (1957), 65-78.
Glans, Ingemar. "Sweden: the 1964 Riksdag
Election," ScPolSt, 1 (1966), 225-30.
Herlitz, Nils. "Proportional Representation
in Sweden," APSR, 19 (1925), 582-92.
Kastrup, Allan. "'Time for a Change' in
Sweden: Will Voters Agree?" ASM, 54
(S 1960), 37-39.
Särlvik, Bo. "The Swedish General Election
of 1960," Paper for UNESCO Seminar,
Bergen, 1961. Mimeographed.
"War-Time Elections and Government in
Sweden," Archive, 1 (1947), 6-7.
Tingsten, Herbert L. G. Political Behavior:
Studies in Election Statistics. Lond.,
1937. 231 p. Reissued U.S.A., 1963.

PARTIES AND PRESSURE GROUPS

Andrén, Nils. The Party System in Sweden.
Stock., 1961. 21 p. Reprinted from his,
Modern Swedish Government.
Angman, Berndt G. "The Early Ideological
Development of the Social Democratic

Workers' Party of Sweden, 1889-1920,"
Northwest Missouri State College Studies,
21 (1957, no. 1), 29 p.
——. "Intra-Party Ideological Debates
Within the Social Democratic Workers'
Party of Sweden During the War Period,
1940-1946," Northwest Missouri State
College Studies, 24 (1960, no. 3), 82 p.
——. "Socialist Theory or Welfare State
Reality — Ideological Conflicts Within the
Social Democratic Workers' Party of
Sweden, 1932-1940," Northwest Missouri
State College Studies, 24 (1960, no. 1),
36 p.
——. A Study of Ideological Development
Within the Social Democratic Workers'
Party of Sweden in Relation to the Ques-
tion of Socialization, 1932-1952. Thesis
(Ph.D.), University of Texas, 1954. 504 p.
Bellquist, Eric C. "Emergency Regulations
and the Press in Sweden," Journalism
Quarterly, 18 (1941), 355-75.
Blake, Donald J. "Swedish Trade Unions
and the Social Democratic Party: the
Formative Years," SEHR, 8 (1960), 19-44.
——. The Trade Unions and the Social
Democratic Party: the Early History of
the Swedish Labor Movement, 1870-1914.
Thesis (Ph.D.), University of California,
1956.
Carlsson, Sten C. O. Lantmannapolitiken
och industrialismen; partigruppering och
opinions förskjutningar i svensk politik,
1890-1902 [Farmers' Politics and Indus-
trialism; Party Groupings and Changing
Opinions in Swedish Politics, 1890-1902].
Stock., 1953. English Summary, 436-50.
Davison, W. Phillips. "A Review of Sven
Rydenfelt's 'Communism in Sweden',"
POQ, 18 (1954/1955), 375-88.
Hancock, M. Donald. Opposition Parties in
Post-War Sweden: Dilemma and Pros-
pects. Thesis (Ph.D.), Columbia Univer-
sity, 1966.
——. Sweden: a Multiparty System in
Transition? (University of Denver Mono-
graph Series in World Affairs). Denver,
1968. 51 p.
Håstad, Elis W. Swedish Party Organization.
Stock., 1951. 38 p. Mimeographed.
Heckscher, Gunnar. "Group Organization in
Sweden," POQ, 3 (1939), 130-35.
——. "Interest Groups in Sweden: Their
Political Role," in Henry W. Ehrmann,
ed., for the International Political Science
Association, Interest Groups on Four
Continents (Pittsburgh, 1958), 154-72.
——. "Pluralist Democracy — The Swedish
Experiment," SocRes, 15 (1948), 417-61.

Heckscher, Gunnar. "The Role of Voluntary Organizations in Swedish Democracy," in J. A. Lauwerys, ed., Scandinavian Democracy (Coph., N.Y., 1958), 126-38.

Johanson, K. E., U. Karlsson, and W. Svensson. "The Swedish Youth and the Communists," World Marxist Review, 9 (1966), 66-67.

Kihlberg, Mats, and Donald Söderlind. Två Studier i Svensk Konservatism, 1916-1922 [Two Studies in Swedish Conservatism, 1916-1922]. Stock., 1961. English Summary, 251-61.

Landsorganisationen. The Postwar Programs of Swedish Labor. Stock., 1946.

Mehlem, Max. "Sweden's Communists on Trial," SRWA, 2 (1952/53, no. 4), 11-13.

Molin, Björn. "Swedish Party Politics: a Case Study," ScPolSt, 1 (1966), 45-58.

Oehman, Gunnar. "Communist Electoral Success in Sweden," World Marxist Review, 9 (1966), 73-75.

Postwar Programme of Swedish Labour: Summary in 27 Points and Comments. Stock., 1946. 151 p.

Severin, F. The Ideological Development of Swedish Social Democracy. Stock., 1956. 57 p.

Sparring, Åke. "Sweden," in William E. Griffith, ed., Communism in Europe (Cambridge, Mass.; London, 1966), 287-319.

Sundstrom, E. "Branting, Father of Swedish Prosperity," Fortnightly (1935), 695-707.

"Swedish Social Democratic Party," Yearbook of the International Socialist Labour Movement 1956-1957 (Lond., 1956), 447-60.

Therborn, Göran. "The Swedish Left," New Left Review, no. 34 (N/D 1965), 50-59.

——. "The Swedish Left," Studies on the Left, 7 (1967), 69-81.

Westerståhl, Jörgen, and Carl-Gunnar Janson. Politisk Press — The Political Press. Gothenburg, 1958. 127 p.

POLITICAL BEHAVIOR

Anderson, Bo. "Opinion Influentials and Political Opinion Formation in Four Swedish Communities," ISSJ (1962), 320-36.

——. "Some Problems of Change in the Swedish Electorate," AcSoc, 6 (1962), 241-55.

Anderson, Bo, and L. O. Mehlen. "Lazarsfeld's Two-Step Hypothesis: Data from Some Swedish Surveys," AcSoc, 4 (1959), 20-34.

Bellquist, Eric C. "Maintaining Morale in Sweden," POQ, 5 (1941), 432-47.

Karlsson, Georg. "Party Differentiating Political Opinions in Male Swedish Youth," AcSoc, 4 (1959), 8-24.

——. "Political Attitudes Among Male Swedish Youth," AcSoc, 3 (1958), 220-41.

——. "Voting Participation Among Male Swedish Youth," AcSoc, 3 (1958), 98-111.

Lägnert. Folke. The Electorate in the Country Districts of Scania 1911-1948. Lund, 1952. 25 p.

Särlvik, Bo. "Political Stability and Change in the Swedish Electorate," ScPolSt, 1 (1966), 188-222.

——. The Role of Party Identification in Voters' Perception of Political Issues: a Study of Opinion Formation in Swedish Politics, 1956-1960. Paper for International Political Science Association Congress, Paris, 1960. Mimeographed.

PUBLIC ADMINISTRATION

Anderman, Steven D. "The Swedish Justitieombudsman," AJCL (1962), 225-38.

Andrén, Nils. "The Swedish Office of 'Ombudsman'," Municipal Review, 33 (1962), 820-21.

——. "The Swedish Ombudsman," Anglo-Swedish Review (1962), 97-103.

Bexelius, Alfred. "The Ombudsman for Civil Affairs," in Donald Rowat, ed., The Ombudsman: Citizen's Defender (Lond., Toronto, Stock., 1965), 22-44.

——. "The Origin, Nature and Functions of the Civil and Military Ombudsmen in Sweden," Annals, 377 (1968), 10-19.

——. "The Swedish Institution of the Justitieombudsman," IRAS, 27 (1961), 243-56. Reprinted in Administration (Dublin), 9 (1961/62), 272-90.

——. The Swedish "Ombudsman," Special Parliamentary Commissioner for the Judiciary and the Civil Administration 1810-1860. Stock., 1961. 34 p. Mimeographed.

Bolang, C. O. "But the Ombudsman Thought Otherwise," ASM, 57 (1963), 22-24.

Chapman, Brian. "The Ombudsman," in his, The Profession of Government: the Public Service in Europe (N.Y., 1959), 245-59.

Heckscher, Gunnar. Swedish Public Administration at Work. Stock., 1955. 24 p.

Henkow, Hugo. Memorandum on the Institution of the Swedish Procurator of Military Affairs (MO). Stock., 1959. 18 p. Mimeographed.

——. "The Ombudsman for Military Affairs," in Donald Rowat, ed., The Ombudsman: Citizen's Defender (Lond., Toronto, Stock., 1965), 51-57.

Herlitz, Nils. "The Civil Service of Sweden," in Leonard D. White, ed., The Civil Service in the Modern State (Chicago, 1930), 487-504.

——. "Swedish Administrative Law," International Comparative Law Quarterly, 2 (1953), 224-37.

——. Swedish Administrative Law, Some Characteristic Features (Studia juridica Stockholmiensia, 7). Stock., 1959. 35 p.

Hesslén, Gunnar A. Public Administration in Sweden. Stock., 1956. 64 p. Mimeographed.

Höök, Erik. "The Expansion of the Public Sector — A Study of the Development of Public Civilian Expenditures in Sweden During the Years 1913-58," PubFin, 17 (1962), 289-312.

Hormell, Orren C. The Control of Public Utilities Abroad: Great Britain, Germany, France, Sweden, Norway, etc. Syracuse, N.Y., 1930. 88 p.

Jägerskiöld, Stig. "The Swedish Ombudsman," University of Pennsylvania Law Review, 109 (1961), 1077-99.

——. "Swedish State Officials and Their Position Under Public Law and Labour Law," ScStL, 4 (1960), 103-23.

Kjellin, Björn, ed. Working Paper on Sweden Prepared for UN Seminar on Judicial and Other Remedies Against Abuse of Administrative Authority (UNDoc. 62-03518). N.Y., 1962. 36 p. Mimeographed.

Löfberg, Olof. "The Recruitment of Civil Servants in the Swedish Administration," IRAS (1957), 487-96.

——. "The Recruitment of Civil Servants in the Swedish Administration," Les Cahiers de Bruges (1957).

Lundvik, Ulf. "Comments on the Ombudsman for Civil Affairs," in Donald Rowat, ed., The Ombudsman: Citizen's Defender (Lond., Toronto, Stock., 1965), 44-50.

Romander, Holger. "The Administrative Organization for Combating Juvenile Delinquency under New Swedish Legislation," IRAS, 29 (1963), 371-77.

Rosenthal, Albert H. "The Ombudsman — Swedish 'Grievance Man'," Public Administration Review, 24 (1964), 226-33.

Rudholm, Sten. "The Chancellor of Justice," in Donald Rowat, ed., The Ombudsman: Citizen's Defender (Lond., Toronto, Stock., 1965), 17-22

Sanders, Marion K. "Sweden's Remedy for 'Police Brutality'," Harper's Magazine, 229 (1964), 132-36.

Skogh, Sven. "The Administration of Social Welfare," Annals (May 1938), 20-24.

Tammelin, Paul. "Rationalization in Swedish Public Administration," IRAS (1962), 415-18.

Verney, Douglas V. Public Enterprise in Sweden. Liverpool, 1959. 132 p.

Wennergren, Bertil. "The Rise and Growth of Swedish Institutions for Defending the Citizen against Official Wrongs," Annals, 377 (1968), 1-9.

Westerståhl, Jörgen, with Bo Särlvik and Esbjörn Janson. "An Experiment with Information Pamphlets on Civil Defense," POQ, 25 (1961), 236-48.

LOCAL GOVERNMENT

Andrén, Nils. Local Government of Sweden. Stock., 1957. 38 p.

Baude, Annika. "Swedish Local Government," APSR, 50 (1956), 1115-16.

Berghult, C. R. Municipal Government of Sweden. Thesis (Ph.D.), Columbia University, 1931.

Gichard, J. Administrative Organization of the City of Stockholm. Stock., 1930.

Hanson, Bertil L. Stockholm Municipal Politics. Thesis (Ph.D.), University of Chicago, 1959. 227 p.

Langenfelt, Per. Principles for a New Division of Sweden's Municipalities. Stock., 1962. 9 p.

Lindstrom, D. E. "The Changing Rural Community in Sweden: a Major Change in Local Governmental Units," RS, 16 (M 1951), 64-68.

Lock, M. "Town Planning in Sweden and Norway," Listener, 52 (1954), 850-52.

Niemi, Donald R. Sweden's Municipal Consolidation Reforms. Thesis (Ph.D.), University of Chicago, 1966.

Olsson, John. The Local Government of Sweden: a Survey, February 1952. Stock., 1952. 15 p.

Peel, Roy V. "Local Government in Sweden," Public Affairs (M 1940).

——. "Stockholm Goes to the Polls," National Municipal Review (1935), 359-61.

Robson, W. A. "My Investigation of City Government in Stockholm," The Municipal Journal and Public Works Engineer (Jl 17, 1936), 1403-1405.

Schalling, Erik. "Swedish Local Government and Some of Its Problems," Public Administration (1926), 19ff.

Zimmerer, P. N. City Planning Policy and Administration: a Comparative Study of England, Sweden, and the United States. Thesis (M.Sc.), London School of Economics, 1953.

Zink, Harold, Arne Wåhlstrand et al. Rural Local Government in Sweden, Italy and India. Lond., 1957; N.Y., 1958. 142 p.

SOCIOLOGY

INTRODUCTION

Quite a bit of Scandinavia's best work in Sociology has appeared in English, and at present there is a great deal of ongoing research, some of it at specialized institutes. Recent work is of high quality, being both methodologically advanced and rigorously executed. The census and other statistics available to researchers have long been among the world's best. *Acta Sociologica*, an English-language journal, is recommended for those wishing to consult the latest research articles. Also, beginning in 1965, the Scandinavian Research Council for Criminology has been publishing a series of volumes, *Scandinavian Studies in Criminology*. For those interested in Finland, the *Transactions of the Westermarck Society* are important; volume XIII (1966) is a *Bibliography of Finnish Sociology 1945-1959*. The Winter 1961 issue of *Sociological Inquiry* is a seven-article special issue on "Current Developments in Scandinavian Sociology." The compilation presented in the following pages excludes travellers' accounts, which are numerous and which tell much about style of life, however impressionistically.

There is no textbook-like introduction to Scandinavia organized around the variables of sociological analysis. For a journalistic, pleasantly biased and most entertaining introduction to the Scandinavian peoples, one might well begin with Donald Connery's *The Scandinavians* (1966). Users of this bibliography wishing to learn about the background of these peoples will find

many entries on the population characteristics of the Finns, Norwegians, and Swedes, and almost peculiarly many on the Lapps. There are many complementary items under History, and, on settlement, population, and migration, under Geography. Those interested in the linguistic struggles of Norway and Finland should consult the works of Einar Haugen on Norway and supplement the entries on Finland by looking at works on nationalism under History. There are relevant entries under Law and under Political Science.

The purpose of providing an introductory overview can at this point be served by dividing the literature into two categories, one policy oriented and one science oriented. The Northern Countries have attracted widespread attention because they have been socially progressive, showing leadership in coping with the problems of modern societies. There are numerous, often repetitive, and largely descriptive works on social problems, policies, and programs such as social security and insurance systems, crime, and alcoholism. The basic work, now out-of-date, is George Nelson, ed., *Freedom and Welfare: Social Patterns in the Northern Countries of Europe* (1953). For Sweden there is a more recent study, Albert Rosenthal's *The Social Programs of Sweden: a Search for Security in a Free Society* (1967). Although there is no landmark successor volume for any of the other countries, subsequent descriptive material is plentiful, often in the form of government booklets. On several topics the country literature is sufficiently parallel to permit extensive comparisons. For complementary items, see the sections on Labor and Housing under Economics and the entries under Education.

With regard to the more scientific literature, most of it is in the form of articles, and probably the best of it concerns social stratification, rural sociology, demography, and migration. On these topics, existing materials will permit comparative analysis. The demography and migration literature on Sweden includes several fine studies, and rural sociology materials on Norway are relatively good. Perhaps the most notable work in urban sociology is Ørjar Øyen's *Ecological Context and Residential Differentiation: Neighborhood Attachment in Four Areas of Oslo* (1964). There is adequate material for comparative analysis of the family; a basic work is Thomas Eliot and Arthur Hillman, eds., *Norway's Families* (1960). The leading work on social stratification is by a professor in Denmark, Kaare Svalastoga, and is entitled *Prestige, Class and Mobility* (1959). Those interested in Denmark may with also to consult Svalastoga's *Where Europeans Meet: a Sociological Investigation of a Border Town* (1960), and the Andersons' *The Vanishing Village; a Danish Maritime Community* (1964). The work of Veli Verkko on suicide in Finland merits special mention. The works on religion in this bibliography generally are more historically than sociologically ori-

ented; convenience dictated however that most entries on religion be placed in this section. Those interested in political sociology and political behavior will find the entries they seek under Political Science.

It is noteworthy that there is virtually nothing on the sociology of religion or the sociology of literature for any of the countries. There has been virtually no comparative research published in English, with the notable exception of Herbert Hendin's *Suicide and Scandinavia* (1964), which won the Association for Psychoanalytic Medicine's annual prize for original research in 1964. There is nothing in comparative urban or rural sociology, and, although there are plentiful descriptive materials on nearly each country's press, there are no comparative treatments of the media. It is curious that there are hardly any American Ph.D. dissertations in Sociology based on research in Scandinavia, apparently none at all since World War II in Denmark, Finland, or Iceland. Only two seem noteworthy: John Flint's *State, Church, and Laity in Norwegian Society: a Typological Study of Institutional Change* (1957); and Anders Lunde's *Norway: a Population Study* (1955). There is a recent British dissertation on population growth: Michael Drake, *Marriage and Population Growth in Norway* (1964). One might add a most impressive dissertation listed under Political Science, Allen Barton's *Sociological and Psychological Problems of Economic Planning in Norway* (1957).

SCANDINAVIA

Agersnap, Torben. "Bibliography on Theodor Geiger," AcSoc, 1 (1955/56), 80-84.

Allardt, Erik. "Scandinavian Sociology," Social Science Information, 6 (1967, no. 4), 223-46.

"Bibliography on Torgny T. Segerstedt," AcSoc, 3 (1958/59), 147-51.

Christie, Nils. "Scandinavian Criminology," Sociological Inquiry, 31 (1961), 93-104.

Connery, Donald S. The Scandinavians. N.Y., 1966. 590 p.

Eckhoff, Torstein. "Sociology of Law in Scandinavia," ScStL, 4 (1960), 29-58.

Friis, Henning K. Scandinavia Between East and West (Publication of the New School for Social Research). Ithaca, N.Y., 1950. 388 p.

Grönbech, Vilhelm P. The Culture of the Teutons. 3 vols. Oxford, 1932.

Jansen, Carl-Gunnar. "Project Metropolitan," AcSoc, 9 (1966), 110-15.

Johnson, Sveinbjorn. "Social and Industrial Progress in Scandinavia," CH, 34 (1931), 858-61.

Kleven, Hans J. "Changes in the Class Structure of the Scandinavian Countries," World Marxist Review, 9 (1966), 32-39.

Leach, Henry G. Scandinavia of the Scandinavians. N.Y., 1915. 346 p.

League of Nations. European Conference on Rural Life, 1939. Geneva, 1939. No. 1, Finland, 59 p.; No. 20, Denmark, 54 p.; No. 21, Sweden, 71 p.; No. 25, Norway, 66 p.

Linnér, Birgitta. "Sexual Morality and Sexual Reality — the Scandinavian Approach,"

American Journal of Orthopsychiatry, 36 (1966), 686-93.

Lundquist, Agne. "Industrial Sociology in Sweden, Norway, and Denmark," Sociological Inquiry, 31 (1961), 60-73.

Persson Blegvad, Britt-Mari. "The Systematic Position of Sociology of Law in Current Scandinavian Research," AcSoc, 10 (1966), 2-19.

Philip, David. "The Originality of Scandinavian Culture," Norseman, 13 (1955), 78-84.

———. "Social Scandinavia," Norseman, 14 (1956), 364-69.

———. "The Social Structure of the Northern Countries," Norseman, 14 (1956), 73-82.

Salvesen, Kaare. "Cooperation in Social Affairs Between the Northern Countries of Europe," ILR, 73 (1956), 334-57.

"Scandinavian Seminar in Rural Sociology," SocRur, 3 (1963), 370-72.

Schlauch, Margaret. "Scandinavia: the Dilemma of the Middle Way," SciS, 9 (1945), 97-124.

Scott, Franklin D. "American Influences in Norway and Sweden," JMH, 18 (1946), 37-47.

Svalastoga, Kaare, and Gösta Carlsson. "Social Stratification and Social Mobility, Scandinavian Contributions," Sociological Inquiry, 31 (1961), 23-46.

Svalastoga, Kaare, and Tom Rishøj. "Social Mobility: the Western European Model," AcSoc, 9 (1966), 175-82.

Svensson, Sten. "Sport and Open-Air Life in Scandinavia," ScPP, III, 255-67.

Vogt, William. "Success Story," in People! Challenge to Survival (N.Y., 1960), 170-207.

Wasberg, Gunnar C. "The Nordic Cultural Commission," ASR, 49 (1961), 169-73.

Westergaard, John H. "Scandinavian Urbanism: a Survey of Trends and Themes in Urban Social Research in Sweden, Norway and Denmark," AcSoc, 8 (1965), 304-23.

———. "The Scope of Urban Social Studies in the Scandinavian Countries: Sweden, Norway and Denmark," Current Sociology, 4 (1955), 77-90; 5 (1956), 77-96.

Williams, Mary W. Social Scandinavia in the Viking Age. N.Y., 1920. 451 p.

THE FAMILY

Bardis, P. "Evolution of the Scandinavian Family," Archelon Oikonomikon Kai Koinonikon Epistemon (Athens), 37 (1957), 31-35.

Beckman, H. G. Married Misery and Its Scandinavian Solution. Lond., 1923.

Brun-Gulbrandsen, Sverre. "Sex Roles and the Socialization Process," in Edmund Dahlström, ed., The Changing Roles of Men and Women (Lond., 1967), 59-78.

Dahlström, Edmund, and Rita Liljeström. "The Family and Married Women at Work," in Edmund Dahlström, ed., The Changing Roles of Men and Women (Lond., 1967), 19-58.

Holter, Harriet. "Rebellion Against the Family: a Discussion of Some Trends in Scandinavian Left-Wing Ideologies," AcSoc, 6 (1962), 185-202.

Karlsson, Georg. "Sociological Studies of the Family in Scandinavia," Sociological Inquiry, 31 (1961), 47-59.

Knudsen, Thora. "The Scandinavian Marriage Law," ASR, 10 (1922), 36-40.

League of Nations, Child Welfare Committee. Child Welfare Councils [Denmark, Norway, Sweden] (Official no: C.8.M.7. 1937, IV, 1), Geneva, 1937.

Schmidt, Folke. "The 'Leniency' of Scandinavian Divorce Laws," ScStL, 7 (1963), 107-21.

Svalastoga, Kaare. "The Family in Scandinavia," Marriage and Family Living, 16 (1954), 374-80.

Tiller, Per Olav. "Parental Role Division and the Child's Personality Development," in Edmund Dahlström, ed., The Changing Roles of Men and Women (Lond., 1967), 79-104.

Tillotson, Harry S. "Scandinavia's Solution of the Divorce Problem," CH, 34 (1931), 551-54.

WOMEN

Anthony, Katherine S. Feminism in Germany and Scandinavia. N.Y., 1915. 260 p.

Ewerlöff, Elsa. "Women's Rights in Scandinavia," ScPP, III, 211-16.

Gloerfelt-Tarp, Kirsten G., ed. Women in the Community. Lond., N.Y., Coph., Oslo, 1939. 301 p.

Langhoff, Johannes. "Women and Hell Stir Scandinavia," Christian Century, 85 (F 5, 1958), 179.

Larsen, Hanna A. "Four Scandinavian Feminists," Yale Review, 5 (1916), 347-62.

RELIGION

Almedingen, Edith M. "The Catholic Church

in the Early North," CHistR, new series, 7 (1927), 383-93.

Almedingen, Edith M. "Vikings and 'Christ's Men,'" ASR, 14 (1926), 525-31.

Andersen, N. K. "The Reformation in Scandinavia and the Baltic," in The New Cambridge Modern History (Cambridge, 1958), v. 2, 134-60.

Bergendoff, Conrad J. L. "The Churches of Scandinavia," ASR, 28 (1940), 295-300.

Berggrav, Eivind J. "Christianity and Democracy," in J. A. Lauwerys, ed., Scandinavian Democracy (Coph., N.Y., 1958), 349-54.

Bumpus, Thomas F. Cathedrals and Churches of Norway, Sweden and Denmark. Lond., 1908. 299 p.

"The Church in Scandinavia," Catholic International Outlook, no. 197 (1959), 1-24.

Flakser, David. "The Jews in Scandinavia," Israel Horizons, 9 (Je/Jl 1961), 25-29.

Hunter, Leslie S. Scandinavian Churches. Minneapolis, 1965. 200 p.

Jenson, Andrew. History of the Scandinavian Mission. Salt Lake City, 1927. 570 p.

Kellett, Ernest E. The Religion of Our Northern Ancestors (Manuals for Christian Thinkers). Lond., 1914. 141 p.

Kerridge, H. J. "Scandinavia not Christian? Letter to the Editor," Norseman, 6 (1948), 209-11.

Koch, Hal H. "Paganism and Christianity," ScPP, I, 130-35.

Lid, Nils. "The Paganism of the Norsemen," in Studies in Folklore in Honor of Prof. Stith Thompson (Bloomington, Ind., 1957), 230-51.

MacCulloch, John A. The Celtic and Scandinavian Religions (Hutchinson's University Library; World Religions, 10). Lond., N.Y., 1948. 180 p.

Mulder, William. Homeward to Zion: the Mormon Migration from Scandinavia. Minneapolis, 1957. 375 p.

Nichols, C. H. "Scandinavia and the Negro," ASR, 45 (1957), 253-57.

Oppermann, Charles J. A. The English Missionaries in Sweden and Finland. Lond., N.Y., 1937. 243 p.

Rasmussen, Carl C. What About Scandinavia? Phila., 1948. 194 p.

Rodhe, Sten. "Swedish and Danish Christianity," Nord, 6 (1943), 104-20.

Roussell, Aage. "Mediaeval Parish Churches and the Geometric Systems," AcAr, 27 (1956), 61-90.

Skovmand, Roar. "Rome and Scandinavia," ScPP, I, 62-63.

POPULATION

Frumkin, Gregory. Population Changes in Europe Since 1939. N.Y., Lond., 1951. 191 p.

Gille, Halvor. "The Demographic History of the Northern European Countries in the 18th Century," PopSt, 3 (1949), 3-65.

Hovde, Brynjolf J. "Notes on the Effects of Emigration upon Scandinavia," JMH, 6 (1934), 253-79.

"Immigration: A Symposium," ASR, 14 (1926), 675-79.

Jenson, Adolph L. O. "Migration Statistics of Denmark, Norway, and Sweden," International Migrations, 2 (1931), 283-312.

League of Nations, Health Organization. The Official Vital Statistics of the Scandinavian Countries and the Baltic Republics (Statistical Handbooks Series, no. 6). Geneva, 1926. 107 p.

Princeton University, Office of Population Research. The Future Population of Europe and the Soviet Union; Population Projections; 1940-1970 (Series of League of Nations Publications, II; Economic and Financial, 1944; II. A.). Geneva, 1944. 315 p.

Wahlund, Sten G. W. "Nordic Demography," ScPP, III, 25-31.

THE LAPPS

Allison, A. C. "The Lapps; Origins and Affinities," GeogJ, 110 (1953), 315-20.

Bergsland, K. and Reidar Th. Christiansen. "Norwegian Research on the Language and Folklore of the Lapps," Journal of the Royal Anthropological Institute, 80 (1950), 79-95.

Bernatzik, Hugo A. Lapland. Lond., 1937. 136 p.

——. Overland with the Nomad Lapps. N.Y., 1938. 136 p.

Bosi, Roberto. The Lapps (Ancient Peoples and Places Series, v. 17). Lond., N.Y., 1960. 220 p.

Brown, Donald W. "A Tour in Swedish Lapland," American Alpine Journal, 3 (1937), 47-56.

Chapman, Olive M. Across Lapland, with Sledge and Reindeer. Lond., 1932. 212 p.

Collinder, Björn. The Lapps. Princeton, 1949. 252 p.

——. "The Lapps and Their Origin," ASR, 37 (1949), 117-23.

Croft, Andrew. "Nomads of the North: Lappish Life Under Modern Administration," GeogM, 7 (1938), 393-404.

Cross, A. L. "A Visit to Lapland," SGM, 27 (1911), 78-87.

Elton, Charles. "Notes on a Traverse of Norwegian Lapland in 1930," GeogJ, 79 (1932), 44-48.

Erixon, Sigurd. "Some Primitive Constructions and Types of Layout, with Their Relation to European Rural Building Practice," Folkliv, 1 (1937), 124-54.

Foye, Isabel. "A Journey thru Lapland in Finland and Norway," JofGeo, 48 (1949), 298-303.

Finnish Lapland. Hels., 1951. 32 p.

Finnish State Commission Report on Lapp Affairs, 1949-1951. Abridg. ed. by Karl Nickul in Fennia, 76, no. 3. Hels., 1953. 60 p.

Fischer, Alfred J. "Encounter with Norwegian Lapps," CR, 190 (1956), 165-68.

Fisher, Clyde. "Nomads of Arctic Lapland: Mysterious Little People of a Land of the Midnight Sun Live Off the Country Above the Arctic Circle," NGeogM, 76 (1939), 641-76.

Gjessing, Gutorm. Changing Lapps: a Study in Culture Relations in Northernmost Norway (London School of Economics and Political Science, Monographs on Social Anthropology, no. 13). Lond., 1954. 67 p.

——. "The Lapps of Norway," Norseman, 12 (1954), 40-45.

——. "Norwegian Contributions to Lapp Enthnography," Journal of the Royal Anthropological Institute, 77 (1950), 47-60.

——. "Prehistoric Social Groups in North Norway," Proceedings of the Prehistoric Society, 21 (1955), 84-92.

Gourlie, Norah. A Winter with Finnish Lapps. Lond., 1939, 243 p.

Haglund, Sven. Life Among the Lapps: On the Spring Trek with the Köngämä Lapps. Lond., 1935. 252 p.

Hatt, Gudmund. "Artificial Moulding of the Infant's Head Among the Scandinavian Lapps," AmAnthro, 17 (1915), 245-56.

Hill, Rowland G. P., ed. [on behalf of the Nordic Lapp Council]. The Lapps To-day in Finland, Norway and Sweden, vol. I [vol. 2 in preparation] (École pratique des hautes études, 6e section; sciences économiques et sociales: Bibliothèque Arctique et Antarctique). Paris, 1960. 227 p.

Hinds, E. M. "Lapland," CG, 26 (1943), 14-25.

Holmqvist, Wilhelm. "On the Origin of the Lapp Ribbon Ornament," AcAr, 5, (1934), 265-82.

Hooton, E. A. "Finns, Lapps, Eskimos, and Martin Luther," Harvard Alumni Bulletin, (F 6, 1930), 545-53.

Høst, Per. The Laplanders, Europe's Last Nomads. Oslo, 1964. 112 p.

Hultkrantz, Åke. "Swedish Research on the Religion and Folklore of the Lapps," Journal of the Royal Anthropological Institute, 85 (1955), 81-100.

Hyne, Cutliffe. Through Arctic Lapland. Lond., 1898. 284 p.

Itkonen, T. I. "The Lapps of Finland," Southwestern Journal of Anthropology, 7 (1951), 32-68.

Jannes, Elly. Nomads of the North. N.Y., 1953. 84 p.

Jenkins, Alan C. "Arctic Boatbuilder," Norseman, 15 (1957), 310-14.

Kallas, Hillar. "A Lapp Wedding in the Finnish Arctic," Norseman, 14 (1956), 335-37.

Karsten, Rafael. The Religion of the Samek; Ancient Beliefs and Cults of the Scandinavian and Finnish Lapps. Leiden, 1955. 136 p.

Koebel, Everard R. O. "Life on the Tracks of the Reindeer Herd," GeogM, 3 (1936), 102-17.

Kokko, Yrjö. The Way of the Four Winds. N.Y., 1954. 286 p.

Kuhne, Jack. "Europe's Northern Nomads," NGeogM, 76 (1939), 657-64.

"Lapland" [Special Issue], Finlandia Pictorial, 14 (N 1959), 1-15.

Leach, Henry G. "Lapland — Sweden's America," ASR, 2 (1914), 28-35.

Lloyd, Trevor. "South to the Circle," CG, 50 (1955), 168-75.

Lowie, Robert H. "A Note on Lapp Culture History," Southwestern Journal of Anthropology, 1 (1945), 447-65.

Lundborg, Herman B. and Sten G. W. Wahlund, eds. The Race Biology of the Swedish Lapps. Uppsala, 1932.

Lundquist, Gösta. Lappland: the Land of Pioneers and Nomads. Stock., 1954. 182 p.

Manker, Ernst M. "The Last of the Reindeer Lapps; Among the Samer, These Herding Nomads Are on the Verge of Extinction Today," Natural History, 67 (1958), 71-81.

——. The Nomadism of the Swedish Mountain Lapps: The Sudas and Their Migratory Routes in 1945 (Acta Lapponica, 7). Stock., 1953. 261 p.

——. People of Eight Seasons: the Story of the Lapps. N.Y., 1963. 214 p.

——. "The Study and Preservation of the Ancient Lapp Culture: Sweden's Contribution Since 1939," Man, 47 (1947), 98-100.

Manker, Ernst M. "Swedish Contributions to Lapp Ethnography," Journal of the Royal Anthropological Institute, 82 (1952), 39-54.

Michie, George H. "Valijoki and Lisma: New Planned Settlements in Finnish Lapland," CG, 5 (1961), 24-36.

Minn, Eeva K. The Lapps (Human Relations Area Files, Inc.; Subcontractor's Monograph, HRAF-3). Prepared by Indiana University Graduate Program in Uralic and Asian Studies. New Haven, Conn., 1955. 137 p.

Morden, Irene. "Arctic Nomads: a Glimpse into the Life of the Lapps — A People Whose Very Existence Is Determined by the Reindeer They Follow Through the Wilderness of the Far North," Natural History, 61 (1952), 24-29.

Nickul, Karl. "The Finnish Lapps in Wartime and After," Man, 50 (1950), 57-60.

——. The Skalt Lapp Community Snenjelsijd During the Year 1938 (Acta Lapponica — Nordiska Muset, v. 5). Stock., 1948. 90 p.

Nordström, Ester B. Tent Folk of the Far North. Lond., 1930. 255 p.

Osborne, John Ball. "The Present Development of Swedish Lapland," Commerce Reports, no. 46 (1929), 398-400; no. 47 (1929), 461-63.

Paine, Robert. Coast Lapp Society I: a Study of Neighborhood in Revsbotn Fjord. Oslo, 1957. 358 p.

——. Coast Lapp Society II: a Study of Economic Development and Social Values. Oslo, 1965. 194 p.

——. "Emergence of the Village as a Social Unit in a Coast Lappish Fjord," AmAnthro, 62 (1960), 1004-17.

Pehrson, Robert N. The Bilateral Network of Social Relations in Könkämä Lapp District (Publication of the Indiana University Research Center in Anthropology, Folklore and Linguistics, 3). Bloomington, Ind., 1957. 128 p.

——. "Culture Contact without Conflict in Lapland," Man, 50 (1950), 156-60.

——. "The Lappish Herding Leader: a Structural Analysis," AmAnthro, 56 (1954), 1076-80.

——. North Lappish Kinship Terminology in Relation to Working Organization. IVth Congrès International des Sciences Anthropologiques et Ethnologiques. Vienna, 1952. Actes (Du IV Congrès etc.) 1954—. v. 3, 81-86.

——. "Reindeer Herding Among the Karesuando Lapps," ASR, 39 (1951), 271-79.

Qvigstad, Just. "The Lapps," Norseman, 4 (1946), 326-31.

Ruong, Israel. The Lapps in Sweden. Stock., 1962. 46 p.

Sariola, Sakari. Drinking Patterns in Finnish Lapland (Alcohol Research in the Northern Countries). Stock., 1956. 88 p.

Shor, Jean, and Franc Shor. "North with Finland's Lapps," NGeogM, 106 (1954), 249-80.

Strunge, Mogens. Lapland. Coph., 1948. 253 p.

Sutherland, Halliday. Lapland Journey. Lond., 1938. 294 p.

Turi, Johan O. Turi's Book of Lappland. Lond., 1931. 293 p.

Virtanen, E. A. "Hunting on Another Man's Ground," WestSocTrans, 1 (1947). 94-112.

Vorren, Ørnulf. "Lapp Settlement and Population," in Norway North of 65 (Oslo, 1960), 122-33.

Vorren, Ørnulf, and Ernst M. Manker. Lapp Life and Customs: a Survey. Lond., N.Y., 1962. 183 p.

Wahlund, Sten G. W. Demographic Studies in the Nomadic and the Settled Population of Northern Lapland. Uppsala, 1932. 133 p. Tables, 93 p.

Walter, L. E. Norway and the Lapps. Lond., 1929. 90 p.

Whitaker, Ian. Social Relations in a Nomadic Lappish Community (Samiske Samlinger 2). Oslo, 1955. 178 p.

Wiklund, K. B. The Lapps in Northernmost Sweden. Stock., 1938.

——. "The Lapps in Sweden," GeoR, 13 (1923), 223-42.

Winslow, E. D. "The Lapps of Sweden," Bulletin of the American Geographical Society, 32 (1900), 430-31.

Wyatt, Colin. "On Ski Through Arctic Lapland to the North Cape," AlpineJ, 50 (1938), 248-56.

FOLKLORE

Bødker, Laurits. "Nordic Folklore. Reports, 1958-59," Arv, 14 (1958), 163-79.

Christiansen, Reidar Th. The Migratory Legends: a Proposed List of Types with a Systematic Catalogue of the Norwegian Variants (FF Communications, no. 175). Hels., 1958. 221 p.

——. Studies in Irish and Scandinavian Folktales (Irish Folklore Commission). Dublin, Coph., 1959. 249 p.

Erixon, Sigurd. "An Introduction to Folklife

Research or Nordic Ethnology," Folk-Liv, 14-15 (1950/51), 5-15.

Erixon, Sigurd. "Surviving Primitive Gatherings in the Nordic Countries," Folk-Liv, 14-15 (1950/51), 95-101.

Kelchner, Georgia D. Dreams in Old Norse Literature and Their Affinities in Folklore. Cambridge, 1935. 154 p.

Lid, Nils. Light-Mother and Earth Mother (Studia norvegica, Ethnologica and Folkloristica, no. 4). Oslo, 1946. 20 p.

Mitchell, P. M. "The Scandinavian Literary Engagement," in Carl Bayerschmidt and Erik Friis, eds., Scandinavian Studies: Essays Presented to Henry Goddard Leach (Seattle, 1965), 331-43.

Primmer, Kathleen. Scandinavian Peasant Costume. N.Y., 1940. 106 p.

Strömbäck, Dag. "Kurt Liestøl, In Memoriam," Arv, 8 (1952), 141-46.

———. "Nils Lid: In Memoriam," Arv, 14 (1958), 115-17.

Tschan, Francis J. "Helmold: Chronicler of the North Saxon Missions," CHistR, 16 (1931), 379-412.

MYTHOLOGY

Branston, Brian. Gods of the North. N.Y., 1955. 318 p.

Craigie, William A. The Religion of Ancient Scandinavia (Religions Ancient and Modern). Lond., 1906. 71 p.

Davidson, Hilda R. E. Gods and Myths of Northern Europe. Baltimore, 1964. 251 p.

Karsten, Rafael. The Religion of the Samek: Ancient Beliefs and Cults of the Scandinavian and Finnish Lapps. Leiden, 1955. 136 p.

Kauffmann, Friedrich. Northern Mythology. Lond., 1903. 106 p.

Nilsson, Martin. "At Which Time of the Year Was the Pre-Christian Yule Celebrated?" Arv, 14 (1958), 108-14.

Pettersson, O. Jabmek and Jalmearino. A Comparative Study of the Dead and the Realm of the Dead in Cappish Religion (Lund University Årsskrift, N.F. Avd. 1, Bd. 52. Nr. 6). Lund, 1957. 253 p.

Rooth, Anna B. Loki in Scandinavian Mythology (Humanistiska vetenskapssamfundet i Lund, Skrifter, 61). Lund, 1961. 266 p.

Steiner, Rudolf. The Mission of Folk-Souls, in Connection with Germanic Scandinavian Mythology. Lond., 1929. 145 p.

Turville-Petre, E. O. Gabriel. Myth and Religion of the North: the Religion of Ancient Scandinavia. N.Y., 1962. 340 p.

Vries, Jan de. The Problem of Loki (FF Communications, no. 110). Hels., 1933. 306 p.

MASS COMMUNICATIONS

Beyer, Nils. "Theater and Cinema," in J. A. Lauwerys, ed., Scandinavian Democracy (Coph., N.Y., 1958). 328-38.

Elvin, Rene. "Advertising Media in Scandinavia," EFTA Bull, 8 (1967, no. 7), 5-10.

Hardy, Forsyth. Scandinavian Film (The National Cinema Series) Lond., 1952. 62 p.

Skautrup, Peter. "Our Common Language," ScPP, I, 136-39.

———. "The Scandinavian Languages," ScPP, II, 1019-22.

Tingsten, Herbert L. G. "The Press," in J. A. Lauwerys, ed., Scandinavian Democracy (Coph., N.Y., 1958), 316-27.

Walker, John. "The Press in Scandinavia," EFTA Bull, 8 (1967, no. 5), 10-13.

SOCIAL PROBLEMS

Block, Jeanne, and Bjørn Christiansen. "A Test of Hendin's Hypotheses Relating Suicide in Scandinavia to Childrearing Orientations," Scandinavian Journal of Psychology, 7 (1966), 267-88.

Croog, Sydney H. "Premarital Pregnancies in Scandinavia and Finland," AJS, 57 (1951/52), 358-65. A correction by Julie E. Backer, AJS, 58 (1952/53), 68.

de Boer, H. A., and F. B. Venema. "General Trends in the Rehabilitation of Disabled Persons in Scandinavia," ISSAssoc, 6 (1953), 155-66.

Gebhard, Paul H., and others. Pregnancy, Birth and Abortion. N.Y., 1958. 282 p.

Harrison, Lawrence W., and others. Report on Anti-Venereal Measures in Certain Scandinavian Countries and Holland (Great Britain, Ministry of Health, Reports on Public Health and Medical Subjects, no. 83). Lond., 1938. 156 p.

Hendin, Herbert. Suicide and Scandinavia. N.Y., 1964. 177 p.

Moss, J. Joel. "Teenage Marriage: Cross-national Trends and Sociological Factors in the Decision of When to Marry," AcSoc, 8 (1965), 98-117.

ALCOHOLISM

Allardt, Erik, T. Markkanen, and Martti

Takala. Drinking and Drinkers; Three Papers in Behavioral Sciences (Alcohol Research in the Northern Countries). Hels., Stock., 1957. 162 p.

Bruun, Kettil. "Alcohol Studies in Scandinavia," Sociological Inquiry, 31 (1961), 78-92.

Bruun, Ketil, Ragnar Hauge, Nils Christie et al. Drinking Habits Among Northern Youth (Alcohol Research in the Northern Countries). Hels., 1963. 97 p.

Henius, Max. Modern Liquor Legislation and Systems in Finland, Norway, Denmark and Sweden. 1931. 18 p.

Pratt, Edwin A. Licensing and Temperance in Sweden, Norway, and Denmark. Lond., 1907. 117 p.

PRISONS

Almquist, Viktor. "Scandinavian Prisons," Annals, 157 (1931), 197-207.

Northern Association of Criminalists Yearbook, 1948-49. Stock., 1949.

Verkko, Veli. "General Theoretical Viewpoints in Criminal Statistics Regarding Real Criminality," WestSocTrans, 2 (1953), 47-75. Uses Scandinavian data.

——. "Survey of Current Practice in Criminal Statistics," WestSocTrans, 3 (1956), 5-33.

SOCIAL POLICY

Armstrong, Barbara N. "Old Age Security Abroad: the Background of Titles II and VIII of the Social Security Act," LCP, 3 (Ap 1936), 175-85.

Bratteli, Olav, and Tore Tallioth. "Social Welfare, Scandinavian Way: Norwegian Welfare State under Labor; Swedish Welfare State Protects Liberty," L&N (1949/50), 36-41.

Denmark, Ministry of Labor and Social Affairs. The Historical Background of Social Welfare in Scandinavia (Danish Social Structure, no. 1). by John Dornstrup. Coph., 1952.

Friis, Henning K. "Social Welfare," in his, Scandinavia Between East and West (Ithaca, N.Y., 1950), 139-68.

Hovde, Brynjolf J. "Social Security in Scandinavia," ASR, 23 (1935), 34-41.

League of Nations, Child Welfare Commission. Child Welfare Councils: Denmark, Norway, Sweden. Geneva, 1937. 96 p.

Mannio, Niilo A. "Trends of Social Security in Nordic Countries," ISSAssoc, 5 (Ja 1952), 3-13.

Nelson, George R. Social Welfare in Scandinavia. Reprinted from Scandinavian Yearbook, 1952. Coph., 1953. 70 p.

Nelson, George R., ed. Freedom and Welfare: Social Patterns in the Northern Countries of Europe. Coph., 1953. 539 p.

Orfield, Lester B. "Scandinavian Health Insurance Legislation," South Carolina Law Quarterly, 12 (1960), 202-344.

Philip, David. "Scandinavian Social Policy," India Quarterly, 11 (1955), 137-58.

Stewart, R. H. M., and L. K. Pallister. Report on a Tour of Hospitals in Scandinavia (including Finland) under the Auspices of the World Health Organization. Newcastle upon Tyne, 1963. 36 p.

DENMARK

Andersen, Helge. "Sports and Games in Denmark in the Light of Sociology," AcSoc, 2 (1956/57), 1-27.

Bendix, Hans. "Denmark: Oasis of Decency," Comm, 4 (1947), 246-50.

Butlin, F. M. Among the Danes. N.Y., 1909. 278 p.

Clausen, Sven. "Language Reform in Denmark," ASR, 34 (1946), 137-42.

"Danish Social Democracy," AmPers, 1 (1948), 567-74.

Egan, Maurice F. "Denmark and the Danes," NGeogM, 42 (Aug 1922), 115-64.

Gosse, Edmund W. Two Visits to Denmark: 1872, 1874. Lond., 1911. 371 p.

Graae, Frederick. "The Danish Society," Nord, 6 (1943), 57-71.

Hackett, Francis. I Chose Denmark. N.Y., 1940. 291 p.

Harvey, William J., and Christian Reppien. Denmark and the Danes: a Survey of Danish Life, Institutions and Culture. Lond., 1915. 346 p.

Jones, Hugh L. Modern Denmark: Its Social, Economic, and Agricultural Life. Lond., 1927. 83 p.

Knight, Edgar W. Among the Danes (University of North Carolina, Social Study Series). Chapel Hill, N.C., 1927. 236 p.

Shankland, Graeme. "How Denmark Lives," GeoM, 30 (1957/58), 484-98.

Svalastoga, Kaare. Where Europeans Meet. A Sociological Investigation of a Border Town. Coph., 1960. 144 p.

SOCIAL STRUCTURE

Agersnap, Torben. Studier over indre vandringer i Danmark; Studies on Internal

Migration in Denmark (Acta Jutlandica. Supplementum B. Samfundsvidenskabelig serie, 5). Coph., 1952. 78 p.

Andersen, Helge. "Knight of the Dannebrog: a Socio-Statistical Study," AcSoc, 4 (1959), 7-15.

Bartels, Erik D. Gipsies in Denmark: a Social-Biological Study. Coph., 1943. 179 p. Also appears in the series Opera ex Domo Brologiae Hereditariae Humanae Universitatis Hafniensis, v. 5.

Clinard, Outten J. "Denmark's Minority Problem," Historian, 4 (1942), 193-216.

Goldstein, Sidney. "The Extent of Repeated Migration: an Analysis Based on the Danish Population Register," Journal of the American Statistical Association, 59 (1964), 1121-32.

Herling, John. "The Golden Rule in Denmark," Survey Graphic, 36 (F 1947), 152-55.

Hvidt, Kristian. "Danish Emigration Prior to 1914: Trends and Problems," SEHR, 14 (1966), 158-78.

Lassen, Aksel. "The Population of Denmark in 1660," SEHR, 13 (1965), 1-30.

——. "The Population of Denmark, 1660-1960," SEHR, 14 (1966), 134-57.

Nellemann, George. "Polish Immigrants in Denmark: the Study of a Migration and Its Effects," Folk, 7 (1965), 89-105.

RURAL AND URBAN SOCIOLOGY

Anderson, Robert T., and Barbara G. Anderson. The Vanishing Village: a Danish Maritime Community. Seattle, 1964. 148 p.

——. "Voluntary Associations and Urbanization: a Diachronic Analysis," AJS, 65 (1958), 265-73.

Bröchner, Jessie. Danish Life in Town and Country. Lond., 1903. 242 p.; N.Y., 1903. 266 p.

Danish Institute. Town Planning in Denmark. Coph., 1956. 34 p.

Dorph-Petersen, K. "The Liberation of the Danish Peasant," ASR, 26 (1938), 320-36.

Goldstein, Sidney. "Rural-Suburban-Urban Population Redistribution in Denmark," RS, 30 (1965), 267-77.

——. "Some Economic Consequences of Suburbanization in the Copenhagen Metropolitan Area," AJS, 68 (1963), 551-64.

Hansen, Viggo. "The Danish Village: Its Age and Form," GT, 58 (1959), 96-102.

League of Nations, European Conference on Rural Life. National monographs drawn up by governments, no. 20: Denmark. Geneva, 1939. 54 p.

Manniche, Peter. "The Rise of the Danish Peasantry," SR, 19 (1927), 35-39, 130-33, 218-22.

Michelsen, Peter. "Danish Rural Culture on Display," ASR, 54 (1966), 44-48.

Sellers, Edith. "The Remaking of Village Life," Living Age, 302 (Jl 1919), 165-72.

Westergaard, Waldemar C. "Farm Life in Jutland," ASR, 4 (1916), 76-83.

THE GREENLANDERS

Brun, Eske. "The Greenlander of Today," Arctic, 2 (1946), 3-12.

Dommelen, David B. van. "Folklore of the Greenland Eskimos," ASR, 50 (1962), 49-52.

"Greenland Today: Progress and Reforms in the World's Largest Island," WT, 13 (1957), 173-82.

Goldschmidt, Verner. "The Greenland Criminal Code and Its Sociological Background," AcSoc, 1 (1955-1956), 217-65.

Moltke, Harald. "An Artist Among the Polar Eskimos," ASR, 9 (1921), 668-79.

Nellemann, George. "Mitârneq: a West Greenland Winter Ceremony," Folk, 2 (1960), 99-114.

Powers, William E. "Polar Eskimos of Greenland and Their Environment," JofGeo, 49 (1950), 186-93.

Rosing, Jens. "Two Ethnological Survivals in Greenland," Folk, 3 (1961), 13-22.

SOCIAL STRATIFICATION

Geiger, Theodore. "A Dynamic Analysis of Social Mobility," AcSoc, 1 (1955/56), 26-38.

——. "An Historical Study of the Origins and Structure of the Danish Intelligentsia," BJS, 1 (1950), 209-20.

——. "Intelligentsia," AcSoc, 1 (1955/56), 49-61.

Hedtoft, Hans. "Denmark — Land of Social Equality," DFOJ (1947, no. 2), 4-9.

Ranulf, Svend. Moral Indignation and Middle Class Psychology: a Sociological Study. Coph., 1938. 204 p.

Streib, Gordon F. "Social Stratification in Denmark: a Review of Kaare Svalastoga's 'Prestige, Class and Mobility, 1959'," NT, 100 (1962), 157-63.

Svalastoga, Kaare. "Four Stratification Problems," EEH (Winter supplement, 1956), 52-57.

——. "Measurement of Occupational Prestige: Methodology and Preliminary Findings Based on Danish Data," in International Sociological Association Congress,

Liège, 1953. Communication and Papers, Sect. 1, "Social Stratification and Social Mobility," Oslo, 1953. 31 p. Mimeographed.

Svalastoga, Kaare. Prestige, Class and Mobility. Coph., 1959. 466 p.

Svalastoga, Kaare et al. "Differential Class Behavior in Denmark," AmSocR, 21 (1956), 435-39.

THE FAMILY

Auken, Kirsten. "Time of Marriage, Mate Selection and Task Accomplishment in Newly Formed Copenhagen Families," AcSoc, 8 (1965), 128-41.

Christensen, Harold T. "Selected Aspects of Child Spacing in Denmark," AcSoc, 4 (1959), 35-45.

Dam, Poul, and Jørgen Larsen, eds. Danish Youth, Work and Leisure. Coph., 1948.

Denmark, Ministry of Labour and Social Affairs, International Relations Division. Danish Care of Children and Young Persons (Danish Social Structure, pamphlet 12). Coph., 1960. 16 p.

———. Family Welfare (Danish Social Structure, pamphlet 2). Coph., 1953. 12 p.

Denmark, Youth Commission. The Danish Government Youth Commission, 1945-52. Coph., 1953. 11 p.

Faurholt, Carl, and Per T. Federspiel. Recent Danish Legislation on the Relation of Husband and Wife (International Law Association, Danish branch). Coph., 1927. 16 p.

Higgins, Anna D. "Making the Danish Child Fit," ASR, 5 (1917), 38-44.

Hoffmeyer, Henrik. Experimental Study on Family Counselling. Coph., 1952.

———. "Medical Aspects of the Danish Legislation on Abortion," Western Reserve Law Review, 17 (1965), 529-52.

Skalts, Vera, and Magne Norgaard. "Abortion Legislation in Denmark," Western Reserve Law Review, 17 (1965), 498-528.

WOMEN

Forchhammer, Henni. "Karen Jeppe and the League of Nations," Nord, 1 (1938), 292-304.

Gloerfeldt-Tarp, Kirsten G., ed. Women in the Community. Lond., N.Y., 1939. 301 p.

Moesgaard, Lizzi. The Legal Status of Married Women in Denmark. Coph., 1953. 18 p.

Social and Economic Conditions of Widows and Unmarried Mothers in Copenhagen. Coph., 1948.

"Some Danish Women," ASR, 5 (1917), 335-40.

RELIGION

Andersen, Johannes Oskar. "Survey of the History of the Church in Denmark," in Det Lutherske Verdenskonvent i København (Coph., 1929), 10-86.

———. Survey of the History of the Church in Denmark. Coph., 1930. 80 p.

Christiansen, Tage. "Denmark's Village Churches," ASR, 44 (1956), 250-55.

Donaldson, Gordon. "The Example of Denmark in the Scottish Reformation," Scottish Historical Review, 27 (1948), 57-64.

Dunkley, E. H. The Reformation in Denmark. Lond., 1948. 188 p.

Hansen, Martin A. "The Master Stonecutter Builds a Danish Parish Church," ASR, 50 (1962), 362-72.

Jarvis, Alexander C. Some Account of the English Episcopal Church in Denmark. Coph., 1934. 183 p.

Jensen, Christian A. The Churches of Praestø County (Danish Churches, published by the Danish National Museum). Coph., 1956. 88 p.

———. The Churches of Tisted County (Danish Churches, published by the Danish National Museum). Coph., 1948. 82 p.

Kjaer, Jens C. History of the Church of Denmark. Blair, Neb., 1945. 127 p.

MASS COMMUNICATIONS

Oldendow, Knud. "Lars Møller: Pioneer Greenland Editor," ASR, 50 (1962), 402-16.

———. "Printing in Greenland," Libri, 8 (1958), 223-62.

Pedersen, A. E., Jr. "A Newspaper-Operated Course in Journalism: Danish Newspapers Sponsor a Three-Month Course in Journalism at the University of Aarhus," Journalism Quarterly, 27 (1950), 310-14.

Persson Blegvad, Britt-Mari. "Newspapers and Rock and Roll Riots in Copenhagen," AcSoc, 7 (1964), 151-78.

Poulsen, Einar. "The Danish Daily Press," DFOJ, no. 5 (1952), 22-25.

Thorsen, Svend. "The Daily Press of Denmark," ScPP, I, 305-10.

———. Newspapers in Denmark (Danish Information Handbook). Coph., 1953. 171 p.

SOCIAL PROBLEMS

"The Care of Cripples in Denmark," ISSAssoc, 4 (1951), 315-20.

Denmark, Komiteen til undersøglse af den danske befolknings sundhedstilstand. The Hospital Survey of Denmark: a Statistical Analysis of the Utilization of Medical Surgical Hospitals in 1952-53, and 1930. Coph., 1959. 201 p.

Denmark, Ministry of Social Affairs. Danish Care of Mental Defectives. Coph., 1955. 31 p.

The Fight Against Tuberculosis in Denmark. Coph., 1950. 133 p.

Fremming, Kurt H. The Expectation of Mental Infirmity in a Sample of the Danish Population (Occasional Papers on Eugenics, no. 7.). Lond., 1951. 53 p.

Kemble, H. S. "Refugee Camps — a Social Dilemma in Denmark," Justice of the Peace, 3 (1947), 624-26.

Kemp, Tage. "Genetic-Hygenic Experiences in Denmark in Recent Years," Eugenics Review, 49 (Ap 1957), 11-18.

Nikolaisen, J. B. "Holböll and the Christmas Seal," ASR, 27 (1939), 295-302.

Svalastoga, Kaare. "Homicide and Social Contact in Denmark," AJS, 62 (1956), 37-41.

United States, President's Panel on Mental Retardation. Report of Mission to Denmark and Sweden By Ernest P. Willenberg et al. Wash., 1963. 48 p.

ALCOHOLISM

Hansen, H. A., and K. Teilmann. "A Treatment of Criminal Alcoholics in Denmark," Quarterly Journal of Studies on Alcohol, 15 (1954), 246-87.

Røgind, Sven. "Alcohol and Temperance in Denmark," ASR, 19 (1931), 85-90.

——. "Alcohol Consumption and Temperance Conditions in Denmark," QJSA, 10 (1949), 471-78.

CRIME, PRISONS

Berntsen, Karen, and Karl O. Christiansen. "The Resocialization of Short-Term Offenders," International Review of Criminal Policy, no. 6 (1954), 25-39.

——. "A Resocialization Experiment with Short-Term Offenders," ScStCrim, 1 (1965), 35-54.

Christiansen, Karl O. "Crime in Denmark from 1937 to 1948," Bulletin of the International Penal and Penitentiary Commission (Berne), 14 (1951), 537-74.

——. "Industrialization and Urbanization in Relation to Crime and Juvenile Delinquency," International Review of Criminal Policy, no. 16 (1960), 3-8.

Christiansen, Karl O., Mimi Elers-Nielsen, Louis Le Maire, and George K. Stürup. "Recidivism Among Sexual Offenders," ScStCrim, 1 (1965), 55-85.

Fenton, Norman. Observations on the Correctional System of Denmark. Under the auspices of the Commission on Personnel Training, Dept. of Corrections, California. Sacramento, 1954. 130 p.

Fremming, Kurt H. "Criminal Frequency in a Danish Rural Area," APNS, 21 (1946), 257-74.

Givskov, Carl G. "The Danish 'Purge-Laws'," Journal of Criminal Law, 39 (1948), 447-60.

Hurwitz, Stephan. "Criminality and Pathology," APNS, 21 (1946), 375-77.

——. Criminology. Coph., 1952. 442 p.

Jacobsen, Otto. Treatment of Criminal Psychopaths in the Detention Institution and Mental Hospital at Nykøbing Seeland, Denmark; Report on the 8th Congress of Scandinavian Psychiatrists 1946. APNS Supplement 47 (Coph., 1947), 42-53.

Jersild, Jens. Boy Prostitution. Coph., 1956. 104 p.

Kampmann, Erik. "Prisons and Punishments in Denmark," Journal of Criminal Law and Criminology, 25 (1934), 115-17.

Kemp, Tage. Prostitution: an Investigation of Its Causes, Especially with Regard to Hereditary Factors. Coph., 1936. 253 p.

Nelson, Alvar. "Sexual Offences and Sexual Offenders in Denmark," Sexual Offences: a Report of the Cambridge Department of Criminal Science (Lond., 1957), 478-92.

Petersen, H. W. "Leisure-Time Arrangements as Part of the Social Rehabilitation of Prisoners," Publication of the International Penal and Penitentiary Foundation (Berne, 1960), 177-82.

Reiter, P. J. "Treatment of Psychopathic Delinquents in Denmark," Journal of Social Therapy, 4 (1958), 16-25.

Riismandel, V. J. Punishments Under the Law of Denmark (Library of Congress, Law Library). Wash., 1955. 14 p. Mimeographed.

Schmidt, Max. "Criteria Governing the Selection of Offenders for Examination," International Review of Criminal Policy, no. 3 (1953), 13-19.

Stürup, George K. "A Psychiatric Establishment for Investigation, Training and Treatment of Psychologically Abnormal Criminals," APNS, 21 (1946), 781-93.
——. "The Treatment of Criminal Psychopaths at Herstedvester," British Journal of Medical Psychology, 25 (1952), 31-38.
——. "Sexual Offenders and Their Treatment in Denmark and the Other Scandinavian Countries," International Review of Criminal Policy, no. 4 (1953), 1-19.
——. "The Observations of Prisoners in Denmark," Herstedvester Papers 1942-1957 (Herstedvester, 1958), 1-12.
——. "Group Therapy with Chronic Criminals," Herstedvester Papers 1942-1957 (Herstedvester, 1958), 13-20.
——. "The Observation of Prisoners in Denmark," Publication of the International Penal and Penitentiary Foundation (Berne, 1960), 29-39.
Tetens, Hans. "To What Extent Can Open Institutions Take the Place of the Traditional Prison?" Proceedings of the 12th International Penal and Penitentiary Congress 1950, v. 4 (1951), 147-60.
——. "The Training of Prisoners in Open Institutions in Denmark" (Select Papers on Penal and Penitentiary Affairs), Bulletin of the International Penal and Penitentiary Commission (Berne, 1950), 11-22.
Waaben, Knud. "Punishment and Treatment in Danish Criminal Law," Bulletin de la Société Internationale de Criminologie (1960), 255-63.
Wolf, Preben. "A Contribution to the Topology of Crime in Denmark," ScStCrim, 1 (1965), 201-26.
——. "Crime and Social Class in Denmark," British Journal of Criminology, 3 (1962), 5-17.
Worm, A. A. "Recent Principles for the Classification of Prisoners in Denmark," Proceedings of the 12th International Penal and Penitentiary Congress 1950, v. 3 (1951), 443-54.

YOUTH

Denmark, Youth Commission. Danish Youth: a Summary of a Statistical Inquiry into the Problems of Danish Youth Undertaken by the Danish Government Youth Commission. Coph., 1953. 18 p.
——. A Study of the Behaviour Problems of 200 Maladjusted Children and Juveniles under the Guardianship of the Child Welfare Board. Coph., 1952.

——. Summary of Report on Maladjusted Youth. Coph., 1953. 8 p.

SEX

Andersen, Helge. "An Analysis of 777 Matrimonial Want Ads in Two Copenhagen Newspapers," AcSoc, 3 (1958/59), 173-82.
Bohm, Ewald. "Sex Life of Scandinavian Countries: Denmark," in Albert Ellis and Albert Abarbanel, eds., The Encyclopedia of Sexual Behavior (N.Y., 1961), v. 2, 910-14.
Christensen, Harold T. "Cultural Relativism and Premarital Sex Norms," AmSocR, 25 (1960), 31-39.
——. "Value-Behavior Discrepancies Regarding Premarital Coitus in Western Cultures," AmSocR, 27 (1962), 66-74.
Croog, Sydney H. "Aspects of the Cultural Background of Premarital Pregnancies in Denmark," Social Forces, 30 (1951), 215-19.
Denmark, National Health Service. The Combating of Venereal Diseases in Denmark. Coph., 1949.
Hartmann, Grethe. The Girls They Left Behind: an Investigation into the Various Aspects of the German Troops' Sexual Relations with Danish Subjects. Coph., 1946. 207 p.
Le Maire, Louis. "Danish Experiences Regarding the Castration of Sexual Offenders," Journal of Criminal Law and Criminology, 47 (1956), 294-310.

SUICIDE

Hendin, Herbert. "Suicide in Denmark," Psychiatric Quarterly, 34 (1960), 443-60.
——. "Suicide in Denmark," ASR, 49 (1961), 399-407.
——. "Suicide in Denmark," Columbia University Forum, 4 (1961), 26-32.
Rudfeld, Kirsten. "Suicides in Denmark 1956," AcSoc, 6 (1962), 203-14.
Weiss, Hilda P. "Durkheim, Denmark, and Suicide: a Sociological Interpretation of Statistical Data," AcSoc, 7 (1964), 264-78.

SOCIAL WELFARE

Bøje, Andreas [and others]. Private Philanthropical Work in Denmark. Coph., 1932. 32 p.
Bruun, Alice. "Securing Freedom from Need: Social Welfare in Denmark," DFOJ, no. 24 (Je 1957), 17-20.
The Danish Mothers' Aid Centers: Review of Their History and Activities. Coph., 1957.

Denmark, Ministry of Social Affairs. "Danish Social Policy in Wartime," ILR, 50 (1944), 185-206.

Friis, Finn T. B. "New Initiative and New Organizations in Wartime Denmark," Nord, 5 (1942), 256-67.

Friis, Henning K. "The Evolution of Social Security Benefits in Denmark," ISSAssoc, 19 (1966), 369-73.

———. "Trends in Social Welfare in Denmark," ISSAssoc, 7 (1954), 228-31.

Gills, H. "Family Welfare Measures in Denmark," PopSt, 6 (1952), 172-210.

Halck, Niels. Social Welfare in Denmark. Coph., 1961. 72 p.

"Important Reforms in Danish National Insurance Legislation," I&L, 25 (1961, no. 3), 97-99.

Jensen, Orla. Social Services in Denmark (Danish Information Handbook). Coph., 1948. 118 p.

Koch, Hal H. The Danish Public Assistance Act. Published under the auspices of the Ministry for Social Affairs. Coph., 1936. 44 p.

Kruse, Margrethe. "The Relief Housewife in Denmark: a New Type of Social Legislation in Helping to Solve Some of the Problems of Family Care in Danish Homes," American Journal of Nursing, 51 (1951), 105-108.

Lassen, R. Social Reform in Denmark. Coph., 1934. 26 p.

League of Nations. Protection of Children and Young People from the Consequences of the Economic Depression and Unemployment. Memorandum submitted by the delegate of Denmark. Geneva, 1934.

Manniche, Peter. "Denmark, A Social Laboratory," IO, 3 (1939), 1-116.

———. Denmark: a Social Laboratory; Independent Farmers, Co-operative Societies, Folk High Schools, Social Legislation. Coph., Lond., 1939. 215 p.

———. Living Democracy in Denmark: Independent Farmers, Farmers' Cooperation, the Folk High Schools, Cooperation in the Towns, Social and Cultural Activities, Social Legislation, a Danish Village. Coph., 1952. 237 p. Rev. ed. of Denmark, a Social Laboratory.

Selley, Edith. Danish Poor Relief System: an Example for England. Lond., 1904, 131 p.

Social Denmark: a Survey of Danish Social Legislation. Coph., 1945; Lond., 1946. 475 p.

"Social Insurance," DFOJ, no. 221 (Je 1939), 96-117.

"Social Welfare for the Worker," DFOJ, no. 224 (S 1939), 151-53.

Steincke, K. K. "The Danish Social Reform Measures," ILR, 31 (1935), 620-48.

———. "The Social Reform Law in Denmark," ASR, 24 (1936), 101-106.

Wechselmann, S. The Danish National Insurance Act. Published under the auspices of the Ministry for Social Affairs. Coph., 1936. 52 p.

"The Working of Social Insurance in Denmark," ILR, 30 (1934), 208-26.

Zeuthen, Fr. Social Legislation in Denmark. Published by the Danish Ministry of Social Affairs. Coph., 1924. 16 p.

HEALTH INSURANCE

Ammentorp, Verner. A Survey of the Voluntary Sickness Insurance in Denmark. Coph., 1950. 23 p.

Armstrong, Barbara N. The Health Insurance Doctor: His Role in Great Britain, Denmark, and France. Princeton, N.J., 1939. 264 p.

Canada, Department of National Health and Welfare, Research Division. Health Insurance in Denmark (Social Security Series, Memo no. 9). Rev. ed., Ottawa, 1952. 67 p.

Denmark, Direcktoratet for sygekassevaesenet. The National Sickness, Invalidity and Funeral Insurance in Denmark. Published by the Commissioner of Recognized Sickness Funds. Coph., 1932. 36 p.

Gibbon, Joan G. Medical Benefits: a Study of the Experience of Germany and Denmark. Lond., 1912. 296 p.

Gordon, Max. "The Danish National Health Service," Social Service Quarterly, 30 (Je/Aug 1956), 14-16.

League of Nations, Health Organisation. Health Organisation in Denmark. Cambery, 1924. 435 p. Supplement, Geneva, 1926. 56 p.

Røgind, Sven. "Danish Sickness Insurance," ASR, 20 (1932), 71-75.

"State Medicine in Denmark, by a Danish Doctor," Municipal Journal, 56 (1948), 2490+.

OLD AGE BENEFITS

Awner, Max. "Freedom and Security in Denmark," Progressive, 22 (1958), 27-29.

Bokkenheuser, Knud. "Where to be Happy though Old," ASR, 14 (1926), 26-32.

"Denmark: Important Reforms in Old-Age

and Invalidity Pensions Scheme," ISSAssoc, 10 (1957), 208-13.

"Developments in Social Security in Denmark," I&L, 22 (1959), 196-98.

Friis, Henning K. "Comparison of Benefits in the Danish Social Security Legislation," ISSAssoc, 12 (1959), 15-18.

Sellers, Edith. "Old Age Pensions in Denmark," CR, 78 (1900), 430-41.

RESEARCH

Christiansen, Karl O. "The Institute of Criminal Science of the University of Copenhagen," British Journal of Delinquency, 10 (1959), 48-50.

——. "The Institute of Criminal Science of the University of Copenhagen," Bulletin de l'association internationale de psychologie appliquée, 10 (1961), 100-107.

"The Danish National Institute of Social Research, Nyhavn," ISSJ, 12 (1960), 112-15.

Friis, Henning K. "The Danish National Institute of Social Research," AcSoc, 4 (1960), 55-60.

Lund, Reinhard and Poul Milhøj. "Social Research on Labour in Denmark," ILR, 87 (1963), 233-46.

"Social Research Undertaken or Sponsored by the Danish Ministry of Labour and Social Affairs," ISSB, 4 (1952), 137-40.

FINLAND

Aaron, Daniel. "The Helsinki the Athletes Didn't See," Reporter, 7 (S 2, 1952), 24-27.

Allardt, Erik. "The Westermarck Society," AcSoc, 5 (1960/62), 50-52.

Bradley, David. Lion Among Roses. N.Y., 1965. 278 p.

Bruun, Ketil. "Institutional Sociological Research in Finland, 1950-1955," Transactions of the Third World Congress of Sociology, v. 7 (Lond., 1956), 65-68.

——. "Sociological Teaching in Finland," Transactions of the Third World Congress of Sociology, v. 7 (Lond., 1956), 23-24.

Finland, Ministry of Education. Youth Services and Organizations in Finland. Hels., 1954. 75 p.

Fry, F. C. "Finland and Poland After One Year of Peace," Religion in Life, 16 (1947), 381-87.

Gilmour, Kay. Finland. Lond., 1931. 182 p.

Ginsberg, Morris. "The Life and Work of

Edward Westermarck," SocR, 32 (1940), 1-28.

Granroth, Leena. "Bibliography of Professor Veli Verkko's Printed Works," West SocTrans, 4 (1958/59), 8-25.

Haavio-Mannila, Elina, and Frank L. Sweetser. "Sociological Research at the University of Helsinki," Boston University Graduate School Journal, 12 (Spring 1964), 89-99.

Hirn, Yrjö. "Edward Westermarck and His English Friends," WestSocTrans, 1 (1947), 39-51.

Holm, Tor W., and Erkki J. Immonen. Bibliography of Finnish Sociology 1945-1959 (WestSocTrans, XIII). Åbo, 1966. 179 p.

Mead, William R. "The Finn in Fact and Fiction," Norseman, 16 (1958), 178-89.

——. "The Image of the Finn," Nenphilologische Mitteilungen, (1963).

Mikkola, Joseppi. "Social Culture of Finland," BC, 1 (1935), 40-44.

Myhrman, Anders M. The Swedish Nationality Movement in Finland. Chicago, 1939. 198 p. Based on thesis (Ph.D.), University of Chicago, 1938.

Nordenskiöld, Erland. "Finland: the Land, the People," GeoR, 7 (1919), 361-76.

"Notes on Finland," NGeogM, 21 (1910), 493-94.

Numelin, Ragnar J. "Edward Westermarck and the Finnish Sociological School," Nord (1941), 268-82.

Owen, John E. "Sociology in Finland," AmSocR, 19 (1954), 62-68.

Ravila, Paavo. "Who Are the Finns?" ASR, 49 (1961), 135-38.

Rob, K., and V. Wikman. "Yrjö Hirn as an Anthropologist of Art and Literature," WestSocTrans, 2 (1953), 1-8.

Seppanen, Paavo. "Industrial Sociology in Finland," Sociological Inquiry, 31 (1961), 74-77.

Smith, George E. K. "Alvar Aalto," ASR, 28 (1940), 313-20.

Söderhjelm, Werner. "Finnish Culture in Finland," ASR, 8 (1920), 421-29.

Takala, Martti. "A Report on the Psychological Institute at Helsinki University," AcPsy, 7 (1950), 110-14.

Waris, Heikki. "Finland," in Arnold M. Rose, ed., The Institutions of Advanced Societies (Minneapolis, 1958), 193-234.

Wikman, V., and K. Rob. "Edward Westermarck as Anthropologist and Sociologist," WestSocTrans, 9 (1962), 7-35.

Willis, Richard H. "Finnish Images of the Northern Lands and Peoples," AcSoc, 7 (1964), 73-88.

SOCIAL STRUCTURE

Eskola, Antti. "Social Influence and Power in Two-Person Groups," WestSocTrans, 6 (1961), 1-153. Uses Finnish data.

Gaier, Eugene L., and Yrjö Littunen. "Modes of Conformity in Two Sub-Cultures: a Finnish-American Comparison," AcSoc, 5 (1960/62), 65-75.

Grönholm, Leo. "The Ecology of Social Disorganization in Helsinki," AcSoc, 5 (1960/62), 31-41.

Hartman, Tor. "Nuptuality and Social Structure, a Study," WestSocTrans, 4 (1958/59), 31-73.

Koli, Paavo. "Ideology Patterns and Ideology Cleavage, a Factual Study," WestSocTrans, 4 (1958/59), 75-140.

POPULATION, MIGRATION

"Finland," Population Index, 6 (1940), 3-6.

Gadolin, Carl A. J. The Solution of the Karelian Refugee Problem in Finland (Publication of the Research Group for European Migration Problems). The Hague, 1952. 47 p.

Hall, Wendy. "Resettlement in Finland," GeoM, 24 (1951/52), 419-28.

Hyppölä, Jorma. "Changes in the Distribution of Population Between 1950 and 1960, By Industry and Industrial Status," BFMB, 36 (1962, no. 11), 18-21.

Inervo, Ilmari. "The Resettlement of Evacuees in Finland," ASR, 55 (1967), 136-42.

Jutikkala, Eino K. "Can the Population of Finland in the 17th Century Be Calculated?" SEHR, 5 (1957), 155-72.

Lento, Reino. Internal Migration. Hels., 1951.

Lindman, Kirsten. "Finland's Swedes: an Introduction and a Bibliography," ScSt, 35 (1963), 123-31.

Mead, William R. "The Seasonal Round: a Study of Adjustment on Finland's Pioneer Fringe," Tijdschrift voor Economische en Sociale Geografie, 49 (1958, no. 7), 157-62.

Oinas, Felix J. The Karelians. Prepared by Indiana University Graduate Program in Uralic and Asian Studies (Human Relations Area Files, Inc.; Subcontractor's Monograph, HRAF-12). New Haven, Conn., 1955. 199 p.

Pihkala, Kaarlo U. "The Land Settlement Program and Its Execution," BFMB, 26 (1952, no. 3/4), 24-31.

"Resettlement of Karelian Refugees" [by J.H.J.], WT, 9 (1953), 249-56.

Rosenberg, Antti. "Mobility of Population in the Finnish County of Uusimaa (Nyland) 1821-1880," SEHR, 14 (1966), 39-59.

Sirelius, Uuno T. The Genealogy of the Finns: the Finns-Ugrian Peoples. Hels., 1925. 77 p.

Smeds, Helmer. "A New Population and Settlement Map of Finland," IGCong, 17th (1952), 505-507.

Soininen, Arvo M. "Burn-Beating as the Technical Basis of Colonization in Finland in the 16th and 17th Centuries," SEHR, 7 (1959), 150-66.

Strömmer, A. "Recent Demographic Developments and Population Policies in Finland," Population Index, 22 (1956), 3-23.

Tunkelo, Aarre. "The Growth of the Population of Finland up to 1975," BFMB, 33 (1959, no. 11), 18-20.

———. "The Structure of Finland's Population in 1950," BFMB, 28 (1954, no. 2), 20-23.

———. "A Survey of the Population of Finland," BFMB, 27 (1953, no. 11/12), 20-24.

Waris, Heikki. "Finland's Solution of Its Displaced Persons Problems," Integration, 1 (1955), 7-9.

Waris, Heikki, and Vieno Jyrkilä. "The Social Adjustment of Displaced People in Finland," ISSB, 3 (1951), 268-72.

Waris, Heikki, and J. Süpi. "Re-settlement of Displaced Persons in Finnish Society," Unitas (1951), 94-99.

RACE AND MINORITIES

Harva, Uno. "The Finno-Ugric System of Relationship," WestSocTrans, 1 (1947), 52-74.

Hildén, Kaarlo. The Racial Composition of the Finnish Nation. Hels., 1932. 29 p.

———. "Some Aspects of the Physical Anthropology of Finland," BSC, 3 (1937), 233-37.

———. "Some Aspects of the Physical Anthropology of Finland" [Summary] in Compte Rendu of the First International Congress of Anthropological and Ethnological Sciences (Lond., 1934), 129-30.

Hitonen, Ensio. "Are Minority Concepts Applicable to Finland?" BSC, 4 (1938), 25-29.

RURAL AND URBAN SOCIOLOGY

Aario, Leo E. The Inner Differentiation of the Large Cities in Finland (Turun Yliopiston Maanticteellisen laitoksen julkaisuja, 22). Turku, 1951. 67 p. Reprinted in Fennia, 74, no. 2, 1951.

Jutikkala, Eino K. "The Borderland: Urban History and Urban Sociology" [Review of Swedish book of Sven-Erik Åström], SEHR, 6 (1958), 191-95.

Jutikkala, Eino K. and Sven-Erik Åström. "The Development of Urban Society in Finland," in Recueils de la Société Jean Bodin pour l'histoire comparative des institutions; 7:La Ville (Bruxelles, 1955), 625-49.

League of Nations. European Conference on Rural Life, 1939. Finland. Geneva, 1939. 59 p.

Sillanpää, F. E. "Culture of the Finnish Peasant," Scandinavian Review, 1 (1938), 50-51.

Sweetser, Dorrian A. "Urbanization and Patrilineal Transmission of Farms in Finland," AcSoc, 7 (1964), 215-24.

Sweetser, Frank L. "Factor Structure as Ecological Structure in Helsinki and Boston," AcSoc, 8 (1965), 205-25.

RELIGION

The Church of Finland. Hels., 1949. 24 p.

The Crusade of the Finns. Ed. by a committee of the Karelian diocese of Viipuri. Hels., 1942.

Kaila, Erkki. Legislation Concerning Liberty of Faith in Finland. Hels., 1923. 10 p.

Kantonen, T. A. "The Finnish Church and Russian Imperialism," ChHist, 20 (1951, no. 2), 3-13.

Lehtonen, Aleksi E. The Church of Finland. Hels., 1927. 56 p.

Sormunen, Eino. The Church of Finland in Pictures. Hels., 1949. 150 p.

Stahlecker, Lotar V. "Finland's Medieval Churches," ASR, 54 (1966), 361-68.

Tiililä, O. A Hundred Years of Systematic Theology in Finland. Hels., 1948. 48 p.

SOCIAL STRATIFICATION

Anderson, C. Arnold. "Social Class as a Factor in the Assimilation of Women into Higher Education," AcSoc, 4 (1960), 27-32.

Åström, Sven-Erik. "Literature on Social Mobility and Social Stratification in Finland: Some Bibliographic Notes," West SocTrans, 2 (1953), 221-27.

Honkala, Kauko. "Social Class and Visiting Patterns in Two Finnish Villages," AcSoc, 5 (1960/62), 42-49.

Sariola, Sakari. "Defining Social Class in Two Finnish Communities," WestSoc Trans, 2 (1953), 134-57.

Waris, Heikki. "Social Stratification and Social Mobility in Eighteenth Century Finland" [Review of Finnish books by Kaarlo Wirilander and by Sven-Erik Åström], SEHR, 2 (1954), 47-49.

THE FAMILY

Allardt, Erik. "The Influence of Different Systems of Social Norms on Divorce Rates in Finland," Marriage and Family Living, 17 (1955), 325-31.

Chambliss, Rollin. "Contributions of the Vital Statistics of Finland to the Study of Factors that Induce Marriage," AmSocR, 22 (1957), 38-48.

Haavio-Mannila, Elina. "Local Homogamy in Finland," AcSoc, 8 (1965), 155-62.

Nieminen, Armas. "Premarital Pregnancy in Finland," AcSoc, 7 (1964), 225-28.

Takala, Annika, and Martti Takala. "Finnish Children's Reactions to Frustration in the Rosenweig Test: an Ethnic and Cultural Comparison," AcPsy, 13 (1957/58), 43-50.

Voipio-Juvas, Anni, and K. Ruohtula. The Finnish Woman. Hels., 1949. 109 p.

LEISURE ACTIVITIES

Aaltonen, Esko. "On the Sociology of the Sauna of the Finnish Countryside," West SocTrans, 3 (1956), 158-70.

——. "The Sociology of the Sauna," West SocTrans, 2 (1953), 158-70.

Allardt, Erik. "Community Activity, Leisure Use and Social Structure," AcSoc, 5 (1962), 67-82.

—— [et al.]. "On the Cumulative Nature of Leisure Activities" [Among Finnish youth], AcSoc, 3 (1959), 165-72.

"The Utilization of Leisure in Finland," ILR, 9 (1924), 573-86.

FOLKLORE

Christiansen, Reidar Th. "A Finnish Fairytale in Norway," Acta Ethnologica (1933) 7-16. Reprinted: Coph., 1936.

Einarsson, Stefán. "Alternate Recital by Twos in Wídsíp, Sturlunga and Kalevala," Arv, 7 (1951), 59-83.

Mansikka, Viljo J. "Parallels Between the Folk-Lore of Finland and Estonia," BSC, 4 (1938), 21-24.

Richmond, W. Edson. "The Study of Folklore in Finland," Journal of American Folklore, 74 (1961), 325-35.

Wikman, K. "Popular Divination: Some Remarks Concerning Its Structure and Function" [Among the Swedish-speaking population of Finland], WestSocTrans, 2 (1953), 171-83.

LANGUAGE

Fougstedt, Gunnar. "Social Factors Affecting the Choice of Language by Children of Finnish-Swedish Mixed Marriages in Finland," WestSocTrans, 3 (1956), 34-55.

Jansson, Jan-Magnus. Bi-Lingualism in Finland. Paper for the Fifth World Congress of the International Political Science Association. Paris, 1961. 24 p. Mimeographed.

Lille, Axel. The New Language Law Passed by the Riksdag of Finland. Hels., 1921. 11 p.

Multilingual Demographic Dictionary. Finnish Section. Hels., 1962. 148 p.

Törnudd, Klaus. "The Language Situation in Finland," ASR, 51 (1963), 27-32.

THE PRESS

Berg, Eero A. "The Newspaper as an Economic and Social Factor," KOPER (1961, no. 2), 65-71.

Grönvik, Axel. The Character of the Finnish Press. Hels., 1953. 8 p.

——. "The Press in Finland," ScPP, III, 315-18.

Littunen, Yrjö. "The Attitude Adopted by the Press during a Labour Strike at Kemi," WestSocTrans, 2 (1953), 206-20.

Ruuskanen, Pentti. "The Press in Finland," EFTA Bull, 7 (1966, no. 8), 18-20.

Waldrop, A. Gayle. "The Daily-Newspaper Press in Finland," Journalism Quarterly, 34 (1957), 228-38.

ALCOHOLISM, PROHIBITION

Bruun, Ketil. Drinking Behaviour in Small Groups: an Experimental Study (The Finnish Foundation for Alcohol Studies). Hels., 1959. 132 p.

Caselius, Ilmari. "New Alcohol Legislation," BFMB, 12 (1932, no. 3), 22-26.

Dorr, Rheta C. "The Other Prohibition Country," Harper's (S 1929), 495-504.

Gadolin, Axel. "The Fate of Prohibition in Finland," ASR, 20 (1932), 216-19.

Kuusi, Pekka. Alcohol Sales Experiment in Rural Finland (Alcohol Research in the Northern Countries). Stock., 1957. 237 p.

Sariola, Sakari. Drinking Patterns in Finnish Lapland. Stock., 1956. 86 p.

Wuorinen, John H. "Finland's Prohibition Experiment," Annals, 163 (1932), 216-26.

——. The Prohibition Experiment in Finland. N.Y., 1931. 251 p.

CRIME, DELINQUENCY

Ahto, Aito K. Dangerous Habitual Criminals: a Psychopathologic and Sociologic Study of 216 Segregated Criminals (Acta psychiatrica et neurologica, Supplementum 69). Hels., 1951. 168 p.

Allardt, Erik. "Veli Verkko as a Criminologist and Sociologist," WestSocTrans, 3 (1956), 77-87.

Anttila, Inkeri, and Achilles Westling. "A Study in the Pardoning of, and Recidivism Among, Criminals Selected to Life Imprisonment," ScStCrim, 1 (1965), 13-34.

Helanko, Rafael. "The Hand-Outs of Boys' Gangs" [in Turku], WestSocTrans, 3 (1956), 77-87.

——. "The Yard Group in the Socialization of Turku Girls," AcSoc, 4 (1959), 38-55.

Leinberg, Georg. "Crime," in Atlas of Finland 1925 (Hels., 1929), 287-90.

Mustala, Paavo. "Prisons and Lock-up Houses," in Atlas of Finland 1925 (Hels., 1929), 290-92.

Soine, Valentin. "Finland's Open Institutions," Federal Probation, 28 (D 1964), 19-23.

Verkko, Veli. "International Comparison in Criminal Statistics," Nordisk tidskrift for kriminal videnskab, 39 (1951), 109-19.

——. Homicides and Suicides in Finland and Their Dependence on National Character; With an Additional Chapter: the Themes of Morselli and Ferri on Homicides and Suicides and the Attitude to Them of Tarde and Durkheim. (Scandinavian Studies in Sociology, 3). Coph., 1951. 189 p.

——. "Supplementary Notes to Some Chapters of My Investigation 'Homicides and Suicides in Finland and Their Dependence on National Character'," WestSocTrans, 2 (1953), 187-202.

HEALTH

Haavio-Mannila, Elina. "Official and Unofficial Expectations Concerning the Care of the Sick," AcSoc, 7 (1964), 105-18.

Institute of Occupational Health. Publications, 1960. Hels., 1961. 15 p.

Jansson, Kurt. The Care of Disabled Ex-Service Men in Finland. Hels., 1949.

——. The Vocational Rehabilitation of Disabled Ex-Service Men in Finland. Hels., 1949.

Mattila, Antti. Features of Public Health in Finland. Hels., WHO, 1961.

Noro, Leo. Institutes of Occupational Health: 10 Years, 1951-1960. Hels., 1961. 16 p.

Savonen, K. Student Health Service in Finland. Hels., 1952. 15 p.

Savonen, Severi [for the Finnish National Anti-Tuberculosis Association]. BCG Vaccination in Finland. Hels., 1949.

—— [for the Finnish National Anti-Tuberculosis Association]. The Battle Against Tuberculosis in Finland. Hels., 1947. 61 p.

—— [for the Finnish National Anti-Tuberculosis Association]. Where Infants Are Won for Life. Hels., 1954. 16 p.

Virtanen, Paavo, et al. Return to Work: Vocational Rehabilitation of the Physically Handicapped in Finland. Hels., 1953. 43 p.

SOCIAL POLICY

Böök, Einar. "Social Administration and Labour Laws," in Finland: the Country, Its People and Institutions (Hels., 1926), 154-68.

Bredenberg, Ulla. "The Employment Pensions Scheme in Finland," BFMB, 38 (1964, no. 11), 18-21.

Eskola, Aarne. The Social Welfare Administration in the Finnish Municipalities and the Finnish Law Relating to the Administration of Social Welfare. Hels., 1954. 20 p.

Finland, Lastensuojelun Keskusliitto-Centralförbundet för Barnskydd. Statistical Survey of Child Welfare Work in the Communes of Finland in 1948. Hels., 1951.

Finland, Ministry of Social Affairs. Measures of Family Support in Finland. Hels., 1950. Mimeographed.

——. Social Legislation and Activity in Finland. By I. V. Laati. Rev. by Niilo Salomaa. Hels., 1953. 189 p. Many previous editions: 1939, 142 p.; 1946, 171 p.; 1949, 179 p.

Finland, National Pension Institution. National Pension Insurance in Finland. Hels., 1950.

——. Old-age and Invalidity Pensions in Finland. Hels., 1957. 11 p.

The Finnish Red Cross: Some Features of the Work of the Society. Hels., 1945. 64 p.

The Finnish Red Cross: the Main Features of the Work during the Decade 1938-1948. Hels., 1948. 38 p.

"Government Declaration on Social Policy in Finland," ILR, 44 (1941), 62-64.

Holiday Policy in Finland. Hels., 1951. 11 p.

Jylhä, Tauno. "On the Burdens of Pensions for the Aged and Invalids," KOPER (1953, no. 2), 51-62.

——. "The Reorganisation of Old Age and Disability Pensions," BFMB, 30 (1956, no. 9), 18-22.

Kuusi, Pekka. Social Policy for the Sixties: a Plan for Finland. Hels., 1964. 295 p.

Mannio, Niilo A. "The New National Pensions Law," BFMB, 17 (1937, no. 8), 22-24.

——. "Proposals for Revising the National Pensions Act," Unitas (1954), 80-82.

——. "Recent Social Developments in Finland," ILR, 57 (1948), 1-14.

"The New Law on Old-Age and Invalidity Pensions in Finland," ISSAssoc, 10 (1957), 340-45.

Owen, John E. "Social Welfare in Finland," Norseman, 14 (1956), 289-93.

——. "Social Welfare in Finland," Social Service, 27 (1954), 180-84.

Pajula, Jaakko. "The Finnish Sickness Insurance Scheme," BFMB, 39 (1965, no. 7), 18-23.

——. "Sickness Insurance in Finland," ISSAssoc, 16 (1963), 393-403.

Salomaa, Niilo. "Social Legislation and Work in Finland," BFMB, 23 (1949, no. 9/10), 25-29; (no. 11/12), 25-29.

Social Welfare in Europe: Finland. Geneva, 1955. 128 p.

The State's Gift to the Mothers of Finland, Ten Years Activity of Maternity Relief. Hels., 1948. 48 p.

United Nations, Department of Social Affairs, Division of Social Welfare. Social Welfare Information series, Current Literature and National Conferences: Finland, January-December, 1950. N.Y., 1951. 20 p.

ICELAND

Bogardus, Emory S. "Social Change in Iceland." [Changes in communications, language, social economy, population, and relations with the U.S. and the world], S&SR, 40 (1955), 117-26.

Briem, Helgi P. Iceland and the Icelanders. Maplewood, N.J., 1945. 96 p.

Finnbogason, Gudmundur. The Icelanders. Rey., 1943. 24 p.

Gesladottir, Anna, and Kristin Einarsdottir.

"Homes and Family Life in Iceland,"
JHE, 42 (1950), 263-65.

Gislason, Gylfi P. "Problems of Icelandic
Culture," ASR, 54 (1966), 241-48.

Kratz, Lawrence A. "The Cultural Progress
of Iceland," JofGeog, 45 (1946), 285-91.

Ogburn, William F. "Malthusian Theory and
the Population of Iceland, 1750," Proceedings of the International Congress
for Studies on Population, Rome, 1931,
9 (1933), 207-15.

Olafsson, Ragnar. "Culture in Changing
Iceland," ASR, 27 (1939), 229-39.

Strömbäck, Dag. "Cult Remnants in Icelandic Dramatic Dances," Arv, 4 (1948),
132-45.

———. "Icelandic Dramatic Dances and
Their West European Background,"
Annen Viking Kongress, Bergen, 1953.
Reprinted in Arctica: Essays Presented
to Åke Campbell (1956).

Thompson, Laura. "Care Values and Diplomacy: a Case Study in Iceland," Human
Organization, 19 (1960), 82-85.

SOCIAL STRUCTURE

Gunnarson, Olafur. "Rural Culture in Iceland," Norseman, 15 (1957), 314-18.

Jackson, Thorstina. "Home Life in Iceland,"
ASR, 16 (1928), 419-26.

Kennedy, June. "Women in Iceland," Norseman, 15 (1957), 318-20.

Nordal, J. "The Recruitment of the Profes-
sions in Iceland," in International Sociological Association, Liège Congress,
Papers. Section I: "Social Stratification
and Social Mobility" (World Congress of
Sociology, Communications, Papers).
Oslo, 1953. 15 p. Mimeographed.

Perkins, Mekkin S. "The Women of Iceland," ASR, 31 (1943), 40-49.

SOCIAL POLICY

Iceland, Félagsmálaráðuneytio. Labour
Legislation and Social Service in Iceland.
Rey., 1949. 101 p.

———, Landlaeknisskrifstofan. Heibrigois-
skryslur; Public Health in Iceland. Rey.
Irregularly issued.

"Iceland: Recent Developments in Social
Security," ISSAssoc, 14 (1961), 268-70.

Jónsson, Vilmundur. Health in Iceland.
Rey., 1940. 29 p.

"A National Insurance Plan for Iceland,"
ILR, 53 (1946), 258-62.

Odhe, Thorsten. Iceland: the Cooperative
Island. 1960. 115 p.

Sigurdsson, Sigurdur. Tuberculosis in Iceland (Epidemiological Studies; Public
Health Service technical monograph no.
2). Wash., 1950. 86 p.

Thorbjörnsson, Sverrir. "Social Services in
Iceland," ScPP, III, 206-10.

NORWAY

Allwood, Martin S. Eilert Sundt, A Pioneer
in Sociology and Social Anthropology.
Oslo, 1957. 109 p.

Aubert, Vilhelm. "Some Social Functions of
Legislation," AcSoc, 10 (1966), 98-120.

Barth, Fredrik, ed. The Role of the Entrepreneur in Social Change in Northern Norway. Oslo, 1963. 83 p.

Castberg, Frede. "National Character and
Ideals of Personality," in his, The Norwegian Way of Life (Lond., 1954), 1-18.

———. The Norwegian Way of Life. Lond.,
Melbourne, 1954. 110 p.

Colbjornsen, Ole. "Norway for the People,"
American Federationist (D 1942), 23-24+.

Eitinger, Leo. Concentration Camp Survi-
vors in Norway and Israel. Oslo, N.Y.,
1964. 199 p.

Graff, Magne. "Eager Young Hands Across
the Seven Seas; the Norwegian Ship Adoption Scheme Popular at Sea and on Shore,"
Norseman (1960, no. 5), 18-20.

Grönseth, Erik. "Research on Socialization
in Norway," Family Process, 3 (1964),
302-22.

Gullvag, Harriet, et al. Attitudes and Perceptions of Representatives and Repre-
sentees in Industry. Oslo, 1953. I-IV,
74; 35; 168; 140 p. Mimeographed.

Harthan, John P. "Norwegian Folk Costumes in the Romantic Age," Norseman,
8 (1950), 252-59.

Hillman, Arthur. "Eilert Sundt: Social Sur-
veyor Extra-ordinary," SR, 43 (1951),
49-56.

Hindal, Berthold. A History of the Y.M.C.A.'s
Boy's Work in Norway. Thesis, International YMCA College, 1940. 69 p.

Malmström, Vincent H. and Ruth M. Life in
Europe: Norway. Grand Rapids, Iowa,
1955. 160 p.

Mead, William R. How People Live in Norway. Lond., 1959. 100 p.

Mortensen, Sverre, and Per Vogt. One Hundred Norwegians: an introduction to Norwegian Culture and Achievement. Oslo,
1955. 206 p.

Norway, Central Statistical Bureau. History
of Social Statistics in Norway during 100

Years, 1850-1950 (Norges offisielle sta-
tistikk, ser. 11, no. 113). Oslo, 1952.

Norway, Ministry of Foreign Affairs, Office
of Cultural Relations. Norway: Land and
People. By Ole Knudsen. Oslo, 1961.
67 p.

Norway, Ministry of Social Affairs. Social
Developments in Norway. Oslo, 1957.
62 p.

Norway, Youth and Sports Office. The State
Office for Sport and Youth Work in Nor-
way: Responsibilities and Activities.
Oslo, 1959. 30 p.

"Norwegian Social Democracy" [by H.O.L.],
AmPers, 1 (1948), 479-94.

Ofstad, Ingmund. "From Football to Science," Norseman, 3 (1961), 11-14.

Ramsøy, Natalie R. "On the Flow of Talent
in Society," AcSoc, 9 (1966), 152-74.

Rodnick, David. The Norwegians: a Study in
National Culture. Wash., 1955. 165 p.

Scott, Franklin D. "Søren Jaabeck, Americanizer in Norway," Norwegian-American
Studies and Records, 17 (1952), 84-107.

Vorren, Ørnulv, ed. Norway North of 65
(Tromsø Museums skrifter, v. 8). Oslo,
1961. 271 p.

Warbey, William et al. Modern Norway: a
Study in Social-Democracy. Lond., 1950.
181 p.

Whyte, Anne. "How the People Live," in
William Warbey, et al., Modern Norway:
a Study in Social Democracy. (Lond.,
1950), 145-72.

Willson, Thomas B. Norway at Home.
Lond., 1908. 227 p.

SOCIAL STRUCTURE

Aubert, Vilhelm and Oddvar Arver. "On the
Social Structure of the Ship," AcSoc, 3
(1958/59), 200-19.

Brackmann, Georg. "The Norwegian Sea-
man," GeoM, 1 (1935), 207-16.

Bull, Edvard. "Autobiographies of Industrial Workers. Sources of Norwegian
Social History," IRSH, 1 (1956), 203-209.

Burchardt, Carl J. B. Norwegian Life and
Literature; English Accounts and Views,
Especially in the 19th Century. Lond.,
N.Y., 1920. 230 p.

Hebert, B. T. "The Island of Bolsö: a Study
of Norwegian L fe," SR, 17 (1925), 307-13.

Jefferson, Mark. "Man in West Norway,"
JofGeo, 7 (1908/9), 86-96.

Sommerfelt, Alf. "The Norwegian Fjords, I:
the People," Geographical Teacher, 13
(1925), 30-41.

POPULATION, MIGRATION

Backer, Julie E. "Norwegian Migration
1856-1960," International Migration, 4
(1966), 172-82.

——. "Population Statistics and Population
Registration in Norway; Part I: the Vital
Statistics of Norway, an Historical Review," PopSt, 1 (1947), 212-26; 2 (1948),
318-38.

Drake, K. Michael. "The Growth of Population in Norway 1735-1855," SEHR, 13
(1965), 97-142.

——. Marriage and Population Growth in
Norway, 1735-1865. Thesis (Ph.D.), Cambridge University, 1964.

International Studies Conference, 10th, Paris,
1937. Memoir on Fluctuations in Migration from Norway Since 1900, Compared
with Other Countries and Causes of These
Fluctuations. Paris, 1937. 194 p.

Jackson, J. N. "Norwegian Colonisation in
an Arctic Village," SR, 44 (1952), 21-38.

Jahn, Gunnar. "Norway's Population Problem," ASR, 25 (1937), 118-21.

Johansen, Leif. "Death Rates, Age Distribution and Average Income in Stationary
Populations," PopSt, 11 (Jl 1957), 64-77.

Ljone, Oddmund. "The Norsemen Live
Longer," Norseman, 2 (1962), 9-12.

Lunde, Anders S. Norway: a Population
Study. Thesis (Ph.D.), Columbia University, 1955. 531 p.

Myklebost, Hallstein. "Population and Set-
tlement North of the Arctic Circle," in
Ørnulf Vorren, ed., Norway North of 65
(Oslo, 1960), 134-46.

Ofstad, Kåre. "Population Statistics and
Population Registration in Norway; Part
III: Population Censuses," PopSt, 3 (1949),
66-75.

Semmingsen, Ingrid. "Norwegian Emigration in the Nineteenth Century," SEHR, 8
(1960), 150-60.

Thompson, S. W. Migration Within Oslo.
Oxford, 1951.

Zavis, William. "Policy of Compassion:
Exiled Hungarians Have Found a Permanent Home in Norway," Norseman, 1
(1962), 9-12.

RURAL AND URBAN SOCIOLOGY

Barth, Fredrik. "Subsistence and Institutional System in a Norwegian Mountain
Valley," RS, 17 (1952), 28-38.

Bremer, Johan. A Social Psychiatric Investigation of a Small Community in Northern

Norway (APNS Supplement 62). Coph., 1951. 166 p.

Ekblaw, W. Elmer. "Fjords and Fjord Life," Home Geographic Monthly, 1 (1932 no. 11), 36-42.

Hornslien, J. "Organization of the General Process on Farms in Western Norway," in Changing Patterns of Rural Organization (Oslo, 1961).

League of Nations, European Conference on Rural Life. National Monographs Drawn up by Government: Norway. Geneva, 1939. 66 p.

Munch, Peter A. "Gård: the Norwegian Farm," RS, 12 (1947), 356-63.

——. "Gård: the Rural Family Homestead," in Thomas D. Eliot et al, Norway's Families: Trends, Problems, Programs (Phila., 1960), 71-80.

——. "The Peasant Movement in Norway," BJS, 5 (1954), 63-77.

——. A Study of Cultural Change, Rural-Urban Conflicts in Norway (Studia Norvegica, no. 9). Oslo, 1956. 103 p.

"The Old Norwegian Peasant Community," Investigations undertaken by the Institute for Comparative Research in Human Culture, Oslo. I: Andreas Holmsen, "General Survey and Historical Introduction," 17-32; II: Halvard Bjørkvik, "The Farm Territories; Habitation and Field Systems, Boundaries and Common Ownership," 33-61; III: Rigmor Frimannslund, "Farm Community and Neighborhood Community," 62-81. All in SEHR 4 (1956), 17-81.

Olsen, Magnus B. Farms and Fanes of Ancient Norway; the Place-names Discussed in their Bearings on Social and Religious History (Instituttet for Sammenlignende Kulturforskning, Serie A, Forelesninger, 9). Oslo; Cambridge, Mass., 1926. 349 p.

Øyen, Ørjar. Ecological Context and Residential Differentiation: Neighborhood Attachment in Four Areas of Oslo. Oslo, 1964. 203 p.

Park, George K., and Lee Soltow. "Politics and Social Structure in a Norwegian Village," AJS, 27 (1961), 152-64.

Ramsøy, Natalie R. "Assertative Mating and the Structure of Cities" [Oslo], AmSocR, 31 (1966), 773-86.

Vine, Margaret W. "Social Change in a Norwegian Valley Community," RS, 22 (1957), 67-77.

Vollaux, Camille. "The Maritime and Rural Life of Norway," GeoR, 14 (1924), 505-18.

RELIGION

Berggrav, Eivind J. The Norwegian Church in Its International Setting (Burge Memorial Lecture). Lond., 1946. 31 p.

Bergstad, Silas E. Hans Nielsen Hauge and Religious Lay Activity in Norway. Thesis (Ph.D.), New York University, 1959. 237 p.

Castberg, Frede. "Home, School and Church," in his, The Norwegian Way of Life (Lond., 1954), 19-43.

Cushman, Robert B. American Religious Societies in Norway. Thesis (Ph.D.), Northwestern University, 1943.

Dahl, Ottar. "Norwegian Clergy," SEHR, 4 (1956), 185-88.

Dehlin, Stene. "Norway's First Woman Pastor," Norseman (1964, no. 6), 170-72.

Eliot, Thomas D. "Norway's Churches and Morals," Christian Century, 69 (Ja 30, 1952), 127-29.

Flint, John T. "The Church in Relation to Family Life," in Thomas D. Eliot, ed., Norway's Families: Trends, Problems, Programs (Phila., 1960), 387-406.

——. State, Church and Laity in Norwegian Society: a Typological Study of Institutional Change. Thesis (Ph.D.), University of Wisconsin, 1957. 397 p.

Hare-Scott, Kenneth. "The Church in Norway," Norseman, 4 (1946), 135-36.

Kaasa, H. E. The Doctrine of the Church in Norway in the Nineteenth Century. Thesis (Ph.D.), University of Durham, 1961.

Michalsen, Fin. "Church Registers in Norway," Archivim, 8 (1958), 43-53.

Molland, Einar. Church Life in Norway, 1800-1950. Minneapolis, 1957. 120 p.

Myklebust, Olav G. "The Strongest Nerve of Christian Life," Norseman (1960, no. 6), 4-7.

Norway, Information Office. The Norwegian Church Struggle. Lond., 1943. 68 p.

Stiansen, Peder. History of the Baptists in Norway. Chicago, 1933. 176 p.; Wheaton, Ill., 1939. 344 p. Based on Thesis (Ph.D.), Northwestern University, 1932.

Tveteraas, R. "The See of Stavanger," ASR, 13 (1925), 222-27.

Willson, Thomas B. History of the Church and State in Norway from the Tenth to the Sixteenth Century. Westminister, 1903. 382 p.

SOCIAL STRATIFICATION

Barnes, J. A. "Class and Committees in a

Norwegian Island Parish," HumRel, 7
(1954), 39-58.

Barth, Fredrik. "The Social Organization of
a Parish Group in Norway," Norveg
(Oslo), 5 (1955), 125-43.

Holmsen, Andreas. "The Transition from
Tenancy to Freehold Peasant Ownership
in Norway," SEHR, 9 (1961), 152-64.

Mathiesen, Thomas. "Aspects of Social
Stratification in a Changing Community"
[Mo, Norway], AcSoc, 4 (1959/60), 42-54.

Pihlblad, C. T., and Dagfinn Aas. "Residential and Occupational Mobility in an Area
of Rapid Industrialization in Norway,"
ASR, 25 (1960), 369-75.

Semmingsen, Ingrid. "The Dissolution of
Estate Society in Norway," SEHR, 2
(1954), 166-203.

Sundt, Eilert. The Conditions and Customs
of the Working Class in Christiania.
Christiania, before 1900.

THE FAMILY

Akman, Fahire. "A Comparative Study of
the Norwegian and Turkish Family
Laws," Women Lawyers Journal, 51
(1965), 14-17, 29-31.

Barth, Fredrik. "Family Life in a Central
Norwegian Mountain Community," in
Thomas D. Eliot, et al., Norway's Fami-
lies: Trends, Problems, Programs
(Phila., 1960), 81-107.

Brox, Ottar. "Natural Conditions, Inheritance and Marriage in a North Norwegian
Fjord," Folk, 6 (1964, no. 1), 35-45.

Daniels, H. K. Home Life in Norway. Lond.,
N.Y., 1911. 298 p.

Eliot, Thomas D. "A Century's Contrasts in
Design for Living: Family Studies in a
Habitat Area," AcSoc, 4 (1959/60), 33-54.

——. "Family Life Education in Norway,"
Marriage and Family Living, 15 (F 1953),
4-8.

——. "Norway's Distribution of Books on
Family Problems," JofDoc, 10 (M 1954),
19-25.

Eliot, Thomas D., and Arthur Hillman, eds.
Norway's Families: Trends, Problems,
Programs. Phila., 1960. 485 p.

Larsen, Cecil E. "The Family in Norwegian
Fiction," S&SR, 36 (1951), 97-102.

Lynn, David B., and William L. Sawrey.
"Effects of Father-Absence on Norwegian
Boys and Girls," Journal of Abnormal
Social Psychology, 59 (1959), 258-62.

Nordland, Eva, et al. "Child Management:
Trends in Urban Middle Classes," in
Thomas D. Eliot, et al., Norway's Fami-

lies: Trends, Problems, Programs
(Phila., 1960), 191-221.

Ramholt, P. "Nuptuality, Fertility, and Reproduction in Norway," PopSt, 7 (Jl 1953),
46-61.

Sørhus, Kjell. "Meet Mr. and Mrs. Norway:
Odds and Ends from the Vital Statistics
about the Average Norwegian Family,"
Norseman (1960, no. 2), 22-24.

Stephenson, John C. "Family Life in an Industrial Community," in Thomas D. Eliot,
et al., Norway's Families: Trends, Problems, Programs (Phila., 1960), 108-29.

Striar, Myles. "The Troupers" [Young
Children], Norseman (1961, no. 6), 20-23.

Tiller, Per Olav. Father Absence and Per-
sonality Development of Children in Sailor
Families (Nordisk Psykologi, Monograph
Series no. 9). Oslo, 1958. 48 p.

WOMEN

Alnaes, A. "Norway Women Organize!"
ASR, 35 (1947), 226-30.

Aubert, Vilhelm. "The Housemaid — an Occupational Role in Crisis" [in Oslo],
AcSoc, 1 (1955/56), 149-58.

Norwegian Joint Committee on International
Social Policy. Facts about Women in
Norway. Oslo, 1960. 42 p.

——. The Status of Women in Norway Today. Oslo, 1953. 68 p.

Voss, Sofie. "Women Leaders in Norway,"
ASR, 20 (1932), 268-75.

THE STUDENT

Lovaas, O. I. "Social Desirability Ratings
of Personality Variables by Norwegian
and American College Students," Journal
of Abnormal Social Psychology, 57 (1958),
124-25.

Sommerfelt, Alf. "Some Reflections on the
Influence of the University on Society in
Norway and France," Norseman, 2 (1944),
192-95.

Simenson, William C. A Comparative Study
of the Social Activities and Attitudes of
Students at the University of Wisconsin
and the University of Oslo. Thesis, University of Wisconsin, 1951.

Simenson, William C. and Gilbert Geis.
"Courtship Patterns of Norwegian and
American University Students," Marriage
and Family Living, 18 (1956), 334-38.

MINORITIES

Østberg, Kristian. "A Norwegian Minority

Problem in the Eighteen Twenties" [Finnish immigrants], NGT, 7 (1938/39), 648-65.

Pelcovits, Nathan A. "A Note on Norway's Jews," Contemporary Jewish Record, 3 (1940), 402-404.

Striar, Myles. "Minority under the Midnight Sun," Norseman (1960, no. 4), 20-22.

MASS COMMUNICATIONS, THEATRE, TELEVISION

Berg, Henrick. "The Municipalisation of the Cinema in Norway," AnColEc, 3 (1927), 130-33.

Brøgger, N. C. "The Norwegian Theater of Today," ASR, 42 (1954), 118-28.

Buraas, Anders. "Northern Outpost of TV," Norseman (1960, no. 3), 6-9.

Geiss, Gilbert L. American Motion Pictures in Norway: a Study in International Mass Communications. Thesis (Ph.D.), University of Wisconsin, 1954.

Klaebo, A. "The Norwegian Broadcasting Corporation," ScPP, III, 327-29.

Marcussen, Elsa B. "Film Production in Norway," ASR, 42 (1954), 309-18.

Norman, Carl. "The Norwegian Rural Cinema," ASR, 50 (1962), 53-57.

Von der Lippe, Frits. "Theatre Goes to the People," Norseman (1960, no. 3), 17-19.

Zavis, William. "Stage, Film and the State," Norseman (1961, no. 5), 12-16.

THE PRESS

Eide, Richard B. "Norway's Post-War Press in the Golden Jubilee Year," Journalism Quarterly, 32 (1955), 335-42.

Rokkan, Stein and Per Torsvik. "The Voter, the Reader and the Party Press: an Analysis of Political Preference and Newspaper Reading in Norway," Gazette, 6 (1960), 311-28.

Taylor, Alfred H. 'Morgenbladet' in Norwegian Press History. Thesis (Ph.D.), University of Missouri, 1955. 545 p.

Torsvik, Per. "Magazines in Norway," Gazette, 6 (1960), 123-30.

Vogt, Per. "The Norwegian Press," ScPP, III, 311-14.

LANGUAGE

Abrahamsen, Samuel. "The Linguistic Controversy of Modern Norway: a Study in Cultural Change," in Carl Bayerschmidt and Erik Friis, eds., Scandinavian Studies: Essays Presented to Henry

Goddard Leach (Seattle, 1965), 125-40.

Berulfsen, Bjarne. "The Language Situation in Norway," Norseman, 10 (1952), 183-92.

Haugen, Einar. "Historical Background of Norwegian," in his, Norsk Engelsk Ordbok/ Norwegian English Dictionary (Oslo; Madison, Wisc., 1965), 20-28.

——. Language Conflict and Language Planning: the Case of Modern Norwegian. Cambridge, Mass., 1966. 393 p.

——. "Language Planning in Modern Norway," ScSt, 33 (1961), 68-81.

——. "Norway's Language Problem," Norseman (1962, no. 3), 17-19.

——. The Origin and Early History of the New Norse Movement in Norway. Thesis (Ph.D.), University of Illinois, 1931.

Huse, Birger. "English on the 6:40 Train," Norseman (1961, no. 4), 8-11.

Sommerfelt, Alf. "Norwegian Languages," Norseman, 15 (1957), 165-72.

SOCIAL PROBLEMS

Allwood, Inga W. Housing Studies in the City of Oslo: a Critical Study of the Development of Psychological and Sociological Orientations in Housing Statistics, 1855-1948. Mullsjö, Sweden, 1952. 38 p.

Bergsgard, Unnliev. "Redevelopment Problems of Two Major Norwegian Towns," Municipal Journal, 69 (1961), 1122-23+.

Evang, Karl, and Otto G. Hansen. An Inquiry into the Diet of 301 Poorly Situated Families in Norway (Acta medica scandinavica, Supplementum, C111). Hels., 1939. 225 p.

Haun, Myrtle L. "Social Problems as Ibsen Found Them and as They Are Today," ScSt, 10 (1928/29), 176-79.

Norwegian Joint Committee on International Social Policy. Measures for Care of Cripples in Norway. Oslo, Aug 1951. Mimeographed.

Ødegård, Ørnulf. "The Distribution of Mental Diseases in Norway," APNS, 20 (1945), 247-84.

ALCOHOLISM, PROHIBITION

"The Failure of Prohibition in Norway," ASR, 15 (1927), 41-44.

Knudsen, Rolf. Public and Private Measures in Norway for the Prevention of Alcoholism (International Bureau Against Alcoholism Booklets, v. 1, no. 2). Geneva, 1958; Lausanne, 1959. 14 p.

Norway, Ministry of Social Affairs in Cooperation with the Norwegian Joint Committee on International Social Policy. Alcohol Problems in Norway; Measures Taken to Prevent the Abuse of Alcohol, by Rolf Knudsen. Oslo, 1952. 21 p.

Norway's Noble Experiment. Wash., 1931. 34 p.

Norwegian Joint Committee on International Social Policy. Alcohol Problems in Norway Today. Oslo, 1957. 21 p.

Seth, James. "The Norwegian System of Liquor Control," CR, 90 (1906), 861-72.

CRIME

Andenaes, Johannes. "Short Term Imprisonment and its Alternatives," in Twelfth International Penal and Penitentiary Congress, The Hague, 1950, Proceedings, v. 5 (The Hague, 1951), 23-36.

Christie, Nils, Johannes Andenaes, and Sigurd Skirbekk. "A Study of Self-Reported Crime," ScStCrim, 1 (1965), 86-116.

Hambro, Cato. "Juvenile Delinquency in Norway," Norseman (1962, no. 1), 17-21.

Hauge, Ragnar. "Crime and the Press," ScStCrim, 1 (1965), 147-64.

Mögelstue, Idar. "Methods of Criminological Analyses," ScStCrim, 1 (1965), 165-72.

Pihlblad, C. T. "The Juvenile Offender in Norway," Journal of Criminal Law and Criminology, 46 (1955), 500-11.

Sveri, Knut. "Criminality and Age," AcSoc, 5 (1960/62), 76-86.

——. "Group Activity," ScStCrim, 1 (1965), 173-85.

SEX

Bremer, Johan. Asexualization: a Follow-up Study of 244 Cases. Oslo, N.Y., 1959. 366 p.

Eliot, Thomas D. "Norway Conquers Venereal Disease," British Journal of Venereal Diseases, 31 (1955), 2-8.

——. "Sex Instruction in the Norwegian Culture," Social Problems, 1 (1953), 44-48.

Gjessing, H. C. "Venereal Diseases Past and Present in Norway with Special Reference to Oslo," British Journal of Venereal Diseases, 32 (1956), 86-90.

Johnstadt, Trygve. "Sex Life of Scandinavian Countries: Norway," in Albert Ellis and Albert Abarbanel, eds., The Encyclopedia of Sexual Behavior (N.Y., 1961), v. 2, 915-18.

SOCIAL POLICY

Hansson, Per M., and Reidar D. Holmsen. "Insurance in Norway," ScPP, III, 843-51.

Lindsay, Inabel B. A Survey of Selected Aspects of Social Welfare in Sweden and Norway. Wash., 1959. Mimeographed.

Nordskog, John Eric. Social Reform in Norway, a Study of Nationalism and Social Democracy (The University of Southern California. Research studies, no. 9). Los Angeles, 1935. 184 p.

Norway, Ministry of Social Affairs. Assistance to Victims of the War. Oslo, 1951. Mimeographed.

——. Norwegian Social and Labor Survey. Oslo, 1958. 147 p. Rev. ed. of Guide for Advanced Students of Social Welfare, Norway, issued by the UN in 1951.

——. Norwegian Social Policy, 1959-1961. Oslo, 1961. 50 p.

——. Public Assistance in Norway. Oslo, 1951. Mimeographed.

——. Social Assistance in Norway. Oslo, 1952. 15 p.

——. Social Development, July 1953-Sept. 1955. Oslo, 1955.

——. Social Developments in Norway. Oslo, 1957. 62 p.

——. Social Developments in Norway, 1957-1959. Oslo, 1959. 38 p.

Norwegian Joint Committee on International Social Policy. Norwegian Social and Labour Survey. Oslo, 1950. 110 p.

Pew, Eileene. "Norway's 'Middle Way' in Health Care," ASR, 53 (1965), 256-68.

"The Question of Family Allowances in Norway," ILR, 40 (1939), 56-63.

Skardal, Dorothy B. Social Insurance in Norway: a Survey. Rev. ed., Oslo, 1956. 115 p.

SWEDEN

Ajo, Reino. An Analysis of Automobile Frequencies in a Human Geographic Continuum (LSG, series B., no. 15). Lund, 1955. 16 p.

Åkesson, Elof. The Tacit Assumptions of Swedish Social Life. Lund, 1939. 21 p.

Ander, Oscar Fritiof. The Cultural Heritage of the Swedish Immigrant (Augustana Library Publications, 27). Rock Island, Ill., 1956. 191 p.

Anderson, Bo. The Märsta Study: Social and Cultural Change in a Central Swedish Community (Research Reports from the Department of Sociology, Uppsala University, 5). Uppsala, 1961. Mimeographed.

Bromstedt, Magnus and Fredrik Böök. Sweden of Today: a Survey of Its Intellectual and Material Culture. Stock., 1930. 402 p.

Borland, Harold H. Nietzsche's Influence on Swedish Literature; With Special Reference to Strindberg, Ola Hansson, Heidenstam and Fröding. Gothenburg, 1956. 177 p.

Carlsson, Gösta. "Swedish Character in the Twentieth Century," Annals, 370 (1967), 93-98.

Dovring, Karin. "Quantitative Semantics in 18th Century Sweden," POQ, 18 (1954), 389-94.

Edström, J. S. "Playgrounds and Sports in Sweden," ASR, 21 (1933), 107-13.

Fleisher, Frederic. The New Sweden: the Challenge of a Disciplined Democracy. N.Y., 1967. 384 p.

Fleisher, Wilfred. Sweden, The Welfare State. N.Y., 1956. 255 p.

Gillespie, James E. "Swedish Co-operatives: How the Widespread System of Co-operatives Affects Swedish Life," CH, 18 (Je 1950), 331-36.

Gustafsson, Lars. Predominant Topics of Modern Swedish Debate. Stock., 1961. 9 p.

Heidenstam, Oscar G. von. Swedish Life in Town and Country (Our European Neighbours, v. 12). N.Y., Lond., 1904. 286 p.

Hodin, J. "Sociology in Sweden," SR, 33 (1941), 85-100.

Hohmann, Helen F. "Social Democracy in Sweden," Social Security Bulletin (F 1940), 3-10.

Korpi, Walter. "A Note on the Ability of Military Leaders to Assess Opinions in Their Units," AcSoc, 8 (1965), 293-303.

Lorénzen, Lilly. Of Swedish Ways. Minneapolis, 1964. 270 p.

Lundbergh, Holger. "Prince Eugen's Waldemarsudde," ASR, 42 (1954), 22-31.

Malmström, Vincent H. and Ruth M. Life in Europe: Sweden. Grand Rapids, Mich., 1956. 160 p.

Ohberg, Hjordis G. A Comparative Study of Selected Types of Organized Camping in Sweden and the United States. Thesis (M.A.), University of Michigan, 1946. 109 p.

Öhman, Ivar. "Swedish Laughter," ASR, 34 (1946), 342-51.

Olson, Grant. "Sweden in 1943," ForComWk (Je 17, 1944), 3-11.

Peel, Roy V. "The Swedish Character," BC, 2 (1936), 243-46.

Posse-Brázdová, Amelie. In the Beginning Was the Light. N.Y., 1942. 410 p.

Schück, Adolf. "Cultural Co-operation Between Sweden and the Baltic States," BSC, 4 (1938), 225-27.

Segerstedt, Torgny T. "The Uppsala School of Sociology," AcSoc, 1 (1956), 85-119.

"The Social Effects of Rationalisation in Sweden," ILR, 4 (Ja/Je, 1940), 72-78.

Strömbäck, Dag. "Åke Campbell: In Memoriam," Arv, 13 (1957), 180-83.

Sweden, Socialstyrelsen. Social Sweden. Rev. ed., Stock., 1952. 462 p.

Tallroth, Tore. Phases of Cultural Life in Sweden. Stock., 1962. 9 p.

Westerblad, C. A. "Per Henrik Ling, His Work and His Importance in the Light of Documents," Nord, 2 (1939), 217-27.

SOCIAL STRUCTURE

Anderson, Bo. "Opinion Influentials and Political Opinion Formation in Four Swedish Communities," ISSB, 14 (1962), 320-36.

Carlson, Sune, and Per Ernmark. A Swedish Case Study on Personnel Relations. Stock., 1951. 67 p.

Eysenck, H. J. "Primary Social Attitudes: a Comparison of Attitude Patterns in England, Germany and Sweden," Journal of Abnormal Social Psychology, 48 (1953), 563-68.

Israel, Joachim. "Self-Evaluation in Groups" [of 29 Stockholm Nurses], AcSoc, 3 (1958-59), 29-47.

Kälvesten, Anna-Lisa. The Social Structure of Sweden. Stock., 1965. 91 p.

Lundborg, Herman B., and F. J. Linders. The Racial Characters of the Swedish Nation. Uppsala, 1926. 182 p., 108 p.

Nyström, Bertil. "The Use of Sparetime in Sweden," ILR, 9 (1924), 845-62.

Westerlund, Gunnar. Group Leadership: a Field Experiment. Stock., 1952. 257 p.

POPULATION, MIGRATION

Beckman, Lars. "A Contribution to the Genetical Demography of North Sweden," Eugenics Quarterly, 4 (1957), 153-56.

Book, J. A. "A Genetic and Neuropsychiatric Investigation of a North Swedish Population," Acta Genetica et Statistica Medica, 4 (1953), 1-100, 133-39; 345-414.

Dahl, Sven. "The Contacts of Västerås with the Rest of Sweden," LSG, Series B, no. 13 (1957), 206-43.

De Geer, Sten. "A Map of the Distribution of Population in Sweden," GeoR, 12 (1922), 72-83.

Edin, Karl A., and Edward P. Hutchison. Studies of Differential Fertility in Sweden (Stockholm Economic Studies, no. 4). Lond., 1935. 116 p.

Essen-Møller, Erik. Individual Traits and Morbidity in a Swedish Rural Population (APNS Supplement 100). Coph., 1956. 160 p.

Forbat, Fred. "Migration, Journey to Work and Planning," LSG, Series B, no. 13 (1957), 310-19.

Freire, Maia. "Inbreeding Levels in Different Countries," Eugenics Quarterly, 4 (1957), 127-38.

Gille, Halvor. "Recent Developments in Swedish Population Policy," PopSt, 2 (1948), 3-70, 129-84.

Godlund, Sven. Population, Regional Hospitals, Transport Facilities, and Regions: Planning the Location of Regional Hospitals in Sweden (LSG, Series B, no. 21). Lund, 1961. 32 p.

Grundström, Måus. "The Journey to Work from the Statistical Point of View," LSG, Series B, no. 13 (1957), 320-25.

Hägerstrand, Torsten. "Migration and Area, Survey of a Sample of Swedish Migration Fields and Hypothetical Considerations on Their Genesis," LSG, Series B, no. 13 (1957), 27-158.

Hannerberg, David, ed. et al. Migration in Sweden: a Symposium (LSG, Series B no. 13), Lund, 1957. 336 p. 10 maps.

Heckscher, Eli F. "Swedish Population Trends Before the Industrial Revolution," EcHistR, 2 new series (1949-50), 266-77.

Hutchison, Edward P. "Internal Migration and Tuberculosis Mortality in Sweden," AmSocR (1936), 273-85.

——. "Swedish Population Theory in the Eighteenth Century," in his, The Population Debate: the Development of Conflicting Theories up to 1900 (Boston, 1967), 69-93.

——. "Swedish Population Thought in the Eighteenth Century," PopSt, 13 (1959), 81-102.

Hyrenius, D. H. "Fertility and Reproduction in a Swedish Population Group Without Family Limitation," PopSt, 12 (1958), 121-30.

——. "The Relation Between Birth Rates and Economic Activity in Sweden," OISB, 8 (Ja 1946), 14-21.

——. "Reproduction and Replacement: a Methodological Study of Swedish Population Changes during 200 Years," PopSt, 5 (1951), 421-31.

Isbell, E. C. "Internal Migration in Sweden and Intervening Opportunities," AmSocR, 9 (1944), 627-39.

Janson, Florence E. The Background of Swedish Immigration, 1840-1930 (University of Chicago Social Service Monograph, no. 15). Chicago, 1931. 517 p.

Johnson, Roy A. "Immigration: a Swedish Dilemma," ASR, 55 (1967), 18-25.

Kaasik, N. "The Baltic Refugees in Sweden — A Successful Experiment," BR I, 2 (1947, no. 1), 55-61.

Kulldorff, Gunnar. Migration Probabilities (LSG, Series B, no. 14). Lund, 1955. 48 p.

Larsson, Tage. A Methodological, Psychiatric, and Statistical Study of a Large Swedish Rural Population (APNS Supplement 89). Coph., 1954. 250 p.

——. Mortality in Sweden. White Plains, N.Y., 1965. 143 p.

Lindberg, John S. The Background of Swedish Emigration to the United States: an Economic and Sociological Study in the Dynamics of Migration. Minneapolis, 1930. 272 p.

Lövegren, Esse. "Mutual Relations Between Migration Fields: a Circulation Analysis" [Data from Stockholm], LSG, Series B, no. 13 (1957), 159-69.

Moore, Jane. Cityward Internal Migration: an Analysis of the 1930 Population of Stockholm Born in Västmanland County, Sweden. Chicago, 1938. 140 p. Based on thesis (Ph.D.), University of Chicago, 1932.

Myrdal, Alva. "Can Sweden Evolve a Population Policy?" ASR, 25 (1937), 114-18.

——. Nation and Family: the Swedish Experiment in Democratic Family and Population Policy. N.Y., Lond., 1941. 441 p.

Myrdal, Gunnar. Population: A Problem for Democracy (Godkin lectures, 1938). Cambridge, Mass., 1940. 237 p.

——. "Population Problems and Policies," Annals, 197 (1938), 200-15.

Nelson, Helge. "Some Remarks on Seasonal Wanderings, Internal Migration and Emigration in and From Sweden in the 19th Century," Folk-Liv, 21-22 (1957/58), 85-100.

Nyblén, G., and Carl-Erik Quensel. Fertility in Sweden 1931-1935 after Duration of Marriage and Order of Birth (Acta Universitatis Lundensis, new series. Lund Universitets Årsskrift, 45, no. 6). Lund, 1950. 45 p.

Odhe, Anna. "More Babies in Sweden," ASM (Aug 1945), 10-11.

Otterland, Anders. A Sociomedical Study of the Mortality of Seafarers: Analysis of Deaths in the Population of Active Seafarers Registered in Sweden (Acta Medica Scandinavica, Supplement 357). Stock., 1960. 300 p.

Population Movements and Industrialization: Swedish Counties, 1895-1930. Lond., 1941. 538 p.

Quensel, Carl-Erik. "Population Movements in Sweden in Recent Years," PopSt, 1 (1947), 29-43.

———. "Tendencies in Swedish Population Development," SBQR 38 (Jl 1957), 55-61.

Scott, Franklin D. "Sweden's Constructive Opposition to Emigration," JMH, 37 (1965), 307-35.

Tarm, Heino. "Estonians in Sweden in 1953," LSG, Series B, no. 13 (1957), 328-36.

Thomas, Dorothy S. "Economic and Social Aspects of Internal Migrations: an Exploratory Study of Selected Swedish Communities," in Economic Essays in Honor of Wesley Clair Mitchell (N.Y., 1935), 447-76.

———. "Internal Migrations in Sweden," AJS, 42 (1936), 345-57.

———. "The Swedish Census of 1935-36," Journal of the American Statistical Association (1936), 541-44.

Thomas, Dorothy S. et al. Social and Economic Aspects of Swedish Population Movements, 1750-1933. N.Y., 1941. 487 p.

United States, Library of Congress. Guide to the Official Population and Vital Statistics of Sweden. By Edward P. Hutchinson. Wash., 1942. 72 p.

Utterström, Gustaf. "Some Population Problems in Pre-Industrial Sweden," SEHR, 2 (1954), 103-65.

Walsh, Francis P. "Immigration Problems in Sweden," CR, 208 (1966), 187-89.

Wargentin, Pehr W. Tables of Mortality Based Upon the Swedish Population, Prepared and Presented in 1766. Stock., 1930. 68 p.

Wendel, Bertil. A Migration Schema [for Sweden] Theories and Observations (LSG, Series B, no. 9). Lund., 1953. 38 p.

———. "Regional Aspects of Internal Migration and Mobility in Sweden, 1946-1950," LSG, Series B, 13 (1957), 7-26.

Wikman, V., and K. Rob. "Linnaeus as Anthropologist and Ethnologist," Arv, 14 (1958), 102-7.

Winberg, Isak P. "Population Investigations Carried Out by the Royal Board of

Agriculture, With Examples from Loftakammas, Kalmar Län and Northern Roslagen, Stockholm Län," LSG, Series B, 13 (1957), 192-205.

RURAL AND URBAN SOCIOLOGY

Barnes, J. A. "Land Rights and Kinship in Two Brimnes Hamlets," Journal of the Royal Anthropological Institute, 87 (1957, no. 1), 31-56.

Beggs, Vera W. "Operation Vallinby — Sweden Experiments with Planned Decentralization," American City, 70 (Jl 1955), 117-19, 163.

Erixon, Sigurd. "Villages and Common Lands in Sweden," WestSocTrans, 3 (1956), 122-34.

Jansson, Carl-Gunnar, and Bengt Rudolfsson. "Ecological and Geographical Distances in Stockholm," AcSoc, 8 (1965), 285-92.

Johnson, Ellen. "Swedish Peasant 'Bonader'," ASR, 31 (1943), 220-30.

Johnson, Hallett. "Peasants of Dalarna," FSJ, 4 (1927), 273-78.

League of Nations, European Conference on Rural Life (Sweden: Publications, no. 21) Geneva, 1939. 71 p.

Leighly, John B. The Towns of Mälardalen in Sweden: a Study in Urban Morphology (University of California Publications in Geography, v. 3, no. 11). Berkeley, 1928. 134 p.

Lindstrom, David E. "The Changing Rural Community in Sweden," RS, 16 (M 1951), 49-55.

Posse-Brázdová, Amelie. "Country-House Life in Sweden: In Castle and Cottage the Land Gentry Gallantly Keep the Old Traditions," NGeogM, 66 (1934), 1-64.

Wilson, Linton. "Old Farmsteads," ASR, 25 (1937), 5-17.

RELIGION

Bergendoff, Conrad J. L. "Lutherans at Lund," ASR, 35 (1947), 297-303.

———. Olavus Petri and the Ecclesiastical Transformation in Sweden, 1521-1552. N.Y., 1928. 264 p.

Block, Marguerite B. "Jesper Svidberg (1653-1735): Watcher on Sion's Walls," ChHist, 13 (1944), 42-55.

Butler, C. M. The Reformation in Sweden. N.Y., 1884. 259 p.

The Church of Sweden, Past and Present. Malmö, 1960. 340 p.

Cnattingius, Hans J. Studies in the Order of St. Bridget of Sweden; Vol. 1: The Crisis of the 1420's (Stockholm Studies in History, 7). Stock., 1963.

Edström, Lennart. Women Clergy in Sweden. Stock , 1962. 4 p.

Ferm, Deane W. "The Role of the Church in Modern Sweden," ASR, 55 (1967), 360-70.

Heldtander, Tore. "Church and State in Sweden," ASR, 50 (1962), 15-24.

Hertzman-Ericson, Gurli. "St. Ansgar's Church," ASR, 18 (1930), 589-97.

Morris, Franklyn K. "The 800th Anniversary of the See of Uppsala," ASR, 52 (1964), 255-60.

Normann, Carl-E. "Swedish Research in Ecclesiastical History During the Last Decade," JofEH, 3 (1952), 201-17.

Oppermann, Charles J. A. The English Missionaries in Sweden and Finland. N.Y., 1937. 221 p.

Paraiso, Valentine. St. Bridget of Sweden (1303-1373). Reprinted with Enlargements and a Foreword by a Bridgettine of Syon Abbey, South Brent, Devon, 1959. 31 p.

Pleijel, Hilding. The Devotional Literature of the Swedish People in Earlier Times (Opuscula instituti hist.-eccl. lundensis. 4). Lund, 1955. 24 p.

Swinstead, J. H. The Swedish Church and Ours. Lond., 1921 128 p.

Toksvig, Signe. Emanuel Swedenborg, Scientist and Mystic. New Haven, Conn., 1948. 389 p.

Waddams, Herbert M. The Swedish Church. Lond., 1946. 70 p.

Wald, Arthur. "The New Bishop of Stockholm," ASR, 30 (1942), 328-31.

Wordsworth, John. The National Church of Sweden (The Hale Lectures, 1910). Lond., Milwaukee, 1911. 459 p.

SOCIAL STRATIFICATION

Anderson, C. Arnold. "Lifetime Inter-Occupational Mobility Patterns in Sweden," AcSoc, 1 (1956), 168-202.

Aronson, Albert. Sub-Communities in Stockholm. Stock., 1957.

Boalt, Gunnar. "Social Mobility in Stockholm: a Pilot Investigation," in International Sociological Association, Transactions of the Second World Congress of Sociology (Lond., 1954), v. II, 67-73.

Carlsson, Gösta. Social Mobility and Class Structure. Lund, 1958. 197 p.

——. "Some Current Research Problems in the Field of Stratification and Mobility in Sweden," EEH, 8 (1955-56), 45-51.

Gehnich, Karl. "A Swedish Study of the

White Collar Class," SRWA, 2 (1952, no. 3), 15-17.

Hanssen, Börje. "Fields of Social Activity and Their Dynamics" [Data from Skåne], WestSocTrans, 2 (1953), 99-133.

Linders, F. J. "Contributions to the Knowledge of Stature and Its Variation Within Different Social Strata in Sweden," GeoA, 12 (1930), 56-71.

McConough, Edward C. et al. "Relative Professional Status as Perceived by American and Swedish University Students," Social Forces, 38 (O 1959), 65-69.

Remity, Uno. Professional Satisfaction Among Swedish Bank Employees: a Psychological Study. Coph., 1960. 422 p.

Söderlund, Ernst F. "The Rural Working Classes in Pre-Industrial Sweden" [Review of Published Swedish Doctoral Thesis by Gustaf Utterström], SEHR, 6 (1958), 98-101.

THE FAMILY

Chambliss, Rollin. "Median Age at First Marriage in Sweden, 1881-1953," Milbank Memorial Fund Quarterly, 35 (1957), 280-86.

Dahlström, Edmund. "Analysis of the Debate on Sex Roles," in Edmund Dahlström, ed., The Changing Role of Men and Women (Lond., 1967), 170-205.

Hanssen, Boye. "Dimensions of Primary Group Structure in Sweden in Studies of the Family," in Papers of the 1st International Seminar on the Family (UNESCO Social Science Institute, Cologne) (Tübingen, 1956), 115-54.

Kälvesten, Anna-Lisa. "Family Policy in Sweden," Marriage and Family Living, 17 (1955), 250-54.

Larson, Carl A. "The Frequency of First Cousin Marriages in a South Swedish Rural Community," American Journal of Human Genetics, 8 (1956), 151-53.

Larsson, Yngve. "Planning for Family Life and Leisure," Town and Country Planning, 26 (1958), 97-102, 137-43.

Lindblom, B. "Swedish Settlements and the Youth Problems," Community Development, 1 (1958), 53-57.

Locke, Harvey J. "Marital Adjustment and Prediction in Sweden," AJS, 60 (1954), 51-53.

Locke, Harvey J., and Georg Karlsson. "Marital Adjustment and Prediction in Sweden and the U.S.," AmSocR, 17 (1952), 10-17.

Moberg, Sven. "Marital Status and Family

Size Among Matriculated Persons in Sweden," PopSt, 4 (1950), 115-27.

Person, Henry A. "The Swedes and Their Family Names," ScSt, 39 (1967), 209-48.

Riemer, Svend. "A Research Note on Sociological Home-Planning" [Based on Research in Stockholm], AJS, 46 (1940-41), 865-72.

Segerstedt, Torgny T., and Phillip Weintraub. "Marriage and Divorce in Sweden," Annals, 272 (1950), 185-94.

Willis, Richard H. "Political and Child Rearing Attitudes in Sweden," Journal of Abnormal Social Psychology, 53 (Jl 1956), 74-77.

WOMEN

Fleisher, Frederic. "The Emerging Women," in his, The New Sweden: the Challenge of a Disciplined Democracy (N.Y., 1967), 224-53.

Fröberg, Gerda. "Sweden's 'Landsturm' Women," ASR, 19 (1931), 611-14.

Gendell, Murray. Swedish Working Wives. Totowa, N.J., 1963. 269 p.

Key-Rasmussen, Essy. "Are Women Losing Ground? A Swedish Woman Writer Analyzed Our Civilization and Woman's Part Therein," ASR, 30 (1942), 337-41.

Larsen, Hanna A. "Sweden's Unique Organization of Women," ASR, 1 (1913), 14-17.

Myrdal, Alva. "Swedish Women in Industry and at Home," Annals, 197 (1938), 216-31.

Svedelius, Julia. "Types of Swedish Women Today," ASR, 17 (1929), 223-29, 287-93.

FOLKLORE

Campbell, Åke. "Notes on a Swedish Contribution to the Folk Culture Atlas of Europe," Laos, 1 (1951), 111-20.

Hagberg, Louise. "Old Time Christmas in Sweden," ASR, 14 (1926), 744-50.

Heurlin, Gustav. "Color and Customs of Sweden's Chateau Country," NGeogM, 66 (1934), 33-40.

———. "Types and Costumes of Old Sweden," NGeogM, 54 (1928), 424-41.

Holme, Charles, ed. Peasant Art in Sweden, Lapland, and Iceland. Lond., 1910. 48 p.

Liljeblad, Sven. "Swedish Folk Tale Collections: the Gustavus Adolphus Academy Edition of Folktales," Folk-Liv, 2 (1938), 77-101.

Nylén, Anna-Maja. Swedish Peasant Costumes. Stock., 1949. 91 p.

Rooth, Anna. B. "The Conception of 'Rulers' in the South of Sweden," Stockholm

Studies in Comparative Religion, 1 (1961).

Sweden, Landsmåls-och folkminnesarkivet i Uppsala. Institute for the Investigation of Swedish Dialects, Folklore and Folklife. Uppsala, 1949. 39 p.

Tillhagen, C. H. "Funeral and Death Customs of the Swedish Gypsies," Journal of the Gypsy Lore Society, 31 (1952), 29-54.

PUBLISHING, COMMUNICATIONS

Ehnmark, Elof, and Henrik Hahr. "Radio and Television in Sweden," ScPP, III, 357-60.

Lundbergh, Holger. "Radio Broadcasting in Sweden," ASR, 29 (1941), 56-59.

Nilsson, Anders. "The Swedish Labour Press," Free Labour World (D 1957), 33-37+.

Pers, Anders Y. "Newspapers in Sweden," ScPP, III, 298-304.

———. Newspapers in Sweden. Stock., 1954. 66 p.

Stolpe, Herman A. "Co-operative Book Publishing in Sweden," RIC, 44 (1951), 22-24.

Thedin, Nils. "Co-operation and Culture: the Co-operative Press as a Means of Raising the Cultural Level of the Members," RIC, 42 (1949), 290-94+.

SOCIAL PROBLEMS

Ballgren, Bertil, and Torsten Shogren. A Clinical and Genetico-Statistical Study of Schizophrenia and Low-Grade Mental Deficiency in a Large Swedish Rural Population (APNS Supplement 140). Coph., 1959. 65 p.

Bellquist, Eric C. "Maintaining Morale in Sweden," POQ, 5 (1941), 432-47.

Björkman, Edwin. "Sweden's Solution of Divorce," Forum, 76 (1926), 543-50.

Fleisher, Frederic. "Temperance and Drinking," in his, The New Sweden: the Challenge of a Disciplined Democracy (N.Y., 1967), 21-28.

Hartelius, H. "Suicide in Sweden, 1925-1950, a Statistical Analysis and Psychodynamic Interpretation," APNS, 32 (1958), 151-81.

Hedström, Birgit Magnusdotter. "Rehabilitating the Crippled," ASR, 29 (1941), 35-40.

Hendin, Herbert. "Suicide in Sweden," Psychiatric Quarterly, 36 (1962), 1-28.

Jonsson, Erland. "Annoyance Reactions to External Environmental Factors in Different Sociological Groups," AcSoc, 7 (1964), 229-63.

Ohlin, Bertil. "Social Problems and Policies of Sweden," Annals, 197 (1938), 1-30.

Sellin, J. Thorsten. Marriage and Divorce
Legislation in Sweden. Also thesis
(Ph.D.), University of Pennsylvania, 1922.
Minneapolis, 1922. 148 p.

Sweden, Royal Social Board. Social Work
and Legislation in Sweden. Stock., 1928.
289 p. 2d ed. (New Sweden Tercentenary
Publication), 1938. 351 p.

Swedish Automobile Manufacturers Association. Motor Traffic in Sweden, 1960.
Stock., 1960. 80 p.

Tec, Nechama. Gambling in Sweden. Totowa, N.J., 1964. 139 p.

ALCOHOLISM, PROHIBITION

Bengtsson, Halfdan. "The Temperance
Movement and Temperance Legislation
in Sweden," Annals, 197 (1938), 134-53.

Bergvall, John. The Liquor Legislation in
Sweden. Stock., 1931.

Bratt, Ivan. "Controlling Alcohol in Sweden," ASR, 7 (1919), 345-52.

———. "How Sweden Does It," Forum, 85
(1931), 195-99.

Fleming, R. "The Management of Chronic
Alcoholism in England, Scandinavia, and
Central Europe," New England Journal of
Medicine (1937), 279-89.

Gebhart, J. C. The Bratt System of Liquor
Control in Sweden. Wash., 1930. 32 p.

Goldberg, Leonard. "Alcohol Research in
Sweden, 1939-1948," Quarterly Journal of
Studies on Alcohol, 10 (1949), 279-88.

Kinberg, Olov. "Temperance Legislation in
Sweden," Annals (S 1932), 206-15.

Malmquist, Sten G. A Statistical Analysis of
the Demand for Liquor in Sweden: a
Study of the Demand for a Rational Commodity. Uppsala, 1948. 135 p.

Mingos, Howard. "A Sober Wet-Land,"
Forum, 73 (1925), 512-20.

Sjöhagen, A. "How a Swedish Temperance
Board Works," Quarterly Journal of
Studies on Alcohol, 14 (M 1953), 69-77.

Thompson, Walter. The Control of Liquor
in Sweden. N.Y., 1935. 244 p.

Wiklund, Daniel. Proposal of the Swedish
Government Committee for Reform of the
Care of the Inebriates. Stock., 1948.
Mimeographed.

Willerding, E. A Memorandum on the Liquor and Licensing — Laws in Sweden,
and on the Old Gothenburg System. Gothenburg, 1894. 25 p.

CRIME

Dahlberg, G. "New Method in Crime Statistics Applied to the Population of Sweden,"
Journal of Criminal Law and Criminology,
39 (1948), 327-41.

Eriksson, Torsten. "Postwar Prison Reform
in Sweden," Annals, 392 (1954), 152-62.

Fleisher, Frederic. "Violence and the Vio-
lent," in his, The New Sweden: the Challenge of a Disciplined Democracy (N.Y.,
1967), 168-95.

Göransson, Hardy. "Treatment of Criminals
and Other Asocial Individuals," Annals,
197 (1938), 120-33.

———. "The Treatment of Offenders in Sweden," Howard Journal, 8 (1949/1950), 21-
26.

Kinberg, Olov. "Criminal Policy in Sweden
in the Last Fifty Years," Journal of
Criminal Law and Criminology (1933),
313-32.

———. "Swedish Organization of Forensic
Psychiatry," Journal of Criminal Law
and Criminology, 44 (1953), 135-50.

Masreliez, Gustaf. "The Swedish Prison
System," Island Lantern (Ja 1930), 1-8.

Rudholm, Sten. "Swedish Legislation and
Practice Concerning Sexual Offences,"
English Studies in Criminal Science, 9
(1957), 445-64.

Saksena, H. C. "Report to the United Nations on Social Defense — Prevention of
Crime and Treatment of Offenders — in
Sweden," Penal Reformer, 8 (1952), 199-
216.

Sellin, J. Thorsten. "Probation and Parole
of Adult Offenders in Sweden," in National
Probation and Parole Association, Bul-
warks Against Crime: 1948 Yearbook
(N.Y., 1949), 239-51.

———. The Protective Code: a Swedish
Proposal. Stock., 1957. 56 p.

———. Recent Penal Legislation in Sweden.
Stock., 1947. 70 p.

———. "The Treatment of Offenders in Sweden," Federal Probation, 12 (Je 1948),
14-18.

Strömberg, Tore. "Some Reflections on the
Concept of Punishment," Theoria, 23
(1957), 71-83.

Törnqvist, Karl-Erik. "Correction and the
Prevention of Crime," ScStCrim, 1 (1965),
187-99.

Towne, Arthur W. "Probation in Sweden,"
Journal of Criminal Law and Criminology,
4 (1913), 599-601.

JUVENILE DELINQUENCY

Ahlander, Björn O. "Juvenile Delinquency in Sweden," AcSoc, 3 (1958/1959), 65-72.

Bolin, Lars. Measures to Combat Juvenile Delinquency in Sweden. Stock., 1961. 15 p.

Elmhorn, Kerstin. "Study in Self-Reported Delinquency Among Schoolchildren in Stockholm," ScStCrim, 1 (1965), 117-46.

Grobe, Hans. "Juvenile Delinquency in Sweden," Kentucky Law Journal, 53 (1964-1965), 247-53.

Nyquist, Ola. Juvenile Justice: a Comparative Study with Special Reference to the Swedish Child Welfare Board and the California Juvenile Court System (Cambridge Studies in Criminology, v. 12). Lond., 1960. 302 p.

Post-war Juvenile Delinquency in Sweden. Stock., 1959. Mimeographed.

Schlyter, Karl. "Trends in Sweden in the Treatment of Youthful Offenders Who Have Reached the Age of Eighteen But Are Not Twenty-one," International Review of Criminal Policy, 11 (1957), 69-88.

Sellin, J. Thorsten. "Sweden's Substitute for the Juvenile Court," Annals, 272 (1950), 137-49.

SEX

Bohm, Ewald. "Sex Life of Scandinavian Countries: Sweden," in Albert Ellis and Albert Abarbanel, eds., The Encyclopedia of Sexual Behavior (N.Y., 1961), v. 2, 919-25.

Fleisher, Frederic. "The New Morality," in his, The New Sweden: the Challenge of a Disciplined Democracy (N.Y., 1967), 254-84.

Höök, Kerstin. Refused Abortion: a Follow-up Study of 249 Women Whose Applications were Refused by the National Board of Health in Sweden (APNS Supplement 168, v. 39). Coph., 1963. 156 p.

Linnér, Birgitta. Sex and Society in Sweden. N.Y., 1967. 204 p.

Sternberg, David. "Sweden Debates Sex Morality," ASR, 54 (1966), 37-43.

Sweden, Medical Board. An Investigation into Questions of Social Hygiene in the Countries of Västerbotten and Norrbotten, Sweden [Conducted with the support of the Royal Medical Board in 1929-1931]. Lund, 1937. 784 p.

Sweden, Population Commission. Report on the Sex Question. Baltimore, 1940. 182 p.

SOCIAL POLICY

Anderson, Mary. "Social Legislation; Progress in the United States and in Sweden," ASR, 33 (1945), 32-40.

Black, Robson. "Youth Hostels in Sweden," American Forests (May 1949), 18-19.

Confederation of Swedish Trade Unions, Swedish Central Organisation of Salaried Employees and Förenade-Framtiden. Social Benefits in Sweden. Stock., 1954. 51 p.

Erlander, Tage. "Swedish Social Policy in Wartime," ILR, 47 (1943), 297-311.

Fleisher, Frederic. "From the Womb to the Tomb: Security and the Long Waits," in his, The New Sweden: the Challenge of a Disciplined Democracy (N.Y., 1967), 196-223.

Hedin, Naboth, ed. Social Welfare in Sweden. N.Y., 1941. 331 p.

Heinig, Peter. "Social Services and Public Expenditures in Sweden: Recent Developments and Problems." ILRR, 13 (1959-60), 533-49.

Höjer, Axel. Some Aspects of Swedish Social Welfare. N.Y., 1939. 102 p.

Höjer, Karl J. "The Care of the Indigent in Sweden," Annals, 197 (1938), 72-79.

——. "Social Reforms in Sweden," ScPP, III, 158-78.

——. Social Welfare in Sweden. Stock., 1949. 155 p.

Larsen, Joseph E. A. Some Aspects of Social Welfare Work in Sweden. Thesis (M.A.), Fordham University, 1935. 53 p.

Larson, Carl A. "Sweden's Modern Social Welfare Structure," JofEdSoc, 25 (1952), 384-400.

Larsson, Yngve, and Göran Tegner. "Community Facilities and Services in Sweden," United Nations, Housing and Town and Country Planning, Bull. no. 5 (1951), 16-30.

Markelius, Sven. "The Structure of Stockholm: Study of the Planning Problems and Policy," TCP, 24 (1956), 575-80, 636-42; 25 (1957), 87-91.

Osborn, F. J. "Sweden and Denmark: a Planning Tour," TCP, 15 (Autumn, 1947), 122-29.

Persson, Konrad. "Social Welfare in Sweden," Social Security Bull. (Ap 1949), 16-18+.

——. Social Welfare in Sweden: a Summary Account. Stock., 1959. 51 p. 1955 ed., 26 p.

Petri, Carl W. "When Every Fifth Swede Has a Car...," Plan (1953), pt. 2.

Rosenthal, Albert H. The Social Programs of Sweden: a Search for Security in a Free Society. Minneapolis, 1967. 193 p.

Schmidt, Carl C. "The Organization and Functions of the Swedish Royal Social Board," AJS (1931), 190-202.

Skogh, Sven. "The Administration of Social Welfare," Annals, 197 (1938), 20-24.

Smith, G. Howard. Swedish Relief. Stock., 1951.

Social Benefits in Sweden. Stock., 1959. 56 p.

"Social Planning in Sweden," ILR, 48 (1943), 308-15.

Social Sweden. Published by the Social Welfare Board. Stock., 1952. 462 p.

"Social Welfare in Sweden; Social Work in Switzerland," Indian Journal of Social Work, 11 (Je 1950), 126-41.

Sweden, Ministry of Social Affairs. National Insurance Act, May 25, 1962. Stock., 1963.

Sweden, Socialstyrelsen. The Cost and the Financing of the Social Services in Sweden in 1954. Stock., 1956. 10 p.

Swedish Institute. Social Benefits in Sweden. Stock., 1957. 49 p.

Swedish Institute, Swedish Employers Federation, the Confederation of Swedish Trade Unions, the Swedish Central Organization of Salaried Employees. Social Benefits in Sweden. Stock., 1959. 56 p.

Wahlund, Sten G. W. Social Work in Stockholm. Uppsala, 1937. 90 p.

FAMILY WELFARE

Craven, Cicely M. "The Child Welfare Boards of Sweden," Journal of Criminal Law and Criminology, 41 (1950), 344-45.

Lundquist, Birger. "Maternity Care in Sweden from the Medical and Social Point of View," AJPH, pt. 2 (N 1951), 20-25.

Malmström, Åke. "Children's Welfare in Family Law," ScStL, 1 (1957), 123-36.

Myrdal, Alva. "A Programme for Family Security in Sweden," ILR, 39 (1939), 723-63.

Nordstrom, Margareta. "Social Homes Help Services in Sweden," ILR, 88 (1963), 366-79.

Social Services for Children and Young People in Sweden. Stock., 1947.

Ström, Justus, and Harald Johansson. Maternity and Child Welfare Work in Sweden. Stock., 1950. 14 p.

Wangson, Otto R. "Maternal and Child Welfare," Annals, 197 (1938), 93-103.

HEALTH BENEFITS

Biörk, Gunnar. Trends in the Swedish Health and Welfare Policy. Stock., 1961. 10 p.

Birch-Lindgren, Gustaf. Modern Hospital Planning in Sweden and Other Countries. Stock., 1951. 109 p.

Canada, Department of National Health and Welfare. Health Insurance in Sweden (Its Social Security Series, memorandum, no. 10). Ottawa, 1952. 76 p.

Engel, Arthur, and Ann-Margaret Lundgren. "Swedish Health and Medical Care," ScPP, III, 179-89.

Heppell, Gordon. "Report on Swedish Hospitals: the International Hospital Federation Tour of Sweden's Hospitals," Municipal Journal, 58 (1950), 2509-11.

Höjer, Axel. "Public Health and Medical Care," Annals, 197 (1938), 104-19.

Lichtenstein, A. Preventive Pediatrics in Sweden. Stock., 1946. Mimeographed.

Maunsbach, Arvid B. Notes on the Public Dental Service of Sweden. Stock., 1947. Mimeographed.

———. "The Public Dental Service in Sweden," Dental Magazine and Oral Topics (Lond.) (O 1948).

"The Medical Examination of Young Persons in Industry in Sweden," ILR, 22 (1930), 816-22.

Myrgård, Arvid. "Sweden's Public Health System," ASR, 35 (1947), 304-20.

"National Sickness Insurance in Sweden," ILR, 76 (1957), 496-512.

Ollén, Lillian. "Health Insurance Plan: Seven Million Swedes are Covered," ASM, 51 (M 1957), 9-11.

Osvald, Olof. The Swedish Public Dental Health Service. Stock., 1962. 12 p.

Samson, A. D. P. The Operation of the Swedish Public Health System. Thesis (Ph.D.), Pennsylvania State University, 1954.

Sieurin, Sven. "Calisthenics With Music Make Swedish Office Happier, Healthier Work Place," NOMA Forum (Je 1949), 5-7.

Sweden, Committee, International Congress on Tuberculosis, 6th, Washington, 1908. The Struggle Against Tuberculosis in Sweden: 1908. Ed. by Sture Carlsson. Stock., 1908. 200 p.

"Sweden: New Act on National Sickness Insurance," ISSAssoc, 6 (1953), 421-25.

Swedish Institute. Public Health and Medicine in Sweden. Stock., 1949. 61 p.

Trott, E. H. "It Pays To Be Sick in Sweden," MT (Aug 1952), 22-25.

Wuorinen, John H. "Socialized Medicine in
Sweden," CH, 44 (1963), 333-38.

INSURANCE AND OLD AGE BENEFITS

Eriksson, Bernhard. "Social Security in
Sweden," ASM (Ap 1945), 8-9+.

Guldberg, S. D. "Staff Pensions in the
Swedish Consumers' Cooperative Movement," RIC, 42 (1949), 98-107.

Hohmann, Helen F. Old Age in Sweden — a
Program of Social Security. Wash., 1940.
305 p.

Hydén, Sven. "The Pensions Scheme in
Sweden," ISSAssoc, 19 (1966), 355-68.

Jerneman, Tor. "Social Insurance in Sweden," Annals, 197 (1938), 80-92.

———. "Sweden's National Pensions," ASR,
24 (1936), 19-23.

"Legislation on Sickness Insurance in Sweden," ISSAssoc, 4 (1951), 28-32.

Liedstrand, Emil. "Social Insurance in Sweden," ILR, 9 (1924), 178-95.

Lindberger, Lars. "The Reform of the Pensions Scheme and Saving," SBQR, 38 (Ap
1957), 34-39.

Lundberg, Erik. "Can the Pension Fund
Rescue Savings?" SBQR, 39 (Ap 1958),
39-47.

Michanek, Ernst. Old Age in Sweden.
Stock., 1962. 37 p.

———. "Sweden's New National Pension Insurance," ISSAssoc, 13 (1960), 413-23.

———. Sweden's New National Pension Insurance. Stock., 1961. 17 p.

Michanek, K. G. Social Insurance in Sweden.
Stock., 1962. 8 p.

New National Pension Scheme in Sweden.
Stock., 1947.

"Pension Funds and Capital Problems of the
Swedish Companies," SBQR, 33 (1952),
37-39.

"Pension Problems," SHI (N 1956), 1-3.

Persson, Konrad. Social Security and Welfare in Sweden. Stock., 1951. 45 p.

"A Proposal for the Reform of Invalidity and
Old-Age Insurance in Sweden," ILR (1934),
528-38.

"Reform of the Swedish National Pension
Scheme," ILR, 54 (1946), 384-87.

"Social Security Convention Between Sweden
and the United Kingdom," ISSAssoc, 10
(1957), 518-23.

Sweden, Ministry of Commerce, Pensions
Commission. Proposal for a General
Pension Insurance in Sweden. Stock.,
1950. 28 p.

Sweden, Official Statistics of Sweden: Insurance. The National Insurance Office:
1 January 1960, 30 June 1961. Stock.,
1962. 26 p.

"The Swedish Act on Pensions Insurance and
Its Application," ILR, 2 (1921), 234-46.

"Swedish Legislation for Increased Pensions," Social Security Bull. (O 1946),
49-50.

Tegner, Göran. Social Security in Sweden.
Stock., Lond., 1956. 140 p.

United States, President's Council on Aging.
Homes for the Aged in Sweden Offer Ideas
to Americans. Wash., 1963. 32 p.

United States, Social Security Board. Old
Age in Sweden: Program of Social Security. Wash., 1940. 305 p.

GENERAL

SCANDINAVIA

Anderson, Burnett, ed. The Northern Countries. Uppsala, 1951. 154 p.

Anderson, Vilhelm. "The Voice of the North," ScPP, I, 28-30.

Braatoy, Bjarne. Northern Nations. Toronto, 1940.

DeMaré, Eric S. Scandinavia: Sweden, Denmark, and Norway. Lond., 1952. 262 p.

Gunther, John. "Scandinavia — the Outer Bastions," in his, Inside Europe Today (N.Y., 1962), 273-86.

Hannah, Ian C. Capitals of the Northlands; Tales of Ten Cities. Lond., 1914. 264 p.

Hendin, Herbert. "National Character," Columbia University Forum, 7 (Winter 1964), 31-35.

Hope, Francis. "North of Europe," New Statesman (N 17, 1967), 666-72.

Innes, Hammond, and the Editors of Life. Scandinavia (Life World Library). N.Y., 1963. 160 p.

Leach, Henry G. Scandinavia of the Scandinavians. Lond., N.Y., 1915. 332 p.

Mohr, Hans. "Scandinavia," Norseman, 4 (1946), 286-90.

Ogrizek, Doré, ed. Scandinavia: Denmark, Norway, Sweden, Finland, and Iceland. N.Y., 1952. 438 p.

Rasmussen, C. C. What About Scandinavia? Phila., 1948. 194 p.

The Scandinavian Year Book 1953: a Comprehensive Guide to Commerce, Industry and Tourism in Denmark, Norway and Sweden. Lond., 1953.

Scott, Franklin D. Scandinavia Today (Foreign Policy Association Headline Series, no. 85). N.Y., 1951. 62 p.

Soloveytchik, George. "The Scandinavians Today," Lloyds Bank Review (1962), 47-58.

Stefánsson, Jón. Denmark and Sweden, with Iceland and Finland. Lond., N.Y., 1917. 378 p.

Tennant, Peter F. D., ed. The Scandinavian Book. Lond., 1951. 314 p.

United Nations World (Aug 1951), contains a special feature on Scandinavia, depicting various aspects of life in Sweden, Norway, Denmark, and Finland.

Young, George G. The Viking Lands. Lond., N.Y., 1949, 1950. 154 p.

DENMARK

Bailhache, Jean. Denmark (Vista Books, W 10). Lond., N.Y., 1961. 191 p.

Clissold, Stephen. Denmark, the Land of Hans Andersen. Lond., 1955. 207 p.

"Denmark," Focus, 11 (May 1961), 1-6.

Denmark, Information Office, New York. Denmark Today. N.Y., 1952. 32 p.

Denmark, Ministry of Foreign Affairs. About Denmark. Coph., 1955. 62 p. 1958 ed., 64 p.

——. Denmark. Ed. by Bent Rying and Mikal Rode. Coph., 1961. 912 p.

——. Facts About Denmark: International Who-What-Where. Ed. by Helge Larsen and Terben J. Meyer. 9th ed., Coph., 1958. 64 p.

——. Life in Denmark. Coph., 1957. 47 p.

Desmond, Shaw. The Soul of Denmark. Lond., N.Y., 1918. 277 p.

Edelberg, Max, ed. Denmark in Word and Picture: a Collection of Monographs. Written by Danish Experts. Coph., 1934. 200 p.

Eppstein, John, ed. Denmark (British Society for International Understanding, British Survey Handbooks, No. 5). Cambridge, N.Y., 1945. 88 p.

Gedde, Knud, ed. This Is Denmark. Coph., 1948. 272 p.

Great Britain, Naval Intelligence Division. Denmark (Geographical Handbook Series, 38). Lond., 1944. 611 p.

Hackett, Francis. I Chose Denmark. N.Y., 1940. 291 p.

Harvey, William J., and Christian Reppien. Denmark and the Danes. Lond., N.Y., 1915. 346 p.

Holland, Clive. Denmark, the Land and Its People. New York: Dodd, 1932. 179 p.

———. Denmark: a Modern Guide to the Land and Its People. Lond., 1927. 179 p.

Lauring, Palle. "Dannebrog, Flag of the Danes," DFOJ (Ap 1962), 33-34.

Miles, Beryl. Candles in Denmark. Lond., 1958. 235 p.

Nielsen, Roger, ed. Denmark. Coph., 1939. 144 p.

Palmer, Paul. Denmark. Lond., 1945. 171 p.

Rothery, Agnes E. Denmark, Kingdom of Reason. N.Y., 1937. 275 p.

Schacke, Erik. "Denmark To-day," SGM, 55 (1939), 97-102.

Sitwell, Sacheverell. Denmark. Lond., N.Y., 1956. 168 p.

Spink, Reginald. The Land and People of Denmark. Lond., N.Y., 1957. 88 p.

Strode, Hudson. Denmark Is a Lovely Land. N.Y., 1951. 304 p.

Thomas, Margaret. Denmark, Past and Present. Lond., 1902. 302 p.

Undset, Sigrid. "Denmark," ASR, 32 (1944), 216-28.

Williams, Ethel C. Denmark and the Danes. Lond., 1932. 242 p.

FINLAND

Ashcroft, Diana. Journey to Finland. Lond., 1952. 292 p.

Bugbee, Willis N. The Spirit of Finland. Syracuse, N.Y., 1940. 157 p.

Butler, Ralph. "The Fourth Scandinavian State," in The New Eastern Europe (N.Y., 1919), 7-20.

"The Civilization of Finland," Round Table, no. 118 (M 1940), 276-95.

De Windt, Harry. Finland as It Is. Lond., 1901. 316 p. 2d ed., 1910.

Facts About Finland. Ed. by J. Miesmaa. Hels., 1952. 64 p. Subsequent editions: 1955, 1957, 1960.

Finland. Suomen osasti New York in maailmannäyttelyssä, 1939-1940. Finland Builds. N.Y., 1940. 111 p.

Finland: the Country, Its People and Institutions. Hels., 1926. 598 p.

Finland: a Democracy of the North [Selected articles from Finland year book, 1947]. Hels., 1947. 137 p.

Finland: its Country and People, a Short Survey. Ed. by K. Blomstedt. Hels., 1919. 89 p.

Finlandia: a Cross Section of Finland, Her Nature, Art and Industry. Hels., 1952. 328 p.

Fox, Frank. Finland To-day. Lond., 1926. 188 p.

Garvin, Viola G. "Finland: Its Land and People," SGM, 56 (May 1940), 49-58.

Great Britain, Admiralty. A Handbook of Finland. Lond., 1919. 208 p.

Gutheim, F. A. "Free Finland: the New Chapter," Survey Graphic, 30 (May 1941), 325-41.

Hall, Wendy. Green Gold and Granite: a Background to Finland. Lond., Toronto, 1953. 190 p.

Hinshaw, David. Heroic Finland. N.Y., 1952. 306 p.

Homén, Viktor T., ed. East Carelia and Kola Lapmark. Described by Finnish Scientists and Philologists. Lond., N.Y., 1921. 264 p.

Järvi, Toivo H. Finland, the Country, its Peoples and Institutions. Hels., 1926. 339 p.

Kihlberg, Jaakko. Speaking of Finland. Hels., 1954. 40 p.

Kovero, Martti. The Official Finnish Statistics. Hels., 1924. 15 p.

Leiviskä, Ilvari, and Lauri Levämäki, eds. Guide to Finland. Hels., 1938. 289 p.

Lyon, Frederick B. "Finland," FSJ, 17 (1940), 121-24 ff.

McBride, Robert M. [by Robert Medill, pseud.]. Finland and Its People. N.Y., 1925. 118 p.

Minn, Eeva K. Finland. Prepared by Indiana University Graduate Program in Uralic and Asian Studies (Human Relations Area Files, Inc.; Subcontractor's Monograph, HRAF-2). New Haven, Conn., 1955. 391 p.

Nickels, Sylvie. Finland. N.Y., 1966. 233 p.

Nordenskiöld, Erland. "Finland: the Land and the People," GeoR, 7 (1919), 361-76.

Olin, Saul C. Finlandia: the Racial Composition, the Language, and a Brief History of the Finnish People. Hancock, Mich., 1957. 198 p.

Pearson, Alfred J. The Land of a Thousand Lakes. Hancock, Mich., 1932. 109 p.

Pirinen, Kauko. "The Coat of Arms of Finland," ASR, 51 (1963), 123-29.

Reade, Arthur. Finland and the Finns. N.Y., 1915. 315 p. 1917 ed., 336 p.

Renwick, George. Finland To-day. Lond., 1911. 348 p.

Rosvall, Toivo D. Finland, Land of Heroes. N.Y., 1940. 272 p.

Rothery, Agnes E. Finland: the Country and Its People. New ed., Lond., 1940. 267 p.

——. Finland, the New Nation. N.Y., 1936. 257 p. Also N.Y., 1937. 257 p.

Scott, Alexander M. Suomi: the Land of the Finns. Lond., 1926. 223 p.

Strode, Hudson. Finland Forever. New ed., N.Y., 1952. 472 p. 1st ed., 1941. 443 p.

Tiovola, Urho, ed. Finland Year Book, 1947. Hels., 1947. 455 p.

——. Introduction to Finland, 1960. Hels., 1960. 312 p.

Tivenhofel, W. H. "Finland," JofGeo, 14 (1917/18), 321-27.

Welle-Strand, Edvard. "An Outpost of Northern Civilization," ASR, 4 (1916), 270-73.

Wright, B. H. "Finnish Solstice," GeoM, 9 (May 1939), 11-30.

ICELAND

Achen, Sven T. "The Coat of Arms of Iceland," ASR, 50 (1962), 355-58.

Ahlmann, Hans W. Land of Ice and Fire. Lond., 1938. 271 p.

Annandale, Nelson. The Faroes and Iceland (Studies in Island Life). Oxford, 1905. 238 p.

Boland, Charles M. Iceland and Greenland. N.Y., 1959. 64 p.

Briem, Helgi P. Iceland and the Icelanders. Maplewood, N.J., 1945. 96 p.

Clark, Austin H. Iceland and Greenland (Smithsonian Institution. War Background Studies, no. 15). Wash., 1943. 103 p.

Directory of Iceland, 1951: Official and Commercial Information. Rey., 1951. 706 p.

Hansson, Ólafur. Facts About Iceland: Information About the People and Country. Tr. by Peter G. Foote. Rey., 1954. 80 p.

Iceland. Statistics Bureau, Iceland, 1946. 4th ed. by Thorsteinn Thorsteinsson.

Rey., 1946. 295 p. 1st ed., 1926; 2d ed., 1930; 3rd ed., 1936.

Iceland Today, the Land, the Nation; the Economy and Culture. Rey., 1961. 489 p.

The Iceland Year Book: a Handbook of General Information. 1st ed., Rey., 1926.

Jensen, Amy Elizabeth. Iceland, Old-New Republic: a Survey of Its History, Life and Physical Aspects. N.Y., 1954. 362 p.

Kemban, Godmundur. "Modern Iceland," GeoR, 5 (1918), 195-207.

Leaf, Horace. Iceland: Yesterday and To-day. Lond., 1949. 205 p.

Lindroth, Hjalmar. Iceland, A Land of Contrasts. Princeton, N.J.; N.Y., 1937. 234 p.

Magnússon, Gudmundur. "The Future of Iceland," ASR, 3 (1915), 73-77.

Priest, George M. "Iceland," ASR, 12 (1924), 221-28.

Reynolds, J. H. "Iceland in 1872 and 1926," GeogJ, 70 (1927), 44-49.

Rothery, Agnes E. Iceland, Bastion of the North. New rev. ed., Lond., 1952. 192 p.

——. Iceland, New World Outpost. N.Y., 1948. 214 p.

——. Iceland Roundabout. N.Y., 1948. 199 p.

Schacke, Erik. "Stepping Stones Across the Atlantic: the Faroes and Iceland," SGM, 57 (1941), 23-29.

Stefansson, Vilhjalmur. Iceland, the First American Republic. N.Y., 1939. 275 p.

Stone, Richard C. "Iceland: Land of Fire," CR, 172 (1947), 165-68.

Terkelsen, Terkel M. "Contrasts in Iceland," Norseman, 16 (1958), 278-82.

NORWAY

Boardman, Philip L. How to Feel at Home in Norway. 3d ed., 1953. 239 p.

——. Northern Paradise: the Intelligent Alien's Guide to Norway. Oslo, 1963. 339 p.

Clough, Ethlyn T., ed. Norwegian Life: an Account of Past and Contemporary Conditions and Progress in Norway and Sweden. Detroit, 1909. 238 p.

Dent, John. Norway (Lands and Peoples Series). N.Y., 1956. 90 p.

Egan, Maurice F. "Norway and Norwegians," NGeogM, 45 (1924), 647-96.

Facts about Norway. 8th ed., Oslo, 1963. 64 p.

Great Britain, Admiralty, Naval Intelligence Division. A Handbook of Norway and Sweden. Oxford, 1920. 476 p.

Harris, Georgine R. Progressive Norway. Wash., 1939. 256 p.

Hølaas, Odd. The World of the Norseman. London, 1949. 96 p.

Lingstrom, Freda. This Is Norway. Lond., 1933. 152 p.

Major, Harlan. Norway — Home of the Norsemen. N.Y., 1957. 195 p.

Martin, Anthony H. Norwegian Life and Landscape. Lond., 1952. 167 p.

Monroe, Will S. In Viking Land: Norway, Its People, Its Fjords and Its Fyelds. Boston, 1908. 332 p.

Norway, Central Bureau of Statistics. Guide to Norwegian Statistics. Oslo, 1963. 61 p.

Norway, Information Office. Norway: a Handbook. Lond., 1943 95 p.

Norway, Ministry of Culture. Official Publication for the Paris Exhibition 1900. Kra., 1900. 626 p.

Norway Yearbook. Oslo. 1st ed., 1924; 2d ed., 1931; 3d ed., 1938. Thereafter, Sverre Mortensen, ed. 4th ed., 1950; 5th ed., 1954; 6th ed., 1962. 423 p.

Rothery, Agnes E. Norway, Changing and Changeless. N.Y., 1939. 294 p.

Vogt, Per. Norway To-day. 5th rev. ed., Oslo, 1951. 160 p.

SWEDEN

Abeel, Neilson. "Sweden and Peace," ASR, 20 (1932), 440-46.

Andersson, Ingvar et al. Introduction to Sweden (Replaces Sweden Year-book of the Ministry for Foreign Affairs). Stock., 1949, 1950. 311 p.

Ashby, Gwynneth M. Sweden (The Lands and Peoples Series). Lond., 1951. 88 p.

Baerlein, Henry. "Sweden, Old and New," Free Europe, 13 (Jl 1946), 204-207.

Blomstedt, Magnus, and Fredrik Böök. Sweden of To-day: a Survey of Its Intellectual and Material Culture. Stock., 1930. 402 p.

Braatoy, Bjarne. The New Sweden: a Vindication of Democracy. Lond., N.Y., 1939. 172 p.

Chessin, Serge De. The Key to Sweden. Stock., 1936. 233 p.

Cole, Margaret, and Charles M. Smith, eds. Democratic Sweden: a Volume of Studies Prepared by Members of the New Fabian Research Bureau. Lond., 1938. 334 p.

Fleisher, Frederic. The New Sweden: the Challenge of a Disciplined Democracy. N.Y., 1967. 384 p.

Fleisher, Wilfred. Sweden: the Welfare State. N.Y., 1956. 255 p.

Fraser, Maxwell. In Praise of Sweden. 3d ed., Lond., 1947. 287 p.

Guinchard, Axel J. J. Sweden: Historical and Statistical Handbook. Vol. 1: Land and People; Vol. 2: Industries. 2d ed., Stock., 1914. 784 p.; 758 p.

Hamilton, Cicely M. Modern Sweden as Seen by an Englishwoman. N.Y., 1939. 236 p.

Heathcote, Dudley. Sweden. Lond., 1927. 228 p.

Heckscher, Gunnar. "Information about Sweden," ScPP, III, 863-66.

Hedin, Naboth. Main Facts about Sweden. N.Y., 1947. 80 p.

Heilborn, Adèle. Travel, Study, and Research in Sweden. Stock., 1957. 243 p.

Höijer, Ernst. "The Organization of Official Statistics in Sweden," BSC (1937), 502-505.

Kastrup, Allan. The Making of Sweden. N.Y., 1953. 128 p.

McBride, Robert M. Sweden and Its People. [by Robert Medill, pseud.]. N.Y., 1924. 114 p.

Nano, Frederic C. The Land and People of Sweden (Portraits of the Nations Series). Phila., 1949. 116 p.

"New Paths for Sweden: a Special Survey," Economist (O 28, 1967), 36 p.

Rothery, Agnes E. Sweden, the Land and the People. N.Y., 1934. 277 p.

Scheffer, C. G. U. "The Coats of Arms of Sweden," ASR, 51 (1963), 237-44.

Steveni, James W. B. Unknown Sweden. Lond., 1927. 327 p.

Strode, Hudson. Sweden, Model for a World. N.Y., 1949. 371 p.

Sundbärg, Axel G., ed. Sweden, Its People and Its Industry. Historical and Statistical Handbook Published by Order of the Government. Stock., 1904. 1141 p.

The Sweden Year Book. Stock., 1921 (1923/24, 1925, 1936, 1938, and others).

Swedish Institute. Facts About Sweden. Stock., 1st ed., 1948. 11th rev. ed., 1964. 52 p.

———. Graphic Sweden: a Survey of This Country's Population, Industry, Commerce and Social Culture. Ed. by Bertil Hydahl. Stock., 1950. 53 p.

———. The Swedish Flag and Sweden's National Coat of Arms. Stock., 1962. 4 p.

The Swedish Institute — What It Is, What It Does, What It Aims At. Stock., 1962. 11 p.

Wilhelm, Prince of Sweden. Something of My Country. N.Y., 1952. 244 p.

———. This Land of Sweden. Stock., 1946 394 p.

William-Olsson, W. Sweden and Finland: Statistical Data. Stock., 1964. 227 p.

SELECTED BIBLIOGRAPHIES

The easiest way to supplement this bibliography with more recent items is to consult the book review sections of *The American Scandinavian Review* or the review and bibliography sections of the specialized journals in one's field of interest, e.g., *The American Historical Review* or *The American Political Science Review*. See also, "The American Scandinavian Bibliography," appearing in each year's May issue of *Scandinavian Studies*. For popular literature, which generally has not been included in this bibliography, one should consult *The Reader's Guide to Periodical Literature* or *The International Index to Periodicals*. Also helpful is *Guide to Historical Literature*. The Swedish Institute, Stockholm, is a source of up-to-date bibliographic listings and literature on Sweden. Most authoritative for books are the catalogues of the Library of Congress and of the British Museum.

Aaltonen, Hilkka. Books in English on Finland; A Bibliographical List of Publications Concerning Finland until 1960, including Finnish Literature in English Translation. Appendix: A Selected List of Books Published from 1961 to 1963 Inclusive (Publications of Turku University Library, 8). Turku, 1964. 276 p.

Afzelius, Nils. A Bibliographical List of Books in English on Sweden and Literary Works Translated into English from Swedish. Stock., 1936. 33 p.; 2d ed., 1938; 3d ed., 1951. 56 p. Title varies; available from the Swedish Institute.

Bay, Jens C. Denmark in English and American Literature: a Bibliography. Chicago, 1915. 96 p.

"Books and Pamphlets on Norway in English Published in England Between April 9, 1940 and May 7, 1945," Norseman, 3 (1945), 299-302.

Cornell University Library. Catalogue of the Icelandic Collection Bequeathed by Willard Fiske. Ithaca, 1960. 755 p.

Dahl, Sven. Danish Theses for the Doctorate and Commemorative Publications of the University of Copenhagen, 1836-1926. Coph., 1929. 412 p.

Frykholm, Lars. "Swedish Legal Publications in English, French, and German 1935-60." ScStL, 5 (1961), 153-217.

Grönland, Erling. Norway in English: Books on Norway and by Norwegians in English 1936-1959. Oslo: Oslo University Press, 1961. 152 p.

Hermannsson, Halldór. "The Ancient Laws of Norway and Iceland: a Bibliography," Islandica, 4 (1911), 83 p.

——. "Bibliographical Notes," Islandica, 29 (1942), 91 p.

Holm, Tor W., and Erkki J. Immonen. Bibliography of Finnish Sociology 1945-1959. Transactions of the Westermarck Society, XIII. Åbo, 1966. 179 p.

The Humanities and the Sciences in Denmark During the Second World War. Coph.: Munksgaard, 1948. 724 p.

Iuul, Stig, Åke Malmström, and Jens Søndergaard. Scandinavian Legal Bibliography Stock., 1961. 196 p.

Julkunen, Martti, and Anja Lehikoinen. A Select List of Books and Articles in English, French and German on Finnish Politics in the 19th and 20th Century. (Publication B:1 of the Institute of Political History, University of Turku). Turku, 1967. 125 p.

Lehtinen, Rauno. "Bibliography of Scandinavian Political Science, 1960-1964," ScPolSt, 1 (1966), 288-336.

Lindberg, Folke, and John I. Kolehmainen. The Scandinavian Countries in International Affairs: a Selected Bibliography on the Foreign Affairs of Denmark, Finland, Norway, and Sweden, 1800-1952 (University of Minnesota Scandinavian Area Studies Publication). Minneapolis, 1953. 17 p.

Mitchell, Philip M. "Scandinavian Bibliography," Sc, 1 (May 1962), 51-62.

Neuvonen, Eero K. A Short Bibliography on Finland (Turku University Library Publications, 7). Turku, 1955. 38 p.

Reinikainen, Veikko. English, French, and German Literature on Finnish Law in 1860-1956 (Library of the Parliament Publications, 2). Hels., 1957. 179 p.

Rintala, Marvin. "Short List of English-Language Studies of Finnish Politics," JCEA, 23 (1963), 77-80.

Rokkan, Stein. "Publications of the Organisation for Comparative Social Research, 1954-1956," Humaniora Norvegica (1955/56), 76-80. And see Humaniora Norvegica generally.

Sandler, Åke, and Ernst Ekman. Government, Politics and Law in the Scandinavian Countries: a Selected, Critical Bibliography (University of Minnesota Scandinavian Area Studies Publication). Minneapolis, 1954. 24 p.

"Selected Bibliography: Publications by Danish Authors (Anthropology)," Folk (1959), 153-68.

Søndergaard, Jens. "Danish Legal Publications in English, French, and German," ScStL, 7 (1963), 167-260.

Swedish Archeological Society. Swedish Archeological Bibliography, 1939-48. Ed. by Sverker Janson and Olof Vessberg. Stock., 1951. 360 p.

——. Swedish Archeological Bibliography, 1949-53. Ed. by Christian Callmer and Wilhelm Holmquist. Stock., 1956. 293 p.

Swedish Institute (Svenska Institutet för Kulturellt Utbyte med Utlandet, Stockholm). Swedish Books and Publications on Science, Medicine and the Humanities, 1939-1947. Prepared by Gösta Ottervik and Sten G. Lindberg. Stock., 1949. 199 p.

Swedish Urban History Institute (Svenska Stadshistoriska Institutet). International Bibliography of Urban History: Denmark, Finland, Norway, Sweden. By Gunnar Olsen. Stock., 1960. 73 p.

United States, Library of Congress. Report on the Scandinavian Collection. By Sigmund Skard. Wash., 1944. 96 p.

Parliamentary Debates of the Scandinavian Countries: Library Holdings

(as of September, 1960)

LIBRARY	Denmark "Folketings- tidende"	Finland "Valtiopäivät: "Pöytäkirjat, or "Riksdags- handlingar"	Iceland "Althingis- tidindi"	Norway "Stortings- forhand- linger"	Sweden "Riksdagens Protokoll"
Cambridge, Massachusetts: Harvard College	1953/54 -	1947 -; S 1947 -	1845-1934		1950 -

Canberra,
  Australia:
The Commonwealth
  National Library
	1958 -	S 1940 -		1954 -	1901 -

Chicago, Illinois: The Midwest Inter- Library Center					1905 -
Decorah, Iowa: Luther College				1814 -	
Geneva, Switzerland: United Nations	1922/23 -	1927 -; S 1927 -	1939 -	1921 -	1924 -
The Hague, Netherlands: Library of the Second Chamber of the Estates General	1874 -	1943 -		1814 -	1874 -

LIBRARY	Denmark "Folketings- tidende"	Finland "Valtiopäivät: "Pöytäkirjat, or "Riksdags- handlingar"	Iceland "Althingis- tidindi"	Norway "Stortings- forhand- linger"	Sweden "Riksdagens Protokoll"
Ithaca, New York: The Fiske Icelandic Collection of Cornell University			1845 -		
Leeds 2, England: Brotherton Library, University of Leeds			1845 -		
London, W.C.1, England: State Paper Room of the British Museum	1848 -	1914, 1917 -; S 1872 -	1845 -	1815 -	1867 -
Los Angeles, Calif.: University of California, Los Angeles		S 1944 -			
Minneapolis, Minn.: University of Minnesota	1850-1918, 1929/30 - 1933/34	S 1907 -	1845-1938	1814, 1845 -	1867 -
New York City: New York Public Library	1850/51 -	S 1864 -	1845 -	1814 -	1868 -
Paris, XVI, France: Bibliothèque de Documentation Internationale Contemporaine, Université de Paris	1914-1938, 1945 -				
Stanford, Calif.: Hoover Library of Stanford University	1914/15 - 1923/24, 1939/40 - 1942/43	1907 -; S 1907 -			1914-1925, 1939 -
Strasbourg, France: Library of the Council of Europe	1949/50 -		1952 -	1948 -	1948 -
Urbana, Illinois: University of Illinois		1920 -; S 1920 -			
Washington, D.C.: Library of Congress	1848 -	1907 -; S 1907 -	1845 -	1814 -	1867 -

"*S*" signifies Swedish-language edition.

Variations in title: The Danish debates were until 1953 entitled "Rigsdagstidende," and the Icelandic were prior to 1875 entitled "Tidini frá alþingi Íslendinga".

Binding of debates: All holdings are bound except parts of the Paris and Stanford Danish collections, part of the Strasbourg Norwegian collection, and the following: Canberra Danish and Norwegian collections, Leeds Icelandic collection.

Time of receiving debates, general comments: Some libraries are two to five years behind in receiving their debates. Holdings are considered current if they include the year 1955. Some libraries have indicated missing volumes which they intend to fill in. Many libraries have other parliamentary documents also.

Notes on holdings listed: The British Museum has most of the proceedings from the Swedish Four Estates from 1786 to 1866. In the case of the Preste-ståndet its set begins in 1809. The Library of Congress has most of the proceedings of these Four Estates 1809-1866 and also has most of the proceedings of the Finnish Four Estates, beginning 1809. Cornell University has the proceedings of many of the pre-1845 sessions of the Alþingi. The University of Leeds holds many of the Alþingi proceedings from the period 1696-1800, some in printed and some in manuscript form. Chicago's Midwest Inter-Library Center has several pre-1905 volumes of Swedish debates. The University of Minnesota has Stortings-efterretninger for the periods 1814-1833 and 1836-1854. It is missing the Danish volume for 1913/14. Its Icelandic collection, more specifically, includes 1845-1873, 1875-1891, 1894-1907, 1912, 1914-1918, 1922-1924, 1926-1938. The University of Illinois' Finnish collections are incomplete for 1925, 1952 and 1953 in the Swedish-language series and for 1924, 1925, 1953 and 1954 in the Finnish-language series. Some few volumes are lacking in the New York Public Library collections.

Other libraries receiving the debates: The parliamentary proceedings of each of the five Northern Countries are available in all five capital cities, either at the parliamentary or the university libraries. The proceedings of some are also available in other European capitals, as well as in other Northern cities.

AUTHOR INDEX

This index includes only the bibliographic listings; it does not provide
pagination for names mentioned in the introductory essays.